Disability Rights Handbook

38th Edition
April 2013 - April 2014

by Ian Greaves

Acknowledgements

We would like to acknowledge the valuable contribution of all the contributors and checkers of this edition of the Handbook.

Thanks also to colleagues at Disability Rights UK for their work on Handbook sales administration and distribution, in particular Steve Newsham.

Thanks also to Paula McDiarmid for her patience and efficiency in co-ordinating the writing and checking of the Handbook and for her copy-editing skill.

Design and print production management is by Deborah Kamofsky, Anderson Fraser Partnership. Typesetting is by Humphrey Weightman. I am most grateful to them for their professional support and high-quality work.

Special acknowledgements go to Judith Paterson who wrote the *Disability Rights Handbook* from the 19th through to the 26th edition and to her predecessor Sally Robertson.

We do our best to ensure the information in the Handbook is correct. However, changes in the law after April 2013 might affect the accuracy of some of the information. Where this could be important to you, you should check the details with a local advice centre or your local Jobcentre Plus office.

If you think anything in the Handbook is incorrect, please write and tell us. Thanks to all those who wrote to us this year with comments and suggestions on the Handbook. Your contributions are always very welcome.

This edition is dedicated to the memory of Peter Townsend, Disability Alliance's founder and President, without whom the *Disability Rights Handbook* would not exist. Peter spent his life working tirelessly to highlight the unacceptable levels of poverty experienced by disabled people and their families and he is sorely missed by all those striving to maintain his impressive legacy.

Contributors
Ken Butler
Paddy Cullen
Lynsey Dalton
Marije Davidson
Helen Dolphin
Barbara Donegan
Mike Ellison
Richard Forrest
Sarah Goldberg
Daphne Hall
Lisa Jennison
Janet Moore
Derek Sinclair
Robbie Spence
Tony Stevens
Rundip Thind
Keith Venables
Rebecca Walker
Helen Winfield
Debbie Witton

and
Norman Kirby
(Low Incomes Tax Reform Group)

Checkers
Kate Fincham
Ann Flint
Philip Gibson
(Criminal Injuries Compensation Authority)
Sandie Lock
Fiona MacConnacher
David Malcolm
(National Union of Students)
Alan Markey
Clive Martin
(Ferret Information Systems)
Chris Parsons
(Tower Hamlets Law Centre)
Judith Paterson
Sarah Powney
(National Assembly for Wales)
Fiona Seymour
Kate Smith
Keith Turner
(Independent Living Fund)
Sally West
Mary Convill, Sarah Cosby,
Martin Inch, Ben Kersey,
Robert Mandelstam, Banane Nafeh
and Michael Paul
(Disability Rights UK)

and staff at
Compensation Recovery Unit
Department for
Work and Pensions
Department of Health
TV Licensing Campaign Office

Disability Rights Handbook
38th Edition
April 2013 - April 2014
ISBN: 978-1-903335-60-4

Published by
Disability Rights UK © 2013

Design by
Anderson Fraser Partnership © 2013

Contents

Benefits checklist

This is a quick guide to help you see which benefits you might be entitled to. More than one of the circumstances below may apply to you and you may qualify for more than one benefit, especially if you have low savings and income. Box A.1 in Chapter 1 tells you which benefits depend on your national insurance (NI) record and which are affected by other income. Benefits marked with an asterisk (*) will be replaced by universal credit over the next few years (see Box J.1 in Chapter 25).

Circumstance	Benefit	Chapter
Problems with walking		
■ disabled child (aged under 16)	disability living allowance (DLA) mobility component	3
■ aged 16 to 64 (inclusive) when you claim	personal independence payment (PIP) mobility component	4
■ hire or buy a car using the DLA or PIP mobility component	Motability	6
■ if you get higher rate of DLA or PIP mobility component	road tax exemption/reduction	6
■ parking concessions	Blue Badge scheme	6
Need help with personal care		
■ aged under 16 when you claim	DLA care component	3
■ aged 16 to 64 (inclusive) when you claim	PIP daily living component	4
■ aged 65 or over when you claim	attendance allowance	5
Caring		
■ you care for a disabled person for at least 35 hours a week	carer's allowance	7
■ you or your partner get carer's allowance or would do but for an overlapping benefit	carer premium with means-tested benefits	25
Limited capability for work		
■ employed	statutory sick pay (SSP)	9
■ not employed or SSP has run out	employment and support allowance (ESA)	10
Unemployed or working less than 16 hours a week		
■ payable for 26 weeks if you've paid enough NI contributions	contribution-based jobseeker's allowance (JSA)	16
■ if you've not paid enough NI contributions, or your contribution-based JSA has run out or is not enough to live on	income-based jobseeker's allowance*	16
■ if you don't have to sign on for work (eg you are a carer or a lone parent with a young child) and any income or savings are low	income support*	15
Working at least 16 hours a week		
■ you have a child, or you have a disability and get a qualifying disability benefit or recently got a qualifying incapacity benefit, or you are aged 60+, or you are 25 or over and working at least 30 hours a week	working tax credit*	19
Housing problems		
■ repairs, adaptations, improvements	housing grants	31
■ help with the mortgage interest (and certain other housing costs), if you are entitled to income support, income-related ESA, income-based JSA, pension credit (guarantee credit) or universal credit (if you are not working)	help with housing costs	26
■ help with the rent	housing benefit*	21
■ help with the council tax	council tax reduction, disability reduction or discount schemes	22
You do not have enough to live on		
■ limited capability for work	income-related employment and support allowance*	13
■ not working, or working less than 16 hours a week, and you do not have to sign on for work (eg you are a carer)	income support*	15
■ if you have to sign on for work	income-based jobseeker's allowance*	16
■ from pension credit qualifying age	pension credit	42
■ working at least 16 hours a week (see above)	working tax credit*	19
■ responsible for a child (see below)	child tax credit*	19
■ paying rent for your home	housing benefit*	21

Circumstance	Benefit	Chapter
You have needs difficult to meet out of regular income		
■ if you've had income-related ESA, income support, income-based JSA or pension credit for at least 26 weeks	budgeting loan*	24
Practical help at home		
■ practical help if you are disabled	care services, eg home care, Meals on Wheels	29
■ equipment and adaptations	help from social care or the NHS	30
Pregnancy		
■ employed	statutory maternity pay (SMP)	36
■ recently self-employed, or employed but not entitled to SMP	maternity allowance	36
■ limited capability for work	employment and support allowance	10
■ if income and savings are low	income support*	15
■ help with maternity expenses for first child	Sure Start maternity grant	23
■ vouchers for milk, fruit and vegetables	Healthy Start	54
Responsibility for children		
■ employed	statutory paternity pay	36
■ employed (responsible for adopted child)	statutory adoption pay	36
■ responsible for a child under 16, or 16-19 in full-time, non-advanced education or approved unwaged training	child benefit	38
	child tax credit*	19
■ responsible for an orphan	guardian's allowance	38
■ disabled child	disability living allowance	3
	Family Fund	37
■ vouchers for milk, fruit and vegetables	Healthy Start	54
Retirement		
■ from state pension age	state pension	43
■ from pension credit qualifying age and income or savings are low	pension credit	42
■ from age 80 and little or no state pension before	non-contributory state pension	43
Injured or contracted disease in work		
■ disabled through an industrial accident or prescribed disease	industrial injuries disablement benefit	44
■ the industrial accident or disease occurred before 1.10.90 and your earnings capacity is reduced	reduced earnings allowance	44
■ replaces reduced earnings allowance when you give up regular employment after state pension age	retirement allowance	44
War disablement		
■ injured because of service in the armed forces (prior to 6.4.05), or a civilian disabled due to World War 2	war disablement pension	45
■ your spouse or civil partner died because of the war, or because of service in the armed forces	widows, widower and surviving civil partners' pensions	45
■ injured because of service in the armed forces on or after 6.4.05	Armed Forces Compensation scheme	45
Disabled due to vaccine damage	vaccine damage payment	47
Injured due to violent crime	criminal injuries compensation	46
Need help with NHS costs, glasses, hospital fares	health benefits	54
Death		
■ widow, widower or surviving civil partner under state pension age, or whose late spouse or civil partner did not get state pension	bereavement payment	53
■ widow, widower or surviving civil partner with a dependent child	widowed parent's allowance	53
■ paid for 52 weeks to a widow, widower or surviving civil partner aged 45 or over but under state pension age when spouse or civil partner dies	bereavement allowance	53
■ help with the cost of a funeral	social fund funeral payment	23

Legal references

The footnotes in this Handbook are references to Acts and Regulations, case law and official guidance. Each footnote applies to the block of text above it. If there are several paragraphs in a block, with just one footnote at the bottom, the footnote applies to all text within the block. If text contains several footnotes, each one refers to the text directly above it, up to the previous footnote. Text that provides tactical advice or discussion on specific points is not generally footnoted.

Acts and Regulations

Acts of Parliament (also known as statutes) contain the basic rules for social security benefits, tax credits and community care administration. Regulations flesh out the law and provide the detail that determines procedure for the rules as laid down in the Acts. These are also known as statutory instruments (SIs) and can be amended at any time using other SIs.

Finding Acts and Regulations

You can buy printed copies of Acts and Regulations from The Stationery Office (0870 600 5522) or find them on the National Archives website (www.legislation.gov.uk).

Most regulations are updated over time with further amending regulations. The consequent consolidated and updated legislation is set out in:
■ *The Law Relating to Social Security* (The Blue Volumes), available via our website: www.disabilityrightsuk.org/links-government-departments (listed under 'department for work and pensions').
Consolidated and updated legislation is also available in:
■ *Social Security: Legislation 2012/13 Volumes I, II, III and IV* (Sweet & Maxwell). These have detailed footnotes explaining the legislation and highlighting relevant case law. They are used by members of appeal tribunals (see Chapter 58).

Case law

Case law is created through decisions or judgments made on points of law by the Upper Tribunal, the Court of Appeal or the Supreme Court (before 1.10.09 this was the jurisdiction of the House of Lords). These decisions clarify any doubt about the meaning of the law or its application to individual cases. When case law sets up a general principal, it also creates a precedent to be followed in similar cases.

The Upper Tribunal (previously the Social Security Commissioners) hears appeals against appeal tribunal decisions (see Box T.7 in Chapter 58), the Court of Appeal against decisions of the Commissioners/Upper Tribunal and the Supreme Court against Court of Appeal judgments.

Finding case law

All Commissioners/Upper Tribunal decisions are available from their office individually on request at a small charge (see inside back cover for their address). Decisions are also available on the website (www.osscsc.gov.uk/Aspx/default.aspx), where reported decisions from 1991 and selected unreported decisions deemed to be of interest from 2002 are published.
Case law summaries – Brief outlines of the main reported decisions can be found in *Neligan's Digest*, available via our website: www.disabilityrightsuk.org/links-government-departments (listed under 'department for work and pensions'). We have produced case law summaries covering disability [al]lowance and attendance allowance, incapacity benefit, [employme]nt and support allowance and decision making and [ww]w.disabilityrightsuk.org/how-we-can-help/benefits-[...]pages/case-law-summaries).Our factsheet [...he]lps you find the law relevant to disability [...di]sabilityrightsuk.org/finding-law).

Official guidance

See www.disabilityrightsuk.org/links-government-departments for the following:
■ *Decision Makers Guide* – Covering all benefits administered by the Department for Work and Pensions (DWP)
■ *Children's A-Z of Medical Conditions* – To help decide disability living allowance for children (see Chapter 3(22))
■ *A-Z of Medical Conditions* – To help decide disability living allowance and attendance allowance (see Chapter 5(17))
See also the boxes entitled 'For more information' in various chapters of the Handbook (and Box L.1 in Chapter 32 for Sections K and L).

Acts

CCH(S)A	Community Care and Health (Scotland) Act 2002
CSDPA	Chronically Sick and Disabled Persons Act 1970
HASSASSA	Health and Social Services and Social Security Adjudication Act 1983
HGCRA	Housing Grants, Construction and Regeneration Act 1996
HSA	Housing (Scotland) Act 2006
JSA	Jobseekers Act 1995
LGFA	Local Government Finance Act 1992
NAA	National Assistance Act 1948
PA	Pensions Act 2007
SPCA	State Pension Credit Act 2002
SSA	Social Security Act 1998
SSAA	Social Security Administration Act 1992
SSCBA	Social Security Contributions and Benefits Act 1992
TCA	Tax Credits Act 2002
TCEA	Tribunals, Courts and Enforcement Act 2007
VDPA	Vaccine Damage Payments Act 1979
WRA 2007	Welfare Reform Act 2007
WRA 2012	Welfare Reform Act 2012

Regulations

AA Regs	Social Security (Attendance Allowance) Regulations 1991 (SI 1991/2740)
AOR Regs	National Assistance (Assessment of Resources) Regulations 1992 (SI 1992/2977)
ARF(CS) Order	Armed Forces and Reserve Forces (Compensation Scheme) Order 2011 (SI 2011/517)
CB Regs	Child Benefit (General) Regulations 2006 (SI 2006/223)
CE Regs	Social Security Benefit (Computation of Earnings) Regulations 1996 (SI 1996/2745)
Cont. Regs	Social Security (Contributions) Regulations 2001 (SI 2001/1004)

C&P Regs	Social Security (Claims and Payments) Regulations 1987 (SI 1987/1968)
Credit Regs	Social Security (Credits) Regulations 1975 (SI 1975/556)
CTC Regs	Child Tax Credit Regulations 2002 (SI 2002/2007)
D&A Regs	Social Security and Child Support (Decisions and Appeals) Regulations 1999 (SI 1999/991)
DLA Regs	Social Security (Disability Living Allowance) Regulations 1991 (SI 1991/2890)
DP(BMV) Regs	Disabled Persons (Badges for Motor Vehicles) (England) Regulations 2000 (SI 2000/682)
ESA Regs	Employment and Support Allowance Regulations 2008 (SI 2008/794)
ESA (WRA) Regs	Employment and Support Allowance (Work-Related Activity) Regulations 2011 (SI 2011/1349)
GB Regs	Social Security (General Benefit) Regulations 1982 (SI 1982/1408)
HB Regs	Housing Benefit Regulations 2006 (SI 2006/213)
HB(SPC) Regs	Housing Benefit (Persons who have Attained the Qualifying Age for State Pension Credit) Regulations 2006 (SI 2006/214)
HB&CTB (D&A) Regs	Housing Benefit and Council Tax Benefit (Decisions and Appeals) Regulations 2001 (SI 2001/1002)
HIP Regs	Social Security (Hospital In-Patients) Regulations 2005 (SI 2005/3360)
HR Regs	Social Security Pensions (Home Responsibilities) Regulations 1994 (SI 1994/704)
HRG Regs	Housing Renewal Grants Regulations 1996 (SI 1996/2890)
(IA)CA Regs	Social Security (Immigration and Asylum) Consequential Amendments Regulations 2000 (SI 2000/636)
ICA Regs	Social Security (Invalid Care Allowance) Regulations 1976 (SI 1976/409)
II&D(MP) Regs	Social Security (Industrial Injuries and Diseases) Miscellaneous Provisions Regulations 1986 (SI 1986/1561)
IIPD Regs	Social Security (Industrial Injuries)(Prescribed Diseases) Regulations 1985 (SI 1985/967)
IS Regs	Income Support (General) Regulations 1987 (SI 1987/1967)
IW Regs	Social Security (Incapacity for Work)(General) Regulations 1995 (SI 1995/311)
JPI Regs	Social Security (Jobcentre Plus Interviews) Regulations 2002 (SI 2002/1703)
JPIP Regs	Social Security (Jobcentre Plus Interviews for Partners) Regulations 2003 (SI 2003/1886)
JSA Regs	Jobseeker's Allowance Regulations 1996 (SI 1996/207)
LATO(EDP) Regs	Local Authorities' Traffic Orders (Exemptions for Disabled Persons)(England) Regulations 2000 (SI 2000/683)
MPL Regs	Maternity and Parental Leave etc Regulations 1999 (SI 1999/3312)
NHS(CDA) Regs	National Health Service (Charges for Drugs and Appliances) Regulations 2000 (SI 2000/620)
NHS(TERC) Regs	National Health Service (Travel Expenses and Remission of Charges) Regulations 2003 (SI 2003/2382)
OB Regs	Social Security (Overlapping Benefits) Regulations 1979 (SI 1979/597)
PA Regs	Social Security Benefit (Persons Abroad) Regulations 1975 (SI 1975/563)
PAOR Regs	Social Security (Payments on Account, Overpayments and Recovery) Regulations 1988 (SI 1988/664)
PIP Regs	Social Security (Personal Independence Payment) Regulations 2013 (SI 2013/377)
SFM&FE Regs	Social Fund Maternity and Funeral Expenses (General) Regulations 2005 (SI 2005/3061)
SMP Regs	Statutory Maternity Pay (General) Regulations 1986 (SI 1986/1960)
SPC Regs	State Pension Credit Regulations 2002 (SI 2002/1792)
SSP Regs	Statutory Sick Pay (General) Regulations 1982 (SI 1982/894)
TC(C&N) Regs	Tax Credits (Claims and Notifications) Regulations 2002 (SI 2002/2014)
TC(DCI) Regs	Tax Credits (Definition and Calculation of Income) Regulations 2002 (SI 2002/2006)
TC(I) Regs	Tax Credits (Immigration) Regulations 2003 (SI 2003/653)
TC(IT&DR) Regs	Tax Credits (Income Thresholds and Determination of Rates) Regulations 2002 (SI 2002/2008)
TC(R) Regs	Tax Credits (Residence) Regulations 2003 (SI 2003/654)
TPEA Regs	Employment and Support Allowance (Transitional Provisions, Housing Benefit and Council Tax Benefit)(Existing Awards)(No.2) Regulations 2010 (SI 2010/1907)
TP(FTT)SEC Rules	Tribunal Procedure (First-tier Tribunal)(Social Entitlement Chamber) Rules 2008 (SI 2008/2685)
TP(UT) Rules	Tribunal Procedure (Upper Tribunal) Rules 2008 (SI 2008/2698)
UC Regs	Universal Credit Regulations 2013 (SI 2013/376)
UCPIP(C&P) Regs	Universal Credit, Personal Independence Payment, Jobseeker's Allowance and Employment and Support Allowance (Claims and Payments) Regulations 2013 (SI 2013/380)
UCPIP(D&A) Regs	Universal Credit, Personal Independence Payment, Jobseeker's Allowance and Employment and Support Allowance (Decisions and Appeals) Regulations 2013 (SI 2013/381)
VDP Regs	Vaccine Damage Payments Regulations 1979 (SI 1979/432)
WBRP Regs	Social Security (Widow's Benefit and Retirement Pensions) Regulations 1979 (SI 1979/642)
WTC(E&MR) Regs	Working Tax Credit (Entitlement and Maximum Rate) Regulations 2002 (SI 2002/2005)

Abbreviations

Most abbreviations used in the Handbook are explained here. If you come across one that isn't listed, you will usually find it explained towards the beginning of the chapter, towards the beginning of the section in a chapter, or in a box headed 'For more information'.

AIP	assessed income period	LBC	London Borough Council
art	article	LHA	local housing allowance
BEL	Benefit Enquiry Line	LHB	local health board
CC	county council	MBC	Metropolitan Borough Council
CCD	Community Care Circular	MDC	Metropolitan District Council
CCLR	Community Care Law Reports	NAfWC	National Assembly for Wales Circular
CEL	Chief Executive Letter	NHS	National Health Service
CLA	Community Legal Advice	NI	national insurance
CoA	Court of Appeal	p./para	paragraph in a schedule to an Act or
CoSLA	Convention of Scottish Local Authorities		set of Regulations, or in a Guidance Manual
CRAG	Charging for Residential Accommodation Guide	PAYE	pay as you earn
CTC	child tax credit	PCT	primary care trust
DEA	disability employment adviser	PEA	personal expenses allowance
DHP	discretionary housing payment	PIP	personal independence payment
DIAL	Disability Information and Advice Line	PPF	Pension Protection Fund
DLA	disability living allowance	REA	reduced earnings allowance
DMG	Decision Makers' Guide	Reg	regulation in a set of Regulations
DSA	disabled students' allowance	S.	section of an Act of Parliament
DWP	Department for Work and Pensions	S2P	state second pension
ECJ	European Court of Justice	SAAS	Student Awards Agency for Scotland
EEA	European Economic Area	SAP	statutory adoption pay
EHRC	Equality and Human Rights Commission	SC	Supreme Court
ESA	employment and support allowance	Sch	schedule, at the end of an Act or a
EU	European Union		set of Regulations
EWHC	High Court (England and Wales)	SDA	severe disablement allowance
FNC	funded nursing care	SDP	severe disability premium
GB	Great Britain (England, Scotland and Wales)	SERPS	state earnings-related pension scheme
GP	general practitioner	SMP	statutory maternity pay
HB	housing benefit	SPP	statutory paternity pay
HMCTS	HM Courts & Tribunals Service	SPVA	Service Personnel and Veterans Agency
HMRC	HM Revenue & Customs	SSP	statutory sick pay
HoL	House of Lords	UK	United Kingdom (England, Northern Ireland,
HRP	home responsibilities protection		Scotland, Wales)
HRT	habitual residence test	WAGC	Welsh Assembly Government Circular
HSC	Health Service Circular	WCA	work capability assessment
HSG	Health Service Guidance	WGC	Welsh Government Circular
IIDB	industrial injuries disablement benefit	WHC	Welsh Health Circular
ILF	Independent Living Fund	WOC	Welsh Office Circular
IS	income support	WPA	widowed parent's allowance
JSA	jobseeker's allowance	WTC	working tax credit
LAC	Local Authority Circular		

This section of the Handbook looks at:

Overview

1 Introduction

1. What does the Handbook include?

This Handbook is a comprehensive guide to social security and related benefits for disabled people, their families and their carers and the many professionals who work with them. It is aimed at disabled people, whether their impairment is physical, mental or sensory. You may find it helpful to start by looking at the benefits checklist on pages 4 and 5.

In addition to social security benefits and tax credits, the Handbook covers practical help and services and other essential matters including community care, income tax, council tax, housing grants and equality legislation.

2. What's new in this edition?

This year sees major changes to the benefits system wrought by the 2012 Welfare Reform Act. As the system has been targeted for £18 billion of public spending cuts, much of the content of the Act will have a negative impact on disabled people. Two key elements of the Act are the introduction of the *'personal independence payment'* and *'universal credit'* in April 2013.

Personal independence payment – This is replacing disability living allowance (DLA) for people of working age (ie people between the ages of 16 and 64 inclusive). The new benefit is described in Chapter 4. For details of the re-assessment process for existing DLA claimants, see Box B.6 in that chapter.

Universal credit – Several means-tested benefits and tax credits (child tax credit, housing benefit, income-related employment and support allowance (ESA), income-based jobseeker's allowance (JSA), income support, working tax credit and parts of the social fund) are being replaced with the universal credit. This is being piloted from April 2013 in north-west England; nationwide roll-out starts in October 2013 on the basis of one district in each Jobcentre Plus region. A new claim for one of the existing benefits may be treated as a claim for universal credit instead, depending on where you live. Universal credit is described in Box J.1 in Chapter 25

Other changes – Other significant changes explained in this Handbook include:

❑ New sanction regimes are in place if you fail to meet the work-related compliance conditions for ESA and JSA. See Chapters 10(17) and 16(9) respectively.

❑ A *'benefit cap'* is being rolled out nationally between 15.7.13 and 30.9.13, which will limit the total weekly benefits that can be claimed by people of working age. See Box H.1 in Chapter 21 for details.

❑ A *'bedroom tax'* reduces the amount of housing benefit that can be claimed if you are a working-age tenant of a local authority or housing association who is considered to have a spare bedroom(s). See Box H.4 in Chapter 21.

❑ Council tax benefit has been replaced with reduction schemes run by local authorities (and a new national scheme in Scotland). See Chapter 22(12) for details.

❑ Most of the discretionary social fund has been abolished. Budgeting loans are in place for the time being (see Chapter 24(2)). A new system of loans (*'short-term advances'*) while you are waiting for a benefit claim to be processed has been introduced (see Chapter 57(6)). Community care grants and crisis loans for all other circumstances have been replaced by a new service delivered by local authorities (see Chapter 24(1)).

❑ A new civil penalty system has been introduced where negligence has resulted in an overpayment. See Chapter 57(8).

❑ A mandatory revision process is being introduced. See Chapter 58(3).

New material – There are extended chapters on DLA for children (Chapter 3) and attendance allowance (Chapter 5), which include guidance on completing the claim-forms. There is extended material on the *'Access to Work'* scheme in Chapter 18(5).

3. Disability and benefits

Few of your rights depend on what your condition is called. In most cases, your entitlement to a benefit or service depends on the effect of the disability on your life. In addition to the disability tests and definitions listed below, there may be other criteria you must satisfy to get a particular benefit or service. Within the benefits and tax credits systems there are several different tests of disability:

■ **limited capability for work** – used for employment and support allowance;

■ **incapacity for work** – used for statutory sick pay, incapacity benefit, severe disablement allowance, income support and the unemployability supplement under the Industrial Injuries and War Disablement schemes. The tests of incapacity differ, depending on the benefit you claim;

■ **degree of disablement** – used for industrial injuries disablement benefit, war disablement pension and vaccine damage payments;

■ **at a disadvantage in getting a job** – used for the disability element of working tax credit.

Disability living allowance, personal independence payment and attendance allowance each has its own tests of disability; see Chapters 3(9), 3(14), 4(10), 4(12) and 5(8).

Two further definitions are in use:

■ **substantially and permanently disabled** – used for registering as disabled with a local authority social care department and for getting a disability reduction in your council tax;

■ **physical or mental impairment that has a substantial and long-term adverse effect on your ability to carry out normal day-to-day activities** – used to define those people covered by the disability sections of the Equality Act 2010.

The different categories of benefits

Benefits can be divided into three broad categories:

■ those that are intended to replace earnings;
■ those that compensate for extra costs;
■ those that help alleviate poverty.

The first category includes benefits that compensate you if you are unable to work because of sickness, disability, unemployment, pregnancy, retirement or caring responsibilities. In general, these benefits are not subject to a means test, but some will depend on your national insurance contribution record (see Box A.1).

Benefits intended to contribute towards the extra costs of disability are not means tested and do not depend on national insurance contributions.

Benefits intended to alleviate poverty by providing a basic income or topping up a low income are means tested.

2 The benefits system

1. Department for Work and Pensions
The Department for Work and Pensions (DWP) is responsible for most of the help available for disabled people. Responsibility for policy making lies with the DWP, while services are delivered and benefits administered by three operational organisations (see 2 below).

The DWP contracts out some of its functions to private companies; for example, Atos Healthcare and Capita are contracted to provide medical advice and examinations.

Tax credits, child benefit and guardian's allowance are administered by HM Revenue & Customs (see 5 below).

2. The structure of the DWP
The day-to-day running of the benefits system is undertaken by three operational organisations: Jobcentre Plus, The Pension Service, and the Disability & Carers Service.

Jobcentre Plus – Jobcentre Plus provides services to people of working age, administering most of the benefits they can claim through a network of local Jobcentre Plus offices. Jobcentre Plus aims to provide a work focus to the benefits system. The benefits it administers include employment and support allowance, income support and jobseeker's allowance.

The Pension Service – This provides services for pensioners and people planning for retirement. It administers the state pension, pension credit and winter fuel payments, through largely telephone-based pension centres. These centres are supported by a local service network that provides appointment-based meetings in such places as libraries and community centres as well as arranging home visits.

Disability & Carers Service – This service provides important benefits for disabled people and their carers. It administers disability living allowance, personal independence payment, attendance allowance, carer's allowance and vaccine damage payments through regional Disability Benefits Centres, plus three central units: the Blackpool Benefits Centre and the Carer's Allowance Unit and the Vaccine Damage Payments Unit in Preston. Initial contact for these benefits will usually be through the Benefit Enquiry Line (see Box A.2).

3. Northern Ireland
The Department for Social Development is responsible for social security matters, and benefits are administered by the Social Security Agency.

A.1 Types of benefit

Entitlement to benefits depends on your circumstances and may be affected by your income, savings and national insurance (NI) contribution record.

Means-tested benefits
The following means-tested or income-related benefits are affected by most other types of income and by the amount of savings you have. However, child tax credit and working tax credit are affected only by income from your savings, not by your actual level of savings. Your NI contribution record does not matter.
- Child tax credit
- Housing benefit
- Income-related employment and support allowance
- Income-based jobseeker's allowance
- Income support
- Pension credit
- Social fund
- Universal credit
- Working tax credit

Non-means-tested benefits
The following non-means-tested benefits are not usually affected by other money you have, although some are dependent on you earning a certain amount, whereas others can be reduced if you have earnings or an occupational or private pension. There are two types of non-means-tested benefits: non-contributory and contributory.

Non-contributory benefits
For these benefits, your NI record does not matter. Those marked (*) are dependent on you earning a certain amount. Carer's allowance can be affected by your earnings or your occupational or private pension. See the relevant chapter for details.
- Attendance allowance
- Carer's allowance
- Child benefit
- Disability living allowance
- Guardian's allowance
- Industrial injuries benefits
- Maternity allowance*
- Personal independence payment
- State pension: Category D
- Statutory adoption pay*
- Statutory maternity pay*
- Statutory paternity pay*
- Statutory sick pay*
- War disablement pensions

Contributory benefits
For these benefits you (or in some cases your partner) must have made sufficient NI contributions. See relevant chapter for details. Those marked (**) can be affected by your earnings or your occupational or private pension.
- Bereavement allowance
- Bereavement payment
- Contribution-based jobseeker's allowance**
- Contributory employment and support allowance**
- State pension: Categories A and B
- Widowed parent's allowance

Northern Ireland has its own legislation, and the structure and organisation of the system are different from that of Great Britain (GB). However, the legislation tends to mirror GB legislation and the rates of benefits and their qualifying conditions are similar.

4. Who's who in the benefits system

The services are organised in slightly different ways. What follows is an outline – you'll find further details in the chapters on the individual benefits. The rules about claims, payments, decision making and appeals are in Chapters 57 and 58.

In all cases, you have the right to expect a good standard of service. If you want to complain about something or have suggestions about how services could be improved, see Chapter 60.

Administrative staff

The people you talk to when you ring or visit a local office are not always legally responsible for making a decision on your claim. They will do the support and maintenance work for claims and may handle many routine claims, particularly for means-tested benefits, but decisions must, in law, be made by a decision maker authorised by the Secretary of State.

The Secretary of State

The Secretary of State for Work and Pensions is responsible for decisions on your social security benefit entitlement. In practice, this responsibility is delegated to decision makers who are officers acting under the Secretary of State's authority. In a few cases, the Secretary of State delegates decision-making responsibility to officers of HM Revenue & Customs (eg for some national insurance credits decisions).

Decision makers

Decision makers are officers acting under the authority of the Secretary of State. They make decisions on your entitlement to benefits but will not always be based in your local office. If you are not satisfied with a decision, you can ask for an explanation of the decision, ask for a revision of the decision, or appeal to an independent tribunal. The letter giving you the decision must always explain what you can do next. See Chapter 58 for more on decisions, revisions and appeals.

5. HM Revenue & Customs

HM Revenue & Customs (HMRC) is responsible for decisions on tax credits, child benefit and guardian's allowance, and these are made by officers based in the Tax Credit Office in Preston or the Child Benefit Office in Washington, Tyne and Wear. HMRC is also responsible for decisions on national insurance contributions and employer-paid benefits (statutory sick/maternity/paternity/adoption pay). Appeals on HMRC decisions are heard by First-tier Tribunals (see 6 below).

6. Ministry of Justice

The Ministry of Justice has responsibility for running the appeals system. It does this through the HM Courts and Tribunals Service, which provides common administrative support to the main central government tribunals: the First-tier Tribunals and the Upper Tribunals.

First-tier Tribunals – In addition to hearing appeals on decisions made by the Secretary of State for Work and Pensions (on benefits such as employment and support allowance, income support and personal independence payment), First-tier Tribunals also hear appeals against local authority decisions on housing benefit and HMRC decisions on tax credits, national insurance contributions and employer-paid benefits. First-tier Tribunals cover a range of other areas, including mental health reviews, care standards, criminal injuries compensation and special educational needs. The role and powers of the First-tier Tribunals are explained in Chapter 58.

Upper Tribunals – Upper Tribunals hear appeals against decisions of the First-tier Tribunals. Their decisions set precedents and form case law. Chapter 58(18) explains more about appealing to the Upper Tribunal.

A.2 Contacting the DWP

Details of local Jobcentre Plus offices are on the website (www.gov.uk/contact-jobcentre-plus). Claims for benefits administered by Jobcentre Plus can be made by contacting their claim-line (0800 055 6688; textphone 0800 023 4888). For details of pension centres, contact The Pension Service (0845 606 0265; textphone 0845 606 0285; www.gov.uk/find-pension-centre). Addresses of DWP central units are listed on the inside back cover of this Handbook.

Northern Ireland

To find your local social security office, look in the phone book under 'Social Security' or on the website (www.dsdni.gov.uk).

Benefit Enquiry Line (BEL)

This is a confidential telephone advice and information line for people with disabilities, their carers and representatives. It covers England, Scotland and Wales. BEL can provide general benefits advice and information, but staff do not have access to claimant records and are therefore unable to give information on the progress of a claim or benefits you are already receiving. It is a confidential service and nothing you ask or say will go on your file.

For certain disability-related benefit claims, staff can arrange to fill in your claim-form over the phone and send it to you to check and sign. The service covers carer's allowance, disability living allowance, personal independence payment and attendance allowance.

Ring the enquiry line on 0800 882 200 or textphone 0800 243 355. Lines are open 8am-6pm Monday to Friday. From a landline your call is free.

Northern Ireland Benefit Enquiry Line (BEL)

Ring 0800 220 674 or textphone 0800 243 787. Staff can provide general advice on benefits for disabled people and offer a forms-completion service. Lines are open 9am-5pm Monday, Tuesday, Thursday and Friday; 10am-5pm Thursday.

A.3. Keeping you up to date

Keep up to date by joining us. *Updates*, our bi-monthly *welfare and disability rights* newsletter includes updates to this Handbook, case law and information about proposed changes to benefits and tax credits.
- **Individual members** receive *Updates* and a 25% discount on the full price of next year's *Handbook*.
- **Member organisations** receive a free copy of the *Handbook*, 30% discount on the cost of our training courses for advice workers, *Updates* and access to our members-only benefits and tax credits advice service.

For information e-mail members@disabilityrightsuk.org or visit www.disabilityrightsuk.org/membership.

Next year's Handbook

The 39th edition of the Handbook will be published in May 2014. Orders can be placed from February 2014.

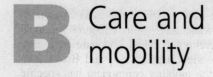

Care and mobility

This section of the Handbook looks at:

3   Disability living allowance

A. GENERAL POINTS

1. What is disability living allowance?
Disability living allowance (DLA) provides help towards the extra costs of bringing up a disabled child. It is paid on top of almost any other income you have and can give you access to other types of help (see Box B.1).

DLA is divided into two parts:
- **a mobility component** – for help with walking difficulties, paid at two rates. See 9 to 13 below.
- **a care component** – for children needing extra personal care, supervision or watching over because of a disability. It is paid at three different rates. See 14 to 19 below.

Your child can be paid either the care component or the mobility component on its own, or both components at the same time.

Adults claiming DLA – Prior to 10.6.13, DLA could also be claimed by people of working age (ie people between the ages of 16 and 64 inclusive). For people in this age group, DLA has now been replaced by the personal independence payment (PIP). Details of this new benefit are in Chapter 4.

If you are of working age and already have an award of DLA, you may continue to receive it for the time being, but will be re-assessed for PIP at some stage. See Box B.6 in Chapter 4 for details of the re-assessment.

If you were aged 65 or over at 8.4.13 and in receipt of DLA, you can continue to receive it as long as you satisfy the entitlement conditions. The PIP re-assessment will not apply.

For details of how DLA claims for adults differ from those of children, see 27 below.

2. Does your child qualify for DLA?
To qualify for DLA, your child must:
- pass at least one of the disability tests (see 9 and 14 below); *and*
- be within the age limits (see 3 below); *and*
- meet the qualifying periods condition (see 4 below); *and*
- pass the residence and presence tests, and not be subject to immigration control (see Chapter 49(2) and (3)).

A claim for DLA must be made (see 20 below). The DWP must also be satisfied there is nothing to prevent payment (see 6 below). If your child meets all these conditions, they will be entitled to DLA. They keep their underlying entitlement to DLA even if other rules mean they are not actually paid it.

3. Age limits
Lower age limit – There is no lower age limit for the DLA care component. However, since a three-month qualifying period usually applies (see 4 below), your child will normally not be paid the care component until they are 3 months old. For example, if your baby has severe feeding problems from birth, the qualifying period means payment can only start from the first pay day on or after the day they reach 3 months. If your child is terminally ill (see Box B.8 in Chapter 4 for the definition) the qualifying period will not apply, and they can be paid the care component from birth.

The higher rate mobility component can start from when your child reaches the age of 3 and the lower rate from the age of 5. Claims for the mobility component can be made earlier, but payment will not start until they have reached the appropriate age.
SSCBA, S.73(1A)

Upper age limit – From 10.6.13, there is an upper age limit of 16 for new claims. After this date, if the young person you care for has reached their 16th birthday and is not already receiving DLA, they will need to claim personal independence payment instead (PIP; see Chapter 4). If they are already receiving DLA and coming up to 16, the benefit they can claim on reaching that age will depend on the date of their 16th birthday.

If they reach 16 before 7.10.13, they will be asked to complete a DLA renewal form (see 28 below for the differences between DLA claims for children and those for adults). Once they are on DLA, they will undergo a re-assessment for PIP after October 2015.

If they reach 16 on or after 7.10.13, they will need to claim

PIP instead (you should be sent a letter explaining what will happen around five months before their birthday).

4. Qualifying periods
Backwards condition
To qualify for DLA, your child must pass the disability test(s) (see 9 and 14 below) throughout the three months before their claim. The claim can be made before the three months are up, but payment will not start until the qualifying period has been served.
SSCBA, Ss.72(2)(a) & 73(9)(a)

Renal dialysis – If your child has passed the dialysis test (see 19 below) during the three months before their claim, they have served the qualifying period. Spells dialysing at least twice a week in hospital or as an outpatient getting help from hospital staff always count for the purposes of this qualifying period.
DLA Regs, reg 7(3)

Linked claims – If your child re-claims DLA within two years of the end of a previous award, the claims are linked. This means if they have a relapse they don't have to re-serve the qualifying period. They can get DLA as soon as they re-claim, but only at the previous rate and component. If they qualify for a different amount, they will have to serve the qualifying period before it is paid.
DLA Regs, Regs 6(1) & 11

Forwards condition
Your child must be likely to satisfy the disability test(s) throughout the six months after their claim.
SSCBA, Ss.72(2)(b) & 73(9)(b)

Terminal illness
There is no qualifying period if your child is awarded DLA because they are terminally ill (see Box B.8 in Chapter 4). They will automatically get the highest rate care component. To get the mobility component they must pass one of the disability tests (see 9 below) from the date of claim.
SSCBA, Ss.72(5) & 73(12)

5. How much is DLA?
Your child can get one of the three rates of care component and one of the two rates of mobility component. They will always get the highest rate to which they are entitled. Payment of DLA is affected by some situations (see 6 below).

Mobility component	per week
Lower rate	£21.00
Higher rate	£55.25

Care component	per week
Lowest rate	£21.00
Middle rate	£53.00
Highest rate	£79.15

The disability tests for the mobility component are explained in 9 to 13 below. The disability tests for the care component are explained in 14 to 19.

6. Does anything affect payment?
Other benefits or help
DLA is usually payable in full on top of other social security benefits or tax credits.

DLA is ignored as income for means-tested benefits and tax credits. If your child is awarded DLA, check to see if you then qualify for housing benefit or child tax credit, or higher amounts of either of these benefits. See Box B.1 for how an award of DLA to your child may help you qualify for other types of help in cash or kind.

The care component may be taken into account in non-social security means tests, such as in charging for local authority services (discretionary rules) and care in a care home (national rules) – see Chapter 29(5) and Box L.2 in Chapter 34. However, the mobility component has specific protection against means testing – it can only be taken into account if the law (not policy or practice) governing such a test of means specifically states that the mobility component should count.
SSCBA, S.73(14)

If your child goes abroad
See Chapter 50(8) for details.

If your child goes into hospital or a care home
See 7 and 8 below.

7. If your child goes into hospital
Generally, payment of both the care component and the mobility component stops after your child has been in hospital for 84 days (12 weeks). Payment starts again from the first benefit pay day after your child leaves hospital. If they leave

---

B.1 DLA and other help

DLA acts as a gateway to other types of help. Listed below are the rates and components of DLA that provide entitlement to further help (if you pass any other tests there are for that help).

If your child gets DLA middle or highest rate care component, your family is also eligible for the help available if your child receives only the lowest rate. Similarly, if your child gets higher rate mobility component, your family is also eligible for the help available if your child receives only the lower rate.

Care component
❑ **Lowest rate**
■ Benefit cap exemption – see Box H.1, Chapter 21
■ Disabled child element (child tax credit) – see Chapter 19(4)
■ Disabled child premium (housing benefit) – see Chapter 25(8)
■ Parental leave from work – see Chapter 36(2)
❑ **Middle or highest rate**
■ Carer's allowance: carer test – see Chapter 7(2)
■ National insurance credits for parents and carers – see Box D.7, Chapter 12
■ Income support: carer's eligibility – see Box E.1, Chapter 15
❑ **Highest rate**
■ Enhanced disability premium: child (housing benefit) – see Chapter 25(4)
■ Severely disabled child element (child tax credit) – see Chapter 19(4)

Mobility component
❑ **Lower rate**
■ Benefit cap exemption – see Box H.1, Chapter 21
■ Disabled child element (child tax credit) – see Chapter 19(4)
■ Disabled child premium (housing benefit) – see Chapter 25(8)
■ Parental leave from work – see Chapter 36(2)
❑ **Higher rate**
■ Exemption from road tax – see Chapter 6(2)
■ Blue Badge – see Chapter 6(1)
■ Motability – see Box B.16, Chapter 6

hospital temporarily and expect to return within 28 days, they can be paid DLA for each day out of hospital (see Chapter 35(6)). If the first claim for DLA is made when your child is already in hospital, it cannot be paid until they leave. But it can then be paid for the full 12 weeks if they return to hospital, even if they do so within 28 days.

Back to hospital within 28 days? – If your child is readmitted to hospital, having been at home for 28 days or less since they were last in hospital, the number of days during each hospital stay are added together and payment of DLA stops after a total of 12 weeks.

You count days in hospital from the day after they are admitted to the day before they come home. Neither the day they go in nor the day they leave count as days in hospital.

Linked spells in a care home – For the care component, if your child goes into hospital straight from a care home, or after having been home for 28 days or less, the two periods are added together, and DLA stops after 12 weeks in total.

DLA Regs, regs 8 & 10, 12A-12C

8. If your child goes into a care home

Normally, your child cannot be paid the care component if they live in a care home but you should apply for it anyway. What counts as a *'care home'* is explained in Chapter 5(8) and usually includes a residential school. Once you establish that they pass the disability tests, they can be paid the care component for any day they stay in your home, including the day they leave and the day they return. For example, if they spend a weekend at home with you, coming home on Friday and returning on Sunday, they will be paid the care component for those three days. This chapter gives the main points about being paid the care component in a care home; Chapter 33(2) gives further details.

The mobility component is not affected by a stay in a care home.

Children entitled to the care component in care homes – Your child can receive the care component while in a care home if:

■ they are terminally ill and residing in a hospice, defined as *'a hospital or other institution whose primary function is to provide palliative care for persons... suffering from a progressive disease in its final stages'* (but not an NHS hospital);

DLA Regs, reg 10(6)&(7)

■ a local authority has accommodated them with someone in a private dwelling and they are under 16 and being looked after by the local authority or under 18 and accommodated due to their disability;

DLA Regs, reg 9(4)(a)&(b)&(5)

■ they are living outside the UK and being funded under the Education Act (such as at the Peto Institute Hungary).

DLA Regs, reg 9(4)(c)

The 28-day concession

If your child has been awarded the care component before they go into a care home, it can continue for up to 28 days. Payment may stop sooner if they have been in a care home within the previous 28 days. In this case, the different periods are added together and treated as one stay, and their care component will stop after a total of 28 days. You count a stay in a care home from the day after they enter to the day before they leave. Box B.13 in Chapter 5 shows how you can plan a pattern of respite care that allows them to keep their care component.

DLA Regs, reg 10(5)

Linked spells in hospital and a care home

Payment of the care component continues for the first 12 weeks in hospital but stops after 28 days in a care home. The following examples show how the linking rule works.

❑ If your child has been in a care home (eg residential school) for, say, six weeks, returns home for a week, and then goes into hospital, the care component is payable for their week at home and the first six weeks in hospital. This is because they have not yet had a linked spell in hospital or a care home of longer than 12 weeks – so they can be paid for the remainder of the 12 weeks they spend in hospital.

❑ If your child had been in a care home for 12 weeks or more and then went into hospital, the two spells are linked and they will not be paid the care component.

❑ If they have spent more than 28 days in your home, they have broken the link with any earlier spells in hospital or a care home (see Box B.13 in Chapter 5). If they go into hospital, they can then be paid for the first 12 weeks. If they go back to a care home they can then be paid for the first 28 days.

B. THE MOBILITY COMPONENT

9. The disability tests
Higher rate

To qualify for the £55.25 higher rate mobility component your child must be aged 3 or over. For tests 1, 2 or 3, they must be *'suffering from physical disablement'* (but if it is accepted that they have severe learning disabilities which have a physical cause, they may also qualify). Their *'physical condition as a whole'* must be such that:

No. 1 they are unable to walk (see below); *or*

No. 2 they are virtually unable to walk (see 11 below); *or*

No. 3 the *'exertion required to walk would constitute a danger to [their] life or would be likely to lead to a serious deterioration in [their] health'* (see below); *or*

SSCBA, S.73(1)(a); DLA Regs, reg 12(1)(a)

No. 4 they have no legs or feet (from birth or through amputation) (see 10 below); *or*

SSCBA, S.73(1)(a); DLA Regs, reg 12(1)(b)

No. 5 they have a severe visual impairment (see below); *or*

SSCBA, Ss.73(1)(ab) and (1AB); DLA Regs, reg 12(1A)

No. 6 they are both deaf and blind (see below); *or*

SSCBA, Ss.73(1)(b)&(2)(a); DLA Regs, reg 12(2)&(3)

No. 7 they are entitled to the highest rate care component and are severely mentally impaired with extremely disruptive and dangerous behavioural problems (see 12 below).

SSCBA, S.73(1)(c)&(3); DLA Regs, reg 12(5)&(6)

Lower rate

To qualify for the £21 lower rate mobility component your child must be aged 5 or over. It doesn't matter if they are able to walk but they must be *'so severely disabled physically or mentally that, disregarding any ability [they] may have to use routes which are familiar to [them] on [their] own, [they] cannot take advantage of the faculty out of doors without guidance or supervision from another person most of the time'* (see 13 below).

SSCBA, S.73(1)(d)

They must also show that either:

■ they require *'substantially more guidance or supervision from another person than persons of [their] age in normal physical and mental health would require'*; or

■ people of their age *'in normal physical and mental health would not require such guidance or supervision'*.

SSCBA, S.73(4A)

Unable to walk?

'Unable to walk' means not being able to take a step by putting one foot in front of the other. If your child has one artificial leg, their walking ability is considered when using it; they are unlikely to count as being unable to walk but they

may qualify on the basis that they are virtually unable to walk (see 11 below).

Effects of exertion
For the third disability test for the higher rate it is the exertion needed to walk that must cause the serious problem. How far your child can walk, were they to do so, is not relevant. What is relevant is the effect of the act of walking on their life or health. Children with serious lung, chest or heart conditions may qualify in this way.

The *'danger'* or *'serious'* deterioration does not have to be immediate (CM/23/1985). Although any deterioration in your child's health would not have to be permanent, their recovery would need to take a significant length of time or need some kind of medical intervention (eg oxygen or drugs) (R(M)1/98). If they would get better without medical intervention after a few days rest, they won't qualify. Danger from other causes besides the effort needed to walk (eg being run over) cannot be taken into account.

Severe visual impairment
Your child will be considered to have a severe visual impairment if their visual acuity (measured on an eye test chart called the Snellen scale) with appropriate corrective lenses if necessary, is:

- less than 3/60; *or*
- less than 6/60 and they have both a complete loss of peripheral vision and severely restricted central vision of no more than 10 degrees.

They must be certified as severely sight impaired or blind by a consultant ophthalmologist. If you have a CVI certificate of visual impairment for your child, this may provide enough information but if not, or if you tell the DWP that your child's eyesight has worsened, they may be referred for a sight test. If your child doesn't qualify for the higher rate on this basis, they may qualify for the lower rate (see 13 below).

Deaf and blind
Your child may qualify for the higher rate if they are blind and also profoundly deaf. It must be the case that because of those conditions in combination with each other, your child is *'unable, without the assistance of another person, to walk to any intended or required destination while out of doors'*. Blind is defined as 100% disablement resulting from loss of vision (with respect to an adult, this means loss of vision such that they are unable to do any work for which eyesight is essential). Deaf is defined as 80% disablement resulting from loss of hearing (where 100% is absolute deafness). An average hearing loss at 1, 2 and 3 kHz of at least 87dB in each ear counts as 80% disablement. Your child will be referred to a DWP healthcare professional to assess their hearing loss and loss of vision.

DLA Regs, reg 12(2)-(3); R(DLA)3/95; GB Regs, Sch 2; IIPD Regs, Sch 3, Part II

10. Other factors
In a coma
If your child's condition is such that they cannot *'benefit from enhanced facilities for locomotion'*, they won't be entitled to the mobility component. This generally only excludes children who are in a coma or whose medical condition means it is not safe to move them. If they can get out from time to time, they are not excluded from the mobility component.

SSCBA, S.73(8); R(M)2/83; CDLA/544/2009

The locality
The first three disability tests for the higher rate ignore the effect of where your child lives on their mobility. Therefore it is irrelevant if they live on a steep hill or far from the nearest bus stop.

DLA Regs, reg 12(1)(a)

Artificial aids and medical treatment
Your child will automatically qualify under the fourth disability test if they have no legs or feet, regardless of their ability to manage with prostheses. However, the first three disability tests for the higher rate do take into account your child's walking abilities when using suitable artificial aids such as a built-up shoe or a prosthesis. If there is an artificial aid or prosthesis that is *'suitable in [their] case'*, and they wouldn't be unable or virtually unable to walk if they used it, they will fail the test.

DLA Regs, reg 12(4)

If your child uses crutches and can only swing through them, rather than use them to walk with each leg able to bear their weight, then they are unable to walk.

R(M)2/89; CDLA/97/2001; [2010] EWCA Civ 962 (CoA 'Sandhu')

Painkillers do not count as an artificial aid. What counts is your child's walking ability under any painkillers or other medication they normally take, if it is reasonable to expect them to take it. For example, it may not be reasonable to expect a bulky nebuliser to be carried around, even though it helps when your child gets breathless (CDLA/3188/02). If you have refused treatment that might have improved your child's condition, that cannot be held against them: it is their ability to walk as they are that counts (R(M)1/95).

Terminal illness
If your child is terminally ill, although they are treated as passing the qualifying period for mobility component, they must actually pass one of the disability tests to be paid mobility component from the time that it is claimed.

11. 'Virtually unable to walk'
There are four factors to be taken into account in deciding whether your child is *'virtually unable to walk'*; the test is whether their *'ability to walk out of doors is so limited, as regards:*

- *the distance over which, or*
- *the speed at which, or*
- *the length of time for which, or*
- *the manner in which [they] can make progress on foot without severe discomfort, that [they are] virtually unable to walk'.*

DLA Regs, reg 12(1)(a)(ii)

Physical cause
The test of being *'virtually unable to walk'* looks only at physical factors that limit your child's walking and only at factors that restrict the act of walking outdoors on a flat surface and level ground, rather than, for example, where or when they walk outdoors.

Children with a severe learning disability who cannot meet the test described in 12 below may qualify for the higher rate as virtually unable to walk if the interruptions to their walking ability can be shown to be physical in origin (see Box B.2). If your child can walk but is often unable or afraid to do so, for example, because of mental illness, they may qualify for the lower rate instead (see 13 below).

If your child's walking is limited by pain or dizziness or some other symptom but their doctors do not know what is causing it or say there is no physical reason for it, it may be difficult for them to get the higher rate. However, a medical diagnosis is not necessary. Nor should decision makers assume that your child's disability must be psychological because no physical cause has been identified. They should consider all the evidence. But to get the higher rate, your child's pain, dizziness or other symptoms must have at least some existing physical cause. If it is entirely psychological, they will not qualify. On the other hand, the physical cause need only contribute a little (more than minimally) towards their walking difficulty. So they could qualify even if the pain

is made much worse by, for example, depression.
R(DLA)4/06; R(DLA)3/06

Severe discomfort

From the point your child starts to suffer severe discomfort walking outdoors, any extra distance they walk should be ignored (R(M)1/81 and CM/267/93). For example, they may be able to walk about 20 metres without too much pain or breathlessness, but this discomfort begins to get worse until eventually they are forced to stop. By the time they stop, they may be in agony. The first question is: at what point do they start to suffer what can be called *'severe discomfort'*? If it is at, say, 40 metres, then any extra walking should be discounted. The second question is whether or not the 40 metres they are capable of walking *'without severe discomfort'* is *'so limited... that [they are] virtually unable to walk'*.

'Severe discomfort' is subjective; different people have different pain thresholds and will show pain in different ways. Severe discomfort does not mean severe pain or distress; severe discomfort is a lesser problem than severe pain and is far from being excruciating agony, which would cause the most stoic person to stop walking.
R(M)2/92 (CoA: 'Cassinelli')

Severe discomfort includes *'pain'* or *'breathlessness'* – factors brought on by the act of walking (R(M)1/83). It does not include the screaming fits of an autistic child or other factors brought on by resistance to the idea of walking. Normally, severe discomfort has to be brought on by walking, not just by being outside (so that, for example, a child whose skin blistered badly on exposure to sunlight would not qualify). However, this does not mean any pain your child suffers must increase when they walk; if they are already in severe discomfort when they start walking, they can still qualify (R(DLA)4/04).

Distance, speed, time and manner

These four factors affect the ability to walk outdoors and will often be closely interrelated. There is no set walking distance to mark the difference between success and failure. The decision maker must look at the speed, time and manner of walking as well as the question of severe discomfort. For example, if your child has to stop, but then after a rest they can walk again without severe discomfort, that extra distance counts, but so does the extra time it takes (R(DLA)4/03).

Intermittent walking ability

If your child's walking ability varies from day to day, they may have difficulty showing that they are virtually unable to walk (including during the two qualifying periods).

It may help to keep a diary of their walking ability over a period of time. The fact that your child can walk on some days might not disqualify them. The question is whether or not the evidence about their walking abilities would allow a decision maker to consider that, looking at your child's physical condition as a whole, it would be true to say they are virtually unable to walk (including for the duration of the two qualifying periods).

12. Severe mental impairment

This way of qualifying for the higher rate mobility component is aimed at children with severe learning disabilities. If your child doesn't pass this test, they may pass the virtual inability to walk test. Box B.2 looks at how that test applies to children with learning disabilities. If your child fails both tests, they will probably pass the disability test for the lower rate (see 13 below).

To be entitled to higher rate mobility component on the basis of severe mental impairment, your child must satisfy all the following conditions:

■ they must be entitled to highest rate care component, even if it cannot be paid because they live in hospital or a care home. (This rules out children who receive only the middle rate care component because they sleep soundly and safely all night. If your child is in this situation, see Box B.2.); *and*
SSCBA, S.73(3)(c)
■ they suffer from *'a state of arrested development or incomplete physical development of the brain, which results in severe impairment of intelligence and social functioning'*; *and*
■ they *'exhibit disruptive behaviour'* that *'is extreme'*; *and*
■ they *'regularly require another person to intervene and physically restrain [them] to prevent [them] causing physical injury to [themselves] or another, or damage to property'*; *and*
■ their behaviour *'is so unpredictable that [they require] another person to be present and watching over [them] whenever [they are] awake'*.
DLA Regs, reg 12(5)&(6)

The DWP will normally obtain a specialist's opinion before awarding the higher rate on the basis of severe mental impairment.

'Arrested development' can apply to a child who has arrested emotional or functional development which has a physical cause, even if this is not related to the development of the brain (CDLA/1621/09). *'Incomplete physical development of the brain'* must take place before the brain is fully developed, which will be before the age of 30 (R(DLA)2/96).

An IQ of 55 or less is generally taken to be *'severe impairment of intelligence'*. But an IQ test is not the only measure of impaired intelligence. Some children, such as those with autism, may do well in abstract intelligence tests but cannot apply their intelligence in a useful way in the real world. For them, an IQ test can give a misleading impression of useful intelligence. Therefore, if IQ is above 55 or there is no IQ test, the decision maker must consider other evidence, including evidence of impairment of social functioning if that has an effect on useful intelligence. For example, having no sense of danger may indicate a severe impairment of intelligence (CDLA/3215/01).
R(DLA)1/00 (CoA: 'M')

You may have to show that the *'physical restraint'* your child needs to prevent them causing injury or damage involves more than just physical contact, such as a hand on the arm, and that they are likely to need restraining on a significant number of the times they walk outdoors.
CDLA/2470/06 but CDLA/2054/98 says otherwise

Your child must need watching over whenever they are awake due to their disruptive behaviour being so unpredictable. Because of this, they might have trouble passing the test if their home or school is structured so that their behaviour is no longer disruptive or they can be safely left alone behind closed doors. Emphasise the way in which their behaviour is disruptive despite such a structured environment. If they cannot be left alone anywhere while awake, but regularly need active intervention only in some places but not others, they can still pass the test (CDLA/2955/2008).

If you think your child satisfies each part of this disability test and is turned down, consider asking for a revision or lodging an appeal (see Chapter 58).

13. The lower rate

The lower rate mobility component is for children who can walk but who generally need someone with them to guide or supervise them on unfamiliar routes. It is particularly aimed at children with learning disabilities or those with a visual impairment not severe enough to qualify for the higher rate. However, other children can qualify, eg a hearing-impaired child may need such guidance or supervision.

Your child must show they need *'substantially more'* guidance or supervision than a child of the same age would require, or show that a child of the same age would not require such guidance or supervision. Although most young children need guidance or supervision in unfamiliar places, what matters is the nature and extent of your child's needs compared with another child of the same age.

SSCBA, S.73(4A)

For example, if a child lacks awareness of danger from traffic and other outdoor hazards, or could not give their

B.2 Learning disabilities

If your child does not qualify for higher rate mobility component on the basis of 'severe mental impairment' (see 12 in this chapter), they are likely to pass the test for the lower rate (see 13). However, some children who are autistic or have a learning disability may qualify for higher rate mobility component on the basis of 'virtual inability to walk' (see also 11).

'Virtually unable to walk'?

The need for help to get from one point to another and the purpose of walking are totally irrelevant to the 'virtually unable to walk' test. Instead, this test is tied to physical limitations on a child's ability to put one foot in front of the other and continue to make progress on foot. These physical limitations can include behavioural problems if they are a reaction to or result of the child's physical disablement (eg genetic damage in the case of Down's syndrome or brain damage).

The virtual inability to walk test looks at interruptions in the ability to make progress on foot. The interruptions must be accepted as physical in origin and part of your child's accepted physical disablement rather than, for example, being under their direct and conscious control. Thus, being able to put one foot in front of the other does not stop your child passing the virtual inability test. But you must be able to show that:

■ their behavioural problems, which may sometimes include a failure to exercise their powers of walking, stem from a physical disability; *and*

■ their walking difficulties, including interruptions in their ability to make progress on foot, happen often enough so that their walking is *'so limited... that [they are] virtually unable to walk'*.

Case law establishes two parts to the 'virtually unable to walk' test:

❏ The decision maker should consider separately the distance, speed, length of time and manner in which your child can make progress on foot (see 11). Any walking achieved only with severe discomfort must be discounted.

❏ If the decision maker finds your child *'virtually unable to walk'*, they must then decide whether that is attributable to some physical impairment such as brain damage, or to a *'physical disability which prevents the co-ordination of mind and body'*.

R(M)3/86

If your child has had a history of behavioural problems since birth, the decision maker *'should provide very clear reasons for attributing the behavioural problems in question to something other than brain damage'* [or Down's syndrome, etc].

CM/98/89

What can you do?

Provide evidence (from a GP, consultant, etc) to show that:

■ the learning disabilities have a physical cause (eg brain damage);

■ all the behavioural problems that interrupt outdoor walking stem directly from that physical cause; *and*

■ there is no deliberate and self-conscious choice to walk or not to walk. The interruptions are reactions to various stimuli and are the result of the brain damage or the genetic damage that caused the learning disabilities, and prevent or interfere with the normal co-ordination of mind and body.

You need to be able to give the decision maker a clear picture of your child's normal walking difficulties and the frequency of interruptions in their ability to make independent progress on foot. The idea is to present an objective picture of how they normally make, or don't make, progress on foot outdoors without active help from another person.

Focus on walking difficulties

In order to get a clear picture of your child's normal walking difficulties, we suggest you carry out a short outdoor walking test. Ensure the surface is reasonably flat. Choose a period of time that you consider long enough to get a good impression of your child's walking difficulties, be it one minute or ten minutes. Ask someone else to take notes if necessary.

For each test:

❏ Describe the place where you carry out the test. Mark the starting point. Note the time.

❏ Let your child loose. Don't actively intervene to help them walk. A gentle hand on the shoulder or words to help them go in the right direction is OK (to help overcome any fear because they cannot see where they are going). But don't give any physical support or restraint you wouldn't routinely expect to give to a non-disabled child of the same age (so you'll need to be sure the test place you choose is a safe one).

❏ Describe exactly what happens. Do they move at all? If yes, then how do they walk? Note what size steps they take; how they lift their legs; the speed of walking; changes in speed and in direction; their balance; and the effect of distractions. This all relates to the manner in which they walk, and the speed at which they walk.

❏ For each stop or interruption in their walking, note the time, mark the place and measure the distance from the starting point (or from the previous stop).

❏ Describe exactly what happened. Why do you think they stopped? Note the time they start to move on again. What made them move on? Or, why do you think they moved on? Give all your reasons.

❏ At the end of the period, mark the place they have reached and note the time. How far, in a straight line, is it from their starting point? If they didn't move in a straight line, also measure how far they walked or ran.

Note: If your child's walking ability is also limited by severe discomfort, do not continue with the test. As soon as they start to suffer what they, or you, consider to be severe discomfort, note the time and mark the place. Describe the severe discomfort that made them stop. Are there any physical changes in their appearance from when they started walking? Any breathing problems? Any outward and visible signs of their discomfort?

name and address if they got lost, or would become more disoriented or distressed than a child of the same age without a disability, all these might suggest a need for guidance or supervision beyond that normally required. A deaf child might need someone within reach watching out for them because they can't hear warnings or dangers (CDLA/2268/99). A non-disabled child may not need such close supervision.

Guidance
This means directing or leading. It can be physical (eg holding your child's elbow or putting a hand on their arm) or it can be verbal (eg telling them which turning to take or helping them avoid obstacles). It can also include persuasion or encouragement if they are feeling panicked and too afraid to continue (CDLA/42/94). If your child is deaf and cannot read enough to follow road maps or signs and cannot easily understand by lip reading, they may need someone with them to ask for directions or tell them which turnings to take (R(DLA)4/01).

Supervision
This means at least monitoring your child or the route for signs of a need to intervene, but can be more active than this (CDLA/42/94). If your child gets the middle rate care component for continual supervision to avoid danger, they could get the lower rate mobility component because of the same problems, but this is by no means automatic: you need to explain what supervision they need outdoors and how this enables them to get about (R(DLA)4/01). They may need supervision when out walking to avoid danger but this need not be the reason for supervision or guidance. What is important is that guidance or supervision enables them to overcome their mobility problems, whatever they are, and to take advantage of their ability to walk, which they would not otherwise be able to do.

Mental or physical disability
Your child's mobility problems must be due to physical or mental disability. If fear or anxiety prevents them from walking on unfamiliar routes, it must be a symptom of a mental disability.

If your child's anxiety is connected to a physical condition, but could nevertheless be described as a symptom of mental disability, they may still qualify. For example, a deaf child needing your reassurance to overcome anxiety about being on an unfamiliar route may qualify if their anxiety is classed as a mental disability.

DLA Regs, reg 12(7)&(8)

C. THE CARE COMPONENT

14. The disability tests
To qualify for the DLA care component your child's care needs must ultimately stem from disability; both physical and mental disabilities may help them qualify. They must need care, supervision or watching over from another person because of their disabilities.

Five different conditions apply to the care component. Your child must be *'so severely disabled physically or mentally that ... they require [from another person]'*:

during the day
No. 1 *'frequent attention throughout the day in connection with [their] bodily functions' or*
No. 2 *'continual supervision throughout the day in order to avoid substantial danger to [themselves] or others' or*
at night
No. 3 *'prolonged or repeated attention in connection with [their] bodily functions' or*
No. 4 *'in order to avoid substantial danger to [themselves]*

or others [they require] another person to be awake for a prolonged period or at frequent intervals for the purpose of watching over [them]' or
part-time day care
No. 5 *'[they require] in connection with [their] bodily functions attention from another person for a significant portion of the day (whether during a single period or a number of periods)'.*
SSCBA, S.72(1)

In each case they must show that *either:*
■ their needs are *'substantially in excess of the normal requirements of persons [their] age'; or*
■ they have *'substantial'* care, supervision or watching-over needs *'which younger persons in normal physical or mental health may also have but which persons of [their] age and in normal physical and mental health would not have'.*
SSCBA, S.72(1A)

The definitions of the words and phrases used here are explained below.

Which rate will they get?
Highest rate care component – Your child will pass the disability test for the £79.15 highest rate if they satisfy:
■ either (or both) No. 1 or No. 2 daytime conditions; *and*
■ either (or both) No. 3 or No. 4 night-time conditions.
Basically, their care or supervision needs are spread throughout both the day and the night. If your child is terminally ill, they qualify automatically for the highest rate (see Box B.8 in Chapter 4 for details).
Middle rate care component – Your child will pass the disability test for the £53 middle rate if they satisfy:
■ either (or both) No. 1 or No. 2 daytime conditions; *or*
■ either (or both) No. 3 or No. 4 night-time conditions.
Basically, their care or supervision needs are spread throughout just the day or just the night.

If they are undergoing dialysis two or more times a week and normally require some help with the dialysis, they may qualify automatically for the middle rate (see 19 below).
Lowest rate care component – Your child will pass the disability test for the £21 lowest rate if they satisfy the No. 5 part-time day care condition.

Definitions
Brief definitions are provided here. More detailed definitions are provided in Chapter 5; the information is applicable to DLA for children, as well as attendance allowance.
Attention – This means any active help from another person that your child needs to do the personal things they cannot do for themselves. To count as 'attention', the help they need because of their disability must be in connection with their *'bodily functions'.*
Bodily functions – These are personal actions such as breathing, hearing, seeing, eating, drinking, walking, sitting, sleeping, getting in or out of bed, dressing and undressing, going to the toilet, getting in or out of the bath, washing, communicating, speech practice, help with medication or treatment, etc. Anything to do with the body and how it works can count. See Chapter 5(9) for more on 'attention' and 'bodily functions'.
R(A)2/80
Continual supervision – *'Supervision'* is when there is a need for someone to be around to prevent accident or injury. *'Continual supervision'* means frequent or regular, but not non-stop; your child does not need to be supervised every single minute; see Chapter 5(10) for details. Supervision and attention tend to overlap; generally speaking, however, attention tends to be active help while supervision is more passive; see Chapter 5(11) for details.
Frequent – This means *'several times – not once or twice'.*
R(A)2/80

Prolonged – This has been interpreted as being at least 20 minutes.
R(A)2/80

Repeated – This means needed two times or more.
R(DLA)5/05

Significant portion of the day – This has been interpreted as being at least an hour, though not necessarily all at once.
CDLA/58/93

Less than one hour's care may still count as a significant portion of the day. In deciding this, your position as carer may be taken into account. If your own life is disrupted by the need to give attention for short periods of time on a considerable number of occasions in the day, then those periods of providing attention taken together may be significant, even though individually they may be relatively insignificant. Periods of intense, concentrated activity may be more significant than more routine tasks.
CSDLA/29/94; R(DLA)2/03 (CoA: 'Ramsden')

Substantial danger – This must be real, not just a remote possibility. But the fact that an incident may be isolated or infrequent does not rule it out. As well as looking at the chances of the incident happening, the decision maker must look at the likely consequences if it does. If the consequences could be dire, then the frequency with which it is likely to happen becomes less relevant.
R(A)1/83

Watching over – This has its ordinary English language meaning, so it includes when you need to be awake and listening, as well as getting up and checking how your child is. See Chapter 5(12) for details.

15. Extra care or supervision needs

Your child's needs must also be *'substantially in excess'* of what is normally required by a child of the same age, or your child must have substantial needs that non-disabled children of the same age would not have. This extra condition does not apply to children who are terminally ill.
SSCBA, S.72(1A)&(5)

Such needs might be 'in excess' of the care and supervision required by a non-disabled child because they are more frequent or take longer to attend to, or your child might need a greater quality or degree of attention or supervision. For example, a child who needs to be fed has needs in excess of a non-disabled child of the same age who just needs food cut up, even though both might need attention for the same length of time during meal times. To take another example, a child with disabilities might need someone watching them, whereas a non-disabled child of the same age might need someone around but it would be enough if they were in another room.

The extra condition demands a comparison between your child and non-disabled children of the same age. Children vary greatly, so comparison is made with an 'average' child. Your child's needs are 'substantially' greater if they are outside the range of attention or supervision normally required by the 'average' child, even though a particularly needy or difficult child might need the same level of attention or supervision. You might find it useful to compare your child's needs with those of school friends or brothers and sisters at that age.
CA/92/92

16. Infants (children under 1 year old)

DWP guidance, the *Children's A-Z of Medical Conditions* (see 22 below), states that because of the amount of care and supervision all infants need, the amount required by an infant with disabilities may not be much greater than that needed by a healthy infant, but may differ in kind. For example, instead of being handled in an ordinary manner, an infant with disabilities may need more specific stimulation or formal passive movements of the limbs in the form of physiotherapy but the amount of care or supervision may not be greater than that given to a healthy infant.
This guidance arguably runs counter to CA/92/92 above

The guidance lists those infants who will require considerable amounts of stimulation, care or supervision in addition to the normal care routine, including infants with:

■ frequent loss of consciousness usually associated with severe fits secondary to birth asphyxia or rare forms of congenital metabolic disease;
■ severe impairment of vision and/or hearing;
■ severe multiple disabilities;
■ severe feeding problems, which are due to physical reasons such as malformations of the mouth (eg cleft palate) or cerebral palsy; *and*
■ some infants with developmental delay or learning disabilities who require prolonged periods to take adequate amounts of each feed.

The guidance states that other categories of infants with disabilities may well require extra care, such as infants with renal failure, cystic fibrosis, asthma, cerebral palsy and survivors of extremely pre-term birth.

From birth
The guidance accepts that infants with disabilities involving the following types of actions or interventions will have attention or supervision needs from birth that may be greatly in excess of that required by a healthy infant. These are:

■ regular mechanical suction because they have a tracheostomy or other upper airway problem;
■ regular administration of oxygen;
■ tube feeding into the stomach or vein; *or*
■ dealing with a gastrostomy, ileostomy, jejunostomy, colostomy or nephrostomy.

17. Older infants and young children

The guidance in the *Children's A-Z of Medical Conditions* (see 22 below) clarifies that with older infants and young children (usually 9-15 months), the gap between the care needs of a healthy child and a child with disabilities may have widened to the extent that the needs of the child with disabilities are now significantly in excess of those of a healthy child of the same age. A child with disabilities may have continued attention needs no longer required by a healthy child of the same age. Alternatively, a child with disabilities may now need more attention for the development of new skills such as crawling, standing or walking.

The guidance goes on to list those groups of children with needs persisting or first appearing at a level greater than the norm for their age. The list includes:

■ children with brittle bones, haemophilia and other severe bleeding disorders at risk of fractures or haemorrhage from bumps and falls;
■ mobile children with hearing or visual problems who cannot respond to a warning shout or see a potential danger;
■ children with cerebral palsy whose mobility is impeded who need to have their position changed frequently in order to reduce the risk of postural deformity;
■ children with severe learning disabilities who need extra stimulation to maximise their potential, or who eat undesirable substances or mutilate themselves; *and*
■ children in whom developmental delay may first become evident because of a need to continue a level of attention appropriate for a much younger baby.

The guidance does not provide exhaustive advice and children with other needs may qualify. For example, it does not mention the care needs created by severe eczema/ichthyosiform erythroderma and similar skin conditions. These can involve a substantial amount of extra care – eg frequent bathing, nappy changing, applying preparations and dressings, and comforting a child whose sleep is disturbed.

Night needs in infants and young children

Guidance in the *Children's A-Z of Medical Conditions* points out that specific, regular attention at night in excess of normal levels may be required by some children with disabilities whose medical condition calls for parental intervention in the form of turning, nebulizer or oxygen therapy, suction, intubation and care during fits, etc.

It goes on to state that where such attention is not needed, if suitable precautions are taken (such as the child being safely placed in a cot), there may be few conditions requiring watching over that is substantially in excess of that needed by a healthy child of the same age. However, the guidance accepts that children with severe learning difficulties may have an abnormal tendency to develop a persistent habit of night wakening, in which case, attention may be required more than once a night for at least an hour each time.

18. Older children

The *Children's A-Z of Medical Conditions* advises that as children develop, both physically and mentally, there may be a reduction in their care needs; on the other hand, some care needs may increase.

A child with a physical disability may become more adept at using mechanical aids to move independently. Increasing maturity may lead some children with a chronic illness, such as diabetes, to assume responsibility for the care of their condition and so require less supervision. Training may help reduce needs, particularly for children with sensory impairments.

On the other hand, physical development may increase care or supervision needs: a child with a learning disability may need more supervision as they get older and become more mobile. Adolescents with disabilities may have to cope with care or mobility needs while undergoing rapid bodily change, often accompanied by the non-conforming or rebellious behaviour common among this age group.

19. Renal dialysis

Special rules for some children undergoing renal dialysis help them to qualify for middle rate care component. Depending on when and where they dialyse, they will be treated as satisfying the disability tests for the day or the night. The conditions are that:

- they undergo renal dialysis two or more times a week; *and*
- the dialysis is of a type which normally requires the attendance or supervision of another person during the period of the dialysis; *or*
- because of their particular circumstances (eg their age) during the period of dialysis they require another person to supervise them in order to avoid substantial danger to themselves, or to give them some help with their bodily functions.

DLA Regs, reg 7

For more details, see Chapter 5(14); the rules are the same for DLA.

D. CLAIMS, PAYMENTS & APPEALS

20. How do you claim?

Starting the claim – You can get a DLA claim-form (the *DLA1A Child*) by ringing the Benefit Enquiry Line (BEL – 0800 882 200; textphone 0800 243 355) or downloading one from the government website (www.gov.uk/dla-disability-living-allowance-benefit/how-to-claim). You can also claim online from that website. For advice on how to complete the claim-form, see Box B.3.

The date of claim – If you phone BEL, your child's DLA can be backdated to the date of your call. A claim-form issued by the DWP will be date stamped and provided with a postage-paid envelope addressed to the Disability Benefits Centre that

will be handling the initial claim. If you return the completed claim-form within the six weeks, the date you asked for the form counts as the date of claim. If you take longer than six weeks to return the completed form, explain why on the form. If the delay is reasonable, the time limit can be extended. If not, the date of claim is the day the completed claim-form reaches the Disability Benefits Centre.

If the claim is made online, you are given six weeks from the date you first accessed the claim online to submit your completed claim. If you submit it within the deadline, the date of claim will be the date you first accessed the online claim. If you download a claim-form from the government website, the date of claim is the day the completed form reaches the Disability Benefits Centre.

21. Keeping a diary

If your child is claiming DLA care component, keeping a diary of their day-to-day needs can improve their chances of success. It can also be important when trying to explain symptoms that fluctuate either during a single day or over a longer period.

One-day diary – The simplest form of diary would be an account of your child's needs over a typical day. Start from the time your child gets up in the morning, through a 24-hour period, ending with the time they get up the following morning. Try to list all the times when they need help from someone else. When you write something down, try to answer the following questions:

- what help do they need?
- why do they need the help?
- at what time do they need help? *and*
- how long do they need the help for?

The notes that come with the DLA claim-form provide an example of such a diary; see Box B.4 for another example.

If your child's needs vary from day to day, it would be worthwhile keeping the diary over a few days to get a clearer picture of their needs.

Long-term diary – Long-term diaries can be useful when explaining more sporadic problems that result from your child's condition, such as falls or fits. If they need continual supervision or watching-over to prevent substantial danger to themselves or others, such a diary can show exactly what happened, or what could have happened, if someone had not been there to stop it. See Box B.15 in Chapter 5 for an example of a long-term diary.

Making use of the diary

Once you have finished the diary, put your child's name and national insurance number at the top and make several copies of it. Attach one copy to the claim-form and keep one copy for yourself. If you are asking someone to complete the 'Statement from someone who knows the child' on the form, give them a copy also. Finally, you should send copies of the diary to anyone else you have listed on the claim-form, such as the paediatrician, GP or specialist nurse.

22. How the claim is assessed

Claims for DLA are handled first by one of the regional Disability Benefits Centres. Decisions are made by DWP decision makers, not by healthcare professionals. To help make decisions, the DWP uses online guidance: the *Children's A-Z of Medical Conditions*, which outlines the main care and mobility needs likely to arise from different illnesses and disabling conditions. It is available via our website (www.disabilityrightsuk.org/links-government-departments).

In the light of this guidance, the completed claim-form may give the decision maker enough information to make a decision. If not, the decision maker may request a short report from your child's paediatrician, GP or specialist nurse (or any other person you mentioned on the claim-form who is involved in your child's treatment or care). If your child is at school, the decision maker may request a copy of a statement of special education needs or an individual education plan from the school.

If any of these still do not provide a complete picture, the decision maker can arrange for a DWP-approved healthcare professional to visit your child at home and carry out a medical examination in order to prepare a medical report. Such a visit can also be arranged as an alternative to getting in touch with the paediatrician, nurse, etc.

The medical examination

Before the healthcare professional visits, read through the notes that came with the claim-form and the copy you made of the completed form.

During the visit, the healthcare professional should ask questions relating to each of the areas covered on the claim-form. This should include questions about your child's walking ability, their care and supervision needs, any difficulties they have seeing, speaking and hearing, whether or not they have fits, if they need extra help with their development, if they need help at school or nursery, and if they need help to take part in hobbies, interests, social or religious activities.

In the case of an infant or young child, the healthcare professional will put the questions directly to you. They may address an older child directly, depending on the nature of their impairment; you can add to what your child has to say in terms of the care you provide.

Ensure that the healthcare professional knows about any pain or tiredness your child feels when carrying out each activity. If you need to encourage or prompt your child to start or complete a task properly, ensure the healthcare professional is aware of this. Let them know about any variation in your child's condition and about both good and bad days. Show them any medical evidence you have confirming your child's problems.

The healthcare professional may then carry out a brief physical examination of your child.

After completing their medical report, the healthcare professional will send it to the decision maker, who will decide whether or not to award DLA and, if it is awarded, at what rate.

Delays

The DWP aims to give you a decision within 40 working days (ie not including weekends or public holidays) of the day they receive your child's DLA claim. If your child is terminally ill and the claim is being made under the 'special rules' (see Box B.8 in Chapter 4) you should get a decision within eight working days. Compensation may be payable for long delays (see Chapter 60(2) for details).

In any case, if the claim is taking too long, complain to the Customer Services Manager at the Disability Benefits Centre dealing with the claim.

23. The award

Once your child's claim is decided, you will be sent a notification of that decision. Any award made will be for a fixed period. This could be for just one year, or for a longer period if it is clear that the condition(s) giving rise to a need for help are likely to continue.

Backdating – DLA cannot be backdated to earlier than the pay day on or after the date of claim (see 20 above). There are only limited situations in which an earlier date can be treated as the date of claim, which are:

❏ If industrial action has caused postal disruption, the day the claim would have been delivered to a Disability Benefits Centre is treated as the date of claim.
C&P regs, reg 6(5)

❏ If a decision maker uses their discretion to treat anything written as being sufficient in the circumstances to count as a valid claim, the date of that earlier document is treated as the date of claim.

24. If you are not happy with the decision

If you are not happy with the decision on your child's claim, you can ask for a revision within one calendar month of the date the DWP sends you the decision. The decision letter should make it clear who to write to. With a revision, a decision maker will reconsider the claim. They can confirm the initial decision, or increase or reduce the rate of the award, or the length of the award. You have a further month to appeal to an independent tribunal if you are still not happy. The one-month time limit to ask for a revision can be extended only if there are special reasons for the delay. Otherwise, if the decision was notified to you more than one month ago, see below.

Asking for a revision – If you want to challenge the decision, you will need to know why it was made. You must also get your revision in on time. Ring the phone number on the decision letter and do the following:

■ request a revision of the decision. State your grounds simply at this stage; for example, *'I believe you have underestimated how my child's disability affects her and how much care and supervision she needs'*;
■ ask them to send you copies of all the evidence that was used in making the decision; *and*
■ ask them not to take any further action until you have had the chance to respond to that evidence.

Put your request in writing as well and send it to the address on the decision letter. Keep a copy for yourself. If you have not received the evidence after two weeks, ring again to remind them to send it. When you do receive the evidence, you should gain a better idea of why the decision was made.

Building a case

Sometimes the only evidence used will be the information you gave on the claim-form. In most cases, however, there will be a medical report as well. This could be a short one from your child's paediatrician, GP or specialist nurse, etc, or a longer one from a healthcare professional who examined your child on behalf of the DWP. Compare the report with the claim-form. Try to find where a difference of opinion arises.

For example: you may have written on the claim-form that your child could not feed themselves or wash and bathe themselves without support but the healthcare professional noted in their report that they considered that your child could manage these tasks unassisted. Now try to get medical evidence that shows that what you said on the claim-form is correct, for example a letter from your child's paediatrician, for example, confirming the difficulties that your child has with washing, bathing and feeding and why you need to provide them with help doing these things.

Once you have obtained some supportive evidence, make a copy of it and send this off to the address on the decision letter. If it is likely to take a while to obtain the evidence, you must tell the DWP how long this is likely to take, so they do not make a decision straight away.

A decision maker will look at any further evidence that you send in. They will then either revise the decision in your child's favour or write back explaining that they have been unable to change the decision. In this case all is not lost, as you now have a month from the date of the new decision to lodge an appeal to an independent tribunal. For more on appeals, see Chapter 58.

If the decision was notified more than one month ago

To challenge a decision notified more than one month ago (or if there has been a change of circumstances), you need to show there are specific grounds, eg:

B.3 Completing the DLA claim-form

The bulk of the DLA claim-form is given over to a series of questions relating to your child's mobility and their care and supervision needs. These questions have a tick box format; in each case there is a list of statements and you are asked to tick the box next to the statement that best describes how your child manages. There is space to give more detail of your child's difficulties. Read the claim-form notes before answering the questions, as they give an idea of what to say and provide examples of answers. We focus below on some of the questions in more detail.

Mobility questions
Do they have physical difficulties walking?
The first questions relate to the higher rate of the mobility component. This is for children aged 3 or over. Read 9 and 11 in this chapter before answering them.

You are asked to tick the boxes that best describe how far your child can walk without severe discomfort, how long it takes them, what their walking speed is and the way they walk. If you are not sure which to tick, you can do a test of your child's walking ability outdoors. Ensure the surface is reasonably flat. Focus on: the distance they can walk, their speed, the time it takes them and the manner of their walking. Ask them to walk until they feel they can no longer continue (if it is safe for them to do so). Record what happens and when in terms of distance and time (the notes that come with the claim-form give you tips for estimating distances correctly). Include factors such as pain, dizziness, coughing, spasms, uncontrollable actions or reflexes, breathlessness or asthma attacks. Note how long it takes them to recover before they can walk again. Transfer your findings to the claim-form.
Severe learning difficulties – If your child has severe learning difficulties and behavioural problems, they may qualify for the higher rate of the mobility component (the conditions are set out in 12 in this chapter). Use this part of the claim-form to describe your child's behaviour when they are walking outdoors and how this limits the distance they can walk. You could carry out the short outdoor walking test described in Box B.2.

Do they need guidance or supervision most of the time when they walk outdoors?
This question relates to the lower rate of the mobility component and is for children aged 5 or over. Read 13 in this chapter before answering. You must be able to show that the help your child needs is additional to other children of the same age. Try to give examples, eg: *"I have to hold their hand all the time because I never know what they're going to do next – my friend's 6-year old can run ahead and knows to wait at the next road."*

You are asked if your child falls due to their disability. A long-term diary may help to show how often your child has fallen recently and what happened when they fell; you can attach a copy of the diary to the claim-form. See Box B.15 in Chapter 5 for an example of a long-term diary.

Care questions
These questions relate to the care component and are for children of all ages. If your child is under the age of one, read section 16 in this chapter before completing the questions; if they are a young child, read 17; if they are an older child, read 18. Also read the notes that come with the claim-form; these explain what is relevant for each question and provide examples of answers.

The first questions relate to different areas of day-to-day life. Each question has a box where you can give more detail, such as why your child needs the help and how their needs vary. Think about all the things you do to help your child and compare this to the help a non-disabled child of the same age would need. For instance, if you have older children, what were they like at that age? Or, compare to a friend's child or others at nursery or school. Write down if things take longer with your child or you have to do more to help them.

If your child's condition is variable, do not focus just on good days. You need to explain what help your child needs on a regular basis. Try to focus on an average day and list the problems your child faces more often than not. Also, explain what your child is like on their worst days and how often these occur. You may find that a diary helps deal with these points (see 21 in this chapter).

Do they have difficulty seeing/hearing?
Two questions focus on seeing and hearing difficulties. If you have a certificate of visual impairment or an audiology test report for your child, you can attach a copy of it to the claim. Because there may be so many different things you need to do for your child if they have visual or hearing problems, it may be easier to write a one-day diary to list them (see Box B.4). If your child has difficulty communicating due to visual or hearing problems, you can explain these in the next but one question.

Do they have difficulty speaking?
Your child may have limited speech, perhaps because of a hearing impairment or learning disability. They may have an odd tone or speed of voice, unusual vocabulary, or limited or no body language which makes it difficult to understand them. You can provide more details of how their speech problems affect their ability to communicate in the next question.

Do they have difficulty and need help communicating?
This question is about difficulties your child has communicating. Here we look at three types of problem:
Understanding others – If your child has a hearing impairment, they may have difficulty understanding others who do not sign, or they may not be able to lip-read people they do not know well. Children with learning disabilities may rely on non-verbal communication and find strangers difficult to understand. They may misread the body language of others; eg they may not be able to tell when someone is angry or upset. If your child is confused by figures of speech (eg *I'm fed up to the back teeth*) or finds long or complex sentences difficult, write this down.

Your child may need someone to interpret what another person is saying or to repeat it several times or rephrase it into simpler language. Try to give an idea of how much longer it takes your child to understand something compared to other children, eg *'David finds lip-reading strangers really tough – they always have to repeat themselves four or five times and even then he only gets about half what's said – he's always doing the wrong thing because he hasn't understood properly.'*
Being understood – Explain the difficulties your child has being understood and how it affects them, for example they may get very frustrated. What do you do to help them be understood and deal with the frustration? For example, you may interpret for them or encourage them to say things again or in different ways or to speak more clearly. Your child may communicate by signing or other non-verbal communication and needs someone to interpret what they are saying.
Unwilling to communicate – Does your child live in their own world and show little inclination to communicate? Do they find it easier to talk to adults and only about their own

limited topics of conversation? Would they like to talk to other children but lack the skills or confidence, or do they get frustrated or angry when they try to communicate?

Write down the help you need to give them. For example, you may encourage your child to talk about different things or help them in conversations with other children to build their skills and confidence. You may do exercises or games at home designed to build their communication skills.

Do they have fits, blackouts, seizures, or something similar?

You could keep a diary over a period of time to show how often your child has fits or blackouts and what happens when these occur; *attach a copy of the diary to the claim-form.* Box B.15 in Chapter 5 has an example long-term diary.

Do they need to be supervised during the day to keep safe?

This question looks at the level of supervision that your child requires; read section 14 in this chapter and Chapter 5(10) before completing it.

All children need some supervision, particularly very young children, so you need to show that your child needs additional supervision; see 15 in this chapter. Write down examples of incidents such as falls, fits or asthma attacks. Were injuries sustained? Was anything broken? Or did your intervention prevent such occurrences. Keeping a long-term diary of such incidents can help, a copy of which you can attach to the claim-form.

You may have to monitor your child's diet more closely because of diabetes, a severe food allergy, or an eating disorder. If your child has a skin condition, they may need monitoring to stop them scratching. With conditions such as diabetes, older children might be expected to monitor themselves, but there can sometimes be a lack of acceptance of the condition, which leads to rebellious behaviour requiring more supervision.

Do they need extra help with their development?

This question is about what you do to help your child understand the world around them and react to it appropriately. Here we look at four areas of development:

Physical or sensory skills – List any difficulties your child has moving around (eg sitting, standing, running, walking or crawling) and any problems with coordination and manipulation (eg holding a pen or cutlery, picking things up, throwing or kicking). Write down if you need to help them with exercises to develop these skills, how long they take and how often they need to be done.

If your child has a visual impairment, it may be more difficult for them to learn about the world around them; you may have to spend more time making physical contact with them and speaking to them to ensure they get enough stimulation. Or, if they have hearing impairment, you may have to teach them sign language and make extra effort to communicate (eg by ensuring you are in the same room, facing them and they can see you clearly).

Learning skills – Write down if your child has difficulty learning everyday skills, such as dressing and washing, learning to read and write, or if they find it difficult to understand or follow instructions. Or maybe they can learn skills, but have difficulty applying them to other appropriate situations, eg; *'He knows how to ask at the newsagents for his comic and to pay for it, but if I ask him to go to the shop and get something else, he can't do it, he can't see that it's the same thing.'* Explain what sort of extra help they need; this may be physical help or verbal encouragement. Say how long it takes and how your child reacts.

Social skills – If your child has difficulty in social situations, write this down. For example, they may spend time on their own and avoid contact, their behaviour to others might be aggressive or inappropriate, they may lack empathy or the ability to read body language, or they may talk to people and not understand the rules of turn-taking. You might encourage them to respond to people when asked a question and to maintain eye contact, or read 'social stories' with them to help them understand people's responses. Explain that it is important for your child to learn these skills to prevent isolation or bullying in the future.

Play – Does your child find it difficult to play with other children or can they be aggressive; do they need adult involvement when they play; do they have physical difficulty holding toys or seeing where they are; do they lack imaginative play and have a tendency to be obsessional; do they have difficulty maintaining their interest in any activity? Explain the help you give them. For example, encouraging your child to keep interest in a particular game, showing them different parts of a toy and helping them hold or feel it, asking questions to develop their imagination, or intervening to prevent them hurting themselves or someone else. Do you have special games to play with them to develop certain skills, eg social, manipulative or language skills?

Two questions follow: *'Do they need encouragement, prompting or physical help at school or nursery?'* and *'Do they need encouragement, prompting or physical help to take part in hobbies, interests, social and religious activities?'* (see the notes that come with the claim-form for a good list of hobbies, etc). Try to provide as much information as you can. You may need to use extra paper; if you do, put your child's name and national insurance number on each sheet. You may want to cross-refer to what you have already written for other questions (particularly the one on development; see above).

Do they wake and need help at night, or need someone to be awake to watch over them at night?

Read 14 in this chapter and the notes that come with the claim-form before answering this question. If your child needs help at night with the sort of things they need help with during the day (eg using the toilet), you can cross-refer to the questions you have already answered.

If you need to do extra checks on your child in the night, say why. Do they get up and wander? What sort of things do they do – could they hurt themselves or others? Are they liable to fits or seizures at night or to have breathing problems? Do you need to check medical equipment? Try to say how often you need to check on your child or, if you sleep in the same room to keep an eye on them, explain why this is necessary.

Statement from someone who knows the child

The claim-form includes an optional part to be completed by someone who knows your child; this could be their paediatrician or specialist nurse. However, if a lot of your child's problems are learning related, a teacher or specialist support worker would be equally appropriate. If possible, make an appointment with them so you can discuss the matter. The Child Poverty Action Group has a useful factsheet listing the points that should be covered in the statement.

B.4 One-day diary

This is a diary for a 10-year-old girl, Ayesha, who has cerebral palsy

6.30-6.40am Wake Ayesha up – doesn't want to get up but has to get up early so time to do her physio before school – watch over her as she gets out of bed – just needs a hand to steady her as she gets up and gets her sticks.

6.48am Bit of trouble getting the toothpaste out – too much – help her clear it up.

7.05am Breakfast – Ayesha pours the cereal into her bowl – bit spilt but not too bad today – I do the milk.

7.25-7.45am Help her get cleaned up after breakfast – she always gets dressed after as can be a bit messy. She gets a bit frustrated getting her clothes on – takes a few attempts – I chat to her to keep her calm and encourage her along. She wants me to do it but I encourage her to do what she can but give her a hand with the buttons on her school shirt and her socks.

7.55–8.20am Help Ayesha with physio – she's not keen but I do it alongside her and put her favourite CD on and try to make it more fun.

8.45-8.55am Off to school – needs a bit of help climbing in the car. Drive up – have to park in the teacher's car park, help her out and see her into school. Most of her friends walk up or get dropped at the gate but that's too far for her. She tries to lean on me as we go in but I encourage her to use her sticks.

9.00am-3.30pm At school. Ayesha has support worker for two hours a day – she helps her with PE and getting dressed and undressed, speech, and handwriting as she has difficulty with fine motor control. She also helps her keeping focused – because she gets tired easily she has difficulty concentrating.

3.30-3.45pm Pick Ayesha and her friend up – help her into car and out again when we get home.

3.50pm Girls watching TV while I make the tea – Ayesha gets really tired at school and finds it hard to do much when she gets in.

5.00-5.25pm Tea – I cut up Ayesha's food for her – she feeds herself but gets a bit frustrated when she keeps dropping it – also she gets embarrassed in front of her friend – I chat away to them both to help the moment pass.

5.40-6.30pm Ayesha's friend goes home and we have to do physio again – she's tired but I push her – by the end she's very tearful so we cut it short – sit and have a cuddle instead.

6.40-7.25pm Homework – takes Ayesha a lot longer – writing takes a lot longer for her and she gets very tired with concentration needed – it's a big effort and she needs lots of encouragement and praise. Do what we can but don't manage to finish it.

7.30-8.00pm Watch Eastenders.

8.05-8.25pm Bath – help Ayesha in – leave her to it and she shouts when she's ready to get out. Help her out of the bath. Give her a hand getting dried – she can do it but it takes a bit longer and she's getting cold. Give her a hand with pyjamas – she's getting tired now.

8.35pm Make her bedtime drink.

8.50pm Ayesha goes up to bed – listens to a story tape – she likes to read but finds turning the pages of a book difficult when she's tired.

2.20am Ayesha calls out – needs toilet – go to help her out of bed and get to the toilet and then back again – she's a bit sleepy to manage with her sticks.

■ there has been a change of circumstances since the decision was made – eg your child's condition has deteriorated and their care needs have increased; *or*
■ the decision maker didn't know about some relevant fact – eg you missed out some aspect of your child's care needs or mobility difficulties when you filled in the claim-form.

See Chapter 58, Box T.5 for more details.

25. How is DLA paid?

DLA is usually paid every four weeks in arrears, on a Wednesday, into your bank, building society or Post Office card account. If your child is terminally ill, DLA is payable once a week.

26. What if your child's condition changes?

If your child's condition gets worse – If your child already receives DLA, give the Blackpool Benefits Centre details of the change (see inside back cover for contact details). They will usually send you a claim-form to complete; similar to that used for new claims (see Box B.3).

Your child's existing award may be superseded to include a higher rate or a new component. A top-up claim for the component they do not already have does not count as a new claim, but rather as a change to their existing award. (See also 24 above under 'If the decision was notified more than one month ago'.)

If your child's condition improves – If your child's need for care or their mobility difficulties lessen, this could mean the rate of their DLA should drop. Contact the Blackpool Benefits Centre to give them details. A decision maker will usually supersede their award.

If your child's rate of DLA drops (or ends) but they have a relapse within two years, they can regain their former rate of benefit in a linked claim without having to serve the qualifying period again.

DLA Regs, regs 6 & 11

E. DLA FOR ADULTS

27. How is DLA different for adults?

The rules for DLA for people aged 16 or over are broadly the same as for children. There are two significant differences.

First, if you are aged under 16, additional tests apply to the care component and the lower rate mobility component. In either case you must show that *either*:
■ your needs are *'substantially in excess of the normal requirements of persons [your] age'*; *or*
■ you have *'substantial'* needs for care, supervision or watching-over *'which younger persons in normal physical or mental health may also have but which persons of [your] age and in normal physical and mental health would not have'*.

These tests no longer apply once you reach the age of 16.

Second, if you are aged 16 or over, there is an additional way of qualifying for the lowest rate of the care component. This is where *'[you] cannot prepare a cooked main meal for [yourself] if [you have] the ingredients'*. Details of the 'cooking test' are in Box B.5.

SSCBA, S.72(1)

There are further differences if you are aged 65 or over, when the rules for DLA replicate those for attendance allowance (see Chapter 5). Attendance allowance has no equivalent to the mobility component or the lowest rate care component. There is a 6-month qualifying period (rather than a 3-month qualifying period; see 4 above). The differences have implications for renewal and top-up claims for DLA.

B.5 The cooking test

Once you reach the age of 16, you can qualify for the lowest rate of the DLA care component on the basis of the 'cooking test'. The upper age limit for starting to qualify for the first time is the day before your 65th birthday. But if you claim before your 65th birthday, the lowest rate can be maintained and renewed.

To satisfy the cooking test you have to show that you are 'so severely disabled physically or mentally that... [you] cannot prepare a cooked main meal for [yourself] if [you have] the ingredients'.
SSCBA, S.72(1)(a)(ii)

The cooking test is intended to be a hypothetical test. It is intended to gauge the level of disability rather than examine your ability to cook. The test looks at whether you can carry out all the activities necessary to prepare a cooked main meal without help from another person.

What does the cooking test involve?

There are a number of different issues involved in the cooking test. The nature of the 'cooked main meal' that you must show you 'cannot prepare' for yourself is crucial. It should be a labour-intensive, reasonable, main daily meal, freshly cooked on a traditional cooker. The main daily meal is intended to be a standard meal for just one person, not for the rest of the household.
R(DLA)2/95

The use of the word 'prepare' in the law puts the emphasis on your ability to prepare all the ingredients ready for cooking. The meal is not intended to be a main meal made up of convenience foods, such as pies and frozen vegetables, that involve no real preparation.

You 'cannot prepare a cooked main meal for [yourself]' if you can only do so with some help. The need for any type of help counts – it doesn't have to involve any effort or be at all substantial. But it must be crucial in enabling you to start or carry on with the tasks you are capable of doing by yourself. The cooking test also covers people whose disabilities mean they cannot cook at all, even if they had help.

What kind of meal is reasonable (eg vegetarian) depends on the community to which you belong. Because this is a hypothetical test, it is irrelevant that you may never wish to cook such a meal or you can't afford to do so. Nor is it relevant that you prepare, cook and freeze a number of main meals on the days you actually have the help you need (and then defrost and heat them up in the microwave on the other days). The test depends on what you cannot do, without help, if you tried to do it on each day.

If you would be limited to cooking a very narrow range of main meals you should pass the test (CDLA/17329/96).

Intermittent disability – You don't have to show you were unable to cook on every day of the three months before your claim and are likely to be unable to cook on every day of the next six months. The test is rather about what can be seen as normal for you over a period of time. Taking the ordinary English language meaning of the words, and applying the test to the effects of your disabilities, is it true to say that (over the 9-month period) you 'cannot prepare a cooked main meal...'?
R(A)2/74; R(DLA)7/03 (HoL: 'Moyna')

The ability to cook a main meal on four out of seven days each week does not mean, in law, that you must fail the test. All depends on the pattern of what you cannot do over the whole of the qualifying period. You may still have difficulties on your good days that can tip the balance your way, in which case you should explain fully what you can't do on both your good and bad days. In practice, if you say

on the DLA claim-form that you need help on one to three days only, your chances of success are much lower.

Reasonableness – The test is one of whether you cannot reasonably be expected to prepare a cooked main meal for yourself. Things like safety, tiredness, pain, nausea, breathing difficulties in a hot, steamy kitchen or the time it would take you to do everything may mean that although you can, in fact, prepare a cooked main meal, it is not reasonable to expect you to do so (see R(DLA)1/97). If you can't stand for long enough, it may be suggested that you could use a stool. This might be reasonable if all you had to do was wait for a pan to boil, but you might not reasonably be able to peel or chop (eg you might only have the strength and leverage to cut vegetables from a standing position), stir or check food or move pans about on the cooker (see R(DLA)8/02 and CDLA/1714/2005).

Special equipment – The cooking test doesn't depend on the type of facilities or equipment you have available. The test is satisfied if you can't perform the tasks necessary to prepare a main meal using normal reasonable facilities and devices (R(DLA)2/95). Whether you could manage by specially adapting the kitchen or making other arrangements is irrelevant. Being able to heat convenience food in a microwave is not relevant. However, if you know how to and do use a microwave to cook main meals with ingredients you prepare yourself, you might not pass the test. If you use a microwave in this way, explain any drawbacks, eg can you only cook a narrow range of meals or do ingredients cooked first need to be kept warm and, if so, are you able to use a low oven?

Practice and process

To produce an edible cooked main meal calls for the ability to carry out, by yourself, all the physical and mental actions, tasks and stages involved in the process. If there is any part of the process you are (or would be) unable to carry out by yourself, you'll pass this test – even if you cope (or would cope) well with the rest. See R(S)11/81 for support.

If you have a severe mental disability and therefore cannot plan ahead or complete complex tasks, you will pass the cooking test. If lack of motivation is caused by, or is a symptom of, a mental disability, so that you cannot begin to prepare a meal or complete the preparations, you could pass the test (CSDLA/80/96).

The process of preparing a cooked main meal includes:
- planning what to prepare for the cooked main meal – eg each type of food and seasoning, and the quantities required. The law says you already have the ingredients for the main meal, so it's debatable whether or not preparation also includes getting them from their usual storage places;
- carrying out all the stages in the correct order and to the required timings;
- washing, peeling and chopping vegetables, meat, etc;
- using taps – eg to fill a saucepan;
- using a cooker – eg lighting the gas, adjusting the heat, opening and closing an oven door;
- putting the food into pans, stirring, tasting, checking whether it's properly cooked;
- lifting and moving full pans on or off a cooker (you are usually expected to use a slotted spoon to drain vegetables, but explain any difficulties moving pans despite this);
- bending to lift pans into or out of the oven (explain why it is reasonable for you to want to use the oven – eg to prepare a reasonable variety of suitable meals – or to use a low-level grill); and
- dishing up your meal.

Renewal and top-up claims from age 65

If a DLA award ends after you reach 65, you can make a renewal claim within one year of your previous award ending. If you leave it longer than a year, you have to claim attendance allowance instead. You can only re-claim your former rate of mobility component under this concession – you cannot switch rates after 65.

Care component – You can maintain or renew the lowest rate if you qualified for it before reaching 65. If your care needs lessen after 65, you cannot drop to the lowest rate – you will lose the care component altogether. You can, however, regain the lowest rate if you re-claim within 12 months of an earlier award for it ending. If your care needs change after you reach 65, you can switch between the middle and highest rates or move up from the lowest rate, but you must satisfy the 6-month qualifying period.

DLA Regs, Sch 1, para 3(2)&(3)

There is an exception that allows the DWP to drop you to the lowest rate even if you pass the disability test after age 65. This applies if the DWP decides you were not entitled to the rate you were getting before you reached 65 because the original decision maker did not know about, or made a mistake about, a fact in your case (rather than because your circumstances have changed).

CDLA/301/2005

If you receive the mobility component, a change in your care needs after you reach 65 enables your DLA award to be 'superseded'. This means you can claim the care component (at middle or highest rate), rather than attendance allowance, even if you are aged, say, 70. You can still claim the lowest rate care component after age 65 if you met the qualifying conditions before 65 and have a current mobility award made before 65.

DLA Regs, Sch 1, para 7; CSDLA/388/00

Mobility component – Once you reach 65 you can only stay on the rate you got before you were 65. You cannot move up or down a rate. But there is an exception: you can switch to the higher rate after age 65 if you can show that you met the higher rate conditions before age 65.

If you have a current award of the care component, made before you were 65, you can claim the mobility component after your 65th birthday if your mobility difficulties began before you were 65. If your mobility problems are such that you can only satisfy the disability test after your 65th birthday, you cannot get the mobility component.

DLA Regs, Sch 1, paras 1, 5 & 6; CSDLA/388/00

Disability Rights UK training

Personal Independence Payment

New for 2013, this course will tell you all you need to know about the new benefit which will affect over 2 million people.

Suitable for new or non-specialist advisers it covers:
- who can claim PIP
- PIP and DLA: similarities and differences
- the points-based assessment
- the PIP timetable and 'migration' from DLA
- PIP and 'passports' to carer's allowance and other benefits

In-house training

Can't come to us? We can come to you.
To discuss in-house training tailored for your organisation contact sarah.cosby@disabilityrightsuk.org

For details visit www.disabilityrightsuk.org

---

4 Personal independence payment

A. GENERAL POINTS

1. What is personal independence payment?

Personal independence payment (PIP) is a new benefit for people who need help participating in everyday life or find it difficult to get around. It replaces disability living allowance (DLA) for people of working age (ie people between the ages of 16 and 64 inclusive). See below for details of when it is being introduced.

PIP is tax free, not means tested and you do not need to have paid national insurance contributions to be entitled to it. It is not affected by earnings or other income. It is almost always paid in full on top of other social security benefits or tax credits. PIP has two components:
- **a daily living component** – for help participating in everyday life;
- **a mobility component** – for help with getting around.

You can be paid either the daily living component or the mobility component on its own, or both components at the same time.

WRA 2012, S.77(2)

Each component is paid at two different levels: a *'standard rate'* and an *'enhanced rate'*.

PIP is for you, not for a carer. You can qualify for PIP whether or not you have someone helping you; what matters is the effects of your disability or health condition and the help you need, not whether you already get that help. You can spend your PIP on anything you like. PIP acts as a 'passport' for other types of help (see Box B.7).

What is the timetable for the introduction of PIP? – From 8.4.13, PIP is being piloted in several areas of the country, including Cheshire, Cumbria, Merseyside, North East England and North West England. In these pilots, only new claims will be treated as claims for PIP; renewal claims and revisions of existing DLA awards will continue to be treated as DLA cases. From 10.6.13, new claims for PIP will be taken from all parts of Great Britain. If you are considering making a new claim between 8.4.13 and 10.6.13 and want to know whether you can claim PIP or DLA, you can use www.gov.uk/pip-checker.

Renewal claims for DLA and revisions of existing DLA awards will be re-assessed under PIP from 7.10.13. Other DLA awards will be re-assessed under PIP from October 2015. For details of the re-assessment process, see Box B.6.

2. Do you qualify?
To qualify for PIP, you must:
- claim PIP (see 14 below); *and*
- pass the PIP assessment (see 9 below); *and*
- be within the age limits (see 3 below); *and*
- meet the required period condition (see 4 below); *and*
- pass the residence and presence tests (see Chapter 49(2)) and not be subject to immigration control (see Chapter 49(3)).

If you meet all these conditions, you will be entitled to PIP. The DWP must also be satisfied there is nothing to prevent payment (see 6, 7 and 8 below). However, you keep your underlying entitlement to PIP even if other rules mean that payment has been suspended. If you are already receiving disability living allowance, you cannot also get PIP at the same time; see Box B.6 for details of the re-assessment process.

3. Age limits
Lower age limit – The lower age limit for claiming PIP is 16. Children under 16 who have either care needs or mobility problems may be able to claim disability living allowance. See Chapter 3 for details.
Upper age limit – PIP can continue to be paid after you reach the age of 65, but you must establish your entitlement by making a successful claim no later than the day before you reach 65. You do not need to pass the 3-month qualifying period condition (see 4 below) but you must satisfy all the other conditions of entitlement no later than the day before you reach 65. If you have reached 65, you cannot claim PIP for the first time unless you count as having made a claim before reaching this age. Otherwise, you should consider claiming attendance allowance; see Chapter 5 for details.
WRA 2012, S.83; PIP Regs, reg 25

Top-up claims and switching rates from age 65
Daily living component – From the age of 65, if you were not already entitled to the daily living component, you can establish a new entitlement to it, as long as you are already entitled to the mobility component.

B.6 Re-assessment of existing DLA claimants

If you are of working age and currently receiving disability living allowance (DLA) you will be re-assessed under the PIP at some stage between 7.10.13 and October 2017 – the *'re-assessment period'*.

Who will be re-assessed?
You will only be re-assessed if you are of working age, ie between the ages of 16 and 64 inclusive. The re-assessment will apply to both fixed-period and indefinite awards.
Coming up to 16 – DLA awards for children under the age of 16 will not be affected. For young people who turn 16 on or after 8.4.13, whether they can renew their DLA or claim PIP will depend on the date of their birthday.

If they turn 16 before 7.10.13, they will be able to renew their claim for DLA; if they are awarded DLA on renewal, they will be re-assessed under PIP at a later date.

If they turn 16 on or after 7.10.13, they will be re-assessed under PIP (unless their existing DLA award was made under the special rules – see Box B.8, in which case they will remain on DLA and be re-assessed under PIP at a later date). The parent or guardian will be sent a letter about this process when the child reaches the age of 15 years and 7 months (which could be from May 2013). See Chapter 39(2) for details.
Aged 65 or over – If you had reached the age of 65 by 8.4.13, your DLA award may continue; the PIP re-assessment process will not apply to you. If the award is for a fixed period, you will be invited to re-apply for DLA, rather than PIP, prior to the current award coming to an end. For details of how DLA applies to adults, including those who are 65 and over, see Chapter 3(27).

If you reach the age of 65 during the re-assessment period, the re-assessment process will still apply to you.

When will the re-assessment take place?
From 7.10.13, your DLA award will be re-assessed under PIP if:
- you report a change in how your health condition or disability affects you;
- you have a fixed-period DLA award that is due to expire (a renewal claim); *or*
- you elect to be re-assessed under PIP of your own accord.
In the case of a fixed-period DLA award that is due to expire, if you have received a renewal letter prior to 7.10.13, your renewal claim will go ahead as a DLA case. If you have not received a renewal letter by 7.10.13, you will be re-assessed under PIP.

Re-assessments will be applied to all other DLA awards of working-age claimants from October 2015. These will generally be selected at random; however, awards for claimants who reached the age of 65 during the re-assessment period will be dealt with first.

What will happen?
Unless your DLA is up for renewal or you have reported a change in your condition or disability, you will first be sent a letter explaining that DLA is ending for people of working age and that you will be invited to claim PIP instead in about two months.

In all cases, you will be sent an invite to make a claim for PIP. You will have four weeks in which to make the claim, which you are normally expected to do by phone (see Chapter 4(14)). The four weeks can be extended in exceptional circumstances (eg if you have recently gone into hospital). If you do not make a claim within this period, your DLA will be suspended for four weeks (a reminder will be sent to you after two weeks, following which the DWP will try to contact you by phone). The DLA will be re-instated once a PIP claim is made. If no claim is made within a further four weeks of the suspension coming into effect, your DLA award will be terminated.

Otherwise, the process for claiming PIP on re-assessment is similar to the normal claims process; see Chapter 4(14). As long as you comply with the process, your existing DLA award will continue until a decision on your PIP entitlement has been made.

The Personal Independence Payment (Transitional Provisions) Regulations 2013

B.7 PIP and other help

PIP acts as a gateway to other types of help. This table lists the rates and components of PIP that entitle you to further help (if you pass any other tests there are for that help).

If you get the enhanced rate of either component, you are also eligible for the help available to people receiving only the standard rate.

'Premiums' are those included in the assessments of income support, income-based jobseeker's allowance (JSA), income-related employment and support allowance (ESA), housing benefit (HB) and health benefits.

'Elements' are those included in child tax credit (CTC) and working tax credit (WTC).

Mobility component
❑ **Standard rate**
■ 50% discount off road tax – see Chapter 6(2)
■ Benefit cap exemption – see Box H.1, Chapter 21
■ Childcare disregard (HB) – see Chapter 27(5)
■ Childcare element (WTC) – see Chapter 19(7)
■ Disabled child element (CTC) – see Chapter 19(4)
■ Disabled child premium (HB) – see Chapter 25(8)
■ Disability element (WTC) – see Chapter 19(8)
■ Disability premium – see Chapter 25(2)
■ No non-dependant deductions (HB and ESA/ income support/JSA housing costs) – see Chapter 21(21)
■ 16-19 Bursary Fund – see Chapter 40(1)
■ Student eligibility for income-related ESA – see Chapter 13(4)

❑ **Enhanced rate**
■ Exemption from road tax – see Chapter 6(2)
■ Motability – see Box B.16, Chapter 6
■ Driving licence at age 16

Daily living component
❑ **Standard rate**
■ Additional amount for severe disability (guarantee credit of pension credit) – see Chapter 42(3)
■ Benefit cap exemption – see Box H.1, Chapter 21
■ Carer's allowance: carer test – see Chapter 7(2)
■ Carer premium test – see Chapter 25(6)
■ Childcare disregard (HB) – see Chapter 27(5)
■ Childcare element (WTC) – see Chapter 19(7)
■ Disabled child element (CTC) – see Chapter 19(4)
■ Disabled child premium (HB) – see Chapter 25(8)
■ Disability element (WTC) – see Chapter 19(8)
■ Disability premium – see Chapter 25(2)
■ National insurance credits for parents and carers – see Box D.7, Chapter 12
■ No non-dependant deductions (HB and ESA/ income support/JSA housing costs) – see Chapter 21(21)
■ Severe disability premium – see Chapter 25(3)
■ 16-19 Bursary Fund – see Chapter 40(1)
■ Student eligibility for income-related ESA – see Chapter 13(4)

❑ **Enhanced rate**
■ Enhanced disability premium – see Chapter 25(4)
■ Severe disability element (WTC) – see Chapter 19(7)
■ Severely disabled child element (CTC) – see Chapter 19(4)

If your care needs change after you reach 65, you can switch between the standard and enhanced rates of the daily living component.

Mobility component – From the age of 65, if you were not already entitled to the mobility component, you cannot establish a new entitlement to it, even if you are already entitled to the daily living component.

Once you reach 65, if your mobility needs increase, you cannot move up from the standard to the enhanced rate.
PIP Regs, reg 27

Renewal claims
If a PIP award ends after you reach 65, you can make a renewal claim within one year of your previous award ending, as long as your claim relates to substantially the same physical or mental condition(s) (or a new condition which developed as a result of the one for which the previous award was made). If you leave it longer than a year or your claim relates to a different condition or conditions, you would need to claim attendance allowance instead.
WRA 2012, S.83(3); PIP Regs, reg 26

4. The required period condition
The 3-month qualifying period
To qualify for PIP, you must pass the PIP assessment throughout the three months before your claim. You can, however, claim (or ask for the award to be superseded) before the three months are up.
WRA 2012, S.81(1)(a); PIP Regs, regs 12(1)(a)&(2)(a) and 13(1)(a)&(2)(a)

Linked claims – If you re-claim PIP within two years of the end of a previous award for substantially the same physical or mental condition(s) (or a new condition which developed as a result of the one for which the previous award was made), the claims are linked. This means if you have a relapse, you don't have to re-serve the 3-month qualifying period. You can get PIP as soon as you re-claim, but only at the previous rate and component; if you qualify for a different amount, you will need to re-serve the 3-month qualifying period before it is paid.

There is no such linking of claims if your claim relates to a different condition or conditions; so you will need to serve the 3-month qualifying period on the new claim before it is paid.
WRA 2012, S.81(4); PIP Regs, reg 15

If you are aged 65 or over, claims can be linked in this way if the gap between them is no more than one year.
PIP Regs, reg 26(2)(b)

The prospective test
You must show you are likely to satisfy the PIP assessment throughout the nine months after your claim.
WRA 2012, S.81(1)(b); PIP Regs, regs 12(1)(b)&(2)(b) and 13(1)(b)&(2)(b)

Terminal illness
If you are terminally ill and have claimed PIP on this ground (see Box B.8), you do not have to meet the required period condition. You will automatically get the enhanced rate of the daily living component. To get the mobility component, you must still satisfy the conditions outlined in 12 below (with the exception of the required period condition).
WRA 2012, S.82

5. How much do you get?
Each component of PIP has two rates, a *'standard rate'* and an *'enhanced rate'*. You will always get the highest rate to which you are entitled. Payment of PIP is affected by some situations (see 6, 7 and 8 below).

Daily living component	per week
Standard rate	£53.00
Enhanced rate	£79.15

Mobility component	per week
Standard rate	£21.00
Enhanced rate	£55.25

PIP Regs, reg 24

6. Does anything affect what you get?

Earnings
PIP is not affected by earnings. It is payable whether you work or not, and no matter how much you earn. However, starting work may suggest your daily living needs or mobility problems have lessened, or you have found a way to cut back on the help you need from another person. Your PIP can be reviewed because of this, but not just because you have started work. You should tell the DWP if you start work, but if your daily living needs or mobility problems are unchanged, you should have little to worry about.

Other benefits or help
PIP is usually payable in full on top of other social security benefits or tax credits. There are two exceptions: constant attendance allowance and war pensioner's mobility supplement. Constant attendance allowance as part of industrial injuries disablement benefit or war pension overlaps with the care component; you will be paid the higher of the two. War pensioners' mobility supplement overlaps with mobility component; so you will get the supplement instead.

OB Regs, Sch 1, para 5

PIP is ignored as income for means-tested benefits and tax credits and may trigger extra benefit or tax credit. If you are awarded PIP, check to see if you then qualify for income support, income-based jobseeker's allowance, income-related employment and support allowance, pension credit, housing benefit, working tax credit or child tax credit, or higher amounts of any of these benefits. See Box B.7 for how getting PIP may help you qualify for other types of help in cash or kind.

Armed forces personnel and veterans – If you are currently serving or have been a member of the armed forces previously, you may be able to get the armed forces Independence Payment instead of PIP. For details, see Chapter 45(8).

If you go abroad
See Chapter 50(8) for details.

If you go into prison
Payment of PIP ceases to be payable once you have been in prison or legal custody for 28 days. This applies to both criminal and to civil offences and whether you have been convicted or are on remand. Payment may stop sooner if you have been in prison or legal custody within the previous year. In this case, the different periods are added together, and your PIP will stop after a total of 28 days in prison or legal custody. Suspended payments are nor refunded, regardless of the outcome of the proceedings against you.

WRA 2012, S.87; PIP Regs, regs 31 & 32

7. If you go into hospital
Usually, neither component of PIP is payable while you are an inpatient of a hospital (or similar institution) in which any of the costs of your treatment, accommodation or related services are met out of public funds. The term *'similar institution'* is not defined in legislation, although you must receive inpatient medical treatment or professional nursing care in the home under specified NHS legislation. What matters is not so much the nature of the accommodation, but whether your assessed needs for care are such that the NHS is under a duty to fund the accommodation free of charge, in which case you will still be treated as an inpatient.

WRA 2012, S.86; R(DLA)2/06

PIP can generally be paid, however, for the first 28 days of a hospital stay; see Chapter 35(4) for details.

Private patients – If you are a private patient paying the whole cost of accommodation and non-medical services in hospital, PIP can still be paid.

8. If you go into a care home
The daily living component is not normally payable while you are a resident of a care home in which any of the costs of your accommodation, board, personal care or other services are met out of public or local funds. The mobility component is not affected by a stay in a care home.

WRA 2012, S.85; PIP Regs, reg 28(1)

Even though the daily living component is not normally payable while you are in a care home, you should apply for it anyway. Once you establish that you are entitled, you can be paid the daily living component for any day you are not in the care home, including the day you leave and the day you return. For example, if you spend a weekend at home with relatives, going home on Friday and returning on Sunday, you will be paid the daily living component for those three days.

What is a care home?
A care home is defined as an *'establishment that provides accommodation together with nursing or personal care'*. The daily living component is not normally payable if any of the costs of your accommodation, board, personal care or other services in the home are met out of public or local funds under any of the following legislation:

■ Part III of the National Assistance Act 1948;
■ sections 59 and 59A of the Social Work (Scotland) Act 1968;
■ Mental Health Act 1983;
■ Community Care and Health (Scotland) Act 2002;
■ Mental Health (Care and Treatment) (Scotland) Act 2003; *or*
■ any other legislation *'relating to persons under a disability'* or to young people or to education or training (with specific exceptions, such as grants in aid of educational services or research).

WRA 2012, S.85(3); PIP Regs, reg 28(2)

People entitled to the daily living component in care homes
See Chapter 33(2) for details, but, in brief, you can receive the daily living component while in a care home if:

■ you are terminally ill (see Box B.8) and residing in a hospice, defined as *'a hospital or other institution whose primary function is to provide palliative care for persons... suffering from a progressive disease in its final stages'* (but not an NHS hospital);

PIP Regs, reg 30(3)&(4)

■ you are under the age of 18 and a local authority has accommodated you with someone in a private dwelling due to your disability; *or*
■ you are living outside the UK and being funded under the Education Act (such as at the Peto Institute Hungary).

PIP Regs, reg 28(3)&(4)

Paying your own fees – If you are paying your own care home fees, you are a self-funder and can receive the daily living component as long as you:

■ do not get any funding from the local authority; *or*
■ are only getting funding on an interim basis from the local authority and will be paying it back in full; ie you

are a 'retrospective self-funder'. This is most likely to apply if you are in the process of selling your home and/ or you have a 'deferred payment agreement' with the local authority (see Chapter 34(9)).

WRA 2012, S.87; PIP Regs, reg 30(5)

The 28-day concession

If you already have an award of the daily living component before you move into a care home, this can continue for up to 28 days of your stay. Payment may stop sooner if you have been in a care home within the previous 28 days. In this case, the different periods are added together and treated as one stay, and your daily living component will stop after a total of 28 days. You count a stay in a care home from the day after you enter to the day before you leave. Box B.13 in Chapter 5 shows how to plan a pattern of respite care that allows you to keep your daily living component.

PIP Regs, reg 30(1)&(2)

Linked spells in hospital and a care home – For the daily living component, spells in hospital and a care home are linked if the gap between them is no more than 28 days. There is no link for the mobility component because payment is not affected when you are in a care home. The daily living component stops being paid after a total of 28 days in hospital or a care home, or both if you've moved from one to the other with a gap of 28 days or less in between.

B. THE PIP ASSESSMENT

9. What is the PIP assessment?

The PIP assessment tests your ability to participate in everyday life. It is a points-related assessment of your physical and mental condition and cognitive functions considered within a range of 12 different types of activity. Within each activity is a list of *'descriptors'* with different scores. The descriptors explain related tasks of varying degrees of difficulty. You score points when you are not able to complete a task described, safely, to an acceptable standard, repeatedly and in a reasonable time period (see below).

The different types of activity are grouped under two broad headings: 'daily living activities' and 'mobility activities', which relate to the daily living component and mobility component respectively. Details of the assessment as it relates to each of these components are described in 10 to 11 below (for the daily living component) and 12 to 13 below (for the mobility component). However, there are common definitions, which apply to both parts of the assessment (see below).

Who delivers the assessment? – The assessment is delivered by two private sector 'provider' organisations: Capita and Atos Healthcare. Each delivers the service across different parts of the UK: Capita across central England, Wales and Northern Ireland and Atos Healthcare across the rest of the UK. There are differences in the way that each of these

---

B.8 Terminal illness

Automatic awards

If you are considered to be terminally ill, you don't have to serve the 3-month qualifying period to get disability living allowance (DLA), personal independence payment (PIP) or attendance allowance. Claims from terminally ill people are given high priority under the *'special rules'*, in which case the DWP aims to send a decision within eight working days.

Depending on which benefit you have claimed, you will qualify automatically for the following if your death *'can reasonably be expected'* within the next six months:

- the highest rate of the DLA care component;
- the enhanced rate of the PIP daily living component; *or*
- the higher rate of attendance allowance care component.

If you pass the 'terminal illness' test, you are treated as satisfying the conditions for one of these components – even if at the time of the claim you don't need nursing-type help from another person.

Living with a terminal illness, particularly with the shock on first diagnosis, is distressing. Claiming benefits and sorting out any financial problems may be the last thing on your mind. In part, claiming DLA, PIP or attendance allowance is an acknowledgement, if not acceptance, of what is happening to you: and you may not be ready to face up to that. Unfortunately, these benefits cannot be backdated to before the day you actually claimed them, and there is no extension of the time limit for claiming. All we can advise is to claim as soon as you feel able.

Note that even if you have a terminal illness, you will fail the test if, at the time you claim, your death cannot reasonably be expected within the next six months. Talk to your doctor to ensure a claim is submitted quickly. If you are turned down, check with your doctor and ask for a revision or lodge an appeal against that decision (see below), or make a fresh claim when your situation changes.

The mobility component – Automatic awards only apply to the benefits listed above, not to the mobility component (payable with DLA or PIP). Consequently, to be entitled to

the mobility component, you must still satisfy the conditions outlined in Chapters 3(9) or 4(12), with the exception of the qualifying period. If you are claiming PIP under the special rules, you will be asked questions about your mobility during the phone call you make to start the claim. This should speed up the decision on the mobility component (as well as ensuring you do not have to complete a further claim-form).

How do you claim?

Claim in the normal way (see the appropriate chapter for details). If you are claiming under the special rules, you are asked to send a factual statement (a DS1500 report) from your doctor or consultant to the DWP when you make the claim. Your doctor should have a supply of DS1500 forms.

The person who is terminally ill does not have to make the claim. Another person, including their doctor, can claim the benefit on their behalf, for example if the terminally ill person is not up to completing the claim-form, or has not yet been told the full nature of their condition. In this box we refer to the terminally ill person as the 'claimant' even though they may not physically make the claim, or even know about the claim. However, payment will be made direct to the claimant.

Hospital – If you are in hospital when you first claim DLA, PIP or attendance allowance, it cannot be paid until you leave hospital.

What happens once you claim?

Once you have claimed the benefit under the special rules, a decision maker decides if you satisfy the test of terminal illness. They will base their decision on advice provided by the healthcare professional assigned to your case. The healthcare professional will consider the evidence on your clinical condition, diagnosis and treatment, which your doctor or consultant gives in the DS1500 report. The report does not ask about prognosis (ie about your life expectancy). The healthcare professional may phone your doctor or consultant to clarify matters.

If the decision maker then decides that you do satisfy the terminal illness test, you will be awarded the appropriate component (listed above). Awards are usually made for three organisations delivers the service on the ground, but the framework of the assessment is the same across the UK.

Definitions

Assistance – This means physical intervention by another person. It does not include speech. The person intervening obviously needs to be in your presence and has to help with some or all of the activity in question. It is not necessary, however, for them to help with the whole activity; as long as they need to intervene for part of the activity, you will be counted as needing assistance.

Prompting – This is where someone needs to remind or encourage you to undertake or complete an activity or explain to you how it is done. Again, if you only need prompting with part of an activity, it will still count.

Supervision – This means someone needs to be continuously with you to ensure your safety.

Unaided – You can perform an activity unaided if you do not use any aids or appliances (see below) or require assistance, prompting or supervision from another person.

PIP Regs, Sch 1, para 1

Aid or appliances

'*Aids or appliance*' means any device that improves, provides or replaces your impaired physical or mental function, including a prosthesis. It could also include items such as walking sticks, glasses or collecting devices (eg colostomy bags). In assessing your ability to carry out a task, you will be assessed as if wearing or using any aid or appliance that you would normally wear or use, or which you could reasonably be expected to wear or use if you do not currently do so. It should not be considered reasonable for you to wear or use an aid or appliance if it is too expensive, difficult to obtain or is culturally inappropriate for you.

PIP Regs, regs 2 & 4(2)

Variable and fluctuating conditions

In the assessment, a descriptor will be deemed to apply to you if it reflects your ability for the majority of days (ie on over 50% of days). This will be considered over a 12-month period; three months looking backwards and nine months forwards (in common with the required period condition; see 4 above).

Where one descriptor is satisfied on over half of the days of the period, that descriptor will apply. Where two or more descriptors are satisfied on over half the days of the period, the descriptor which scores the highest number of points will apply. If no single descriptor is satisfied on over half the days of the period, but two or more descriptors, when added together, do, the descriptor which is satisfied for the most days over the period will apply.

Unlike disability living allowance, PIP does not separate your needs into daytime and night-time needs. Instead, your ability to complete each activity will be considered over the

years so they can be looked at again if you live longer than originally expected.

If the decision maker considers that you do not satisfy the terminal illness test, they will go on to consider your claim under the ordinary assessment for the benefit (see the relevant chapter for details).

What if you already get the benefit?

If you are already getting DLA, PIP or attendance allowance (but not at one of the three higher rates listed above), you don't have to make a separate claim under the terminal illness provisions. Instead, contact the Blackpool Benefits Centre (see inside back cover for contact details) and ask for the award to be superseded on the basis that you are now terminally ill. You don't have to send a DS1500 report (see above) immediately, but it will speed up the decision if you do.

If you are successful, the new higher rate of the benefit should be backdated to the date you first counted as terminally ill if you told the Blackpool Benefits Centre within one month. If it has been longer than one month, the higher rate can still be fully backdated if special circumstances caused the delay, so when you first contact the Blackpool Benefits Centre, explain why it has taken you longer (eg you were too ill or distressed to cope).

The legal definition of terminal illness

You count as being terminally ill at any time '*if at that time [you suffer] from a progressive disease and [your] death in consequence of that disease can reasonably be expected within 6 months*'.

SSCBA, S.66(2)(a); WRA 2012, S.82(4)

The diagnosis question should be straightforward. Do you have a progressive disease? Is the disease one which, by its nature, develops and gets worse, perhaps in identifiable stages? AIDS, for example, counts as a progressive disease because it involves a progressive breakdown of the body's immune system.

What is crucial for qualifying for benefit automatically is the question of prognosis – that your '*death in consequence of that disease can reasonably be expected within 6 months*'. The prognosis test looks forwards, not backwards. It may be that, given your progressive disease alone, your death could not reasonably be expected within six months: but your age or general physical condition may, for example, make respiratory infections more likely. You may be more prone to complications associated with, but not part of, your progressive disease. As long as the progressive disease plays the key role in whether your death can reasonably be expected within six months, you should succeed in your claim for an automatic award.

This test does not put an upper limit on life expectancy: it is not a matter of what is the longest period you can reasonably be expected to live. Clearly, no one can predict death six months ahead to the day, nor even to the month. It is quite possible that your death could reasonably be expected at any time within a period of five to ten months ahead. In that case, the upper limit of your reasonable life expectancy would be ten months ahead, with death at that stage fairly certain; while five months ahead would be the start of the period during which your death could reasonably be expected, rather than just being a possibility.

Appeals

Decisions on whether or not you satisfy the terminal illness test can be revised or appealed in the normal way (see Chapter 58). An existing award under the special rules can also be superseded if your prognosis changes so that you no longer count as terminally ill. If your benefit has been paid under the special rules for over three years, you may be sent an enquiry form asking for up-to-date information on your condition.

Harmful medical information – On appeal, if the claimant has not been told about specific medical evidence or advice about their condition or prognosis, and the tribunal considers that disclosure of that evidence or advice '*would be likely to cause [her or him] serious harm*', it won't be included in any papers sent to the claimant. If you consider that such evidence or advice should be kept from the claimant, you should say in your appeal letter why you think it would be harmful.

TP(FTT)SEC Rules, rule 14

24-hour period of each day during the period.

PIP Regs, reg 7

If you are awaiting medical treatment (such as an operation), the result of which is difficult to predict, descriptor choices should be based on your continued condition as if the treatment were not taking place.

PIP Assessment Guide, para 3.2.10 (www.dwp.gov.uk/docs/pip-assessment-guide.pdf)

Epilepsy – The DWP accepts that someone with epilepsy can go from having no functional limitation one minute, to having a considerable limitation the next. Guidance to the draft regulations emphasised that the key to assessing individuals with epilepsy is the consideration of risk: '*Within each activity, the relevant descriptor should apply to a person with epilepsy if there is evidence that a serious adverse event is likely to occur if the person carried out the activity in that descriptor. It is essential to consider the likely effects of any seizure – type and frequency of fit, associated behaviour, the post-ictal phase* (ie the altered state of consciousness after a seizure) *and whether there is likely to be sufficient warning to mitigate any risk of danger.*'

Personal Independence Payment: second draft of assessment criteria, Annexe A, para 7.17

Safely, to an acceptable standard, repeatedly and in a reasonable time period

If you cannot complete an activity safely, to an acceptable standard, repeatedly and in a reasonable time, you should be treated as unable to complete it.

'*Safely*' means in a fashion that is unlikely to cause harm to you or anyone else, either during or after the completion of the activity. The DWP considers that a serious adverse event must be '*likely to occur*' rather than '*may occur*' for it to count.

An example of someone not completing an activity to an acceptable standard would be where someone washes themselves but does not realise they have done so inadequately and are still not clean after they have finished.

'*Repeatedly*' means being able to repeat the activity as often as is reasonably required. Consideration should be given to the cumulative effects of symptoms such as pain and fatigue. The DWP should take into account the fact that the effort of completing an activity can adversely affect your ability to repeat it or to undertake other activities. For instance, if you are able to prepare a meal once unaided, but the exhaustion from doing this would mean that you could not prepare another meal that day, you should be treated as being unable to prepare a meal unaided. This is because it is reasonable to expect someone to be able to prepare more than one meal a day.

PIP Regs, reg 4(4)-(5)

10. The daily living component

You are entitled to the daily living component at the standard rate if:

■ your ability to carry out daily living activities is limited by your physical or mental condition; *and*
■ you meet the required period condition (see 4 above).

You are entitled to the daily living component at the enhanced rate if:

■ your ability to carry out daily living activities is severely limited by your physical or mental condition; *and*
■ you meet the required period condition (see 4 above).

WRA 2012, S.78(1)-(2); PIP Regs, reg 12

11. What are daily living activities?

Your ability to carry out daily living activities is assessed by focusing on ten types of such activity. These are:

■ preparing food;
■ taking nutrition;
■ managing therapy or monitoring a health condition;
■ washing and bathing;
■ managing toilet needs or incontinence;
■ dressing and undressing;
■ communicating verbally;
■ reading and understanding signs, symbols and words;
■ engaging with other people face to face;
■ making budgeting decisions.

Scoring – Within each activity is a list of descriptors with scores ranging from 0 to 12 points. The descriptors explain related tasks of varying degrees of difficulty. You score points when you are not able to complete a task described safely, to an acceptable standard, repeatedly and in a reasonable time period. If more than one descriptor applies to you, you only include the score from the one with the highest points within each activity.

B.9 Daily living activities

Add together the highest score from each activity that applies to you.

Activity	Points
1. Preparing food	
a Can prepare and cook a simple meal unaided.	0
b Needs to use an aid or appliance to be able to either prepare or cook a simple meal.	2
c Cannot cook a simple meal using a conventional cooker but is able to do so using a microwave.	2
d Needs prompting to be able to either prepare or cook a simple meal.	2
e Needs supervision or assistance to either prepare or cook a simple meal.	4
f Cannot prepare and cook food.	8
2. Taking nutrition	
a Can take nutrition unaided.	0
b Needs – (i) to use an aid or appliance to be able to take nutrition; *or* (ii) supervision to be able to take nutrition; *or* (iii) assistance to be able to cut up food.	2
c Needs a therapeutic source to be able to take nutrition.	2
d Needs prompting to be able to take nutrition.	4
e Needs assistance to be able to manage a therapeutic source to take nutrition.	6
f Cannot convey food and drink to their mouth and needs another person to do so.	10
3. Managing therapy or monitoring a health condition	
a Either – (i) does not receive medication or therapy or need to monitor a health condition; *or* (ii) can manage medication or therapy or monitor a health condition unaided.	0
b Needs either – (i) to use an aid or appliance to be able to manage medication; *or* (ii) supervision, prompting or assistance to be able to manage medication or monitor a health condition.	1
c Needs supervision, prompting or assistance to be able to manage therapy that takes no more than 3.5 hours a week.	2
d Needs supervision, prompting or assistance to be able to manage therapy that takes more than 3.5 but no more than 7 hours a week.	4

To be entitled to the standard rate of the daily living component, you need to score at least 8 points; to be entitled to the enhanced rate, you need to score at least 12 points. These points can be scored in one activity or from any of the activities added together. The descriptors and the points assigned to each one are listed in Box B.9. We look at the descriptors in more detail below.

PIP Regs, reg 5

Preparing food

This activity focuses on your ability to prepare and cook a simple meal. Any problems you have must be due to your physical or mental condition, rather than reflecting a basic inability to cook (eg because you have never been taught how to). The majority of the descriptors focus on your ability to prepare *and* cook a meal; if you can do one, but not the other,

the descriptor will still apply.

A *'simple meal'* is a cooked, one-course meal for one using fresh ingredients. *'Preparing'* food means making the food ready for cooking or eating. This could include opening packaging (including opening tins with a tin opener), checking the food is not out of date, peeling and chopping the food, serving the meal and pouring a drink. 'Cooking' food means heating food safely at or above waist height (eg using a cooker hob or a microwave oven); the activity does not consider any difficulties you may have in bending down to use an oven.

When considering whether or not you need an aid or appliance to prepare and cook a meal, the sort of things that could count include: perching stools, lightweight pots and pans, easy grip handles on utensils, single lever arm taps and liquid level indicators. Pre-chopped vegetables are not

e Needs supervision, prompting or assistance to be able to manage therapy that takes more than 7 but no more than 14 hours a week. — 6

f Needs supervision, prompting or assistance to be able to manage therapy that takes more than 14 hours a week. — 8

4. Washing and bathing

a Can wash and bathe unaided. — 0

b Needs to use an aid or appliance to be able to wash or bathe. — 2

c Needs supervision or prompting to be able to wash or bathe. — 2

d Needs assistance to be able to wash either their hair or body below the waist. — 2

e Needs assistance to be able to get in or out of a bath or shower. — 3

f Needs assistance to be able to wash their body between the shoulders and waist. — 4

g Cannot wash and bathe at all and needs another person to wash their entire body. — 8

5. Managing toilet needs or incontinence

a Can manage toilet needs or incontinence unaided. — 0

b Needs to use an aid or appliance to be able to manage toilet needs or incontinence. — 2

c Needs supervision or prompting to be able to manage toilet needs. — 2

d Needs assistance to be able to manage toilet needs. — 4

e Needs assistance to be able to manage incontinence of either bladder or bowel. — 6

f Needs assistance to be able to manage incontinence of both bladder and bowel. — 8

6. Dressing and undressing

a Can dress and undress unaided. — 0

b Needs to use an aid or appliance to be able to dress or undress. — 2

c Needs either:
(i) prompting to be able to dress, undress or determine appropriate circumstances for remaining clothed; *or*
(ii) prompting or assistance to be able to select appropriate clothing. — 2

d Needs assistance to be able to dress or undress their lower body. — 2

e Needs assistance to be able to dress or undress their upper body. — 4

f Cannot dress or undress at all. — 8

7. Communicating verbally

a Can express and understand verbal information unaided. — 0

b Needs to use an aid or appliance to be able to speak or hear. — 2

c Needs communication support to be able to express or understand complex verbal information. — 4

d Needs communication support to express or understand basic verbal information. — 8

e Cannot express or understand verbal information at all even with communication support. — 12

8. Reading and understanding signs, symbols and words

a Can read and understand basic and complex written information either unaided or using spectacles or contact lenses. — 0

b Needs to use an aid or appliance, other than spectacles or contact lenses, to be able to read or understand either basic or complex written information. — 2

c Needs prompting to be able to read or understand complex written information. — 2

d Needs prompting to be able to read or understand basic written information. — 4

e Cannot read or understand signs, symbols or words at all. — 8

9. Engaging with other people face to face

a Can engage with other people unaided. — 0

b Needs prompting to be able to engage with other people. — 2

c Needs social support to be able to engage with other people. — 4

d Cannot engage with other people due to such engagement causing either –
(i) overwhelming psychological distress to the claimant; *or*
(ii) the claimant to exhibit behaviour which would result in a substantial risk of harm to the claimant or another person. — 8

10. Making budgeting decisions

a Can manage complex budgeting decisions unaided. — 0

b Needs prompting or assistance to be able to make complex budgeting decisions. — 2

c Needs prompting or assistance to be able to make simple budgeting decisions. — 4

d Cannot make any budgeting decisions at all. — 6

PIP Regs, Sch 1, Part 2

considered an aid or appliance. However if you can only prepare a meal using them, this could indicate that you would need an aid or appliance or assistance from someone else to peel and chop food in order to properly complete the activity.

Taking nutrition
This looks at your ability to eat and drink. *'Taking nutrition'* means:
■ cutting food into pieces;
■ conveying food or drink into your mouth;
■ chewing and swallowing food or drink; *or*
■ taking nutrition by using a therapeutic source (a parenteral or enteral tube feeding, using a rate limiting device such as a delivery system or feed pump).

Managing therapy or monitoring a health condition
This activity focuses on the support you need from another person (excluding a healthcare professional, such as your GP) to manage your medication or therapy or monitor your health condition. It also looks at the amount of time that you need such support. *'Managing medication or therapy'* means taking medication (in the right way and at the right time) or undertaking therapy, where a failure to do so is likely to result in a deterioration in your health.

To count, the therapy needs to be undertaken at home and needs to have been prescribed or recommended by a registered doctor, nurse or pharmacist or a health professional regulated

---

B.10 Mobility activities

Add together the highest score from each activity that applies to you.

Activity	Points
1. Planning and following journeys	
a Can plan and follow the route of a journey unaided.	0
b Needs prompting to be able to undertake any journey to avoid overwhelming psychological distress to the claimant.	4
c Cannot plan the route of a journey.	8
d Cannot follow the route of an unfamiliar journey without another person, assistance dog or orientation aid.	10
e Cannot undertake any journey because it would cause overwhelming psychological distress to the claimant.	10
f Cannot follow the route of a familiar journey without another person, an assistance dog or an orientation aid.	12
2. Moving around	
a Can stand and then move more than 200 metres, either aided or unaided.	0
b Can stand and then move more than 50 metres but no more than 200 metres, either aided or unaided.	4
c Can stand and then move unaided more than 20 metres but no more than 50 metres.	8
d Can stand and then move using an aid or appliance more than 20 metres but no more than 50 metres.	10
e Can stand and then move more than 1 metre but no more than 20 metres, either aided or unaided.	12
f Cannot, either aided or unaided, – (i) stand; *or* (ii) move more than 1 metre.	12

PIP Regs, Sch 1, Part 3

---

by the Health Professions Council. It could include home oxygen supply, home dialysis, nebulisers and exercise regimes designed to prevent your condition getting worse (eg stretching exercises to prevent muscle contraction).

The medication must have been prescribed or recommended by a registered doctor, nurse or pharmacist and could include tablets, inhalers, nasal sprays and creams.

'Monitoring' your health condition means:
■ detecting significant changes in your health condition which are likely to lead to a deterioration in your health; *and*
■ taking action advised by a registered doctor, registered nurse or a health professional who is regulated by the Health Professions Council, without which your health is likely to deteriorate.

This would include, for example, monitoring your blood-sugar levels if you have insulin dependent diabetes. It could also include the support you need if you are at risk of accidental or deliberate overdose or deliberate self-harm.

Washing and bathing
'Bathing' includes getting into or out of an un-adapted bath or shower.

Managing toilet needs or incontinence
In this activity *'toilet needs'* are defined as:
■ getting on and off an un-adapted toilet;
■ evacuating your bladder and bowel; *and*
■ cleaning yourself afterwards.
'Managing incontinence' means managing involuntary evacuation of your bowel or bladder, including using a collecting device (such as a bottle or bucket) or self-catheterisation and cleaning yourself afterwards. You will be considered as incontinent if you use a collecting device or catheter.

Dressing and undressing
Dressing and undressing looks at your ability to select, put on, and take off un-adapted clothing (which could include fastenings such as zips or buttons). It includes putting on and taking off socks and shoes. The activity also looks at your ability to select clothing that is appropriate (eg in the right order and suitable for the weather and time of day). The clothing should also be culturally appropriate for you.

Communicating verbally
This activity focuses on your ability to convey and understand verbal information. Two types of information are covered in the descriptors: basic and complex. *'Basic verbal information'* means information in your native language conveyed verbally in a single sentence (such a asking for a drink of water). *'Complex verbal information'* means information in your native language conveyed verbally in either more than one sentence or one complicated sentence. In either case, a lack of understanding of English, if this is not your first language, will not be relevant.

Three of the descriptors refer to *'communication support'*. This is support from a person trained or experienced in communicating with people with specific communication needs, including interpreting verbal information into a non-verbal form and vice versa (eg using sign language). The *'experienced'* person could potentially include a family member or close friend.

Reading and understanding signs, symbols and words
Two types of written information are covered in the descriptors of this activity: basic and complex. *'Basic written information'* means signs, symbols and dates of written or printed standard sized text in your native language. *'Complex written information'* means more than one sentence of written or printed standard-sized text in your native language, eg a gas

bill or bank statement. In either case, a lack of understanding of English, if this is not your first language, will not be relevant. *'Reading'* in the context of this activity includes the reading of signs, symbols and words but does not include the reading of Braille (thus if you could not read signs, symbols or words at all, but could read Braille, you would satisfy the descriptor providing you with the maximum 8 points).

Engaging with other people face to face

This activity considers your ability to engage socially, which means to interact with others in a contextually and socially appropriate manner, understand body language and establish relationships. Your inability to engage socially must be due to your condition, rather than to shyness. One descriptor deals with whether or not you need social support to be able to engage with other people. *'Social support'* means support from someone trained or experienced in assisting people to engage in social situations. The *'experienced'* person could potentially include a family member or close friend. Another descriptor refers to an inability to engage with other people due to such engagement causing *'overwhelming psychological distress'*. This is defined as distress related to an enduring mental health condition or an intellectual or cognitive impairment. This condition may have a physical root cause.

Making budgeting decisions

This activity looks at your ability to spend and manage your money. Two types of decision are considered: complex and simple. *'Simple budgeting decisions'* involve calculating the cost of goods and calculating the change required after a purchase. *'Complex budgeting decisions'* are those that involve calculating household and personal budgets, managing and paying bills and planning future purchases.

PIP Regs, Sch 1, Parts 1 & 2

12. The mobility component

You are entitled to the mobility component at the standard rate if:
■ your ability to carry out mobility activities is limited by your physical or mental condition; *and*
■ you meet the required period condition (see 4 above).
You are entitled to the mobility component at the enhanced rate if:
■ your ability to carry out mobility activities is severely limited by your physical or mental condition; *and*
■ you meet the required period condition (see 4 above).

WRA 2012, S.79(1)-(2); PIP Regs, reg 13

13. What are mobility activities?

Your ability to carry out mobility activities is assessed by focusing on two types of such activity. These are:
■ planning and following journeys;
■ moving around.
Scoring – Within both of these activities is a list of descriptors with scores ranging from 0 to 12 points. The descriptors explain related tasks of varying degrees of difficulty. You score points when you are not able to complete a task described safely, to an acceptable standard, repeatedly and in a reasonable time period. If more than one descriptor applies to you, you only include the score from the one with the highest points within each activity.

To be entitled to the standard rate of the mobility component, you need to score at least 8 points; to be entitled to the enhanced rate, you need to score at least 12 points. These points can be scored in one activity or from either of the activities added together.

The descriptors and the points assigned to each one are listed in Box B.10. We look at the descriptors in more detail below.

PIP Regs, reg 6

Planning and following journeys

This activity assesses your ability to work out and follow a route safely and reliably. Two types of route are considered: familiar and unfamiliar. You should only be considered able to journey to an unfamiliar destination if you are able to use public transport such as a bus or train.

Two of the descriptors refer to *'overwhelming psychological distress'*. This is defined as distress related to an enduring mental health condition or an intellectual or cognitive impairment. The mental health condition may have a physical root cause (eg if you have unmanageable incontinence, you may have anxiety about making journeys).

Two descriptors consider whether or not you need an assistance dog or an orientation aid. An *'assistance dog'* is one trained to guide or assist someone with a sensory impairment. An *'orientation aid'* is a specialist aid designed to assist disabled people to follow a route safely.

PIP Regs, Sch 1, Parts 1 & 3

Moving around

This activity focuses on your physical ability to stand and then move around without severe discomfort (such as breathlessness, pain or fatigue). *'Stand'* means stand upright *'with at least one biological foot on the ground'* (therefore if you have had both your legs or feet amputated, you would be deemed unable to stand, regardless of any ability you may have using prostheses). The words *'... and then move'* mean that you need to be able to move independently while remaining standing. So if you could only cover, say 20 metres, by standing, transferring to a wheelchair and then completing the journey, you will not be considered capable of moving that distance.

PIP Assessment Guide, p.97 (www.dwp.gov.uk/docs/pip-assessment-guide.pdf)

A number of different distances are covered by the descriptors. However, unless you also pick up points in the previous activity, you would only get the 12 points required for the enhanced rate of mobility component (the equivalent of the higher rate mobility component of disability living allowance) if you:
■ cannot, either aided or unaided, stand or move more than 1 metre; *or*
■ can stand and then move more than 1 metre but no more than 20 metres, either aided or unaided.
Your ability to move around should be judged in relation to the type of surface normally expected out of doors, such as pavements, roads and kerbs.

The use of aids or appliances that you normally use to support your physical mobility without assistance (eg walking sticks or frames, crutches and prostheses) will be considered.

Factors such as pain, breathlessness, abnormalities of gait and fatigue should be taken into account. If you can only move a certain distance in a state of excessive fatigue, you should be regarded as unable to move that distance. You must also be able to move the distance concerned safely and in a reasonable time period. This only refers to the actual act of moving around; any dangers posed by traffic, etc are considered in the previous activity.

PIP Regs, Sch 1, Parts 1 & 3

C. CLAIMS, PAYMENTS & APPEALS

14. How do you claim?
Starting your claim

You can start your PIP claim by ringing 0800 917 2222 (textphone 0800 917 7777). The lines are open 8am to 6pm Monday to Friday and are free on BT landlines and most mobiles. Someone else can make the call on your behalf (eg a support worker), but you need to be with them when they do so. During this call, which should last about 15 minutes, basic details will be obtained from you, including:

■ your personal and contact details and national insurance number;

■ information about your nationality (see Chapter 49(2)-(3)) and whether you have spent time abroad over the last three years (see Chapter 50(8));

■ whether you are in hospital, a hospice or a care home or have been in one of these over the last 28 days (see 7 and 8 above);

■ which healthcare professional supporting you would be the best to contact? It would help if this person is aware of your day-to-day problems; if you have kept a diary (see below) you could provide them with a copy of it;

■ details of your bank or building society, for payment purposes;

■ questions relating to the special rules if you are claiming under these (see Box B.8); these will include questions on your mobility (see 12 and 13 above); *and*

■ whether you find it difficult to return forms because of a mental health or behavioural condition, learning disability, developmental disorder or memory problems.

It will speed things up if you have all this information ready when you make the call. Once the call is completed, you will be asked to agree a declaration.

Your date of claim – The date of your claim will be the date of this phone call.

Paper and online claims – You can ask for a paper claim-form instead if you are unable to start the claim by phone. An online service should be available from 2014.

How your disability affects you

If it is clear from the information you have provided above that you do not satisfy the basic entitlement conditions for PIP, the DWP will send you a letter stating that your claim has been disallowed. Otherwise, you will be sent a form to complete: *'How your disability affects you'*. This form aims to give you the chance of describing how your condition affects your daily life. For advice on completing this form, see Box B.11.

You have one month in which to return the form from the date it was sent out. If you do not return the form within the month without good reason (taking into account your state of health and the nature of any disability) your claim will be disallowed.

PIP Regs, regs 8 & 10

Once you have completed this form, make a copy of it for future reference, and send it in the freepost envelope provided with the form.

Keeping a diary

If your condition varies from day to day, you may wish to keep a diary over a few days, focusing on the tasks described in 11 and 13 above. This can help provide a picture of what your abilities are like over time. For instance, in a diary over a typical week, you may note down that you need assistance managing your toilet needs over four days, and can manage your toilet needs unaided on the other three days. This will help you correctly answer the questions on toileting in the form *How your disability affects you*.

Long-term diaries can be useful when explaining more sporadic problems that result from your condition such as stumbles, falls or fits. If your condition is getting slowly worse, such a diary can help pinpoint the date that you start to satisfy the appropriate disability test (see 10 and 12 above). See Box B.15 in Chapter 5 for an example of a long-term diary.

Once you have completed the diary, make a copy of it, which you can attach to the form *How your disability affects you* before posting it.

15. How your claim is assessed

Claims for PIP are handled first by one of the regional Disability Benefits Centres. Decisions are made by DWP decision makers (referred to as *'case managers'*) at these centres. However, the assessment itself will be carried out by one of two *'provider'* companies: Capita or Atos Healthcare (see 9 above).

Once the DWP has received your completed form *How your disability affects you*, they will refer your case to the provider that deals with assessments in your part of the country. Once the provider receives your case, they will allocate it to one of the healthcare professionals working for them. This healthcare professional may initially contact your doctor, consultant or other medically qualified person treating you for further information. They may ring them or they may ask them to produce a report. The healthcare professionals are advised to seek such information where there is an appointee dealing with the claim (see Chapter 57(4)) or where there is evidence of a previous suicide attempt or self-harm. In most cases, however, the healthcare professional will arrange to see you at a face-to-face consultation.

The face-to-face consultation

The face-to-face consultation will be carried out by the healthcare professional assigned to your case. The consultation will normally take place in an Examination Centre in those parts of the country where the assessments are delivered by Atos Healthcare. Capita aims to deal with the majority of assessments in claimants' own homes.

If you are not able to attend an Examination Centre and need the consultation to take place in your home, you should inform the office arranging the consultation as soon as possible, explaining why you cannot attend the centre.

You must be provided with at least seven days' notice of the time and place for the consultation, unless you agree to accept a shorter notice period. If you cannot attend, you should inform the office that arranged the consultation as soon as possible.

PIP Regs, reg 9

If you fail to attend or participate – If you do not attend or participate in the consultation without good reason (taking into account your state of health and the nature of any disability) your claim will be disallowed. You will be contacted and asked to explain your reasons. If the case manager refuses to accept that you had good reason, you can appeal. For more on appeals, see Chapter 58.

PIP Regs, regs 9(2) & 10

At the face-to-face consultation

At the face-to-face consultation, the healthcare professional will identify the descriptors that they consider apply to you with respect to the PIP assessment (see 9 to 13 above). To do this, they will ask questions about your day-to-day life, your home, how you manage at work if you have a job, and about any social or leisure activities that you engage in (or have had to give up). They will often ask you to describe a 'typical day' in your life.

When answering the healthcare professional, explain your abilities as fully as you can. You should tell them about any pain or tiredness you feel, or would feel, while carrying out tasks, both on the day of the examination and over time. Consider how you would feel if you had to do the same task repeatedly. Tell them if you need reminding or encouraging to do the tasks. Try not to overestimate your ability to do things. If your condition varies, let them know about the variability and what you are like on bad days as well as good days. The healthcare professional's opinion should not be based on a snapshot of your condition on the day of the consultation; they should consider the effects of your condition over time.

At the consultation the healthcare professional will be able to observe your ability to stand, sit and move around. They may watch you getting on and off the examination couch and bending down to pick up your belongings. They will check whether you have any aids or appliances, and the extent to which you use them. They will also be able to assess your levels of concentration and your ability to understand them and express yourself, if these matters are at issue.

The healthcare professional may carry out a brief physical examination.

Once the healthcare professional has completed their report, they will send it to the case manager who will decide whether or not to award you PIP and, if it is awarded, at what rate and for how long.

Support – If you have a carer, you could ask them to attend the consultation with you. Your carer will not be able to answer questions on your behalf (unless the healthcare professional cannot understand your speech or you cannot understand their questions), but they will be able to add to what you have to say, particularly with respect to their role as carer.

16. The decision
If your claim is disallowed
If a decision is made to disallow or reduce your claim, the DWP will send you a notification of that decision. The letter should indicate briefly their reasons for choosing the descriptors that they consider apply to you, but unfortunately will not include details of the scores you obtained from these. Scores may be included from October 2013.

The notification letter will be shortly followed by a phone call to you so that they can talk through the decision with you.

If you are unhappy with the decision, you can ask for it to be reconsidered; see 17 below.

If you are awarded PIP
If a decision is made to award you PIP, you will be sent a notification of that decision. You will usually be awarded PIP for a fixed term. This may be for a short period such as one or two years. Alternatively, a longer award of five or 10 years may be considered appropriate. An ongoing award (ie one that does not have a fixed term) would only be considered where improvements in your condition (either over time or in response to treatment) or rehabilitation are unlikely and where your needs are likely to remain broadly the same. If you do not agree with the level of the award or the period for which it has been granted, you can ask for it to be reconsidered; see below.

17. If you are not happy with the decision
Reconsiderations
If your claim for PIP is disallowed, you have one calendar month from the date of the decision in which to ask the DWP for a *'reconsideration'* of the decision. You can also ask for a reconsideration if you are unhappy with the level of the benefit that has been awarded (eg if you are awarded the standard rate of the daily living component but believe you are entitled to the enhanced rate) or the period for which it has been granted. Be careful, however, because when you ask for a reconsideration, they will look at the whole award and they can take away the rate already granted. If you are in any doubt, seek advice.

Asking for a reconsideration – You should have the opportunity of asking for a reconsideration when the DWP contacts you by phone to talk through the decision (see 16 above). If you do not get this call, you should phone the number on the decision letter. In either case, you should do the following:
- request a reconsideration of the decision. State your grounds simply at this stage, such as, *'I believe that you have underestimated the degree of my disability and*

consequently underestimated the extent of my mobility problems and/or the difficulties I have in carrying out daily living activities';
- ask them to send you copies of all the evidence that was used in making the decision; *and*
- ask them not to take any further action until you have had the chance of responding to that evidence.

Put your request in writing as well and send it to the address on the decision letter. Keep a copy for yourself. If you have not received the evidence after two weeks, ring them again to remind them to send it. When you do receive the evidence, you should have a better idea of why the decision was made.

Building a case
Sometimes the only evidence used will be the information you gave on the form *How your disability affects you* (see 14 above). In most cases, however, there will be a report produced by the healthcare professional at the face-to-face consultation (see 15 above). Compare the report with your account on the form. Try to find where a difference of opinion arises. For example, you may have written on the form that you could not get on and off the toilet without support but the healthcare professional noted in their report that they thought you could manage by yourself. Now try to get medical evidence showing that what you said on the form was correct – eg a letter from your doctor or consultant confirming the difficulties and risks you have getting on and off the toilet unassisted.

Once you have obtained evidence to support your case, send it to the address on the decision letter. If it is likely to take a while to obtain the evidence, you must inform them how long this is likely to take, so they do not make a decision straight away.

A case manager will look at any further evidence you send. They will then either revise the decision in your favour or write back explaining that they have been unable to change the decision. In this case all is not lost, as you now have a month from the date of the new decision to lodge an appeal to an independent tribunal. For more on appeals, see Chapter 58.

If the decision was notified more than one month ago
To challenge a decision notified more than one month ago in relation to an ongoing award of PIP, you need to show there are specific grounds, eg:
- there has been a change of circumstances since the decision was made – eg your condition has deteriorated and your mobility has reduced;
- the case manager didn't know about some relevant fact – eg you missed out some aspect of your daily living needs or mobility difficulties when you filled in the form *How your disability affects you*.

See Chapter 58, Box T.5 for more details.

18. How are you paid?
PIP is usually paid every four weeks in arrears, into your bank, building society or Post Office card account.

Appointees – If you cannot manage your own affairs, the DWP can appoint another person to act on your behalf (see Chapter 57(4)). But PIP is your benefit, not your appointee's benefit. If you don't want someone else formally appointed to act for you, but cannot collect your PIP yourself, you can arrange with the bank, building society or Post Office for someone to do this for you.

19. What if your condition changes?
If your condition gets worse – If you already receive PIP, give the Blackpool Benefits Centre details of the change (see inside back cover for contact details). Your existing award may be superseded to include a higher rate or a new component. A top-up claim for the component you do not

B.11 Completing the form 'How your disability affects you'

Question 1

The first question asks for details of the professional(s) who are best placed to provide advice on your circumstances. Examples are given, which include social workers, counsellors and support workers, as well as medical professionals, such as your GP. If possible, make an appointment with the professionals that you list to discuss the claim with them. They will need to know about your daily living needs and any mobility problems you have. If you have written a diary (see section 14 in this Chapter), give them a copy of it.

Question 2

The second question asks about your health conditions or disabilities and approximately when each of these started. You do not need to go into detail about how they affect you; there is room later in the form for that. You are asked to list any tablets or medicines you are taking or treatments you are having; if you have a printed prescription list, you can attach that. If you have any side effects as a result of the medication, you should list these.

Questions 3 to 12

The next ten questions relate to the activity headings of the daily living component. When you are completing each question, you should refer to section 11 in this chapter, as this contains the definitions that are relevant to each activity. Note that the wording in the form is sometimes different from the wording in section 11 (and Box B.9 in this chapter), in which we use the exact wording of the law.

Each question occupies a couple of pages. The first page introduces the activity and explains what is relevant. A tick box section follows, which follows a similar format for questions 3 to 10:

First, you are asked if you use an aid or appliance to complete the activity. If it is accepted that you do and it is necessary, you will be awarded at least two points under that activity, except with 'managing treatments' where you just get one point.

Second, you are asked if you need help from someone with that activity. If it is accepted that you do need help, you will be awarded at least two to eight points under the activity, depending on the activity concerned and the nature of the help that you need (from just prompting, encouragement or reminding, to supervision or physical assistance).

In each case, you are offered one of three boxes to tick: 'yes', 'no' or 'sometimes', the last being helpful if your condition is variable.

The second page of each question has a box where you can explain what difficulties you face with each activity. Examples are provided above the box and in the information booklet that comes with the form. Unfortunately, the form does not indicate the descriptors that are relevant for each activity or the number of points allocated to each one. Consequently, when you fill in each box, you should use Box B.9 in this chapter, which lists the descriptors and the points allocated to each one.

You should clarify in the box which descriptor applies to you and explain why it applies. In each case you need to consider whether or not you can do the activity safely, to an acceptable standard, as often as you need to and in a reasonable time (see section 9 in this chapter).

3 Preparing food

Write down if there is any aspect of preparing or cooking a simple meal that is a risk to you. List any incidents that may have happened in the past. Have you cut yourself mishandling knives or burnt yourself on hot pans? Write down if you are not able to ascertain sell-by dates or read (or understand) cooking instructions on packets. If you use any aids or appliances to cook, do you need some help even when you use them? Write down if you have difficulty timing the cooking correctly. Let them know if you are so exhausted after cooking a meal that you could not do it again that day.

4 Eating and drinking

This activity is called 'Taking nutrition' in section 11 of this chapter. Write down if you need someone to encourage you to eat the right portion sizes. If you can cut up some food, but cannot cut up tougher items, such as meat, write this down. If you need an appliance such as a feed pump to eat, let them know if you need any help to use it properly.

5 Managing treatments

This activity is called 'Managing therapy or monitoring a health condition' in section 11 of this chapter. Write down if there have been any times in the past when you have forgotten to take your medication, or have taken too much. Let them know if you have taken a deliberate overdose, or if you self-harm. Write down if you need someone to keep an eye on you because you are not aware that your condition is getting worse; sometimes this is the case with conditions such as diabetes or epilepsy.

If you need supervision, prompting or assistance to be able to manage therapy, write down how many hours on average each week you require this. You may find it helpful to keep a diary over a typical week to answer this correctly (see section 14 in this chapter). Box B.9 in this chapter shows what points you get for particular time periods; eg if you need such help for more than seven hours, but no more than 14 hours a week, you would receive 6 points.

6 Washing and bathing

Write down any aids or adaptations you use to wash or bathe yourself. These could include a long-handled sponge, shower seat or bath rail. Let them know if there are any parts of your body that you cannot reach even using such aids (eg if you could not wash your back properly).

7 Managing toilet needs

This activity is called 'Managing toilet needs or incontinence' in section 11 of this chapter. Write down if you need to use any aids or appliances, such as a commode, raised toilet seat, bottom wiper, bidet, incontinence pads or a stoma bag. Write down if you need help even when you use an aid, or if you need help with an appliance (eg securing the stoma bag, or washing around it to prevent infection). If there is an aid that could help, but which you do not use, explain why. For instance you may not use a commode during the day because there is no private space on the level where you spend the day.

8 Dressing and undressing

List any aids you use to dress, such as modified buttons, zips, front fastening bras, trousers, velcro fastenings and shoe aids. Write down if you still need assistance, despite using such aids, even if this does not take long. Let them know if you need someone to choose clothing that is clean and appropriate (eg if you have a visual impairment and cannot see stains or marks on clothing).

9 Communicating
This activity is called *'Communicating verbally'* in section 11. Write down if you cannot speak so that others can understand you properly or hear and understand what people are saying to you. Let them know if you have a support worker (such as a sign language interpreter) who helps you to communicate or if a family member or friend helps you. Write down if you have nobody to help you, and what difference such help would make.

10 Reading
This activity is called *'Reading and understanding signs, symbols and words'* in section 11. Write down if you need to use aids to help you read, eg a large magnifier or magnifying glass. If you can manage indoors, but cannot adequately read signs, symbols and words outdoors, let them know.

11 Mixing with other people
This activity is called *'Engaging with other people face to face'* in section 11. If you avoid mixing with other people because you have nobody to help you, write this down. How would you feel mixing with others without any support? Write down how you would feel; would you get panicky, angry or paranoid, or do you have difficulty understanding the behaviour of others?

12 Making decisions about money
This activity is called *'Making budgeting decisions'* in section 11. Write down if you would have problems in buying a few items from your local shop. Would you be able to give the shop assistant the right amount of money for the items? Would you know if the change was correct?

If going to the local shop would pose no problems, but you would have problems with more complex budgeting decisions, such as working out the household budget for the month or sorting out a gas bill, write this down. Let them know if you can do most of the task by yourself, but would still need some support to finish it properly.

Questions 13 and 14
The next two questions relate to the activity headings of the mobility component. When you are completing each question, you should refer to section 13 in this chapter, as it contains definitions that are relevant to each activity. Note that the wording in the form is sometimes different from the wording in section 13 (and Box B.10 in this chapter), in which we use the exact wording of the law.

Each question occupies a couple of pages. The first page introduces the activity and explains what is relevant. A tick box section follows. The second page of each question has a box where you can explain what difficulties you face with each activity. Examples are provided above the box and in the information booklet that comes with the form. When you fill in each box, use Box B.10 in this chapter, which lists the descriptors and the points allocated to each one.

You should clarify in the box which descriptor applies to you and explain why it applies. In each case you need to consider whether or not you can do the activity safely, to an acceptable standard, as often as you need to and in a reasonable time (see section 9 in this chapter).

13 Going out
This activity is called *'Planning and following journeys'* in section 13. Write down if you are unable to use public transport due to stress or anxiety – eg if you get claustrophobic on buses or trains. Let them know if you would find small disruptions or unexpected changes difficult to deal with – eg roadworks where you normally cross the road or if your bus stop has been moved.

Write down if you need to have someone with you to get somewhere, or if you would need an assistance dog or aid (such as a long cane or a white stick). Would you need such support only on unfamiliar routes, or would you also need it in places you know well?

14 Moving around
The tick box section for this question gives you the opportunity to identify how far you can walk, using, if necessary, any aids such as a walking stick, frame or crutches. It is important that you identify how far you can walk safely, reliably and without severe discomfort. If you could walk 50 metres, but would be in severe discomfort over the last 30 metres, then your walking ability will be considered to be limited to 20 metres.

Only tick the box *'It varies'* if none of the other boxes apply for at least 50% of the time. If you do tick the 'It varies' box, clarify matters in the box on the next page (eg *'On an average week, I can manage to walk about 40 metres before I can go no further on three days; another three days this distance is 20 metres, and on one day I cannot walk at all without severe discomfort.'*). A diary kept over a week, identifying your walking limit on each day, may help clarify matters.

List any symptoms that you feel on walking, such as pain, fatigue or breathlessness. Once the symptoms come on, how long do they take to subside. Write down if you are at risk of falling; give examples of falls you have had in the past outdoors. Were you injured? Were you able to get up again? Describe your gait, and give an idea of your speed; if you walk slowly, and were to cover 20 metres, what distance would someone without a disability or health condition cover in that time?

If you are not sure how limited your mobility is, you can do a time and motion study on your outdoor walking ability. Find a safe location on level ground. Walk until you feel that you are unable to continue (if it is safe for you to do so). Record what happens and when in terms of distance and time (you may find it helpful to have someone with you to record both of these). Include factors such as pain, dizziness, coughing, spasms, uncontrollable actions or reflexes, breathlessness, angina or asthma attacks. Note how long it takes you to recover before you feel able to walk again.

Question 15
Additional information
The box provides more space to explain your problems. If you run out of space here, you can use extra sheets of paper, which you need to write your name and national insurance number on.

Declaration
Once you are satisfied that what you have written on the form is a true and accurate reflection of your situation, sign the declaration. Attach to the form any evidence that you may have, such a letter from your consultant outlining your condition, a report from an occupational therapist or a certificate of visual impairment. If you have written a diary (see section 14 in this chapter), attach a copy of that.

You should make a copy of the form before sending it off.

already have does not count as a new claim, but rather as a change to your existing award. (See also 17 above under 'If the decision was notified more than one month ago'.)

If your condition improves – If your need for assistance or your mobility difficulties lessen, this could mean your rate of PIP should drop. Contact the Blackpool Benefits Centre to give them details. The case manager will usually supersede your award.

20. Checking of awards

Whether you have been awarded PIP for a fixed period, or if the award is ongoing, you must continue to satisfy all the qualifying rules throughout the award. Although the DWP tells you the main changes in circumstances that you must report, it is up to you to let the DWP know if *anything* changes that might affect your existing award, such as improvements or deterioration in your condition.

All PIP awards will be reviewed from time to time, whether or not they are for fixed periods or are ongoing. How often your award is reviewed will depend on the likelihood of your condition changing or improving and the chances that aids or appliances could result in an improvement in your ability to manage in future. The information for these reviews may be gathered in a number of different ways. You may be sent a self-assessment form similar to the form *How your disability affects you* that you completed originally (see Box B.11), a questionnaire may be sent to one of the health professionals treating you, or you may receive a phone call from the DWP or be asked to attend a face-to-face consultation (see 15 above).

PIP Regs, reg 11

B.12 Attendance allowance and other help

Attendance allowance acts as a gateway to other types of help. This table lists the rates of attendance allowance that entitle you to further help (if you pass any other tests there are for that help).

If you get higher rate attendance allowance, you are also eligible for the help available to people receiving only the lower rate.

'Premiums' are those included in the assessments of housing benefit and health benefits.

'Elements' are those included in child tax credit and working tax credit.

❑ **Lower rate**
■ Benefit cap exemption – see Box H.1, Chapter 21
■ Additional amount for severe disability (guarantee credit of pension credit) – see Chapter 42(3)
■ Carer's allowance: carer test – see Chapter 7(2)
■ Childcare disregard in housing benefit – see Chapter 27(5)
■ Childcare element in working tax credit – see Chapter 19(7)
■ Disability element – see Chapter 19(8)
■ Disability premium – see Chapter 25(2)
■ National insurance credits for parents and carers – see Box D.7, Chapter 12
■ No non-dependant deductions (housing benefit) – see Chapter 21(21)
■ Severe disability premium – see Chapter 25(3)

❑ **Higher rate**
■ Severe disability element – see Chapter 19(7)

---

5 Attendance allowance

A. GENERAL POINTS

1. What is attendance allowance?
Attendance allowance is a tax-free benefit for people aged 65 or over who are physically or mentally disabled and need help with personal care or supervision to remain safe. You do not actually have to be getting any help. It is the help you need that is relevant, not what you get. You can get attendance allowance even if you live alone; you do not need to have a carer. Attendance allowance is not means tested, there are no national insurance contribution tests, and it is paid in addition to other money in most cases (see 3 below).

Attendance allowance acts as a 'passport' for other types of help (see Box B.12).

Attendance allowance is not affected by the introduction of the personal independence payment, which is replacing disability living allowance for people aged 16 to 64 (see Chapter 4).

2. Do you qualify?
To qualify for attendance allowance, you must:
■ claim attendance allowance (see 15 below); *and*
■ be aged 65 or over (if you have not yet reached your 65th birthday you should claim personal independence payment instead – see Chapter 4); *and*
■ satisfy one of the disability tests (see 8 below); *and*
■ meet the qualifying period condition (see 3 below); *and*
■ pass the residence and presence tests, and not be subject to immigration control (see Chapter 49(2) and (3)).

The DWP must also be satisfied there is nothing to prevent payment (see 5 below). If you meet all these conditions, you will be entitled to attendance allowance. You keep your underlying entitlement to attendance allowance even if other rules mean you are not actually paid it.

Kidney patients - There are special rules for some kidney patients to help them qualify for attendance allowance at the lower rate (see 14 below).

3. Qualifying period

New claim – You must have been in need of care for six months before your award can begin, but you can make your claim before the six months have passed. It does not matter if during the six months you could not receive attendance allowance in any case – eg if you were in hospital. Make a claim to establish your entitlement, even if you cannot be paid at that time.
SSCBA, S.65(1)(b)&(6)

Renal dialysis – If you've passed the dialysis test (see 14 below) during the six months before your claim, you have served the qualifying period. Spells dialysing at least twice a week in hospital or as an outpatient getting help from hospital staff always count for the purposes of this qualifying period.
AA Regs, reg 5(4)

Terminal illness – There is no qualifying period if you are awarded attendance allowance because you are terminally ill (see Box B.8 in Chapter 4). Nor do you have to pass the 26-week presence test. You will automatically get higher rate attendance allowance.
SSCBA, S.66 & AA Regs, reg 2(3)

Current award – If you already have lower rate attendance allowance, you can qualify for the higher rate after you have needed the greater level of attention or supervision for six months. You can put in your request for the higher rate before the six months have passed.
SSCBA, S.65(3)

Linked claim
If you previously received attendance allowance (or dropped to the lower rate) and have a relapse no more than two years from the end of that award, you do not have to re-serve the 6-month qualifying period to regain your former rate. You still need to claim (or ask for your current lower award to be superseded), but you do not have to have needed the help or extra help for six months to be paid. For example, you previously received higher rate attendance allowance but this was reduced to the lower rate because your condition improved. You have a relapse within two years and ask for your award to be superseded to include the higher rate. Your higher rate can be paid from the date you make your request, or from the date of your relapse if you tell the DWP within one month.
SSCBA, S.65(1)(b) & AA Regs, reg 3

4. How much do you get?
Attendance allowance has two rates, a lower and a higher. Payment of attendance allowance is affected by some situations (see 5 below).

Attendance allowance	per week
Lower rate	£53.00
Higher rate	£79.15

The rate you are awarded is determined by the disability tests described in 8 below.

5. Does anything affect what you get?
Attendance allowance can be paid in addition to almost any other benefit – eg state pension or pension credit. It is not affected by earnings. It is payable whether you work or not, and no matter how much you earn.

Attendance allowance is ignored as income for means-tested benefits, so does not reduce the amount of any pension credit or housing benefit you receive. It may, however, be taken into account in the means test for charging for local authority services, and for local authority-arranged care in a care home (see Chapter 29(5) and Box L.2, Chapter 34).

You will not get attendance allowance if you are entitled to disability living allowance. If you get constant attendance allowance with industrial injuries disablement benefit or war pension, this overlaps with attendance allowance and you will be paid whichever is higher.

Check your benefits – Getting attendance allowance can trigger extra help with means-tested benefits. You might qualify for a severe disability premium with your housing benefit, or a severe disability addition with your pension credit guarantee credit. If you have not been able to get these benefits before because your income was too high, you might qualify now. Contact The Pension Service and your local authority to make sure they know you are getting attendance allowance.

If you go abroad
See Chapter 50(8) for details.

If you go into hospital or a care home
See 6 and 7 below.

If you go into prison
Payment of attendance allowance is suspended if you go into prison on remand to await trial. If you do not receive a custodial sentence, including a suspended sentence, you'll be paid arrears of attendance allowance for the time you spent on remand.
SSCBA, S.113(1)(b)

6. If you go into hospital
Generally, payment of attendance allowance stops after you've been in hospital for 28 days. Payment starts again from the first benefit pay day after you leave hospital. If you leave hospital temporarily and expect to return within 28 days, you can be paid attendance allowance for each day out of hospital (see Chapter 35(6)).

If you first claim attendance allowance when you are already in hospital, you cannot be paid until you leave. But you can then be paid for the full 28 days if you return to hospital, even if you do so within 28 days.

Back to hospital within 28 days? – If you are readmitted to hospital, having been at home for 28 days or less since you were last in hospital, the number of days during each hospital stay are added together and payment of attendance allowance stops after a total of 28 days.

You count days in hospital from the day after you are admitted to the day before you go home. Neither the day you go in nor the day you leave count as days in hospital.

Linked spells in a care home – If you go into hospital straight from a care home, or after having been home for 28 days or less, the two periods are added together, and attendance allowance stops after 28 days in total.
AA Regs, regs 6 & 8

7. If you go into a care home
Normally, you cannot be paid attendance allowance if you live in a care home, but you should apply for it anyway. Once you establish your entitlement, you can be paid attendance allowance for any day you are not in a care home, including the day you leave and the day you return. For example, if you spend a weekend at home with relatives, going home on Friday and returning on Sunday, you will be paid attendance allowance for those three days.

What is a care home?
A care home is defined as an *'establishment that provides accommodation together with nursing or personal care'*. Attendance allowance is not normally payable if any of the costs of your accommodation, board, personal care or other services in the home are met out of public or local funds under any of the following legislation:

- Part III of the National Assistance Act 1948;
- sections 59 and 59A of the Social Work (Scotland) Act 1968;
- Mental Health (Care and Treatment) (Scotland) Act 2003;
- Community Care and Health (Scotland) Act 2002;
- Mental Health Act 1983; *or*
- any other legislation *'relating to persons under disability'*.

SSCBA, s.67(2)-(4); AA Regs, reg 7(1)&(2)

People entitled to attendance allowance in care homes
See Chapter 33(2) for details, but, in brief, you can receive attendance allowance while in a care home if:
- you are terminally ill (see Box B.8) and residing in a hospice, defined as *'a hospital or other institution whose primary function is to provide palliative care for persons... suffering from a progressive disease in its final stages'* (but not an NHS hospital);

AA Regs, reg 8(4)&(5)

- you are living in a care home and paying the fees for accommodation, board and personal care in full with or without the help of benefits such as pension credit. In Scotland, if you are 65 or over and get free personal care payments from the local authority, you are not paid attendance allowance in a care home even if you are

B.13 Respite care

This box explains how disability living allowance (DLA), personal independence payment (PIP) and attendance allowance are affected if you go in and out of hospital or a care home more than once and how you could keep your benefit if you plan a pattern of respite care.

The linking rule
Payment of DLA, PIP and attendance allowance stops after you've been in hospital for 28 days (or 84 days for children under 16). If you go back into hospital after being at home for 28 days or less, the two (or more) hospital stays are linked. Adding together the number of days in hospital in each linked stay, benefit stops after a total of 28 (or 84) days. You are still paid for days at home.

Similarly, payment of the DLA care component, the PIP daily living component and attendance allowance stops after you've been in a care home for a total of 28 days (adults and children) in one stay, or in linked stays where the gaps at home are 28 days or less.

If you go into hospital then into a care home, or the other way round, payment of DLA care component, the PIP daily living component and attendance allowance stops after 28 days, adding together days spent in hospital and in the care home. Stays in hospital and a care home are linked if they follow on from each other or if you spend 28 days or less at home in between. If a child under 16 has linked spells in hospital and a care home, see Chapter 3(8).

You count a stay in hospital or a care home from the day after you enter to the day before you leave.

Careful counting
If you keep a careful count of the days you (or your disabled child) are in hospital or a care home, you can establish a pattern of respite care that will allow you to keep the benefit. But even if you can't keep your benefit for all the days in respite care, you can be paid for days at home.
Example: If you have two full days of respite care every weekend, you can continue like this for 14 weeks (2 x 14 = 28 days). For 14 weekends, you can go into respite care on a Friday and return home on a Monday. Only Saturday and Sunday count as days in hospital or a care home – the day you enter and the day you leave count as days at home.

If your respite care is provided in a care home, the DLA care component, the PIP daily living component and attendance allowance will not be paid for days of respite care (Saturday and Sunday) after the 14 weeks unless you break the link (see below) – although you can be paid for days at home (Monday to Friday). The DLA or PIP mobility component is not affected by a stay in a care home so continues to be paid as usual.

If your respite care is provided in hospital, DLA, PIP and attendance allowance will not be paid for days of respite care after the 14 weeks unless you break the link. You will continue to be paid benefit for days at home.

If a child under 16 is in hospital, you could continue this pattern for 42 weeks (2 x 42 = 84 days) before losing payment of DLA for further days in hospital until you break the link.

Break the link
If you spend 29 days in your own home, you will break the link between respite care stays. The next time you go into respite care in a care home, your DLA care component, PIP daily living component or attendance allowance can be paid for another 28 days, in one stay or in linked stays. Similarly, the next time you go into respite care in hospital, your DLA, PIP or attendance allowance can be paid for another 28 days (or 84 days for children).

A pattern of respite care interrupted by spells of at least 29 days in your own home will allow you to keep the benefit. Direct payments of benefit into a bank or other account will continue, but you must give the Blackpool Benefits Centre details of all dates you enter or leave respite care.

In the example above, you can break the link and at the same time continue to have some respite care. For the next four weekends, instead of going into respite care on a Friday and leaving on a Monday, you go in on the Saturday morning and return home on the Sunday evening. Because the day you enter and the day you leave hospital or a care home count as days at home, you'll have spent more than 28 days in a row at home and so you'll have broken the link. For the next 14 weekends, you can return to your main Friday to Monday pattern of respite care.

Informing the Blackpool Benefits Centre
When you first go into respite care, always write to the Blackpool Benefits Centre (see inside back cover), giving the name and address of the home or hospital you are going to, the date you will be entering it and the date you will be leaving to return to your own home. If you have planned a specific pattern of respite care in advance, let the Centre have details. Keep a copy of your letter. If there are any changes from your planned pattern of care, write and let the Centre know.

Arranging or keeping to a pattern of respite care that allows you to keep your benefit (by breaking the link every 28 days) will not always be possible. Until that link is broken, you will not be entitled to the DLA care component, the PIP daily living component or attendance allowance (or the DLA or PIP mobility component in the case of hospital stays) for any further days spent in respite care from the 29th day onwards. However, you will be entitled for the days spent in your own home. When you tell the Centre the dates you will be entering and leaving care, the Centre adjusts each payment to your bank or other account as necessary.

otherwise self-funding. If you are self-funding except for nursing care payments, you can be paid attendance allowance;

AA Regs, reg 8(6)

■ the local authority is paying your fees only until you are able to repay them in full (eg once you sell your house) – see Chapter 34(9).

The 28-day concession

If you have been awarded attendance allowance before you go into a care home, it can continue for up to 28 days. Payment may stop sooner if you have been in a care home within the previous 28 days. In this case, the different periods are added together and treated as one stay, and your attendance allowance will stop after a total of 28 days. You count a stay in a care home from the day after you enter to the day before you leave. Box B.13 shows how you can plan a pattern of respite care that allows you to keep your benefit.

AA Regs, reg 8(2)

Linked spells in hospital and a care home – Spells in hospital and a care home are linked if the gap between them is no more than 28 days. Attendance allowance stops being paid after a total of 28 days in hospital or a care home, or both if you've moved from one to the other with a gap of 28 days or less in between.

B. THE DISABILITY TESTS

8. The disability tests

To pass the disability tests, you must meet at least one of these four conditions. You must be *'so severely disabled physically or mentally that... [you require] from another person'*
during the day

■ *'frequent attention throughout the day in connection with [your] bodily functions, or*

■ *continual supervision throughout the day in order to avoid substantial danger to [yourself] or others' or*
during the night

■ *'[you require] from another person prolonged or repeated attention in connection with [your] bodily functions, or*

■ *in order to avoid substantial danger to [yourself] or others [you require] another person to be awake for a prolonged period or at frequent intervals for the purpose of watching over [you]'.*

SSCBA, S.64(2)&(3)

The meanings of the words and phrases used here are explained in 9 to 12 below.

Lower or higher rate

The higher rate is for people who need help day and night. If you meet one of the day conditions and one of the night conditions, you will qualify for the higher rate. The lower rate is for people who need help only during the day or only during the night. If you meet one of the day conditions or one of the night conditions, you will get the lower rate.

The starting point

The starting point for your attention, care, supervision and/or watching-over needs must be that you are *'so severely disabled physically or mentally that [you require]...'*. In most cases this poses no problem.

If you do not have a specific diagnosis of your condition, your needs can still be taken into account. What matters is that you have a disability (ie some impairment in your ability to perform activities) and it affects the way you can care for yourself.

If you have a mental or physical disability (eg depression or cirrhosis) because of alcohol or drug misuse, your care needs should be taken into account even if you could control your habit. If you *choose* to drink alcohol, the short-term

effects of intoxication (eg incontinence) should not be taken into account. If, however, you are dependent on alcohol, these effects can count, although you may need to provide evidence that rehabilitation programmes do not cure your dependence or are not suitable for you.

R(DLA)6/06

There is no extra test of the severity of your disability.

9. What is 'attention'?

'Attention' means active help from another person to do the personal things you cannot do for yourself. It does not matter whether you actually get the help; what counts is the help you need. It must also be help that would need to be given in your presence, not, for example, over the telephone.

To count as 'attention', the help you need because of your disability must be in connection with your 'bodily functions' and it must be 'reasonably required'.

Help with bodily functions

'Bodily functions' are personal actions such as breathing, hearing, seeing, eating, drinking, walking, sitting, sleeping, getting in or out of bed, dressing and undressing, going to the toilet, getting in or out of the bath, washing, shaving, communicating, speech practice, help with medication or treatment, etc. Anything to do with your body and how it works can count.

R(A)2/80

Indirect or ancillary attention counts but is often forgotten. Think about the beginnings and ends of particular activities. If there are other tasks involved during the course of attending to a bodily function, these can count if they are done on the spot. For example, if you need help to change bedding because of incontinence, then rinsing out the bedclothes if done straight away also counts, as can soothing you back to sleep. If you need help with eating, then cleaning up spills may also count.

R(A)2/98 (HoL: 'Cockburn'); R(A)2/74; R(DLA)2/03 (CoA: 'Ramsden')

If there is part of an activity you need help with (and could not carry on without it) that also counts. For example, you may be able to dress yourself, but you cannot get your clothes, or you need to be prompted to dress. It is irrelevant that you can manage most of the activity by yourself. If it takes you a long time to do something, eg getting dressed, you may reasonably require help even though you persevere and eventually manage by yourself.

If you are deaf, the help of an interpreter to communicate counts (including translating into another language to allow you to lip-read – CDLA/36/2009), as does assistance in developing communication skills. Extra effort attracting your attention may count (R(DLA)1/02). The extra effort involved in two-way communication if one of you is not adequately skilled in sign language may also be included as 'attention' (R(DLA)3/02).

Help to overcome problems communicating or interacting with others may count if, for example, you have a learning disability. This is because brain function also counts as a bodily function. This help can include someone prompting you or keeping you motivated if your concentration is impaired (R(DLA)1/07).

Domestic duties and other kinds of help

You might need help with things that can't easily be seen as bodily functions, such as reading, guiding, shopping, cooking, housework, etc. But if your disability is such that there is one bodily function that is 'primarily impaired', then whatever activities you need help with in connection with that impaired bodily function can count (as long as it is *'reasonably required'*). For example, if you are blind, the 'primarily impaired' function is seeing. So help reading correspondence or labels can count; the help would be attention in connection with the bodily function of seeing, not reading, which is not a bodily function. Similarly, if you are deaf or paralysed, the primarily impaired function is hearing or movement. Once you have identified the impaired bodily function, think of all the help you need from other people to do things you could do for yourself if you did not have that disability. You don't actually have to be getting help, it is enough that the help is *'reasonably required'* (see below).

R(A)3/94 (HoL: 'Mallinson')

In each case, the help you need must be carried out in your presence and involve some personal contact with you – this can be physical contact, talking or signing. Generally, this rules out domestic tasks like cooking, shopping and cleaning – they are not bodily functions nor would they normally need to be carried out in your presence. However, while it would not count if someone does the cooking for you, if someone helps you to do the cooking *for yourself*, eg reading labels and recipes, checking cooker settings, this could count if it is reasonably required (see below). You might argue it is reasonable for you to develop or maintain a level of independence; try to link the help you need to the bodily function that is impaired – and be prepared to appeal.

CDLA/3711/95, CDLA/12381/96 & CDLA/8167/95, although there are conflicting decisions: CSDLA/281/1996 & CSDLA/314/1997; see also CDLA/3376/05

'Reasonably required'

The attention you need must be *'reasonably required'* rather than medically required.

R(A)3/86

You may reasonably require more attention than you actually get. For example, if the only help you get is over the telephone, perhaps to encourage you to dress or eat or to check on you, you could argue that your needs would be more reasonably met by direct help in your presence, or more direct help than is currently available to you. If you are deaf, communication might be easier if you had an interpreter (see R(DLA)3/02). Think about activities you manage only with difficulty or in an unsafe way, even if you don't actually get help from another person.

The test is whether *'the attention is reasonably required to enable [you] as far as reasonably possible to live a normal life'*. This includes social, recreational and cultural activities – what is reasonable depends on your age, interests and other circumstances.

R(A)2/98 (HoL: 'Fairey')

Refusing medical treatment

If you refuse medical treatment that would reduce the help you need from others, you may find this help is consequently not taken into account. You should explain why your refusal is reasonable. You cannot be expected to undergo invasive surgery nor should it count against you if treatment would have unwanted side effects or if a psychiatric condition leads you to avoid treatment (R(DLA)10/02).

During the day

You must need *'frequent attention throughout the day'*, ie during the middle of the day, as well as in the morning and evening. The fact that you can manage most of your bodily functions without help does not mean you fail this test; it depends on the pattern of your accepted care needs.

'Frequent' means *'several times – not once or twice'* (R(A)2/80), and the pattern of help must be such that, looking at all the facts about your accepted care needs as a whole, it is true to say you need *'frequent attention throughout the day'*.

If your care needs vary because your condition fluctuates, give an idea of the pattern of those needs over, say, a month or whatever period of time accurately reflects your circumstances; it may help to keep a diary (see 16 below). The decision maker must then focus on what care you need and the pattern of those needs, rather than the length of time it

takes to meet your needs and the gaps between the attention.

See R(A)4/78, CA/140/85

During the night

During the night, the help you need must be *'prolonged'* (normally at least 20 minutes) or *'repeated'* (needed two times or more).

R(A)2/80, R(DLA)5/05

There is no fixed time for the start of the night. It depends on when your household closes down for the night. It normally starts when your carer goes to bed and ends when they get up in the morning. On the other hand, if a carer stays up late or gets up early to attend to you, that should count as night-time attention. If you live alone and keep unusual hours, like getting up at 4.30am, your care needs may count as night-time care between the more usual bedtime hours of 11pm to 7am.

R(A)4/74, CDLA/2852/02, CDLA/997/03, R(A)1/04 & CDLA/3242/03

10. What is 'continual supervision'?

Supervision means you need someone around to prevent accidents to yourself or other people. The words used are *'continual supervision'*. This means frequent or regular, but not non-stop; you don't need supervision every single minute. The supervision doesn't have to prevent the danger completely, but it must be needed *'in order to effect a real reduction in the risk of harm to the claimant'* (R(A)3/92).

The supervision must be *'reasonably required'*, rather than medically required (R(A)3/86). For example, you may be mentally alert and know what you should not do without someone on hand to help. Medically speaking, you could supervise yourself. But the question is whether or not you reasonably require supervision from someone else. In practice, supervising yourself might mean that to avoid the risk of danger you would have to do nothing but stay in bed or an armchair. If you would have to restrict your lifestyle in order to supervise yourself without help from someone else, the question is whether or not those restrictions are reasonable. Do they allow you to carry on anything approaching a normal life? If the restrictions on your lifestyle are not reasonable, then you reasonably require help from another person to live a normal life (CA/40/1988).

The next question is whether you satisfy the rest of the continual supervision test, which has four parts.

❑ You must show that your medical condition is such that it may (not will) give rise to substantial danger to yourself or to others. The danger to you could arise from your own actions or from the actions of other people. The danger to others could be wholly unintended (eg if you are unable to care for a young child safely).

❑ The substantial danger must not be too remote a possibility. But the fact that an incident may be isolated or infrequent does not rule this out. As well as looking at the chances of the incident happening, the decision maker must look at the likely consequences if it does. If the consequences could be dire, then the frequency with which it is likely to happen becomes less relevant.

❑ You must need supervision from someone else to avoid the substantial danger.

❑ The supervision must be continual, but the person providing the supervision need not always be alert, awake and active. Standby supervision, and being ready to intervene and help, can also count.

R(A)1/83

If you have epilepsy and the onset of an attack is unpredictable, with not enough warning for help to arrive or for you to put yourself in a place of safety, you may qualify for attendance allowance, certainly at the lower rate for your daytime supervision needs. The same applies to others whose needs for supervision and attention are unpredictable, and if the

consequences of an unsupervised attack would be grave, including those who are mentally alert and can supervise themselves between attacks but not during attacks.
R(A)1/88 (CoA: 'Moran')

Supervision and falls
If you are mentally alert and sensible, it is sometimes said you could supervise yourself and so avoid the risk of falling without help from another person. But it is not enough just to say you are sensible (R(A)3/89 and R(A)5/90); decision makers must identify precautions you could take and/or activities you should not do to avoid the risk of falls without help from someone else. It is only if it is *possible to isolate one or two activities which alone might give rise to a fall, and which could be avoided except for one or two occasions during the course of the day, and [you would] still be left to enjoy a more or less normal life, [that] it would be justifiable to say that continual supervision was not required. Everything will depend upon the facts of the case'* (CA/127/88, para 8). However, there is a close overlap between supervision and attention. Even if your need for help to avoid the risk of falls does not amount to continual supervision, it is possible that particular help could count as attention (see below).

11. Attention or supervision?
Attention tends to be active help, while supervision is more passive. Sometimes both can be given at the same time; for example, if you are deaf and don't have much traffic sense, someone walking beside you could be supervising you (ready to stop you walking) and giving attention in connection with hearing (informing you what you need to know to continue walking in safety).

Similarly, if you are unsteady on your feet and liable to fall, you might need both supervision and attention when walking. The supervision could be a matter of looking out for any unexpected obstacles or uneven surfacing, and being on hand to catch you if you fell. The attention might involve telling you what is in front of you, or it could be a hand on your arm to steady you.

There are many other possibilities where the help you need can amount to both attention and supervision. Keeping a 24-hour diary, listing all your needs throughout a typical day, may help you think about the types of help that could count as both.

If the decision maker does not look at the same needs under both the attention and supervision conditions, you may fail both sets of conditions. A long gap during the middle of the day might mean the pattern of help you need does not amount to *'frequent... throughout the day'*. Under the supervision condition, the risk of danger and the situations of potential danger may not be great or frequent enough to warrant continual supervision. Yet if some of the needs considered only under the supervision condition were also considered under the attention condition, the combination of needs could well amount to frequent attention throughout the day. This argument only works if some of the supervision also amounts to active attention in connection with a bodily function.

Use the attendance allowance claim-form to explain all your care needs. If you are unsuccessful, you can ask for a revision or you can appeal (see 19 below). In either case, ask that all your needs are considered under both conditions. If you can, list those needs that could count as both attention and supervision.

12. What is 'watching over'?
'Watching over' has its ordinary English language meaning, so it includes needing to have someone else being awake and listening, as well as getting up and checking how you are.
Decision Makers Guide, para 61161

You do not need to show that you need watching over every night in the week. It depends on the normal pattern of your needs – three or four nights a week may be sufficient, perhaps less if the dangers would be very grave.

A *'prolonged period'* is normally at least 20 minutes.
Decision Makers Guide, para 61165

'Frequent intervals' means at least three times. But it's worth trying if someone has to check on you twice a night.

The test is based on what you reasonably require, not on what is actually done for you. If you have had a fair number of accidents or incidents at night (or even just one bad accident), that might suggest you need more watching-over than you've been getting. If you've had few accidents, etc, the chances are that the watching-over you get is the watching-over you need.

13. Simpler methods
It may be suggested that you would need less attention or supervision from another person if you used certain aids or tried simpler methods. A typical simpler method is the use of a commode or portable urinal. If you could use one without help, it is usually concluded that you do not reasonably require help with trips to the toilet.

Sometimes an assumption is made that you can use a commode, but all the practical issues involved (eg privacy, hand washing, etc) have not been considered, nor the effect on your morale or general health if trips to the toilet are your only regular exercise. In any case, you might actually need help using the commode. Emptying and cleaning the commode can count as attention if it needs to be done right away (as it generally would be during the day if not necessarily at night) (CSDLA/44/02).

14. Renal dialysis
Special rules for some kidney patients undergoing renal dialysis help them to qualify for the lower rate of attendance allowance. Depending on when and where you dialyse, you will be treated as satisfying the disability tests for the day or the night. You must show that:
- you undergo renal dialysis two or more times a week; *and*
- the dialysis is of a type which normally requires the attendance or supervision of another person during the period of the dialysis; *or*
- because of your particular circumstances (eg age, visual impairment or loss of manual dexterity) during the period of dialysis you require another person to supervise you in order to avoid substantial danger to yourself, or to give you some help with your bodily functions.
AA regs, reg 5

Hospital
If you are dialysing as an outpatient and getting help from hospital staff, you won't automatically satisfy the disability tests, but it does help you to satisfy the qualifying period (see 3 above). This is helpful if you alternate between outpatient dialysis and dialysis at home. You will be treated as satisfying the disability tests for the period you dialyse at home (if this is at least twice a week and you need assistance as above) even if it is only for a short period. If the help you get as an outpatient is from someone who doesn't work for the hospital, this passes the disability test. Inpatient dialysis counts for both the qualifying period and the disability test, but payment of attendance allowance is affected by a spell in hospital (see 6 above).

Other types of dialysis
Continuous ambulatory peritoneal dialysis (CAPD) and automated peritoneal dialysis (APD) are designed to be done without help. You can only be covered by the above rules if your disabilities or frailty mean you need help. If you are

fully independent in dialysing you are not covered. But if you need even a small amount of help (eg to change the bag) you should pass the day or night disability test. You do not need to show that attention needed is frequent or supervision required is continual.

C. CLAIMS, PAYMENTS & APPEALS

15. How do you claim?
Starting your claim
You can get the attendance allowance claim-form (the *AA1A*) by ringing the Benefit Enquiry Line (BEL – 0800 882 200; textphone 0800 243 355) or downloading it from the government website (www.gov.uk/attendance-allowance/how-to-claim). You can also claim online from the website. For advice on how to complete the claim-form, see Box B.14.

Your date of claim
If you phone BEL, attendance allowance can be backdated to the date of your call. A claim-form issued by the DWP will be date stamped and provided with a postage-paid envelope addressed to the Disability Benefits Centre that will be handling the initial claim. If you return the completed claim-form within the six weeks, the date you asked for the form counts as the date of claim. If you take longer than six weeks to return the completed form, explain why on the form. If the delay is reasonable, the time limit can be extended. If not, the date of claim is the day the completed claim-form reaches the Disability Benefits Centre.

If the claim is made online, you are given six weeks from the date you first accessed the claim online to submit your completed claim. If you submit it within the deadline, the date of claim will be the date you first accessed the online claim. If you download a claim-form from the website, the date of claim is the day the completed form reaches the Disability Benefits Centre.

16. Keeping a diary
Writing a short diary of your day-to-day needs can lend support to your attendance allowance claim. It can help you remember things you would otherwise forget because

B.14 Completing the attendance allowance claim-form

The bulk of the claim-form is given over to a series of questions relating to your care and supervision needs. These questions have a tick-box format. Each question looks at a different area of day-to-day life. They generally follow a similar pattern. You are first asked to tick 'yes' or 'no' to confirm whether or not you have difficulties or need help with that area of day-to-day life; read the whole page before answering this. You are then asked more specific questions on each subject, including how often you need help.

Some questions ask if you have difficulty concentrating or motivating yourself and therefore need encouragement to carry out a task. You might need such encouragement because of a mental health problem (such as depression) or a condition affecting your mental capacity (such as dementia).

At the end of each question there is space to provide details of your difficulties. You may live alone and manage because you have no choice, but it is important to describe what help you would ask for if someone was there to help. You might be managing by yourself at the moment, but some of the tasks may be difficult (eg painful, time consuming or risky) without assistance from someone else.

Your condition may be variable. Many people claiming attendance allowance focus on good days. But you need to explain what help you need on a regular basis. Try to focus on an average day and list the problems you face more often than not. Explain what you are like on your worst days and how often such days occur. A diary may help with these points (see 16 in this chapter).

In each case, if you have tried an aid or simpler method that has not helped (see 13 in this chapter), explain why it wasn't practical or reasonable for you or didn't fit in with your abilities, agility and normal domestic arrangements (R(A)1/87).

We now look at some of the questions in more detail.

Help with your care needs during the day
Do you usually have difficulty or do you need help with your toilet needs?
This is one of the most difficult subjects to write about, because the questions are of such a personal nature. Try to put as much information down as you can; the claim-forms are treated with strict confidentiality.

If you have difficulty walking, the most difficult part of toileting may be getting to and from the toilet, especially if there are stairs involved. If this is the case, explain on the form why using a commode would not be easier; for instance, there may be no private space for one on the level you live in.

Mention any difficulties you have using the toilet, including sitting down or getting back up from it, wiping yourself, adjusting your clothing and washing afterwards. If you need to visit the toilet more often than is usual, explain why; it might be due to the medication you are on. If you are incontinent, you may need help changing your clothes and washing yourself.

Do you fall or stumble because of your illnesses or disabilities?
You may fall or stumble because of poor co-ordination, maybe your legs are weak or your ankle, knee or hip joints give way. The falls could be a result of dizzy spells, perhaps brought on by the medication you take, or you could fall during a fit or blackout. You may stumble into things because of a visual impairment. Whatever the reason, write down why you fall and what happens when you fall. Can you get up without help? Have you ever been stuck on the floor for any length of time, unable to get up? Have you hurt yourself; if so, have the injuries needed treatment? How often do you fall or stumble? Is it happening more frequently? These questions may be easier to answer if you keep a long-term diary of your falls and stumbles. See Box B.15 for an example. Also see 'Supervision and falls' in 10 in this chapter.

Do you usually need help from another person to communicate with other people?
You may have difficulties communicating with people if you have hearing or speech problems. If you have a mental health problem or a learning difficulty, you may have difficulty concentrating during conversations or remembering what has been said. If you hear voices, this may make it more difficult to have a conversation. If any of these circumstances apply to you, list examples where you might need help either understanding or being understood when having a conversation. This could be if someone comes to the door, calls on the telephone or when you need to communicate in shops, buses or taxis, etc.

If you have a visual impairment, list all the situations where you need someone to read things to you. These could include checking labels on medication and sell-by dates on food, reading your post, dealing with official letters, reading radio and TV listings or a newspaper.

they are so much a part of your everyday life. It can also be important when trying to explain symptoms that fluctuate either during a single day or over a longer period. The simplest form of diary would be an account of your needs over a typical day.

One-day diary

Start from the time you get up in the morning, through a 24-hour period, ending with the time you get up the following morning. Try to list all the times when you need help from someone or you have difficulties doing something because there is nobody around to give you a hand. When you write something down, try to answer the following questions:

■ what help do you need?
■ why do you need the help?
■ at what time do you need help? *and*
■ how long do you need the help for?

If your needs vary from day to day, keep the diary over a few days to get a clearer picture of your needs. See Box B.4 in Chapter 3 for an example of a one-day diary (in this case, for a child).

Long-term diary

Long-term diaries can be useful when explaining more sporadic problems that result from your condition such as stumbles, falls or fits. If you need continual supervision or watching-over to prevent substantial danger to yourself or others, such a diary can show exactly what happened, or what could have happened, if someone had not been there to intervene. If your condition is getting slowly worse, a long-term diary can help pinpoint the date that you start to satisfy the appropriate disability test (see 8 above). See Box B.15 for an example of a long-term diary.

Making use of the diary

Once you have finished the diary, write your name and national insurance number on it and make several copies of it. Attach one copy to the claim-form and keep one copy for yourself. If you are asking someone to complete the 'Statement from someone who knows you' on the attendance allowance claim-form, give them a copy. Finally, you should send copies of the diary to anyone else who you have listed on the claim-form, such as your GP, consultant or specialist nurse.

If you are deaf, write down if you need help from an interpreter to communicate, or if you need help developing your communication skills.

Do you usually need someone to keep an eye on you?
This question relates to any need you may have for *'continual supervision'* (defined in 10 in this chapter). You may need such supervision because you get confused. Confusion can arise from a mental health problem, learning disabilities, dementia or memory loss. It can also arise as a side affect of certain types of medication. List examples of potential dangers that could result from the confusion, such as turning on the gas and not lighting it, or allowing strangers to come into the house without checking who they are. Write down if such incidents have already taken place.

If your condition is likely to deteriorate or relapse, you may not be able to recognise the symptoms or take any action once they have come on. Write down if, as a consequence, you need someone to keep an eye on you to make sure you get help quickly in order to stem the deterioration or prevent too bad a relapse.

You might be at risk of hurting yourself or someone else. List any occasions when this has happened. Try to remember what brought on the incidents. State if you have any phobias that affect your daily life, such as claustrophobia or agoraphobia. Mention if you get anxious or panicky and need someone to calm you down.

If you have fits or seizures, say whether you get any warning. Can anyone else see warning signs and consequently take steps to ensure you are safe? List times you have fallen in the past during a fit or seizure. Give examples of any injuries you suffered and treatment you have received as a result. Write down how long it takes for you to recover from the fit or seizure and what other people might have to do to keep you safe in the meantime. If you were to keep a long-term diary before completing the claim-form (see 16 in this chapter and Box B.15), these points might be easier to answer.

Help with your care needs during the night
Do you usually need someone to watch over you?
This question relates to any need you may have for *'watching over'* (defined in 12 in this chapter). You need to show how your disability or medical condition is such that it may give rise to substantial danger. Outline the nature of the danger(s). Explain the basis for your fears of danger; refer to anything that supports your fears – eg the previous pattern and course

of attacks, wandering at night, falls, etc. Explain why you cannot avoid the substantial danger without help from another person – eg because of a mental disorder or an inability to administer medication, oxygen, etc during an attack. Relate the danger(s) to the need to have another person awake and watching over you. Do the dangers warrant having another person watching over you for 20 minutes or longer, or to wake up to listen out for you or get up to check on you two, three, or more times in the night? On how many nights a week?

Think about simpler methods (see 13 in this chapter) that may bypass the need to have another person watching over you. Explain fully how and why they have not worked, or do not or would not work. Are they reasonable in your circumstances?

If you need any active help at night (eg soothing back to sleep, rearranging bedding), state that your night-time care needs are both attention and supervision – you might pass the attention test more easily than the watching-over test.

Statement from someone who knows you
The claim-form includes an optional section to be completed by someone who knows you; this could be your doctor or another professional involved in your care. The best person to complete this section is the one who is most involved with your treatment or care. It would be better if this person is medically qualified, such as your GP, consultant or specialist nurse. If possible, make an appointment with them to discuss the matter. They will need to know about your care or supervision needs. If you have written a diary (see 16 in this chapter), give them a copy of it.

What to do next
Once you have completed the claim-form make a copy of it, which you should keep. If you have kept a diary of your care needs (see 16 in this chapter), attach a copy of that to the claim-form. Also attach copies of a prescription list if you have one, and any other medical evidence that could support the claim. Then send the claim-form in the postage-paid envelope that came with the form.

If you are claiming online, state on the online claim that you are going to forward them copies of any diaries you have produced or further evidence you have obtained. Send this to them as soon as you can; if it is likely to be delayed, let the DWP know roughly when they can expect to receive it.

17. How your claim is assessed

If you are claiming attendance allowance for the first time or after a break, a decision maker at one of the regional Disability Benefits Centres will make the initial decision on every aspect of your claim. If you are making a renewal claim, a decision maker at the Blackpool Benefits Centre makes the decision on your claim.

To help make decisions, the DWP produces online guidance called the *A-Z of Medical Conditions* available via our website (www.disabilityrightsuk.org/links-government-departments). The guidance outlines the main care and supervision needs likely to arise from a number of different illnesses and disabling conditions.

In the light of this guidance, your completed claim-form may give the decision maker enough information to make a decision. If not, the decision maker may request a short report from your doctor or another medical person you named on the claim-form. If this does not provide a complete picture, the decision maker can arrange for a DWP-approved healthcare professional to visit you at your home and carry out a medical examination in order to prepare a medical report. Such a visit can also be arranged as an alternative to getting in touch with your doctor, consultant, etc.

Refusing the medical – If you refuse to undergo the medical, the claim will be decided against you unless you have 'good cause' for your refusal.

SSA, S.19

The medical examination

If you have a carer, try to ensure they are in when the healthcare professional visits. Your carer will not be able to answer questions on your behalf (unless the healthcare professional cannot understand your speech or you cannot understand their questions), but they will be able to add to what you have to say, particularly with respect to their role as carer. Before the healthcare professional comes, read through the copy that you made of your attendance allowance claim-form.

During the visit, the healthcare professional should ask questions relating to each of the areas covered on the claim-form. You should let the healthcare professional know about any pain or tiredness you feel when carrying out each activity. Let them know about any variation in your condition and about both good and bad days. Show them any medical evidence you have confirming your problems. Try to make sure that what you tell the healthcare professional is consistent with what you put on the claim-form, unless of course there has been a significant change in your condition.

The healthcare professional may then carry out a brief physical examination.

Once the healthcare professional has completed their medical report, they will send it to the decision maker, who will decide whether or not to award you attendance allowance and, if it is awarded, at what rate.

Delays

The DWP aims to give you a decision within 22 working days (ie not including weekends or public holidays) of the day your attendance allowance claim is received. If you are claiming under the 'special rules' (see Box B.8 in Chapter 4) you should get a decision within eight working days. Compensation may be payable for long delays (see Chapter 60(2) for details).

In any case, if your claim is taking too long, complain to the Customer Services Manager at the Disability Benefits Centre dealing with your claim.

18. The award

Attendance allowance may be awarded for a fixed period or indefinitely. If your award is for a fixed period, the Blackpool Benefits Centre will invite you to make a renewal claim about four months before the end of your current award.

Backdating – Attendance allowance cannot be backdated to earlier than the pay day on or after your date of claim (see 15 above). There are only limited situations in which an earlier date can be treated as your date of claim. These are:

❑ If industrial action has caused postal disruption, the day your claim would have been delivered to a Disability Benefits Centre is treated as your date of claim.

C&P regs, reg 6(5)

❑ If a decision maker uses their discretion to treat anything written as being sufficient in the circumstances to count as a valid claim, the date of that earlier document is treated as your date of claim.

19. If you are not happy with the decision

If you are not happy with the decision on your claim, you can ask for a revision within one calendar month of the date the DWP sends you the decision. The decision letter should make it clear who to write to. With a revision, a decision maker will reconsider your claim. They can confirm the initial decision, or increase or reduce the rate of your award, or the length of your award. You have a further month to appeal to an independent tribunal if you are still not happy. The one-month time limit to ask for a revision can be extended only if there are special reasons for the delay. Otherwise, if the decision was notified to you more than one month ago, see below.

Asking for a revision

If you want to challenge the decision, it will help to know why it was made. You must also get your revision in on time. Ring the phone number on the decision letter and do the following:

■ request a revision of the decision. State your grounds simply at this stage, eg, *'You have underestimated how my disability affects me and how much care and supervision I need'*;

■ ask them to send you copies of all the evidence that was used in making the decision; *and*

B.15 Long-term diary

This is a diary kept over a 3-month period by a 73-year old man with rheumatoid arthritis:

04/03/13 Fell in the front room. My left ankle gave way. (I use a frame to walk, which helps me to steady myself, but when my ankles or knees give way I cannot bear my weight with my arms, which are weak at the elbow, and I usually end up on the floor.) I bruised my left hip. It took me five minutes to get up again.

17/03/13 Tripped in the hall. My left ankle again. This time fell against the cupboard. No injury or damage.

26/03/13 Stumbled on patio, carrying small plant pot. My right knee gave way. Banged my head on the door. Small cut above left eyebrow.

12/04/13 Fell in shower. Early in the morning – just due to general stiffness and weakness. Badly bruised right shoulder. Took ten minutes to get out. Scalded my right thigh. I rang my GP, who sent nurse round to look at the injuries. Not too serious; could have been much worse. She dressed the scald.

24/04/13 Stumbled in hall. Right knee again. Didn't hurt myself, but trod on the cat.

13/05/13 Fell on the patio again, left ankle this time. My son was there. Badly sprained my right ankle. My son suspected I might have broken something and took me to casualty, where the ankle was cold-compressed and dressed.

■ ask them not to take any further action until you have had the chance to respond to that evidence.

Put your request in writing as well and send it to the address on the decision letter. Keep a copy. If you have not received the evidence after two weeks, ring them again to remind them to send it. When you do receive the evidence, you should have a better idea of why the decision was made.

Building a case
Sometimes the only evidence used will be the information you gave on the attendance allowance claim-form. In most cases, however, there will be a medical report as well. This will be either a short report from your GP, consultant or nurse for instance, or a longer one from a healthcare professional who examined you on behalf of the DWP. Check the report and your claim-form. Try to find where a difference of opinion arises.

For example, you may have written on the claim-form that you could not get up and down the stairs without support, but the DWP-approved healthcare professional noted in their report that they considered you could manage by yourself. Now try to get medical evidence showing that what you said on the claim-form is correct: eg a letter from your doctor or consultant, confirming the difficulties and risks you have in getting up and down stairs, possibly detailing any falls you have had that they are aware of.

While good medical evidence is usually the most effective, a letter from someone who knows the help you need, such as a carer, can also be useful.

Once you have evidence to support your case, send it to the address on the decision letter. If it is likely to take a while to get the evidence, you must inform the DWP how long this is likely to take, so they do not make a decision straight away.

A decision maker will look at any further evidence you send in. They will then either revise the decision or write back to you explaining that they have been unable to change the decision. Either way, if you are not satisfied with the result, you now have a month from the date of the new decision to lodge an appeal to an independent tribunal. For more on appeals, see Chapter 58.

If the decision was notified more than one month ago
To challenge a decision notified more than one month ago (or if there has been a change of circumstances), you need to show there are specific grounds, eg:
■ there has been a change of circumstances since the decision was made – eg your condition has deteriorated and your care needs have increased; *or*
■ the decision maker didn't know about some relevant fact – eg you missed out some aspect of your care needs when you filled in the claim-form.

See Chapter 58, Box T.5 for more details

20. How are you paid?
Attendance allowance is paid to you, not to a carer, to spend as you wish. It is usually paid on a Wednesday, every four weeks in arrears, into your bank, building society or Post Office card account or paid with your state pension.

Appointees
If you cannot manage your own affairs, the DWP can appoint another person to act on your behalf (see Chapter 57(4)). But attendance allowance is your benefit, not your appointee's benefit. If you don't want someone else formally appointed to act for you, but cannot collect your attendance allowance yourself, you can arrange with the bank, building society or Post Office for someone to do this for you.

21. What if your condition changes?
If your condition gets worse – If you already receive attendance allowance at the lower rate, give the Blackpool Benefits Centre details of the change (see inside back cover for contact details). Your existing award may be superseded to award the higher rate.

If your condition improves – If your need for assistance lessens, this could mean your rate of attendance allowance should drop. Contact the Blackpool Benefits Centre to give them details. The decision maker will usually supersede your award.

If your rate of attendance allowance drops (or ends) but you have a relapse within two years, you can regain your former rate of benefit in a linked claim without having to serve the qualifying period again.

AA regs, reg 3

6 Help with mobility

1. Blue Badge scheme
The Blue Badge scheme of parking concessions allows people with severe mobility problems, registered blind people, and those with severe disabilities in both arms to park close to places they wish to visit.

You should not be wheel-clamped or towed away if you are displaying a current badge, although your vehicle may be moved if it is causing an obstruction. The badge does not apply to parking on private roads and land. The badge does not automatically confer exemption from car park charges.

The entire side of the badge showing the wheelchair symbol must be visible from outside the vehicle; displaying the wrong side (the photo) can result in a penalty charge notice.

DP(BMV) Regs, regs 11 & 12

It is an offence not to allow a police officer, traffic warden, parking attendant or civil enforcement officer to fully examine a badge.

For more information about the Blue Badge in England, ring 0844 463 0213.

Where can you park?
The scheme allows a vehicle displaying a valid badge in the correct place to park:
■ without charge or time limit at on-street parking meters and in Pay and Display bays, unless signs show a time limit for badge holders;
■ without time limit in streets where otherwise waiting is allowed for only limited periods;
■ for a maximum of three hours in England, Wales and Northern Ireland, or without any time limit in Scotland, on single or double yellow lines.

In England and Wales, a parking disc must also be displayed showing the time of arrival if you are parked on yellow lines or in a reserved parking place for badge holders that has a time limit (if you are visiting England or Wales from Scotland or Northern Ireland, ask your local authority for a disc). The time limit only applies during the operating hours of the restriction.

It is required that:
■ the badge holder is in the vehicle when it arrives at or when it leaves the parking place;
■ the vehicle is not parked in a bus or cycle lane during the lane's hours of operation;
■ the vehicle is not parked where there is a ban on loading or unloading; *and*

■ all other parking regulations are observed.
LATO(EDP) Regs, regs 7-9

Red routes are subject to special controls on stopping, but there are usually parking bays for badge holders.

Where does the scheme apply?

The scheme applies in England, Northern Ireland, Scotland and Wales, but there are major differences in the scheme's operation in certain London boroughs (City of London, Westminster, Kensington and Chelsea, and part of Camden). Contact the local authority for details. The scheme does not apply in security zones, eg at airports.
LATO(EDP) Regs, reg 5(2)

Do you qualify?

You qualify automatically for a Blue Badge if you are aged 2 or over *and*:

■ receive the higher rate mobility component of disability living allowance; *or*
■ receive war pensioners' mobility supplement; *or*
■ are registered blind; *or*
■ have received a lump sum payment from the Armed Forces and Reserve Forces Compensation scheme (within tariff levels 1-8); *or*
■ (in England) have been awarded 8 points or more in the 'moving around' activity of personal independence payment (PIP) or (in Scotland and Wales) have been awarded 8 points or more in the 'moving around' activity or 12 points in the 'planning and following journeys' activity.

You may also qualify through the 'assessed route' if you are aged 2 or over *and*:

■ have a *'permanent and substantial disability which causes inability to walk or very considerable difficulty in walking'*; *or*
■ drive regularly, have a severe disability in both arms and are unable to operate, or have considerable difficulty in operating, all or some types of parking meter; *or*
■ (in Scotland only) are unable to walk or virtually unable to walk because of a temporary but substantial disability which is likely to last for a period of at least 12 months but less than three years.

In these three cases, you may be assessed by your local authority.

Special rules allow children under the age of 3 to qualify for a Blue Badge if they have a specific medical condition which means they:

■ must always be accompanied by bulky medical equipment that cannot be carried around with the child without great difficulty; *and/or*
■ need to be kept near a motor vehicle at all times so that they can, if necessary, be treated in the vehicle or quickly driven to a place where they can be treated.

'Bulky medical equipment' includes in particular any of the following:

■ ventilators;
■ suction machines;
■ feed pumps;
■ parenteral equipment;
■ syringe drivers;
■ oxygen administration equipment;
■ continual oxygen saturation monitoring equipment; *and*
■ casts and associated medical equipment for the correction of hip dysplasia.
DP(BMV) Regs, reg 4

Applications are processed by local authorities, or the Roads Service in Northern Ireland (028 6634 3700). In England, you may be charged a statutory maximum fee of £10; in Scotland, up to £20; in Northern Ireland the fee is £2; in Wales it is free of charge. The badge will last up to three years. You can apply online at www.gov.uk/apply-blue-badge if you live in England or Wales, or www.directscot.org/article/blue-badge-scheme if you live in Scotland.
DP(BMV) Regs, reg 6

Appeals

If your local authority refuses to issue you with a Blue Badge, you have no formal right of appeal. As many authorities have internal procedures for dealing with appeals, it is worth writing to request a review. Alternatively, your councillor or a disability group or advice agency might help change their mind. You only have a formal right of appeal (to the Secretary of State for Transport) if you have been denied a badge on grounds of misuse.
DP(BMV) Regs, reg 10

Congestion charging exemption

Exemption from congestion charging in Central London is available to Blue Badge holders for an initial £10 administration fee if they apply to the Congestion Charging Office (for an application form ring 0845 900 1234 or visit www.tfl.gov.uk). This exemption can be used on any two vehicles. Vehicles with an exempt 'Disabled' class tax disc are automatically exempt if they are registered at DVLA, Swansea.

European concessions

Blue Badge holders visiting European Union countries that provide disabled parking concessions can take advantage of those by displaying their badge. Concessions vary. Details can be found in the European Commission booklet *Parking card for people with disabilities in the European Union* (http:// tinyurl.com/6p2dtyw).

For more information

Contact Disabled Motoring UK (01508 489 449). The *Blue Badge Parking Guide for London* contains information on how the scheme operates in London (£6.99 including postage, PIE Enterprises 0844 847 0875; www.thepieguide.com).

2. Exemption from road tax (VED)

Who can get exemption? – All vehicles on the road are liable to Vehicle Excise Duty (VED), better known as road tax. However, exemption from VED (including the first registration fee) for one car is given to some disabled people. If you receive one of the following qualifying benefits:

■ higher rate mobility component of disability living allowance (DLA);
■ enhanced rate mobility component of personal independence payment (PIP);
■ armed forces independence payment (AFIP); *or*
■ war pensioners' mobility supplement,

you (or your appointee or someone you choose to nominate in your place) can apply for exemption from VED. Long-stay

---

Disability Rights UK publications

Get Motoring

A practical guide to help disabled people find and finance a suitable car. It includes information on:

■ getting a driving licence
■ driving lessons and tests
■ finding the right car
■ the Motability Scheme

Free download available from
www.disabilityrightsuk.org

hospital patients with transitional protection can still get the exemption.

If you receive the standard rate mobility component of PIP, you will be entitled to a 50% discount off your VED.

Vehicle Excise & Registration Act 1994, Sch 2, para 19

The Act states that *'A vehicle is an exempt vehicle when it is being used, or kept for use, by or for the purposes of a disabled person'*. What exactly this means has never been defined. The use of an exempt car for purposes totally unconnected with the disabled person is unlawful.

When you are awarded DLA higher rate or PIP enhanced rate mobility component, you should receive a re-usable *'Certificate of Entitlement'*, which lasts for the duration of your mobility award. It will only be issued once and will be required each time you need to renew your tax disc. If you have not been sent the certificate (or want guidance on it), write to the Blackpool Benefits Centre (see inside back cover).

If you are getting war pensioners' mobility supplement or the AFIP, you need to apply for an exemption certificate: WPA0442. To do this, contact the Service Personnel and Veterans Agency (0800 169 2277; textphone: 0800 169 3458).

Motability contract hire customers enjoy the same exemptions, but the process is handled by Motability.

Nominating another person's vehicle – If you receive a qualifying benefit, you can nominate another person's vehicle to be exempt from road tax. This may also apply to a company car registered in the name of the company; the person receiving mobility component should nominate the company for exemption. In order to qualify for exemption, the vehicle should be used *'by or for the purposes of'* the disabled person. The named person who gets the exemption may be changed at any time. For example, if you have nominated someone else for exemption and then get your own car, the exemption can be returned to you.

If you are refused exemption – Even if you have an Certificate of Entitlement from the DWP, it is within the discretion of the DVLA to refuse to grant exemption from road tax if they think the vehicle will not be used *'solely by or for the purposes of'* the disabled person. They are unlikely to do this unless your intended use of the vehicle would blatantly breach this condition.

If you are refused exemption, there is no formal procedure for appealing. However, you can write, giving full details of why you think you qualify for exemption, the purposes for which the vehicle will be used, etc to: Specialist Casework, DVLA Swansea SA99 1ZZ (030 0790 6802).

B.16 Mobility checklist

It is important to choose the car and adaptations that are best suited to you. Contact the Forum of Mobility Centres (www.mobility-centres.org.uk) for practical advice.

Motability

Motability is an independent charity set up to help people with disabilities use one of the following qualifying benefits to improve their mobility:

■ higher rate mobility component of disability living allowance;
■ enhanced rate mobility component of personal independence payment;
■ armed forces independence payment; *or*
■ war pensioner's mobility supplement.

The scheme offers cars (including cars adapted to carry a driver or passenger seated in their wheelchair), powered wheelchairs and mobility scooters. Many car adaptation costs can be included.

People receiving a qualifying benefit (or the parents of children who receive it), who need adaptations to their car or help with the initial deposit can apply to Motability for additional discretionary help.

To use the Motability scheme, your qualifying benefit must usually have at least 12 months still to run. The DWP (or the Service Personnel and Veterans Agency) will make payments direct to Motability.

You cannot start or renew a Motability car agreement if you are in hospital.

Motability can sometimes help towards the cost of driving lessons if the applicant receives a qualifying benefit and is aged under 25.

For enquiries about either scheme, contact Motability Operations, City Gate House, 22 Southwark Bridge Road, London SE1 9HB (0845 456 4566; www.motability.co.uk).

Concessions on cars and wheelchairs

Some car companies offer discounts to disabled people; ask the dealership for details.

The NHS can supply and maintain wheelchairs free of charge in some circumstances, and may provide a voucher towards the cost of a more expensive wheelchair of your choice (see Chapter 30(5)).

If you are working, you may be able to get financial help towards a mobility solution through Access to Work (see Chapter 18(5)).

For details on VAT exemption on car purchase price or the cost of adaptations to the car, see Chapter 52. This must be claimed before you purchase the car.

Concessions on public transport

You can buy a Disabled Person's Railcard (£20 for one year or £54 for three years), which entitles you and a companion to one-third off the cost of most train journeys. The scheme is for people with a wide range of disabilities; check the claim-form or website for a full list. You can get details from www.disabledpersons-railcard.co.uk or by ringing 0845 605 0525 (textphone 0845 601 0132).

In England, people who have reached the qualifying age for pension credit (see Chapter 42(2)) and eligible disabled people are entitled to free off-peak travel on all local buses anywhere in England. Application forms are available from local authorities. In Wales, there is a similar concession for any time of day.

In Scotland, older and disabled people are entitled to free Scotland-wide bus travel on most services. You need to apply for a National Entitlement Card; application forms are available from local authorities or SPT Travel Centres.

For travel concessions in Northern Ireland, enquire at Translink bus and rail stations or ring 028 9066 6630.

Concessions are available on some ferry routes and Eurotunnel for disabled people travelling with a car. Contact Disabled Motoring UK (01508 489 449; www.disabledmotoring.org).

Help with travel to work – see Chapter 18(5).

Assessment services and information

A network of accredited mobility centres, members of the Forum of Mobility Centres, offers professional assessment, advice and recommendations for drivers and passengers with mobility needs. For information about accredited centres, ring 0800 559 3636. Advice, information and contact details for Mobility Centres can also be found on the website (www.mobility-centres.org.uk).

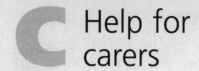

Help for carers

7 Carer's allowance

1. What is carer's allowance?

Carer's allowance is a benefit for people who regularly spend at least 35 hours a week caring for a severely disabled person. You don't have to be related to, or live with, the disabled person. You can get carer's allowance even if you've never worked. You are not prevented from getting carer's allowance if you are disabled yourself and also need care. If you are entitled to carer's allowance, a carer premium of £33.30 will be included in your applicable amount for means-tested benefits (see 9 below).

Carer's allowance is not means tested and does not depend on national insurance (NI) contributions. It is taxable and counts as income for tax credits. Carer's allowance gives you Class 1 NI contribution credits (see Box D.7, Chapter 12) and helps you qualify for additional state pension (see Chapter 43(6)).

The severe disability premium – If you are paid carer's allowance, the person you are caring for cannot get the severe disability premium included in their applicable amount for means-tested benefits (or the equivalent amount used in pension credit). Because of this, it is not always advantageous to claim carer's allowance even if you are eligible. See Chapter 25(3). The person you care for will not lose the severe disability premium (or the pension credit equivalent) if you are entitled to carer's allowance but cannot be paid it because of the overlapping benefits rule (see 6 below).

The benefit cap – Carer's allowance is included in the list of benefits to which the 'benefit cap' applies. This cap, which will be rolled out nationally between 15.7.13 and 30.9.13, limits the total weekly benefits that can be claimed. See Box H.1 in Chapter 21 for details (including exemptions).

2. Do you qualify?

❑ You must regularly spend at least 35 hours a week (see below) caring for a person who receives one of the following *'qualifying benefits'*:
- disability living allowance (DLA) care component (at the middle or highest rate only); *or*
- attendance allowance (at either rate); *or*
- personal independence payment (PIP) daily living component (at either rate); *or*
- constant attendance allowance (of £64.70 or more) paid with the Industrial Injuries/War Pensions schemes; *or*
- armed forces independence payment.

❑ You must be aged 16 or over.
❑ You must not be in full-time education. You are generally treated as being in full-time education if your course is described as such by your educational establishment, although there can be exceptions, eg you have been granted exemptions from parts of your course or your course is not a traditional university-type course. Even if your course is not described as full time you will be treated as in full-time education if the course involves supervised study of 21 hours a week or more.
❑ If you work, you must not earn more than £100 a week (see 5 below).
❑ You must pass the UK residence and presence tests, and must not be subject to immigration control (see Chapter 49(2) and (3)).
SSCBA, S.70 & ICA Regs, regs 3, 5, 8 & 9

Carer's allowance can continue for up to eight weeks after the person you look after dies. You must continue to satisfy all the rules other than those related to the care of a disabled person or that person's receipt of a qualifying benefit.
SSCBA, S.70(1A)

If someone else gets carer's allowance to look after the same person you look after, you cannot also get carer's allowance to look after them. You can get national insurance credits (see Box D.7, Chapter 12) to help protect your entitlement to a state pension and you may get income support as a carer (but not the carer premium). You and the other carer can decide who should claim carer's allowance. You can only get one award of carer's allowance, even if you care for more than one person.
SSCBA, S.70(7)

If you were aged 65 or over and entitled to carer's allowance on 27.10.02 (then called invalid care allowance), you can continue to get carer's allowance even if you stop caring for 35 hours a week or if the DLA, attendance allowance or PIP of the person you look after stops or if you start full-time work. You must, however, continue to meet the other carer's allowance rules.
Regulatory Reform (Carer's Allowance) Order 2002, art 4

Caring for 35 hours a week – If you are caring for more than one person, you can't add together the time you spend caring for each of them. You have to show that for at least 35 hours each week you are caring for one person. If you meet the 35-hours test during part of the year (eg in school holidays) you may qualify for carer's allowance during that period.

Carer's allowance benefit weeks run from the start of Sunday to the end of the following Saturday. The hours of caring in any given week must total at least 35: you cannot average the hours over a number of weeks. If, for example, you provide care on alternate weekends, it may be difficult to show you provide care for 35 hours in any given benefit week, as the care you provide on Saturday will fall within one benefit week and Sunday's care will fall into the next. The time you spend caring includes preparing for the visit of the person you care for on the day they arrive, clearing up after they leave, and collecting them from or taking them back to the place where they usually live (CG/6/1990).
ICA Regs, reg 4

3. How much do you get?

Carer's allowance	per week
For yourself	£59.75
For an adult dependant*	£35.15
Extra for dependent children**	
For the oldest child	£8.10
For each other child	£11.35

* available only on claims made before 6.4.10
** available only on claims made before 6.4.03

4. How do you claim?

Claim on form DS700, or on DS700(SP) if you get a state pension. These forms are available from a Jobcentre Plus office or Pension Centre or from the Carer's Allowance Unit (0845 608 4321; 0800 220 674 in Northern Ireland). You can also claim online (www.dwp.gov.uk/carersallowance/). The claim-form includes a statement to be signed by the cared-for person. This asks them to confirm that they know a claim for carer's allowance is being made, that the carer provides them with at least 35 hours' care a week and that they are aware their own benefits could be affected by the claim (ie if they receive the severe disability premium – see Chapter 25(3)). If the cared-for person is incapable of signing the statement themselves, it can be done by someone acting on their behalf.

Once you claim carer's allowance you may be offered the option of attending a voluntary interview to discuss work prospects. However, if you are also claiming certain other benefits, eg income support, you may be obliged to attend an interview as a condition of receiving that other benefit (see Box T.1, Chapter 57).

Backdating – If you were entitled to carer's allowance prior to claiming it, you can ask that it be backdated for up to three months. If you have been waiting for the person you are caring for to be awarded a qualifying benefit (see 2 above), and you claim carer's allowance within three months of the date the qualifying benefit is awarded, your claim for carer's allowance can be treated as having been made on the first day of the benefit week in which the qualifying benefit became payable. Thus carer's allowance can be fully backdated to that time if you satisfied the other conditions of entitlement throughout that period.

C&P Regs, reg 6(33)

If entitlement to carer's allowance means you can start receiving a benefit such as income support because of the award of a carer premium, you should claim the benefit at the same time that you claim carer's allowance to ensure it is also backdated.

What happens next? – You will be sent a written decision on your claim. If you disagree with the decision, you have one month in which to dispute it, either by asking a decision maker in the Carer's Allowance Unit to revise the decision or by lodging an appeal (see Chapter 58). From October 2013, you must seek a revision before you will have the option of an appeal.

5. How do earnings affect carer's allowance?

You cannot get carer's allowance if your net earnings are more than £100 a week – the 'earnings limit'. See below for the way in which earnings are calculated.

ICA Regs, reg 8

Your partner's earnings do not affect your basic benefit but can affect any addition(s) for a dependent adult or children. If you get an adult dependant's addition, it will not be paid in any week that your partner earns more than £35.15. If you are still entitled to any child dependant's addition(s) and your partner earns £220 or more in any week, you will lose an addition for one child in the next week. For each extra

£29 earned, you lose another child dependant's addition.

Social Security Benefit (Dependency) Regs 1977, Sch 2, para 2B

Occupational and personal pensions count as earnings for adult and child dependants' additions, but not for the basic rate of carer's allowance. Earnings of £100 a week or less do not affect carer's allowance, but any means-tested benefit you also receive may be reduced (see Chapter 27(3)-(5)).

Calculating earnings

In working out how much of your earnings are taken into account, certain deductions and disregards can be made from gross earnings. Count any payment from your employer as earnings (eg bonus, commission, retainer). If you stop work and then claim carer's allowance, most payments made at the end of your job are ignored, eg pay in lieu of notice or holiday pay. If you are self-employed, the rules on working out net profit follow the rules for means-tested benefits (see Chapter 27(4)).

From your gross weekly earnings (or net profit) deduct:

- income tax, national insurance contributions (Class 1, 2 or 4) and half of any contribution you make to an occupational or personal pension;
- expenses *'wholly, exclusively and necessarily incurred in the performance of the duties of the employment'*, eg equipment, special clothing, travel between workplaces (but not travel between home and work);
- advance of earnings or a loan from your employer;
- fostering allowance;
- payments from a local authority, health authority or voluntary organisation for someone temporarily in your care;
- the first £20 of rent paid to you by a subtenant(s);
- the first £20 a week plus half the rest of the income from a boarder;
- the whole of any contribution towards living and accommodation costs from someone living in your home (other than boarders and subtenants);
- earnings from employment payable abroad where transfer to the UK is prohibited;
- charges for currency conversion;
- annual bounty paid to part-time members of the fire brigade or lifeboat service, or to auxiliary coastguards or members of a territorial or reserve force;
- payments for expenses related to participation in a public body service user group.

CE Regs, regs 9 & 10 & Sch 1

If earnings paid in one week are over the limit, carer's allowance is lost the following week. Monthly earnings are worked out on a weekly basis and affect benefit for the month ahead. If earnings fluctuate, they may be averaged over a recognisable cycle of work or over five weeks, but this is discretionary. One-off payments that are not for any specific period are divided by the relevant weekly earnings limit to work out the number of weeks your benefit will be affected.

CE Regs, reg 8

Care costs – For basic carer's allowance, if because of your work you pay someone other than a 'close relative' to look after the person you care for or to look after a child aged under 16, these payments are deducted from your earnings. A maximum of half your net earnings can be ignored in this way. A 'close relative' is the parent, son, daughter, brother, sister or partner of either yourself or the disabled person you care for.

CE Regs, regs 10(3)(b) & 13(3)(b) and Sch 3

For dependant additions in carer's allowance, or for calculating earnings in other non-means-tested benefits, more restrictive rules apply. Childcare costs of up to £60 a week can be deducted from earnings for children under 11. You must be paying a registered childminder or other registered childcare provider (or paying for childcare provided on Crown premises or by schools, hospitals, etc where childcare is exempt from registration) or paying an out-of-school-hours scheme (run on school premises or provided by a local authority) to look after at least one child aged eight or over but under 11. In addition, you can only have childcare costs counted if you are a lone parent, or one of a couple and either you are both working or one of you is working and the other is *'incapacitated'*.

CE Regs, regs 10(2)(b) & 13(2)(b) and Sch 2

You are treated as incapacitated if you get disability living allowance, personal independence payment or attendance

C.1 Caring away from your home

Seek legal advice
If you have to leave your own home to care for a disabled or elderly relative or friend, seek advice before you go (see Chapter 59). Consider what you will do if the need for that care stops, if your relationship with the cared-for person deteriorates, or if they die, go into a care home or become mentally incapable of looking after their own affairs.

Housing costs
If you leave your main home temporarily, you remain liable for housing costs, including the rent or mortgage. If the absence is for up to 13 weeks, you can claim help with rent from housing benefit (see Chapter 21(6)) or help with mortgage interest from income-related employment and support allowance, income support, income-based jobseeker's allowance or pension credit (see Chapter 26). That help continues for up to 52 weeks if the care you provide is medically approved. If you think your absence might be for longer than 13 weeks, ask a doctor or other medical professional (eg a nurse) involved in the disabled person's care to provide a letter approving the care you provide.

Housing benefit and help with mortgage interest stop after a continuous absence of 13 or 52 weeks. However, if you return home (perhaps with the disabled person) for even a very short stay, a new period of absence should then start, allowing you to continue getting benefit beyond those initial limits. Tell the office dealing with your claim of each visit to your home and keep a record of the dates of the visits. If you leave your home permanently, help with housing costs will stop immediately.

Council tax
If you have left your home empty to live elsewhere to care for someone, your former home may be exempt from council tax. The person you care for must need that care because they are elderly, ill or disabled, or have a mental disorder or a drug or alcohol problem. For the exemption to apply, the empty property must have ceased to be your sole or main residence.

If the home of the person you care for becomes your sole or main residence, you may be counted as living there for council tax purposes. However, your presence in their home will be disregarded if:
■ they are not your child under 18 or your partner;
■ they are entitled to a 'qualifying benefit' (see section 2 in Chapter 7); *and*
■ you spend at least 35 hours a week on average caring for them.
This means council tax for the home will be the same as if you were not resident there. See Chapter 22(9).

allowance (or the equivalent for War Pensions or Industrial Injuries schemes), long-term incapacity benefit or severe disablement allowance, or you are getting housing benefit and either childcare costs have been allowed under the rules for this benefit (see Chapter 27(5)) or a disability premium or higher pensioner premium has been awarded based on your (not your partner's) disability. Note that employment and support allowance is not on this list.

CE Regs, Sch 2, para 8

6. How do other benefits affect carer's allowance?
You cannot be paid carer's allowance while you are receiving the same amount or more from:
■ state pension;
■ maternity allowance;
■ incapacity benefit or unemployability supplement;
■ contributory employment and support allowance;
■ contribution-based jobseeker's allowance;
■ widows' benefits and bereavement benefits;
■ a state training allowance.
This is known as the overlapping benefits rule. If you get less than the basic rate of carer's allowance from one of the above benefits, that benefit is paid and topped up with carer's allowance to the amount you would get from carer's allowance alone. Only the basic rate of these benefits overlaps with carer's allowance. Carer's allowance can be paid in addition to any earnings-related or age-related addition to the other benefit.

If your partner is entitled to a dependency addition for you with one of these benefits, the addition cannot be paid if you get the same amount or more from carer's allowance. If carer's allowance is less than the addition, you receive carer's allowance and your partner gets the difference between carer's allowance and the standard rate of the addition. If you get an adult dependant's addition with your carer's allowance, it will stop if your dependant gets an overlapping benefit of £35.15 a week or more.

OB Regs, regs 4, 6 & 9

You can get carer's allowance at the same time as disability living allowance, attendance allowance or personal independence payment.

If the person you look after gets the severe disability premium included in the calculation of a means-tested benefit, this will stop once you get carer's allowance. If you cannot be paid carer's allowance because of the overlapping benefit rules, the person you care for will not lose the severe disability premium, even if you get a carer premium.

Severe disablement allowance (SDA) – SDA and carer's allowance also overlap. Normally, carer's allowance is paid in full, topped up with any balance of SDA. However, if your SDA is the same amount or more than carer's allowance, you can ask for your SDA to be paid in full. The person you care for is then not excluded from the severe disability premium and you can still claim a carer premium.

7. Carer's allowance and income support
You may be entitled to both carer's allowance and income support (see Box E.1, Chapter 15). Because income support is means tested, it is reduced by the amount of your carer's allowance (although any additional carer's allowance paid for a dependent child is ignored if you also receive child tax credit). The advantages of claiming carer's allowance are outlined in 9 below. If you are paid carer's allowance, the person you care for is excluded from the severe disability premium, but only once carer's allowance is actually paid; arrears of carer's allowance do not affect entitlement to the premium.

IS Regs, Sch 2, para 13(3ZA)

8. Carer's allowance and state pension

If you begin receiving a state pension that is more than carer's allowance (not including age- or earnings-related additions), payment of carer's allowance will stop due to the overlapping benefit rules (see 6 above). If your state pension is less than carer's allowance, state pension is paid and topped up with carer's allowance to the basic weekly rate of carer's allowance. If all that prevents payment of carer's allowance is your state pension, a carer addition (£33.30) is included in the calculation of your pension credit (see Chapter 42(3)), and a carer premium (£33.30) is included in the calculation of housing benefit (see Chapter 25(6)).

If you defer claiming your state pension (see Chapter 43(7)) you will not receive increased pension payments for any period in which you get carer's allowance instead.

9. Why claim carer's allowance?

Your household income might not be higher after claiming carer's allowance, since it overlaps with other benefits. But if you are entitled to carer's allowance, even if it can't be paid because of other benefits, you might get:

- a carer premium included in your income-related employment and support allowance, income support, income-based jobseeker's allowance, housing benefit or health benefits. The premium is included if you get carer's allowance or have an underlying entitlement to carer's allowance but receive an overlapping benefit instead (see 6 above). An addition equivalent to the carer premium can be included in the calculation of pension credit. See Chapter 25(6);
- Class 1 national insurance contribution credits (see Box D.7, Chapter 12) or help towards satisfying the national insurance contribution conditions for contributory employment and support allowance (see Chapter 12(6)) and jobseeker's allowance (see Chapter 16(15));
- help to qualify for additional state pension (see Chapter 43(6)).

10. Time off from caring

Carer's allowance rules allow breaks in care of up to 12 weeks in any 26-week period. Carer's allowance is payable for up to 12 weeks if you or the person you look after goes into hospital (but see below). Up to four of the 12 weeks can be for other temporary breaks in care – eg a holiday or short-term stay in a care home for the person you look after. After this, you cannot be paid carer's allowance for any week in which you do not provide care for at least 35 hours.

ICA Regs, reg 4(2)

Going into hospital – If you are in hospital, your carer's allowance will stop after 12 weeks. It may stop sooner if you have been in hospital or had a break in care within the last 26 weeks.

If the person you look after goes into hospital, the 12-weeks-off rule still applies, but in practice your carer's allowance may stop sooner. Your carer's allowance depends on the disabled person receiving a *'qualifying benefit'* (see 2 above). If they go into hospital and the stay is arranged by the NHS, payment of the qualifying benefit stops after 28 days if they are aged 16 or over, or after 12 weeks for children under 16. Your carer's allowance will stop when their qualifying benefit stops. If the person can arrange a pattern of respite care that allows them to keep their qualifying benefit, carer's allowance may continue to be paid (see Box B.13, Chapter 5).

Arranging care breaks – A week off is a week in which you care for the disabled person for less than 35 hours, so odd days or weekends away are unlikely to affect your carer's allowance entitlement. A weekend straddles two carer's allowance weeks: a carer's allowance week runs from Sunday to Saturday. This means if you arrange respite care from midweek to midweek, you may still care for the required 35 hours both in the week the disabled person goes into respite care and the week they come home. These weeks won't count as weeks off and carer's allowance will be paid even though you've had a full week of respite care.

New carers – To get paid carer's allowance for breaks in care, new carers must have been caring for the disabled person for at least 35 hours a week for an initial period of at least 22 weeks and the disabled person must also have been in receipt of a qualifying benefit (see 2 above). However, it is not necessary for the carer to have actually been in receipt of carer's allowance during this initial period. You can include up to eight weeks of hospital stays in those 22 weeks if you would have cared for the disabled person had they (or you) not been in hospital.

Tell the DWP – Report any of these changes in writing to the Carer's Allowance Unit as soon as possible to avoid having to repay overpaid benefit.

Keep a diary – If all this seems confusing, keep a diary.

8 Other help for carers

1. Introduction

This chapter covers some of the financial and practical help available for carers. Parents of disabled children should also look at Chapter 37. Some of the help depends on you getting carer's allowance (see Chapter 7). See Chapter 22(9) for details of the council tax discount scheme as it affects carers caring in their own home. Other help depends on your circumstances: eg whether you have given up work, have a low income or have a disability yourself. See the benefits checklist (pages 4-5) for other benefits to which you may be entitled.

2. Giving up work

You may be entitled to carer's allowance if you spend at least 35 hours a week caring for someone who gets a qualifying disability benefit (see Chapter 7(2)). You are eligible for carer's allowance even if you have a partner who is working.

If your income and savings are low and you are under pension credit qualifying age, claim income support. If you have other income or savings, you may be better off claiming contribution-based jobseeker's allowance (JSA) for the first six months (see below). If you have a limited capability for work, you may be able to claim employment and support allowance (see 4 below). If you have reached pension credit qualifying age, you may be able to claim pension credit (see Chapter 42). If you have dependent children, claim child tax credit (see Chapter 19). You may be eligible for housing benefit (see Chapter 21) or help with NHS costs (Chapter 54).

Income support

Income support (IS) is a means-tested benefit for people under pension credit qualifying age. It can be paid on its own if you (and your partner, if you have one) have no other income, or it can top up your carer's allowance or other income. You normally cannot get IS if you have capital over £16,000 or a partner who works for 24 hours a week or more. See Chapter 15 for details.

You are eligible for IS if you get carer's allowance. You can also get IS if you are *'regularly and substantially engaged in caring for a disabled person'* who gets a qualifying benefit (see Chapter 7(2)); it is possible to get IS under this rule even if you provide less than 35 hours' care a week. You can claim IS as a carer for up to six months while you are waiting for a claim for disability living allowance or attendance allowance to be processed. If you stop being treated as a carer for IS, you continue to be eligible for IS for eight weeks if you satisfy all of the other IS rules. Otherwise, you may need to claim JSA instead.

Carer premium – If you or your partner get carer's allowance, a carer premium of £33.30 a week is included in the assessment for IS and other means-tested benefits (see Chapter 25(6)). You can get this premium included if all that prevents the payment of carer's allowance is the overlapping benefits rule (see Chapter 7(6)).

Mortgage interest – There is normally a 13-week waiting period before mortgage interest is included in your IS assessment. If you are planning to claim IS, but your income is too high if the mortgage interest is not included, consider making your claim now. The claim will be turned down, but your waiting period will have started. You will need to make a further claim for IS after 13 weeks, in which case the waiting period for the new claim can run from the date of your first claim. See Chapter 26(5).

Jobseeker's allowance
Contribution-based JSA of up to £71.70 a week (less if you are under 25) is payable for up to six months if you have paid enough national insurance contributions. You are eligible even if you have a partner who works. The amount may be reduced if you have earnings or an occupational pension. It is not affected by other income or savings. You might be better off claiming JSA instead of IS for the first six months if you have other household income or savings. Carer's allowance overlaps with contribution-based JSA – if you claim both you'll be paid JSA, perhaps topped up with carer's allowance if that is higher (see Chapter 7(6)).

JSA is for people who are available for, and actively looking for, work. Usually, you are expected to look for a full-time job even if you have given up work to be a carer. However, if you care for a person who is a close relative or member of your household, you can restrict the hours you are available for work. Carers are also allowed to ask for one week's notice before taking up a job offer from Jobcentre Plus and 48 hours' notice to attend other employment opportunities (eg an interview). If you have caring responsibilities for a child aged under 16, these notice periods can be extended in certain circumstances. See Chapter 16(4) for details.

JSA is not payable for a fixed sanction period if you leave your job voluntarily without 'good reason'. You should not be sanctioned in this way if your caring responsibilities meant it was no longer reasonable for you to continue working, although you are expected to look for alternatives before giving up work. See Chapter 16(12) for details.

3. Working part time or full time
If you are eligible for income support as a carer, you can work without limit on your weekly hours. However, you can only keep £20 a week of your net earnings (or of joint earnings if your partner also works); anything over that reduces your income support penny for penny (see Chapter 27(5)). You cannot get income support if your partner works 24 hours or more a week.

Your carer's allowance will stop if your earnings after allowable deductions go over £100 a week (see Chapter 7(5)). If your earnings are at or below £100 a week, the amount you receive is unaffected.

4. Limited capability for work
If you have a limited capability for work due to disability or ill health and are under state pension age, you may be able to claim employment and support allowance (ESA – see Chapter 10). Payment of carer's allowance usually stops when you get contributory ESA because these benefits overlap, but you keep an underlying entitlement. This means the carer premium continues to be included in any income-related ESA assessment (see Chapter 25(6)). Because carer's allowance is not actually paid, the person you care for may still get the severe disability premium (see Chapter 25(3)).

5. Over state pension age
If you don't have enough contributions for a basic state pension of at least £59.75, it can be topped up to that figure with carer's allowance. If you were 65 or over and entitled to invalid care allowance on 27.10.02, you can continue to be entitled to carer's allowance even if you cease to care for at least 35 hours a week, or the person you care for stops getting a qualifying benefit (see Chapter 7(2)).

Pension credit is a means-tested benefit to provide for basic living expenses for older people (see Chapter 42). If you claim carer's allowance and it cannot be paid because your state pension is higher, an 'additional amount for carers' is still included in your pension credit calculation.

If you are disabled, you may be eligible for disability living allowance (DLA), attendance allowance or personal independence payment (PIP) even though you are caring for another person (see Chapters 3, 4 and 5). If you and your partner get attendance allowance, middle or highest rate DLA care component or PIP daily living component, or you live alone and get one of these benefits, you may be entitled to an 'additional amount for severe disability' to be included in the pension credit calculation.

6. National insurance credits
For each week that you are entitled to carer's allowance, you get a Class 1 national insurance contribution credit (as long as you have lost, given up or never had the right to pay reduced-rate contributions). But if you already get 'credits for unemployment' or 'credits for limited capability or incapacity for work' for that week, you cannot get carer's allowance credits for that same period. Carer's allowance credits can give you a better deal than these other credits. For instance: if you were entitled to carer's allowance for the 2010/11 and 2011/12 tax years, your credits for those years may mean that if you fall sick in 2013 you'll pass the second contribution condition for employment and support allowance; at the same time, carer's allowance entitlement helps you pass the first contribution condition.

Each tax year in which you have 52 Class 1 credits is a qualifying year for state pension (see Box O.1, Chapter 43). **Credits for parents and carers** – Even if you do not get carer's allowance you may still be able to protect your

entitlement to a state pension. From 1978 to April 2010, home responsibilities protection could protect a carer's state pension record. In April 2010 this was replaced by 'credits for parents and carers'. See Box D.7 in Chapter 12 and Box O.2 in Chapter 43 for details.

Additional state pension (state second pension) – For each complete tax year between 2002/03 and 2009/10 in which you got carer's allowance or home responsibilities protection, you are treated as though you have earned enough to have made full contributions towards the state second pension for that year. From 6.4.10, weekly credits for parents and carers, paid contributions and other credits can be combined to build up an entitlement to the state second pension. See Chapter 43(6) for details.

7. Practical help

The person you care for is entitled to an assessment from the social care department (social work department in Scotland) of their need for services. Social care must also assess your support needs as a carer and look at your continuing ability to provide care if you ask them to do so (see Chapter 29(3)). See Box K.2 in Chapter 29 for a checklist of services that might be available in your area. Contact your social care department for information about short breaks and other practical help.

There might be a local carers' support group where you can share information with other carers. Contact Carers UK for details (0808 808 7777; www.carersuk.org).

8. If the person you care for dies

Your benefit entitlement may depend on the benefits of the person you care for. This is the case if you receive carer's allowance or income support as a carer. Carer's allowance can continue for up to eight weeks following the death of the person you cared for. Throughout those eight weeks you must continue to satisfy all of the conditions for carer's allowance not related to caring or payment of a qualifying benefit to the person you cared for (see Chapter 7(2)). If you were 65 or over and entitled to invalid care allowance on 27.10.02, you can continue to be entitled to carer's allowance indefinitely after the person you cared for has died.

You continue to be eligible for income support with a carer premium and/or to claim income support as a carer for eight weeks following the death. You continue to be eligible for the additional amount for carers in pension credit for eight weeks following the death, or indefinitely if you were 65 or over and entitled to invalid care allowance on 27.10.02.

If you are under pension credit qualifying age, you may be expected to claim jobseeker's allowance from eight weeks after the death. If you gave up work to be a carer, you may qualify for contribution-based jobseeker's allowance based on national insurance contributions paid when you were working (see Chapter 16(15)). Check first to see if you might be eligible for income support (see Box E.1, Chapter 15) or employment and support allowance (see Chapter 10). Even if you hadn't claimed income support before the death, you may be able to claim it now, either as a carer for up to eight weeks following the death, or on other grounds after the eight weeks has ended.

You may be eligible for bereavement benefits if it was your spouse or civil partner who died (see Chapter 53).

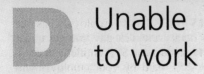

Unable to work

9 Statutory sick pay

1. What is statutory sick pay?
Statutory sick pay (SSP) is paid to employees by their employers for up to 28 weeks in any period of sickness lasting for four or more days. SSP does not depend on national insurance contributions. You can work full or part time but must earn at least the lower earnings limit (£109 from April 2013). SSP is taxable. There are no additions for dependants.

SSP is primarily the responsibility of employers. The scheme is operated by HMRC. Information for employers is provided in *E14 Employer Help Book for Statutory Sick Pay* (www.hmrc.gov.uk/helpsheets/e14.pdf). Help is also available from the National Insurance helpline: 0845 302 1479.

SSP is payable to agency workers if they satisfy the qualifying conditions. Unemployed and self-employed people cannot get SSP, but may be able to claim employment and support allowance (see Chapter 10).

If your SSP, plus any other income you get, is below your income support (IS) 'applicable amount', you can claim IS to top it up (see Chapter 15). If you don't get IS, you may still get housing benefit because SSP is treated more generously under that scheme (see Chapter 27(6) and Chapter 21).

2. Do you qualify?
Three key terms describe the qualifying conditions for SSP:
■ SSP period of incapacity for work;
■ period of entitlement;
■ qualifying days.
You can be paid SSP only if you are sick on a qualifying day and your days of sickness form part of an SSP period of incapacity for work that comes within a period of entitlement. The three qualifying conditions are explained in 3 to 5 below.

3. SSP period of incapacity for work
The first qualifying condition for SSP is that there must be an SSP *'period of incapacity for work'* (PIW). This means you must be incapable of doing the job you are employed to do because of sickness or disability for at least four days in a row. Weekends and public holidays count – therefore, every day of the week can count towards a PIW, including days when

you wouldn't have worked even if you had been fit. PIWs separated by eight weeks or less are linked and count as one PIW. Further spells of sickness must be at least four or more days in a row to link with a previous SSP PIW.
SSCBA, S.152

There are some situations when you will qualify even if you are not actually sick on a particular day. You can be treated as incapable of work for days when you are under medical care in respect of some specific disease or bodily or mental disablement and a doctor has advised you not to work for precautionary or convalescent reasons, provided you do not work on those days. You are also treated as incapable of work if you are excluded, abstain from or are prevented from working (having received the due notice in writing) because it is known or reasonably suspected that you are infected or contaminated by, or have been in contact with a case of, a relevant infection or contamination (including certain types of food poisoning).
SSP Regs, reg 2

4. Period of entitlement
The second qualifying condition for SSP is that there must be a *'period of entitlement'*, meaning the actual period of time when you are entitled to SSP. It begins with the start of the SSP period of incapacity for work (PIW) and ends when your employer's liability to pay you SSP ends.

Your employer's liability to pay SSP ends if:
■ you are no longer sick; *or*
■ you have had 28 weeks of SSP, either in one time period or linked; *or*
■ your contract of employment comes to an end (unless your employer has dismissed you solely or mainly to avoid paying you SSP); *or*
■ for pregnant women, you are at the start of the *'disqualifying period'*, which is the 39 weeks during which you are entitled to statutory maternity pay or maternity allowance. If you are entitled to neither, there are two possibilities, depending on whether or not you are already getting SSP:
  – if you are getting SSP, it cannot be paid after the day your baby is born or, if earlier, after the first day you are off work sick with a pregnancy-related illness on or after the start of the 4th week before the expected week of confinement;
  – if you are not getting SSP, it cannot be paid for a period of 18 weeks, which starts from the earlier of either the start of the week your baby is born or the start of the week you are first off sick with a pregnancy-related illness if this is after the beginning of the 4th week before your expected week of confinement; *or*
■ you are taken into legal custody; *or*
■ your linked SSP PIW has spanned three years.
SSCBA, Ss.153(2) and SSP Regs, reg 3(1) & (3)-(6)

SSP will also end if your employer no longer considers you to be incapable of work. In this case, you can appeal against the decision (see 10 below).
People who cannot get SSP – In some circumstances, you won't be entitled to SSP at all (so no period of entitlement can start). These circumstances are listed in Box D.1 – but

they must apply on the first day of an SSP PIW for you to be excluded from SSP altogether.

5. Qualifying days

SSP is paid only for *'qualifying days'*. These are normally the days you would have been required to work under the terms of your contract if you hadn't been sick – but they don't have to be.

If your working pattern varies from one week to another, you and your employer can come to some other arrangement as to which days will be qualifying days. If you and your employer reach agreement, you have a free choice of qualifying days – as long as they are not fixed by reference to the actual days you are off sick and there is at least one qualifying day in each week.

If you can't reach agreement with your employer, the qualifying days are the days your contract would have required you to work if you hadn't fallen sick. If it isn't clear which days would be working days in a particular week, the law says every day of that week except days you and your employer agree are rest days should be SSP qualifying days.

If you would not normally have worked in a particular week and do not have an agreement on qualifying days with your employer, the Wednesday of that week will be a qualifying day regardless.

If there are any doubts about qualifying days, it is important to sort this out with your employer.

SSCBA, S.154 & SSP Regs, reg 5

Waiting days – SSP is not paid for the first three qualifying days of an SSP period of incapacity for work – the *'waiting days'*. However, you do not need to wait another three days if you re-claim SSP and your second spell of sickness (which must last for at least four days) starts no more than eight weeks after the end of the first period of incapacity for work.

SSCBA, Ss.152(3) & 155(1)

6. How much do you get?

SSP is £86.70 a week. There are no additions for dependants. If you are due SSP for a part-week, your employer will work out the daily rate by dividing the weekly rate by the number of qualifying days in that week. To qualify, your average weekly earnings must be at least the level of the lower earnings limit (£109 from 6.4.13). You can qualify even if you are on a short-term contract, provided your earnings are sufficient. To get an average weekly figure, gross earnings are averaged over the eight weeks ending with the last pay day before the start of the SSP period of incapacity for work.

SSCBA, S.157 & Sch 11, para 2(c) and SSP Regs, reg 19

SSP is subject to deductions for income tax and national insurance (NI) contributions. However, no NI deductions are due if SSP is the only payment you receive because SSP is below the primary threshold for NI contributions (but you can get credits – see Chapter 12(5)). Other normal deductions, eg union subs, can be made from SSP. It is important to make sure your payslip shows details of SSP payments you have received, together with deductions made by your employer, so you can check that it's all correct.

SSCBA, S.151(3)

Payment of SSP – You should normally be paid SSP at the same time and in the same way as you would have been paid wages for the same period. SSP cannot be paid in kind or as board and lodging or through a service.

If there has been some disagreement with your employer about your entitlement to SSP, and HMRC states you are entitled to it (provided you pass all the other tests), your employer must pay SSP within a certain time limit. In certain circumstances, if your employer defaults on payment of SSP or becomes insolvent, liability for any outstanding SSP transfers to HMRC (see 11 below).

SSP Regs, regs 8, 9 & 9A

Occupational sick pay – If your employer has an occupational sick pay scheme, any sick pay you get under that scheme will count towards your SSP entitlement for a particular day. Similarly, SSP paid by your employer will count towards any pay due to you for a particular day. But if the occupational scheme pays less than your full SSP, your employer must make up the balance so that you get all the SSP you are due. Employers are not obliged to operate the SSP scheme rules provided they pay remuneration or occupational sick pay at or above the SSP rate. Employees retain an underlying right to SSP. If your employer has their own sick pay scheme, they may have different rules, which you must keep to get payment.

SSCBA, Sch 12, para 2

7. Does anything affect what you get?

Other benefits – You cannot get SSP while you are receiving employment and support allowance, incapacity benefit, severe disablement allowance, contribution-based jobseeker's allowance, statutory maternity pay, maternity allowance, statutory paternity pay or statutory adoption pay. Other benefits do not affect your entitlement to SSP. See Box D.1 for other circumstances in which you cannot get SSP.

Earnings from another job – If your employer accepts you are incapable of doing the work they employ you to do, you can earn money from a different type of work while receiving SSP. There is no limit on what you can earn from a different type of job while receiving SSP. However, doing

---

D.1 Who cannot get SSP?

You are not entitled to SSP if, on the first day of your SSP period of incapacity for work (PIW), any of the following apply.

❏ You are not treated as an employee.
❏ Your average earnings are less than £109 a week. But remember the PIW linking rule – the first day of the first linked PIW should be used when working out your average earnings. If a new tax year starts while you are receiving SSP, this makes no difference (but you will get any increase in payment).
❏ You were entitled to employment and support allowance (ESA) within the previous 85 days or incapacity benefit or severe disablement allowance (SDA) within the previous 57 days.*
❏ There is a stoppage of work at your workplace due to a trade dispute, unless you can prove you have no direct interest in the dispute.
❏ You have received SSP from your employer for 28 weeks in the same PIW.
❏ You are pregnant and into the 'disqualifying period' (see 4 in this chapter).
❏ You are employed in another country; however, you may be entitled if your employer is liable for Class 1 contributions in the UK for you, or would be if your earnings were high enough (see Chapter 50(4)).
❏ You are in legal custody.
❏ You have not yet done any work for your employer. Remember that PIWs with the same employer which are separated by eight weeks or less count as one continuous PIW (ie they are linked together).

Once you have been off sick for four days in a row and your employer decides you cannot get SSP, they must give you form SSP1 so that you can claim ESA (see 13).

* If you were previously entitled to incapacity benefit or SDA you will not be able to return to that benefit. You will need to claim ESA instead.

SSCBA, S.153(3) & Sch 11 and SSP Regs, reg 3

other work may lead an employer to doubt you are genuinely incapable of doing your usual job.

Going into hospital – This will not affect entitlement to SSP.

8. How do you get SSP?

To obtain SSP, you must notify your employer that you are off sick; you may be asked to provide evidence that you are incapable of work. Your employer can decide what kind of evidence is needed, but cannot ask for a doctor's certificate (see 9 below) for the first seven days. If your employer does not have a special form, you can get a self-certificate SC2 from your GP or at www.hmrc.gov.uk/forms/sc2.pdf.

Notification of sickness absence

This means letting your employer know you are sick and incapable of work. To get SSP, you must provide evidence that you are incapable of work if your employer requires you to do so (see 9 below).

These are the rules on notification of sickness laid down in the law and your employer's SSP procedures must conform to them. If you also get occupational sick pay, you will have to keep to the rules of that scheme to safeguard those payments.

❏ Your employer has to make the rules clear to all the workforce in advance.

❏ Your employer cannot demand notification before the end of the first qualifying day of a period of incapacity for work.

❏ Your employer cannot demand notification in the form of medical evidence. But if you use medical evidence to notify your employer, it should be accepted.

❏ Your employer cannot insist you use a special form.

❏ If you post your notification, your employer should treat it as having been given on the day it was posted.

❏ Your employer cannot demand notification more than once a week during a spell of sickness.

❏ Your employer must accept notification from someone else on your behalf.

❏ If your employer does not make any rules about notification of sickness absence or the rules do not conform with SSP law, your employer must nevertheless accept notification of sickness on a qualifying day, if it is given in writing no later than seven days after that day.

SSP Regs, reg 7

Late notification

If your notification of sickness is late according to your employer's rules (and these rules comply with SSP law) you could be disqualified from SSP for any day of incapacity notified late. But SSP can be paid if your employer accepts you have 'good cause' for late notification, provided it is given within one month of the normal time limit. This can be extended to 91 days from the day of incapacity if the employer accepts it was not reasonably practicable for you to contact them within the month. After that time, your employer need not pay SSP for that day even if you have good cause for late notification. If your employer withholds SSP because they do not accept there is good cause for late notification, you can ask HMRC for a decision (see 10 below).

SSP Regs, reg 7(2)

9. Supporting evidence

HMRC employer's handbook E14 says a doctor's certificate is *'strong evidence of incapacity and should usually be accepted as conclusive unless there is more compelling evidence to the contrary'*. Medical evidence may be accepted from someone who is not a registered medical practitioner – eg an osteopath, acupuncturist or herbalist.

The GP's certificate is called the 'statement of fitness for work' (or *'fit note'*). On this, GPs can indicate that either you are not fit for work or you may be fit for work after taking into account certain advice, eg a phased return to work, altered hours or duties, or workplace adaptations.

It is up to your employer to decide whether to accept the evidence that you are not fit for work. If they do not accept it, SSP can be withheld. But you can write and ask HMRC for a formal decision (see 10 below).

Employers can either use their own self-certificates as evidence of incapacity or accept a written note from you as evidence for the first seven days of sickness. It is important that you agree what type of evidence will be acceptable.

For SSP purposes, your employer cannot require initial notice of your sickness in the form of medical evidence, private or otherwise. But after your first seven days of a spell off sick, they can ask for supporting medical evidence.

If your employer wants more medical evidence they must arrange and pay for it – unless HMRC agrees to help (see Box D.2). They can only do this with your consent.

Frequent short spells of sickness

If you are frequently off sick for periods of four to seven days, you may not have seen your doctor and all your absences will probably be self-certificated. If you've had at least four sickness absences over 12 months and your employer is not satisfied you have been incapable of work, they should discuss the matter with you and try to resolve any problem internally. This could involve sending you (with your consent) to a company doctor. If your employer still has doubts, they can refer your case to HMRC for help, but only with your consent. HMRC will then forward your case to their Medical Services, who will either ask for a report from your doctor or arrange for you to attend an examination by one of their doctors. In either case, an opinion will be sought as to whether there are reasonable grounds for your frequent absences. Your employer would take this opinion into account on the next occasion you were off sick.

See Box D.2 if, given the cause of your sickness, you have been off sick for a long time.

10. Fit for work?

If your employer does not accept you are incapable of work, you have the right to ask them for a written statement setting out the reasons for this and the dates you will not receive SSP. You also have the right to apply to HMRC for a formal decision.

Applying for a decision

Write to HMRC Statutory Payments Disputes Team, National Insurance Contributions Office, Room BP2002, Benton Park View, Newcastle upon Tyne NE98 1ZZ (0191 225 5221). They will expect you to have discussed the matter with your employer if it is reasonable to do so, and to have gone through the agreed grievance procedure, if one exists where you work.

Both you and your employer will be asked to send comments in writing to HMRC. You can provide other evidence – eg further medical statements. A copy of the decision will be sent to you and your employer. If the decision says you are incapable of work, your employer must pay you the correct amount of SSP within fixed time limits, providing that you pass the other tests for SSP.

Both you and your employer have the right to appeal against the decision to a First-tier Tribunal (Tax Chamber). If your employer appeals, they do not have to pay SSP until a final decision has been given.

11. Enforcing a decision

If HMRC has issued a formal written decision that you are entitled to SSP, and your employer doesn't pay it within the time laid down by law and has not appealed, inform HMRC Statutory Payments Disputes Team (see 10 above). In this situation, responsibility for paying SSP transfers to HMRC, who will pay any SSP to which you are entitled.

SSP Regs, reg 9A

12. What information will Jobcentre Plus give?

To decide if you are entitled to SSP, your employer can ask Jobcentre Plus for limited information about you. Before disclosing it, Jobcentre Plus should be satisfied that the enquiry comes from your employer and no one else. Employers are told that detailed personal information about employees will not be disclosed.

13. What happens when SSP ends?

If you are still sick at the start of the 23rd week of your period of entitlement to SSP and likely to remain sick beyond the 28th week, you will need to claim employment and support allowance (see Chapter 10). Your employer must complete and send you form SSP1. On the form, your employer must state why SSP is ending and the last day it will be paid. You will need this form to support your claim for employment and support allowance, but if your employer delays issuing it, you should register your claim for employment and support allowance so you do not lose benefit.

The employer must issue the SSP1 if you are not entitled to SSP or whenever they stop paying it. The form should be issued within seven days of your request for it or, if payroll arrangements make this impracticable, by the first pay day in the following tax month.

If your employer is holding any of your doctor's fit notes covering days beyond the last day of your SSP entitlement, these should be returned to you with form SSP1. Send them to your local Jobcentre Plus office with the completed form.

SSP Regs, reg 15(3) & (4)

14. What if your job ends?

If your job ends and you have had less than 28 weeks' SSP from your last employer and are still incapable of work, you can claim employment and support allowance – see Chapter 10. You will need to send form SSP1 (see 13 above) to support your claim.

But if your employer is found to have dismissed you solely or mainly to avoid paying SSP, they remain liable to pay it until liability ends for some other reason. Whatever the reason for your dismissal, you should claim employment and support allowance. Seek advice if you have difficulties or would not qualify for employment and support allowance.

SSP Regs, reg 4

D.2 Lengthy absences

If you are off work for a long time, your employer may ask HMRC for an opinion on your continuing incapacity for work, although employers are expected to try to resolve any problem themselves and make their own arrangements to get more medical advice. HMRC will assist only you give your consent and if they agree that the absence seems unduly long.

The table below is the HMRC guide on the more common and less serious illnesses (from booklet E14). This suggests the time by which your employer should have started some form of control action – although there is nothing in law to stop them taking action sooner.

If HMRC agrees to help, they will refer the case to their Medical Services, who will ask your doctor for a report on your incapacity to work. They may further arrange for you to attend an examination by one of their doctors, who will produce a similar report. The Medical Services will reach an opinion on whether or not you are incapable of work on the basis of these reports. The reports will not be sent to your employer, who will only be told whether or not you are considered to be capable of work. This is not a decision, it is only to help your employer decide whether payment of SSP should continue. If your employer stops SSP and you disagree, see 10.

Illness or diagnosis	Control (by weeks)
Addiction (drugs or alcohol)	10
Anaemia (other than in pregnancy)	4
Anorexia	10
Arthritis (unspecified)	10
Back and spinal disorders – PID (prolapsed intervertebral disc), sciatica, spondylitis	10
Concussion	4
Debility – cardiac, nervous, post-op, post-partum	10

Illness or diagnosis	Control (by weeks)
Fainting	4
Fractures of lower limbs	10
Fractures of upper limbs	10
Gastro-enteritis, gastritis, diarrhoea and vomiting	4
Giddiness	4
Haemorrhage	4
Headache, migraine	4
Hernia (strangulated)	10
Inflammation and swelling	4
Insomnia	10
Joint disorders, other than arthritis and rheumatism	10
Kidney and bladder disorders, cystitis, UTI (urinary tract infection)	4
Menstrual disorders, menorrhagia, D&C (dilation and curettage)	10
Mouth and throat disorders	4
No abnormality detected	Immediate
Nervous illnesses	10
Obesity	Immediate
Observation	4
Post-natal conditions	10
Respiratory illness – asthma	10
– bronchitis	4
– cold, coryza, influenza, URTI (upper respiratory tract infection)	4
Skin conditions, dermatitis, eczema	10
Sprains, strains, bruises	4
Tachycardia	10
Ulcers – corneal	4
– peptic, gastric, duodenal	4
– perforated	10
– varicose	10
Wounds, cuts, lacerations, abrasions, burns, blisters, splinters, FB (foreign bodies)	4

10 Employment and support allowance

1. What is employment and support allowance?

Employment and support allowance (ESA) is a benefit paid to people whose ability to work is limited by either ill health or disability. Your eligibility for the benefit is tested under a *'work capability assessment'*.

ESA has two elements: contributory ESA and income-related ESA. You can receive either of these elements or both together, depending on your circumstances.

The benefit cap – ESA is included in the list of benefits to which the 'benefit cap' applies. This cap, which will be rolled out nationally between 15.7.13 and 30.9.13, limits the total weekly benefits that can be claimed. The cap will not apply if you have been placed in the 'support group' (see 7 below). See Box H.1 in Chapter 21 for details.

2. Contributory ESA

Contributory ESA is linked to your national insurance contribution record. To be entitled, you must have paid national insurance contributions over a certain number of years. Most awards of contributory ESA are limited to 12 months. For details, see Chapter 12.

3. Income-related ESA

Income-related ESA is the means-tested element of ESA. It provides for your basic living expenses (and those of your partner, if you have one). It can be paid on its own or as a top-up to contributory ESA. Income-related ESA can help with mortgage interest payments and some other housing costs (see Chapter 26). For details, see Chapter 13.

4. Assessment phase

A 13-week assessment phase applies to all new ESA claimants, with the exception of those listed below. During this phase you are paid a basic allowance of ESA. If you are under 25, it is paid at a lower rate.

During the assessment phase you undergo the work capability assessment (see below). The assessment phase can be extended beyond 13 weeks if there is a delay in completing this assessment.

The assessment phase does not apply if:

■ you are terminally ill and claiming ESA for that reason;

■ your claim links to an earlier ESA award (see 14 below) during which the assessment phase was completed; *or*

■ you are a lone parent previously on income support with a disability premium and within the last 12 weeks you have been moved off income support because of the age of your youngest child.

ESA Regs, regs 4 & 7

5. Work capability assessment

There are two parts to the work capability assessment:

Limited capability for work assessment – The first part looks at whether you have a *'limited capability for work'*. You are not entitled to ESA unless you have a limited capability for work.

Limited capability for work-related activity assessment – The second part looks at whether you have a *'limited capability for work-related activity'*. It determines which of two different groups you are placed in: the *'work-related activity group'* or the *'support group'* (see 6 and 7 below). The group you are placed in determines the amount of ESA you receive, the responsibilities you must meet to retain the benefit and whether or not your ESA award may be time limited.

See Chapter 11 for details of the work capability assessment.

6. Work-related activity group

If you are found not to have a limited capability for work-related activity, you are placed in the work-related activity group. In this group you must meet work-related conditions, including attending work-focused interviews (see 15 below) and possibly undertaking work-related activity (see 16 below). If you fail to meet the conditions, your ESA payment may be reduced (see 17 below).

If you are placed in the work-related activity group, you receive a lower level of ESA than if placed in the support group. Furthermore, if you are entitled to contributory ESA, the award of it will be limited to just 12 months (see Chapter 12(3)) although you may be able to claim income-related ESA instead (see Chapter 13).

7. Support group

If you are found to have a limited capability for work-related activity, you are placed in the support group. In this group you do not have to undertake work-related activities, although you can volunteer to do so.

If you are placed in the support group, you receive a higher rate of ESA than if placed in the work-related activity group. If you are entitled to contributory ESA, your award may continue for as long as you continue to satisfy the entitlement conditions and remain in the support group; it will not be limited to 12 months.

8. ESA rates

ESA is paid at different rates depending on your circumstances. You may be entitled to contributory ESA or income-related ESA, or a combination of the two. The levels of payment for these two elements are detailed in Chapters 12(9) and 13(5)-(8) respectively.

The level of ESA you receive (whether contributory or income-related) is also determined by whether you are in the 13-week *'assessment phase'* or the *'main phase'* of your claim.

Assessment phase – During the assessment phase, ESA is paid at a lower level: the *'basic allowance'*. If you are aged under 25 during the assessment phase, you are paid a lower rate of the basic allowance.

Main phase – After the assessment phase, you receive an additional component on top of the basic allowance: either the *'work-related activity component'* or the *'support component'*. Which one you receive will depend on whether you are placed in the work-related activity group or the support group (see 6 and 7 above). If you are under 25, the lower rate basic allowance will no longer apply; you will be paid the same rate as someone aged 25 or over.

The different levels of payment during the two phases are illustrated in the diagram below.

9. Do you qualify?

The following rules apply to all ESA claims. To be entitled to ESA, you need to satisfy all the following basic qualifying conditions. You must:

■ have a limited capability for work – see Chapter 11(2);
■ be aged 16 or over;
■ be under state pension age (see Chapter 43(2));
■ be in Great Britain (GB) – see below;
■ not be in work – see below;
■ not be entitled to income support;
■ not be entitled to jobseeker's allowance (and not a member of a couple entitled to joint-claim jobseeker's allowance); *and*
■ not be within a period of entitlement to statutory sick pay.

WRA, Ss.1(3) & 20(1); ESA regs 40(1)

You must also meet at least one of the following conditions:

■ you satisfy the national insurance contribution conditions – see Chapter 12(6); *or*
■ you satisfy the conditions for income-related ESA – see Chapter 13(2).

WRA, S.1(2)

You can be entitled to both contributory ESA and income-related ESA at the same time (see Chapter 13(5)).

Work

You are generally not entitled to ESA in any week in which you work. This means any work you do, whether or not you expect to be paid for it.

ESA Regs, reg 40(1)

However, there are certain types of work that you can undertake and still be entitled to ESA. For details see Chapter 17(3).

Presence in Great Britain

To be entitled to ESA, you must be in GB, which means England, Scotland and Wales. You can, however, continue to be entitled to ESA during a temporary absence from GB in the circumstances set out in Chapter 50(3).

10. Making a claim

You are usually expected to start your claim for ESA by ringing the Jobcentre Plus claim-line (0800 055 6688; textphone 0800 023 4888). The claim-line should put you through to your nearest Jobcentre Plus contact centre. The contact centre will confirm your identity, then ask if you want to claim under the 'special rules' that apply to terminally ill claimants (see below). The contact centre then takes the details of your claim over the telephone. Once they have finished, a 'customer statement' is sent to you confirming the details so you can check they are correct. The contact centre may ring back for additional information if you do not have it to hand.

Alternatively, you can ask for a paper claim-form, ESA1, to make a written claim at Jobcentre Plus offices, or a local authority housing benefit office in some circumstances.

Who should claim?

If you are a member of a couple and both of you could claim income-related ESA, you must decide which of you will make the claim. If one of you would be more likely to be assessed as having a limited capability for work (and thus remain entitled to ESA) or having a limited capability for work-related activity (and thus be placed in the support group, where a higher level of ESA will be payable), it would be sensible if they were the claimant.

For anyone who cannot claim for themselves because of mental incapacity, Jobcentre Plus can appoint someone to act on their behalf (see Chapter 57(4)).

No claim necessary

If you are appealing against a decision that you do not have a limited capability for work, you do not need to submit a new claim in order to continue receiving ESA while your appeal is dealt with, but you should let Jobcentre Plus know that you want to continue receiving ESA while appealing.

C&P Regs, reg 3(j)

Medical evidence

For the first seven days of any period of limited capability for work, you do not need a medical certificate (the 'fit note' – see Chapter 9(9)). Once you have had a limited capability for work for more than seven days, you must forward a fit note from your doctor to the office dealing with your ESA claim

ESA: Levels of payment during the two phases

13-WEEK ASSESSMENT PHASE	MAIN PHASE (FROM WEEK 14)	
	Work-related activity group	Support group
		Support component
	Work-related activity component	
Extra premiums and housing costs Income-related ESA only		
Basic allowance Lower rate for under-25s	Standard rate regardless of age Reductions may apply	Standard rate regardless of age

£

(Jobcentre Plus should send you an envelope to do this when you first claim).

Social Security (Medical Evidence) Regs 1976, regs 2 & 5 & Sch 1

If you work for an employer and do not get statutory sick pay (or it is ending), you will also need to send in form SSP1, which you get from your employer, as well as a fit note from the first day of your claim.

C&P Regs, reg 10(1A)-(2)

It is important to keep your fit notes up to date; ask your doctor for a new fit note well before the old one runs out. If you are not covered by a note for each day of your claim, benefit could be withheld. Until you have passed (or are treated as having passed) the limited capability for work assessment in the work capability assessment, you must carry on sending in fit notes. Jobcentre Plus will let you know if this is no longer required.

Special rules

If you are terminally ill, your claim can be dealt with under the *'special rules'*. You count as terminally ill if

ESA: Claim route

On the basis of information provided with the claim, if Jobcentre Plus is satisfied that you have a limited capability for work-related activity, you will be placed in the support group.

A CLAIMING ESA
Start by contacting Jobcentre Plus.
You will need to answer some questions and may be asked to send further information.
The 13-week assessment phase begins.

B WORK CAPABILITY ASSESSMENT (WCA)
During the 13-week assessment phase, the WCA will be applied.
First you will be sent form ESA50 to complete and return.
You may then be asked to attend a face-to-face assessment.

The WCA is made up of two elements:

1 Limited capability for work?
This assessment determines whether you have a limited capability for work and are therefore eligible for ESA.

No → Claim jobseeker's allowance or challenge the decision (see Chapter 11(11)).

Support group
You have a limited capability for work-related activity.

You do not have to undertake work-related activity unless you volunteer to do so.

Claimants in this group receive a higher rate of ESA than those in the work-related activity group.

← Yes

2 Limited capability for work-related activity?
This assessment looks at whether you could undertake work-related activity.

This determines whether you are placed in:
■ the support group; *or*
■ the work-related activity group.

No →

Work-related activity group
You do not have a limited capability for work-related activity.

You must attend the work-focused interviews. Failure to attend may result in your ESA being reduced.

Claimants in this group receive a lower rate of ESA than those in the support group.

If you receive contributory ESA, this will be limited to 12 months.

C WORK-FOCUSED INTERVIEWS
If you are in the work-related activity group, you will be expected to take part in a series of work-focused interviews with a personal adviser. These will usually be monthly.

At the work-focused interviews, a personal adviser will discuss:
■ your views on work;
■ barriers that prevent you working; *and*
■ the package of support that may be needed to help you move into work.

The action plan
During the work-focused interviews you will complete an action plan containing a list of agreed steps to enhance your job prospects.

you *'suffer from a progressive disease and [your] death can reasonably be expected within 6 months'*. Under the special rules, your ESA claim will be fast-tracked. Once you have made the claim, Jobcentre Plus will normally contact your GP, consultant or specialist nurse to confirm that you are terminally ill. Once Jobcentre Plus receives such confirmation, they will automatically treat you as having a limited capability for both work and work-related activity (thus putting you in the support group – see 7 above). If, however, your GP, consultant or specialist nurse has given you a DS1500 form, you should give this to Jobcentre Plus as they may be able to deal with your claim immediately.

Jobcentre Plus should be able to make a decision under the special rules within five working days of your initial claim.

When a claim is made on the grounds of terminal illness, you do not have to serve the 13-week assessment phase before being put in the support group and the support component (see 8 above) can be paid from the beginning of your ESA award.

ESA Regs, regs 2 & 7(1)(a)

11. Date of claim

For telephone claims, your date of claim is the date of the initial telephone call to the Jobcentre Plus claim-line, as long as you provide the required information during that call and approve the customer statement (see 10 above).

For written claims, your date of claim is the date you inform Jobcentre Plus of your intention to claim, as long as that office receives a properly completed claim-form from you within a month of your first contact (this period can only be extended if the decision maker considers it reasonable to do so). The same time limit applies if you are making an ESA claim at the housing benefit office.

C&P Regs, reg 6(1F)

Advance awards – A decision maker can make an advance award of income-related ESA when you have income that exceeds your applicable amount (see Chapter 13(6)) and the decision maker considers that you would only become entitled to ESA once one of the additional components (see 8 above) becomes payable.

WRA, S.5(1); ESA Regs, reg 146

Advance claims – If you are receiving statutory sick pay (SSP) you cannot claim ESA (but you can claim income support – see Chapter 15). However, if you know your SSP will be running out, you can make an advance claim for ESA up to three months before your SSP expires. This can help to ensure minimal delays in receiving any ESA to which you may be entitled.

12. Late claims

Your award of ESA can be backdated for up to three months prior to the date of your claim (see 11 above) if you claim for that earlier period and meet all the entitlement conditions during it. You will need to ask your doctor to confirm on the fit note that you were not fit for work during this period.

C&P Regs, Sch 4, para 16

13. Payments

Waiting days – You are not normally entitled to ESA for the first three days of your claim (these are called *'waiting days'*), unless:

■ your claim links to an earlier ESA award (see 14 below); *or*
■ you claim expressly on the grounds that you are terminally ill; *or*
■ your entitlement to ESA begins within 12 weeks of a previous entitlement to carer's allowance, income support, incapacity benefit, jobseeker's allowance, maternity allowance, pension credit, severe disablement allowance or statutory sick pay; *or*

■ you are a member of a couple, your partner was already in receipt of income-related ESA (having already served the waiting days) and you have decided to become the claimant; *or*
■ you have been discharged from the armed forces and for at least three days immediately prior to discharge were absent from duty through sickness.

ESA Regs, reg 144

How you are paid – ESA is paid fortnightly in arrears, but if this causes you problems, Jobcentre Plus can consider a different arrangement. If your ESA payment is less than £1 a week, it may be paid in arrears at intervals of no more than 13 weeks. The minimum payment of ESA is 10p a week; an entitlement of less than 10p a week is not payable.

C&P Regs, reg 26C

Your benefit is normally paid into a bank, building society, credit union or Post Office card account (see Chapter 57(5)).

14. Linking rule

Any two periods of limited capability for work (ie days in which you have a limited capability for work) that are separated by no more than 12 weeks are treated as a single period. Therefore, if you have to reclaim ESA within 12 weeks of a previous award, you will not have to serve any waiting days (see 13 above). Additionally, if you had already served the 13-week assessment phase (see 4 above) in the previous award, you can go back onto the rate of payment of the earlier ESA award straightaway (as long as your previous award was not terminated because you were found not to have a limited capability for work). If you had served part of the 13-week assessment phase in the previous award, you only have to serve the remaining weeks before you can move into the main phase (see 8 above).

ESA Regs, reg 145(1)

15. Work-focused interviews

If you are placed in the work-related activity group, you will be required to attend a *'work-focused interview'* shortly after the work capability assessment. You will then be expected to take part in a series of five further work-focused interviews at monthly intervals. Further work-focused interviews can be triggered by: a new work capability assessment, other changes of circumstance, or if you have not had a work-focused interview for three years.

At each interview, you meet a *'personal adviser'* who should help you to explore barriers and identify support to assist you to move towards work. At the initial work-focused interview, the personal adviser will be an officer from Jobcentre Plus. At follow-up interviews, the personal adviser may be from a private or voluntary sector organisation contracted to do this work.

A work-focused interview has the following functions:

■ to assess your prospects and assist or encourage you to remain in or obtain work;
■ to identify activities, training, education or rehabilitation you could undertake to improve your job prospects; *and*
■ to identify current or future work opportunities (including self-employment) that are relevant to your needs and abilities.

ESA Regs, reg 55

If you do not attend or take part in a work-focused interview as required, your benefit can be reduced (see below).

Who is not required to take part

You are not required to take part in a work-focused interview if you:

■ have been placed in the support group (see 7 above); *or*
■ have reached the qualifying age for pension credit (see Chapter 42(2)); *or*
■ are a lone parent responsible for a child under the age of one; *or*

■ are only entitled to limited capability for work national insurance credits (see Box D.7 in Chapter 12).

ESA Regs, reg 54

The requirement to take part can be waived altogether in limited circumstances or deferred to a later date at the discretion of the personal adviser. If the adviser declines your request to defer or waive the interview, you cannot appeal against such decisions (although you can appeal against any benefit reduction applied as a result).

D&A Regs, Sch 2, para 26

Attendance is waived – The personal adviser can waive the requirement to take part in an interview if they believe the interview would not be of assistance to you because you are likely to be starting or returning to work soon.

ESA Regs, reg 60

Attendance is deferred – The requirement to take part can be deferred if the personal adviser believes it would not be of assistance or appropriate in the circumstances at that particular time. A decision to defer can be backdated if the date of the work-focused interview has already passed, at the discretion of the personal adviser. If the interview is deferred, the personal adviser will seek agreement with you for another appropriate date to hold the interview.

ESA Regs, reg 59

At the interview

Jobcentre Plus (or the private or voluntary sector contractor) must notify you of the requirement to take part in the work-focused interview. They will usually phone you to arrange the date, time and, if you are required to attend in person, the place for the interview. If they are not able to do this, they will write to you with details of the appointment.

If they are persuaded that attending a work-focused interview elsewhere would cause you undue inconvenience or endanger your health, they can arrange for it to take place in your own home.

ESA Regs, reg 56

Taking part in the interview – To meet the interview requirement, you must not only attend the interview at the right time and place, but also must 'take part' in it. Taking part involves participating in discussions with the personal adviser on:

■ any activity you are willing to undertake to improve your job prospects;
■ any such activity that you may have done previously;
■ any progress you may have made towards remaining in or obtaining work; *and*
■ your opinion on the extent to which your condition restricts your ability to remain in or obtain work.

ESA Regs, reg 57(3)

What are you asked at the interview? – When taking part in the interview, you are expected to answer questions about any of the following:

■ your educational qualifications and vocational training;
■ your work history;
■ any paid or unpaid work you are doing;
■ your aspirations for future work;
■ your work-related skills and abilities; *and*
■ any caring or childcare responsibilities you may have.

ESA Regs, 57(2)

What if you do not take part in the interview?

If you fail to take part in a work-focused interview, your ESA may be reduced (see 17 below). This reduction will not take place if you can show *'good cause'* for your failure to attend or participate. You will be notified that you have failed to take part. You then have five working days to show good cause. If the notification is sent by post, the five-day period is counted from the second working day after posting.

ESA Regs, reg 61(1)-(2) & 65

16. Work-related activity

If you are required to take part in a work-focused interview, you may also be expected to undertake *'work-related activity'*. This is defined as: *'activity which makes it more likely that the person will obtain or remain in work or be able to do so'*. What this actually entails is left to the personal adviser. It can include work experience and work placements (see below). However, you cannot be required to:

■ apply for a job or undertake work; *or*
■ undergo medical treatment.

WRA, S.13; ESA(WRA) Regs, reg 3(4)(b)

Who is not required to undertake work-related activity

You will not be required to undertake work-related activity if you are:

■ a lone parent and responsible for a child under 5;
■ entitled to carer's allowance or a carer premium; *or*
■ in the support group (see 7 above).

If you are a lone parent and responsible for a child under 13, you would be required to undertake work-related activity only during your child's normal school hours.

ESA(WRA) Regs, reg 3

The action plan

When you are notified that you are required to undertake work-related activity, you will be provided with a written *'action plan'*. This will specify what work-related activity you are expected to undertake. If an action plan already applies to you, and you consider that its instructions are no longer relevant to you, you can ask for it to be reconsidered.

ESA(WRA) Regs, regs 5 & 7

Work experience and work placements – You will not be required to take part in work experience as part of your action plan; participation will be voluntary. You may be required to take part in a work placement as part of your action plan. Such a placement will not be deemed to be paid or unpaid work. Any placement must be appropriate to your condition, given its location, content and the expected hours of attendance.

What if you do not undertake work-related activity?

If you fail to undertake work-related activity, your ESA may be reduced (see below). This reduction will not take place if you can show *'good cause'* for your failure within five working days of having been notified of it. Your ESA cannot be reduced if you fail to take part in work experience, as this is voluntary.

ESA(WRA) Regs, reg 8

17. Reductions

A reduction will be made to your ESA if you fail to meet a *'compliance condition'*. Two of these conditions relate to work-focused interviews. These are, that you fail to:

■ take part in a work-focused interview; *or*
■ make an agreement with your personal adviser to take part in a work-focused interview at a later date.

Three more conditions relate to work-related activity. These are, that you fail to:

■ undertake activity specified in your action plan (see 16 above); *or*
■ undertake an alternative activity notified by your personal adviser; *or*
■ make an agreement with your personal adviser to undertake such activity a later date.

ESA Regs, regs 63(11)

How much is the reduction?

The reduction is £71.70 a week (equal to the prescribed amount of ESA for a single person).

ESA Regs, regs 63(2)

If you are entitled to both contributory and income-related ESA (see Chapter 13(5)) the reduction will first be applied to contributory ESA. The reduction is only applied to income-related ESA if the reduction has resulted in the complete removal of contributory ESA and there is still some reduction outstanding.
ESA Regs, reg 63(4)

A reduction will never result in the complete removal of ESA; you will always be left with at least 10p a week. This allows claimants receiving income-related ESA to retain their entitlement to ESA while the reduction is in place, thus preserving their rights to benefits such as free prescriptions and housing benefit.
ESA Regs, reg 63(3)(a)

If a reduction is applied, you may be entitled to claim a hardship payment in some circumstances (see 18 below).

How long will the reduction be imposed?
The period over which the reduction is imposed is made up of two parts: one open ended; one fixed. The open-ended reduction will apply until the compliance condition has been met. This will be followed by a fixed-period reduction, which will apply as follows:
■ one week, if this is your first failure to meet a compliance condition;
■ two weeks, if this is your second failure, having already received a 1-week fixed-period reduction within the last year;* *and*
■ four weeks, if this is your third or subsequent failure, having already received a 2- or 4-week fixed-period reduction within the last year.*
*But not within two weeks of the current failure. The previous failure must also have occurred on or after 3.12.12. If you fail to meet a compliance condition for a period of less than one week, only the fixed-period reduction will apply.
ESA Regs, reg 63(6)-(10)

A reduction ceases if you move into one of the groups of people who do not have to undertake work-related activity, for example, if you are placed in the support group.
ESA Regs, reg 64

The reduction will take effect from the first day of the benefit week after the one for which you were last paid ESA.
D&A Regs, reg 36

Safeguards
The government has indicated that Jobcentre Plus will seek to telephone or visit ESA claimants with a mental health condition, learning disability or condition affecting communication or cognition before applying a reduction.

Challenging decisions
You can appeal against decisions that you failed to take part in a work-focused interview or that you failed to undertake the work-related activity agreed in your action plan. You can also appeal against a decision that you did not show good cause for your failure in either case within the 5-day time limit. You can appeal using form GL24, available from the Jobcentre Plus office. You have one month from the date of the decision to lodge the appeal.

Alternatively, you can ask Jobcentre Plus to reconsider and revise their decision. You have one month from the date of the decision in which to do this.

Chapter 58 covers the process of challenging decisions.

18. Hardship payments
If your ESA is reduced following a failure to meet a compliance condition, you may be entitled to a reduced-rate hardship payment for the duration of the reduction. Payment is not automatic; you must show that you or your family will suffer hardship unless a hardship payment is paid and you must be entitled to income-related ESA (see Chapter 13). The rate of the hardship payment is set at £43 a week (60% of the prescribed amount of ESA for a single person). You must complete an application for a hardship payment.
What is 'hardship'? – In deciding whether or not you will suffer hardship if no payment is made, the decision maker must take into account any resources likely to be available to you (excluding child benefit and child tax credit). They must look at whether there is a substantial risk that you will have much-reduced amounts of, or lose altogether, essential items such as food, clothing, heating or accommodation. The length of time that any such risk will apply will be relevant. It is also relevant whether a severe disability premium, enhanced disability premium or disabled or severely disabled child element of child tax credit is payable. The decision maker may take other factors into account.
ESA Regs, regs 64A-64D

19. Disqualification
You can be disqualified from receiving ESA for up to six weeks if you:
■ have a limited capability for work through your own misconduct (but not if your limited capability is due to pregnancy or a sexually transmitted disease). Misconduct is a wilful act, eg recklessly and knowingly breaking accepted safety rules;
■ do not accept medical or other treatment (not including vaccination, inoculation or major surgery) recommended by a doctor or hospital that is treating you – but only if the treatment would be likely to remove the limitation on your capability for work and you do not have good cause for your refusal;
■ behave in a way calculated to slow down your recovery, without having good cause; *or*
■ are absent from home without leaving word where you can be found, without having good cause.
A disqualification will not apply if you are considered to be a *'person in hardship'*. In that case your ESA will be reduced instead. A 20% reduction will be imposed on your basic allowance (if you get contributory ESA) or your prescribed amount (if you get income-related ESA).
ESA Regs, reg 157 & Sch 5, para 14

Hardship – You are considered to be a person in hardship if you:
■ or a member of your immediate family are pregnant;
■ are under 18 (or if you have a partner, you are both under 18).
You will also be considered to be a person in hardship if you or your partner:
■ are responsible for a child or young person who lives with you;
■ have been awarded attendance allowance, disability living allowance (DLA) care component or personal independence payment (PIP) daily living component (or have claimed one of these benefits within the last 26 weeks and the claim has not yet been determined);
■ devote a considerable portion of each week to caring for another person who has been awarded attendance allowance, DLA care component or PIP daily living component (or has claimed one of these benefits within the last 26 weeks and the claim has not yet been determined); *or*
■ have reached the qualifying age for pension credit (see Chapter 42(2)).
Even if one of the above grounds is not satisfied, you can still be considered a person in hardship if a decision maker is satisfied that unless ESA is paid, you or a member of your family will suffer hardship. The decision maker must take into account any resources likely to be available to you. They must also look at whether there is a substantial risk that you will have much-

reduced amounts of, or lose altogether, essential items such as food, clothing and heating, and if so for how long.

If you have been disqualified from receiving ESA and you believe one of the above categories applies to you, you must tell Jobcentre Plus which one applies.

ESA Regs, reg 158

11 The work capability assessment

1. What is the work capability assessment?

The *'work capability assessment'* (WCA) is a key element of employment and support allowance (ESA) and has two parts. The first part determines whether or not you may be entitled to ESA (see 2 below). The second determines whether you are placed in the *'work-related activity group'* (see Chapter 10(6)) or the *'support group'* (see Chapter 10(7)).

When will the WCA take place? – The first WCA takes place during the 13-week assessment phase that follows your initial claim (see Chapter 10(4)). Once it has taken place, and your entitlement to ESA has been established, you may be required to attend further WCAs at intervals in the future to determine whether you are still entitled to ESA and, if so, whether you should remain in the same group.

Universal credit – The WCA also determines entitlement to the capability for work elements in universal credit and the requirements you must meet to continue receiving the benefit (see Box J.1 in Chapter 25).

2. Limited capability for work assessment

The first part of the WCA looks at whether you have a *'limited capability for work'*. You are not entitled to ESA unless you have (or can be treated as having) a limited capability for work. This part of the WCA is a points-related assessment of your physical and mental health and cognitive functions considered within a range of activities. Points are awarded on the basis of any limitations with respect to each activity and totalled up. If the total reaches 15 points or more, you are assessed as having a limited capability for work.

ESA Regs, reg.19(3)

Some 'specific' disease or disablement – In assessing your capability or otherwise in performing each activity, it must be clear that an inability to do an activity arises:

■ from a specific bodily disease or disablement (in the case of the physical descriptors listed in Box D.3);

■ from a specific mental illness or disablement (in the case of the mental, cognitive and intellectual functions descriptors listed in Box D.4); *or*

■ as a direct result of treatment provided by a registered medical practitioner for such a disease, illness or disablement.

ESA Regs, reg 19(5)

'Specific' is not the same as 'specified', so it may not be essential that the cause of the disease or disablement is identified (CS/7/82). For example, you may suffer pain, the cause of which has not yet been diagnosed. A normal pregnancy does not count as a disease or disablement, but conditions such as high blood pressure arising because of the pregnancy do count. Symptoms such as the pain experienced by those with chronic pain syndrome or by those who are showing 'illness behaviour' are likely to be taken into account, as there is sufficient medical consensus that these are 'specific' conditions (CIB/5435/2002).

The physical descriptors

The physical descriptors in the limited capability for work assessment are grouped into ten types of activity (abbreviated here):

■ mobilising;
■ standing and sitting;
■ reaching;
■ picking up and moving things;
■ manual dexterity (using your hands);
■ making yourself understood;
■ understanding communication;
■ navigation and maintaining safety;
■ absence or loss of control… of the bowel or bladder;
■ consciousness.

Under each activity heading is a list of descriptors with scores ranging from 0 to 15 points. The descriptors explain related tasks of varying degrees of difficulty. You score points when you are not able to perform a task described, with the highest points you score under each activity added together.

ESA Regs, reg 19(6)

If you score 15 points, you are assessed as having a limited capability for work. These points can be scored in just one activity or from any of the activities (in both the physical and the mental parts of the assessment) added together.

ESA Regs, reg 19(3)

The descriptors and the points assigned to each one are listed in Box D.3.

The mental, cognitive and intellectual function descriptors

The descriptors relating to mental, cognitive and intellectual functions in the limited capability for work assessment are grouped into seven types of activity (abbreviated here):

■ learning tasks;
■ awareness of everyday hazards;
■ initiating and completing personal action;
■ coping with change;
■ getting about;
■ coping with social engagement;
■ appropriateness of behaviour with other people.

As with the physical descriptors, there is a list of descriptors under each activity heading and the scoring follows the same pattern. You score points if you cannot perform the task described, with the highest points you score under each activity added together. If you score 15 points, you are assessed as having a limited capability for work. These points can be scored in just one activity or from any of the activities (in both the physical and the mental parts of the assessment) added together.

ESA Regs, reg 19(3) & (6)

The descriptors and the points assigned to each one are listed in Box D.4.

Treated as having a limited capability for work
You can automatically be treated as having a limited capability for work, without having to score 15 points, in the following circumstances:

■ you are terminally ill. This is defined as *'a progressive disease and death in consequence of that disease can reasonably be expected within six months'*;

■ you are receiving treatment for cancer (or are likely to receive it within six months) by way of chemotherapy or radiotherapy, or you are recovering from that treatment and Jobcentre Plus is satisfied that you should be treated as having a limited capability for work;

■ you have been requested or given notice, under specific legislation, to refrain from work because it is known or reasonably suspected that you have been infected, contaminated or been in contact with an infectious disease or contamination;

■ you are pregnant and there would be a serious risk to the health of you or your child if you did not refrain from work;

■ you are pregnant or have recently given birth, are entitled to maternity allowance and are within the maternity allowance payment period;

■ you are pregnant or have recently given birth but are not entitled to maternity allowance or statutory maternity pay from six weeks before the baby is due to two weeks after the birth;

■ you satisfy either descriptor 15 (conveying food or drink to the mouth) or 16 (chewing or swallowing food or drink) in the 'limited capability for work-related activity assessment' – see Box D.5;

ESA Regs, reg 20

■ you are a student in full-time education (and not a 'qualifying young person' for child benefit purposes) entitled to income-related ESA by virtue of the fact that you are entitled to disability living allowance or personal independence payment.

ESA Regs, reg 33(2)

Hospital inpatients – You are treated as having a limited capability for work on any day you are receiving medical or other treatment in a hospital or similar institution (including residential rehabilitation for treatment of drug or alcohol addiction), having been advised by a healthcare professional to stay there for a period of 24 hours or longer. You are also treated as having a limited capability for work on any day you are recovering from such treatment and Jobcentre Plus is satisfied that you should be treated as having a limited capability for work.

ESA Regs, reg 25

Renal failure and certain other regular treatments – You are treated as having a limited capability for work during any week in which you are receiving:

■ regular weekly treatment by way of haemodialysis for chronic renal failure, *or*

■ treatment by way of plasmapheresis, *or*

■ regular weekly treatment by way of total parenteral nutrition for gross impairment of enteric function.

You are also treated as having a limited capability for work during any week in which you have a day of recovery from such treatment and Jobcentre Plus is satisfied that you should be treated as having a limited capability for work.

However, you are only treated as having a limited capability for work from the first week in which at least two days of that week are days of treatment or recovery. The two days need not be consecutive.

ESA Regs, reg 26

Treated as not having a limited capability for work
You are treated as not having a limited capability for work, even if you have been assessed as having a limited capability for work, in the following circumstances:

■ you are, or were, a member of the armed forces and are absent from duty through sickness;

■ you attend a training course that day for which you are paid a state training allowance or premium (unless this is only paid to cover travelling or meals expenses);

■ you are treated as not entitled to ESA because you have done work in that week;

■ you have been disqualified from receiving contributory ESA for at least six weeks during a period of imprisonment or detention in legal custody.

ESA Regs, regs 32, 44 & 159

3. Limited capability for work-related activity assessment
The second part of the WCA considers whether you have a *'limited capability for work-related activity'*. Although the wording is similar to that of the first part of the WCA, the second part has a different function. It determines whether you are placed in the work-related activity group (see Chapter 10(6)) or the support group (see Chapter 10(7)). The group you are placed in determines the level of ESA you receive, the responsibilities you must meet to retain the benefit and whether or not your ESA award may be time limited.

The assessment has a list of descriptors relating to both physical and mental/cognitive functions. If you meet at least one of these descriptors, you are placed in the support group of claimants, in which case your ESA can be paid at a higher level, you will not be required to undertake work-related activities and any contributory ESA awarded will not be limited to just 12 months.

The descriptors are grouped together under the following 16 activity headings (abbreviated here):

■ mobilising;
■ transferring from one seated position to another;
■ reaching;
■ picking up and moving things;
■ manual dexterity;
■ making yourself understood;
■ understanding communication;
■ continence;
■ learning tasks;
■ awareness of hazard;
■ initiating and completing personal action;
■ coping with change;
■ coping with social engagement;
■ appropriateness of behaviour with other people;
■ conveying food or drink to the mouth;
■ chewing or swallowing food or drink.

The descriptors are listed in Box D.5.

Some 'specific' disease or disablement – In assessing your capability or otherwise in performing each activity, it must be clear that an inability to do an activity arises:

■ from a specific bodily disease or disablement, in the case of descriptors 1 to 8, 15(A)-(B) and 16(A)-(B);

■ from a specific mental illness or disablement, in the case of descriptors 9 to 14, 15(C)-(D) and 16(C)-(D); *or*

■ as a direct result of treatment provided by a registered medical practitioner for such a disease, illness or disablement.

ESA Regs, reg 34(3A)

Treated as having a limited capability for work-related activity
You can automatically be treated as having a limited capability for work-related activity if you:

■ have a terminal illness, which is defined as *'a progressive disease and death in consequence of that disease can reasonably be expected within six months'*;

■ are receiving treatment (or are likely to receive it within six months) by way of chemotherapy or radiotherapy, or you are recovering from that treatment and Jobcentre Plus is satisfied that you should be treated as having a limited capability for work-related activity;

■ have a specific disease or bodily or mental disablement and consequently there would be a substantial risk to the mental or physical health of any person if you were found not to have a limited capability for work-related activity; *or*

■ are pregnant and there would be a serious risk to the health of you or your child if you did not refrain from work-related activity.

ESA Regs, reg 35

4. How is the WCA applied?

A Jobcentre Plus decision maker looks at the information you have provided with your ESA claim to see, without having to make further enquiries, if there is evidence that you have a limited capability for work and for work-related activity. They should also see if there is evidence that you can be 'treated' as having a limited capability for work and for work-related activity (see 2 and 3 above). If the decision maker considers they do not have such evidence, they will send you a questionnaire, the ESA50, to complete.

5. ESA50 questionnaire

The questionnaire begins by asking for general personal details (name, address, etc). It then asks about any help you may need to attend a face-to-face assessment, if one is arranged (see 9 below), and any times or dates that you would not be able to attend. You are asked to tell them about your illness or disability and the medication or treatment you are receiving (including side effects). You are asked to provide details of your GP and any other professionals who are giving you care, support or treatment (eg a physiotherapist, community psychiatric nurse, social worker, occupational therapist, support worker or hospital consultant). There are also questions relating to any hospital or clinical treatment you may be receiving and whether or not your health problems are linked to drug, alcohol or other substance abuse.

The rest of the questionnaire is an assessment of how your illness or disability affects you. It is divided into two parts: the first part asks about physical functions, the second about mental, cognitive and intellectual functions.

D.3 Limited capability for work assessment – physical functions

Activities 1 to 10 cover physical functions and must arise from a physical condition. To be assessed as having a limited capability for work, you need to score 15 points or more. Add together the highest score from each activity that applies to you. The scores from these activities can be added to those in the mental, cognitive and intellectual function activities (see Box D.4). If any task marked with an underlined A applies (see activities 1,2,3,4,5,6 and 7) you will also satisfy the 'limited capability for work-related activity assessment' (see Box D.5).

Activity	Points

1. Mobilising unaided by another person with or without a walking stick, manual wheelchair or other aid if such aid is normally, or could reasonably be worn or used

A Cannot either:
(i) mobilise more than 50 metres on level ground without stopping in order to avoid significant discomfort or exhaustion; *or*
(ii) repeatedly mobilise 50 metres within a reasonable timescale because of significant discomfort or exhaustion. 15

B Cannot mount or descend two steps unaided by another person even with the support of a handrail. 9

C Cannot either:
(i) mobilise more than 100 metres on level ground without stopping in order to avoid significant discomfort or exhaustion; *or*
(ii) repeatedly mobilise 100 metres within a reasonable timescale because of significant discomfort or exhaustion. 9

D Cannot either:
(i) mobilise more than 200 metres on level ground without stopping in order to avoid significant discomfort or exhaustion; *or*
(ii) repeatedly mobilise 200 metres within a reasonable timescale because of significant discomfort or exhaustion. 6

E None of the above apply. 0

2. Standing and sitting

A Cannot move between one seated position and another seated position located next to one another without receiving physical assistance from another person. 15

B Cannot, for the majority of the time, remain at a work station, either:
(i) standing unassisted by another person (even if free to move around); *or*
(ii) sitting (even in an adjustable chair) *or*
(iii) a combination of (i) and (ii)
for more than 30 minutes, before needing to move away in order to avoid significant discomfort or exhaustion 9

C Cannot, for the majority of the time, remain at a work station, either:
(i) standing unassisted by another person (even if free to move around); *or*
(ii) sitting (even in an adjustable chair) *or*
(iii) a combination of (i) and (ii)
for more than an hour before needing to move away in order to avoid significant discomfort or exhaustion. 6

D None of the above apply. 0

3. Reaching

A Cannot raise either arm as if to put something in the top pocket of a coat or jacket. 15

B Cannot raise either arm to top of head as if to put on a hat. 9

C Cannot raise either arm above head height as if to reach for something. 6

D None of the above apply. 0

4. Picking up and moving or transferring by the use of the upper body and arms

A Cannot pick up and move a 0.5 litre carton full of liquid. 15

B Cannot pick up and move a one litre carton full of liquid. 9

C Cannot transfer a light but bulky object such as an empty cardboard box. 6

D None of the above apply. 0

6. Completing the ESA50 – physical functions

Part 1 of the questionnaire is divided into ten activity headings. These headings relate to the activities listed in Box D.3. Note that the wording in the questionnaire is sometimes different from the wording in Box D.3 (in which we use the exact wording of the law).

Under each heading, you are first asked whether you can do that particular activity without any difficulty. Read all the text relating to the activity before ticking the box, as you will find out more about what is meant by having difficulty with that activity.

You are then usually asked about specific tasks related to each activity. In each case, you are usually offered one of three boxes to tick: *'no'*, *'yes'* or *'it varies'*, the last being helpful if your condition is variable. When deciding which box to tick, bear in mind that the question is whether you reasonably can or cannot do the particular task both reliably and repeatedly. Things like safety, tiredness, pain and discomfort may mean that it is not reasonable to expect you to do a task, or although you could do it occasionally you could not repeat it with reasonable regularity.

There is a box in each section where you can give extra information on the difficulties you have with each task. Use the box to give details of how you are affected if you attempt to do a task. Are there any risks involved in attempting the task? Have you previously had any injuries or accidents attempting it? Explain how often you would need to rest and whether you take painkillers, and explain the cumulative effects of exhaustion or pain on your ability to perform the tasks. If you take pain-killing medication, say whether it affects your ability to complete tasks effectively. If your condition varies, try to give an idea of how many days each week you would be able to do the task and how many you would not.

This is a points-related test (see 2 above). To see how many points your answers in this part can potentially score, see Box D.3. We look at each activity heading in more detail below.

Risk – When a certain task would be a risk to your health, enough to put off any reasonable person from doing it, you should be treated as not able to do it. If you've been advised by a doctor, physiotherapist or other health professional to avoid an activity, be sure to note this in the box.
CSIB/12/96

Pain and fatigue – Pain, tiredness, stiffness, breathlessness, nausea, dizziness or balance problems might affect how difficult you find it to do things. If doing a particular task causes you too much pain or discomfort, you should be

---

5. Manual dexterity

A Cannot either:
(i) press a button, such as a telephone keypad; *or*
(ii) turn the pages of a book with either hand.   15

B Cannot pick up a £1 coin or equivalent with either hand.   15

C Cannot use a pen or pencil to make a meaningful mark.   9

D Cannot single-handedly use a suitable keyboard or mouse.   9

E None of the above apply.   0

---

6. Making self understood through speaking, writing, typing, or other means which are normally, or could reasonably be used, unaided by another person

A Cannot convey a simple message, such as the presence of a hazard.   15

B Has significant difficulty conveying a simple message to strangers.   15

C Has some difficulty conveying a simple message to strangers.   6

D None of the above apply.   0

---

7. Understanding communication by
(i) verbal means (such as hearing or lip reading) alone
(ii) non-verbal means (such as reading 16-point print or Braille alone, *or*
(iii) a combination of (i) and (ii)
using any aid that is normally, or could reasonably be, used, unaided by another person

A Cannot understand a simple message due to sensory impairment, such as the location of a fire escape.   15

B Has significant difficulty understanding a simple message from a stranger due to sensory impairment.   15

C Has some difficulty understanding a simple message from a stranger due to sensory impairment.   6

D None of the above apply.   0

---

8. Navigating and maintaining safety, using a guide dog or other aid if either or both are normally, or could reasonably be, used

A Unable to navigate around familiar surroundings, without being accompanied by another person, due to sensory impairment.   15

B Cannot safely complete a potentially hazardous task such as crossing the road, without being accompanied by another person, due to sensory impairment.   15

C Unable to navigate around unfamiliar surroundings, without being accompanied by another person, due to sensory impairment.   9

D None of the above apply.   0

---

9. Absence or loss of control whilst conscious leading to extensive evacuation of the bowel and/or bladder, other than enuresis (bed-wetting) despite the wearing or use of any aids or adaptations which are normally, or could reasonably be, worn or used

A At least once a month experiences:
(i) loss of control leading to extensive evacuation of the bowel and/or voiding of the bladder; *or*
(ii) substantial leakage of the contents of a collecting device sufficient to require cleaning and a change in clothing.   15

B The majority of the time is at risk of loss of control leading to extensive evacuation of the bowel and/or voiding of the bladder, sufficient to require cleaning and a change in clothing, if not able to reach a toilet quickly.   6

C None of the above apply.   0

---

10. Consciousness during waking moments

A At least once a week, has an involuntary episode of lost or altered consciousness resulting in significantly disrupted awareness or concentration.   15

B At least once a month, has an involuntary episode of lost or altered consciousness resulting in significantly disrupted awareness or concentration.   6

C None of the above apply.   0

ESA Regs, Sch 2, part 1

treated as not able to do it.

CIB/14587/96

Similarly, if you find it so tiring or painful to do a particular task that you could not repeat it within a reasonable time, or could only do it so slowly that you could not effectively complete the task, you should be treated as unable to do it. **Artificial aids** – In each case, you are assessed as if:

■ fitted with or wearing any prosthesis with which you are normally fitted or normally wear; *or*
■ wearing or using any aid or appliance which is normally, or could reasonably be expected to be, used or worn (eg a walking stick or glasses).

D.4 Limited capability for work assessment – mental, cognitive and intellectual functions

Activities 11 to 17 cover mental, cognitive and intellectual functions and must arise from a mental illness or disablement (although this, in turn, could arise from a underlying physical cause). To be assessed as having a limited capability for work, you need to score 15 points or more. Add together the highest score from each activity that applies to you. The scores from these activities can be added to those in the physical function activities (see Box D.3). If any task with an underlined A applies (see activities 11, 12, 13, 14, 16 and 17) you will also satisfy the 'limited capability for work-related activity assessment' (see Box D.5).

Activity	Points

11. Learning tasks

A Cannot learn how to complete a simple task, such as setting an alarm clock. 15

B Cannot learn anything beyond a simple task, such as setting an alarm clock. 9

C Cannot learn anything beyond a moderately complex task, such as the steps involved in operating a washing machine to clean clothes. 6

D None of the above apply. 0

12. Awareness of everyday hazards (such as boiling water or sharp objects)

A Reduced awareness of everyday hazards leads to a significant risk of:
(i) injury to self or others; *or*
(ii) damage to property or possessions
such that they require supervision for the majority of the time to maintain safety. 15

B Reduced awareness of everyday hazards leads to a significant risk of:
(i) injury to self or others; *or*
(ii) damage to property or possessions
such that they frequently require supervision to maintain safety. 9

C Reduced awareness of everyday hazards leads to a significant risk of:
(i) injury to self or others; *or*
(ii) damage to property or possessions
such that they occasionally require supervision to maintain safety. 6

D None of the above apply. 0

13. Initiating and completing personal action (which means planning, organisation, problem solving, prioritising or switching tasks)

A Cannot, due to impaired mental function, reliably initiate or complete at least 2 sequential personal actions. 15

B Cannot, due to impaired mental function, reliably initiate or complete at least 2 personal actions for the majority of the time. 9

C Frequently cannot, due to impaired mental function, reliably initiate or complete at least 2 personal actions. 6

D None of the above apply. 0

14. Coping with change

A Cannot cope with any change to the extent that day-to-day life cannot be managed. 15

B Cannot cope with minor planned change (such as a pre-arranged change to the routine time scheduled for a lunch break), to the extent that overall day-to-day life is made significantly more difficult. 9

C Cannot cope with minor unplanned change (such as the timing of an appointment on the day it is due to occur), to the extent that overall, day-to-day life is made significantly more difficult. 6

D None of the above apply. 0

15. Getting about

A Cannot get to any space outside of the claimant's home with which the claimant is familiar. 15

B Is unable to get to a specified place with which the claimant is familiar, without being accompanied by another person. 9

C Is unable to get to a specified place with which the claimant is unfamiliar without being accompanied by another person. 6

D None of the above apply. 0

16. Coping with social engagement due to cognitive impairment or mental disorder

A Engagement in social contact is always precluded due to difficulty relating to others or significant distress experienced by the individual. 15

B Engagement in social contact with someone unfamiliar to the claimant is always precluded due to difficulty relating to others or significant distress experienced by the individual. 9

C Engagement in social contact with someone unfamiliar to the claimant is not possible for the majority of the time due to difficulty relating to others or significant distress experienced by the individual. 6

D None of the above apply. 0

17. Appropriateness of behaviour with other people, due to cognitive impairment or mental disorder

A Has, on a daily basis, uncontrollable episodes of aggressive or disinhibited behaviour that would be unreasonable in any workplace. 15

B Frequently has uncontrollable episodes of aggressive or disinhibited behaviour that would be unreasonable in any workplace. 15

C Occasionally has uncontrollable episodes of aggressive or disinhibited behaviour that would be unreasonable in any workplace. 9

D None of the above apply. 0

ESA Regs, Sch 2, part 2

If an aid or appliance has been prescribed or recommended to you by a suitable expert, you will be assessed as if you were using it, unless it would be unreasonable for you to do so. If an aid or appliance has not been prescribed or recommended in your case, you may still be assessed as if using one, if it would normally be used by someone in your circumstances and it would be reasonable for you to do so. In assessing what is 'reasonable', the decision maker needs to take into account whether or not such an aid or appliance is widely available and if you can afford it, use it and store it. They need to consider if your physical or mental condition would mean you are unable to make use of the aid or appliance (eg you could not use a walking stick to improve your mobility because of arthritis in your elbows). They also need to take into account how long your condition is likely to last; ie would it be reasonable to expect you to purchase an aid if your condition is unlikely to last long.

ESA Regs, regs 19(4) & 34(3); CE/1217/11 [2011]UKUT 449 (AAC)

Moving around and using steps

Two tasks are considered under this heading (activity 1 in Box D.3; the heading is differently worded).

First, you are asked how far you can move safely and repeatedly on level ground without needing to stop (with choices of 50 metres, 100 metres or 200 metres or more). 'Moving' in this case includes using aids such as crutches, a walking stick or a manual wheelchair (but not an electric wheelchair); it is not simply about walking. If you have difficulty walking, but do not use a manual wheelchair because it would not make getting around any easier for you, explain why.

Think carefully before ticking the boxes. If you are unsure how far you can move before you need to stop, then you should test yourself on an average day. It would help if you had someone with you to measure the distance in paces; one pace of an average healthy male adult is about three-quarters of a metre. Time how long it takes you to cover the distance.

Second, you are asked whether or not you can go up or down two steps without help from another person if there is a rail to hold onto. Even if you can do this once, if fatigue, pain or co-ordination or balance difficulties prevent you from being able to perform the task repeatedly (after reasonable rest periods), you should state that you are incapable of doing it. If you have fallen when trying to negotiate steps in the past, write down what happened.

Standing and sitting

Two tasks are considered under this heading.

First, you are asked if you can move from one seat to another right next to it without help from someone else. This may apply if you are a wheelchair user and are unable to transfer from the wheelchair without help. Simple aids such as a transfer board will be taken into account, but the use of more elaborate apparatus, such as a hoist, will be ignored. Write down if you have problems with similar activities, such as getting on and off the toilet or getting in and out of the car.

Second, you are asked how long you can stay in one place (defined in Box D.3 as a 'work station'), either standing, sitting, or a combination of the two, without help from another person, without pain or exhaustion. You are not expected to remain still, and you can change position. With standing, you would be expected to use aids such a walking stick, if they help. However, if you can stand only using two sticks, you will be treated as unable to stand because this would severely limit the sort of work you could do while standing (such as using the phone).

Although you are expected to alternate between sitting and standing if this would help you to stay in one place, there may be situations in which you have to alternate so much between the two positions that you cannot 'remain at a work station' in

any meaningful way. Let them know if this is the case.
CE/1516/07 [2012]UKUT 324 (AAC)

Reaching

This activity focuses on your ability to raise yours arms above waist height. It is about reaching upwards, not about manual dexterity (which is covered later). To obtain points, you must have problems with both arms.

When answering whether you can or cannot do the task described, you need to consider whether you can do it repeatedly, not just once.

If you cannot raise either arm to the top of your head as if to put on a hat, you should write this down. Such a limitation would provide you with 9 points in the assessment, but the questionnaire omits to ask you this question.

Picking up and moving things

This activity focuses on your ability to pick up and move light objects (specifically: a half-litre carton of liquid, a litre carton of liquid and an empty cardboard box). You are not asked if you can pick up the objects from the ground, so it is assumed that you are moving the object at waist level; neither are you asked if you can do each task with just one hand.

Remember to focus on whether or not you can do the task described repeatedly (after a reasonable rest period in each case), not whether you can do it just once.

If you have dropped objects of a similar size in the past when trying to move them, write down what happened. In this way, you may be able to show that you cannot perform the task in question 'reliably'.

Manual dexterity (using your hands)

This activity focuses on your ability to use your hands and wrists in relation to the kind of things you would be expected to do at work. A number of different tasks are suggested, such as using a pen or pencil or a computer keyboard. It is the problems you have in being able to press, turn, pick up or manipulate the object in question that matters here, not whether you are literate or understand how to use a computer.

You are asked if you can manage the tasks with either hand. So, if you can manage to do something effectively with one hand, but not the other, you will not pick up any points for that task. Bear in mind that it is your ability to perform each task repeatedly and reliably that matters.

Communicating with people

This activity (activity 6 in Box D.3) looks at your ability to express yourself, either by talking or by other methods. It may be relevant to you if your condition affects your speech and you also have difficulties writing or typing because of reduced dexterity. It is assumed you are using the same language as the person with whom you are communicating and that they will be able to understand your accent or dialect.

You are asked if you can communicate a simple message to other people (such as the presence of something dangerous) by speaking, writing, etc but without the help of another person (with the usual answers of 'yes', 'no' and 'it varies').

You would get 15 points if you cannot convey a simple message by speaking, writing, etc. Fifteen points could also be obtained if you have 'significant difficulty' conveying a simple message to strangers and 6 points if you have 'some difficulty' doing so. Therefore, if any of these apply, you should make this clear on the questionnaire. You will also need to explain why you cannot write or type the message; if you have dexterity problems, you can cross-refer to the previous activity.

Other people communicating with you

This activity (activity 7 in Box D.3) is relevant if you have hearing or visual problems. You are asked two questions.

D.5 Limited capability for work-related activity assessment

If one or more of the following descriptors applies to you, you will be assessed as having a limited capability for work-related activity and will be placed in the support group of claimants.

1. Mobilising unaided by another person with or without a walking stick, manual wheelchair or other aid if such aid is normally, or could reasonably be, worn or used

Cannot either:

A mobilise more than 50 metres on level ground without stopping in order to avoid significant discomfort or exhaustion; or

B repeatedly mobilise 50 metres within a reasonable timescale because of significant discomfort or exhaustion.

2. Transferring from one seated position to another

Cannot move between one seated position and another seated position located next to one another without receiving physical assistance from another person.

3. Reaching

Cannot raise either arm as if to put something in the top pocket of a coat or jacket.

4. Picking up and moving or transferring by the use of the upper body and arms (excluding standing, sitting, bending or kneeling and all other activities specified in this Schedule [ie this box])

Cannot pick up and move a 0.5 litre carton full of liquid.

5. Manual dexterity

Cannot either:

A press a button, such as a telephone keypad; or

B turn the pages of a book
with either hand.

6. Making self understood through speaking, writing, typing, or other means which are normally, or could reasonably be, used, unaided by another person

Cannot convey a simple message, such as the presence of a hazard.

7. Understanding communication by
(i) verbal means (such as hearing or lip reading) alone
(ii) non-verbal means (such as reading 16-point print or Braille) alone, or
(iii) a combination of (i) and (ii)
using any aid that is normally, or could reasonably be, used, unaided by another person

Cannot understand a simple message due to sensory impairment, such as the location of a fire escape.

8. Absence or loss of control whilst conscious leading to extensive evacuation of the bowel and/or voiding of the bladder, other than enuresis (bed-wetting) despite the wearing or use of any aids or adaptations which are normally, or could reasonably be, worn or used

At least once a week experiences:

A loss of control leading to extensive evacuation of the bowel and/or voiding of the bladder; or

B substantial leakage of the contents of a collecting device, sufficient to require the individual to clean themselves and change clothing.

9. Learning tasks

Cannot learn how to complete a simple task, such as setting an alarm clock, due to cognitive impairment or mental disorder.

10. Awareness of hazard

Reduced awareness of everyday hazards, due to cognitive impairment or mental disorder, leads to a significant risk of:

A injury to self or others; or

B damage to property or possessions

such that they require supervision for the majority of the time to maintain safety.

11. Initiating and completing personal action (which means planning, organisation, problem solving, prioritising or switching tasks)

Cannot, due to impaired mental function, reliably initiate or complete at least two sequential personal actions.

12. Coping with change

Cannot cope with any change, due to cognitive impairment or mental disorder, to the extent that day-to-day life cannot be managed.

13. Coping with social engagement, due to cognitive impairment or mental disorder

Engagement in social contact is always precluded due to difficulty relating to others or significant distress experienced by the individual.

14. Appropriateness of behaviour with other people, due to cognitive impairment or mental disorder

Has, on a daily basis, uncontrollable episodes of aggressive or disinhibited behaviour that would be unreasonable in any workplace.

15. Conveying food or drink to the mouth

A Cannot convey food or drink to the claimant's own mouth without receiving physical assistance from someone else;

B Cannot convey food or drink to the claimant's own mouth without repeatedly stopping, experiencing breathlessness or severe discomfort;

C Cannot convey food or drink to the claimant's own mouth without receiving regular prompting given by someone else in the claimant's physical presence; or

D Owing to a severe disorder of mood or behaviour, fails to convey food or drink to the claimant's own mouth without receiving:
i) physical assistance from someone else; or
ii) regular prompting given by someone else in the claimant's presence.

16. Chewing or swallowing food or drink

A Cannot chew or swallow food or drink;

B Cannot chew or swallow food or drink without repeatedly stopping, experiencing breathlessness or severe discomfort;

C Cannot chew or swallow food or drink without repeatedly receiving regular prompting given by someone else in the claimant's presence; or

D Owing to a severe disorder of mood or behaviour, fails to:
i) chew or swallow food or drink; or
ii) chew or swallow food or drink without regular prompting given by someone else in the claimant's presence.

ESA Regs, Sch 3

First, whether or not you can understand simple messages (such as the location of a fire escape) from other people by hearing or lipreading without the help of another person. Second, whether or not you can understand simple messages from other people by reading large size print or using Braille.

You would get 15 points if you cannot understand a simple message due to sensory impairment; 15 points could also be obtained if you have *'significant difficulty'* understanding a simple message from a stranger and 6 points if you have *'some difficulty'* doing so. If any of these apply, you should make this clear on the questionnaire.

Getting around safely
This activity (activity 8 in Box D.3) focuses on your ability to navigate and get around safely. It may apply if you have visual problems.

If your vision has only recently deteriorated, this may have affected your confidence; this should also be taken into account. If your vision varies from day to day, describe what you are like on both bad days and good days and how frequently the former occur.

Provide details of any incidents that may have occurred when you have tried to get around without someone with you, such as bumping into things or people, getting lost, or incidents with traffic. Write down if your driving licence has been withdrawn because of your visual problems.

If you are unable to get around a *'familiar'* place without someone else (due to sensory impairment), you would get 15 points. If you cannot safely cross the road (or deal with a similar hazard) without someone else, 15 points would also apply. You would get 9 points if you are unable to get around an *'unfamiliar'* place without someone else.

Controlling your bowels and bladder and using a collective device
This activity (activity 9 in Box D.3) concerns your ability to control your bowels or bladder (or use a stoma device or catheter without leakage). This is one of the most difficult parts of the questionnaire to complete because the questions are of such a personal nature. Try to put as much information down as you can; the questionnaire is treated with strict confidentiality.

Bladder incontinence that occurs when you are asleep will be ignored, as will minor leakage that can be contained by the use of pads.

You would get 15 points if the loss of control of your bowel or bladder leads to an extensive evacuation or voiding at least once a month. Fifteen points also apply if at least once a month there is substantial leakage of a collecting device which means you need to clean yourself and change your clothing.

If there is an extensive evacuation, voiding or substantial leakage once a week, you will also satisfy the 'limited capability for work-related activity assessment' (see Box D.5).

If you risk the loss of control of your bowel or bladder (leading to an extensive evacuation or voiding where you need to clean yourself or change your clothing) if you are not able to reach a toilet quickly, you would get 6 points.

If any of these apply to you, make this clear on the questionnaire. Explain what precautions you have tried to take and why these may not always work.

Staying conscious when awake
This activity (activity 10 in Box D.3) covers fits, seizures or absences. It should cover *'any involuntary loss or alteration of consciousness resulting in significantly disrupted awareness or concentration'* that occurs during the hours when you are normally awake. The DWP describes *'altered consciousness'* as *'... a definite clouding of mental faculties resulting in loss of control of thoughts and actions'*. It does not currently consider giddiness, dizziness or vertigo (in the absence of an epileptic or similar seizure) to be states of altered consciousness.

7. Completing the ESA50 – mental, cognitive and intellectual functions
Part 2 of the questionnaire relates to a number of different conditions, including mental illness, learning difficulties, the effects of head injuries and autistic spectrum disorders. You are asked broad questions about how your illness or disability affects your daily life. The questions are grouped into seven headings relating to the activities listed in Box D.4. Note that the wording in the questionnaire is sometimes different from the wording in Box D.4 (in which we use the exact wording of the law).

Under each heading, you are first asked whether you can manage that particular area of daily life without any difficulty. Read the text under the heading before ticking the box. Each heading is usually broken down into two or three further questions. You are given a number of options in each case, such as *'no'*, *'yes'* and *'it varies'*. There is a box within each heading where you can give extra information on the difficulties you have with each area of daily life.

This is a points-related test (see 2 above). To see how many points your answers in this part can potentially score, see Box D.4. We now look at each activity heading in more detail.

Learning how to do tasks
This activity (activity 11 in Box D.4) focuses on your ability to learn (and remember) how to do things. If you can learn a task one day, but have forgotten how to do it the next day, you will not be considered to have learnt it.

Two types of task are considered: *'simple'* and *'moderately complex'*. A simple task is one involving one or two steps; the example given is the setting of an alarm clock. A moderately complex task may involve three or four steps; the example given is the operating of a washing machine. Other examples could include playing CDs on a stereo, using a microwave oven or using a PlayStation.

If you are able to learn a moderately complex task, but cannot learn anything more complex than this (a task involving five or more steps – such as setting up a DVD player and programming the channels), you should make this clear on the questionnaire. If you are not able to learn anything *'beyond'* a moderately complex task, you would get 6 points in the assessment. Write down examples of the kind of tasks you would have problems learning, perhaps ones you have tried to learn recently but not succeeded.

Awareness of hazard or danger
This activity (activity 12 in Box D.4) may be relevant if your condition (or the medication you take for it) has affected your concentration such that your awareness of the risks posed by common hazards has been reduced. It may also be relevant if you have a learning disability or a brain injury, or if depressive illness or a psychotic disorder has affected your attention or concentration.

If you consequently need supervising to maintain your safety for the *'majority of the time'* (ie you need daily supervision, according to the DWP), you would get 15 points. If you *'frequently'* require supervision (ie several times a week) you would get 9 points. If you *'occasionally'* require supervision, you would get 6 points. Mention any accidents you have had because you were not aware of a danger and list any injuries you sustained as a consequence.

Starting and finishing tasks
This activity (activity 13 in Box D.4) looks at your ability to start and complete *'personal actions'*, without needing prompting from someone else. To be relevant, the problems must stem from an *'impaired mental function'* (such as autism or severe depression), rather than from any physical symptoms you may have. Examples of personal actions could include: making travel arrangements; sorting out the

laundry and using a washing machine; writing shopping lists; and dealing with finances. In each case your ability to complete the task in question reliably and repeatedly must be considered.

If you are unable to complete two such actions following on from each other, you would get 15 points. If you are not able to complete two such actions *'for the majority of the time'* you would get 9 points. If you *'frequently'* are unable to do so, you would get 6 points. Provide examples of the kind of things you are no longer able to finish because of your mental condition.

Coping with changes

This activity focuses on your ability to cope with minor changes to your daily routine. Two types of change are considered: *'planned'* and *'unplanned'*. The activity may be relevant if you have a moderate or severe learning disability, an autistic spectrum disorder, a brain injury, an obsessive compulsive disorder, severe anxiety or a psychotic illness.

The activity is not intended to reflect a simple dislike of any changes to your routine, but rather your inability to cope with it. If you are unable to cope with any change, such that your day-to-day life would grind to a halt, you would get 15 points. If a minor planned change made your life *'significantly more difficult'*, you would get 9 points; if a minor unplanned change had the same affect, you would get 6 points.

Going out

This activity (activity 15 in Box D.4) considers your ability to go out on your own. It is concerned with the problems posed by disorientation or agoraphobia (rather than by visual problems, which are dealt with by activity 8 in Part 1 of the questionnaire; see 6 above). This activity may also be relevant if you have a learning disability.

If you would be unable to get to a place you know well even if you had someone with you, you would get 15 points. If you need to be accompanied in order to get to a place you know well, you would get 9 points. If you need to be accompanied in order to get to a place that is unfamiliar to you, you would get 6 points. In each case, the way that you arrive at the destination is not relevant (eg if you cannot use public transport, but could manage to get there by another means, you would not score points).

If you do become disorientated or agoraphobic outdoors, explain on the questionnaire what is likely to happen to you were you go out alone. Provide details of any incidents that may have occurred (and what you felt like) if you have attempted to go somewhere alone in the past.

Coping with social situations

This activity (activity 16 in Box D.4) focuses on any problems you may have in meeting people because of a *'significant lack of self confidence'*, rather than shyness or reticence. If you have severe anxiety or autism, suffer panic attacks or have agoraphobia, this heading may apply.

If you are never able to meet with people you know because of difficulty relating to them or because of significant distress, you would get 15 points. If you are never able to meet with people you do not know (for the same reason), you would get 9 points. If you are sometimes able to meet with people you do not know, but for the majority of the time would be unable to do so, you would get 6 points.

Behaving appropriately with other people

This activity (activity 17 in Box D.4) focuses on the way you behave socially, whether or not you have episodes of *'aggressive or disinhibited behaviour'* that you are not able to control and, if so, how often these occur. It may be relevant if you have a psychotic illness or an autistic spectrum disorder. It particularly looks at whether behaviour would be unreasonable *'in the work place'* where expectations may be higher than in general.

8. Returning the ESA50 questionnaire

Once you have completed the ESA50, sign and date the declaration at the end of the questionnaire. Before you post it, photocopy it for future reference. You should return the questionnaire in the addressed envelope provided within three weeks from the day after it was sent to you. If you have not returned it within the time limit, you should be sent a reminder. If you do not return the ESA50 within a week of receiving the reminder, you will be treated as not having a limited capability for work, and thus not entitled to ESA, unless you can show you had *'good cause'* for failing to return it.

ESA Regs, regs 22 & 37

Good cause – When deciding whether you had good cause for failing to complete and send back the ESA50, Jobcentre Plus must take into account your health, your disability and whether you were outside Great Britain. However, other reasons could be valid. You have a right of appeal against a decision that you failed to send back a completed ESA50 but you cannot be paid the basic allowance of ESA pending an appeal on this matter (see 11 below).

ESA Regs, regs 24 & 39

What happens next? – Your completed ESA50 is assessed by a DWP-approved healthcare professional. The healthcare professional considers all the evidence on your claim and may request further information from your own GP (or any other professional providing you with treatment) and/or ask that you attend a face-to-face assessment.

9. Face-to-face assessment

The face-to-face assessment will take place at an Examination Centre. It is carried out by a healthcare professional working for Atos Healthcare, the organisation delivering the WCA on behalf of the DWP. You must be provided with at least seven days' notice of the time and place for the assessment, unless you agree to accept a shorter notice period. This may be arranged over the phone. If you cannot attend, you should inform the office that arranged the assessment as soon as possible.

ESA Regs, regs 23(3) & 38(3)

If you fail to attend – If you do not attend, you will be treated as not having a limited capability for work unless you can show you had 'good cause' for not attending (see 8 above). You will be contacted and asked to explain your reasons. If the decision maker refuses to accept that you had good cause, you can appeal – but you cannot be paid the basic allowance of ESA pending an appeal on this matter (see 11 below). You should also make a new claim for benefit in case your appeal is unsuccessful, but ESA will not be paid until you have attended a face-to-face assessment.

ESA Regs, regs 23(2) & 24

At the assessment

When the healthcare professional is ready to see you, they will come to the waiting area to take you into the examination room. This gives them a chance to watch how you manage to rise from a chair, walk and sit down again or how you manage with a wheelchair.

During the assessment, the healthcare professional will identify the descriptors that they consider apply to you with respect to both the limited capability for work assessment and the limited capability for work-related activity assessment. To do this, they will ask questions about your daily activities, including hobbies or leisure activities. They will observe how you manage during the assessment itself and may give you a clinical examination.

Physical functions – When answering the healthcare professional, explain your abilities as fully as you can. You should tell them about any pain or tiredness you feel, or would feel, while carrying out tasks, both on the day of the examination and over time. Consider how you would feel if you had to do the same task repeatedly. Try not to overestimate your ability to undertake tasks. If your condition varies, let them know about the variability; and what you are like on bad days as well as on good days. The healthcare professional's opinion should not be based on a snapshot of your condition on the day of the examination; they should consider the effects of your condition over time.

Mental, cognitive and intellectual functions – The healthcare professional needs to consider a number of different disabilities and conditions that may apply to you, including mental health, learning disability and autistic spectrum disorders. To do this, they should ask you how your condition affects your day-to-day abilities (eg going to the shops, cooking food and travelling on your own), whether you can understand and remember things, whether you can concentrate on tasks, how you cope with change and unexpected situations, and how you get on with other people.

When you explain how your condition affects your day-to-day abilities, tell the healthcare professional how you are on an average day. If your condition varies over time or from day to day, tell them how often it varies and for how long at a time. Answer the questions as honestly and fully as you can. If you do not understand a question, ask the healthcare professional to explain what they mean or to repeat the question.

You may find it helpful to have someone with you at the assessment. This could be a relative, friend or care worker. They can help to fill in any gaps in what you tell the healthcare professional.

Who makes the decisions?
The decisions (technically called *'determinations'*) on whether or not you have a limited capability for work or a limited capability for work-related activity are not made by the healthcare professional. They will produce a report of the assessment, the ESA85 (see Box D.6), and send it to a Jobcentre Plus decision maker, who will decide whether you have a limited capability for work and for work-related activity. The decision maker may ring you prior to making the decisions, to ensure they have all the available evidence. They will then write to you, to inform you of their decisions.

10. Exceptional circumstances
If the decision maker decides you do not meet the limited capability for work assessment, they can still treat you as having a limited capability for work if one of the *'exceptional circumstances'* applies. These are, that you are suffering from either:
■ a life-threatening disease, in relation to which there is medical evidence that the disease is uncontrollable or uncontrolled by a recognised therapeutic procedure, and in the case of a disease that is uncontrolled there is a reasonable cause for it not to be controlled by a recognised therapeutic procedure; *or*
■ some specific disease or bodily or mental disablement, and because of that there would be a substantial risk to any person's mental or physical health if you were found not to have a limited capability for work. The risk should be linked to the work, and any work considered should be work you could realistically do according to your education or skills (R(IB)2/09). This circumstance will not apply to you if the risk could be significantly reduced by making reasonable adjustments to your workplace or by you taking medication as prescribed.

ESA Regs, reg 29

Decisions on exceptional circumstances – The decision maker decides if any of the exceptional circumstances apply, based on the report from the healthcare professional who examined you. If there is medical evidence from your own doctor, they must consider this as well and decide on the basis of *'the most reliable evidence available'*. You can appeal against the decision made.

11. Challenging the decision
You can appeal against most decisions that are made during the work capability assessment. You can appeal against a decision:
■ based on a determination that you do not have a limited capability for work;
■ based on a determination that you do not have a limited capability for work-related activity;
■ that you do not have good cause for failing to send back the ESA50 questionnaire or to attend the face-to-face assessment;
■ on exceptional circumstances.
The appeals process is described in Chapter 58.
Reconsiderations – You do not have to appeal straight away. You can ask the decision maker to reconsider the decision instead, which you can do within one calendar month of the date of the decision letter. However, if it is determined that you do not have a limited capability for work, you would not be entitled to ESA while your request for a reconsideration was being dealt with. If this is the case, you should appeal straightaway, in which case ESA could be paid up to the appeal hearing (see below).

Unfortunately, from October 2013 the government intends to introduce mandatory reconsiderations. Once it does this, you would need to claim jobseeker's allowance (see Chapter 16) while the reconsideration was being dealt with, unless you can show that your condition has worsened or you have a new condition, in which case you can re-claim ESA (see 12 below). See Chapter 58(3) for more on reconsiderations (also known as 'any grounds' revisions)

Appeals on the limited capability for work assessment
If it is determined that you do not have a limited capability for work and none of the exceptional circumstances apply (see 10 above), you will not be entitled to ESA. You can appeal against this decision. The appeal tactics you can use in such cases are described in Box D.6.
While you are appealing – You can continue to receive the basic allowance of ESA (see Chapter 10(8)) and any appropriate premiums in the case of income-related ESA (see Chapter 25) while appealing against a decision on your limited capability for work (but see below for an exception). This applies if you are making a new claim for ESA or if your existing entitlement to ESA has been reassessed. In either case, you will need to send in 'fit notes' (see Chapter 9(9)) until the appeal has been heard or otherwise dealt with. If your appeal is successful, you will receive full arrears for any additional component that has not been paid.
ESA Regs, regs 5(4) & 147A

You cannot automatically receive ESA pending the appeal if you are appealing against a decision that you do not have good cause for failing to send back the ESA50 questionnaire or attend the face-to-face assessment. In these situations, you will need to submit a new claim pending your appeal; payment of this may be suspended until you return an ESA50 or attend a face-to-face assessment. Alternatively, you can claim jobseeker's allowance pending the appeal (see Chapter 16).
What if you get worse before the appeal is heard? – A tribunal can look at your situation only as it was at the time of the decision you are appealing against. If your condition has deteriorated since then, or you have a new condition,

the tribunal cannot take this into account. To make sure you do not lose out while your appeal is pending, you should inform Jobcentre Plus that your condition has deteriorated or that you have a new condition and you would like them to reconsider the decision. If you have medical evidence to support your request, forward it to them. A fresh WCA would normally then be arranged. If, following the new WCA, it is determined that you still do not have a limited capability for work, you should appeal against the new decision. You can request that an appeal tribunal hears both appeals together.

Appeals on the limited capability for work-related activity assessment

If it is determined that you do not have a limited capability for work-related activity, you will be placed in the work-related activity group. In that case, you receive a lower level of ESA than if placed in the support group and, if you are entitled to contributory ESA, the award of this will be limited to 12 months. If you consider that at least one of the descriptors listed in Box D.5 applies to you, or alternatively one of the circumstances where you can be treated as having a limited capability for work-related activity applies to you (see 3 above), then you may wish to appeal against the decision.

If you appeal against the decision to place you in the work-related activity group, you will continue to be paid the lower level of ESA for claimants placed in that group. If the appeal tribunal decides that you do have a limited capability for work-related activity, you can be placed in the support group and become entitled to the higher level of

---

D.6 Appeal tactics – limited capability for work assessment

If a decision maker finds that you do not have a limited capability for work you will be sent a decision notice. You have one calendar month from the date the decision was sent to you to lodge an appeal (although from October 2013 you must first ask for a reconsideration of the decision – see 11 in this chapter).

Your appeal will be heard by a First-tier Tribunal, the members of which are independent of the DWP. Details of the appeal process are covered in Chapter 58. This box explains ways you can maximise your chances of success with appeals over the limited capability for work assessment.

Get the ESA85 – Attached to the decision will be a summary of the face-to-face assessment, telling you the activities in which it was decided you had some limitation and the total number of points allocated. (For lists of descriptors and points, see Boxes D.3 and D.4.) Unfortunately, this does not necessarily identify where there are areas of dispute. You should ask Jobcentre Plus to send you a copy of the DWP healthcare professional's assessment report, the ESA85. This will contain a *personalised summary statement* that will justify their recommendations on which activities and descriptors should apply to you and clarify where their recommendations conflict with your views. This will allow you to see where you might need to dispute the findings, or point out misunderstandings. It is also worth checking the report for inconsistencies or inaccuracies – make a list of any and send it to Jobcentre Plus.

Opt for a hearing – Your chances of success are much higher if you go in person to the appeal hearing. You can take someone with you and it is a good idea to do this. When you receive the 'pre-hearing enquiry form', make sure you opt for a hearing.

Prepare your case – Seek advice from a Citizens Advice Bureau, DIAL or other advice centre, if you haven't already done so. They can help you prepare your case and may be able to represent you at the tribunal.

Here are some general guidelines to start with:
❑ Use Box D.3 and/or Box D.4 to see which descriptors apply to you and add up the points. Remember to think about your ability to perform the task reliably, safely, repeatedly and at reasonable speed, and the effects of pain, fatigue, etc. You can use this information to gather good medical evidence (see below) and to help you clarify to the tribunal exactly where in the assessment you should score points.
❑ If you think one of the circumstances applies in which you can be treated as having a limited capability for work (see Chapter 11(2)) seek medical evidence to confirm which one applies.

❑ If your medication affects your ability to complete tasks, or your physical condition affects your alertness, check whether this has been properly assessed under the mental, cognitive and intellectual functions assessment. Perhaps you have a mental health problem that has not been taken into account. For example, you may suffer from depression or anxiety but have not seen your GP about it. If so, you will stand more chance of having this taken into account if you have evidence, preferably medical evidence, to back you up.

Get medical or other supportive evidence – Seek medical evidence in advance of the hearing. An advice centre may be able to help you with this. Your doctor may want to charge a fee for providing evidence for you, so check on this first. If you cannot get medical evidence, check whether there is any other professional you could get evidence from (eg a support worker).

Ask your doctor, consultant, physiotherapist, etc to comment on the practical and functional problems you have regarding each descriptor that is at issue in your appeal.
❑ Where there is a dispute, what descriptors do they think should apply?
❑ Is your assessment of your limitations consistent with their understanding of your condition?
❑ Do any of the circumstances apply in which you can be treated as having limited capability for work?
It is important that your evidence focuses on these things, not simply on what condition you have and the treatment you receive.

If your condition has changed since the decision that you are appealing against was made, the tribunal cannot take that into account. So make sure that your evidence is about your condition as it was at the time of the decision.

Remember, however, that you know your abilities better than anyone. The DWP healthcare professional will only have seen you briefly so cannot know everything about you. What you say will count as evidence as long as it is not self-contradictory or implausible (R(I)2/51, R(SB)33/85). Your statements will, however, carry more weight when supported by medical evidence.

At the tribunal hearing – The tribunal should be conducted in an informal manner and should consider all the medical and other evidence in making its decision, and reach its own conclusions on each descriptor that is at issue in the appeal, not simply adopt the report of the DWP healthcare professional (CIB/14722/96). If you think you need more evidence from your own doctor, ask for an adjournment. However, you do not have an automatic right to an adjournment for this reason, so it is best to get all of your medical evidence ready before the hearing.

ESA. The difference between the two levels of benefit can be backdated to the time that the additional component for the support group would have become payable (which would normally be once the ESA assessment phase was completed – see Chapter 10(4)).

The general advice provided in Box D.6, which applies to appeals on the limited capability for work assessment, also applies to appeals on the limited capability for work-related activity assessment. Any medical evidence you obtain should focus on confirming which Box D.5 descriptor(s) apply to you or which circumstance where you can be treated as having a limited capability for work-related activity applies. In the former case, you could ask your doctor, consultant or physiotherapist, etc to comment on the practical and functional problems you have with respect to the descriptor(s) in question.

Note that when you appeal against a determination that you do not have a limited capability for work-related activity, the tribunal can look at the whole decision, including whether or not you also have a limited capability for work. Potentially, you could lose your entitlement to ESA. If in doubt, seek advice.

12. If your condition deteriorates
After a decision on limited capability for work – If you re-claim ESA within six months of a determination that you do not have (or can be treated as having) a limited capability for work, fit notes from your doctor (see Chapter 9(9)) will be sufficient evidence of your limited capability until you are assessed under a WCA, provided:

■ you have a different condition; *or*
■ your condition has significantly worsened since the decision.

It would be helpful if your fit notes clearly showed this was the case. This allows benefit to be paid pending a new decision under the WCA.

ESA Regs, reg 30

If you re-claim within six months for the same condition and it has not significantly worsened, you will not get paid while waiting to be assessed. The decision maker may decide not to reassess you immediately. This cannot be appealed, but after six months you may be paid on the basis of your fit notes. Alternatively, the decision maker may decide, without obtaining any further evidence, that you do not have a limited capability for work. This is a new decision, so you have the right to appeal against it. If you missed the deadline for appealing against the earlier decision, this gives you another chance, although you may not get full arrears if successful.

After a decision on limited capability for work-related activity – If you have been placed in the work-related activity group and your condition has recently got worse, it is possible you will now satisfy one (or more) of the descriptors that will allow you to be placed in the support group (see Box D.5).

If you are still in receipt of ESA, you will need to contact your local Jobcentre Plus office, explain that your condition has recently got worse and tell them which of the descriptors in Box D.5 now apply to you. If you do this by phone, follow it with a letter to the office confirming your request. If you can, obtain medical evidence to back up your case, eg a letter from your doctor, consultant or specialist nurse, confirming the descriptor that applies to you. Attach a copy of this evidence to your request.

If you are not in receipt of ESA as your 12-month contributory ESA has ended, you may need to make a new claim for ESA. See Chapter 12(3) for details.

You can appeal against a decision to place you in the work-related activity group. For details of the appeals process, see Chapter 58.

12 Contributory ESA

1. What is contributory ESA?
You can qualify for contributory employment and support allowance (ESA) if you have paid sufficient national insurance contributions. Contributory ESA is not affected by savings or most other income, except for occupational or personal pensions. It is taxable.

You should claim contributory ESA if you cannot get statutory sick pay (SSP) because, for example, you are not in employment, you are self-employed or your SSP entitlement has run out. You cannot normally work and receive contributory ESA; for exceptions, see Chapter 17(3).

2. Do you qualify?
To be entitled to contributory ESA, you must satisfy the national insurance contribution conditions (see 6 below) as well as the basic conditions laid out in Chapter 10(9).

WRA, S.1(2)(a)

Contributory ESA in youth – Prior to 1.5.12, the requirement to satisfy the contribution conditions could be waived if your limited capability for work began before the age of 20 (or 25 in some cases). This would enable you to receive 'contributory ESA in youth' (CESA(Y)). For details, see the *Disability Rights Handbook* 36th edition, page 63.

If you were already receiving CESA(Y) by 1.5.12 and had been placed in the support group (see Chapter 10(7)) at that date, you can continue to receive it for as long as you continue to satisfy the eligibility conditions and remain within the support group. If in future you are moved from the support group to the work-related activity group (following a new work capability assessment), the 12-month time limit will be imposed (see below).

3. Time limits
Since 1.5.12 contributory ESA is payable for a maximum of 12 months for anyone placed in the work-related activity group (see Chapter 10(6)). The 12 months can be in one spell, or in separate 'linked' periods of limited capability for work (see 6 below). The 13-week assessment phase you have served (see Chapter 10(4)) will form part of the 12-month payment period if it was immediately followed by you being in the work-related activity group. It does not count if it was immediately followed by you being in the support group (see Chapter 10(7)).

If you are placed in the support group, the time limit does not apply and you will continue to receive contributory ESA for as long as you satisfy the eligibility conditions. If in future you are moved from the support group to the work-related activity group (following a new work capability assessment), the time limit will be imposed. The time you spent in the support group will not form part of the 12-month payment period nor will the 13-week assessment period if it was immediately followed by you being in the support group.

Once your 12-month payment period is exhausted, you can usually only re-qualify for contributory ESA when you begin a new period of limited capability for work (which must

be separated from the earlier period of limited capability for work by more than 12 weeks) and your new claim is based on different tax years (see 6 below).
WRA, S.1A

If your condition gets worse
If your contributory ESA is terminated at the end of the 12-month payment period, you should ask Jobcentre Plus to continue to assess you as having a limited capability for work. This will allow you to be credited with national insurance contributions; see 5 below. More importantly, if your condition deteriorates in the future, it is possible that you will begin to satisfy the conditions for the support group (see Chapter 10(7)). In this case, you should make a new claim for ESA. You will probably be referred for a work capability assessment (see Chapter 11). If it is accepted at this assessment that you have a limited capability for work-related activity (and can thus be moved into the support group) and provided that you continued to have (or can be treated as having) a limited capability for work from the time that the first ESA award was terminated, you can be awarded contributory ESA once more. You will not have to serve any waiting days (see Chapter 10(13)) or the assessment phase (see Chapter 10(4)).

This route back onto the benefit applies in a similar fashion to awards of 'contributory ESA in youth'.
WRA, S.1B

Income-related ESA
The time limit does not apply to income-related ESA. If you are receiving only time-limited contributory ESA, Jobcentre Plus should contact you before the benefit ends to ask if you want to be considered for income-related ESA. If your contributory ESA is due to end, you want to be considered for income-related ESA and you have not heard from Jobcentre Plus, contact them directly (0800 055 6688; textphone 0800 023 4888). See Chapter 13 for details of income-related ESA.

4. National insurance contributions
There are six different classes of national insurance (NI) contributions, but only Classes 1 and 2 count towards contributory ESA. Voluntary Class 3 contributions only count towards bereavement benefits and the basic state pension. Classes 1A and 1B are paid by employers only and do not count towards benefit entitlement. Class 4 contributions are normally paid by self-employed people on profits or gains above a certain level.

Class 1 contributions
Class 1 contributions are paid by employees and employers. You pay these, and hence build up entitlement to contributory ESA, on any earnings above the *'primary threshold'* of £149 a week (for the tax year 2013/14).

If you are not contracted out of the state second pension scheme, your contribution will be 12% on earnings between £149.01 and £797 a week. The contribution on earnings over £797 a week, the *'upper earnings limit'*, is just 2%.

If you earn less than the primary threshold, but more than the *'lower earnings limit'* of £109 a week (for the tax year 2013/14), you will be treated as having paid Class 1 contributions even though you do not actually have to pay any contributions.
SSCBA, Ss. 6(1), 6A & 8(1)-(2)

Earnings per week	level of NI contribution
Below £109	Nil
From £109 – £149	Nil (but treated as paid)
From £149.01 – £797	12%
£797.01 and above	2%

Reduced rate for married women – If you are a married woman or widow and have kept your right to pay reduced-rate contributions and you earn over £149 a week, you will pay Class 1 contributions of 5.85% on your earnings between £149.01 and £797 and 2% on earnings above £797.
SSCBA, S.19(4) & Cont. Regs, regs 127(1)(a) & 131

Reduced-rate contributions do not count towards contributory ESA, so it is worth considering giving up your right to pay reduced-rate contributions, particularly if you are not contracted out of the state second pension. Ask for advice from a Citizens Advice Bureau or the NI Contributions Office (see inside back cover).

Class 2 contributions
Class 2 contributions are flat-rate contributions of £2.70 a week (2013/14) paid by self-employed people.

If your net profits or gains are below (or you expect them to be below) £5,725 in the 2013/14 tax year, you can apply for a certificate of exception on form CF10, available from the HMRC helpline (0845 915 4655) or website (www.hmrc.gov.uk/forms/cf10.pdf). If (and only if) you get this certificate, you do not have to pay Class 2 contributions. However, even if your net profits are below £5,725 and you have the certificate, you still have the right to pay Class 2 contributions. You may wish to do this to protect your contribution record for contributory ESA, state pension and bereavement benefits. If you have low earnings from self-employment and want to pay contributions voluntarily, it is sensible to pay Class 2 rather than Class 3 contributions.
SSCBA, S.11 & Cont. Regs, reg 46

A married woman or widow who has kept her reduced-rate election does not have to pay Class 2 contributions. But if her taxable profits from self-employment are £7,755 a year or more, she will be liable to pay Class 4 contributions.
Cont. Regs, reg 127(1)(b)

Class 3 contributions
Class 3 contributions are voluntary, flat-rate contributions. In the 2013/14 tax year they are £13.55 a week. You may want to pay them if the other contributions you have paid (or been credited with) in a tax year are not enough to make that year count as a 'qualifying year' for state pension or bereavement benefits (see Box O.1, Chapter 43).
SSCBA, S.13

5. Contribution credits
There are situations when you are not in a position to pay national insurance (NI) contributions but are awarded NI *'credits'* instead. These only count towards the second contribution condition for contributory ESA (see 8 below). There are different ways of receiving such credits. For instance, you are awarded a Class 1 credit for each week you receive jobseeker's allowance or are entitled to carer's allowance. If you are awarded a Class 1 credit, you are treated as if you had earnings equal to the lower earnings limit for that week. If you are a married woman and have kept your right to pay reduced-rate NI contributions, you cannot get Class 1 contribution credits (except 'credits for parents and carers' and bereavement credits).

The different ways that you can be awarded NI credits are listed in Box D.7.

6. Contribution conditions
There are two national insurance (NI) contribution conditions, both of which you must meet to be entitled to contributory ESA. The first condition depends on the NI contributions that you have actually paid in the relevant tax year (see 7 below). For the second condition, credited NI contributions, as well as paid NI contributions, count (see 8 below). In both cases, there is a relationship between 'tax years' and 'benefit years',

so it is important to know the difference between them.

Tax years – A tax year runs from 6 April to 5 April the following year.

Benefit years – Benefit years start on the first Sunday in January and end on the Saturday before the first Sunday in January the following year. The 2013 benefit year started on Sunday 6.1.13 and will end on Saturday 4.1.14.

SSCBA, S.21(6)

The *'relevant benefit year'* is usually the year that includes the start of your *'period of limited capability for work'*.

WRA, Sch 1, para 3(1)(f)

However, if you have already made a claim for contributory ESA which was unsuccessful because you did not satisfy the contribution conditions at that time and you re-claim in a subsequent year, then that year can be treated as the relevant benefit year if it would now enable you to satisfy the contribution conditions.

ESA Regs, reg 13

Period of limited capability for work – This is the period throughout which you have, or are treated as having, a limited capability for work. It usually begins once you have made a claim for ESA. There is a linking rule that means, in some circumstances, your period of limited capability for work begins before you actually claim.

The linking rule – Any two periods of limited capability for work separated by no more than 12 weeks are treated as one single period. This is important because it is the beginning of the period of limited capability for work that determines which tax years are relevant.

ESA Regs, reg 145

7. First condition: paid contributions

You must have paid, or be treated as having paid, at least 26 weeks of Class 1 or Class 2 national insurance (NI) contributions on earnings at the lower earnings limit in one of the last two complete tax years before the start of the relevant benefit year. For instance, if you make your ESA claim in the 2013 benefit year, you need to have paid 26 weeks' contributions in one of the following tax years: 2010/11 or 2011/12 (unless one of the exceptions listed below applies).

WRA, Sch 1, para 1; ESA Regs, reg 7A

Lower earnings limits – These are uprated each year. For the last nine years they were:

Lower earnings limits

2005/06	**£82**	2008/09	**£90**	2011/12	**£102**
2006/07	**£84**	2009/10	**£95**	2012/13	**£107**
2007/08	**£87**	2010/11	**£97**	2013/14	**£109**

Example: If you claim ESA in the 2013 benefit year, you pass the first condition if you earned at least £97 a week for 26 weeks between April 2010 and April 2011; or at least £102 a week for 26 weeks between April 2011 and April 2012.

Exceptions

There are exceptions for some people whose circumstances may have prevented them from working or paying enough contributions in the usual 2-year period. If you are in one of the following groups, you will satisfy the first condition if you have paid, or can be treated as having paid, sufficient NI contributions in *any* complete tax year:

❑ **Carers** – You were entitled to carer's allowance for at least one week in the last complete tax year before the start of the relevant benefit year. For example, if you claim ESA in the 2013 benefit year and you were getting carer's allowance at any time between 6.4.11 and 5.4.12, you can pass the first condition based on contributions paid in any tax year.

❑ **Low-paid disabled workers** – You were working and entitled to the disability or severe disability element of

working tax credit. You must have been working for at least two years immediately before the first day of your period of limited capability for work. This helps you claim contributory ESA when your earnings were below the limit for NI contributions.

❑ **Spouses and civil partners of members of HM forces** – You were entitled to an NI credit to cover a period of assignment outside the UK (see Box D.7) for at least one week in the last complete tax year before the start of the relevant benefit year.

❑ **In prison or detention but conviction or offence quashed** – You were entitled to an NI credit for a period in prison or detention, or would be if you applied, for at least one week in any tax year before the relevant benefit year.

ESA Regs, reg 8

8. Second condition: paid or credited contributions

You must have paid or been credited with Class 1 or Class 2 national insurance contributions on earnings 50 times the lower earnings limit in each of the last two complete tax years before the start of the relevant benefit year. For example, if your benefit year is 2013, you meet this condition if you paid contributions on earnings of £4,850 in the 2010/11 tax year, and of £5,100 in the 2011/12 tax year.

WRA, Sch 1, para 2

9. How much do you get?

For the first 13 weeks of your claim, you are paid the basic allowance, which depends on your age.

Contributory ESA (assessment phase)	per week
Aged under 25 years	£56.80
Aged 25 years or over	£71.70

Following the 13-week assessment phase, if you are assessed as having a limited capability for work, you receive the basic allowance plus an additional component depending on whether you are placed in the work-related activity group or the support group (see Chapter 10(8)).

Contributory ESA (main phase)	per week
Basic allowance	£71.70
Work-related activity component	£28.45
Support component	£34.80

ESA Regs, reg 67(2)-(3) & Sch 4, paragraph 1(1) & Part 4

10. Does anything affect what you get?
Other benefits

To be entitled to ESA you must not be entitled to either income support or jobseeker's allowance. Additionally, you cannot receive contributory ESA as well as state pension, maternity allowance, carer's allowance, bereavement benefits and unemployability supplement, as these are *'overlapping benefits'*. This means you cannot receive more than one of any of these benefits, but you receive an amount equal to the highest amount of whichever benefit you are entitled to.

WRA, S.1(3)(e)-(f) & OB Regs, reg 4

You can receive other benefits such as disability living allowance, personal independence payment and industrial injuries disablement benefit without contributory ESA being affected. You may also be entitled to income-related ESA to top up contributory ESA if you are on a low income (see Chapter 13(5)).

Employer-paid benefits

Statutory maternity pay, statutory adoption pay and statutory paternity pay also 'overlap' with contributory ESA.

Consequently, if you are entitled to contributory ESA and claim one of these employer-paid benefits, you will receive whichever is the higher (which will usually be the employer-paid benefit).

ESA Regs, regs 80-82

Occupational and personal pension

If you receive an occupational or personal pension (including permanent health insurance payments, Pension Protection Fund periodic payments and Financial Assistance Scheme payments – but see below) that pays more than £85 a week, then your contributory ESA payment is reduced by half of the amount over this limit. For example, if you receive £105 a week before tax from a personal pension, your ESA is reduced by £10 a week, ie half of the excess figure of £20. If you receive more than one pension, they are added together for this calculation.

Some payments are ignored for this purpose, ie:

D.7 Contribution credits

Credits for limited capability or incapacity for work

You will be credited with a Class 1 national insurance (NI) contribution for each complete week you have a limited capability for work – ie on each day of the week you are entitled to employment and support allowance (ESA). If your contributory ESA is terminated because of the 12-month time limit (see Chapter 12(3)) and you are not entitled to income-related ESA, you can protect your NI contribution record by continuing to claim limited capability for work credits. You will get a credit for each week in which you meet the basic ESA rules (other than the specific contributory or income-related conditions for receipt of the benefit).

You will be credited with a Class 1 contribution for each complete week of incapacity for work – ie on each day of the week you are entitled to incapacity benefit, statutory sick pay (SSP), severe disablement allowance, income support on the grounds of incapacity for work or maternity allowance.

The rules for assessing limited capability for work are described in Chapter 11(2); the rules for assessing incapacity for work are described in Chapter 13, *Disability Rights Handbook*, 35th edition.

You should apply for your credits before the end of the benefit year after the tax year in which you had a limited capability for work or were incapable of work.

If you were getting SSP, you will have paid or been treated as having paid Class 1 contributions if your employer also has an occupational sick pay scheme that brings your SSP up to the lower earnings limit. But if you only got SSP, and therefore did not earn enough to pay or be treated as paying contributions and your contribution record is deficient, you should apply for credits.

You can also get a credit for each week for any part of which you received a war pensions or industrial injuries unemployability supplement.

A week for NI contribution purposes begins on a Sunday and ends on a Saturday.

Incapacity and limited capability for work credits can help meet the second contribution condition for any benefit.

Credit Regs, reg 8B

Credits for unemployment

You will be credited with a Class 1 contribution for each complete week you are paid jobseeker's allowance (JSA).

If you cannot be paid JSA (eg because your 6-month award of contribution-based JSA has come to an end), you can protect your NI contribution record by signing on at the Jobcentre Plus office for credits only. You will get a credit for each week in which you meet the basic JSA rules (other than the specific contribution-based or income-based conditions for receipt of the benefit) – see Chapter 16(2). If you have a limited capability for work or are incapable of work for part of the week, you are still entitled to a credit.

However, you may not get a credit for any week in which your JSA is not paid (or joint-claim JSA reduced) because of a sanction, or you get JSA hardship payments or you are on strike. If consequently there is a gap in your contribution record, you can protect your state pension entitlement by paying voluntary Class 3 contributions.

Unemployment credits help meet the second contribution condition for any benefit.

Credit Regs, reg 8A

Credits for caring

Carer's allowance credits – You get a Class 1 credit for each week in which you are paid carer's allowance, or in which you would be paid carer's allowance were you not receiving a bereavement benefit instead. Carer's allowance credits count for any benefit.

Credit Regs, reg 7A

Credits for parents and carers – From 6.4.10, to help meet the second contribution condition for basic state pension and bereavement benefits, you get a Class 3 credit for each week in which you:

- are caring for one or more disabled people for at least 20 hours a week and either they get attendance allowance, disability living allowance middle or highest rate care component (or the equivalents under the War Pensions or Industrial Injuries schemes) or the daily living component of personal independence payment, or that level of care has been certified as appropriate by a health or social care professional. The credits can continue for a period of 12 weeks after you cease to satisfy these conditions for any reason; or
- are entitled to income support as a carer (see Box E.1, Chapter 15); or
- (or your partner, if they have already met the contributory conditions for a Category A or B state pension that tax year) are awarded child benefit for a child under the age of 12; or
- are an approved foster carer.

You also get these credits to cover the 12-week period before or after an award of carer's allowance.

At the same time, in each case you will be credited with qualifying earnings for the state second pension (see Chapter 43(6)).

Prior to 6.4.10 similar provision was met by home responsibilities protection (see Box O.2, Chapter 43).

You will usually need to apply for these credits. Ring the Benefit Enquiry Line (see Box A.2, Chapter 2) for a CC1 claim-form (for carers) or HMRC (0845 302 1479; www.hmrc.gov.uk/forms/cf411A.pdf) for a CF411A (for parents and carers of children).

SSCBA, S.23A(2)-(3); Social Security (Contributions Credits for Parents & Carers) Regs 2010

Credits for providing care for a child under 12 – From 6.4.11, to help meet the second contribution condition for basic state pension and bereavement benefits, you can get a Class 3 credit for each week in which you provide care to a child under the age of 12. These credits may apply if you are the child's parent, (great- or great-great-) grandparent, brother, sister, aunt, uncle, nephew or niece (or partner or former partner of any of these).

The credits will apply only if you are not entitled to a credit

- a pension payment (or Pension Protection Fund periodic payment or a Financial Assistance Scheme payment) that you receive as the beneficiary upon the death of the pension scheme member;
- a pension payment in respect of death due to military or war service;
- any shortfall, if a full pension cannot be paid because the pension scheme is in deficit or has insufficient funds;
- any guaranteed income payment made under the Armed Forces Compensation scheme;
- a permanent health insurance payment if you paid more than 50% of the premium.

ESA Regs, regs 72, 72A, 74 & 75

Existing incapacity claimants – If you have been claiming incapacity benefit or severe disablement allowance since 2001, your occupational or personal pension will still be fully disregarded.

If you are 'migrated' onto ESA (see Chapter 14), the full

---

for parents and carers (as above) and someone else is in receipt of child benefit for the child (and they have already met the contributory conditions for a Category A or B state pension that tax year). Only one person can apply for these credits in respect of the same child.

Credit Regs, reg 9F & Sch

Credits for tax credits

You get a Class 1 credit for each week in which you receive the disability element or severe disability element of working tax credit (WTC). These credits count for any benefit. You may also get a Class 1 credit, which counts for state pensions and bereavement benefits, for any week you receive WTC. (If you are a couple, the credit is awarded to the one who is earning; if both of you are earning, it is awarded to the one being paid WTC.) In each case you must be either:

- employed and earning less than the lower earnings limit for that year; *or*
- self-employed and exempt from having to pay Class 2 contributions (see Chapter 12(4)).

Credit Regs, regs 7B & 7C

Training and education credits

Termination of full-time education/training credits – To help meet the second contribution condition for contribution-based JSA or contributory ESA only, you can get Class 1 credits for one of the two tax years before your benefit year if in that tax year you were aged 18 or over and in full-time education or on a full-time training course (or a part-time course of at least 15 hours a week if you are disabled) or in an apprenticeship, and the course or apprenticeship, which must have begun before you became 21, has now ended. In the other year, you must have passed the second contribution condition in a different way.

Credit Regs, reg 8

Approved training credits – To help you meet the second contribution condition for any benefit, you can get Class 1 credits for each week you are on an approved training course. The course must be full time, or 15 or more hours a week if you are disabled, or be an introductory course to one of those courses. It must not be part of your job. It must be intended to run for no longer than one year (unless it is a course provided by or on behalf of Jobcentre Plus and a longer period is reasonable because of your disability). You must have reached 18 before the start of the tax year in which you require the credits.

Credit Regs, reg 7

Others

Maternity, additional paternity and adoption pay period credits – If you receive statutory maternity pay (SMP), additional statutory paternity pay (SPP) or statutory adoption pay (SAP) and do not earn enough to pay or be treated as paying contributions on your SMP, SPP or SAP, you can apply for Class 1 credits if you need them. These credits count for any benefit.

Credit Regs, reg 9C

Jury service credits – If you are on jury service for all or part of any week, you can apply for Class 1 credits if you need them. These credits count for any benefit.

Credit Regs, reg 9B

Spouses and civil partners of members of HM forces – From 6.4.10, if you were accompanying (or treated as accompanying) your spouse or civil partner who is a member of HM forces on an assignment outside the UK, you can apply for Class 1 credits to cover the period of the assignment. These credits count for any benefit.

Credit Regs, reg 9E

Credits following official error – Due to an error in passing information between the DWP and HMRC between 1993 and 2007, some people have been over-credited with contributions for incapacity or approved training. If you are in this position, you can be awarded with credits to take the place of those incorrectly awarded. This can help you meet the second contribution condition for contribution-based JSA and state pension.

Credit Regs, reg 8E-8F

Starting credits – To help meet the second contribution condition for basic state pension and bereavement benefits, you can get Class 3 credits for the tax year in which you reached 16 and for the two following years (for tax years between 6.4.75 and 5.4.10).

Credit Regs, reg 4

Credits for men approaching state pension age – Men can get credits automatically for the tax year in which they reach pension credit qualifying age (see Chapter 42(2)) and for the following tax years up to the year they reach the age of 65, provided they are not out of the UK for six months or longer in the year. These credits cover gaps in your NI record for these years and count for all benefits.

Credit Regs, reg 9A

Bereavement credits – To help meet the second contribution condition for contribution-based JSA or contributory ESA when your bereavement benefit ceases, you can get Class 1 credits for each year up to (and including) the year in which your bereavement benefit ended, except where your benefit stopped because of remarriage, forming a civil partnership or cohabitation. Women who were getting widow's allowance or widowed mother's allowance can similarly get credits to help meet the second contribution condition for contributory ESA and will also be deemed to have satisfied the first condition (again, except where the benefit stopped because of remarriage, etc).

Credit Regs, reg 8C & Statutory Instrument 1974/2010, reg 3(1)

Credits for periods in prison – You can apply for credits for any weeks in which you were imprisoned or detained in legal custody for convictions or offences which were subsequently quashed by the courts, provided there were no other reasons for you being in prison or custody at that time. These credits count for all benefits.

Credit Regs, reg 9D

disregard will be protected, ie the above £85 limit will not be applied to you.

Sick pay
Any contractual sick pay paid by your employer will not affect your entitlement to contributory ESA.

ESA Regs, reg 95(2)(b)

Hospital and care homes
You can continue to receive contributory ESA while in hospital or a care home.

Prison
You are generally disqualified from receiving contributory ESA for any period during which you are in prison or legal custody.

WRA, S.18(4)(b)

Payment of contributory ESA is suspended if you are on remand awaiting trial or sentencing. Full arrears of benefit are payable if you do not receive a penalty (such as a fine or imprisonment) at the end of proceedings. No arrears are payable if you do receive a penalty.

If you are detained in a hospital or similar institution following a criminal conviction as a person *'suffering from a mental disorder'*, contributory ESA is payable for the length of the sentence unless you are detained under sections 45A or 47 of the Mental Health Act 1983 (or equivalent Scottish legislation).

ESA Regs, regs 160 & 161

Councillor's allowance
If you receive a councillor's allowance that pays more than £99.50 a week (excluding expenses), an amount equal to the extra money will be deducted from your contributory ESA.

ESA Regs, reg 76

13 Income-related ESA

1. What is income-related ESA?
Income-related employment and support allowance (ESA) is the means-tested element of ESA. It provides for basic living expenses for you and your partner, if you have one. Income-related ESA does not depend on your national insurance contributions. It can be paid on its own if you have no other income, or it can top up contributory ESA (see 5 below and Chapter 12).

Income-related ESA reflects contributory ESA in that it is paid at a higher rate after the 13-week assessment phase, when one of two additional components can be included in the calculation. The component you are eligible for is determined by whether you are placed in the work-related activity group or the support group (see Chapter 10(8) and 7 below).

Income-related ESA can help towards mortgage interest payments and certain other housing costs. If you get income-related ESA, you may also be eligible for housing benefit and will not have to go through a separate means test (see Chapter 21(20)).

Getting income-related ESA may entitle you to other types of benefit, eg:
- free prescriptions and dental treatment (Chapter 54);
- housing grants (Chapter 31);
- help from the social fund (Chapter 23) and budgeting loans (Chapter 24(2));
- free school meals (Chapter 37);
- help with hospital fares (Chapter 35).

Income-related ESA only covers the needs of you and your partner. If you have dependent children, you can claim child tax credit to cover their needs (see Chapter 19).

The government is replacing income-related ESA with 'universal credit'. This is being piloted from April 2013 in north-west England; nationwide roll-out starts in October 2013 on the basis of one district in each Jobcentre Plus region. A new claim for income-related ESA may be treated as a claim for universal credit instead, depending on where you live. See Box J.1 in Chapter 25 for more on universal credit.

2. Do you qualify?
To be entitled to income-related ESA you must satisfy all the following conditions, as well as the basic qualifying conditions laid out in Chapter 10(9).
- ❑ You must have no income, or your income is below your 'applicable amount' (a set amount that depends on your circumstances) – see 6 below.
- ❑ Your capital must be no more than £16,000. See Chapter 28(3).
- ❑ You must not be entitled to pension credit.
- ❑ If you are a member of a couple, your partner must not be entitled to income-related ESA, pension credit, income support or income-based jobseeker's allowance.
- ❑ You must not be in remunerative work (see 3 below).
- ❑ If you are a member of a couple, your partner must not be working for 24 hours or more a week (see 3 below).
- ❑ You must not be in full-time education (see 4 below).
- ❑ You must not be subject to immigration control (see Chapter 49(3)).
- ❑ You must satisfy the habitual residence test (see Chapter 49(2)).

WRA, Sch 1, para 6(1) & Sch 3, para 19; ESA Regs, reg 70 & Sch 5, para 11

Couples
You are treated as a couple if you and your partner are in any of the following categories:
- a man and woman who are married to each other and living in the same household;
- an unmarried man and woman who are living together as husband and wife;
- two people of the same sex who have entered into a civil partnership and live in the same household;
- two people of the same sex who have not entered a civil partnership but who live together as if they were civil partners.

ESA Regs, reg 2

3. Full-time or part-time work
You are excluded from income-related ESA if you or your partner are in *'remunerative work'*, which is work done for payment or in expectation of payment. You are not entitled to income-related ESA if you, the claimant, do any such work (except in some limited circumstances – see Chapter 17(3)). If you have a partner, you are not entitled to income-related ESA if they work for 24 hours or more a week, unless one of the exceptions listed in Chapter 15(6) applies to them (the same rules apply to income-related ESA). If one of these exceptions does apply, earnings are taken into account in the usual way (see Chapter 27(3)-(5)).

ESA Regs, regs 41(1) & 42(1)

4. Full-time education

You cannot usually undertake full-time education and receive income-related ESA (unless you are entitled to disability living allowance or personal independence payment). You are treated as receiving such education if you are a 'qualifying young person' for child benefit purposes (see Chapter 38(1)). Otherwise, whether your course is classed as full time or part time usually depends on the academic institution you attend.

If you are on a government-funded further education course in England or Wales, it is full time if it involves more than 16 hours of guided learning a week.

If you are on a government-funded further education course in Scotland that is not a course of higher education, it is full time if it involves more than 16 hours a week of classroom-based or workshop-based programmed learning under the direct guidance of a teacher. Hours including structured learning packages supported by teaching staff can be included, if the total adds up to more than 21 hours a week.

ESA Regs, regs 14, 15 & 18

Under 19

If you are aged under 19 but not a qualifying young person for child benefit purposes, you are not treated as in full-time education unless the course of study is:

■ a course leading to a first degree or postgraduate degree (or comparable qualifications), a higher education or higher national diploma; *or*
■ any other course of a standard above advanced GNVQ or equivalent.

ESA Regs, reg 16

Any student grants, loans or bursaries you receive while in education can be taken into account as income when determining how much income-related ESA you will be entitled to. See Chapter 40(3) for details.

5. How is income-related ESA worked out?

Income-related ESA is worked out by comparing your needs with your resources (ie any income or capital you may have). If you are a single person, only your needs and resources are relevant. If you are one of a couple (see 2 above), the needs and resources of both of you are relevant.

Set amounts for different needs are added together to reach the total amount the law says you need to live on. This is called your *'applicable amount'*. Any income you have (worked out under set rules) is deducted from your applicable amount. This leaves the amount of income-related ESA you are entitled to. The calculation is as follows:

Step 1: Add up your total capital resources – See Chapter 28. You will not be entitled to income-related ESA if your capital, and any capital belonging to your partner, is more than £16,000.

Step 2: Work out your applicable amount – See 6 below.

Step 3: Add up your total income resources – See Chapter 27. Do not forget the tariff income if you have capital over £6,000, or £10,000 if you live permanently in a care home (see Chapter 28(4)).

Step 4: Deduct your income from your applicable amount – If your income is less than your applicable amount, income-related ESA makes up the difference in full, provided you meet the other qualifying conditions (see 2 above and Chapter 10(9)).

WRA, S.4, ESA Regs, reg 67

If you are also entitled to contributory ESA

If you have no other income that should be taken into account, the amount of ESA you get will be whichever is the higher: contributory ESA or the applicable amount (see 6 below).

If you do have income that should be taken into account, the amount of ESA you get will be whichever is the higher: contributory ESA or the amount by which your applicable

amount exceeds your income (the result of Step 4 above).

In each case, if ESA is payable at a rate greater than the contributory ESA rate, your ESA payment will consist of two combined elements:

■ contributory ESA; *and*
■ a top-up of income-related ESA.

WRA, S.6

If your contributory ESA ends once the 12-month payment period is completed (see Chapter 12(3)) your income-related ESA should be adjusted to take this into account. The income-related ESA can then continue for as long as you satisfy the eligibility conditions.

6. What is your applicable amount?

Your applicable amount is the amount of money the law says you need to live on. It consists of:

■ a prescribed amount – for either a single claimant or a couple (see 7 below);
■ an additional component, depending on whether you are in the work-related activity group or support group (see 7 below);
■ premiums – flat-rate extra amounts if you satisfy certain conditions (see 8 below);
■ certain housing costs (see Chapter 26).

ESA Regs, reg 67

7. Prescribed amount and additional components

Prescribed amount

The prescribed amount is part of your applicable amount. The rate that applies to you depends on your age and whether or not you are part of a couple. There are lower rates of prescribed amount for people aged under 25, although these only apply during the 13-week assessment phase. After that, if you have established your entitlement to ESA, the higher rate applies regardless of your age.

Prescribed amount		per week
Single person	25 or over	£71.70
	under 25 (assessment phase)	£56.80
	under 25 (main phase)	£71.70
Lone parent	18 or over	£71.70
	under 18 (assessment phase)	£56.80
	under 18 (main phase)	£71.70
Couple	both 18 or over[1]	£112.55
	both under 18 (assessment phase)[2]	£85.80
	both under 18 (main phase)[2]	£112.55
	one 25 or over[3]	£71.70
	one 18-24 (assessment phase)[3]	£56.80
	one 18-24 (main phase)[3]	£71.70

ESA Regs, Sch 4, Part 1

Couples (where one partner is aged under 18) – In the table of rates above, the reference numbers mean:

1: includes couples where one is under 18 but would be eligible for either income-related ESA or income support if they were single, or is eligible for income-based jobseeker's allowance (JSA) or severe hardship payments;

2: only if one is responsible for a child; or each would be eligible for income-related ESA if they were single; or the claimant's partner would be eligible for income support if they were single or is eligible for income-based JSA or severe hardship payments. If none of these conditions are met, the single person's amount will apply (£56.80 during the assessment phase, £71.70 after this);

3: only if the other is under 18 and would not be eligible for either income-related ESA or income support (even if they were single), income-based JSA or severe hardship payments.

The additional component

Following the 13-week assessment phase, you are paid an additional component depending on whether you are placed in the work-related activity group or the support group (see Chapter 10(8)).

Components	per week
Work-related activity component	£28.45
Support component	£34.80

ESA Regs, Sch 4, Part 4

8. Premiums

There are four different premiums, each with specific qualifying conditions, as detailed in Chapter 25. The premiums are included as part of your applicable amount (see 6 above). Unless otherwise specified in Chapter 25, each premium to which you are entitled is added to the total of your applicable amount.

Premiums		per week
Severe disability	single	£59.50
	couple (one qualifies)	£59.50
	couple (both qualify)	£119.00
Enhanced disability	single	£15.15
	couple	£21.75
Pensioner (single)	work-related activity group	£45.25
	support group	£38.90
	assessment phase	£73.70
Pensioner (couple)	work-related activity group	£81.05
	support group	£74.70
	assessment phase	£109.50
Carer		£33.30

ESA Regs, Sch 4, Part 3

9. Other matters

Care homes – For how income-related ESA is calculated for care home residents, see Chapter 33(4).

Hospital – For how income-related ESA is affected by a stay in hospital, see Box M.1, Chapter 35.

Going into prison – You are generally disqualified from receiving income-related ESA for any period during which you are in prison or legal custody. However, if you are detained in custody awaiting trial or sentence you can continue to receive an amount of income-related ESA to cover housing costs.

ESA Regs, Sch 5, Part 1, para 3

14 Existing incapacity claimants

1. What will happen to existing claimants of incapacity benefits?

Between February 2011 and April 2014 the following benefits are being phased out:
■ incapacity benefit (see Box D.8);
■ severe disablement allowance (SDA) for those under state pension age (see Box D.9); *and*
■ income support paid on the grounds of incapacity (see Chapter 15).

If you are in receipt of one of these benefits, at some point prior to April 2014 you will be asked to take part in a work capability assessment (see 2 below). If you are found to have a limited capability for work in this re-assessment, you will be moved (or 'migrated') onto ESA.

Are there any exemptions? – If you reach state pension age (see Chapter 43(2)) before 6.4.14, the re-assessment will not apply to you; you will remain on your existing benefit until you reach state pension age. If you have already reached state pension age and are continuing to receive SDA, the re-assessment will not apply to you. Otherwise, no exemptions will apply.

TPEA Regs, reg 4(5)

2. Work capability assessment

First contact – Jobcentre Plus will write to you to inform you of the changes and that you are to be re-assessed. Shortly afterwards, they will ring to confirm that you have received the letter and understand what is going to happen.

TPEA Regs, reg 4

The assessment – You will then be sent a questionnaire to complete: the ESA50. This is the first stage of the work capability assessment (WCA), which is covered in Chapter 11. The process for claimants undergoing the re-assessment will be similar to that of new ESA claimants. Read Chapter 11(5)-(7) carefully before completing the ESA50 questionnaire. Your completed ESA50 will be assessed by a DWP-approved healthcare professional. They may request further information from your GP, or they may ask you to attend a face-to-face assessment (see Chapter 11(9)).

If you fail to send back the questionnaire, or attend the face-to-face assessment, without good cause (see Chapter 11(8)), a decision will be made that you do not have a limited capability for work and that your existing award of benefit does not therefore qualify for conversion to ESA. The existing award will be terminated. If you think that you have good cause for not sending back the questionnaire or attending the assessment, you can appeal against the decision.

TPEA Regs, Sch 2, para 7; ESA Regs, regs 22(1), 23(2) & 24

3. Moving onto ESA

Following the work capability assessment, if you are found to have (or can be treated as having) a limited capability for work, you will be moved onto ESA.

If you were previously getting incapacity benefit or SDA, this will be converted into contributory ESA (see Chapter 12). Payment of this may be limited to 12 months (see below).

If you were previously getting income support, this will be converted into income-related ESA (see Chapter 13).

If you were previously getting incapacity benefit or SDA topped up with income support, they will be converted into a single award of ESA, consisting of both the contributory and income-related elements.

You will not be required to make a claim for ESA, nor will you be required to serve any waiting days (see Chapter 10(13)) or the 13-week assessment phase (see Chapter 10(4)).

TPEA Regs, regs 5(1)-(2)(a), 7 & 8(1)(b)

Jobcentre Plus will ring you to advise on your ESA entitlement and explain the next steps in the process. They will then send a decision letter, notifying you of your ESA award and providing you with details of the benefit. They will let you know if you are entitled to contributory ESA, income-related ESA or both together. They will also let you know if you have been placed in the work-related activity group (see Chapter 10(6)) or the support group (see Chapter 10(7)).

TPEA Regs, regs 5(3)&(5)

Contributory ESA time limit – Since 1.5.12 contributory ESA has been payable for a maximum of 12 months for anyone in the work-related activity group. This time limit will be applied to the claims of those moved onto ESA from incapacity benefit or SDA. The 12-month period will run from the point that the previous benefit is converted into ESA. For details of how the time limit is applied, see Chapter 12(3).

What if ESA is paid at a higher rate?
If the level of ESA you are entitled to is greater than that of your previous benefit, the amount you receive will be increased as soon as you are migrated onto ESA.

What if ESA is paid at a lower rate?
Transitional addition – If the level of ESA you are entitled to is lower than that of your previous benefit, your ESA will be topped-up by a *'transitional addition'* to the rate of your previous benefit and frozen at that level. There are a number of circumstances in which your ESA entitlement may be lower than that of your previous benefit, including where:
- you received incapacity benefit or SDA that included an addition for an adult or child dependant;
- you received incapacity benefit that included an age addition;
- you received income support that included a disability premium (unless you are a single claimant placed in the ESA support group);
- you were transferred from invalidity benefit to incapacity benefit in 1995, and your incapacity benefit included an invalidity allowance (see Box D.10).

TPEA Regs, regs 9-12

If there is a substantial difference between the level of ESA you are entitled to and that of your previous benefit, you may find that the level of your ESA is effectively frozen for several years (unless there is a change of circumstances). Once the level of ESA you are actually entitled to has reached the same level as your previous benefit (eg through annual upratings), your ESA can start to be increased each April. The transitional addition will not extend beyond 5.4.20.

TPEA Regs, regs 18-21

If there is a break in your ESA claim of up to 12 weeks, your transitional addition is protected and it can be included in your new claim (as long as your previous award was not terminated because you were found not to have a limited capability for work).

TPEA Regs, regs 21(4)-(5); ESA Regs, reg 145

D.8 Incapacity benefit

Incapacity benefit was abolished for new claims from 27.10.08 and replaced by contributory employment and support allowance (ESA) – see Chapter 12.

Staying on incapacity benefit
If you were already in receipt of incapacity benefit on 27.10.08, you can remain on it for the time being if you continue to satisfy the rules of entitlement. At some point before 2014 you will be re-assessed under the 'work capability assessment' (see Chapter 11) unless you reach state pension age before 6.4.14. If you are found to have a 'limited capability for work' under this assessment, you will be moved onto ESA. For details, see Chapter 14.

How much do you get?

Incapacity benefit		per week
Long-term basic rate		£101.35
Adult dependant		£58.85
Child dependant	first child	£8.10
Child dependant	each other child	£11.35
Age addition	under 35	£10.70
Age addition	35-44	£6.00

SSCBA, S.30B & Sch 4(Parts I & IV)

You can qualify for an addition for an adult dependant only if you were already receiving the increase on 6.4.10, and for a dependent child or young person only if you were already receiving the increase on 5.4.03.

Work and earnings – Generally, if you do any work you are treated as capable of work and cannot get incapacity benefit. But some work is exempt from this rule (see Chapter 17(3)). Your partner's earnings do not affect your basic benefit, but can affect additions for children and dependent adults.

Other benefits – You cannot get incapacity benefit as well as maternity allowance, carer's allowance, bereavement benefits and unemployability supplement, as these benefits 'overlap'; you can only receive an amount equal to the highest of any of these benefits to which you are entitled. State pension and jobseeker's allowance cannot be paid at the same time as incapacity benefit.

Other benefits can be paid on top, including disability living allowance, attendance allowance and industrial injuries disablement benefit. Working tax credit can be paid on top, but incapacity benefit is taken into account in the tax credit assessment (unless you previously got invalidity benefit and are still in the same period of incapacity for work).

The benefit cap – Incapacity benefit is included in the list of benefits to which the benefit cap applies. This cap limits the total weekly benefits that can be claimed. See Box H.1 in Chapter 21 for details (including exemptions).

Occupational and personal pensions – Occupational and personal pensions affect your incapacity benefit in a similar way to contributory ESA (see Chapter 12(10).

Other incapacity benefit rules – More information about incapacity benefit can be found in Chapter 14, *Disability Rights Handbook*, 33rd edition. If you don't have a copy, send us an A4-sized, stamped addressed envelope and we'll send a photocopy.

National insurance credits only

If you are entitled only to national insurance (NI) credits (see Chapter 12(5)), ie you are incapable of work but not entitled to incapacity benefit, SDA or income support, you will be moved onto limited capability for work NI credits (see Box D.7 in Chapter 12). This will help towards your entitlement to a state pension. You will not be expected to meet work-related conditions to remain entitled to these credits.

ESA Regs, reg 54(2)(d)

If you have children

ESA does not include extra money for any children or young people for whom you are responsible. If you are responsible for a child or young person and you have previously been getting extra for them in your income support, Jobcentre Plus will send your details to HMRC, who will assess you for child tax credit. You do not need to make a claim for child tax credit, but Jobcentre Plus will try to contact you by phone to seek your agreement to the move. The process should take place prior to your migration onto ESA to ensure there is minimal disruption to your payments. See Chapters 19 and 20 for more on tax credits.

Payment

It is intended that there should be a continuity of payment when you move from your previous benefit onto ESA. You should be paid in the same way, at the same intervals. If deductions were being made from your previous benefit (eg to cover a social fund loan), these will continue to be made from your ESA. There may be a short delay in transferring such deductions.

Tax credits

If you were previously receiving severe disablement allowance (see Box D.9) or your incapacity benefit included an invalidity allowance (see Box D.10), these will have been disregarded as income in the tax credit calculation. If you are transferred onto contributory ESA from one of these benefits, the contributory ESA will now be taken into account in the tax credit calculation, thus reducing the amount of tax credit payable.

4. If you are found not to have a limited capability for work

Following the work capability assessment (WCA), if you are found not to have a limited capability for work and are therefore not entitled to ESA, your incapacity benefit, income support or SDA will be terminated (along with any award of national insurance credits you were getting on account of your illness or incapacity). You will receive a phone call informing you of the decision and asking if you want to claim jobseeker's allowance (JSA). If you want to challenge the decision, you can appeal, in which case you do not need to claim JSA as you can be paid the basic allowance of ESA until the appeal is decided (see below).

The phone call will be followed up by a decision letter, informing you of the outcome of the WCA, that your existing award of benefit has not qualified for conversion to ESA and of the date from which your existing award will be terminated.

TPEA Regs, regs 5(1) & (2)(b) & 15

Challenging the decision

If you want to challenge the decision (based on the WCA) that you are not entitled to ESA, you can appeal against it

---

D.9 Severe disablement allowance

Severe disablement allowance (SDA) was abolished for new claims on 6.4.01. If you are still on SDA, your entitlement may continue for the time being if you continue to satisfy the rules of entitlement. However, at some point before April 2014 you will be re-assessed under the 'work capability assessment' (see Chapter 11), unless you reach state pension age before 6.4.14. If you are found to have a limited capability for work under this assessment, you will be moved onto employment and support allowance: for details, see Chapter 14.

How much do you get?

SDA rates		per week
For yourself		£71.80
Age addition	higher rate	£10.70
	middle rate	£6.00
	lower rate	£6.00
Adult dependant		£35.35
Child dependant	first child	£8.10
	each other child	£11.35

Earnings – Your partner's earnings do not affect your basic benefit but can affect entitlement to dependants' additions. The rules are the same as for incapacity benefit (for details see the *Disability Rights Handbook* 33rd edition, page 87). SDA is not affected by any wages, sick pay or occupational or personal pension you get. However, it is only possible to do limited work and still be counted as incapable of work for SDA (see Chapter 17(3)).

Other benefits – If you get SDA, you may get a disability premium included in income support or housing benefit. SDA overlaps with other benefits such as carer's allowance, maternity allowance, state pension, bereavement benefits and unemployability supplement. If you are entitled to more than one, you are paid the one worth most.

The benefit cap – SDA is included in the list of benefits to which the benefit cap applies. This cap limits the total weekly benefits that can be claimed. See Box H.1 in Chapter 21 for details (including exemptions).

Other SDA rules – There is more information about SDA in Chapter 15, *Disability Rights Handbook*, 25th edition. If you don't have a copy, send us an A4-sized, stamped addressed envelope and we'll send you a photocopy.

D.10 Transferred from invalidity benefit

Invalidity benefit was abolished on 13.4.95 and replaced by incapacity benefit (itself now replaced by employment and support allowance). If you were entitled to invalidity benefit on 12.4.95, the amount of your benefit is protected (your award is a 'transitional award').

Social Security (Incapacity Benefit)(Transitional) Regs 1995, reg 17(1)

Amounts for 2013/14		per week
Long-term incapacity benefit		£101.35
Invalidity allowance	higher rate	£10.70
	middle rate	£6.00
	lower rate	£6.00
Dependants' addition		£58.85
Additional pension (SERPS) – the amount is based on your contribution record and frozen at your 1994/95 level.		

once you have received the written decision. Once you have lodged the appeal, you can be paid the basic allowance of ESA (see Chapter 10(8)), and any appropriate premiums in the case of income-related ESA (see Chapter 25), until the appeal is decided. If you win the appeal, you will receive arrears for the additional component that applies to you (see Chapter 10(8)) and any transitional addition that may apply (see 3 above). You will need to supply Jobcentre Plus with 'fit notes' while you are appealing (see Chapter 9(9)).

You cannot be paid the ESA basic allowance if you simply ask for the decision to be reconsidered (or 'revised' – see Chapter 58(3)). Consequently, it is advisable to appeal straight away. Unfortunately, from October 2013 the government intends to introduce mandatory reconsiderations. Once it does this, you would need to claim JSA (see below) while the reconsideration is being dealt with.

You cannot be paid the ESA basic allowance if you are appealing against a decision that was made solely because you failed to either send back the ESA50 questionnaire or attend the face-to-face assessment without good cause.

WCA appeals are covered in Chapter 11(11). See Box D.6 for methods you can use to ensure you have a fair hearing. For general information on appeals, see Chapter 58.

Claiming JSA
JSA is for people who are unemployed (or working less than 16 hours a week) and seeking work. There are two types of JSA: contribution-based JSA (based on your national insurance record) and income-based JSA (which is means tested). To get either type of JSA, you must be available for and actively seeking work. For details, see Chapter 16.
Making the claim – When you receive the phone call from Jobcentre Plus to inform you that you are not entitled to ESA, you should be asked if you want to claim JSA. If you say that you do, you will be transferred to someone who can take details of your claim.
If you are appealing – You can claim JSA when you are appealing against the decision not to award you ESA. If you win the appeal, you will become entitled to ESA rather than JSA, and will receive arrears for the additional component that applies to you (see Chapter 10(8)) and any transitional addition that may apply (see 3 above), back to the date from which ESA should have first become payable.

Staying on income support
If you were getting income support paid on the grounds of incapacity and have been found not to have a limited capability for work, you may be able to remain on income support if you are eligible in another way. You may be eligible for income support if you:
■ are a lone parent and your youngest child is under 5; *or*
■ are caring for someone and either you get carer's allowance or they get a qualifying benefit.
IS Regs, Sch 1B, paras 1 & 4
The full list of categories is set out in Box E.1 in Chapter 15. Jobcentre Plus should already have enough information to make a decision on your continued eligibility for income support. If they do, they will inform you of the decision in writing. Contact Jobcentre Plus if your income support is terminated following a WCA and you consider that you satisfy one of the other eligibility grounds, which they have not taken into account.
Disability premium – Even if you are eligible for income support through another route, the amount may be substantially reduced if the disability premium (see Chapter 25(2)) is removed. The disability premium is £31 for a single person and £44.20 for a couple. You will lose the premium if you only qualified for it on the basis that you were considered

incapable of work. You will not lose the premium if you still qualify for it another way, eg you receive disability living allowance. If you continue to get income support but lose the disability premium, you may wish to challenge the ESA decision (see above).

5. Ending linked claims
Until 31.1.11, there were linking rules that applied to incapacity benefit, severe disablement allowance and income support paid on the grounds of incapacity that would allow you to come off the benefit for a certain period (eg to try out work) and re-claim it later under the same conditions and at the same rate. From 31.1.11, a claim for any of those incapacity benefits will automatically be treated as a new claim for ESA.
TPEA Regs, reg 24

6. Housing benefit
Your housing benefit may be recalculated when you are migrated onto ESA. In some circumstances, your entitlement to this benefit may be reduced. This could be the case if:
■ your housing benefit included a disability premium (see Chapter 25(2)) prior to re-assessment; *and*
■ following the work capability assessment you are placed in the work-related activity group (see Chapter 10(6)); *and*
■ you are entitled to contributory ESA but not income-related ESA.
If you are moved from income support onto income-related ESA, your housing benefit award should remain unchanged.
Transitional addition – If your housing benefit entitlement is reduced, you may be awarded a 'transitional addition', which will restore your housing benefit to the level it was prior to the re-assessment. This transitional addition will be eroded each April when benefits are uprated, until it is reduced to nothing. Consequently, the level of your housing benefit may be effectively frozen for a number of years (unless there is a change of circumstances).
HB Regs, Sch 3, paras 27-31

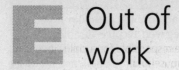

Out of work

This section of the Handbook looks at:

15 Income support

1. What is income support?

Income support is a means-tested or income-related benefit intended to provide for basic living expenses for you (and your partner, if you have one). It does not depend on your national insurance contributions. It can be paid on its own if you have no other income or can top up other benefits or earnings from part-time work to the basic amount the law says you need to live on. If you have children, their basic living expenses can be met by child tax credit (see Chapter 19).

Income support is available only to limited groups of people; Box E.1 lists the eligible groups. If you are not in one of these groups, you should consider claiming an equivalent means-tested benefit instead. If you have a limited capability for work, claim income-related employment and support allowance (see Chapter 13). If you are looking for work, claim income-based jobseeker's allowance (see Chapter 16). If you have reached the qualifying age for pension credit, that will be the equivalent benefit (see Chapter 42).

Income support can help with mortgage interest payments and some other housing costs. If you get income support, you may be eligible for housing benefit to help with rent and will not have to go through a separate means test (see Chapter 21(20)). Getting income support may entitle you to other types of benefit, eg:
■ free prescriptions and dental treatment (Chapter 54);
■ housing grants (Chapter 31);
■ help from the social fund (Chapter 23)) and budgeting loans (Chapter 24(2));
■ free school meals (Chapter 37);
■ help with hospital fares (Chapter 35).
This chapter deals with the conditions of entitlement to income support, the way it is calculated and how to claim it. The premiums that make up part of the calculation of income support are covered in Chapter 25. The way in which housing costs can be met by income support is covered in Chapter 26. For the way income, including part-time earnings, is treated for income support purposes, see Chapter 27; for the way capital and savings are treated, see Chapter 28.

The government is replacing income support with 'universal credit'. This is being piloted from April 2013 in north-west England; nationwide roll-out starts in October 2013 on the basis of one district in each Jobcentre Plus region. A new claim for income support may be treated as a claim for universal credit instead, depending on where you live. See Box J.1 in Chapter 25 for more on universal credit.

The benefit cap – Income support is included in the list of benefits to which the 'benefit cap' applies. This cap, which will be rolled out nationally between 15.7.13 and 30.9.13, limits the total weekly benefits that can be claimed. See Box H.1 in Chapter 21 for details (including exemptions).

2. Qualifying conditions

In order to be entitled to income support you must satisfy all the following conditions.
❑ You must be in Great Britain (see 3 below).
❑ You must be aged 16 or over (see 4 below).
❑ You must be under the qualifying age for pension credit (see Chapter 42(2)); once you have reached this age, claim pension credit instead. If your partner receives pension credit, you are not entitled to income support.
❑ You must not be claiming either jobseeker's allowance (JSA) or employment and support allowance (ESA). If you have a partner, they must not be claiming income-based JSA or income-related ESA. (You can switch claims if you find you have made the wrong choice – see 13 below.)
❑ You must not be in full-time education, though there are exceptions (see 4 and 5 below).
❑ You must not be working 16 or more hours a week (see 6 below).
❑ If you have a partner, they must not be working 24 or more hours a week (see 6 below).
❑ You must have no income, or your income is below your 'applicable amount' (a set amount that depends on your circumstances) – see 8 below.
❑ Your capital (and any belonging to a partner, but not to a dependent child) must be no more than £16,000 (see Chapter 28).
❑ You must not be subject to immigration control (see Chapter 49(3)).
❑ You must be in one of the categories of people who can claim income support (see Box E.1).
SSCBA, S.124
For the rules for people in care homes, see Chapter 33(4).

3. Presence in Great Britain (GB)

Income support can only be paid for the first four or eight weeks of a temporary absence from GB (see Chapter 50(5)). As well as being present in GB, you must also be 'habitually resident' in the UK, Channel Islands, Isle of Man or Republic of Ireland (see Chapter 49(2)).

4. Aged 16 or over

If you are under 16 you cannot get income support in your own right in any circumstances.

If you are under 20 and still at school or doing a non-advanced course at college or certain types of approved, unwaged training, you are usually excluded from income support; your parents can claim child benefit and child tax credit for you instead. But in some circumstances you can

E.1 Who can claim income support?

You can claim income support only if one of the categories below applies to you. You are eligible for the whole benefit week if the category applies for at least one day. You must also pass the qualifying conditions listed in (2).

The categories marked with an asterisk*, which allowed income support claims to be made on the grounds of disability, do not apply to new claims from 27.10.08.

Disability
❏ You are entitled to statutory sick pay (SSP).
❏ You are incapable of work.* This was tested under the 'personal capability assessment' (for details, see the *Disability Rights Handbook* 35th edition, page 67). If you are claiming income support in this category, at some stage prior to April 2014 you will be asked to take part in the 'work capability assessment'. If you are found to have a limited capability for work in this re-assessment, you will be migrated onto income-related ESA. See Chapter 14 for details.
IS Regs, Sch 1B, para 7
❏ You have appealed against a decision under a determination that you are capable of work following a personal capability assessment. This category continues to apply until the final decision on your appeal. Income support will be reduced by 20% of the single person's personal allowance for your age group (unless you are eligible for income support under one of the other categories in this box, eg you are a carer). If you win your appeal, the reduction will be repaid.
IS Regs, reg 22A & Sch 1B, para 25
❏ You are registered (or, in Scotland, certified) as blind, or it is less than 28 weeks since you were taken off the register (on regaining your sight).*
❏ You are mentally or physically disabled and are not treated as being in remunerative work because your hours or earnings are 75% or less than that of a person without your disability in the same job.
❏ You are in employment while living in (or temporarily absent from) a care home, an Abbeyfield Home or an independent hospital in which you receive care.
IS Regs, Sch 1B, paras 13, 8 & 9
The last two categories can only apply if you were already entitled to income support on that basis on 24.1.10.

Caring
❏ You are looking after your partner or a child or qualifying young person (see Chapter 38(1)) who is *'temporarily ill'* and for whom you are responsible.
❏ You are *'regularly and substantially engaged in caring for another person'* and either you are receiving carer's allowance or the person you are caring for gets a 'qualifying benefit' (see Chapter 7(2)). If the person you are looking after has claimed disability living allowance or attendance allowance, you'll be eligible for up to 26 weeks while you are waiting for their claim to be processed. You are also eligible if they have an advance award of a qualifying benefit but are still in the qualifying period. If carer's allowance entitlement stops, or the person you are looking after stops getting the qualifying benefit, you continue to be eligible for eight weeks.
❏ If you would have been eligible for income support as a carer had you made a claim for income support, then you are eligible for income support for eight weeks from the date your carer's allowance and/or the disabled person's qualifying benefit stops.
IS Regs, Sch 1B, paras 3(b), 4-5 & 6

Childcare responsibility
❏ You are a lone parent and are responsible for a child under 5 who is a member of your household.
❏ You are single or a lone parent and are fostering a child under 16 through a local authority or voluntary organisation or are looking after a child placed with you by an adoption agency prior to adoption.
❏ You are looking after a child under 16 because the child's parent, or the person who usually looks after the child, is temporarily ill or away from their home.
IS Regs, Sch 1B, paras 1, 2-2A & 3(a)
❏ You are taking unpaid parental leave to look after a child who lives with you. You must have been entitled to housing benefit (HB), council tax benefit (CTB), working tax credit (WTC) or child tax credit (CTC – payable at a higher rate than the family element) on the day before your leave began.
❏ You are taking paternity leave and you do not receive statutory paternity pay or any payment from your employer, and/or you were entitled to HB, CTB, WTC or CTC (payable at a higher rate than the family element) on the day before your leave began.
❏ Your partner is temporarily outside the UK and you are responsible for a child under 16 who is a member of your household.
IS Regs, Sch 1B, paras 14A, 14B & 23

Education and training
❏ You are on a full-time course and eligible for income support as a disabled or deaf student (see Chapter 40(2)).*
❏ You are a 'qualifying young person' (see Chapter 38(1)) and in one of the categories not excluded from income support (see 5).
❏ You are under 22, have no parents or are living away from your parents (see 5) and are undertaking a full-time non-advanced course that you started before your 21st birthday.
❏ You are a refugee and start attending an English course for over 15 hours a week during your first year in Great Britain (to help you obtain employment); you are eligible under this category for up to nine months only.
❏ You are not a 'qualifying young person' (see Chapter 38(1)), are under 24, and are undergoing Work-Based Learning for Young People.
IS Regs, Sch 1B, paras 10-12, 15, 15A, 18 & 28

Pregnancy
❏ You are pregnant and incapable of work because of your pregnancy.
❏ You are pregnant and due to have your baby within the next 11 weeks.
❏ You have had a baby within the last 15 weeks.
IS Regs, Sch 1B, para 14

Other
❏ You have started work and are eligible for the first four weeks of housing costs run-on (see Chapter 17(4)).
❏ You are required to attend a court or tribunal as a JP, juror, witness, defendant or plaintiff.
❏ You are held to be involved in a trade dispute.
❏ You are remanded or committed in custody for trial or sentencing (but you can only get income support to cover housing costs; see Chapter 26).
IS Regs, Sch 1B, paras 9A, 19, 20 & 22

claim income support in your own right while you are at school (see 5 below).

If you are under 20 and on a full-time advanced course, see Chapter 40(2) for details of income support entitlement.

Once you've left school, you can claim income support from the 'terminal date' (see Chapter 38(1)) if you fit into one of the groups listed in Box E.1. If you don't fit into one of these groups, claim employment and support allowance (if you have a limited capability for work) or jobseeker's allowance (JSA) instead. There are additional conditions for 16/17-year-olds claiming JSA (see Chapter 16(21)).

Care leavers – If you are a care leaver, your local authority has a duty to support you until your 18th birthday. Generally, you would be excluded from income support but this does not apply if you are a lone parent or single foster carer.

Children (Leaving Care) Social Security Benefits Regs 2001, reg 2

5. Full-time education

You are normally excluded from income support if you are aged 16-19 and are at school or doing a non-advanced course at college for 12 or more hours a week or participating in approved unwaged training (and thus treated as a qualifying young person for child benefit purposes – see Chapter 38).

IS Regs, reg 12

However, you won't be excluded from income support in this way if you:
■ have limited leave to enter or remain in the UK and you are dependent on funds from abroad that have been temporarily disrupted; or
■ get child benefit for a child living with you; or
■ are a refugee on an English course (see Box E.1); or
■ are an orphan and no one is legally responsible for you or acting in place of your parents; or
■ are living away from your parents (and anyone acting in their place) and they cannot support you as they are chronically sick or disabled (mentally or physically), in custody, or prohibited from coming into Great Britain; or
■ have to live away from your parents (and anyone acting in their place) because:
– you are estranged from them; or
– you are in physical or moral danger; or
– there is a serious risk to your physical or mental health; or
■ have left local authority care and have to live away from your parents (and anyone acting in their place).

IS Regs, reg 13

If you are aged 20 or over and on a full-time course, you will be treated as a student whether your course is advanced or non-advanced. Chapter 40(2) explains which students are entitled to income support.

6. Full-time or part-time work

You are excluded from income support if you or your partner are in *'remunerative work'*. This means you are not entitled to income support if you, the claimant, work for 16 hours or more a week or if your partner works for 24 hours or more a week. But there are exceptions (see below).

To count as 'remunerative' it must be work *'for which payment is made or which is done in expectation of payment'*.

Lunch breaks, if you are paid for them, count towards the 16 or 24 hours.

Some people may be treated as being in full-time work, eg if they are off work because of a holiday. But if you are off work because you are ill or on maternity leave, you are not treated as being in remunerative work, even if you are getting sick pay or maternity pay from your employer. You are also not treated as being in remunerative work if you are off work because you are on paternity or adoption leave.

IS Regs, reg 5

Exceptions to the 16-hour/24-hour rule

If you come within one of the exceptions listed below, you can qualify for income support even if you are working for 16 hours or more a week. If your partner is working 24 hours or more a week, they must come within one of these exceptions.

Although you are not excluded from income support on account of the number of hours you work in these cases, any earnings are taken into account in the usual way (see Chapter 27(3)).

Unless you are a carer (see below), if you have an additional occupation that is not in one of these exceptions, the hours you work in that occupation count towards the 16-hour or 24-hour remunerative work limit.

You are not treated as being in remunerative work in the following circumstances.

❏ **Volunteering** – You are a volunteer or working for a charity or voluntary organisation, but only if the payment you receive or expect to receive is solely a payment to cover your expenses. If you are paid anything else, even if it is below your earnings disregard, all your hours of work count. If your average hours are 16 or more a week, you'll be excluded from income support. If the decision maker is not *'satisfied that it is reasonable for [you] to provide [your] service free of charge'*, they may treat you as having 'notional' earnings (see Chapter 27(20)).

❏ **Caring** – You are eligible for income support because you are caring for a person who gets a 'qualifying benefit', or you get carer's allowance (see Box E.1). If this exception applies, you are not excluded from income support even if you have another job. For example, if you care for your mother during the day and she gets attendance allowance, and you also work 20 hours a week in a supermarket in the evenings, because you are a carer none of your hours count, not even the 20 hours' evening work.

❏ **Foster or respite care** – You are a foster carer or you are paid by a health body, local authority or voluntary organisation to provide respite care in your own home for someone who does not normally live with you.

❏ **Childminding** – You are working as a childminder in your home.

❏ **Other** – You are not treated as being in remunerative work if you are:
■ engaged on a scheme for which a training allowance is being paid;
■ on a government scheme for helping people into self-employment;
■ starting work and eligible for the first four weeks' housing costs run-on (see Chapter 17(4));
■ working as councillor;
■ engaged as a part-time firefighter, auxiliary coastguard or lifeboat person, or a member of the territorial or reserve forces;
■ held to be involved in a trade dispute (but not during the first seven days after the day you stopped work);
■ engaged in an activity in respect of which a sports award has been, or is to be, made and no other payment is expected.

IS Regs, reg 6

Prior to 25.1.10 there were two further categories:
■ you are mentally or physically disabled and your earnings or hours of work are 75% or less than that of a person without your disability in the same or comparable work;
■ you are in employment while living in (or temporarily absent from) a care home, Abbeyfield Home or independent hospital in which you receive certain types of care.

These categories can continue to apply if you were already entitled to income support on this basis on 24.1.10.

7. How is income support worked out?
Income support is worked out by comparing your needs with your resources (ie any income or capital you have). If you are a single person, only your needs and resources are relevant. If you are one of a couple, the needs and resources of both of you are relevant. You are considered to be one of a couple if you are married, in a civil partnership, or cohabiting (whether with someone of the opposite or the same sex).

If you have dependent children living with you, their needs and resources will be ignored, unless your claim for income support began before April 2004 and you continue to receive support for your children through income support rather than child tax credit (see below). For details on child tax credit, see Chapter 19.

Set amounts for different needs are added together to reach the total amount the law says you need to live on. This is called your *'applicable amount'*. Your income (worked out under set rules) is deducted from your applicable amount. This leaves the amount of income support you are entitled to. The calculation is as follows:

Step 1: Add up your capital resources – See Chapter 28. You will not be entitled to income support if your capital, and any capital belonging to your partner, is more than £16,000.
Step 2: Work out your applicable amount – See 8 below.
Step 3: Add up your income resources – See Chapter 27. Include the tariff income if you have capital over £6,000, or £10,000 if you live permanently in a care home (see Chapter 28(4)).
Step 4: Deduct your income from your applicable amount – If your income is less than your applicable amount, income support makes up the difference in full, provided you meet the other qualifying conditions (see 2 above).

Example: Mr Porter, aged 37, cares for his mother, who lives with him. Mr Porter receives carer's allowance.

His applicable amount is:
Personal allowance	£71.70
Carer premium	£33.30
Applicable amount	*£105.00*

His income is:
Carer's allowance	£59.75

Applicable amount	£105.00
Less income	£59.75
Income support entitlement	*£45.25*

Mr Porter will be paid income support of £45.25 as well as carer's allowance of £59.75.

Special groups
In some circumstances your income support may be worked out differently or paid at a reduced rate.
Children: pre-April 2004 claims – If your claim for income support began before April 2004 and you have dependent children living with you, your income support may still include amounts payable for the children. These will include a personal allowance of £65.62 for each child (or qualifying young person – see Chapter 38(1)) for whom you are responsible, as well as a family premium, and possibly disabled child premiums and enhanced disability premiums for disabled children. These premiums are covered in Chapter 25.
Care homes – If you live permanently in a care home, the lower capital limit is higher (see Chapter 28(3)).
Hospital – If you or a member of your family are in hospital, your applicable amount may be reduced (see Box M.1, Chapter 35).

Incapacity appeals – Generally, income support is reduced while you are appealing against a decision under the 'personal capability assessment' that you are capable of work (see Box E.1).
Jobcentre Plus interviews – You (or your partner) may be asked to attend a work-focused interview with a personal adviser. If you fail to attend without good cause, your income support will be paid at a reduced rate. See Box T.1 in Chapter 57.
Housing costs run-on – For the first four weeks after starting work, you may continue to get housing costs, including mortgage interest, met by income support (see Chapter 17(4)).
Sanctions – Income support can be paid at a reduced rate for 13 weeks through sanctions, which can be applied if either you or your partner are convicted of more than one benefit offence within a 5-year period.

8. What is your applicable amount?
The *'applicable amount'*, set by Parliament, is the amount the law says you need to live on. It consists of the sum total of:
■ personal allowances – for a single claimant or for a couple (see 9 below);
■ premiums – flat-rate extra amounts if you satisfy certain conditions (see 10 below);
■ certain housing costs (see Chapter 26).
IS Regs, reg 17

9. Personal allowances
Personal allowances are part of your applicable amount (see 8 above). For income support, the decision maker takes into account your age and whether you are part of a couple.

Personal allowances		per week
Single person	aged 25 or over	£71.70
	aged under 25	£56.80
Lone parent	aged 18 or over	£71.70
	aged under 18	£56.80
Couple	both aged 18 or over [1]	£112.55
	both under 18 [2]	£85.80
	one aged 25 or over [3]	£71.70
	one aged 18-24 [3]	£56.80

Couples (where one partner is under 18) – In the table of rates above, the reference numbers mean:
1: includes couples where one is under 18 but is: eligible for income support or income-related employment and support allowance (ESA), or would be if they were single; or eligible for income-based jobseeker's allowance (JSA) or severe hardship payments (see Chapter 16(21));
2: only if one is responsible for a child; or each would be eligible for income support or income-related ESA if they were single; or the claimant's partner is eligible for income-based JSA or severe hardship payments. If only one of the couple is eligible for income support, etc, the single person's allowance of £56.80 would apply;
3: only if the other is under 18 and would not be eligible for income support or income-related ESA (even if they were single), income-based JSA or severe hardship payments.
IS Regs, Sch 2, Part I

10. Premiums
There are five premiums, each with specific qualifying conditions. These are detailed in Chapter 25. The premiums are part of your applicable amount (see 8 above). Unless otherwise specified in Chapter 25, each premium to which you are entitled is added to the total of your applicable amount.

Premiums		per week
Disability	single	£31.00
	couple	£44.20
Enhanced disability	single	£15.15
	couple	£21.75
Severe disability	single	£59.50
	couple (one qualifies)	£59.50
	couple (both qualify)	£119.00
Pensioner	couple	£109.50
Carer		£33.30

IS Regs, Sch 2, Parts III & IV

11. How do you claim income support?

You start your claim for income support by ringing the Jobcentre Plus claim-line (0800 055 6688; textphone 0800 023 4888). The claim-line will put you through to your nearest Jobcentre Plus contact centre. The contact centre will take your details and go through your claim over the phone. In some cases, they may need to ring you back for additional information. They may also arrange a date for you to attend a Jobcentre Plus interview with a personal adviser about work prospects (see Box T.1, Chapter 57).

You will then be sent a statement containing the information you provided over the phone. You need to sign to confirm the statement is correct and return it in the envelope provided or take it to the Jobcentre Plus interview, if one has been arranged. You may be asked to provide supporting documents, such as payslips or proof of savings, with the statement; these will be necessary for your claim to be accepted as properly made. If you do this within one month of the date you first notified the Jobcentre Plus of your intention to claim, your date of claim will be the date of that first contact. If you have problems getting the necessary information or evidence within one month, tell Jobcentre Plus straightaway and send the statement anyway. If your difficulty is for certain specified reasons, your claim can still be treated as made on the date of your first contact. For more details see Chapter 57(2).

C&P Regs, reg 6(1A)

If you are not able (or it is inappropriate for you) to use the telephone, a claim can be made on a paper form – the A1, obtainable from your local Jobcentre Plus office.

If you re-claim income support after a break in benefit of no more than 26 weeks, you can re-claim the benefit under a rapid reclaim process using a much shorter claim-form.

12. Backdating

If you think you were entitled to income support before you put in your claim, ask, in writing, for your claim to be backdated. Income support can be backdated for up to three months if there are 'special reasons' why you couldn't reasonably have been expected to claim earlier (see Chapter 57(3)).

Waiting for a decision on another benefit?
Entitlement to another benefit may entitle you to income support, or to more income support, because your applicable amount (see 8 above) goes up. For example, if you or your partner get personal independence payment (PIP), you will qualify for a disability premium.

If you already get income support – Ask for your award to be revised or superseded once you get the decision on PIP or other qualifying benefit. Arrears of any extra income support you are entitled to are paid for the same period as the award of the qualifying benefit.

If you do not already get income support – To make sure you do not miss out on benefit, you may need to make two income support claims. (We use the example of PIP here, but the process is the same for any other benefit that allows you to qualify for income support.)

Do not delay making an income support claim while you are waiting for a decision on the PIP claim, as PIP claims can sometimes take a while to be decided. This income support claim will be turned down if entitlement depends on PIP being awarded (eg without a disability premium, your income is higher than your applicable amount). If you are later awarded PIP, and then claim income support again within three months of the date of the decision to award PIP, income support can be backdated to the date from which PIP was first payable (or the date of the first income support claim if that is later).

If the PIP claim is made more than ten working days after your first income support claim, the second income support claim cannot be backdated in this way. If you did not make an income support claim at the right time, claim as soon as you can and ask for it to be backdated for up to three months if there are 'special reasons' (see Chapter 57(3)).

C&P Regs, reg 6(16)-(18)

If your income support is stopped – Where income support entitlement depends on getting another qualifying benefit like PIP, and the qualifying benefit is stopped, your income support will also stop. But if you challenge the decision on the qualifying benefit and it is reinstated, claim income support again within three months of the reinstatement and it will be fully backdated.

C&P Regs, reg 6(19)-(22)

Conversely, if your income support is stopped and following this a decision is made to award you a qualifying benefit, a further income support claim can be backdated to the date the earlier claim was stopped (or the date the qualifying benefit became payable, if that is later), as long as it is made within three months of the decision on the qualifying benefit.

C&P Regs, reg 6(30)

13. Who should make the claim?

You should normally make the claim yourself. If you are unable to act for yourself, a decision maker can appoint someone else (eg a parent, carer or close friend) to take over the management of your claim (see Chapter 57(4)).

Couples
A married couple, a man and woman living together as husband and wife, and same-sex partners (whether registered as civil partners or not), all count as couples for income support.

If one is eligible for income support – If you are eligible for income support but your partner would be required to sign on for benefit, you can choose which of you should make a claim. Either you claim income support or your partner claims jobseeker's allowance (JSA). However, if you are in the joint-claim age group for JSA (see Chapter 16(2)) either you claim income support or you both claim JSA jointly. You can't get income support and JSA at the same time unless your partner is only claiming contribution-based JSA. In this case, you can claim income support to top up the JSA.

Whether you claim income support or JSA, the amount of benefit is usually the same. However, income support is tax free (whereas JSA is taxable) and JSA carries a greater risk of sanctions (see Chapter 16(9)). If you claim income support, your partner can sign on voluntarily at the Jobcentre Plus office to secure national insurance credits.

If you find you've made the wrong choice, simply put in a claim for income support. Jobcentre Plus will stop the JSA award if your income support claim is successful.

If you are eligible for income support and your partner is eligible for employment and support allowance (ESA), you can choose which of you should make the claim; ie either you claim income support or your partner claims income-related ESA. If a disability premium is payable with the income support (which, for instance, would be the case if your partner is in receipt of personal independence payment – see Chapter 25(2)), you will usually be better off claiming income support. If a disability premium is not payable with the income support, you will probably be better off if your partner claims income-related ESA.

If both are eligible for income support – You can choose which of you should make the claim. You can switch roles at any time. Your partner just has to put in a claim for income support with your agreement that they should make the claim, or vice versa.

C&P Regs, reg 4(3) & (4)

14. How is income support paid?

Income support is paid fortnightly in arrears. If your income support payment is less than £1 a week, it may be paid in one sum at intervals of no more than 13 weeks. The minimum payment is 10p a week; entitlement of less than 10p a week is not payable unless it can be paid with another benefit.

C&P Regs, reg 26(4) & Sch 7, para 5

Your benefit is normally paid into a bank, building society, credit union or Post Office card account (see Chapter 57(5)).

16 Jobseeker's allowance

A. GENERAL CONDITIONS

1. What is jobseeker's allowance?

Jobseeker's allowance (JSA) is for people who are unemployed or working less than 16 hours a week and who are seeking work. People with a limited capability for work due to illness or disability should claim employment and support allowance instead (see Chapter 10). Others who do not have to sign on for work (eg carers or lone parents with responsibility for young children) should claim income support instead (see Chapter 15). There are two forms of JSA.

❑ **Contribution-based JSA:** This is a personal flat-rate allowance with entitlement based on your national insurance contribution record; it is payable for up to six months (182 days) and is taxable.

❑ **Income-based JSA:** This is means tested, taxable and payable if you have no income or a low income and no more than £16,000 in savings. If you have a partner, they cannot work 24 hours a week or more.

One set of jobseeking conditions applies to JSA as a whole, so you must be available for work, take active steps to look for work and have a current jobseeker's agreement.

The benefit cap – JSA is included in the list of benefits to which the 'benefit cap' applies. This cap, which will be rolled out nationally between 15.7.13 and 30.9.13, limits the total weekly benefits that can be claimed. See Box H.1 in Chapter 21 for details (including exemptions).

2. Qualifying conditions

You are entitled to jobseeker's allowance if you:
■ are available for work (see 4 below); *and*
■ are actively seeking work (see 5 below); *and*
■ have entered into a jobseeker's agreement that remains in force (see 6 below); *and*
■ are not working 16 hours or more a week (see 7 below); *and*
■ do not have a limited capability for work (see 8 below); *and*
■ are under state pension age (see Chapter 43(2)); *and*
■ are not in full-time education – see Chapter 40(4) for exceptions; *and*
■ are in Great Britain (GB) – see Chapter 50(7) for exceptions; *and*
■ for contribution-based JSA, pass the contribution-based conditions (see 15 below); *or*
■ for income-based JSA, pass the income-based conditions (see 19 below).

You may be entitled to contribution-based JSA topped up with income-based JSA if you satisfy the conditions for both (see 22 below).

JSA, S.1(1)-(2B)

Couples

You are considered to be one of a couple if you are married, in a civil partnership, or cohabiting (whether with someone of the opposite or the same sex). For contribution-based JSA, both members of a couple can claim separately based on their own contribution records. For income-based JSA, unless you are in a joint-claim couple (see below), one of you must claim for both partners. The person who claims must sign on as available for work and meet all the other conditions for benefit.

Joint-claim couples – Some couples must make a joint claim for income-based JSA. This applies to couples without dependent children, where one or both members of the couple is aged at least 18. If you are one of a joint-claim couple, both you and your partner must be available for work and meet all the other qualifying conditions above, unless one of you is 'excused'. You and your partner need to decide which one of you receives payment of JSA.

If one of you does not meet all the conditions, JSA is paid at the single person rate. But if one of you would be eligible for income support (see Box E.1, Chapter 15) or employment and support allowance (ESA – see Chapter 10) instead, that person is excused from meeting the JSA conditions. In this case, there is a choice: the eligible partner can claim income support or income-related ESA for both of you (and the other can sign on voluntarily for national insurance credits), or you claim JSA jointly and get paid the full couple rate but only one of you needs to meet the JSA conditions.

There are a few further circumstances in which only one member of the couple is expected to meet JSA conditions, including if one of you is a full-time student, or is not habitually resident in GB, or is working at least 16 hours but less than 24 hours a week.

JSA Regs, regs 3A, 3D, 3E & Sch A1

3. How do you claim?

On the first day you become unemployed, you should make a claim for JSA. Don't delay, otherwise you will lose benefit unless you can show you have 'special reasons' for delaying (see Chapter 57(3)).

JSA is administered by Jobcentre Plus. Most contact will be with a personal adviser at the local office where you sign on. Decisions on your claim will normally be made at a processing centre, which you can contact by phone.

Waiting days – The first three days of your claim are 'waiting days', during which you cannot usually be paid either type of JSA. You do not have to serve waiting days if your claim is linked to a previous 'jobseeking period' (see 15 below), if a decision maker elects to move you to JSA from income support, or if you claim within 12 weeks of the end of a previous entitlement to employment and support allowance, incapacity benefit, income support or carer's allowance.

JSA, Sch 1, para 4 & JSA Regs, reg 46

Starting your claim – To make a claim, ring the national claim number (0800 055 6688; textphone 0800 023 4888). Call centre staff will take your details and book an appointment for you to see a personal adviser at a work-focused interview. This interview will take place at your local Jobcentre Plus office, normally within a week. The call centre will usually send you a 'customer statement', a computer printout of the information you provided over the phone, which you need to check, sign and bring to the interview. You can also claim online (www.gov.uk/jobseekers-allowance/overview). If you find it hard to use the phone or claim online, you can ask for a paper claim-pack to be sent to you.

The work-focused interview – At the interview the personal adviser will discuss your benefit entitlement and confirm the information on your customer statement or completed claim-pack. They will ask questions to check whether you are capable of and available for work and what you intend to do to look for work. You will also be asked to discuss, agree and sign the jobseeker's agreement (see 6 below).

Once it has been established that you meet the jobseeking conditions for benefit, your claim will be assessed for both contribution-based and income-based JSA. If your health or disability means you need specialist advice and help, you can be referred to a disability employment adviser.

Payment – JSA is paid every two weeks in arrears, usually into a bank or building society account (see Chapter 57(5)).

Signing on

Normally, you will have to sign on at Jobcentre Plus every fortnight (although sometimes you may be required to do so more frequently). If you fail to attend your signing-on day, your benefit entitlement will stop, unless you can show Jobcentre Plus within five working days that you had a good reason for not attending.

JSA, S.8 & JSA Regs, reg 24(6), 25(1)(c) & 27

Each time you sign on you will be asked to explain what you have done to look for work or improve your prospects of finding work. Keep a record of your jobseeking steps (including any use of the internet and email) so you can show that you are 'actively seeking work' (see 5 below).

In-depth interviews

There will also be more in-depth interviews at regular intervals where your jobseeker's agreement will be reviewed and updated if necessary. These interviews can take place over the phone or at Jobcentre Plus offices. If you do not participate or are late (having previously been warned, in writing, about lateness) your benefit entitlement will stop, unless you can show within five working days that you had a good reason for failing to participate or being late. If you

contact Jobcentre Plus within five days but are unable to show good reason for your failure, a sanction will be applied (see 10 below).

JSA Regs, regs 23, 25(1)(a)-(b) & 70A(2)(b)-(4)

Jobseeker's direction – At an in-depth interview, your personal adviser may issue a 'jobseeker's direction' requiring you to take a specific step to improve your job prospects. For example, you could be directed to attend a course or to improve the way you present yourself to employers. If you don't comply with a jobseeker's direction that is reasonable in your circumstances, a sanction will be applied unless you have a good reason (see 10 below).

JSA, S.19A(2)(c)

You may be referred onto the Work Programme (see Chapter 18(2)) or the Mandatory Work Activity scheme (see Chapter 18(4)).

4. Available for work

You must be willing and able to take up immediately any paid employment of at least 40 hours a week (see below for restrictions you are allowed to make).

JSA, S.6 & JSA Regs, reg 6

Treated as unavailable for work – You are not regarded as available for work and therefore not entitled to JSA if you:
- get maternity allowance or statutory maternity pay; or
- are on paternity or adoption leave; or
- are a full-time student – there are limited exceptions (see Chapter 40(4)); or
- are a prisoner on temporary release.

JSA Regs, reg 15

The permitted period – For a 'permitted period' of up to 13 weeks from the beginning of your claim, you may be allowed to restrict your availability and jobseeking to your usual occupation and/or to your usual pay. After this you must be prepared to widen your availability for work and job searching activity.

JSA Regs, reg 16

Can you restrict the hours you are available for work?

The 40-hours rule – You must be prepared to take up employment of at least 40 hours a week, or less than 40 if required to do so. In most cases, you do not have to accept a job of less than 24 hours a week unless it has been agreed that you may restrict the hours you are available for work to less than 24 hours a week (eg due to caring responsibilities; see below).

JSA is a 7-day benefit, so you must fulfil the conditions of entitlement on each day of the week. This does not mean you must be prepared to work seven days a week. You can restrict the times in the week you are available to take up work (eg Monday to Saturday, 9am to 6pm) provided your 'pattern of availability' would give you 'reasonable prospects of securing employment' (see below), your job prospects are not considerably less than they would be if you were available at all times, and your available hours are at least 40 a week.

JSA Regs, regs 6 & 7

You can specify fewer than 40 hours a week if that is reasonable in the following situations:

Carers – If you care for a child or an elderly person or someone 'whose physical or mental condition requires [him or her] to be cared for' who is a close relative or a member of your household, you may restrict the hours you are available for work to less than 40 hours, but not less than 16 hours a week. A 'close relative' means a partner, parent, parent-in-law, step-parent, son, daughter, son/daughter-in-law, stepson/daughter, grandparent, grandchild, brother or sister, or the partner of any of those. You must be available for as many hours and at the times that your caring responsibilities allow, taking into account: the times you spend caring; whether

the caring is shared; and the age and physical and mental condition of the person you care for. You must normally show you have *'reasonable prospects of securing employment'* (see below). However, if you care for a child, Jobcentre Plus may accept that you do not need to have reasonable prospects of securing employment in light of the type and number of employment vacancies within daily travelling distance of your home.
JSA Regs, regs 4 & 13(4)-(7)

Lone parents – If you are a lone parent responsible for a child under the age of 13, you can restrict your availability for employment to the child's normal school hours.
JSA Regs, reg 13A

Laid off or short-time working – For the first 13 weeks you are treated as available for work, provided you are available to take on casual employment to top up any hours you actually work to at least 40 a week, and you are prepared to resume immediately the work you were laid off from, or return full time to the job in which you are being kept on short time. After 13 weeks, you must show you have reasonable prospects of employment if you want to continue to restrict the hours you are available for work.
JSA Regs, reg 17

Disability – You can restrict your hours of availability if it is reasonable given your physical or mental condition (see 'Disability-related restrictions' below).
JSA Regs, reg 13(3)

Can you put any other restrictions on the type of work you'll accept?
Provided you can show you have 'reasonable prospects of securing employment' (see below), you can restrict:
■ the nature of the employment (eg due to sincerely held religious or conscientious objections);
■ the terms and conditions of employment;
■ the rate of pay – but only for the first six months of your claim (after six months you can't insist on a rate of pay higher than the relevant national minimum wage);
■ the areas you will work in – generally, you are expected to be prepared to travel for up to 1½ hours both to and from work.
JSA Regs, regs 8, 9 & 13(2)

Disability-related restrictions – You can restrict your availability in any way (eg pay, hours, travel time, type of work), providing the restrictions are reasonable given your physical or mental condition. It is not relevant whether the restrictions affect your employment prospects, providing you do not also put non-disability-related restrictions on your availability. If you do, you will have to show you have reasonable employment prospects given all the restrictions. If you restrict the rate of pay you are prepared to accept, this is not subject to the general 6-month limit, but applies for as long as the restriction is reasonable given your physical or mental condition.

If you refuse a job offer where the hours of work or other conditions of the job are beyond your agreed restrictions, you won't generally be sanctioned for this (see 9 below for more on sanctions).
JSA Regs, reg 13(3)

Reasonable prospects of employment
If you put any restrictions on your availability, unless these are solely disability-related, you must show you have reasonable prospects of securing employment. The decision maker must consider all the evidence, and in particular:
■ your skills, qualifications and experience;
■ the type and number of vacancies within daily travelling distance;
■ how long you have been unemployed;
■ your job applications and their outcome; *and*

■ if the restrictions are on the nature of the work, whether you are prepared to move home to take up work.
It is important to think carefully before you put restrictions on your availability. If you can't show you have reasonable employment prospects, your benefit could be disallowed.
JSA Regs, reg 10

Can you delay taking up an offer of employment?
Generally, you must be able to take up employment immediately. However, if you are a carer (see above) or a volunteer, you must be able to take up employment given one week's notice and attend any employment opportunity interview given 48 hours' notice. If you care for a child, you can be given up to 28 days' notice to take up employment and seven days' notice to attend an interview, as long as you can show this is reasonable.

If you are providing a service (paid or unpaid) you must be able to take up work given 24 hours' notice. If you are employed for less than 16 hours a week, you must be able to take up work immediately after the statutory minimum notice period (rather than any contractual notice) that your employer is entitled to – usually one week.
JSA Regs, reg 5

Absences, emergencies and other circumstances
You may be treated as available for work in the following situations. You are also treated as actively seeking work for the week if the situation applies to you for at least three days in the week (unless marked *).
❏ **Absences from home**
■ you are at a work camp – for up to two weeks, once in 12 months;
■ you are on a Venture Trust programme – for up to four weeks, once in 12 months;
■ you are on an Open University residential course – for up to one week per course;
■ you are absent from Great Britain (GB) to attend a job interview (up to one week), or for a child's medical treatment (up to eight weeks), or your partner has reached the qualifying age for pension credit or is disabled and you are both abroad (up to four weeks) – see Chapter 50(7).
❏ **Emergencies**
■ you need time to deal with the death, serious illness or funeral of a close relative or close friend, or a domestic emergency affecting you, a close relative or close friend; or the person you have been caring for has died – for up to one week, no more than four times in 12 months (or, if you care for a child, in the case of a death, serious illness or domestic emergency, up to eight weeks once every 12 months);
■ you are working as a part-time firefighter or helping to run or launch a lifeboat;
■ you are part of a group of people organised to respond to an emergency – eg part of a search for a missing person.
❏ **Other circumstances**
■ you are sick for a short while and treated as capable of work or not having a limited capability for work (see 8 below);
■ you are a full-time student on an employment-related course and have prior approval from the employment officer – for up to two weeks, once in 12 months;
■ you are looking after your child while your partner is temporarily absent from the UK – for up to eight weeks;
■ you are temporarily looking after a child because the usual carer is ill, temporarily away from home, or looking after a member of the family who is ill – for up to eight weeks;
■ you are looking after your child during the child's school holidays (or similar vacations) and it would be unreasonable to make other care arrangements;*
■ you are looking after your child who has been excluded

from school and it would be unreasonable to make other care arrangements;*

■ you are a party to court or tribunal proceedings and have prior approval from the employment officer – for up to eight weeks;

■ you are engaged in annual continuous training as a member of any territorial or reserve force for up to 15 days in any calendar year;

■ you are temporarily detained in police custody – for up to 96 hours;

■ you have been discharged from prison – for one week from the date of release;

■ you have been threatened with, or subjected to, domestic violence during the previous 26 weeks by a partner, former partner or a family member (or their partner) – for up to four weeks after you have notified Jobcentre Plus of the situation (which can be extended to 13 weeks if you are able to provide evidence of the violence or threats). For this to apply, you must no longer be living with the person who inflicted or threatened the violence. It can only apply once during any 12-month period.

JSA Regs, regs 14 & 14A

If you are on holiday in GB, you must still be available for work (although you might not have to be actively seeking work – see below). Contact Jobcentre Plus before you go. You must show you can be contacted regularly while away and be willing to return at once to start work. If you go abroad on holiday, you are not usually entitled to JSA (see Chapter 50(7)).

5. Actively seeking work

As well as being available for work, you are expected to take such steps, usually at least three a week, as you can *'reasonably be expected to have to take'* in order to have the best prospects of getting employment, eg:

■ applying for jobs;
■ looking for vacancies, including via the internet;
■ registering with an employment agency;
■ on referral from an employment officer, seeking specialist advice on improving your prospects with regard to your particular needs or disability;
■ drawing up a CV or getting a reference;
■ drawing up a list of relevant employers and seeking information from them;
■ seeking information on an occupation.

Even if you've taken reasonable steps to look for work, they can be disregarded if, by your *'behaviour or appearance [you] otherwise undermined [your] prospects of securing the employment in question'*, or you acted in a violent or abusive way or spoiled a job application. But it can't be held against you if these were due to circumstances beyond your control (eg because of mental health problems).

JSA, S.7(1) & JSA Regs, reg 18

Absences, emergencies and other circumstances

In some circumstances for a limited time, you can be treated as actively seeking work. The circumstances in which you are treated as both actively seeking work and available for work are listed in 4 above, under 'Absences, emergencies and other circumstances'. There are other times when you are not expected to take any steps to look for work, although you must still be available to take up work.

JSA Regs, reg 19

If you are absent from home – In any 12-month period, you may be treated as actively seeking work for a maximum of:

■ two weeks for any reason (eg a holiday) as long as you are away from home for at least one day each week; *or*
■ six weeks if you are blind: the six weeks consists of a maximum of four weeks during which you are attending, for at least three days a week, a training course in using a

guide dog, and a further two weeks for any reason as long as you are away from home for at least one day each week; *or*

■ three weeks if you are attending an Outward Bound course for at least three days a week.

In each case, you must give written notice that you intend to stay away from home for at least one day in each week and that you do not intend to actively seek work in that week.

The weeks don't have to be consecutive. You can't use more than one provision in any one 12-month period.

For the 2-week 'any reason' provision, once you've notified your intention, you'll be treated as actively seeking work. If you change your mind and don't go anywhere, you must give written notice withdrawing your intention before the start of the week you were due to be away to make sure you don't use up a week unnecessarily.

JSA Regs, reg 19(1)(p) & (2)

Training – You are treated as actively seeking work in any week in which you spend at least three days on a government employment or training programme (other than the 'Work Experience' programme) for which a training allowance is not payable.

JSA Regs, reg 19(1)(q)

Becoming self-employed – You are treated as actively seeking work for up to eight weeks during which you are taking steps to establish yourself in self-employment, starting with the week you are accepted on a government scheme for helping people into self-employment.

JSA Regs, reg 19(1)(r)

You are treated as actively seeking work while you are participating in the new enterprise allowance scheme.

Jobseeker's Allowance (Schemes for Assisting persons to Obtain Employment) Regulations 2013, reg 7(1)

6. Jobseeker's agreement

This describes the type of work you're looking for, the hours you are available and any 'pattern of availability', the action you're expected to take to look for work and improve your job prospects, details of restrictions on your availability for work and the dates of any 'permitted period' (see 4 above). You are expected to spend several hours a day achieving your weekly job-search goals. It is a condition of entitlement to JSA that you and your personal adviser agree and sign the jobseeker's agreement (joint-claim couples must each sign a jobseeker's agreement).

If you don't accept the proposed agreement, you have the right to ask your personal adviser to refer it to a decision maker, who should make a decision *'so far as practicable'* within 14 days. In the meantime, you are not entitled to benefit. You may qualify for hardship payments (see 13 below). The decision maker may decide to backdate the jobseeker's agreement, but not necessarily back to your date of claim.

JSA, S.9 & JSA Regs, regs 31 & 32

Varying an existing jobseeker's agreement – Either you or the adviser can propose to vary the agreement. If there is a dispute, the proposed agreement may be referred to a decision maker as above. Your benefit will continue to be paid while the decision maker is considering a variation. If the agreement is varied, you must sign within 21 days, otherwise the jobseeker's agreement may be terminated and your entitlement to benefit will stop.

JSA, S.10 & JSA Regs, regs 37-40.

7. Working full time or part time

You are excluded from JSA if you are in *'remunerative work'* of (on average) 16 hours or more a week. Work counts if you are paid or if you work *'in expectation of payment'*. The rules closely follow the income support rules and provide for specific circumstances in which work can be ignored or, conversely, in which you can be treated as working even when you're not (see Chapter 15(6)).

You are not treated as working if you are on certain government employment schemes, including: the new enterprise allowance, the sector-based work academy, the Work Programme, the 'Work Experience' programme or the Mandatory Work Activity scheme.

If you stop work because of a trade dispute at your workplace, you are not eligible to claim JSA; your partner could claim income-based JSA or you could claim income support, but payment will be at a reduced rate.

JSA Regs, regs 51, 52 & 53 and JSA, S.14

Partners – For contribution-based JSA it makes no difference to your entitlement whether or not your partner works or how much they earn. For income-based JSA, see 20 below.

8. Limited capability for work

Generally, you only need to state that you do not have a limited capability for work, which is sufficient to satisfy the entitlement condition.

If you are disabled or ill – If you have a limited capability for work through ill health (unless it is a short illness – see below) or disability, you are not entitled to JSA, but you may be able to claim employment and support allowance (ESA) (see Chapter 10).

JSA, S.1(2)(f)

What if you are ill for a short while? – If you fall ill, you may choose to stay on JSA for up to two weeks: you must fill in a form to declare that you are unfit for work and for how long. You may only do this twice in each 'jobseeking period' (ie period of entitlement to JSA – see 18 below). Or, if you are entitled to JSA for over a year (ignoring breaks in entitlement of 12 weeks or less) you can only choose this option twice a year. If you fall ill a third time or are ill for longer than two weeks, you should claim ESA instead.

If you fall ill within eight weeks of the end of an entitlement to statutory sick pay, you cannot stay on JSA but need to claim ESA instead.

JSA Regs, reg 55

9. Sanctions

Sanctions can be applied if you fail to comply with the conditions relating to JSA. These failures are referred to as *'sanctionable failures'*. Three levels of sanctions apply: lower, intermediate and higher. In each case, payment of JSA will normally cease for a fixed sanction period of between four and 156 weeks. In the case of intermediate-level sanctions, your JSA claim may also be disallowed. See 10 to 12 below.

If a sanction is applied, you may be eligible for hardship payments (see 13 below).

For a joint-claim couple, if just one of you is subject to a sanction, JSA is reduced to the single person rate (a lower reduction will be made if you are eligible for hardship payments).

If JSA is already being reduced due to the application of one of these sanctions, and you commit another sanctionable failure, a further reduction is not imposed.

JSA, Ss.19(7), 19A(10) & 19B(8); JSA Regs, reg 70

If a sanction period has been imposed, you come off JSA before the sanction period has ended and then re-claim it at a later date, the outstanding sanction period will be applied to the new claim. However, since the sanction period starts from the date of failure, any time spent off JSA is treated as time served and deducted from the sanction period.

Any outstanding sanction period will not be applied in this way if you have been in employment for at least 26 weeks in the intervening period (in one or several spells).

JSA Regs, reg 70C

You can appeal against a decision to impose a sanction (see Chapter 58).

Good reason – In several of the circumstances that could lead

to a sanction, you can avoid one if you can show there was a *'good reason'* for your actions. This is not defined in law. Decision makers are under guidance to establish three points when deciding whether or not you had a good reason:

■ what would it be reasonable to expect someone to do in the particular circumstances (ie was the action or failure to act preventable);

■ what did you do or fail to do that was different from the expected action; *and*

■ what were your reasons for your action or failure to act.

Examples of circumstances that should be treated as contributing to good reason for an action or failure to act include where you:

■ are a victim of domestic violence;

■ have a mental health condition or disorder;

■ are the victim of bullying or harassment;

■ are homeless; *or*

■ lose or leave a work experience opportunity or placement other than for reasons of gross misconduct.

Decision Makers' Guide Memo 37/12, paras 76 & 81 (see also Appendices 2-5 for other circumstances that may be taken into account)

10. Lower-level sanctions

Lower-level sanctions relate to failures to comply with conditions relating to employment programmes, training schemes and jobseeker's directions. They can be applied in the following circumstances:

❑ You fail to participate in an interview with your personal adviser (see 3 above).

❑ You fail to participate in a particular employment programme (such as the Work Programme – see Chapter 18(2)).

❑ You do not comply with a reasonable jobseeker's direction (see 3 above).

❑ You do not take the opportunity of a place on a training scheme or employment programme.

❑ You refuse or fail to apply for, or accept if offered, a place on a training scheme or employment programme notified to you by your adviser.

❑ You give up, fail to attend or lose through misconduct, a place on a training scheme or employment programme.

In any case other than misconduct, a sanction will not be applied if you can show you had good reason for your action (see 9 above). If a failure could incur both a lower and a higher-level sanction, only the higher-level sanction will apply (see 12 below).

JSA, S.19A

How long is the sanction applied?

In the case of a first sanctionable failure, the sanction will apply for a fixed period of four weeks. However, if this is the second sanctionable failure within 52 weeks (but not within the first two weeks) and the previous failure resulted in a 4-week sanction, the fixed sanction period will be 13 weeks. In the case of joint-claim couples (see 2 above), both failures must have been by the same claimant for the longer sanction period to apply. Any subsequent failure that occurs within 52 weeks of a previous failure will also incur a 13-week sanction.

The sanction period runs from the beginning of the benefit week following the decision to apply the sanction if JSA is already in payment. If JSA is not already in payment, the sanction period runs from the beginning of the week in which the sanctionable failure took place.

JSA Regs, reg 69A

11. Intermediate-level sanctions

Intermediate-level sanctions relate only to failures to fulfil the JSA jobseeking conditions. JSA is disallowed (or paid at a single person's rate if one member of a joint-claim couple fails to meet the conditions – see 2 above) if:

■ you are not available for work (see 4 above); *or*
■ you do not actively seek work (see 5 above).

If you reclaim JSA following such a failure, a sanction of four weeks may apply to your new JSA award if this is your first sanctionable failure. However, if this is the second sanctionable failure within 52 weeks (but not within the first two weeks) and the previous failure resulted in a 4-week sanction, your new JSA award may have a sanction applied for 13 weeks. Any subsequent failure that occurs within 52 weeks of a previous failure will also incur a 13-week sanction.

The sanction period runs from the date of claim for the new JSA award. However, the 4- or 13-week sanction period will be reduced by the period of time starting from the day after the end of the benefit week in which you were last paid JSA and ending with the day before the date of claim for the new JSA award.

If you were previously treated as being available for work or actively seeking work (see 4 and 5 above under 'Absences, emergencies and other circumstances') and your failure is a result of this status coming to an end, Jobcentre Plus can choose not to apply the sanction.

JSA, S.19B; JSA Regs 69B & 70

12. Higher-level sanctions

Higher-level sanctions relate to failures to comply with conditions relating to employment. They can be applied in the following circumstances:

❑ You lose your job through misconduct (see below).
❑ You voluntarily leave your job (see below).
❑ You refuse or fail to apply for a vacancy or accept a job offer notified to you by your personal adviser.
❑ You do not take up a reasonable job opportunity.
❑ You fail to participate in Mandatory Work Activity (see Chapter 18(4)).

JSA, S.19

In any case other than misconduct, a sanction will not be applied if you can show you had good reason for your action (see 9 above). In the third and fourth cases, if your reason for not applying or accepting the offer (or availing yourself of the opportunity) relates to the travel time to and from work, it won't count as a good reason if the travel time is normally less than 1½ hours each way (or one hour during the first 13 weeks of your claim), unless the time is unreasonable due to your health or caring responsibilities.

JSA Regs, reg 72

How long is the sanction applied?

In the case of a first sanctionable failure, the sanction will apply for a fixed period of 13 weeks. However, if this is the second sanctionable failure within 52 weeks (but not within the first two weeks) and the previous failure resulted in a 13-week sanction, the fixed sanction period will be 26 weeks. In the case of joint-claim couples (see 2 above), both failures must have been by the same claimant for the longer sanction period to apply. During the sanction period you will still technically be entitled to JSA; since entitlement to contribution-based JSA lasts for a maximum of 26 weeks, you could be left with no payment at all if the 26-week sanction is applied.

For a third (and any subsequent sanctionable failure) within 52 weeks of a previous failure, the sanction period will be set at 156 weeks.

If JSA is already in payment, the sanction period runs from the beginning of the benefit week following the one for which you were last paid JSA. If JSA is not already in payment, the sanction period runs from the beginning of the week in which the sanctionable failure took place.

JSA Regs, reg 69

A sanction will not be imposed when a sanctionable failure has taken place prior to the JSA date of claim and the relevant sanction period is the same as, or shorter than, the period between the sanctionable failure and the date of claim.

JSA Regs, reg 70A(1)

If you lose your job through misconduct

Being dismissed does not necessarily lead to a benefit sanction. When you claim JSA, you will be asked for details of the dismissal at the work-focused interview (see 3 above). It is important to provide as much detail as you can, and take along any evidence that could assist your argument (such as a letter from your GP or consultant if your condition may have a bearing on the case).

Jobcentre Plus will then contact your former employer to get their side of the story. You can ask Jobcentre Plus to provide you with a copy of the employer's account. Once you have read this, you may wish to respond to it. Do this in writing, and send the response to the Jobcentre Plus office.

You may also be making a claim of unfair dismissal to an Employment Tribunal. If someone is helping with this (eg your union representative) you should ask them for advice. If a sanction is applied, you can appeal (see Chapter 58).

If you leave your job voluntarily

The decision maker has to show that you left your job voluntarily. If they do this, you must show you had a good reason for leaving if you want to avoid a sanction. If you can, show that handing in your notice was the only thing you could do given all the circumstances, including your attempts to resolve the problems. This may enable you to avoid a sanction. You should therefore try to resolve work-related problems (using the firm's grievance procedures if they have any) before handing in your notice. You should also look for other work before leaving, or find out if you can be transferred to lighter work. If possible, discuss your personal or domestic difficulties with your employer to see if you can resolve the difficulty without handing in your notice.

You should not normally be sanctioned for agreeing to take voluntary redundancy, as you are not regarded as having left your job voluntarily. Nor should you be sanctioned if you left because your employer paid you less than the national minimum wage and you had tried unsuccessfully to get them to pay it.

JSA, S.19(3); JSA Regs, reg 71 & Decision Makers Guide, Vol 6, Chap 34, para 34284

Employment on Trial

This allows you to leave a job and still claim JSA without the risk of being sanctioned if you were in the job at least four weeks and one day, and left before you had been there for 13 weeks. You must have worked at least 16 hours in each complete week. In the 13 weeks before you took on the job, you must not have worked (including self-employment) or been a full-time student. Dismissal or leaving the job through misconduct could still lead to sanctions. Jobcentre Plus can provide more details.

JSA, S. 20(3) & JSA Regs, reg 74

13. Hardship payments

If your benefit is sanctioned, suspended or disallowed, or there is a delay in making a decision on your claim, you may be entitled to reduced-rate hardship payments of income-based JSA. Payment is not automatic, and in most cases you must show that you or your family will suffer hardship unless benefit is paid. Unless you fall into a particular vulnerable group, no benefit will be paid for the first two weeks.

The applicable amount is calculated as normal (see 23 below) but is then reduced by 40% of the single person's personal allowance. If you, your partner or your child are seriously ill or pregnant, the reduction is just 20%. If your partner is entitled to income support, they can claim it for both of you. It is not subject to any reduction.

JSA Regs, regs 145 & 146G

You may be entitled to hardship payments if you have no JSA in payment for one of the following reasons.

❑ There is a delay in the decision on your claim for JSA because of a question about whether you satisfy the availability, actively seeking work or jobseeker's agreement conditions for benefit.

❑ Your benefit has been sanctioned.

❑ Your benefit has been suspended because of a doubt about whether you satisfy the availability, actively seeking work or jobseeker's agreement conditions.

❑ If you are not available for work or actively seeking work or do not have a current jobseeker's agreement, you may still get hardship payments, but you must be considered to be vulnerable (see below) even after the first two weeks. However, this reason will not apply if you are 'treated' as unavailable for work (see 4 above).

JSA Regs, regs 141 & 146C

For the first two weeks – Hardship payments are not payable for the first two weeks unless you or your partner are considered to be *'vulnerable'*, ie:

■ are responsible for a child or qualifying young person (see Chapter 38(1)); *or*

■ are pregnant; *or*

■ are a carer looking after someone who gets attendance allowance, disability living allowance middle or highest rate care component (or has claimed and is waiting for a decision or payment) or personal independence payment daily living component, and you cannot continue to care for them unless you receive hardship payments. In this case you need not show hardship would result; *or*

■ qualify for a disability premium; *or*

■ are suffering from a *'chronic medical condition which results in functional capacity being limited or restricted by physical impairment'* that has lasted, or is likely to last, for at least 26 weeks, and during the first two weeks the disabled person's health would probably decline more than that of a healthy person; *or*

■ are under 18 and eligible for JSA at that age (see 21 below); *or*

■ are under 21 and have recently left local authority care.

In each case, other than the exception for carers, you must satisfy the decision maker that the vulnerable person will suffer hardship unless payments are made.

JSA Regs, regs 140(1) & 146A(1)

After two weeks – If you are not considered 'vulnerable', you are eligible for hardship payments only after the first two weeks after the sanction has been applied, or suspension made, etc. You must show that you or your partner will suffer hardship unless payment is made.

JSA Regs, regs 142 & 146D

What is 'hardship'? – You must complete a 'hardship statement' setting out your grounds for applying for a hardship payment. In deciding whether or not you will suffer hardship if no payment is made, the decision maker must take into account any resources likely to be available to you. They must also look at whether there is a substantial risk that you will have much-reduced amounts of, or lose altogether, essential items such as food, clothing, heating and accommodation. It is also relevant whether a disability premium, or disabled or severely disabled child elements of child tax credit, are payable. The decision maker may take other factors into account.

JSA Regs, regs 140(5) & 146A(6)

B. CONTRIBUTION-BASED JSA

14. Do you qualify?

To qualify for contribution-based JSA you must meet the national insurance conditions (see 15 below). You must also satisfy the qualifying conditions for JSA (see 2 above).

Contribution-based JSA is a flat-rate personal benefit payable for a maximum of six months (182 days). If you don't meet the national insurance conditions, you may be entitled to income-based JSA instead. You may also be entitled to income-based JSA to top up your contribution-based JSA (eg if you have a dependent partner or certain housing costs such as a mortgage) – see 19 below.

15. National insurance contribution conditions

There are two national insurance (NI) contribution conditions, both of which you must meet to be entitled to contribution-based JSA. The first condition depends on NI contributions you have actually paid in the relevant tax year. For the second condition, credited NI contributions, as well as paid NI contributions, count. The different classes of NI contribution are covered in Chapter 12(4). Credited contributions are covered in Chapter 12(5).

With both conditions, there is a relationship between 'tax years' and 'benefit years', so it is important to know the difference between them.

Tax years – A tax year runs from 6 April to 5 April the following year.

Benefit years – Benefit years start on the first Sunday in January and end on the Saturday before the first Sunday in January the following year. The 2013 benefit year started on Sunday 6.1.13 and will end on Saturday 4.1.14.

SSCBA, S.21(6)

The 'relevant benefit year' is usually the benefit year that includes the start of your 'jobseeking period' (see below).

JSA, S.2(4)(b)

The first condition – paid contributions

You must have paid, or be treated as having paid, at least 26 weeks of Class 1 NI contributions on earnings at the lower earnings limit (see Chapter 12(7)) in one of the last two complete tax years before the start of the relevant benefit year. For instance, if you claim JSA in the 2013 benefit year, you need to have paid 26 weeks' contributions in one of the following tax years: 2010/11 or 2011/12.

JSA, S.2(1)(a), (2) & (4)

If you are the spouse or civil partner of a member of HM forces, you will satisfy the first condition with sufficient NI contributions paid in *any* complete tax year if you were entitled to an NI credit to cover a period of assignment outside the UK (see Box D.7) for at least one week in the last complete tax year before the start of the relevant benefit year.

JSA Regs, reg 45(B)

The second condition – paid or credited contributions

You must have paid or been credited with Class 1 NI contributions on earnings 50 times the lower earnings limit (see Chapter 12(7)) in each of the last two complete tax years before the start of the relevant benefit year. For example, if you claim JSA in the 2013 benefit year, you meet this condition if you paid, or had been credited with, contributions on earnings of £4,850 in the 2010/11 tax year and £5,100 in the 2011/12 tax year. A credited contribution counts as having earnings at the amount of the lower earnings limit for that tax year. You can combine credits and paid contributions.

JSA, S.2(1)(b), (3), (3A) & (4)

Jobseeking period and linking rules

The *'jobseeking period'* is any period for which you claim and satisfy the qualifying conditions for JSA (see 2 above), or

you get a hardship payment (see 13 above), or you are signing on to protect your NI contribution record. A period in which you lose entitlement because of failure to sign on or attend an appointment, or you are not entitled because you are involved in a trade dispute, is not included in the jobseeking period.
JSA Regs, reg 47

Two jobseeking periods link together and are treated as one single jobseeking period if they are separated by:

- 12 weeks or less; or
- one or more linked periods – periods when you are (or treated as) incapable of, or having a limited capability for, work, or entitled to maternity allowance, or training and getting a training allowance, or on certain Work Programme options; or
- a period on jury service.

Gaps of 12 weeks or less between jobseeking periods and linked periods, or between linked periods, are ignored.
JSA Regs, reg 48

For JSA, the beginning of the jobseeking period or any linked period is used to decide the tax years for which you must satisfy the contribution conditions. For example, if your employment and support allowance (ESA) ends and you sign on for JSA instead, and you claim JSA within 12 weeks of the end of your ESA award, the relevant tax years for your JSA claim will be the same as the ones used for your earlier ESA claim.

Carers – Another linking rule helps people who give up work to care for someone to qualify for JSA on the basis of the contributions they paid when they were working. If you were getting carer's allowance and this ended within 12 weeks of the beginning of your jobseeking period (or linked period), the period of carer's allowance entitlement also links to the jobseeking period, if this would help you satisfy the contribution conditions for JSA. So your benefit year would be the year in which your carer's allowance entitlement began.
JSA Regs, reg 48(2)(a)&(3)

Linking rules before 7.10.96 – Jobseeking periods were introduced on 7.10.96. For a note on linking rules before this, see *Disability Rights Handbook* 25th edition, page 80.

16. How much do you get?

Contribution-based JSA	per week
Aged under 25	£56.80
Aged 25 or over	£71.70

JSA Regs, reg 79

17. Does anything affect what you get?

The amount you get may be affected by earnings or by an occupational or personal pension. Only your earnings (not those of your partner or other family members) are taken into account. Payment is not affected by other income or savings you have.

If one or more of these sources of money mean you are not paid benefit, you will still remain 'entitled' (unless your earnings exceed your 'prescribed amount' – see below). Any day for which you are entitled but not paid will count towards your 182 days of entitlement (see 18 below).

Earnings – Your weekly earnings from employment or self-employment are deducted in full from the amount of benefit due, apart from an earnings disregard of £5 (or £20 if you are working as a part-time firefighter, auxiliary coastguard, lifeboat operator or member of a territorial or reserve force).

If you receive earnings from any annual continuous training as a member of a territorial or reserve force for a maximum of 15 days in any calendar year, an earnings disregard ensures that you are still entitled to at least 10 pence contribution-based JSA after the earnings have been taken into account. This is to ensure that a new claim for benefit is not necessary

after the training has been completed.

In other respects, the assessment of earnings is essentially the same as for means-tested benefits – see Chapter 27(3)-(4).
JSA Regs, regs 98-102 & Sch 6

On days in any week when your earnings exceed your *'prescribed amount'* (which is the amount of contribution-based JSA payable for your age plus your earnings disregard minus one pence) you are not entitled to contribution-based JSA and these days do not count towards your 182 days of entitlement (see 18 below).
JSA, S.2(1)(c) & JSA Regs, reg 56

Occupational or personal pensions – Income of over £50 a week from an occupational or personal pension, the Pension Protection Fund or the Financial Assistance Scheme is deducted from the amount of benefit due – eg, if your pension is £55 a week, £5 is deducted from your benefit. Days when no contribution-based JSA is payable because the level of your pension reduces it to nil count towards your 182 days of entitlement. A one-off lump-sum payment does not affect your benefit.
JSA Regs, reg 81(1)

Other benefits – You cannot get more than one contributory benefit at the same time, nor can you get income support or income-related employment and support allowance (ESA) while claiming contribution-based JSA, although you may be entitled to income-based JSA paid as a top-up. However, if you have a partner they may be entitled to claim income support (if they come within one of the groups listed in Box E.1) or income-related ESA (if they have a limited capability for work) for both of you, provided you only get contribution-based JSA. If this applies, you should check whether you will be better off if you claim income-based JSA or if your partner claims income support or ESA.

18. How long does contribution-based JSA last?

Entitlement to JSA lasts for a total of six months (182 days). This can be one spell of unemployment lasting for six months or more than one spell of unemployment where you make shorter claims for JSA but your entitlement in each of those claims is based on the same two tax years. Once your 182 days are exhausted, you can only re-qualify when you begin a new 'jobseeking period' and your new JSA claim is based on different tax years (at least one of which is a later year). See 15 above for details of the tax years on which your claim is based.
JSA, S.5

Jobseeking period – This is the period when you meet the conditions for JSA or a hardship payment, including time when you are sanctioned. Two jobseeking periods can be linked in certain circumstances (see 15 above). If your new claim is linked to your previous jobseeking period, you will not have to wait another three waiting days but will only be entitled to what remains of your 182 days of contribution-based JSA.
JSA Regs, regs 47(1)&(2)

C. INCOME-BASED JSA

19. Do you qualify?

To qualify for income-based JSA, you must satisfy the basic qualifying conditions for JSA set out in 2 above. In addition you must satisfy the following income-based conditions.

❏ You must have no income, or your income is below your 'applicable amount' (see 22 below).

❏ You (or your partner) must not be claiming income support, income-related employment and support allowance or pension credit.

❏ Your savings or capital must be no more than £16,000.

❏ If you have a partner, they must not be working for 24 hours or more a week (see 20 below).

❏ You must be aged 18 or over; or aged 16 or 17 and pass other tests (see 21 below).
❏ You must be 'habitually resident' and not subject to immigration control (see Chapter 49(2 and 3)).

JSA, Ss.3, 3A & 13

Income-based JSA is means tested and taxable. You claim for yourself and your partner, if you have one. If you are one of a couple, you can choose who should make the claim. The one who claims must sign on and satisfy all the basic qualifying conditions. (If you are part of a joint-claim couple, see 2 above.) Income-based JSA can be paid in addition to contribution-based JSA.

Income-based JSA can help towards mortgage interest payments and certain other housing costs (see Chapter 26). If you get income-based JSA, you may be eligible for housing benefit and won't have to go through a separate means test (see Chapter 21(20)).

Getting income-based JSA may entitle you to:
■ free prescriptions and dental treatment (Chapter 54);
■ housing grants (Chapter 31);
■ help from the social fund (Chapter 23) and budgeting loans (Chapter 24(2));
■ free school meals (Chapter 37);
■ help with hospital fares (Chapter 35).

The government is replacing income-based JSA with 'universal credit'. This is being piloted from April 2013 in north-west England; nationwide roll-out starts in October 2013 on the basis of one district in each Jobcentre Plus region. A new claim for income-based JSA may be treated as a claim for universal credit instead, depending on where you live. See Box J.1 in Chapter 25 for more on universal credit.

20. If your partner is working

You are not entitled to income-based JSA if your partner is in *'remunerative work'* of (on average) 24 hours or more a week. Work counts if it is paid or done *'in expectation of payment'*. The rules closely follow the income support rules (see Chapter 15(6)) and provide for specific circumstances in which work can be ignored or, conversely, in which your partner can be treated as working even when they're not. If your partner's work does not exclude you from entitlement, their earnings are taken into account in the assessment of your benefit.

JSA Regs, regs 51(1)(b) & (2)-(3), 52 & 53

21. If you are aged 16 or 17

If you are aged 16 or 17, you are entitled to JSA only if you are in certain specified groups (see below). You must register for work and training as directed by Jobcentre Plus. You must also satisfy the qualifying conditions (see 2 above) including being available to take up work and taking active steps to look for work and training. Provided you haven't been subject to a JSA sanction in the past, you can restrict your availability to jobs where the employer is providing suitable training – ie you can turn down a job if no such training is offered.

JSA Regs, regs 62 & 64

Who is eligible? – You are eligible for income-based JSA while aged 16/17 if you fall into one of the specified groups of people who are eligible for income support (see Box E.1, Chapter 15) or employment and support allowance (see Chapter 10(9)), but you choose to claim JSA instead. You are eligible if you are one of a couple and treated as responsible for a child who lives with you, or if you are laid off or on short-time working (up to a maximum of 13 weeks).

JSA Regs, reg 61

Severe hardship payments – If you don't fit into any of the circumstances outlined above in which JSA can be paid to people aged 16/17, you can be paid JSA on a discretionary basis if you would otherwise suffer severe hardship. The direction to pay JSA will be for a temporary period (usually eight weeks) and you must also satisfy the basic qualifying

conditions (set out in 2 above). Factors such as your health, vulnerability, threat of homelessness, training or job prospects should be taken into account. In some situations (eg if you fail to complete a course of training without good reason) the amount you get is reduced for the first two weeks by 40% of the personal allowance (or 20% if you are seriously ill or pregnant).

JSA, Ss.16 & 17 and JSA Regs, reg 63

22. How is income-based JSA worked out?

Income-based JSA is worked out by comparing your needs with your resources (ie any income or capital that you have). If you are a single person, only your needs and resources are relevant. If you are one of a couple, the needs and resources of both of you are relevant.

Set amounts for different needs are added together to reach the total amount the law says you need to live on. This is called your *'applicable amount'*. Your income (worked out under set rules) is deducted from your applicable amount. This leaves the amount of JSA you are entitled to. The calculation is as follows:

Step 1: Add up your capital resources – See Chapter 28. You will not be entitled to income-based JSA if your capital, and any capital belonging to your partner, is more than £16,000.
Step 2: Work out your applicable amount – See 23 below.
Step 3: Add up your income resources – See Chapter 27. Include the tariff income if you have capital over £6,000, or £10,000 if you live permanently in a care home (see Chapter 28(4)).
Step 4: Deduct your income from your applicable amount – If your income is less than your applicable amount, income-based JSA makes up the difference in full, provided you meet the other qualifying conditions (see 2 above).

If you satisfy the contribution-based conditions

You are paid contribution-based JSA if you satisfy the conditions (see 15 above). Your entitlement to income-based JSA is also calculated and if this amount exceeds the contribution-based JSA, the extra amount is paid as a top-up.

23. What is your applicable amount?

The applicable amount, set by Parliament, is the amount of money the law says you need to live on. It consists of the sum total of:
■ **a personal allowance:** for yourself or for a couple (these are the same as those for income support – see Chapter 15(9)); *plus*
■ **premiums:** see below; *plus*
■ **certain housing costs** (eg mortgage interest) – see Chapter 26.

JSA Regs, reg 83, Sch 1 & Sch 2

Premiums – There are five premiums, each one with specific qualifying conditions (see Chapter 25 for details). Unless otherwise specified in Chapter 25, each premium to which you are entitled is added to the total of your applicable amount.

Premiums		per week
Disability	single	£31.00
	couple	£44.20
Enhanced disability	single	£15.15
	couple	£21.75
Severe disability	single	£59.50
	couple (one qualifies)	£59.50
	couple (both qualify)	£119.00
Pensioner	single	£73.70
	couple	£109.50
Carer		£33.30

JSA Regs, Sch 1, Parts III & IV

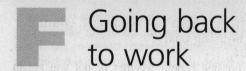

Going back to work

17 Benefits and work

1. Going back to work
This chapter looks at the effect on benefit entitlement of doing paid or voluntary work and the linking rules that can help you return to benefit without losing out.

2. What happens to your disability benefits?
Disability living allowance (DLA), personal independence payment (PIP) and attendance allowance are payable whether or not you are working. They are not means tested, so earnings do not affect the amount of your benefit.
Note: Starting a job may suggest that your care or mobility needs have changed, so your benefit entitlement could be reconsidered. The DWP views starting or leaving work as a potential 'change of circumstances' for DLA and PIP. You may be asked to explain your care needs in work.

3. Can you work while claiming ESA or benefits for incapacity?
Generally, if you do any work, whether or not you expect to be paid, you are treated as capable of work for the week in which you do the work (Sunday to Saturday) and thus are not entitled to the following benefits:
- employment and support allowance (ESA);
- incapacity benefit or severe disablement allowance (SDA);
- income support based on incapacity for work (see Box E.1, Chapter 15);
- disability premium under the 'incapacity condition' (see Chapter 25(2));
- national insurance incapacity or ESA credits (see Box D.7 in Chapter 12).

IW Regs, reg 16(1); ESA Regs 40(1)

If you come off ESA to start paid work, you can protect your right to return to benefit for up to 12 weeks (see 14 below).
Exempt work – You are allowed to do the kinds of work described below while remaining on benefit, although that work might not be ignored completely. The sort of activities or tasks you can do, whether connected with the work or not, could be taken into account when deciding whether you pass the work capability assessment (see Chapter 11) for ESA. When you start work, your case may be referred to a DWP healthcare professional for an opinion and you may be subject to a face-to-face assessment (see Chapter 11(9)), but this should not happen routinely. You do not have to undergo a face-to-face assessment just because you are doing permitted work, but any assessment that may be due during a period of permitted work will go ahead.

Permitted work
Permitted work allows you to try out work within certain limits. You do not need to obtain permission from Jobcentre Plus to do permitted work. However, as you should notify Jobcentre Plus of any change of circumstances that may affect your benefits, it is best to let them know as soon as you start the work. There are three types of permitted work.
Permitted work lower limit – You can earn no more than £20 a week. You can do such work even between periods when you are on the other forms of permitted work described below. The £20 limit means that such work should not interfere with your entitlement to income support if you qualify for the disability premium. There is no limit as to how long you can do this type of permitted work, provided your earnings are no higher than £20 a week.
Supported permitted work – This is work that is:
- carried out as part of your treatment programme under medical supervision while you are an inpatient or a regular outpatient of a hospital or similar institution; *or*
- done under the supervision of a person employed by a public or local authority or voluntary or community-interest organisation that provides or arranges work opportunities for disabled people.

In the latter case, you do not need the person to be working alongside you. The support must be ongoing and regular, but the frequency of contact can vary depending on the needs. The means of contact can vary and be face to face or by phone. The work can be in the community or a sheltered workshop.

There is no limit as to how long you can do this type of permitted work, provided your earnings are no higher than £99.50 a week.
Permitted work higher limit – This is designed to test your ability to work before you move permanently into employment. You can earn up to £99.50 a week and must work less than 16 hours a week.

If you have been placed in the support group of ESA claimants (see Chapter 10(7)) or are an incapacity claimant exempt from the personal capability assessment (PCA), you can do this work for an unlimited period.

If you are in the work-related activity group of ESA claimants (see Chapter 10(6)) or if you are an incapacity claimant not exempt from the PCA, you can do this work only for a period of up to 52 weeks. If you have a break in your claim of more than eight weeks (or 12 weeks for ESA), you can repeat the 52-week period of permitted work higher limit. Otherwise, you can do further permitted work higher limit only after a gap of more than 52 weeks since you last did it.

IW Regs, reg 17(2)-(4); ESA Regs, reg 45(2)-(4)

16-hour limit – You must work for less than 16 hours a week. Your hours are averaged over the current week and the four preceding weeks, or over the period of a *'recognisable cycle'* of work.

IW Regs, reg 17(8); ESA Regs, reg 45(8)

Effect of earnings – For ESA, earnings for permitted work are calculated in the same way as they are under the income assessment for income-related ESA (see Chapter 27(3) and (4)). For benefits paid for incapacity, earnings for permitted work are calculated in the same way as they are for carer's allowance dependant's addition (see Chapter 7(5)).

ESA Regs, reg 88; R(IB)1/06 (CoA: 'Doyle') & CE Regs

If your earnings from permitted work are no more than the £20 or £99.50 limit (whichever is appropriate), your ESA, incapacity benefit or SDA will not be affected. If you get housing benefit while claiming one of these benefits (or national insurance incapacity or ESA credits) your earnings from permitted work will be disregarded. If you get income support, only £20 of your earnings can be disregarded. See Chapter 27(5) for more on earnings disregards.

Other kinds of work
The following kinds of work are also allowed:
■ work as a councillor. If you receive a councillor's allowance of more than £99.50 a week (excluding expenses), the excess will be deducted from your contributory ESA, incapacity benefit or SDA;
■ care of a relative or domestic tasks carried out in your own home. A *'relative'* is a parent (or in-law or step-parent), son/daughter (in-law/step), brother, sister, or the partner of any of them; or a spouse or partner, grandparent, grandchild, uncle, aunt, nephew or niece;
■ any activity carried out during an emergency to protect another person or to prevent serious damage to property or livestock;
■ an approved work trial arranged in writing with the employer by Jobcentre Plus (or an organisation providing services to them) for which you will receive no wages;

IW Regs, reg 16(3)(a),(b),(c)&(d); ESA Regs, regs 40(2)(a),(c)&(e) & 45(7)

■ self-employed work done while you are 'test trading' for up to 26 weeks with help from a self-employment provider arranged by Jobcentre Plus;
■ voluntary work (not for a relative) – see 12 below;
■ duties undertaken as an appeal tribunal disability member – but only one full day or two half days a week is allowed;

IW Regs, reg 17(5),(6)&(7), ESA Regs, regs 45(5)-(6) & 40(2)(b)

■ work which is so minimal that it can be regarded as trivial or negligible – eg someone who occasionally does small jobs for a business (eg signing cheques).

Decision Makers Guide, Vol 3, Chap 13, para 13857

Dialysis, radiotherapy and other treatments
If you receive certain specified types of treatment for two or more days in a week, you can work on the other days and continue to receive incapacity benefit or SDA for the days of treatment (including days of preparation and recuperation specified as part of the treatment). If you receive such treatment and can thus be treated as having a limited capability for work for the week (see Chapter 11(2)) you can work on the other days and continue to receive contributory ESA for the days of treatment and recovery.

IW Regs, reg 13, ESA Regs, reg 46

If your partner works
Your partner's earnings do not affect the basic amount of contributory ESA, incapacity benefit or SDA you get, but for incapacity benefit and SDA they can affect an adult dependant's addition. Your partner's earnings affect income support, income-related ESA and income-based jobseeker's allowance (see Chapter 27(3)-(5)).

4. Can you still get help towards rent, council tax or other housing costs?
Housing benefit
You can claim housing benefit whether or not you are in work (see Chapter 21). It is means tested, so the amount you get depends on the level of your (and your partner's) income and savings. See Chapter 27(3)-(5) for the way earnings are assessed.

Extended payments – If your income-related employment and support allowance (ESA), income-based jobseeker's allowance (JSA) or income support stops because you (or your partner) start work or increase your hours or earnings, your housing benefit may carry on for an extra four weeks at the existing rate. To qualify, you must have been on income-related ESA, income-based JSA or income support (or a combination of these) for at least 26 weeks immediately prior to starting work. Time spent on contribution-based JSA will count towards the 26 weeks but if you were receiving only contribution-based JSA immediately prior to starting work, you will not qualify for this run-on.

An extended payment of housing benefit can also be made if you have received contributory ESA, incapacity benefit or severe disablement allowance (or a combination of these benefits) for at least 26 weeks before you start work or increase your hours or earnings.

In either case, you do not have to make a separate claim. Simply inform Jobcentre Plus or the local authority within four weeks that you or your partner have started or are about to start work or that your earnings or hours have increased.

HB Regs, reg 72-73

Once the extended payments end, housing benefit is based on your new circumstances. You do not have to make a new claim. Your benefit entitlement will be continuous.

Housing costs run-on
If your income-related ESA, income-based JSA or income support stops because you or your partner start work or increase your hours or earnings, any housing costs (including payments to cover mortgage interest) you were getting may be paid for an extra four weeks at the existing rate whatever your earnings, provided your job is expected to last at least five weeks. You can get this help if you or your partner were getting benefit continuously for at least 26 weeks and you received housing costs immediately before starting (or extending) the work. You do not have to make a separate claim. Simply inform Jobcentre Plus that you are starting work or increasing your hours/earnings.

IS Regs, reg 6(5)-(8)

Council tax support
You may get help towards your council tax bills whether or not you are in work. Such support is provided by your local authority (see Chapter 22).

5. What about carer's allowance?
You can work and claim carer's allowance at the same time if your earnings (less any allowable deductions) are no more than £100 a week. There is no limit on the number of hours you can work, although you must continue to provide care for at least 35 hours a week. Work during breaks from caring (see Chapter 7(10)) does not affect carer's allowance.

Carer's allowance is not means tested. Provided your earnings do not exceed the limit, the full amount of carer's allowance is payable. Caring costs of up to half your net earnings can be disregarded if you pay someone other than a close relative to look after the disabled person you care for or a child under 16 (for whom you get child benefit). Your partner's earnings do not affect the basic amount of carer's allowance you get but can affect an adult dependant or child dependant's addition. See Chapter 7(5) for details.

Income support to top up your carer's allowance is affected in a different way. For carers, there is no limit on the number of hours you work, but only £20 of your net earnings can be disregarded (see Chapter 27(5)).

6. What happens to income support?

If you get income support on the grounds of incapacity for work, you may do permitted work of less than 16 hours a week or other exempt work (see 3 above). If you get income support on any other grounds (eg because you are a carer) you can work for less than 16 hours in any job.

If you are the claimant and your partner works, their hours must be less than 24 a week, although there are some exceptions (see Chapter 15(6)).

In each case, you can keep only a maximum of £20 of your earnings or joint earnings for a couple (see Chapter 27(5)).

If your income support stops because you or your partner start work or increase your hours or earnings, you may continue to get housing costs paid for up to four weeks (see 'Housing costs run-on' in 4 above).

7. Jobseeker's allowance

If you are working less than 16 hours a week, you are eligible for jobseeker's allowance (JSA). If your partner works and you get income-based JSA, they must work less than 24 hours a week. You must still sign on for work and actively look for, and be available to take up, a full-time job. Earnings above the earnings disregard affect the amount you get. For income-based JSA only, your partner's earnings also affect the amount of your benefit (see Chapter 27(3)-(5)).

If your income-based JSA stops because you or your partner start work or increase your hours or earnings, you may continue to get housing costs paid for up to four weeks (see 'Housing costs run-on' in 4 above).

8. Tax credits

You may qualify for tax credits if you are in work or have dependent children and have a low income (see Chapter 19). If you qualify for tax credits you are unlikely to be worse off in work, but it is worth getting advice before taking a job so you know just how your income would be affected. Although tax credits include elements that reflect individual and family needs, including disabilities, they do not help with mortgage interest.

For all working tax credit (WTC) awards, if you stop work or your normal working hours fall below the minimum required for a WTC claim, which is either 16 or 30 hours a week (or 24 hours a week for some couples with children), you will be treated as being in work for a further four weeks, allowing for a 4-week run-on of WTC. You must report your change of circumstances to the Tax Credit Office within one month to receive the run-on.

9. Universal credit

Universal credit will be replacing several means-tested benefits for people of working age. See Box J.1 in Chapter 25 for details. Universal credit does not provide for 'permitted work' (as described in 3 above) but you will be encouraged to do some work, even if only for a few hours a week, if you are able to. There will be no time limit to how many weeks you may work.

If your disability or health condition limits your ability to work, additional support is provided in universal credit via two elements: the 'limited capability for work element' and the 'limited capability for work and work-related activity element'. These may not be payable if you move into full-time work (defined by an earnings threshold of 16 times the national minimum wage), depending on whether or not you have had a work capability assessment (see Chapter 11).

❏ If you have been found to have a limited capability for work/work-related activity at a work capability assessment (WCA) before you start the full-time work, you will continue receiving the appropriate element. You will lose it only if at a future WCA you are found not to qualify.

❏ If you have not had a WCA before you start the full-time work, you will not be referred to a WCA to assess whether you are entitled to one of the elements unless you are also entitled to attendance allowance, disability living allowance or personal independence payment.

UC Regs, reg 41

10. In-work assistance

Return-to-work credit – If you take a job of at least 16 hours a week after claiming employment and support allowance, incapacity benefit, income support (paid on the basis of incapacity) or severe disablement allowance for at least 13 weeks, you may be paid a 'return to work credit' of £40 a week for up to 52 weeks. Your earnings (but not other income) must be less than £15,000 a year (£288.46 a week) and the job should be expected to last at least five weeks. The credit is disregarded for tax credits and means-tested benefits.

Return-to-work is being phased out in 2013. New claims can be made until 1.10.13. From 2.7.13, new claimants will not be able to build up eligibility. Payments in progress on 1.10.13 will continue for their full entitlement period or until a change of circumstances bring them to a close.

In-work credit – This is paid to lone parents who move from benefits to working at least 16 hours a week. It is £40 a week (£60 in London) for the first year of the new job and is disregarded for tax credits and means-tested benefits. To be eligible, you must have been in receipt of a qualifying benefit for a set period before starting the job.

In-work credit is being phased out in 2013. New claims can be made until 1.10.13. New claimants have not been able to build up eligibility since 2.10.12. Payments in progress on 1.10.13 will continue for their full entitlement period or until a change of circumstances bring them to a close.

New enterprise allowance – You may get help under the new enterprise allowance scheme if you claim jobseeker's allowance or are a lone parent on income support and want to start a business. It includes help from business mentors to develop a business plan. If you are regarded as having a viable business idea you may be able to get loans of up to £1,000 to help with start-up costs. The scheme can also provide a weekly allowance for up to 26 weeks of your business venture. It is not available to those on the Work Programme.

11. Health benefits

You may qualify for help with prescription charges, hospital travel costs, dental treatment and glasses. If your income and savings are low, claim on form HC1, available from the doctor, dentist or optician or by ringing 0845 850 1166. You qualify automatically if you get income-related employment and support allowance, income-based jobseeker's allowance or income support. If you get tax credits you may qualify, depending on the level of your earnings. See Chapter 54.

12. Industrial injuries benefit

Industrial injuries disablement benefit is not affected by any work or earnings you might have.

13. Voluntary work

If you get incapacity benefit or severe disablement allowance you are allowed to do voluntary work for anyone other than a close relative (parent (or in-law or step-parent), son/daughter (in-law/step), brother, sister or the partner of any of these). If you get employment and support allowance or income support, you are allowed to do voluntary work for anyone other than a relative (see 3 above). You must not be paid for your work, other than expenses 'reasonably incurred *by [you] in connection with that work'*. Permitted expenses could include travel, meals, childminding, the costs of caring for a dependant, equipment needed for work and use of a telephone. There is no limit on the number of hours you can volunteer.

IW Regs, regs 2 & 17(6); IS Regs, reg 6(1)(c); ESA Regs, regs 2 & 45(6)&(10)

See Chapter 15(6) for more on income support and voluntary work.

F.1 Going back to work – a checklist

This is a guide to the main help available if you are in work or looking for work. Where there is more information in this or other chapters, we refer you to the right place in the Handbook. For information about other kinds of help, ask at your Jobcentre Plus office. A disability employment adviser can provide specialist advice on employment and training.

It is worth asking for a 'better-off' calculation before taking a job. Ask an advice agency or a Jobcentre Plus adviser. They can work out how much benefit you might get at a given level of earnings or other income. You can then compare your income in and out of work.

Working 16 hours a week or more
Tax credits – Top up earnings if you are in low-paid work. See Chapter 19.
Income support – You can stay on income support in some circumstances – eg, you are a carer. Keep up to £20 a week of earnings. Income support helps with mortgage interest (tax credits do not). See Chapter 15(6).
Housing benefit – Help with rent. See Chapter 21.
Council tax reduction – Help with council tax. See Chapter 22 (12).

Working under 16 hours a week
Permitted work – Employment and support allowance (ESA), incapacity benefit and severe disablement allowance (SDA) can be paid on top of permitted work earnings of up to a maximum of £99.50 a week (see Chapter 17(3)).
Income support – You can stay on income support if work is permitted or you are eligible for a reason other than incapacity for work. Keep up to £20 a week of earnings. See Chapter 17(6).
Jobseeker's allowance (JSA) – Keep up to £20 a week of earnings. You must still look for full-time work. See Chapter 16.
Housing benefit – Help with rent. See Chapter 21.
Council tax reduction – Help with council tax. See Chapter 22 (12).

When you start work
Housing benefit extended payments – Existing rate paid for first four weeks of coming off ESA, incapacity benefit, income-based JSA, income support or SDA. See Chapter 17(4).
Housing costs run-on – Existing housing costs paid for the first four weeks of coming off income-related ESA, income-based JSA or income support. See Chapter 17(4).
Benefit linking rules – Various linking rules help you reclaim benefit on the same terms as before if you have to stop work again. See Chapter 17(14).

Equipment and support at work
Access to Work – Can help pay for equipment and adaptations at work and cover extra disability-related costs such as travel to work and support workers. See Chapter 18(5).
Work Programme – Provides support to overcome barriers that prevent people finding and staying in work. See Chapter 18(2).

Work Choice – Provides job support for disabled people who face more complex barriers to finding and keeping work. See Chapter 18(3).
Youth Contract – Provides support to help unemployed people aged 18 to 24 find work. See Chapter 18(6).

Trying out a job
Benefit linking rules – Various linking rules help you reclaim benefit without losing out after a trial period at work. See Chapter 17(14).
Work trials – Allow you to remain in receipt of benefit and receive travel and meal allowances for up to 30 working days while you and the employer see whether you will be suitable for a job.
Work Choice – For people out of the job market for some time due to ill health or disability, this programme can improve confidence and work skills. See Chapter 18(3).
Employment on Trial – Your JSA will not be sanctioned for leaving a job voluntarily during the trial period. See Chapter 16(12).
Return-to-work credit or in-work credit – £40 or £60 weekly, payable for a year to help people on benefits move into work. See Chapter 17(10).

Starting a business
Contact: Businesslink in England (helpline: 0845 600 9006), Business Gateway in Scotland (www.business.scotland.gov.uk) or Business Wales (helpline: 0300 060 3000; www.business.wales.gov.uk). There is useful information on starting a business at www.gov.uk/browse/business.
New enterprise allowance – Financial help for unemployed people who are out of work and entering self-employment. See Chapter 17(10).

Looking for work
JSA – Weekly benefit providing a basic income if you have to sign on as available for work. See Chapter 16.
Access to Work – Help with the cost of travel, support workers and communication support at interviews paid through the Access to Work scheme. See Chapter 18(5).
Social fund budgeting loan – This is a loan to help with the expenses of looking for work or starting work if you have been getting income-related ESA, income-based JSA or income support for at least 26 weeks. See Chapter 24(2).

Childcare costs
Working tax credit – Includes a childcare element covering up to 70% of eligible childcare costs. See Chapter 19(7).
Housing benefit – Certain childcare costs can be disregarded from your earnings in the benefit assessment. See Chapter 27(5).

Employment rights
Equality Act – See Chapter 55.
Minimum wage – £6.19 an hour for workers aged 21 and over, £4.98 if aged 18-20 and £3.68 if aged 16/17. There is an apprentice minimum wage of £2.65 an hour for apprentices under 19 and those aged 19 or over in their first year of an apprenticeship.
Other rights at work – Contact your trade union or ACAS (Advisory, Conciliation and Arbitration Service): 0845 747 4747, Minicom 0845 606 1600.

14. Stopping work again

If you stop claiming benefits to begin work, but then stop working and re-claim benefit, there are linking rules that may allow you to go back to your previous benefit on the same terms as before.

Rapid re-claim – If you were claiming income support or jobseeker's allowance (JSA) before starting work, the job ends within 26 weeks, and your circumstances are broadly the same as when you made the previous claim, you can fill out a rapid re-claim form, which should speed up the processing of your new claim. Rapid re-claim also applies to housing benefit if you are making a rapid re-claim for income support or JSA. For employment and support allowance (ESA), you can only use rapid re-claim within 12 weeks of a previous claim.

Incapacity-related benefits

New claims for incapacity benefit, income support paid on the grounds of incapacity or severe disablement allowance can no longer be made. Consequently, the linking rules which allowed you to re-claim these benefits after a break in entitlement have been abolished. You will have to make a new claim for ESA instead. If you claim ESA within 12 weeks of a previous award of one of these benefits, you will not have to serve any 'waiting days' (see Chapter 10(13)).

Employment and support allowance

12-week linking rule – Any two periods of limited capability for work (ie days when you have a limited capability for work) separated by no more than 12 weeks are treated as a single period. So if you re-claim ESA within 12 weeks of a previous award, you will not have to serve any waiting days (see Chapter 10(13)). If you had served the 13-week assessment phase in the previous award, you can go onto the rate of payment of the earlier ESA award straightaway (as long as the previous award was not terminated because you were found not to have a limited capability for work; see Chapter 11(2)).

ESA Regs, regs 7, 35A & 145(1)

Other linking rules

Housing costs – For linking rules and other help, see Chapter 26(5).

Housing benefit – If you have been claiming housing benefit continuously since before 1996, you are exempt from the rent restrictions described in Chapter 21(8). To keep the exemption, any break in claim must be no longer than four weeks.

Disability Rights UK membership

Keep your Handbook up to date all year

Available only to members, *Disability and Welfare Rights Updates* is our bi-monthly PDF magazine written in plain English by benefits specialists. It includes page-by-page updates to the Handbook.

Other information in each issue includes:
■ policy updates on disability and welfare rights issues
■ disabled students training and progress
■ independent living and disability equality
■ Q&As from our helplines
■ a digest of recent case law
■ a timetable of future benefit and tax credit changes

To find out more and to see a free sample magazine email members@disabilityrightsuk.org or visit
www.disabilityrightsuk.org/membership

---

18 Employment and training

1. Introduction

This chapter covers some of the services and programmes designed to help you get and remain in work. Some schemes pay allowances or provide services to make finding work easier, others seek to compel you to find work by cutting or removing your benefit if you do not take particular actions recommended by your personal adviser.

Jobcentre Plus – Jobcentre Plus is the DWP organisation providing benefits and services for people of working age (ie between the ages of 16 and pension credit qualifying age (see Chapter 42(2)). Everyone who claims benefits from Jobcentre Plus has a *'personal adviser'* to deal with claims and provide information on work and training opportunities.

Disability employment advisers (DEAs) – DEAs can be contacted through your Jobcentre Plus office and can provide employment assessment, jobseeking advice and referral to training courses, as well as specialist advice and information on Jobcentre Plus programmes for disabled people. The personal adviser and DEA roles are complementary. If you wish to have a DEA make this clear; your request should not be refused. Advice and support from a DEA is not dependent on receipt of benefits.

2. Work Programme

The Work Programme is the main programme under the welfare to work provisions. The Work Programme is delivered by organisations called 'providers', who aim to help people find, prepare for and stay in work through activities such as work experience, work trials, help to become self-employed, voluntary work, training and further support. The way they do this varies and should depend on your individual needs and circumstances. Referral is normally through Jobcentre Plus.

Is it mandatory? – The programme is generally mandatory if you are considered capable of some kind of work.

If you receive jobseeker's allowance (JSA), you will have to take part in the Work Programme after nine months (if you are aged 18 to 24) or 12 months (if you are aged 25 or over). If your personal adviser agrees, you may join earlier than this if you wish. Some JSA claimants are required to take part after just three months on the benefit, eg those who have recently been moved from incapacity benefit to JSA. Ex-offenders who claim JSA within 13 weeks of their release are referred to the programme straightaway.

For some JSA claimants opting for early entry, participation will then be mandatory.

If you receive employment and support allowance (ESA) and have been placed in the work-related activity group (see Chapter 10(6)), you may have to take part in the Work Programme when you are considered close to being fit for work. Exactly when you are referred onto the programme will depend on your prognosis. Exceptions to this include lone parents with a child under 5 and full-time carers.

Other groups of people can volunteer for the Work Programme, including ESA claimants placed in the support group (see Chapter 10(7)).

Sanctions – If you receive JSA, your benefit could be suspended under a 'lower-level' sanction if you do not comply with the programme requirements (see Chapter 16(10)). If you cannot attend a training or employment scheme because of your disability, this may be accepted as a good reason for failure to comply. In some cases ESA can be reduced if you do not participate in the Work Programme (see Chapter 10(17)).

3. Work Choice

Work Choice is a programme aimed at people who are experiencing complex barriers to work arising from a disability or who are in work but at risk of losing their job as a result of disability. Participation in Work Choice is voluntary. Usually, you must be referred by a disability employment adviser (see 1 above). In some cases other specified organisations can refer, though this varies from area to area.

You will only be accepted for Work Choice if you cannot be helped through other Jobcentre Plus programmes and you must expect to be able to work at least 16 hours a week in the long term.

Work Choice consists of three modules. The modules you are offered, and the help provided in each, should be tailored to your specific situation and needs:

- **Work Entry Support** – up to six months' help with vocational guidance, confidence building, job-search advice, support with job applications and job retention skills;
- **In-Work Support** – up to two years' support once in employment. The Work Choice provider will work with you and the employer to identify the support needed and help you develop the necessary skills and knowledge to move to unsupported employment;
- **Longer-term In-Work Support** – long-term support with a focus on supporting your development through your career.

4. Mandatory Work Activity and Mandatory Work-Related Activity

Mandatory Work Activity – Under this programme, if you are receiving jobseeker's allowance (JSA) you can be required to work for up to 30 hours a week for four weeks (with no payment apart from your usual JSA). Benefit sanctions will apply if you fail to complete or participate in the activity without a *good reason* (see Chapter 16(12)).

Mandatory Work-Related Activity – Under this programme, if you are receiving employment and support allowance and are in the work-related activity group, you can be referred to a Community Benefit Work Placement if your work capability assessment is to be reviewed in 12 months. A reduction can be made to your ESA if you fail to undertake such work-related activity (see Chapter 10(17)).

5. Access to Work

Access to Work is designed to help overcome the barriers disabled people face in getting and staying in work. It provides practical advice and gives grants towards extra employment costs arising from your disability, including:

- special aids or equipment for employment;
- adaptations to existing (but not to new) premises and existing equipment;
- help with travel to work if public transport can't be used because you are disabled (a medical opinion is required before this support is granted); or support with travel training or 'buddying' to help you adapt to using public transport if you have recently become disabled;
- a support worker (eg support with training on the job if you have a learning disability, or a reader) to provide help in the workplace;
- a communicator for support at job interviews;
- an interpreter or lip speaker when you need to be meeting or communicating with others.

Excluded expenditure
Certain types of expenditure might not be covered and it is important to get clarification on this during the application process (see below). Until recently, guidance issued by Jobcentre Plus included a list of items that Access to Work would not provide grants for, as these were regarded as standard equipment. This no longer applies and Access to Work advisers have flexibility in deciding which equipment should be funded through the scheme. See Box F.2 for examples of situations where Access to Work can help.

Access to Work will not cover costs that should be met by your employer as a *'reasonable adjustment'* under the Equality Act (see Chapter 55(3)). In such cases, the adviser may discuss this with you and your employer.

Repairs and maintenance – Repairs and maintenance of equipment are not covered by Access to Work. You could check whether your employer has a duty to cover them under the Equality Act as a reasonable adjustment. Even if this duty does not apply, you could ask the employer if they would share maintenance and insurance costs, and agree that you can take the equipment if you move to another job. If you are self-employed, contact the Business Link Helpline (0845 600 9006) to see if there are other resources available.

Who can get help?
You may be eligible if you are employed (including as an apprentice), self-employed or unemployed and have a job to start, and you are disabled. Access to Work defines disability as in the Equality Act (see Chapter 55(2)) but extends it to include impairments and health conditions that are only apparent in the workplace.

Access to Work can provide help to take part in a Jobcentre Plus work trial or voluntary work experience on the Youth Contract. For others doing voluntary work, help through Access to Work is not available. In these situations it may be worth checking whether the employer will provide any disability-related support and if they need to make *'reasonable adjustments'* for you under the Equality Act (see Chapter 55(3)).

Access to Work is available if you are setting up your own business and enrolled on the new enterprise allowance (see Chapter 17(10)).

Help available for people with mental health conditions – Traditionally, Access to Work mainly helped people with sensory or physical impairments, but it is increasingly becoming available for people with mental health conditions or learning disabilities. The Mental Health Support Service is provided by Remploy and is accessed through Access to Work. The service provides a wide range of support for a period of six months for people with mental health conditions and includes:

- work-focused mental health support tailored to the individual;
- assessment of an individual's needs to identify coping strategies;
- a personalised support plan, detailing the steps needed to remain in, or return to, work;
- advice and guidance to enable employers to fully understand mental health and how they can support employees who have a mental health condition; *and*
- identifying reasonable adjustments within the workplace or within the confines of working practice.

Exclusions – You might not qualify for Access to Work if you are claiming certain benefits while working. Check this with Access to Work.

How much support can you get?

If you have been in a job for less than six weeks, are self-employed or are about to start work, Access to Work will cover 100% of approved costs. If you have been employed for six weeks or more when you apply for help, Access to Work may pay only some of the costs of certain types of support; this is called *'cost sharing'*. Whether cost-sharing applies and the exact share of the costs will depend on the number of employees in the organisation you work for. See our Access to Work factsheet for further information (www.disabilityrightsuk.org/access-work).

Access to Work funding is available for up to three years. At the end of this period your needs will be reviewed to assess if it will be continued or if further funding is required.

Applications

Contact Access to Work on 020 8426 3110 (textphone 020 8426 3133). Normally there will be a telephone interview by an Access to Work adviser to assess your eligibility. General details will be obtained, such as the employer's contact details, a brief description of the job, details of your disability or health condition and how this will affect your work (before contacting them, think about the tasks involved in the job and how your disability may impact on these).

Following this, you should be sent the completed application form (AtW1) to check, sign and return within a fixed period. An adviser may contact you for further discussion upon receipt of the form. Access to Work guidance states that the employer should normally be involved at an early stage of the application; this can only happen with your agreement. Once the assessment process is completed, you should be sent a letter confirming the amount of grant approved.

Delays – If there is a delay in the application, ask the Access to Work adviser to explore temporary alternatives. If you are employed, speak to your employer to explore what help they may give. Some cases can be processed under new fast-track procedures. When applying, check with the adviser to see if these might apply to you.

Claiming ongoing costs

You should get support approved by Access to Work before incurring costs, as otherwise it is not usually possible to claim them. You will normally need to claim costs on a 4-weekly basis, but ask Access to Work if you want to claim at different intervals. Ensure you claim costs promptly; currently this has to be done within six months, but you should check the time limits with your adviser in case this changes. If there is undue delay in getting reimbursement, check the reasons for this. In some cases, a complaint may be made (see below).

F.2 Access to Work: examples

Anne

Anne is registered blind, and has had bilateral congenital cataracts and undeveloped retinas since birth. She has some residual vision but is unable to read printed documents or see her computer screen. She works as a rehabilitation officer, working two days a week in the office and three days visiting service users in their homes. Access to Work provides Anne with funding for:

- a support worker;
- specialist software to enhance the content of her computer screen; *and*
- a large computer screen to afford the best opportunity of viewing her work.

The support worker acts as her driver, her facilitator when she is teaching orientation and mobility, and her assistant when she has lengthy reports and departmental documents to read. Anne uses Zoomtext, specialist software that enables her to use a computer in the same way as her sighted peers. The large computer screen complements the software being used, allowing her to see as much as possible.

Nicola

Nicola has bipolar disorder and experiences episodes of depression and mania. She lost her job as a management consultant following a mental breakdown and was unemployed for four years. Nicola started part-time employment as a project administrator for a mental health organisation. She needed specific support to help her return to the workplace. Her symptoms and the loss of her previous job meant it was important the support was delivered by someone she trusted.

Through Access to Work, Nicola receives a grant for a support worker/counsellor, who helps her with her job alongside managing her condition. She receives 2-hour monthly meetings and unlimited phone calls, texts and email support. She is able to discuss anxieties and regain confidence in her abilities and can manage her symptoms at work.

Danielle

Danielle works for the local hospital trust as an assistant in medical records. Her job involves tracking hospital notes, filing, merging and moving data and records and using standard office equipment. Danielle has Asperger's syndrome and needs intensive support to learn to do tasks. She also experiences difficulties with travel to and from work.

Access to Work has provided funding for a support worker to help her learn tasks and then allow her to work independently. Her role has been analysed and broken down into bite-sized chunks so she can use them as a prompt. She also gets help with travel to and from work.

Peter

Peter is deaf and uses British Sign Language (BSL) as his preferred language to communicate with others. He is a software engineer and his job involves going out to customers, having one-to-one meetings, as well as bigger meetings that frequently last for more than an hour. Peter applied to Access to Work for funding for a BSL/English interpreter for his one-to-one meetings and two BSL/English interpreters for the bigger meetings. Access to Work said that he could use a communication support worker – ie someone who is not qualified as an interpreter; and that he did not need more than one interpreter for the bigger meetings.

Peter argued that he would not be able to communicate effectively if he did not have a qualified interpreter who could interpret complex situations (including the use of technical terminology) and thus would not be able to do his job well. Furthermore, interpreting is a physically and mentally intensive job and having just one interpreter for longer and complex meetings would adversely affect the interpreting quality, and thus his ability to participate effectively in meetings.

Access to Work agreed to fund qualified interpreters and enabled Peter to use two sign language interpreters in a meeting. Also, because Peter needs more communication support in one week and less in another week, they agreed that Peter could have a budget for a certain number of hours over a year, rather than a fixed number of hours per week or per month.

Challenging decisions

Although there is no formal appeal procedure, you can ask the Access to Work manager to look at your decision again. The notification letter about the Access to Work decision should include brief information on this, although you may wish to ask the adviser for full details of the review process.

Complaints – If you want to make a complaint, write to your adviser or Access to Work regional manager. See www.gov. uk/contact-jobcentre-plus for more on the complaints process.

6. Training

There are many government training programmes and new initiatives are often launched, which you can find out about at your local Jobcentre Plus office. If you have a disability, various types of help are available to enable you to participate in government training programmes, including individually tailored programmes, aids, equipment, adaptations to premises and equipment, a readership service for blind people and an interpreter service for deaf people. Contact a disability employment adviser at your Jobcentre Plus office or ring the National Career's Service helpline (0800 100 900).

Work-Based Learning (WBL) – WBL, or Skillseekers in Scotland, is the name generally used for government schemes that allow you to achieve recognised vocational qualifications at the same time as gaining relevant, practical experience in work situations. WBL covers a number of programmes and courses, such as apprenticeships or combining a job with study towards a vocational qualification. In WBL, you can be an employed or unemployed trainee. If you are not employed while training, a training allowance might be available.

Youth Contract – This is a package of support (including wage incentives for employers) to help young unemployed people to prepare for work and find a job. It focuses on improving opportunities for 18-24-year-olds through apprenticeships, sector-based work academy opportunities, careers guidance and voluntary work placements.

Apprenticeships – An apprenticeship is a real job with training. Apprentices work alongside experienced staff to gain job-specific skills. Off the job, usually on a day-release basis, apprentices receive training to work towards a nationally recognised qualification. If you are employed on an apprenticeship scheme, you must be paid at least the national minimum wage for apprentices (see Box F.1). If you are aged 19 or over and have completed the first year of an apprenticeship, the full national minimum wage for your age must be paid. For information, including vacancy and registration details, go to www.apprenticeships.org.uk or www.skillsdevelopmentscotland.co.uk.

Time to Train – If you work in an organisation with 250 or more employees you have the statutory right to request time for study or training. To qualify, you must have worked for your employer continuously for at least 26 weeks. You only have the right to request time for training leading to a qualification or training to help develop skills relevant to your job or workplace. Your employer does not have to pay for the training. However, if they recognise the benefit of the training to their business they may choose to pay for it. Your employer may pay you for the training time but they do not have to.

Residential training programme – This programme aims to help long-term unemployed adults overcome disability-related barriers to employment. It provides a combination of guidance, learning in the workplace, work experience and training. The programme will be tailored to your needs and can run for a maximum of 52 weeks, although it will usually be much shorter. You can apply if you are unable to get training in your local area and are in receipt of any benefit, or just signing on for national insurance credits. Referral to residential training can only be made by a disability employment adviser.

7. Benefits and training allowances

Disability living allowance (DLA) and personal independence payment (PIP)

DLA and PIP are not usually affected if you get a training allowance. However, DLA care component and PIP daily living component will not usually be paid for any days that you stay in a care home to attend a residential training programme, although there is a 28-day concession available (see Chapter 4(8)). You can get the care component or daily living component for any days spent at home.

Although DLA and PIP can be paid at the same time as a training allowance, your ability to start a training programme may suggest a lessening in your care or mobility needs, so your benefit may be reconsidered.

Income support and jobseeker's allowance

If you are under 24, are on Work-based Learning for Young People and are not a *'qualifying young person'* (see Chapter 38(1)) you can claim income support to top up your training allowance. See Chapter 27(11) for how the training allowance is treated in the income support calculation.

IS Regs, Sch 1B, para 28

Once you leave the programme, you are no longer eligible for income support unless you are covered by one of the other situations listed in Box E.1, Chapter 15. You should claim jobseeker's allowance (JSA) instead. Sanctions to JSA may apply if you do not complete the programme and do not have *'good reason'* for leaving (see Chapter 16(9)). If you are an employee, and you are not paid a training allowance, you may qualify for tax credits (see Chapter 19).

Disability premium – If you were getting a disability premium before beginning the programme, it will not be withdrawn even though you may no longer be receiving the qualifying benefit. At the end of the programme, you will continue to receive the disability premium only if you satisfy the entitlement criteria (see Chapter 25(2)).

IS Regs, Sch 2, para 7(1)(b)

Employment and support allowance (ESA) and incapacity benefits

A day in receipt of a state training allowance (other than just travel and meals expenses) cannot count as a day of incapacity for work or limited capability for work. This means that on starting a programme that includes a state training allowance you will cease to be entitled to ESA, incapacity benefit or severe disablement allowance.

IB Regs, reg 4(1)(c) & (2)(c); ESA Regs, reg 32(2)&(3)(b)

If you do not find a job at the end of your programme, and are fit for work, you can sign on and claim jobseeker's allowance (JSA) – see Chapter 16.

Non-government training courses

On a non-government training course you may be paid an allowance, but it is treated differently from a state training allowance. It will be taken into account in full as income for income support and other means-tested benefits unless some or all of it can be disregarded under the normal rules.

You may be regarded as a student for benefit purposes. Most full-time students are excluded from income-related ESA, income support and JSA (see Chapter 40). The rules are complicated, so seek advice. There are no rules to prevent someone from studying or training on a non-government course and receiving contributory ESA, incapacity benefit or severe disablement allowance. However, the assessment of your ability to undertake the activities in the work capability assessment will take into account how you manage on your course. Starting a course may lead to your incapacity or limited capability for work being reassessed. If your course is funded by the European Social Fund, seek advice.

Tax credits

This section of the Handbook looks at:

19 Tax credits

1. What are tax credits?

Tax credits are means-tested or income-related tax-free payments administered by HMRC at the Tax Credit Office (see inside back cover for contact details). They consist of one or more elements (see 4 and 7 below). All the elements you are eligible for are added together. The total is compared to your income (see 9 below) and any reduction due to this income is calculated (as explained in Chapter 19). The resulting amount, if any, is your actual tax credit award. The elements fall into two types:

Child tax credit (CTC) – CTC is for people, whether working or not, who are responsible for children. It replaced child allowances in income support and income-based jobseeker's allowance (JSA), and the increases for child dependants paid with non-means-tested benefits. See Box G.1 for transitional rules.

Working tax credit (WTC) – WTC is for those in low-paid work, whether or not they are responsible for children.

The benefit cap

CTC is included in the list of benefits to which the 'benefit cap' will apply. This cap, which will be rolled out nationally between 15.7.13 and 30.9.13, limits the total weekly benefits that can be claimed. It will not apply if you qualify for WTC. See Box H.1 in Chapter 21 for details.

Future plans

The government is replacing tax credits with universal credit. This is being piloted from April 2013 in north-west England; nationwide roll-out starts in October 2013 on the basis of one district in each Jobcentre Plus region. A new claim after April 2013 may be treated as a claim for universal credit instead of tax credits, depending on where you live.

If you already receive tax credits, in which case your claim has to be renewed every tax year, there will come a point between April 2014 and 2017 when you will have to claim universal credit instead (at the time of publication, it is not clear when this will be). See Box J.1 in Chapter 25 for more on universal credit.

Will you be better off going back to work?

Going back to work usually means some benefits will stop (eg employment and support allowance (ESA)), some carry on as normal (eg the new personal independence payment) and others continue at a reduced rate depending on income (eg housing benefit). Box F.1 in Chapter 17 outlines benefits and other help available when you start work. To work out whether you might be better off on tax credits, note the following points.

❑ You may be able to earn up to £99.50 a week from 'permitted work' on top of ESA, incapacity benefit or severe disablement allowance. You may be better off doing this (see Chapter 17(3)).

❑ Income-related ESA, income-based JSA and income support may include an amount to cover mortgage interest payments, while tax credits do not.

❑ Depending on your level of tax credits, you may be entitled to free prescriptions and other health benefits (see Chapter 54), free legal help (see Chapter 59(2)) and disabled facilities grants (see Chapter 31).

❑ Tax credits (WTC that includes a disability or severe disability element, or CTC above the family element) may give you access to the Sure Start maternity grant and social fund funeral payment (see Chapter 23).

❑ Income-related ESA, income-based JSA and income support entitle your children to free school lunches, and vouchers for milk, fruit and vegetables under the Healthy Start scheme if they are under 4 (see Chapter 54(6)). You are generally not entitled to these if you receive tax credits. (In England or Wales you are entitled, however, if you get CTC *without any* WTC and have annual taxable income of £16,190 or less. The rules differ in Scotland.)

2. Do you qualify for CTC?

You can get CTC if you meet all the following conditions when you make your claim:

■ you are at least 16 years old;

■ you (or your partner) are responsible for a child or qualifying young person who normally lives with you (see 3 below);

■ you satisfy the residence and presence conditions and are not subject to immigration control (see Chapter 49);

■ your income (see 9 below) is low enough for CTC to be paid. See Chapter 20 for the calculation.

If you are one of a couple you claim jointly and your claim is called a *'joint claim'*. Otherwise, you claim as a single person. Your entitlement will end immediately if you are part of a couple who separate or one of you dies, or if you are a single claimant who becomes part of a couple. Your entitlement will also usually end if you cease to be responsible for any children or qualifying young people (see 3 below). A *'couple'* is defined as: a married couple or civil partners (unless separated under court order or separation is likely to be permanent), or two people living together as though they were a married couple or civil partners. See Chapter 20(8) if you have an overpayment because you delayed reporting a change in status (going from a joint to single claim or the other way round).

TCA, S.3

3. Responsible for a child or qualifying young person

A child is someone aged under 16. Between their 16th birthday and the following 31st August, they will be treated as a *'qualifying young person'* without the requirement to be in full-time non-advanced education or approved training. To continue to be treated as a qualifying young person after that date, they must be under 20 and in full-time, non-advanced education or approved training. If they are 19, they must have been accepted or enrolled onto the education or training course *before* the age of 19. Non-advanced education includes anything up to A-level or equivalent.

Following their 16th birthday, young people will no longer count for tax credit purposes once they:

■ cease full-time education or approved training and start work (of at least 24 hours a week);
■ undertake training provided under a contract of employment; *or*
■ claim employment and support allowance (ESA), jobseeker's allowance or income support in their own right.

Young people can continue to count for tax credit purposes for the first 20 weeks after they leave the education or training if they are under the age of 18 and registered for work or training with a 'qualifying body' (ie the Careers or Connexions Service, the Ministry of Defence or in Northern Ireland, the Department for Employment and Learning or an Education and Library Board).

CTC Regs, regs 2, 4 & 5

If two or more households make a claim for the same child (eg the child of separated parents spends time with both), the two households may agree who will receive CTC for that child. If they cannot agree, HMRC will decide for them.

You do not count as responsible for a child or young person who:

■ has been placed by a local authority in certain types of care accommodation;
■ has been placed for adoption with you by a local authority that is making specific payments in respect of their accommodation or maintenance;
■ is serving a custodial sentence of more than four months;
■ is 16 or older and claiming CTC for their own child, WTC or contributory ESA; *or*
■ is living with a spouse or partner (opposite or same sex) who is not in full-time education or approved training.

CTC is not payable if you are the partner of the young person and you live together.

CTC Regs, reg 3

If a child or young person dies during the period of an award, CTC will normally continue for eight weeks following their death.

CTC Regs, reg 6

4. CTC elements

CTC is made up of the following elements.

Family element – one element per family.

Child element – one element per child or qualifying young person (see 3 above) in the family.

Disabled child element – This is included if any child or qualifying young person:

■ receives either component of disability living allowance (DLA), or personal independence payment (PIP) at any rate (or would do but for the fact that they are a hospital inpatient), or armed forces independence payment (AFIP) *or*
■ is registered as blind, or has ceased to be registered within 28 weeks of the claim for CTC being made.

Severely disabled child element – This is included if any child or qualifying young person receives DLA highest rate care component or PIP enhanced rate daily living component (or would do but for the fact that they are in hospital) or AFIP.

CTC Regs, regs 7 & 8

Backdating the elements – If you have been waiting for a child or young person to be awarded DLA or PIP, as long as you inform the Tax Credit Office within one month of the date it is awarded, the disabled and/or severely disabled child element(s) can be backdated to the date that DLA or PIP became payable (or to the date of the CTC claim, if that is later).

TC(C&N) Regs, regs 26A

5. Do you qualify for WTC?

You can get WTC if you are at least 16 years old and either you or your partner are working for 16 or more hours a week, provided that at least one of the following conditions apply:

■ you are single parent responsible for a child or qualifying young person; *or*
■ you are a couple, one or both of you are responsible for a child or qualifying young person, one of you works at least 16 hours a week and you work at least 24 hours a week between you; *or*
■ you are a couple, one or both of you are responsible for a child or qualifying young person and one of you works at least 16 hours a week where the other partner is:
  – in hospital; *or*
  – in prison; *or*
  – entitled to carer's allowance; *or*
  – 'incapacitated' (see 7 below under 'Childcare element' for the definition); *or*
■ you or your partner qualify for the disability element (see 8 below); *or*
■ you are aged 60 or over.

Otherwise, you can only qualify if you are aged 25 or over and work at least 30 hours a week.

You must also satisfy the residence and presence conditions (see Chapter 49(2)), not be subject to immigration control (see Chapter 49(3)) and your income (see 9 below) must be low enough for WTC to be paid. See Chapter 20 for the calculation.

If you are part of a couple, you claim WTC jointly and your claim is called a joint claim. Otherwise you claim as a single person. Your entitlement will end immediately if you are part of a couple who separate or one of you dies, or you are a single claimant who becomes part of a couple.

G.1 Child tax credit: transitional rules

CTC replacing child allowances and premiums

For many years, the government has planned that CTC would replace the child allowances and premiums within income support and income-based jobseeker's allowance – ie, the personal allowances for dependent children, the family premium, disabled child premiums and enhanced disability premiums for children. The deadline for the changeover has been put back to 31.12.14, by which time universal credit will have been introduced (see Box J.1, Chapter 25). This means many claimants will be transferred onto universal credit without ever claiming CTC.

TCA(FCTP)O reg 3

Child dependant increases

Child dependant increases within non-means-tested benefits (such as incapacity benefit, severe disablement allowance, bereavement benefits and state pension) were abolished for new claimants from 6.4.03. After that date, you claim CTC instead. However, if you were receiving a child dependant increase on 5.4.03, you will continue receiving it until you no longer meet the qualifying conditions.

See Chapter 20(8) if you have an overpayment because you delayed reporting a change in status (going from a joint to single claim or the other way round). WTC will also usually end if you cease working the right number of hours to qualify (see above and 6 below).

TCA, S.10 & WTC(E&MR) Regs, reg 4(1)

6. What does and does not count as work?

In order to be treated as being in *'qualifying remunerative work'* you must *either*:

■ be working at the date of your claim, and the work must be expected to continue for at least four weeks after you claim; *or*

■ have an offer of work which you are expected to start within seven days of making your claim, and the work must be expected to last for at least four weeks.

'Work' means work done for, or in expectation of, payment. If you are an employee, the number of hours that count are the number of hours you normally work each week, including any regular overtime. If you are self-employed, the number of hours that count are those you work in your self-employed capacity, including time on *'activities necessary to'* your self-employed activity, eg bookkeeping or distributing advertising flyers. In calculating the number of hours you work, disregard time spent on unpaid meal breaks or periods of customary or paid holiday.

WTC(E&MR) Regs, reg 4

Exceptionally, if you work in a school, college, university (or otherwise work on a seasonal basis) and you have a recognisable pattern of employment over the year which includes periods when you do not work, you may ignore the school holidays or other holiday periods. This rule benefits people like school lunches staff who might otherwise be found not to be working enough hours to qualify.

WTC(E&MR) Regs, reg 7

When you are not treated as being in work

Some kinds of work do not count:

■ work for a charitable or voluntary organisation or otherwise as a volunteer if you are only paid expenses;

■ work on a training scheme where you are paid a training allowance (unless taxable as trade profit);

■ work while you are in prison;

■ activities when you are in receipt of a sports award and no other form of payment is made to you;

■ caring for someone who is temporarily living with you if the only payment you get is from a local authority, health authority, primary care trust, voluntary organisation or the cared-for person, and your income is below the taxable limit for this sort of work. However, foster carers, adult placement carers and other shared-lives carers are able to claim WTC in respect of their care work.

WTC(E&MR) Regs, reg 4(2)

When you are treated as being in work

You can qualify for WTC during certain interruptions or after you have stopped working, provided you were in qualifying remunerative work immediately beforehand. Your working hours will be treated as the same as before in the following circumstances.

❑ You are not working because you are sick. You continue to be treated as being in work for a period of up to 28 weeks while you receive statutory sick pay (SSP), employment and support allowance or limited capability for work national insurance credits. If you are self-employed and off sick, you will be treated as being in work if you would have got SSP but for the fact that self-employed people are not entitled to it.

WTC(E&MR) Regs, reg 6

❑ You have recently finished working (or started to work for less than the required hours each week). You are treated as being in qualifying remunerative work for four weeks, allowing for a 4-week run-on of WTC.

WTC(E&MR) Regs, reg 7D

❑ You are off work and getting maternity allowance or statutory maternity pay (SMP) or statutory adoption pay (SAP), or you are on ordinary maternity or adoption leave, including the first 13 weeks of any additional maternity or adoption leave. If you are self-employed and off work due to birth or adoption, you will be treated as being in work if you would have met these rules but for the fact that self-employed people are not entitled to SMP/SAP or maternity leave.

❑ If you worked less than 30 hours and only satisfy the remunerative work rule after the birth or adoption of your first child, you are treated as in qualifying remunerative work during such leave from the date of the birth or adoption.

❑ You are off work and getting ordinary statutory paternity pay (SPP) or additional SPP, or you are on ordinary paternity leave or additional paternity leave (providing, in the latter case, that you would have been paid additional SPP if you had met the conditions of entitlement).

WTC(E&MR) Regs, regs 5 & 5A

❑ You are temporarily suspended from work while complaints or allegations against you are being investigated.

WTC(E&MR) Regs, reg 7B

❑ You are on strike, but only for a period of up to ten consecutive days on which you would normally work.

WTC(E&MR) Regs, reg 7A

7. WTC elements

WTC is made up of a number of elements. If you are a couple and qualify for more than one disability element or severe disability element they will all be included in the calculation.

Basic element – This will be included in the calculation for all who qualify for WTC.

TCA, S.11(2)

Couple element – This will be included if you are one of a couple (see 2 above). If you are not responsible for a child or qualifying young person (see 3 above), this element is not included where one partner is subject to immigration control or is in prison.

WTC(E&MR) Regs, reg 11

Lone parent element – This will be included if you are single and responsible for a child or qualifying young person.

WTC(E&MR) Regs, reg 12

30-hour element – This will be included if you:

■ work at least 30 hours a week; *or*

■ are part of a couple and:
  – you are responsible for a child or qualifying young person; *and*
  – between you, you work at least 30 hours a week; *and*
  – at least one of you works at least 16 hours a week.

Note: you can only get one 30-hour element, even if you are a couple who both work at least 30 hours a week.

WTC(E&MR) Regs, reg 10

Disability element – See 8 below.

Severe disability element – This will be included if you get higher rate attendance allowance or disability living allowance highest rate care component, or personal independence payment enhanced rate daily living component (or would but for the fact that you are in hospital) or armed forces independence payment. If you are part of a couple and one of you meets this test, you get one severe disability element. If both of you meet this test, you get two. The person who meets this test does not have to be the person who is working.

WTC(E&MR) Regs, reg 17

Childcare element

This is 70% of eligible childcare costs, up to a maximum of £175 a week for one child and £300 a week for two or more children. Therefore the highest childcare element you can get is £122.50 a week for one child or £210 for two or more children.

You include the childcare element if you are:

- a lone parent working at least 16 hours a week; *or*
- one of a couple and you both work at least 16 hours a week; *or*
- one of a couple and one of you works at least 16 hours a week and the other is 'incapacitated' (see below), entitled to carer's allowance, in hospital or in prison.

If you are on maternity, paternity or adoption leave, you can be treated as being in work and may get help with childcare costs for a new child (see 6 above).

You count as *'incapacitated'* if you receive:

- housing benefit that includes a disability premium or higher pensioner premium, or if you have already been counted as 'incapacitated' for the purposes of housing benefit childcare costs; *or*
- incapacity benefit, contributory employment and support allowance (providing you have been entitled to it for at least 28 weeks – including linked periods and periods on statutory sick pay when you otherwise satisfied the contribution conditions), attendance allowance, severe disablement allowance, disability living allowance, personal independence payment, constant attendance allowance (payable with the Industrial Injuries or War Pensions schemes), or war pensions mobility supplement (or would get one of these benefits but for the fact that you are a hospital inpatient) or armed forces independence payment.

In order for you to qualify, your child(ren) must be aged 15 or younger, or aged 16 or younger if they meet the rules for the CTC disabled child element (see 4 above). You can claim a childcare element up to the last day of the week containing the 1st September following their 15th birthday, or following their 16th birthday if they are disabled.

Childcare must be provided by a registered or approved provider. If you have arranged the childcare but it hasn't started by the time you make your claim, the amount is based on an estimate provided by the childcare provider.

If your childcare costs vary (eg you pay more during school holidays), it is your average weekly costs that will be taken into account in the calculation. If you pay childcare only for a short period (eg only for the 6-week summer holiday) you can choose to average the costs over that period. If there is a change while you are getting WTC and your average weekly childcare charges go down by £10 a week or more, or stop, you must report this promptly (see Chapter 20(4)). Your WTC will then be recalculated.

WTC(E&MR) Regs, regs 13-16. See also booklet WTC5 (www.hmrc.gov.uk/ leaflets/wtc5.pdf)

8. WTC disability element

This element is a significant one for disabled people. In addition to working at least 16 hours a week, you have to satisfy two other tests, one relating to your disability and one to your receipt (or recent receipt) of a qualifying benefit. For couples, the partner who works must meet the disability and qualifying benefit tests. So, if you are working and not disabled, but have a disabled partner who is not working, you will not receive the disability element. You may, however, receive the severe disability element (see 7 above). Conversely, if both you and your partner meet the rules about working and about disability and qualifying benefits, you can receive two disability elements.

G.2 The 'disability' test

Disability that puts you at a disadvantage in getting a job

You will pass the disability test for working tax credit (WTC) if:

- on an initial claim, any one (or more) of the conditions in Parts 1 or 2 apply to you;
- on a renewal claim, any one (or more) of the conditions in Part 1 apply to you.

Part 1

❑ When standing you cannot keep your balance unless you continually hold on to something.

❑ Using any crutches, walking frame, walking stick, prosthesis or similar walking aid which you habitually use, you cannot walk a continuous distance of 100 metres along level ground without stopping or without suffering severe pain.

❑ You can use neither of your hands behind your back as in the process of putting on a jacket or of tucking a shirt into trousers.

❑ You can extend neither of your arms in front of you so as to shake hands with another person without difficulty.

❑ You can put neither of your hands up to your head without difficulty so as to put on a hat.

❑ Due to lack of manual dexterity you cannot with one hand pick up a coin which is not more than 2.5 cm in diameter.

❑ You are not able to use your hands or arms to pick up a full jug of one litre capacity and pour from it into a cup, without difficulty.

❑ You can turn neither of your hands sideways through 180 degrees.

❑ You are registered as blind or partially sighted.

❑ You cannot see to read 16-point print at a distance greater than 20 centimetres, if appropriate, wearing the glasses you normally use.

❑ You cannot hear a telephone ring when you are in the same room as the telephone, if appropriate, using a hearing aid you normally use.

❑ In a quiet room you have difficulty hearing what someone talking in a loud voice at a distance of 2 metres says, if appropriate, using a hearing aid you normally use.

❑ People who know you well have difficulty in understanding what you say.

❑ When a person you know well speaks to you, you have difficulty in understanding what that person says.

❑ At least once a year during waking hours you have a coma or fit in which you lose consciousness.

❑ You have a mental illness for which you receive regular treatment under the supervision of a medically qualified person.

❑ Due to mental disability you are often confused or forgetful.

❑ You cannot do the simplest addition and subtraction.

❑ Due to mental disability you strike people or damage property or are unable to form normal social relationships.

❑ You cannot normally sustain an 8-hour working day or a 5-day working week due to a medical condition or intermittent or continuous severe pain.

Part 2

❑ As a result of an illness or accident you are undergoing a period of habilation or rehabilitation.

WTC(E&MR) Regs, Sch 1

The 'disability' test

To get the disability element of WTC included in your assessment, you must have a *'physical or mental disability which puts [you] at a disadvantage in getting a job'*. How this is assessed depends on whether you are making an initial claim or a renewal claim.

Initial claims – If you are claiming WTC for the first time you need to meet the rules set out in *either* Part 1 *or* Part 2 of Box G.2.

Renewal claims – When making a WTC renewal claim you need to meet the rules set out in Part 1 of Box G.2.

The 'qualifying benefit' test

To get the disability element of WTC included in your assessment, you must also meet *one* of the following conditions.

❏ **Condition A** – At any time in the last 26 weeks before your claim, you were getting: employment and support allowance (ESA) or limited capability for work national insurance credits (providing in either case you had been entitled to it for at least 28 weeks, including linked periods and periods on statutory sick pay (SSP)) or incapacity benefit or severe disablement allowance (SDA).

❏ **Condition B** – At any time in the last 26 weeks before your claim, you were getting the disability premium or higher pensioner premium in income support, income-based jobseeker's allowance, housing benefit or council tax benefit.

❏ **Condition C** – You get disability living allowance (DLA – either component, any rate) or personal independence payment (PIP – either component, either rate) or attendance allowance (or an Industrial Injuries or War Pensions scheme equivalent) or armed forces independence payment. You must meet this condition throughout the period of your claim, not just at the start of it (R(TC)1/06).

❏ **Condition D** – On the date of your claim, and throughout your claim (R(TC)1/06), you have a Motability car.

❏ **Condition E** – This route to the disability element is referred to as the *'Fast Track'* because it allows some of those who have been off work for a while to return to work without having either to have been off sick for a prolonged period or to fit the qualifying rules for DLA, PIP, etc (as in Conditions A to D). At the date of claim:

■ you have a disability likely to last at least six months (or for the rest of your life if your death is expected within six months); *and*

■ your gross earnings are less than they were before your disability began, by at least 20% or £15 a week, whichever is greater; *and*

■ at any time in the last eight weeks before you claim, you had been getting, for at least 20 weeks: ESA, SSP, occupational sick pay, incapacity benefit, income support paid on the basis of incapacity, or national insurance credits on the basis that you were incapable of work or had a limited capability for work.

❏ **Condition F** – At any time in the last eight weeks before you claim, you:

■ had been undertaking training for work (which means certain government training courses or a course of 16 hours or more a week learning occupational or vocational skills); *and*

■ within the eight weeks prior to the start of the training course, had been getting incapacity benefit, SDA, contributory ESA or limited capability for work national insurance credits (providing in the latter two cases, you have been entitled to it for at least 28 weeks – including linked periods and periods on SSP when you otherwise satisfied the contribution conditions).

❏ **Condition G** – You will be treated as qualifying for the disability element if, within the eight weeks before your

claim (including renewal claims), you were entitled to the disability element of tax credits by virtue of Condition A, B, E or F. This allows those who were getting a qualifying benefit, such as ESA, to continue to get the WTC disability element long after they stopped receiving that benefit. If you got the disability element because you met Condition C or D, as you were in receipt of, for example, DLA or PIP, you must be currently receiving that benefit.
WTC(E&MR) Regs, reg 9

9. Income and savings

CTC and WTC have no 'capital limits', that is, there is no upper limit on savings above which they are not payable. However, income from savings is taken into account in the calculation (see below).

The rules on what income is taken into account for tax credits are largely based on income tax legislation. The general rule is that taxable income is taken into account and other income is ignored, although there are some exceptions.
TC(DCI) Regs 2002

Income that has the first £300 ignored

The following will be included in the calculation except that the first £300 a year of the total is ignored:

■ pension income, but excluding war disablement pensions, war pensioners mobility supplement and certain other war service pensions that are exempt from income tax;

■ investment income;

■ property income;

■ most foreign income, although some foreign income is ignored entirely, eg payments to victims of Nazi persecution;

■ notional income; the rules are similar, but not identical, to those for means-tested benefits – see Chapter 27(20).
TC(DCI) Regs, regs 5, 10, 11, 12 & 13-17

Employment income

All taxable income from employment is usually taken into account. In contrast to means-tested benefits, income from employment is taken into account gross, that is, before income tax and national insurance contributions have been deducted. Such income includes:

■ PAYE income from employment, including pay, holiday pay, bonus and commission;

■ payment for expenses not *'wholly, exclusively and necessarily incurred'* in your job;

■ cash vouchers, non-cash vouchers or credit tokens (but not if for eligible childcare – see 'Disregarded employment income' below);

■ the value of a car for private use and the fuel (but not if you are a disabled employee with an adapted or automatic company car);

■ goods or assets your employer gave you that you could sell for cash (eg gifts of food) or payments made by your employer that you should have paid yourself (eg if they paid your rent or gas bill);

■ redundancy payments to the extent they are subject to income tax;

■ statutory sick pay;

■ statutory maternity, paternity or adoption pay – but only the amount in excess of £100 a week;

■ certain retainer fees;

■ strike pay;

■ taxable gains from security options (eg company shares, bonds, government gilts) acquired as a result of your employment.

Some tax exempt payments made from your earnings are ignored in calculating your gross income, including:

■ gross contributions to a pension scheme or retirement annuity contract;

- fees and subscriptions to professional bodies, employee liabilities and indemnity insurance;
- contributions to charity under Gift Aid or Give-As-You-Earn.

Disregarded employment income
All the following income from employment is disregarded:
- payments for expenses *'wholly, exclusively and necessarily incurred'* in your job;
- qualifying travelling expenses for tax purposes;
- the provision of transport to a disabled employee, if it is exempt from income tax;
- car parking at work;
- certain overnight expenses or removal expenses;
- cash vouchers or equivalents for childcare costs of the sort that would be included for WTC (see 7 above);
- meal vouchers received as an employee;
- certain taxable benefits provided by an employer that do not have to be reported for tax credit purposes, eg the provision of living accommodation and cheap loans;
- operational allowances paid to members of HM forces in respect of service in certain areas, eg Afghanistan;
- the provision of one mobile phone to an employee, if it is exempt from income tax.

TC(DCI) Regs, reg 4

Self-employment income
Your taxable profit for income tax purposes, as a sole trader or a partner in a business, is taken into account. You can deduct the following items from your taxable profit:
- gross contributions to a pension scheme or retirement annuity;
- current year trading losses and in some cases those brought forward from a previous year;
- gross Gift Aid payments.

If your business made a loss, contact the Tax Credit Helpline (see 10 below), as there are special rules dealing with losses.

TC(DCI) Regs, reg 4

Benefit income
All benefit income is taken into account in full as income, except:
- Armed Forces Compensation scheme payments;
- attendance allowance;
- bereavement payment;
- child benefit;
- Christmas bonus;
- disability living allowance;
- guardian's allowance;
- housing benefit and discretionary housing payments;
- incapacity benefit for people previously in receipt of invalidity benefit and still in the same period of incapacity for work;
- industrial injuries benefits (except industrial death benefit);
- income-based jobseeker's allowance (JSA);
- income-related employment and support allowance;
- income support, except to strikers;
- in-work credit;
- maternity allowance;
- pension credit;
- personal independence payment;
- return to work credit;
- severe disablement allowance;
- social fund payments;
- certain compensation payments, including compensation payments for the non-payment of income support, JSA or housing benefit;
- payments in lieu of milk tokens or vitamins.

TC(DCI) Regs, reg 7

Student grants
Student grants and loans are ignored (except grants for adult dependants and lone parents).

TC(DCI) Regs, regs 8 & 9

Other income
Most other forms of taxable income are counted for tax credits. The following are ignored:
- mandatory top-up payments (and discretionary payments to help meet special needs) to those taking part in certain training or employment programmes;
- payments made to disabled people to help them obtain or retain employment;
- adoption allowances;
- fostering allowances and allowances paid to adult placement carers and other shared-lives carers, to the extent that they do not exceed certain tax-exempt limits;
- maintenance payments;
- income of any child or qualifying young person for whom you claim CTC.

This is not an exhaustive list.

TC(DCI) Regs, reg 19

10. Claiming tax credits
Claims for CTC or WTC are made on claim-form TC600, available from the Tax Credit Helpline (0345 300 3900 or textphone 0345 300 3909).

You must provide a valid national insurance number, or information or evidence to enable one to be traced. If you are unable to make a claim on your own behalf, it can be done by your appointee or someone empowered to act on your behalf.

TC(C&N) Regs, regs 5, 17 & 18

Backdating claims – If you meet the qualifying conditions, tax credits can be backdated for one month – or longer if entitlement to WTC is dependent on the disability or severe disability element being included in the calculation. If you claim WTC within one month of the decision awarding a qualifying benefit for one of these elements, the claim can be backdated to the date on which the qualifying benefit became payable or, if later, the first day on which your eligibility for WTC is dependent on receipt of the qualifying benefit. You must satisfy all the other conditions for WTC throughout this backdated period.

TC(C&N) Regs, regs 7 & 8

Renewal claims – If you got tax credits in 2012/13, HMRC will send renewal papers early in the 2013/14 tax year. The renewal process involves establishing your final entitlement for 2012/13 by establishing your actual income and circumstances in that year. Your 2012/13 income and current circumstances are used as the basis for your initial award in 2013/14. If you are required to complete and return the forms, you must do so by 31.7.13. If you have difficulty giving final income details for 2012/13 (eg because you were self-employed and your accounts are not yet available), you should still provide an estimate by 31.7.13 and provide the actual figure by 31.1.14. If you miss the deadline, but renew within 30 days of the notice stating that your payments will stop, your renewal is treated as if made on time. Alternatively, HMRC may allow you until 31.1.14 to renew if you had good cause for not renewing on time. Otherwise, you may have to make a new claim, which can be backdated by one month only.

You can withdraw from the tax credit system by finalising your previous year's income and responding to the final notice stating that you no longer wish to claim tax credits for the new tax year. However, it is important to act quickly, as you may have to pay back any provisional payments you receive between 6.4.13 and the withdrawal date. Either partner of a couple who separate during the renewal period will be able to complete the renewal process by responding to the final notice.

TC(C&N) Regs, regs 11 & 12

11. Payment of tax credits

In the case of couples, CTC and help with childcare costs are normally paid to the main carer, while WTC, apart from help with childcare costs, is normally paid to the worker.

Payments are normally made by credit transfer to a bank account or similar account. Payments into your account will be made weekly or 4-weekly; this is generally your choice, but HMRC has the power to change it.

The Tax Credits (Payments by the Board) Regulations 2002

12. Penalties

Tax credits contain a system of financial penalties. (Note: the new £50 'civil penalty', see Chapter 57(8), applies only to DWP benefits, not to tax credits.)

A penalty of up to £3,000 can be imposed if you *'fraudulently or negligently'* make an incorrect statement or declaration or give incorrect information or evidence either in connection with your claim or when you are informing HMRC of a change of circumstances. If you claim as a couple, the penalty can be imposed on either of you, unless one of you can show you were not aware and could not *'reasonably have been expected'* to be aware that your partner was making a false statement or providing incorrect information or evidence about your claim. You can also be subject to this penalty if you make a false statement when you are acting for someone else.

A penalty of up to £300 can be imposed if you fail to provide information or evidence that HMRC has asked you to provide in connection with your claim, or if you fail to notify HMRC of a change of circumstances which it is obligatory to report. This penalty can be increased by up to £60 a day for each day that you continue to fail to provide the required information, but will not be imposed if you have a reasonable excuse for not providing it.

TCA, Ss.31 & 32

13. Revisions, appeals and complaints

HMRC can end or amend your tax credit award at any time. They can do so if you have told them of a change of circumstances (see Chapter 20(4)) or if they have *'reasonable grounds'* for believing you should be getting a different or nil amount. If there has been an official error by HMRC or the DWP, HMRC can revise a decision in your favour up to five years after the date of the decision.

The rules on appeals are similar but not identical to those for other social security benefits. Chapter 58 gives details of how to challenge a decision. Some specific differences are:

❏ You have 30 days to appeal to the First-tier Tribunal against a tax credit decision.
❏ Notice of appeal must be sent to the Tax Credit Office.
❏ Appeals up to a year late may be allowed in some cases.
❏ Your notice of appeal must state your grounds of appeal. The tribunal may allow you to put forward grounds that were not specified in your notice if they think the omission was *'not wilful or unreasonable'*.
❏ There is no right of appeal against a decision to recover an overpayment, so arguments about *'failure to disclose'* or *'misrepresentation'* are irrelevant. However, you may be able to appeal against the underlying decision(s) that led HMRC to believe they overpaid you.

It is standard practice for the Tax Credit Office to contact you by phone to settle with you if you submit a valid appeal. You may persist with your appeal if you do not wish to negotiate in this way.

TCA 2002, Ss.38 & 39; The Tax Credits (Appeals) Regs 2002; The Tax Credits (Notice of Appeals) Regs 2002

Complaints – The HMRC complaints procedure is set out in the factsheet *Complaints* (www.hmrc.gov.uk/factsheets/complaints-factsheet.pdf). If you are not satisfied with the internal HMRC process, you can refer the matter to the Adjudicator's Office (www.adjudicatorsoffice.gov.uk; 0300 057 1111). Beyond the Adjudicator, you can approach the Parliamentary and Health Service Ombudsman (see Chapter 60(5)) through your MP, but the Ombudsman will normally expect you to have exhausted all other routes, including the Adjudicator, before considering your complaint.

20 Calculating tax credits

1. Introduction

Child tax credit (CTC) and working tax credit (WTC) calculations are based on the maximum annual amount that you could receive in the tax year (6 April to the following 5 April). Entitlement is based on daily, not annual, rates. You can be entitled to tax credits at different rates for different periods (known as *'relevant periods'*) during the tax year, in which case entitlement is calculated separately for the number of days in each relevant period.

Initially, the income taken into account is your income in the previous tax year. So, if you are awarded WTC/CTC in 2013/14, it is initially based on your income in 2012/13. Your award can be based on current tax year income instead if your income has gone up by more than a certain amount (see 5 below) or down (see 6 below) since the previous tax year.

The final decision on your entitlement is made after the end of the tax year and is normally based on the lower of either your actual income for that year or the previous year (subject to the 'disregards' at 5 and 6 below).

2. Rates of CTC and WTC

The elements described in Chapter 19(4) and (7) are:

CTC elements 2013/14	yearly amount
Family element	£545
Child element	£2,720
Disabled child element	£3,015
Severely disabled child element	£1,220

WTC elements 2013/14	yearly amount
Basic element	£1,920
Couple element	£1,970
Lone parent element	£1,970
30-hour element	£790
Severe disability element	£1,220
Disability element	£2,855
Childcare element*	(weekly amount)
– maximum eligible cost for one child	£175
– maximum eligible cost for two or more children	£300

* Childcare element is paid at 70% of actual childcare costs – the maximum you can receive is £122.50 for one child or £210 for two or more children.

CTC Regs, reg 7; WTC(E&MR) Regs, reg 20 & Sch 2

3. Steps in the tax credit calculation

To work out your tax credits for a whole tax year, use the steps below and see the example in Box G.3. To work out your tax credits for part of a tax year, calculate the 'relevant period' amounts at each step and see the example in Box G.4.

Step 1: Work out maximum tax credits for you and your family – This is the sum of the CTC and WTC elements that apply to you (see 2 above).

Step 2: Work out your income (see Chapter 19(9)) – Remember that the income taken into account is normally your income in the previous tax year but it can be current tax year income instead: see 1 above and the 'disregards' at 5 and 6 below. There is no income calculation for periods when you are receiving income-related employment and support allowance, income-based jobseeker's allowance, income support or pension credit. Receipt of these benefits is a 'passport' to (ie, it automatically entitles you to) an award of your maximum tax credits. The exception to this is where you receive one of these benefits during the 4-week run-on of WTC (see Chapter 19(6)), in which case the calculation is done as normal.

Step 3: Find the appropriate income threshold (see below).

Step 4: Compare your income to the threshold – If your income is below or the same as the threshold, you'll get maximum tax credits. If your income is above the threshold, deduct the threshold from your income, to work out the *'excess income'*. Then apply the 41% taper to your excess income.

Step 5: Deduct the result at Step 4 from your maximum tax credits at Step 1 – The amount you are left with is your tax credit entitlement.

Note: This calculation gives only a provisional entitlement figure, as your actual entitlement is based on a comparison of your actual income in the year of the award and your income in the previous tax year. This will not be known until after the year has ended. See 7 below.

TC(IT&DR) Regs, reg 7

Income thresholds and tapers

There are two thresholds for 2013/14 and they depend on whether you qualify for either CTC or WTC or both:

- WTC and CTC £6,420;
- WTC only £6,420;
- CTC only £15,910.

The taper is 41%.

Note: HMRC must apply the taper in the following order: first to the WTC adult elements, then to the WTC childcare elements, then to the CTC child elements and finally to the CTC family element. The effect of this on a couple is that payments made to the partner who is working (the non-childcare elements of WTC) are reduced before those made to the main carer (the childcare elements of WTC and CTC).

TC(IT&DR) Regs, regs 7 & 8

4. Changes in your circumstances

CTC and WTC awards normally run to the end of the tax year but if you stop meeting the qualifying conditions, your entitlement ends and you should tell the Tax Credit Office immediately. On the other hand, if your income goes up or down, even substantially, you don't usually need to tell the Tax Credit Office right away, although it may sometimes be in your interest to do so (see 'When you should ask for a reassessment' at 5 and 6 below).

You *must* tell the Tax Credit Office within one month if:

- you change your status from a single person to a couple, or the other way round;
- you cease to meet the residence conditions (eg you move abroad);
- your childcare costs end, or your average childcare costs go down by £10 a week or more;

- your work hours change and you no longer meet a 16- or 24- or 30-hours a week qualifying rule: see Chapter 19(5);
- you cease to be entitled to the 30-hour element;
- you stop being responsible for a child or qualifying young person, or one you are responsible for dies, or a qualifying young person stops counting as such (eg because they leave college and start work).

If you don't report the change within one month of becoming aware of it, you may face a penalty (see Chapter 19(12)).

TC(C&N) Regs, Reg 21

A change of circumstances that increases your maximum tax credits (such as the birth of a child) should be reported within one month to allow full backdating.

5. The £5,000 disregard if your income rises

For 2013/14, your income can increase by up to £5,000 a year, compared to the previous year, before it affects your tax credit entitlement for the current year. (The annual disregard was £2,500 until April 2006; then it was £25,000 until April 2011. It was reduced to £10,000 for 2011/12 and has been reduced again this year.)

The £5,000 disregard is applied in the following way.

- ❏ If current year income is greater than the previous year income by £5,000 or less, the lower previous year income is used to work out current year entitlement.
- ❏ If current year income is greater than previous year income by more than £5,000, current year income less £5,000 is used.

G.3 Calculating tax credits

Shirley is a lone parent with two children aged 4 and 10. She works 20 hours a week and her gross annual income is £9,000. She gets disability living allowance highest rate care component for one child. Childcare costs are £30 a week (£1,560 a year).

Step 1: work out maximum tax credits

WTC basic element	£1,920.00
WTC lone parent element	£1,970.00
WTC childcare (£1,560 x 70%)	£1,092.00
CTC child element (£2,720 x 2)	£5,440.00
CTC disabled child element	£3,015.00
CTC severely disabled child element	£1,220.00
CTC family element	£545.00
Maximum tax credits	*£15,202.00*

Step 2: annual income

Annual income	£9,000.00

Step 3: find income threshold

Income threshold (WTC)	£6,420.00

Step 4: compare income to threshold

Excess income (Step 2 result less Step 3 result)	£2,580.00
Tapered at 41%	*£1,057.80*

Step 5: Step 1 result less Step 4 result

£15,202 less £1,057.80	
Tax credit entitlement	*£14,144.20*

Note: For simplicity, this example is based on annual, not daily rates. HMRC uses daily rates of each element, which are calculated by dividing the annual rates by 365 and rounding up to the nearest penny. The relevant income and threshold figures are also apportioned over the relevant period, with the resulting income figure rounded down and threshold figure rounded up to the nearest penny. After rounding, the claimant's actual entitlement will be slightly higher than shown in this example. The discrepancy is more marked when there are more 'relevant periods' and more rounding. See the example in Box G.4.

Example 1: If your income last year was £10,000 but this year is £14,000, your award this year will be based on last year's income of £10,000.

Example 2: If your income last year was £10,000 but this year is £18,000, your award this year will be based on your income of £18,000 less the disregard of £5,000, ie £13,000.

When you should ask for a reassessment

If your current year income is likely to be higher than last year's by more than £5,000 (eg if you get a better-paying job), you should ask for a reassessment right away so that your award is based on your estimated current year income. This will avoid you building up a recoverable overpayment. The second example above illustrates this: HMRC will base your initial award on last year's income of £10,000 and will only

G.4 Change of circumstances calculation

Farouk is single, 35, works full time and has a disability. His salary is £10,220 a year. At the start of the year he does not meet the conditions for WTC disability element, but after 150 days (about five months) he is awarded personal independence payment mobility component. He is not entitled to WTC disability element for the first relevant period, but is for the second.

First relevant period (150 days)
Step 1: work out maximum tax credits at daily rates

WTC basic element: £5.27* x 150	£790.50
WTC 30-hour element: £2.17* x 150	£325.50
Maximum tax credits	*£1,116.00*

Step 2: income

Income: £10,220 x 150/365	**£4,200.00

Step 3: income threshold

Income threshold (WTC) £6,420 x 150/365	*£2,638.36

Step 4: compare income to threshold

Excess income (Step 2 result less Step 3 result) £1,561.64	
Taper excess income by 41%	**£640.27

Step 5: Step 1 result less Step 4 result

£1,116.00 less £640.27	
Tax credit entitlement for first period	*£475.73*

Second relevant period (215 days)
Step 1: work out maximum tax credits at daily rates

WTC basic element: £5.27* x 215	£1,133.05
WTC disability element: £7.83* x 215	£1,683.45
WTC 30-hour element: £2.17* x 215	£466.55
Maximum award	*£3,283.05*

Step 2: income

Income: £10,220 x 215/365	**£6,020.00

Step 3: income threshold

Income threshold (WTC) £6,420 x 215/365	*£3,781.65

Step 4: compare income to threshold

Excess income (Step 2 result less Step 3 result) £2,238.35	
Taper excess income by 41%	**£917.72

Step 5: Step 1 result less Step 4 result

£3,283.05 less £917.72	
Tax credit entitlement for second period	*£2,365.33*

Actual tax credits payable for both relevant periods

First relevant period	£475.73
Second relevant period	£2,365.33
Total	*£2,841.06*

* Figures rounded up to nearest penny (see note in Box G.3)
** Figures rounded down to the nearest penny

use the actual £13,000 figure after the year end. Unless you ask for a reassessment sooner, you will be overpaid.

6. The £2,500 disregard if your income falls

Normally, income disregards work in your favour: you can receive a higher award because less income is taken into account. This disregard, on the other hand, can work against you. If your current year income is less than your previous year's, the first £2,500 of the decrease is ignored. Where the fall is less than £2,500, the higher previous year figure will apply. If the fall is more than £2,500, the figure used is the lower current year figure plus £2,500.

Example 1: If your income last year was £13,000 and your estimated income for this year is £12,000, your award will be based on last year's income of £13,000. Although your income has gone down, the disregard of £2,500 means the fall is ignored.

Example 2: If your income last year was £13,000 and your estimated income for this year is £10,000, your award will be based on income of £12,500. Although your income has gone down by £3,000, the disregard of £2,500 means that only £500 of the fall is counted.

When you should ask for a reassessment

As with other changes of income, you don't have a duty to tell the Tax Credit Office about these changes right away. If you do, however, you may get an increase in your ongoing payments, which may be better than waiting for a lump-sum of underpaid tax credits after the end of the tax year.

7. Overpayment or underpayment of tax credit

Because tax credits are assessed by reference to the tax year and are provisional in nature, being paid throughout the year but not finalised until the year-end, overpayments or underpayments will sometimes arise. Also, as the system is designed to be flexible and respond to changes in your household circumstances, a change in circumstances that affects the tax credits to which you are entitled is bound to give rise, even if only for a limited period, to 'in-year' overpayments or underpayments. Finally, errors – whether they are yours or official ones (ie by HMRC or another government department) – can lead to too much or too little tax credit being paid.

8. Overpayments

An overpayment arises when the amount of tax credit paid to you for a tax year is more than you are or were entitled to. For the reasons given in 7 above, it is not until after the end of a tax year that your award(s) for that year can be seen to be under or over the right amount.

If it appears to the Tax Credit Office during a tax year that you are likely to be overpaid, they may adjust your ongoing award to reduce or avoid the overpayment. This is generally a computer-generated operation, triggered by you reporting a change of circumstances that reduces entitlement.

TCA, S.28(1)&(5)

Methods of recovery

The two usual methods of recovery are by:

■ direct assessment; *or*
■ deduction from payments under future awards.

TCA, S.29(1), (3)&(4)

Under the second method, the rate at which payments can be reduced varies according to the type of award. Your payments are usually reduced by 10% if you receive maximum tax credits; by 25% if you receive less than the maximum award but more than the family element of CTC; or by 100% if you receive only the family element of CTC.

If you do not have an ongoing award because you no longer qualify or you have to make a new claim because your household unit has changed, the Tax Credit Office will send you a demand for payment within 30 days. HMRC allows repayment in 12 monthly instalments or, if you have little disposable income, up to ten years. In cases of hardship it is possible for overpayments to be written off.

If you are already paying back an overpayment on an ongoing award and are asked to pay back another overpayment by direct assessment, you should ask the Tax Credit Office to suspend recovery of the overpayment by direct assessment until the ongoing recovery is finished. You must ask the Tax Credit Office for this as it is not an automatic process.

Where HMRC is recovering an overpayment from a couple who have split up, each partner has 'joint and several' liability, which means HMRC can pursue either one for the whole amount. However, in practice HMRC will recover only 50% from each one (unless a different split is agreed by the couple); you must ask the Tax Credit Office for this as it is not an automatic process.

When will an overpayment not be recovered?
Official error – HMRC has discretion whether or not to recover an overpayment in whole or in part and they generally opt for recovery. There is no right of appeal against a decision by HMRC to recover an overpayment, but there is a right of appeal against an award notice showing an overpayment (eg whether it has been calculated incorrectly). HMRC practice on recovery is set out in code of practice COP26 (available at www.hmrc.gov.uk/leaflets/cop26.pdf). If you fulfil all your responsibilities as listed in COP26, but HMRC has not fulfilled theirs, overpayments generated by official error are generally written off.

While you cannot generally avoid HMRC recovering an overpayment from you, you can try to avoid overpayments arising by:

- comparing the payment schedules on your award notice with your bank statements and raise any queries within 30 days of the award notice being issued; *and*
- reporting changes of circumstances (see 4, 5 and 6 above) as soon as they happen.

If you dispute recovery of an overpayment on grounds of official error, you must do so in writing, preferably on form TC846 (available at www.hmrc.gov.uk/forms/tc846.pdf). On receiving your written dispute, the Tax Credit Office should immediately suspend collection of the overpayment. Suspension continues while HMRC considers your case, but ends if they find against you, even if you subsequently complain to them or to the Adjudicator or the Ombudsman: see Chapter 19(13).

Since most dealings with the Tax Credit Office are via their telephone Helpline (see Chapter 19(10)), keep detailed notes of calls, including the date and time, who you spoke to and what was said. HMRC generally records calls to the Helpline,

and either the Tax Credit Office or the HMRC Data Protection Unit will send you the recordings on request.

Hardship – If repaying the overpayment would cause hardship to you or your family, you can ask the Tax Credit Office to reduce it or write it off.

Change of status – If you delay reporting a change of status (going from a joint to a single claim or the other way round) and incur an overpayment, you may be able to have the overpayment reduced by the amount you would have received had you made a fresh claim at the correct time. This is called notional entitlement or *'offsetting'*. You must make a new claim under the correct status and ask the Tax Credit Office for the offsetting, as it is not an automatic process.

The effect of overpayments on other benefits
If your tax credit award goes down because of overpayment recovery, your means-tested benefit (income-related employment and support allowance, income support or income-based jobseeker's allowance) won't necessarily be increased to make up for the drop in tax credits. This could leave you living on a net income below your normal means-tested benefit level. Remember that if they are recovering an overpayment from an ongoing award, HMRC should pay CTC to people in receipt of a means-tested benefit with only a 10% reduction to recover the overpayment.

By contrast, the tax credits that count for housing benefit are the amounts you actually receive. So, while you are being overpaid tax credit you may receive less housing benefit than if you were getting the correct tax credits. Then, when your tax credit award is lowered to recover an overpayment, you should ask for your housing benefit to be increased to compensate.

9. Underpayments
If you are underpaid tax credit (eg because your income goes down) and the underpayment comes to light during that tax year, the award can be changed to reflect your new circumstances, but any accrued underpayment may be held back until the end of the year. If the underpayment comes to light after the end of the year, the award will be corrected to reflect your circumstances: if there are no outstanding overpayments, you will get a lump sum to make good the underpayment.

The effect of underpayments on housing benefit
If you receive a lump sum of accumulated underpayment, you will most likely have received a higher award of housing benefit during the underpayment period. Had you opted to correct the underpayment during the course of the year, 65% of the additional tax credits would most likely have been lost due to being taken into account as income for your housing benefit.

Help with rent and council tax

This section of the Handbook looks at:

Housing benefit	Chapter **21**
Council tax	Chapter **22**

21 Housing benefit

1. What is housing benefit?

Housing benefit (HB) helps people pay their rent. It can also be known as rent rebate or rent allowance. In nearly all cases, local authorities run the HB scheme. But in a few cases, other organisations run the scheme and some authorities have contracted out part of the administration to private firms. In Northern Ireland, the Northern Ireland Housing Executive administers the scheme.

The benefit cap – A *'benefit cap'* will be rolled out nationally between 15.7.13 and 30.9.13, which will limit the total amount of weekly benefits that can be paid. If the cap applies to you, your HB will be reduced to ensure that the total amount of benefit you receive is not more than the cap level. The cap will apply to people of working age (16 to 64 inclusive). See Box H.1 for details.

Future plans – The government is replacing HB with universal credit. This is being piloted from April in northwest England; nationwide roll-out starts in October 2013 on the basis of one district in each Jobcentre Plus region. See Box J.1 in Chapter 25 for more on universal credit.

2. Who can get housing benefit?

You can get HB if you satisfy all the following conditions:

■ you are not excluded from getting HB (see below and Box H.2);

■ you are liable to pay rent on your normal home (see 5 below);

■ with the exception of some people who have reached pension credit qualifying age, your capital is no more than £16,000 (see 22 below);

■ you are on income-related employment and support allowance, income-based jobseeker's allowance, income support or the guarantee credit of pension credit, or you have a fairly low income (see 20 & 23 below); *and*

■ you claim and provide the information requested (see 13 below).

People who cannot get housing benefit
If you are in any of the groups below, you cannot get HB.

❑ **Care leavers under 18 if social care are responsible for accommodating you** – There are rare exceptions: seek further advice if you are in this situation.

❑ **People in care homes** – There are rare exceptions (see Chapter 33(3)).

❑ **'Persons from abroad' or 'subject to immigration control'** – This does not cover every non-UK national, but it does cover some UK nationals who do not habitually reside in the UK. See Chapter 49 for details.

❑ **Many full-time students** – Full-time students cannot get HB unless they fall within certain groups – eg disabled students (see Chapter 40(2)). If you are in a couple and only one of you is a full-time student, the other one can get HB for you both.

❑ **Members of religious orders** – if you are maintained by the order.

See Box H.2 for details of other people who cannot get HB.

3. What is rent?

You can get HB towards almost any kind of rent, whether paid to a local authority (including a health authority), the Northern Ireland Housing Executive, a housing association, a co-op, a hostel, a bed and breakfast hotel, a private company or a private individual (including a resident landlord – but see Box H.2). This is true whether your letting is a 'tenancy' or 'licence', whether your payments are for 'rent', 'use and occupation', 'mesne profits' or 'violent profits', or whether you have a written or a verbal letting agreement. If you are buying a share of your home through a shared ownership scheme but still pay rent, you can get HB towards the rent (and you may get help with mortgage interest through another means-tested benefit – see Chapter 26). You can also get HB towards the following, which count as 'rent' for HB purposes:

■ mooring charges and/or berthing fees for a houseboat (as well as your rent, if you do not own it);

■ site fees for a caravan or mobile home (as well as your rent, if you do not own it);

■ payments to a charitable almshouse;

■ payments under a 'rental purchase' agreement;

■ payments (in Scotland) on a croft or croft land.

HB Regs, reg 12(1)

4. Housing costs that HB cannot meet

You cannot get HB towards any of the following, but some may be met by another means-tested benefit (see Chapter 26):

- payments you make on your home if you own it or have a long tenancy (over 21 years or a life tenancy created in writing), except for a shared ownership lease;
- payments you make in a co-ownership scheme where, if you left, you would be entitled to a sum based on the value of your home;
- rent if you are a Crown tenant (there is a separate scheme for Crown tenants), although tenants of the Crown Estate Commissioners and the Duchies of Cornwall and Lancaster can get HB;
- hire purchase or credit sale agreements;
- conditional sale agreements (unless for land);
- payments on a tent;
- payments in respect of a dwelling owned by your partner.

HB Regs, reg 12(2)

5. Liability for rent on your normal home

To get HB, the general rule is that you must be personally liable to pay the rent on your home. You can usually get HB on only one home at a time, which is the dwelling *'normally occupied'* by yourself and any members of your family. (Seek advice if you live in more than one dwelling due to the size of your family.) However, there are exceptions to these points, as described in the next few paragraphs.

Couples – Either one of you can get HB towards the rent on your normal home. Even if the letting agreement is in one name only, the other person is treated as liable to make payments. If one of you is excluded from HB (see 2 above), the other partner should be the one to make the claim.

HB Regs, Reg 8(1)(b)

If you take over paying someone else's rent – If the person liable for the rent on your home stops paying it and you take over the payments to continue living there, you can get HB even though you are not legally liable for the rent. This applies if the person liable is your former partner, and in any other reasonable case.

HB Regs, Reg 8(1)(c)

Repairs to your home – If your landlord agrees not to collect rent while you do repairs to your home, you can carry on getting HB for the first eight weeks. After that, you cannot get HB until you start paying rent again.

HB Regs, Reg 8(1)(d)

If you have to move into temporary accommodation while essential repairs are carried out to your normal home, you

H.1 The benefit cap

From 15.4.13 a cap on the total amount you can receive from the main out-of-work benefits and children's benefits is being introduced. If your total income from the relevant benefits is greater than the cap level, your housing benefit will be reduced so that your total benefit does not exceed the cap. There are exemptions (see below). You can ring the government helpline for further details: 0845 605 7064; textphone 0845 608 8551. A similar cap will be applied to universal credit.

Which benefits are taken into account?
The *'relevant'* benefits that are taken into account when calculating the cap are:
- Bereavement allowance
- Carer's allowance
- Child benefit
- Child tax credit
- Employment and support allowance (ESA; however, you will be exempt from the cap if you receive the support component)
- Guardian's allowance
- Housing benefit (HB is not included in the cap calculation if you are in supported accommodation that is exempt from the rules on rent restrictions; see 11 in this chapter)
- Incapacity benefit
- Income support
- Jobseeker's allowance (JSA)
- Maternity allowance
- Severe disablement allowance
- Widowed mother's allowance
- Widowed parent's allowance
- Widow's pension.

All other benefits are ignored when calculating the cap.

How much is the benefit cap?
The weekly amount of the cap is:
- £500 for couples (with or without children) and lone parents
- £350 for single people.

Who is exempt?
You are exempt from the benefit cap if you, your partner or your children (or qualifying young people; see Chapter 38(1)) receive any of the following:

- Armed Forces Compensation scheme guaranteed income payment;
- Attendance allowance
- Disability living allowance
- ESA support component
- Industrial injuries benefit
- Personal independence payment
- War pension
- War widow's, widower's or surviving civil partner's pension
- Working tax credit

or would get one of these benefits were you (or they) not in hospital.

The benefit cap will not be applied during a *'grace period'* if you were previously working for 50 weeks out of the last 52 weeks, were not claiming income support, ESA or JSA while you were working and you lost your job through no fault of your own. The grace period lasts for 39 weeks.

The cap will not be applied if you have reached the qualifying age for pension credit (see Chapter 42(2)), unless you or your partner are continuing to claim income support, income-related ESA or income-based JSA.

When does the cap apply?
The cap is being applied from 15.4.13 to households in the London boroughs of Bromley, Croydon, Enfield and Haringey. The cap will be introduced across the rest of the country between 15.7.13 and 30.9.13.

How does the cap work?
If your total income from the relevant benefits is above the cap, your HB will be reduced until your income equals the cap. However, you will always be left with at least 50p of HB so you will retain eligibility for discretionary housing payments (see 16 in this chapter) and any passported benefits. An online calculator can be found at www.gov.uk/benefit-cap.

Example
John and Mary are a couple with children. Their income from the relevant benefits is £550 a week, including £240 HB. As a couple, the benefit cap that applies to them is £500 a week. Their HB will be reduced by £50 to £190 a week. Their total relevant benefit income will be £500.

HB Regs, regs 75A-75G

can get HB on the property for which you are liable to make payments – but only if you are not liable for payments (of either rent or mortgage interest) on the other home.

HB Regs, Reg 7(4)

Joint occupiers – *'Joint occupiers'* means two or more people (other than a couple) who are jointly liable to pay rent on their home. If you are a joint occupier and not subject to the local housing allowance (LHA; see 9 below), you can get HB towards your share of the rent. This share is assessed by taking into account the number of joint occupiers, how much each of you pays and how many rooms you each occupy. (If the LHA rules apply, rent is not apportioned but joint tenants are not included in the size criteria.)

HB Regs, reg 12(5) (as still in force for non-LHA cases)

Bail or probation hostels – If you are required to reside in a bail or probation hostel, you will not be treated as occupying that dwelling as your home, and so will be unable to claim HB for any rent charged.

HB Regs, reg 7(5)

6. Temporary absence

You can continue to get HB while you are temporarily absent from your normal home in the circumstances described below.

The 13-week rule

You can get HB for up to 13 weeks during a temporary absence from your normal home if:

- you intend to return to occupy it as your home; *and*
- the part you normally occupy has not been let or sub-let; *and*
- your absence is unlikely to exceed 13 continuous weeks.

This rule applies to all absences (including absences outside the UK). Calculation of the length of a prison sentence should include periods of temporary release, but should be reduced by any remission allowable for good behaviour.

HB Regs, reg 7(13)-(15)

The 52-week rule

You can get HB for up to 52 weeks during a temporary absence from your normal home if:

- you intend to return to occupy it as your home; *and*
- the part you normally occupy has not been let or sub-let; *and*
- your absence is unlikely to exceed 52 weeks or, in exceptional circumstances, is unlikely to substantially exceed 52 weeks; *and*
- your absence is for any of the reasons listed below.

You can get HB under this rule if you are:

- a patient in a hospital or similar institution;
- receiving medical treatment or medically approved care or convalescence (other than in a care home) in the UK or abroad;
- accompanying your child or partner who is receiving the above (but not care);

H.2 Who cannot get HB?

The rules in this box apply in addition to those in the main text (see 2). If you have difficulty getting HB because of these rules, seek advice.

Your letting is not on a commercial basis – You cannot get HB if your letting is not on a commercial basis. This rule applies whether you live with your landlord or somewhere else. Factors to be considered when deciding this include: the relationship and agreement between the parties; the living arrangements; the amount of rent; and whether the agreement contains terms enforceable by law.

You live with your landlord who is a close relative – You cannot get HB if you live with your landlord and they are a close relative. Sharing just a bathroom, toilet, hallway, stairs or passageways does not count as living with your landlord, but sharing other rooms might. A *'close relative'* means only a parent, parent-in-law, step-parent, son, daughter, son/daughter-in-law, stepson/daughter, sister, brother or the partner of any of those.

Your landlord is an ex-partner – You cannot get HB if you rent your home from:

- your ex-partner, and you used to live there with that ex-partner; *or*
- your (current) partner's ex-partner, and your (current) partner used to live there with that ex-partner.

Your landlord is the parent of your child – You cannot get HB if you or your partner are responsible for a child whose father or mother is your landlord. You (or your partner) count as 'responsible' for any child who is included in your HB assessment.

Your landlord is a company or a trust connected with you – You cannot get HB if your landlord is a company or a trust of which any director or employee (of the company), or any trustee or beneficiary (of the trust) is:

- you or your partner, or an ex-partner of either of you; *or*
- a person who lives with you and who is a 'close relative' of you or your partner (see above).

This rule does not apply if your letting agreement was created for a genuine reason (rather than to take advantage of the HB scheme). What counts as 'taking advantage of the HB scheme' can be open to argument.

Your landlord is a trust connected with your child – You cannot get HB if your landlord is a trust of which your, or your (current) partner's, child is a beneficiary. For this rule, you cannot get HB even if your letting agreement was created for a genuine reason.

You used to be a non-dependant – You cannot get HB if:

- you lived in your home before you began renting it; *and*
- at that time you were a non-dependant (see 21) of a person who then lived in your home; *and*
- that person still lives in your home.

This rule does not apply if your letting agreement was created for a genuine reason (rather than to take advantage of the HB scheme). What counts as 'taking advantage of the HB scheme' can be open to argument.

You used to own or have a long tenancy of the home you rent – You cannot get HB if you or your partner used to own or have a long tenancy of the home you are now renting. But this rule only applies if you owned it or had a long tenancy of it within the past five years and have lived there continuously since you owned or had a long tenancy of it. It does not apply if you or your partner would have to have left your home if it was not sold or the tenancy given up. For example, this rule should not apply if you are renting your home under a 'mortgage rescue scheme' after exploring all other options.

Tied accommodation – You cannot get HB if you or your partner are employed by your landlord and have to live in your home as a condition of that employment.

Contrived lettings – In addition to all the above rules, you cannot get HB if your or your landlord's principal or dominant purpose in creating your letting agreement was to take advantage of the HB scheme. The motives and intentions of landlord and tenant may be considered in order to determine this.

HB Regs, reg 9

- providing care to a child whose parent or guardian is absent from home due to receiving medically approved care or medical treatment;
- providing medically approved care to anyone in the UK or abroad;
- receiving care in a care home (but not for a trial period – see below);
- on an approved training course in the UK or abroad;
- on remand awaiting trial or sentencing or required to reside in a hostel or property other than your home as a condition of bail;
- a student who is eligible for HB and not covered by the 'two homes' rule (see Chapter 40(2));
- in fear of violence but only if you are not liable for rent on your other home (the conditions are the same as in the rule for getting HB on two homes in such cases – see 7 below).

HB Regs, reg 7(16) & (17)

Your period of absence

If your absence is likely to exceed 13 or 52 continuous weeks, you cannot get HB for any time you are away. If you cannot estimate the length of the absence, you are unlikely to get HB during any of it so give the local authority an estimate if possible. Your intention to return must be a realistic possibility.

Any re-occupation of the home (other than a prisoner's temporary release) will break the period of absence – a stay of 24 hours is usually enough, although the authority has to be satisfied that your stay at home was genuine.

As soon as it becomes likely that the absence will exceed the 13- or 52-week limit, your HB entitlement will stop.

Trial periods in care homes

You can get HB for up to 13 weeks during an absence if:

- you are trying out a care home to see whether it suits your needs; *and*
- at the point you enter the care home, you intend to return to your normal home if the care home does not suit your needs; *and*
- the part that you normally occupy has not been let or sub-let.

You can have further trial periods so long as the total absence does not exceed 52 weeks.

HB Regs, reg 7(11) & (12)

7. Moving home and getting HB on two homes

The general rule – When you move from one rented home to another, you can get HB on both homes for up to four weeks if you have moved into the new home but the local authority agrees you could not reasonably have avoided liability for rent on both the new and the old home (eg because you had to accept the new tenancy and move quickly and had to give notice on your old home). This general rule applies only if you have actually moved into the new home. Exactly what it means to *'move in'* can be interpreted in different ways. It could be enough if you have moved some furniture and personal possessions into the property (R(H)9/05). This 4-week rule also applies if you move to a new home where you are not liable for rent but continue to have a rental liability on your old property.

HB Regs, reg 7(6)(d) & (7)

Different rules apply in the following cases.

Fear of violence – This rule applies if you move because of fear that violence may occur in your old home (regardless of who might cause the violence) or in the locality (in which case, only if the violence would be caused by a former member of your family). In either case, you can get HB on both homes for up to 52 weeks as long as you intend to return to your old home at some point and the local authority agrees it is reasonable to pay HB on both. You do not have to say exactly when you intend to return: it should be sufficient if you

intend to return when it is safe to do so. If you do not intend to return, you continue to get HB on your former property for up to four weeks if the continuing liability was unavoidable.

HB Regs, reg 7(6)(a) & (10)

Waiting for your new home to be adapted – If you do not move into a new rented home straight away because it is being adapted to meet your disablement needs or those of a member of your family, and the local authority agrees the delay is reasonable, you can get HB for up to four weeks before you move in. If you are liable for rent on your old home, you can get HB on both during those four weeks.

HB Regs, reg 7(6)(e) & (8)(c)(i)

Waiting for a loan or grant before moving – If you do not move into a new rented home straight away because you have asked for a social fund payment or local authority loan or grant to help with the move or with setting up home, and the local authority agrees the delay is reasonable, you can get HB for up to four weeks before you move in. However, this rule only applies if there is a child under the age of 6 in your family, or if you or your partner have reached pension credit qualifying age, or if you qualify for one of the HB disability, severe disability or disabled child premiums (see Chapter 25(2), (3) and (8)) or an employment and support allowance additional component (see 24 below). Under this rule you cannot get HB on your old home at the same time.

HB Regs, reg 7(8)(c)(ii)

When you leave hospital or a care home – If you do not move into a new rented home straight away because you are waiting to leave hospital or a care home, and the local authority agrees the delay is reasonable, you can get HB for up to four weeks before you actually move in.

HB Regs, reg 7(8)(c)(iii)

Claiming on time – In the above three cases, you must claim straight away; do not wait until you have moved in. If the authority rejects the claim, but you re-apply within four weeks of moving in, the rejected claim must be reconsidered. If you move within a local authority area, you will qualify if you notify them of the new tenancy before the move.

HB Regs 7(8)(a) & (b)

Large families – If your local authority has arranged for you to be housed in two homes, you can get HB on both.

HB Regs, reg 7(6)(c)

Students – Some students with partners who have to maintain two homes can get HB on both (if they are eligible for HB in the first place) – see Chapter 40(2).

HB Regs, Reg 7(6)(b)

8. How much rent is taken into account?

Eligible rent – The HB calculation is based on your weekly *'eligible rent'*. This may be less than your actual rent if a restriction applies (see below). If a restriction does not apply, your eligible rent will be:

- the actual rent on your home;
- plus in some cases the rent on a garage;
- minus amounts for water, fuel, meals and certain other services (see 12 below).

To convert monthly rent to a weekly figure, multiply by 12 then divide by 52. If you jointly occupy your home with others, see 5 above.

Restrictions

Whether or not a restriction applies, and the nature of the restriction, depends on whether you rent from the local authority, a housing association or any other landlord (including a private landlord).

If you rent from the local authority – The authority will administer your HB claim and ineligible charges (see 12 below) will be deducted from your contractual rent. If it is considered that you have spare bedrooms, your eligible rent may be reduced (see Box H.4).

If you rent from any other authority (such as a non-metropolitan county council), see below 'If you rent from any other landlord, including a private landlord'.

If you rent from a housing association – If you rent from a registered housing association or private registered provider of social housing, ineligible charges (see 12 below) will be deducted from your contractual rent. If it is considered that you have spare bedrooms, your eligible rent may be reduced (see Box H.4). Your eligible rent may also be restricted if the local authority considers the rent is unreasonably high or the accommodation unreasonably large; if this happens, the authority will refer your details to the rent officer.

If you rent from an unregistered housing association or private provider of social housing, all the rules about renting from a private landlord will apply to you (see below).
HB Regs, Sch 2, para 3

Note: The exceptions shown in 11 below may mean you qualify for more HB.

If you rent from any other landlord, including a private landlord – Your eligible rent is restricted to a figure called your *'maximum rent'*, unless you fall within certain protected groups (see 9 and 11 below). If you moved or started to claim HB on or after 7.4.08, your maximum rent will be set at a standard rate: the local housing allowance (see 9 below). Before 7.4.08, maximum rents were set at rates that followed determinations by rent officers (see 10 below).

9. Local housing allowance

If you moved or started to claim HB from 7.4.08, your *'maximum rent'* will be set at a standard rate, the *'local housing allowance'* (LHA). The LHA is a standard amount of maximum HB, set according to where you live and who is in your household, including non-dependants (see 'Rate of LHA' below). The figure is used whatever the actual amount of your rent. From 1.4.11, the amount is restricted to the 'cap' rent (your contractual rent), so it can never be more than the rent you pay. This means your HB may be a lesser amount than your rent, even if you are entitled to maximum benefit. Claimants are expected to make up any shortfall or seek cheaper accommodation.
HB Regs, regs 12D & 13D

The LHA rules apply to most private sector tenancies. They may not apply to you if:
■ your HB claim is backdated to earlier than 7.4.08; *or*
■ your tenancy is exempt (see below); *or*
■ you are in a protected category and your LHA would be less than your eligible rent (see 'Protections for certain people' below).

Exempt tenancies – These are:
■ registered social landlord tenancies (eg local authority or housing association);

■ protected cases – such as supported housing provided by certain local authorities, housing associations, registered charities or voluntary organisations;
■ protected tenancies with a registered fair rent;
■ exceptional cases (eg caravans, houseboats and hostels);
■ board and attendance cases if the rent officer judges that a substantial part of the rent is for board and attendance.
HB Regs, reg 13C(5)

See 11 below for details of other tenancies that are exempt from both the LHA and rent officer rules.

Rate of LHA

If the LHA applies, the amount of eligible rent is the standard LHA, initially determined by a local authority rent officer according to the *'broad rental market area'* where the dwelling is situated, the size of the household and the number of bedrooms required. From 1.4.13, these rates are adjusted annually each April.
HB Regs, reg 13D(1)

Broad rental market area – This is an area within which a person could reasonably be expected to live, having regard to facilities and services, and including a variety of accommodation and tenancy.

Maximum amounts – Since April 2011, LHA rates have been based on the 30th percentile of rents for properties of the relevant size within the broad rental market area, which means around three in ten properties in that area would be affordable. LHA rates have also been subject to an overall maximum cap for each size category since April 2011 (£250 a week for a one-bedroom property, £290 for two bedrooms, £340 for three and £400 for four bedrooms). Existing claimants may have transitional protection for up to nine months after their LHA is reviewed if their HB would otherwise be reduced under the April 2011 rules.

Getting information before you sign up for a letting

LHA rates for each size category of property should be available from every local authority. These rates can help you find out how much HB you would receive if you moved to a new address. Details of the LHA rates for any area are at lha-direct.voa.gov.uk/search.aspx.
HB Regs, reg 13E

Size criteria

The LHA is based on the number of occupants in the benefit household. Restrictions apply to single claimants under 35 and those in shared accommodation. One bedroom is allowed for:
■ every adult couple (including civil partners);
■ any other adult aged 16 or over (this can include a son, daughter, stepson or stepdaughter of you or your partner who was living with you as a non-dependant (see 21 below) and is now serving away on operations as a member of the armed forces, who intends to move back in with you when they return);
■ any two children of the same sex (unless it is inappropriate for them to share a room because of disability – see below);
■ any two children regardless of sex if under the age of 10 (unless it is inappropriate for them to share a room because of disability – see below);
■ a foster child or children, if you are an approved foster carer (or kinship carer in Scotland);
■ any other child; *and*
■ a non-resident carer who regularly provides overnight care for a disabled claimant or their partner.

A further bedroom is allowed for a period of up to 52 weeks, if you have been approved as a foster carer but do not currently have a child or qualifying young person (see Chapter 38(1)) placed with you.

H.3 Why HB may not cover all your rent

Your HB may not cover all of your rent. This could be because:
■ your rent includes service charges or other ineligible charges that must be deducted in the calculation of HB (see 12);
■ you have one or more non-dependant(s) in your home and a deduction must be made because of this (see 21);
■ your HB is restricted (eg because a standard local housing allowance or 'maximum rent' applies) (see 8-11);
■ the level of your income means you do not qualify for the whole of your rent to be met (see 20);
■ a benefit cap has been applied (see Box H.1).

From 1.4.11, the LHA is capped at the 4-bedroom rate from the date of claim for new claimants and for pre-existing claimants from up to nine months after the first annual review date.

HB Regs, reg 13D(2)(c), (3)-(3B) & (12)

Disabled children – If your children are unable to share a bedroom due to disability, the local authority must consider not only the nature and severity of the disability, but also the nature and frequency of care required during the night, and the extent and regularity of the disturbance to the sleep of the child who would normally be required to share the bedroom.

The government had lodged an appeal against a Court of Appeal judgment on this matter, which they have now dropped. If your local authority has suspended part of your HB award that allowed for an extra room pending the outcome of this appeal, the suspension can now be lifted and arrears paid as appropriate.

Burnip, Trengove, Gorry v SSWP [2012] EWCA Civ 629; Housing Benefit & Council Tax Benefit Urgent Bulletin HB/CTB U/2013

Young people – Single claimants under 35 have an LHA based on one bedroom in shared accommodation. This does not apply if they qualify for a severe disability premium or are a care leaver aged under 22. Neither does it apply to those aged 25 or over who have been in a hostel for the homeless for three months and received support to resettle in the community, or to some recent offenders who are deemed a risk to the public.

Prior to 1.1.12, a claimant was classed as a young person under these rules only if they were under 25 – there may be transitional protection for those who were aged 25 to 34 and receiving HB prior to this date.

HB Regs, reg 13D(2)(a)

Single claimants aged 35 or over and couples without children – Single claimants aged 35 or over and all couples without children are allowed the normal one-bedroom rate unless they live in shared accommodation, in which case the one-bedroom rate in shared accommodation is used.

HB Regs, reg 13D(2)(b)

Protections for certain people
Local authorities may not use the maximum rent figure described above in the following two cases. (For how eligible rent is calculated in these cases, see 8 above.)

❑ If you and/or any member of your household could afford the financial commitments of your home when you first entered into them, and you (or your partner) have not received HB during the 52 weeks before your current claim, the authority may not use the maximum rent figure for the first 13 weeks of your claim.

❑ If a member of your household has died, and you have not moved since then, the authority may not use the maximum rent figure until a year after the date of that death (unless there was already a maximum rent figure that applied before that death, in which case that continues).

However, if your LHA rate would be higher than your 'protected' rate, you can receive the LHA rate instead.

Although your local authority may not use the maximum rent figure in the above two cases, it can restrict your eligible rent if it considers it is unreasonable in all the circumstances of your case. If this happens, seek advice.

For the purposes of the above protections, all the following count as members of your household:

■ each member of your family: you, your partner, children under 16 and young people aged 16-19 for whom child benefit is payable (see 24 below, under 'Your family');

■ any other relative of yours (or your partner) who lives with you but does not have an independent right to do so. A *'relative'* means a parent, parent-in-law, step-parent, son, daughter, son- or daughter-in-law, stepson or stepdaughter, sister, brother or the (married or unmarried)

partner of any of those, grandparent, grandchild, uncle, aunt, niece or nephew.

HB Regs, regs 12D & 2(1)

10. Rent officers' determinations
Before 7.4.08, maximum eligible rents were set at rates that followed determinations by rent officers. Rent officers are independent of the local authority; they look at your rent and various other factors before providing the authority with various figures that are used to calculate your maximum rent. Once your maximum rent has been set at a rate following

---

H.4 The 'bedroom tax'

From 1.4.13 your HB will be reduced if you are a working-age tenant of a local authority or housing association and are considered to have one or more spare bedrooms. This rule has been dubbed the *'bedroom tax'*. One bedroom is allowed for:

■ every adult couple (including civil partners);
■ any other adult aged 16 or over (this can include a son, daughter, stepson or stepdaughter of you or your partner who was living with you as a non-dependant (see 21 in this chapter) and is now serving away on operations as a member of the armed forces, who intends to move back in with you when they return);
■ any two children of the same sex (unless it is inappropriate for them to share a room because of disability – see below);
■ any two children regardless of sex if under the age of 10 (unless it is inappropriate for them to share a room because of disability – see below);
■ a foster child or children, if you are an approved foster carer (or kinship carer in Scotland);
■ any other child; *and*
■ a non-resident carer who regularly provides overnight care for a disabled claimant or their partner.

A further bedroom is allowed for a period of up to 52 weeks if you have been approved as a foster carer but do not currently have a child or qualifying young person (see Chapter 38(1)) placed with you.

Your eligible rent will be reduced by 14% if you have one spare bedroom, or 25% if you have two or more spare bedrooms.

HB Regs, reg B13

Disabled children – If your children are unable to share a bedroom due to disability, the local authority must consider not only the nature and severity of the disability, but also the nature and frequency of care required during the night, and the extent and regularity of the disturbance to the sleep of the child who would normally be required to share the bedroom.

Burnip, Trengove, Gorry v SSWP [2012] EWCA Civ 629

Protection for certain people
Local authorities may not apply the reduction if:

■ you and/or any member of your household could afford the financial commitments of your home when you first entered into them, and you (or your partner) have not received HB during the 52 weeks before your current claim; the authority may not apply the reduction for the first 13 weeks of your claim.
■ a member of your household has died, and you have not moved since then; the authority may not apply the reduction until a year after the date of that death (unless there was already a reduction that applied before that death, in which case that continues).

HB Regs, reg 12BA

such a determination, it will continue to be based on this determination until it is referred back to the rent officer because:

■ there has been a relevant change of circumstances; *or*
■ 52 weeks have passed since the last referral.

For details on this type of rent restriction, see *Disability Rights Handbook* 32nd edition, page 41. Note, however, that from 5.1.08, the criteria for establishing the local reference rent relates to a 'broad rental market area' rather than 'locality'. The definition of broad rental market area is the same as for the local housing allowance (see 9 above).

The Rent Officer (Housing Benefit Functions) Order 1997, Sch 1

11. Exceptions to rent restrictions

If one of the following exceptions applies to you, neither the local housing allowance nor the rent officer rules will apply. If you fall within more than one exception, just look at the first one that applies to you.

The exceptions can be complicated in some cases and it is often worth seeking advice. Also check the points under 'Protections for certain people' in 9 above.

Pre-January 1989 tenancies – This applies if your letting began before 15.1.89 in England and Wales or 2.1.89 in Scotland. In these cases it is very unlikely that the local authority will restrict your eligible rent.

HB Regs, Sch 2, para 4

People in accommodation where care, support or supervision is provided – This applies if:

■ your home is provided by a non-metropolitan county council, housing association, registered social landlord, registered charity, non-profit-making voluntary organisation or certain similar bodies; *and*
■ your landlord provides you with 'care, support or supervision' or has arranged for you to be provided with this. For this to apply there must be some contractual obligation between the landlord and care provider.

This exception also applies to you if your home is a resettlement hostel.

In these cases, your local authority can only restrict your eligible rent if it has evidence that your rent is unreasonably high or your home unreasonably large.

There are further rules that give protection to certain vulnerable people. If you have difficulties, seek advice.

HB & CTB (Consequential Provisions) Regs 2006, Sch 3, para 4(1)(b) & (10)

If you have been on HB since 1.1.96 – This applies if you:

■ were getting HB on 1.1.96 (in Northern Ireland on 1.4.96); *and*
■ have been on HB continuously since that date, ignoring gaps of no more than four weeks; *and*
■ have not moved since that date (unless as a result of a fire, flood, explosion or natural catastrophe).

If your partner or another member of your household previously satisfied these conditions, you may be able to take advantage of these rules. Seek further advice.

In the above cases, the local authority can only restrict your eligible rent if it has evidence that your rent is unreasonably high or your home unreasonably large.

HB & CTB (Consequential Provisions) Regs 2006, Sch 3, para 4(1)(a), (2) & (3)

People who pay caravan/mobile home site rent or mooring fees – This applies if you:

■ pay a county council for the rent of a caravan or mobile home or its site for Gypsies and Travellers; *or*
■ pay a housing authority for the rent of a site for a caravan or mobile home or for houseboat mooring charges, and HB is payable as a 'rent allowance'.

From 6.4.09 these tenancies should only be referred to the rent officer if the accommodation is considered to be unreasonably large or expensive.

HB Regs, Sch 2, para 3

12. Ineligible charges

The following apply only to tenancies exempt from the local housing allowance (LHA) and those HB awards not subject to the LHA. For a list of LHA exempt tenancies, see 9 above.

Garages

If you rent a garage, it is included as part of the rent on your home only if you were obliged to rent the garage from the beginning of your letting agreement, or you are making (or have made) all reasonable efforts to stop renting it.

HB Regs, reg 2(4)(a)

Water charges and council tax included in your rent

If your rent includes water or sewerage charges, the actual amount of the charge for your home (or if your water is metered, an estimate) is deducted, unless you are separately liable to pay the charge. If your rent includes a contribution towards the council tax because your landlord pays it, this is included as part of your eligible rent.

HB Regs, reg 12B(2)(a) & (5)

Service charges: general conditions

The rules for several types of service charge are given below, saying whether they can be taken into account as part of your eligible rent. But even when they can, there are two further conditions.

❏ The amount of the charge must be reasonable for the service provided. If it is not, the unreasonable part is deducted.
❏ Payment of the charge must be a condition of occupying your home, whether from the beginning of your letting agreement or from later on. If it is not a condition, the whole charge is deducted.

HB Regs, reg 12(1)(e); Sch 1, para 4

Exception – If the rent officer fixes a maximum rent for your home (see 10 above), they also fix a value for some services.

Fuel and related charges

If your rent includes fuel of any kind, the fuel charge is deducted if there is evidence of the amount (eg in your rent book or letting agreement). If there is no evidence of the amount, flat-rate amounts are deducted for various fuel costs; the amounts are given below.

Whenever your local authority makes flat-rate deductions, it must write inviting you to provide evidence of the actual amount. If you can provide reasonable evidence (which need not be from your landlord), the authority must estimate the actual amount and deduct that instead of the flat rates.

Exceptions – A fuel charge for a communal area (including communal rooms in sheltered accommodation) is included as part of your eligible rent if it is separately specified in your rent book or letting agreement. The same is true for a separately specified charge for providing a heating system.

Flat-rate deductions – If you rent more than one room (not counting any shared accommodation), these are:

Deductions	per week
Heating	£25.60
Hot water	£2.95
Lighting	£2.05
Cooking	£2.95

If you rent only one room (not counting a shared kitchen, bathroom or toilet), the flat-rate deduction for heating is £15.25. If you get a flat-rate deduction for heating, there is no further deduction for hot water or lighting, but the figure for cooking is as above.

HB Regs, Sch 1, paras 5 & 6

Meal charges

If your rent includes meals (the preparation of food or the provision of food) a flat-rate amount is deducted for these. The flat rate is always used, regardless of how much you are actually charged. One flat-rate deduction is made for each person (even if not a member of your family) whose meals are included in your rent.

Weekly deductions per person	aged 16+	under 16
For at least 3 meals every day	£25.85	£13.10
For breakfast only	£3.15	£3.15
For any other arrangement	£17.20	£8.65

For these purposes, a person counts as aged 16+ from the first Monday in the September following their 16th birthday.

HB Regs, Sch 1, paras 1(a)(i) & 2

Other services

Cleaning and window cleaning – A charge for cleaning and window cleaning of communal areas is included in your eligible rent; so is a charge for exterior window cleaning if neither you nor anyone in your household can do it. A charge (estimated if necessary) is deducted for any other cleaning and window cleaning.

Furniture and household equipment – A charge for these is included in your eligible rent unless your landlord has agreed they will become your personal property.

General support charges – Before April 2003, 'support charges' could be included in your eligible rent if you lived in supported accommodation. This has now ceased but you may be able to get help from the Supporting People scheme (see Chapter 29(4)).

Medical, nursing and personal care – A charge for any of these (estimated if necessary) is deducted.

Communal or accommodation-related services – Most charges for these are included in your eligible rent. Examples are: TV/radio aerial and relay, refuse removal, lifts, communal telephones, entry phones, children's play areas, garden maintenance necessary for the provision of adequate accommodation and communal laundry facilities.

Day-to-day living expenses, etc – Charges for these (estimated if necessary) are deducted. Examples are: TV rental, subscription and licence fees, laundering (ie if washing is done for you), transport, sports facilities, leisure items and any other service not related to the provision of adequate accommodation.

Staffing and administration charges – These are covered only if they are connected to the provision of adequate accommodation. To determine this, it is necessary to look at the number of hours a week that employees spend on providing accommodation-related services.

HB Regs, Sch 1, para 1(g)

13. How to claim housing benefit

Paper claims

If you request a claim-form for income support or jobseeker's allowance (JSA), you will be sent a claim-form for HB as well. Complete the form and send it to your local authority. (For pension credit and employment and support allowance (ESA) claims, see 'Telephone claims' below.)

If you are not claiming one of these benefits, ask your local authority for a HB claim-form, complete it and send it back to them within one month. You can phone and ask for the form. If you cannot easily get the claim-form, write to the authority: give your name and address, say you wish to claim HB, and date it. The authority should then send you the claim-form. Make sure you get it back to the authority within one month of the date it was sent to you.

Keeping a record – If possible keep a copy, or at least a record including the date you send the claim-form or any information you have been asked for. If you take in forms instead of posting them, get a receipt or written acknowledgement from whoever you give them to.

What do you need to send with the claim? – The claim-form asks you to provide various documents (eg your rent book). If you do not have all the information or documents requested, send the form back as soon as possible, and write on it that you will send the further information or documents as soon as you can. Explain any reasons for the delay. Sometimes the authority writes with further questions. Always ensure your reply reaches them within one month of when they sent the letter to you.

If you do not keep to the one-month time limit for sending information to your local authority (or for sending in the form if you originally sent a letter), they can agree a delay of whatever period is *'reasonable'*. This will mean you are treated as having claimed within the time limits (see below).

HB Regs, reg 86(1)

Telephone claims

You can claim HB over the phone at the same time that you claim ESA, income support, JSA or pension credit. The relevant DWP office will take your details over the phone, and for income support and JSA will send you a statement of your circumstances to sign and return to them. They will then forward the details to your local authority. For pension credit and ESA, you can claim these benefits and HB simultaneously (without having to sign a statement of circumstances) and your details will be forwarded to the local authority.

Claims for HB can be made by phone direct to the local authority if it has a number for this purpose. However, authorities are not required to do so and must continue to accept paper claims.

Electronic claims

Some local authorities have introduced email or online claiming. However, they are not required to do so and must continue to accept paper claims.

Date of claim

If you make a claim for a means-tested benefit (income-related ESA, income support, income-based JSA or the guarantee credit of pension credit) that is successful, and your HB claim is received within one month of this claim, your HB will start from the same date as the means-tested benefit.

If you notify either the HB office or an authorised DWP office of your intention to claim HB, your date of claim will be that date if you return the form within one month. The one-month time limit can be extended if the HB office thinks it is 'reasonable'.

If you have separated from your partner or your partner has died, and they were receiving HB, your claim for HB will start from the date of the separation or death as long as you claim within one month.

In all other cases, your claim begins on the day your claim-form is received by the HB office. However, it may be possible for your claim to be backdated (see 16 below).

HB Regs, reg 83(5)

Appointees

If you are unable to manage your affairs, an appointee can take over the responsibilities of claiming for you and dealing with further matters relating to your claim. That person (who must be aged 18 or over) should write to your local authority to request approval to act as your appointee. Permission should not be withheld unreasonably.

14. When HB starts, changes and ends

Your first day of entitlement – HB usually starts on the Monday after the date of your claim (this date is described above). Even if that date was itself a Monday, HB starts the following Monday.

The exception is if the date of your HB claim is in the same benefit week (Monday to Sunday) as you moved into your home (or first became liable for rent for any other reason). In that case, your HB starts on the day your rent liability began (whether your rent is due daily, weekly or monthly).

HB Regs, reg 76

When HB ends – You cease to be entitled if a change in your circumstances means you no longer qualify.

Change of circumstances

You have a duty to notify your local authority about any change in circumstances that may affect your entitlement. The authority will advise you of changes you should notify.

HB Regs, reg 88(1)

If a change in circumstances means you qualify for more HB, write to the authority promptly. If you take more than one calendar month and you have no good reason for the delay, you will lose money because the increase will only be given to you from the Monday following the day your letter reached them. If you have a good reason for delaying more than a month, explain this in your letter, as otherwise it may not be taken into account. In all cases, 13 months is the absolute limit for notifying changes.

HB&CTB(D&A) Regs, regs 8(3) & 9

If a change in your circumstances means you qualify for less HB, write to the authority promptly, or you will probably be asked to repay any overpayment (see 18 below).

You normally need to let the local authority know of a change of circumstances in writing, but some authorities give a telephone number you could use instead. Jobcentre Plus offices often give you a number to contact if you find work. You will have discharged your duty to inform the authority of your change of circumstances if you ring that number and provide the authority with the information or evidence it needs to process a new 'in-work' HB claim within one month of the authority requesting it (if you fail to do so and an overpayment occurs, it will be recoverable from you).

HB Regs, reg 88(6)

15. How housing benefit is paid

If you pay rent to the local authority

HB is awarded as a rebate towards your rent account, which is why it is also called a 'rent rebate'. In other words, the rent you have to pay will be reduced. This also applies if you pay rent to the Northern Ireland Housing Executive.

Payment for everyone else

HB is usually paid into your bank account, although it can be paid by cheque, which is why it is also called a 'rent allowance'. The local authority must take into account your *'reasonable needs and convenience'* in choosing the method of payment, so should not insist on paying you by cheque if you do not have a bank account.

Your first payment – The local authority should make your first payment within 14 days of receiving your properly completed claim or *'if that is not reasonably practicable, as soon as possible thereafter'*. This must be either the correct amount of your entitlement or, if that is not yet known, an estimated amount, known as a *'payment on account'*, which will be adjusted when the correct amount is known. You should not have to ask the authority for a payment on account, but if you do not get one, contact them and remind them of their duties. Authorities do not, however, have to make a payment on account if you have not supplied the information and documents they have requested, unless you can show

that your failure to do so is 'reasonable' (eg if the delay in providing these is outside your control).

HB Regs, regs 91(3) & 93,

Payment to your landlord – HB is paid direct to your landlord if:

■ you request or consent to it; *or*

■ it is in your or your family's best interests; *or*

■ you have left the dwelling with rent arrears (but payment will only be made up to the level of rent owing); *or*

■ an amount of income support, jobseeker's allowance, employment and support allowance or pension credit is being paid direct to the landlord to cover rent arrears; *or*

■ you have at least eight weeks of rent arrears (six weeks in Northern Ireland) unless it is in your overriding interest not to make direct payment to the landlord.

In the first three cases, the authority does not have to agree. In the fourth and fifth cases, they must pay the landlord unless the landlord is deemed not to be a 'fit and proper' person to receive payment. The authority can also choose to pay your first payment of HB to your landlord (regardless of whether you agree) if they consider it appropriate.

HB Regs, regs 95 & 96(1)-(2)

Local housing allowance (LHA) payments – These are normally made to you, but can be made to the landlord if:

■ the authority believes you are likely to have difficulty managing your affairs; *or*

■ the authority considers it improbable that you will pay your rent; *or*

■ for eight weeks, if the authority suspects that either of the above may apply and is considering this; *or*

■ the authority has previously had to pay the landlord; *or*

■ you have left the property and there are rent arrears (but payment will only be made up to the level of rent owing); *or*

■ the authority considers that it will assist you in securing or retaining a tenancy.

The local authority must pay LHA direct to the landlord when you have rent arrears of at least eight weeks (unless it is in your overriding interest not to make payments direct to the landlord) or when an amount of a means-tested benefit is being paid to the landlord to cover rent arrears.

HB Regs, regs 95(1)(b), 96(3A) & (3B)

16. Getting more benefit

Discretionary housing payments

Discretionary housing payments (DHPs) are technically not a kind of HB, but are administered by the same authorities and can only be given to people who qualify for at least some HB.

The local authority can give you a DHP if you *'appear to [the] authority to require some further financial assistance… in order to meet housing costs'*. DHPs are discretionary (no one has a right to one) – as is the amount of DHP and the period it is granted for. The combined amount of your HB and DHP in any one week cannot usually exceed your 'eligible rent' (see 8 above). However, a DHP can exceed the current amount of eligible rent in some circumstances, eg if you have rent arrears and the DHP covers the past period.

DHPs cannot be used if benefit has been reduced or suspended (eg for failure to attend a work-focused interview), or for ineligible service charges (see 12 above) or water and sewage charges.

In Northern Ireland, a DHP is paid only to claimants whose rent has been restricted and who seem to need further financial assistance. It is intended to meet only the shortfall between the rent being requested by a landlord and the restricted rent. It does not apply to the rate rebate scheme.

Most local authorities have a form on which to request a DHP. If your authority does not, write a letter instead. The authority may ask for detailed information about your circumstances and those of your household. Explain these fully, in particular your disability needs, as otherwise the authority could take into account the fact that you receive state benefits, such as disability living allowance, when deciding on your DHP request (even if the HB rules would normally ignore these). The availability of DHPs varies widely from authority to authority. The HB appeals system does not apply to DHPs, but you have the right to ask the authority to look again at its decision if you are dissatisfied. It is your duty to report changes in your circumstances that could affect the payment of a DHP.

The Discretionary Financial Assistance Regs

Getting your benefit backdated
If you are under pension credit qualifying age (see Chapter 42(2)), HB can be backdated for up to six months if you have continuous *'good cause'* for the delay in claiming. If you have reached pension credit qualifying age, HB can be backdated for up to three months without you having to show good cause.

HB Regs, reg 83(12), HB(SPC) Regs, reg 64(1)

Good cause – This means some fact or facts which *'having regard to all the circumstances (including the claimant's state of health and the information which he had received and that which he might have obtained) would probably have caused a reasonable person of his age and experience to act (or fail to act) as the claimant did'.*

R(S)2/63(T)

For example, you may have good cause if you are ill and have no one to help you make the claim, or if you are unable to manage your affairs and don't have an appointee. Ignorance of the law is not normally good cause unless there are exceptional circumstances (eg mental health or learning disabilities, educational limitations, youthfulness, language difficulties, or a combination of these and other factors). Generally, you are expected to make reasonable enquiries about your right to benefit. You will normally be able to show good cause if you ask the DWP or local authority for advice and act on the basis of their wrong or misleading advice or if you reasonably misunderstood the advice.

Ex-gratia payments – If your claim was delayed for over three or six months and the delay was the local authority's fault, you can ask for an ex-gratia compensation payment to cover the period remaining after the maximum 3- or 6-month backdate.

17. Underpayments
If your local authority has awarded you less HB than they should have, due to official error, they must make up the difference. An *'official error'* means a mistake by the local authority, DWP or HMRC. There is no limit to the period for which arrears may be paid in these cases. However, if you were awarded less HB because you failed to tell the authority something, see 14 above.

HB&CTB(D&A) Regs, reg 4(2)

18. Overpayments
Overpayments are amounts of HB you were awarded but which you weren't entitled to – perhaps because you did not tell the local authority something you should have, or because the authority or Jobcentre Plus office made a mistake, or for some unavoidable reason. Different rules apply to different types of overpayment, as follows.

Overpayments of payments on account – If you were granted a payment on account (see 15 above) and it turned out to be greater than your actual entitlement to HB, the overpayment will be recovered from your future HB entitlement. If it turns out you were not entitled to any HB, the following rules apply.

HB Regs, reg 93(3)

Overpayments due to official error – An *'official error'* means a mistake, to which you did not contribute, by your local authority, the DWP or HMRC.

If your Jobcentre Plus office does not tell your local authority that you have come off income support, income-based jobseeker's allowance or income-related ESA (or started receiving any other benefit), this may count as an official error. However, because the law says it is your duty to tell the authority about changes in your circumstances, Jobcentre Plus will not be deemed as having caused the overpayment and it will be recoverable from you.

Your local authority must not recover an overpayment due to official error unless you (or someone acting for you, or the person who received the payment, eg your landlord if your HB is paid to them) could *'reasonably have been expected to realise that it was an overpayment'* at the time the payment or any notification about it was received. The authority should take into account what you (or the other person) personally could have been expected to realise.

HB Regs, reg 100(2)-(3)

Overpayments due to a mistake about capital – An overpayment of more than 13 weeks of HB due to a mistake about capital may not be recoverable in full. There are 'diminution of capital' rules that treat the capital as gradually reducing (described in Chapter 57(7)).

All other overpayments – Any overpayment of HB not mentioned above may be recovered by your local authority. This includes overpayments due to a failure or mistake by you, and even overpayments that were unavoidable (such as overpayments due to a backdated pay rise or a backdated social security benefit).

HB Regs, reg 100(1)

How much is the overpayment?
If you qualified for at least some HB during the period for which you were overpaid, your local authority should allow you to keep it (even if you didn't claim it or tell them everything you should have at the time). It should normally only recover the difference between what you were paid and what you should have been paid. If the authority does not do this, seek advice.

HB Regs, reg 104

How are overpayments recovered?
An overpayment can be recovered from you or you partner (but where recovery is by deductions from ongoing HB, only if you were a couple at the time of both the overpayment and the recovery) or (in most cases) the person who received the payment (eg your landlord) or the person who caused the overpayment. It can be recovered as follows:
- by reducing your future HB entitlement (including HB entitlement on a new address when you move within the same local authority area). The most the authority can recover in this way is £10.80 a week (although this can be increased in certain cases if you are working or receive a war widow's or war disablement pension or charitable or voluntary income, have committed fraud or have moved);
- if the above method is not possible, by making deductions from almost any other social security benefit you receive;
- if HB was paid direct to your landlord, by deduction from another tenant's (or the landlord's own) HB.
In all cases, you can negotiate with the authority over how to re-pay the overpayment. As a last resort, the authority can take action in the courts to recover an overpayment.

HB Regs, regs 101-102 & 104A

If an HB overpayment is recovered from your HB paid to your landlord, then (unless you rent your home from the local authority or Northern Ireland Housing Executive), the landlord is legally allowed to treat the amount repaid as rent arrears due from you (but seek housing advice about possible rent arrears).

Discretion and hardship – Even if an overpayment is recoverable, your local authority can exercise its discretion not to recover it (eg if you can show that you would otherwise suffer hardship).

SSAA, S.75(1)

Notifications and appeals – In all cases, if your local authority decides to recover an overpayment, it must write notifying you of the details and your appeal rights. You can use the appeal procedure if you are dissatisfied with its decision.

19. Decisions, revisions and appeals
The following rules apply to HB. For details, see Chapter 58.

Notice of decisions
Your local authority has a duty to send you a written notice about the decision it makes on your HB claim. If you do not qualify, the notice will say why not. If the authority makes further decisions during the course of your claim (eg about a change of circumstances or an overpayment), it must send you a written notice about each one. In each case, it will also explain your right to get more information and to appeal.

Written statement – If you want more information about how your entitlement to HB (or lack of it) was worked out, write to the authority and ask for a written statement. You must do this within one month of notification of the decision. You can ask about specific things or ask for full details of how your claim was assessed. The authority should reply in writing within 14 days, or as soon as possible after that.

HB Regs, reg 90

Exceptions – In certain circumstances, the authority does not have to make a decision, and the tribunal does not have to deal with an appeal. This is called 'staying' a decision or appeal. It arises when a test case is pending, the result of which could affect your case (see Chapter 58(6)).

Asking the authority to revise their decision
You have the right to ask your local authority to revise its decision on almost any matter relating to an HB claim (eg, how much you qualify for, whether you should have to repay an overpayment, etc). If your request is made within the 'dispute period' (see below), the authority must reconsider its decision, taking account of what you say. It should give you a written notice saying whether it is revising or sticking to its original decision, and giving the reasons.

HB&CTB(D&A) Regs, reg 4

Appeals to a tribunal
Either instead of, or after, asking your local authority to revise a decision (see above), you can appeal to an independent appeal tribunal; see Chapter 58 for details.
Exceptions – There is no right of appeal to a tribunal about:
- most administrative decisions about HB claims and payments, although you can appeal to a tribunal about when the benefit should begin and about backdating.
- whether the authority should run a disregard scheme for a war pension (see Chapter 27(6) under 'Benefits that are partly disregarded');
- your maximum rent, if the rent officer or Northern Ireland Housing Executive fixed one, or the level of local housing allowance (see 9 and 10 above);
- discretionary housing payments (see 16 above).

HB&CTB(D&A) Regs, reg 16 and Sch

The dispute period
Whether you are asking the local authority to revise a decision or asking for an appeal, your letter should reach the authority within one calendar month of the day it sent the decision notice. If you are asking for a revision of the decision and have asked for a written statement (see above), the time the authority took to deal with that is ignored when calculating the month. If you are appealing the decision, you have 14 days from the date the written statement is sent out to ask for an appeal.

Your local authority (or the tribunal, in the case of an appeal) can agree to extend the one-month time limit if the delay was caused by special circumstances (or, if you are appealing, the tribunal judge agrees; see Chapter 58(7)). In this case, explain what your special circumstances are when you request the revision/appeal, as otherwise they may not be taken into account. In all cases, 13 months is the absolute limit for asking for the decision to be changed.

HB&CTB(D&A) Regs, regs 4(1), 5, & 19; TP(FTT)SEC Rules, rule 23

The Ombudsman
You can make a complaint to the Ombudsman if you feel the local authority or Northern Ireland Housing Executive administered your claim unfairly or caused unreasonable delays. See Chapter 60(5).

20. How much benefit?
Follow the steps below to work out your entitlement to HB. We first give the steps if you are on a means tested benefit (income support, income-based jobseeker's allowance, income-related employment and support allowance or the guarantee credit of pension credit), then the steps for if you are not.

If you are on a means-tested benefit
If you (or your partner) are on a means-tested benefit:
Step 1: Work out your eligible rent
HB is worked out on your weekly eligible rent; this can be less than your actual rent (see 8 above).
Step 2: Deduct amounts for non-dependants
If you have one or more non-dependants in your home, your HB is reduced by flat-rate amounts (though there are exceptions to this). For who counts as a non-dependant and the other details, see 21 below.
Step 3: Amount of benefit per week
HB equals your weekly eligible rent minus any amounts for non-dependants.

Example
If your weekly eligible rent is £90 and you have no non-dependants, the weekly amount of your HB is £90. But if you have one non-dependant, and a flat-rate deduction of £70.20 applies, the weekly amount of your HB is £19.80.

If you are not on a means-tested benefit
If you (or your partner) are not on a means-tested benefit:
Step 1: Your capital
If your capital (including your partner's) is more than £16,000 you cannot get HB. Not all capital counts. For how to work out your capital, see 22 and 25 below.
Step 2: Your eligible rent
HB is worked out on your weekly eligible rent; this can be less than your actual rent (see 8 above).
Step 3: Deduct amounts for non-dependants
If you have one or more non-dependants in your home, your HB is reduced by flat-rate amounts (though there are exceptions to this). For who counts as a non-dependant and other details, see 21 below.
Step 4: Work out your weekly income
This includes your (and your partner's) income from some, but not all, sources. For how to work out your weekly income, see 23 and 25 below.
Step 5: Work out your applicable amount
This figure represents your weekly living needs. For how to work out your applicable amount, see 24 and 25 below and Chapter 25.
Step 6: Have you got 'excess income'?
If your income is *less* than, or equal to, your applicable amount, you do not have *'excess income'*. See Step 7.

If your income is *greater* than your applicable amount, you have 'excess income'. The amount of the excess income is the difference between your income and your applicable amount. See Step 8.

Step 7: Amount of benefit per week if you do not have 'excess income'
HB equals your weekly eligible rent less any amounts for non-dependants. This is exactly the same as for people who are on a means-tested benefit. For an example, see above.

Step 8: Amount of benefit per week if you have 'excess income'
HB equals your weekly eligible rent less any amounts for non-dependants and less 65% of your excess income. If the result is less than 50p you will not be awarded benefit. See below.

Example if you have excess income
If your weekly eligible rent is £90, you have no non-dependants and you have excess income of £20, the weekly amount of your HB is:

Eligible rent	£90.00
Less 65% of £20 excess income	£13.00
Weekly housing benefit	*£77.00*

But if you have one non-dependant and a flat-rate deduction of £13.60 applies, the weekly amount of your HB is:

Eligible rent	£90.00
Less non-dependant deduction	£13.60
Less 65% of £20 excess income	£13.00
Weekly housing benefit	*£63.40*

The 65% figure is also called a *'taper'*: as your excess income goes up, your benefit goes down. You can have so much excess income that you do not qualify for any benefit. The amount(s) of your non-dependant deduction(s) can also mean you do not qualify for any benefit.
HB Regs, reg 71

If the calculation comes out at less than 50p (the minimum HB award), you will not get any benefit.
HB Regs, Reg 75

21. Non-dependants
Deductions are made from your HB if you have one or more non-dependants, even if you are on income-related employment and support allowance (ESA), income support, income-based jobseeker's allowance (JSA) or the guarantee credit of pension credit. The law assumes they will contribute towards your rent, whether or not they do. A deduction cannot be cancelled on the grounds that your non-dependant pays you nothing. But there are cases when no deduction can be made.
HB Regs, reg 74

Who is a non-dependant?
A non-dependant is someone who normally lives in your home on a non-commercial basis – usually an adult son, daughter, friend or relative. None of the following are your non-dependants (so there is no deduction for any of them):
■ your *'family'* (see 24 below). For example, an 18-year-old who is included in your family is not your non-dependant;
■ foster children;
■ someone with whom you share just a bathroom, toilet, communal area (or in sheltered accommodation, a communal room);
■ any joint occupier(s), tenant(s) or sub-tenant(s), resident landlord (and members of their households);
■ your or your partner's carer if they are provided by a charity or voluntary organisation that charges you for this (even if someone else pays the charge for you).
Almost anyone else who lives with you is your non-dependant.
HB Regs, reg 3

No non-dependant deduction
Your (or your partner's) circumstances – There is no deduction for your non-dependants (no matter how many you have) if you or your partner:
■ are registered as blind or ceased to be registered within the last 28 weeks; *or*
■ get the care component of disability living allowance (DLA; any rate), the daily living component of personal independence payment (PIP; any rate) or attendance allowance or constant attendance allowance.

Your non-dependant's circumstances – There is no deduction for a non-dependant if they:
■ are under 18; *or*
■ are under 25 and on income support, income-based JSA or assessment-phase income-related ESA; *or*
■ are on pension credit; *or*
■ get a Work-Based Learning for Young People training allowance; *or*
■ have been in an NHS hospital for over 52 weeks; *or*
■ are detained in prison or a similar institution; *or*
■ have their normal home elsewhere; *or*
■ are not residing with you because they are a member of the armed forces away on operations; *or*
■ are a full-time student (see Chapter 40(2)); there is a deduction in the summer vacation if they take up remunerative work (see below), unless they (or their partner) are 65 or over.
HB Regs, reg 74(6)-(8) & (10)

The amounts of the deductions
❏ **Non-dependants aged 25 or over on income-related ESA, income support or income-based JSA** – The weekly amount is £13.60.
❏ **Non-dependants on pension credit** – No deduction.
❏ **Other non-dependants not in remunerative work** – Regardless of your non-dependant's income, the weekly amount is £13.60.
❏ **Non-dependants in remunerative work (excluding those on pension credit)** – The weekly amount depends on your non-dependant's weekly gross income.

Weekly gross income	Weekly deduction
£401 or more	£87.75
£322 to £400.99	£79.95
£242 to £321.99	£70.20
£186 to £241.99	£42.90
£126 to £185.99	£31.25
Under £126	£13.60

HB Regs, reg 74(1)-(2)

If you cannot provide evidence of your non-dependant's gross income (and they are in remunerative work and not receiving pension credit), your local authority must consider all the circumstances of the case before making the highest of the above deductions. If you later provide evidence showing the deduction should have been lower, they should award you arrears of HB as you have been underpaid (see 14 above).

Which non-dependants are in remunerative work?
'Remunerative work' means work that averages 16 or more hours a week. If your non-dependant is on maternity, paternity, adoption or sick leave, they do not count as being in remunerative work (even if paid full pay or statutory maternity, paternity, adoption or sick pay). If your non-dependant gets income-related ESA, income support or income-based JSA for more than three days in any benefit week (Monday to Sunday) they do not count as being in remunerative work.
HB Regs, reg 6

Your non-dependant's gross income

Your non-dependant's income is relevant if they are in remunerative work. It is assessed gross, which, in the case of earnings, means before tax, national insurance and other deductions are made. All other income is counted, except DLA, PIP, attendance allowance, constant attendance allowance and payments from the Macfarlane Trusts, the Eileen Trust, MFET Ltd, the Independent Living Fund and the Fund. If your non-dependant has capital, only the interest is counted as gross income. If your non-dependant is in a couple, add their partner's gross income (but see below).

HB Regs, reg 74(9)

Other points about non-dependants

You usually get a deduction for each non-dependant you have (apart from those for whom no deduction applies). But if you have non-dependants who are a couple, you get only one deduction for the two of them. This is the higher figure of the two amounts that would have applied to them if each was single and each had the income of both.

If you are a joint occupier (see 5 above), and your non-dependant is also a non-dependant of the other joint occupier(s), the deduction is shared between you and the other joint occupier(s).

HB Regs, reg 74(3)-(5)

Concession if you are aged 65 or over

If you or your partner are 65 or over, special non-dependant deduction rules apply. If a non-dependant comes to live with you, their income will be ignored for HB purposes for 26 weeks. If you already have a non-dependant living with you and their circumstances or income change (meaning a higher deduction applies), the local authority will not increase the amount of the deduction for a 26-week period. If changes occur more than once, the 26-week period runs from the date of the first change. If your non-dependant's income decreases, the authority should reduce the deduction immediately if appropriate.

HB(SPC) Regs, reg 59(10)-(12)

22. Capital

Your local authority needs to assess your capital if you are not on income-related employment and support allowance, income support, income-based jobseeker's allowance or the guarantee credit of pension credit. If you are in a couple, your partner's capital is included with yours. For how capital is assessed, see Chapter 28. There are different capital rules for claimants who have reached pension credit qualifying age (see 25 below).

If your capital is over £16,000, you cannot get HB. If your capital is £6,000 or less, it is ignored in assessing your HB. If it is a higher figure (but not over £16,000), you are treated as having income – known as 'tariff income' (see Chapter 28(4). In rare cases, some people in care homes are entitled to HB (see Chapter 33(3)), and the first £10,000 (instead of £6,000) of their capital is ignored.

If a child in your family has capital of their own, it is disregarded.

23. Income

Your local authority needs to assess your income if you are not on income-related employment and support allowance, income support, income-based jobseeker's allowance or the guarantee credit of pension credit. If you are in a couple, your partner's income is included with yours. For how income is assessed, see Chapter 27. There are different income rules for claimants who have reached pension credit qualifying age (see 25 below).

If your income is greater than your applicable amount, this affects the amount of HB you get (see 20 above).

24. Applicable amounts

Your local authority needs to assess your applicable amount if you are not on income-related employment and support allowance (ESA), income support, income-based jobseeker's allowance (JSA) or the guarantee credit of pension credit. An *'applicable amount'* is a figure set by Parliament that is intended to reflect your weekly living needs and those of your family. If you (or your partner) have reached pension credit qualifying age, see 25 below. If you are under pension credit qualifying age, your applicable amount is made up of:

■ **personal allowances** – you get one or more of these for various members of your family, including children; *plus*

■ **premiums** – many people, but not all, get one or more premiums to take account of family responsibilities, disabilities and responsibilities as a carer; *plus*

■ **additional components** – apply only if you are entitled to main-phase ESA.

HB Regs, reg 22

You must satisfy conditions for each part of the applicable amount. You can ask for a written statement from the authority about what premiums you have been awarded and why. If you think any have been missed, you should ask for a revision or lodge an appeal (see 19 above).

Your family

Applicable amounts are based on the circumstances of your family. *'Family'* is used in a technical sense and means:

■ you (the claimant); *and*

■ your partner. This can be your spouse or civil partner, as long as you are living in the same household. It can also include your partner if you are unmarried or have not entered into a civil partnership if you are effectively living together as husband and wife or civil partners; *and*

■ any dependent child(ren) or young people who are members of your household and under the age of 16 (or under the age of 20 if they are a 'qualifying young person' for child benefit purposes – see Chapter 38(1)). The definition of a dependent child includes your natural or adopted children and others for whom you are responsible (eg a grandchild). Foster children are not usually included. If a child who is normally in local authority care spends time with you at home, the authority can include that child or not as a member of your family for the benefit week(s) (Monday to Sunday) when the child stays with you. This is an 'all or nothing' rule: the authority cannot give you just part of a personal allowance or family premium.

HB Regs, regs 19-21

Personal allowances

Lower personal allowances can apply to people under 25, unless the claimant is entitled to main-phase ESA.

Allowances for children have been retained in the applicable amount for HB. They are paid for each dependent child or qualifying young person under the age of 20 for whom you are responsible (see above).

Personal allowances		per week
Single person	aged 25 or over	£71.70
	aged 16-24	£56.80
	entitled to main-phase ESA*	£71.70
Lone parent	aged 18 or over	£71.70
	aged under 18	£56.80
	entitled to main-phase ESA*	£71.70
Couple	one or both aged 18 or over	£112.55
	both under 18	£85.80
	entitled to main-phase ESA*	£112.55
Dependent child		£65.62

HB Regs, Sch 3, Part 1

* Includes claimants receiving national insurance credits only.

Premiums

There are six premiums, each with specific qualifying conditions (see Chapter 25). Unless otherwise specified in that chapter, each premium to which you are entitled is added to the total of your applicable amount.

Premiums		per week
Family	ordinary rate	£17.40
	lone parent rate*	£22.20
Disability**	single	£31.00
	couple	£44.20
Disabled child		£57.89
Severe disability	single	£59.50
	couple (one qualifies)	£59.50
	couple (both qualify)	£119.00
Enhanced disability	single	£15.15
	couple	£21.75
	child	£23.45
Carer		£33.30

* Applies in limited circumstances (see Chapter 25(7)).
** Does not apply when there is an entitlement to main-phase ESA.

Additional components

If you are entitled to main-phase ESA (or 'credits only' ESA – see Box D.7, Chapter 12), you are entitled to an additional component depending on whether you are placed in the work-related activity group or the support group (see Chapter 10(6) and (7)):

- work-related activity component: £28.45 a week;
- support component: £34.80 a week.

25. Rules for people who have reached pension credit qualifying age

The rules for claimants who have reached pension credit qualifying age (see Chapter 42(2)) are different (unless you or your partner receive income support, income-based jobseeker's allowance or income-related employment and support allowance). The main differences are listed below.

Applicable amount

Your personal allowance is based on the pension credit *'standard minimum guarantee'* (see Chapter 42(3)) and, if you or your partner are aged 65 or over, the maximum *'savings credit'* (see Chapter 42(4)). For a single claimant the personal allowance is £145.40, or £163.50 if you are 65 or over. For a couple it is £222.05, or £244.95 if either of you is 65 or over.

The following extra sums can be included in your applicable amount following the usual HB rules:

- personal allowances for dependent children and young people (see 24 above);
- family premium (see Chapter 25(7));
- severe disability premium (see Chapter 25(3));
- enhanced disability premium (for any qualifying dependent child or young person, but not for yourself or your partner) (see Chapter 25(4));
- disabled child premium (see Chapter 25(8));
- carer premium (see Chapter 25(6)).

Income and capital

There are different rules about how income and capital affect the amount of HB you get, depending on whether you receive pension credit and which elements are in payment.

Guarantee credit – If you or your partner receive the guarantee credit of pension credit, all of your capital and income will be disregarded and you will receive full HB. This applies even if your capital exceeds the usual HB limit of £16,000. Since there is no capital limit for pension credit,

it is possible to receive the guarantee credit even though your savings would exceed the HB limit.
HB(SPC) Regs, reg 26

Savings credit only – If you or your partner are 65 or over and receive the savings credit but not the guarantee credit of pension credit and do not have more than £16,000 capital, the local authority will use the assessment of your income and capital that The Pension Service used to calculate your savings credit (see Chapter 42(4)). The authority will then adjust this figure by adding:

- any of your partner's income or capital that was not taken into account in the pension credit calculation;
- in very limited circumstances, any income of a non-dependant that is treated as yours under HB rules; *and*
- any pension credit savings credit.

They will then subtract (if applicable):

- the higher HB disregard of lone parent's earnings and the 'additional earnings disregard' (see Chapter 27(5));
- the normal HB disregard of childcare costs (see Chapter 27(5));
- earnings from permitted work (see Chapter 17(3)); *and*
- any discretionary disregard of war pensions allowed by your local authority.

HB(SPC) Regs, reg 27(4)

No pension credit payable – If you or your partner have reached pension credit qualifying age but do not receive pension credit, your income and capital will be assessed by the local authority in much the same way as it is for pension credit (see Chapter 42(5) and (6)).
HB(SPC) Regs, reg 28

22 Council tax

1. What is council tax?

Council tax is a domestic property-based tax paid to the local authority to help pay for the services it provides. It applies only in England, Scotland and Wales. Domestic rates are payable in Northern Ireland.

2. Your dwelling

Council tax is only charged on domestic properties or 'dwellings'. A *'dwelling'* is a self-contained unit of living accommodation, such as a house, flat, bungalow, houseboat or mobile home. It does not matter whether the dwelling is owned or rented. One council tax bill is due on each dwelling, unless it is exempt (see 4 below). If a property is divided into self-contained units (eg flats), each unit is a separate dwelling and gets a separate bill (unless exempt). If a property contains non-self-contained units (eg a house with a number of rooms with different people in each, but they all share some accommodation) the property is one dwelling and gets one bill (unless exempt). A self-contained unit is defined as *'a building or part of a building which has been constructed or adapted for use as separate living accommodation'*. If a property contains living and business accommodation, council tax is due for the domestic part (unless exempt) and the business part is subject to non-domestic rates.

LGFA, S.72(2); Council Tax (Chargeable Dwellings) Order

3. How much council tax?
Council tax valuation bands
Every property in each local authority area is placed into a valuation band, labelled from A (the lowest) to H (the highest) (or A to I in Wales), depending on its value. The higher the band, the more council tax you are liable to pay.

The value of a dwelling does not relate to its current market value. In England and Scotland, it is based on 1991 property values; in Wales, 2003 property values.

In England and Wales, dwellings are valued by the Valuation Office Agency (VOA), and in Scotland by the local assessor. These bodies also decide what counts as a dwelling and how many dwellings there are in a property.

LGFA, Ss.5(2)-(3) & 74(2)

Challenges and appeals
You have the right to challenge the valuation of your dwelling if within six months you have become newly liable for council tax there (eg through moving) or if there has been a material reduction in its value (eg through partial demolition or its adaptation for use by a disabled person). You can also ask for a change if part of the property begins to be used for business purposes. In England and Wales, if the VOA does not agree to the change, an appeal can be made to the independent Valuation Tribunal. An appeal must be made within three months of receiving the decision. In Scotland, if the local assessor does not agree to the change, they will refer the proposal to the Valuation Appeal Committee.

You can also appeal within six months of a successful challenge on a comparable dwelling (eg another property on the same street or on a new estate) if this suggests that the value of your own property should be changed.

In other circumstances, you can ask the VOA or local assessor to reconsider the band for your dwelling and, if it is wrong, they may alter it. But if they do not agree, you do not have the right of appeal.

4. Exempt dwellings
If a home is an exempt dwelling, no council tax is due on it. Most exemptions are for unoccupied dwellings. The main conditions for exemptions are given in Box H.5.

If your local authority has not awarded an exemption, you can ask for one. An exemption can be backdated to the date it should have first applied. There is no time limit and no need to show 'good cause' for applying late but you will need to produce evidence that the exemption has applied throughout the period. You can appeal against a decision on exemption (see 11 below).

H.5 Summary of council tax exemptions for dwellings

Note: Local authorities are required to take reasonable steps to check whether any discounts apply before deciding on the chargeable amount.

❏ **A substantially unfurnished, unoccupied dwelling is exempt if:**
■ structural or major repair works are needed, are in hand, or have been completed recently (for up to 12 months in total); *or*
■ it is unoccupied for any other reason (which could be that it has just been built) and has been for less than six months.

❏ **An unoccupied dwelling (whether furnished or not) can be exempt if it is:**
■ left empty by persons in prison or a similar institution;
■ left empty by persons now resident in a hospital, a care home or a hostel where personal care is provided;
■ left empty by persons now resident elsewhere for the purpose of receiving or providing personal care due to old age, disablement, illness, past or present alcohol or drug dependence, or past or present mental illness or disorder;
■ left empty by deceased persons where probate or letters of administration have not been granted, or less than six months have passed since the granting of probate or letters of administration;
■ left empty by a student owner;
■ the responsibility of a bankrupt's trustees;
■ to be occupied by ministers of religion; *or*
■ a pitch or mooring that is not occupied by a caravan or boat.

❏ **A dwelling is also exempt if it is:**
■ wholly occupied by a person (or persons) who is *'severely mentally impaired'* (see Box H.6) and no one else could be liable. (Note: You do not lose the exemption if a student or students also occupy the dwelling);
■ wholly occupied by people under the age of 18;

■ unoccupied, and is part of a single property containing another dwelling where someone resides, and letting it separately would be a breach of planning control (or, in Scotland, the dwelling would be difficult to let separately);
■ in Scotland and is a housing association trial flat for pensioners or for people with disabilities;
■ unoccupied and occupation is prohibited by law (eg it is unfit for habitation or subject to a compulsory purchase order);
■ unoccupied and a planning condition prevents occupancy;
■ under charitable ownership and has been unoccupied for less than six months;
■ an armed forces barracks or married quarters or used as visiting forces accommodation;
■ a repossessed property where the property is unoccupied;
■ a student hall of residence; *or*
■ currently wholly occupied by students (including students temporarily absent from their course).

❏ **In England and Wales only**
There is a further exemption where there are at least two dwellings (ie two self-contained units) within a single property and one occupant is a *'dependent relative'* of someone who is resident in another part of the property. The exemption applies only to the part of the property where the dependent relative is resident. The definition of 'relative' is quite straightforward and includes quite distant relatives (eg great-great-grandchild) and common-law relations. If there is a dispute about your status as a relative you should seek advice. The dependent relative must be:
■ aged 65 or over; *or*
■ *'severely mentally impaired'* (see Box H.6); *or*
■ *'substantially and permanently disabled'*, the definition of which is open to wide interpretation.

Council Tax (Exempt Dwellings) Order 1992 (as amended); &
Council Tax (Exempt Dwellings)(Scotland) Order 1997, Sch 1

5. Who is liable to pay?

Unless a dwelling is exempt, someone will be liable to pay council tax on it. This usually depends on who is resident there (see 6 below). The rules for the dwelling in which you are resident are given below. If you own or rent a dwelling that has no residents, you are usually liable for council tax there (whether or not you are also liable on the dwelling in which you are resident).

Backdating – If you were liable for council tax in the past but were not billed, a bill can be backdated. There is no time limit, but local authorities must issue bills as soon as is reasonably practicable.

Appeals – See 11 below.

General rules for the dwelling in which you reside

The following rules apply to the dwelling in which you are resident (see 6 below). A partner as referred to below includes a partner of the same sex.

If you own it, you are liable for council tax. Your partner, if resident with you, is jointly liable with you (even if not a joint owner). Any other joint owners resident with you are also jointly liable.

If you rent it and do not have a resident landlord, you are liable for council tax. Your partner, if resident with you, is jointly liable with you (even if not included on the letting agreement). Any other residents who rent it on the same letting agreement are also jointly liable.

The landlord is liable in the following cases:

- if you rent from a resident landlord;
- if it is a care home, or (in most cases) a hostel;
- if you rent non-self-contained accommodation and/or any others who rent it have separate letting agreements (even if the landlord is not resident there); *or*
- if you are an asylum seeker receiving asylum support (other than temporary support) from either the government or the local authority.

LGFA, Ss.6, 8, 75 & 76

Special cases

If you and any other occupiers are *'severely mentally impaired'* (see Box H.6) or are students, the dwelling in which you are resident is exempt (see Box H.5). If anyone else lives with you, including carers, the property will not be exempt, but you may be eligible for a discount (see 9 below).

If you are under 18 you are not liable for council tax on any dwelling in which you are resident. Other resident(s) aged 18 or over are liable instead. If there are none, the dwelling is exempt (see Box H.5).

6. Who is a resident of a dwelling?

You are a *'resident'* of a dwelling if it is your *'sole or main residence'*. You can only be a resident of one dwelling at a time. Deciding where you are resident is usually straightforward. In difficult cases, the local authority should take into account how much time you spend at different addresses, where you work, where your children go to school, how much security of tenure you have at different addresses, and other relevant information. You can appeal against a decision about where you are resident (see 11 below).

LGFA, Ss.6(5) & 99(1)

7. How to pay less council tax

There are three schemes for reducing council tax bills. You can get help through all three at the same time if you satisfy the conditions for all of them. They are:

- the Disability Reduction scheme (see 8 below);
- the discount scheme (see 9 below);
- the council tax reduction scheme (see 12 below).

Some dwellings are exempt from council tax (see 4 above).

8. Disability Reduction scheme

You can get a disability reduction if you or any other *'resident'* (see 6 above) in your dwelling is *'substantially and permanently disabled'*. This can be an adult or a child of any age, whether or not they are related to you. At least one of the following three conditions must also be met:

- you have an additional bathroom or kitchen needed by the disabled person; *or*
- you have a room (other than a bathroom, kitchen or toilet) needed by and predominantly used by that person; *or*
- you have enough space in your dwelling for that person to use a wheelchair indoors.

Disability reductions are available in all types of dwellings, including care homes and hostels.

In Scotland, water charges (collected with the council tax) can also be reduced under this scheme.

Council Tax (Reductions for Disabilities) Regs

There is no general test of who counts as *'substantially and permanently disabled'*, although it is clear that it includes people who have been disabled for life and also those who have become disabled later in life. There is also no general test of what it means for the disabled person to 'need' the room or the wheelchair, except that they must be *'essential or of major importance to [his or her] well-being by reason of the nature and extent of [his or her] disability'*.

However, it is clear that disability reductions are not limited to dwellings specially constructed or adapted to provide a room or wheelchair space.

The *Sandwell* High Court judgment has been misinterpreted by many authorities as denying a reduction to disabled people who use another room instead of a dedicated bedroom. In fact, the judgment simply emphasised that there must be an *'appropriative causative link between the disability and the requirement of the use of the room, because the use has to be essential or of major importance, because of the nature and extent of the disability'*. This has been further clarified in a more recent decision, which states that the room must be extra or additional, in the sense that it would not be required for the relevant purpose if the person were not disabled.

R (Sandwell MDC) v Perks [2003] 1749 (Admin) (EWHC); South Gloucestershire Council v Titley & Clothier [2006] 3117 (Admin) (EWHC)

How much is it worth? – If you qualify for a disability reduction, your council tax bill is reduced to the amount payable for a dwelling in the valuation band below yours. If your dwelling is in band A, you get a reduction of one-sixth of your bill.

Getting a reduction and backdating – The person liable for council tax (not necessarily the disabled person) has to make an application. The authority may have a standard form for this (and in some areas you may have to make a separate application for each financial year). If you should have been given a disability reduction in the past, but were not, it should be backdated. There is no time limit.

Council Tax (Reductions for Disabilities) Regs, reg 3(1)(b)

You can appeal against a decision on disability reductions (see 11 below).

9. Discount scheme

The council tax discount scheme is applied to dwellings where fewer than two adults are resident (see 6 above). You can get a discount if:

- there is only one resident in your dwelling: in this case your discount equals 25% of your council tax liability; *or*
- there are no residents in your dwelling: in this case your discount may be up to 50% of your council tax liability (but see 10 below). If your home is empty, you may be able to qualify for exemption instead of a discount (see 4 above).

LGFA, Ss.11 & 79

Counting the residents – Several groups of people are

'disregarded' when counting the number of residents in your dwelling; they are sometimes called 'invisible'. See Box H.6. This is important because it can mean you qualify for a discount even if there are several people in your dwelling, as long as enough of them are disregarded.

Example: If you are in a couple and have two children aged 17 and 20 at home, you might not expect to get a discount. But if your partner is severely mentally impaired or is a carer (as defined in Box H.6), and the 20-year-old is a student, they will both be 'disregarded'. So will the 17-year-old (because of being under 18). That will leave you as the only resident who will be counted. Your council tax bill will be reduced by 25%.

Getting a discount and backdating – Your local authority may automatically grant a discount, but you can also apply for one. They may have a standard form. A discount can be backdated to the date it should have first applied. There is no time limit within which you can apply for the discount. You can appeal against a decision on discounts (see 11 below).

10. Second homes and long-term empty properties

In England and Scotland, local authorities have the power to reduce the discount offered on furnished second homes from 50% to just 10%. In Wales, authorities have discretion to

---

H.6 People who are disregarded for council tax discount purposes

People who are 'severely mentally impaired'
This means anyone who:
- *'has a severe impairment of intelligence and social functioning (however caused) which appears to be permanent'; and*
- has a certificate from a registered medical practitioner confirming this (which may cover a past, present or future period); *and*
- is entitled to one of the following benefits:
  - disability living allowance (DLA) middle or highest rate care component;
  - personal independence payment (PIP) daily living component (either rate);
  - attendance allowance, constant attendance allowance (or an equivalent benefit);
  - employment and support allowance;
  - incapacity benefit (any rate);
  - severe disablement allowance;
  - income support including a disability premium due to incapacity, or whose partner has a disability premium for them included in their income-based jobseeker's allowance;
  - the disability element of working tax credit; *or*
  - is over state pension age and would have been entitled to one of the above benefits if under state pension age.

Carers
There are two different types of carer who are disregarded.
First type of carer – All the following conditions must be met. The carer:
- provides care for at least 35 hours a week on average. The law refers to *'care'*, not *'support'*;
- is 'resident' (see 6 in this chapter) in the same dwelling as the person cared for;
- is not the partner of the person cared for;
- is not the parent of the person cared for, if the person cared for is aged under 18;
- cares for a person who is entitled to one of the following: the highest rate of DLA care component, the higher rate of attendance allowance or constant attendance allowance, either rate of PIP daily living component.

Second type of carer – All the following conditions must be met. The carer must be:
- providing *'care or support'* on behalf of a local authority, government department or charity, or through an introduction by a charity where the person being cared for is the carer's employer;
- employed for at least 24 hours a week;
- paid no more than £44 a week;
- resident where the care is given or in premises that have been provided for the better performance of the work.

More than one person in the same dwelling can count as a carer, including where caring responsibilities are being shared.

People in hospital, a care home or certain kinds of hostel
People whose sole or main residence is a hospital or care home are disregarded (ie a short stay does not count). People in hostels who have no residence elsewhere are also disregarded; this includes bail or probation hostels along with night shelters and other similar accommodation.

Anyone whose 'sole or main residence' is elsewhere
People whose sole or main residence is with someone else or who are living in another institute (not a hospital or care home) in order to receive care are disregarded. For where someone is 'resident', see 6 in this chapter.

Young people, students, student nurses, youth trainees, apprentices and others
The following individuals or groups are ignored:
- everyone aged 17 or under;
- 18/19-year-olds for whom child benefit is payable (see Chapter 38);
- education-leavers under 20 (but only if they left on or after 1 May, and then only until 31 October inclusive that year);
- school or college-level students aged under 20, if their term-time study normally amounts to 12 or more hours a week;
- students, if their study amounts to at least an average of 21 hours a week for periods of at least 24 weeks a year;
- student nurses whose academic course means they count as a 'student', or who are studying for their first nursing registration;
- foreign language assistants;
- trainees under the age of 25 on training funded by the Skills Funding Agency or Education Funding Agency;
- apprentices undertaking training that leads to an accredited qualification (eg an NVQ), subject to limitations on pay;
- people in prison or similar institutions;
- members of a religious community that provides for all the individuals' needs;
- members of some international organisations or visiting forces;
- foreign spouses and dependants of students;
- diplomats and their spouses.

Council Tax (Discount Disregards) Order 1992;
Council Tax (Additional Provisions for Discount Disregards) Regs 1992;
Council Tax (Discounts)(Scotland) Order 1992;
Council Tax (Disregards)(Scotland) Regs 1992 – each as amended

reduce the discount below 50% or to offer no discount at all. Armed forces personnel who have a home in Wales and are required to live in alternative accommodation provided by the Ministry of Defence receive an automatic discount of at least 50% on their Welsh home.

Properties that have been unoccupied and substantially unfurnished for more than two years do not qualify for a discount and the council tax due may be increased by up to 50%.

LGFA, S.11B; The Council Tax (Prescribed Classes of Dwellings) Regs; The Council Tax (Discount for Unoccupied Dwellings) (Scotland) Regs 2005

11. Appeals

You have the right to appeal against decisions on:
- whether a dwelling is exempt from council tax;
- who is liable to pay council tax;
- where you are resident;
- whether a disability reduction applies; *and*
- whether a discount applies.

In each case the appeal should first go to the local authority. There is no time limit for lodging the appeal. If it is refused you can appeal to the Valuation Tribunal for England or the Valuation Tribunal for Wales (within two months of receiving the decision, or within four months of your original appeal if the local authority has not responded) or Valuation Appeal Committee in Scotland (within four months of your original appeal).

12. Council tax reduction scheme

From April 2013 a new *'council tax reduction scheme'* is being introduced, replacing council tax benefit (see *Disability Rights Handbook 37th edition*, Chapter 20). Since the new scheme comes with a UK-wide 10% drop in funding, many claimants will be substantially worse off; others, in particular those over pension credit qualifying age, will be protected (see below). There are different arrangements in England, Scotland and Wales.

England and Wales

In England and Wales, each local authority is required to have a council tax reduction scheme in place, subject to certain conditions. Because each authority has a different scheme, we cannot describe each one in detail. Below, we describe the general requirements of local schemes, but you should contact your local authority, or a CAB or other advice agency, for details of the scheme adopted in your area.

Each local authority must publish details of its scheme and review it every year. If an authority does not adopt a scheme by 31st January each year, a default scheme (based on the old council tax benefit) will be used instead.

The Council Tax Reduction Schemes (Default Scheme)(England) Regulations 2012; The Council Tax Reduction Schemes (Default Scheme)(Wales) Regulations 2012

How do the schemes operate? – Local schemes operate either by allowing a percentage discount or by calculating an amount of money to be allowed as a discount. The discount can be for the full amount of the council tax or for a lower amount. In England, most authorities have chosen to require all liable people under pension credit qualifying age (see Chapter 42(2)) to pay something. In Wales, authorities are likely to be more generous as the Welsh government is making up for the 10% drop in funding. More generous rules apply if you have reached pension credit qualifying age (see below).

If you have capital over £16,000, you are not eligible for council tax reduction. Nor are you eligible if you are subject to immigration control (see Chapter 49(3)), are not habitually

resident, or do not have the right to reside in the UK (see Chapter 49(2)).

The reduction scheme applies after any reductions have been applied under the Disability Reductions scheme (see 8 above) or the discount scheme (see 9 above).

If you are over pension credit qualifying age – The government has set out detailed rules which English and Welsh local authorities must follow. These are similar to the rules for housing benefit (HB). A maximum council tax reduction is calculated, based on the council tax you are liable for, minus any deductions for non-dependants (see Chapter 21(21); although lower figures are used). An applicable amount is calculated and your income and capital assessed (see Chapter 21(25)). If your income is less than the applicable amount, you are entitled to maximum council tax reduction. If your income is greater than your applicable amount, you are entitled to a reduction equal to your maximum council tax reduction minus 20% of your excess income.

The Council Tax Reduction Schemes (Prescribed Requirements) (England) Regulations 2012; The Council Tax Reduction Schemes and Prescribed Requirements (Wales) Regulations 2012

Claims, reviews and appeals – Local authorities must accept claims in writing, and can accept them by electronic methods or by phone. If you are already in receipt of council tax benefit, you will not need to apply for council tax reduction and will be migrated onto the new scheme by your local authority. All decisions on council tax reduction have to be put in writing.

If you are unhappy with a decision, you can ask the authority to review it. If you are not satisfied with the outcome of the review, you can appeal to the Valuation Tribunal for England or the Valuation Tribunal for Wales.

H.7 For more information

Your local Citizens Advice Bureau has information on housing benefit and council tax reduction schemes and should be able to advise you. If you want to look at the law, see CPAG's *Housing Benefit and Council Tax Benefit Legislation*. For further information see the *Guide to Housing Benefit and Council Tax Benefit* and other publications listed in Chapter 61.

Scotland

The Scottish government has sought to protect claimants from the UK-wide 10% drop in funding, by making up the difference. Hence in Scotland, a single system replicates the old council tax benefit system. As such it is similar to HB.

A maximum council tax reduction is calculated based on the council tax you are liable for, minus any deductions for non-dependants (see Chapter 21(21); although lower figures are used). An applicable amount is calculated (see Chapter 21(24)) and your income and capital assessed (see Chapter 21(22) and (23)). There is similar provision if you are over pension credit qualifying age (see Chapter 21(25)). If your income is less than the applicable amount, you are entitled to maximum council tax reduction. If your income is greater than your applicable amount, you are entitled to a reduction equal to your maximum council tax reduction minus 20% of your excess income.

The Council Tax Reduction (Scotland) Regulations 2012

Grants and loans

23 The social fund

1. What is the social fund?

The social fund makes payments to people in need to cover specific costs. It provides Sure Start maternity grants and funeral, cold weather and winter fuel payments. You are legally entitled to a payment if you satisfy the regulations. If you disagree with a decision relating to the social fund, you can ask for a revision or appeal to a tribunal (see Chapter 58).

2. Sure Start maternity grants

You are entitled to a Sure Start maternity grant of £500 if:

■ you (or a member of your family) are pregnant, have given birth in the last three months (including stillbirth after 24 weeks of pregnancy), have been appointed as a guardian, adopted (including a recognised adoption outside the UK), or been granted a residence order for a child under the age of one, or have been granted a parental order for a child born to a surrogate mother, or are the parent (but not the mother) of a child under the age of one, and are responsible for the child; *and*

■ there is no other member of your family who is under 16, although a grant can be awarded for each child of a multiple birth where there is no other child under 16. If you have a multiple birth and you have another child under 16, a grant can be awarded for each child in that multiple birth less the number of children born to a single pregnancy already in your household: eg if you have triplets but already have twins under 16 you can be awarded just one grant. If you are claiming for someone under 20 who is the parent of the child, the grant is payable provided the parent has no other children under 16; *and*

■ you or your partner have been awarded one of the following *'qualifying benefits'* in respect of the day you claim the maternity grant: income support, pension credit, income-based jobseeker's allowance, income-related employment and support allowance, child tax credit paid at a rate that exceeds the family element, working tax credit that includes the disability or severe disability element, or universal credit; *and*

■ you have received health and welfare advice about child health matters and, if applying before the birth, advice about maternal health; *and*

■ you claim within the time limits (see below).

SFM&FE Regs, regs 5 and 5A

Claim on form SF100, available from Jobcentre Plus or your antenatal clinic. You must claim in the 11 weeks before your expected week of confinement, or in the three months following the date of the birth or adoption, guardianship, residence or parental order. In the case of adoption, guardianship and residence orders, the child must be under the age of one at the date of claim. If you are waiting for a decision on a qualifying benefit, you must still claim within the time limit and if your claim is refused because you are not yet getting the qualifying benefit, re-claim within three months of it being awarded.

C&P Regs, Sch 4, para 8

3. Funeral payments

You are entitled to a funeral payment if:

■ you or your partner accept responsibility for the costs of a funeral (ie you have paid or are liable to pay them) that takes place in the UK (or in another European Economic Area country (see Chapter 49(1)) or Switzerland, if you or a member of your family are classified as a 'worker' or have the right to reside in the UK under European Community law – see Chapter 49(2)); *and*

■ you or your partner have been awarded a 'qualifying benefit' in respect of the day you claim a funeral payment. These are the same as for Sure Start maternity grants (see 2 above) but also includes housing benefit; *and*

■ the deceased was ordinarily resident in the UK when they died; *and*

■ you claim within the time limits (see below); *and*

■ you fall into one of the groups of people who are eligible to claim (see below).

SFM&FE Regs, reg 7

Who can claim? – You must fall into one of the following groups.

❑ You were the partner of the deceased when they died or immediately before either of you moved permanently into a care home. 'Partner' includes opposite and same-sex couples whether or not you were married or civil partners.

❑ The deceased was a child for whom you were responsible and there is no 'absent parent' (unless they were getting one of the above qualifying benefits when the child died), or the deceased was a stillborn child.

❑ You were a close relative or close friend of the deceased and it is reasonable for you to accept responsibility for the funeral costs, given the nature and extent of your contact with the deceased. 'Close relative' means parent (or parent-in-law), son (-in-law), daughter (-in-law), brother (-in-law), sister (-in-law), stepson/daughter (-in-law) or step-parent.

You cannot get a payment as a close relative or friend of the deceased if:

■ the deceased had a partner when they died; *or*

■ there is a parent, son or daughter of the deceased who is not:

– getting a qualifying benefit (see above); *or*

– in prison or hospital immediately following a period on a qualifying benefit; *or*

– under 18, or aged 18 or 19 and a qualifying young person for child benefit (see Chapter 38(1)); *or*

– aged 18 or over and in full-time education; *or*

– a fully maintained member of a religious order; *or*

– someone who was estranged from the deceased; *or*

– receiving asylum support; *or*

– ordinarily resident outside the UK; *or*

■ there is a close relative (see above) of the deceased, other than a person who falls into one of the groups above, who was in closer contact with the deceased than you were, or had equally close contact and is not getting a qualifying benefit.

SFM&FE Regs, reg 7 & 8

How much do you get? – The following costs can be met:
- the necessary costs of purchasing a new burial plot with exclusive rights plus necessary burial fees, or the necessary costs of cremation including medical fees;
- the cost of documentation required to release the deceased's assets;
- the reasonable costs of transport for the portion of journeys in excess of 50 miles undertaken to transport the body within the UK to a funeral director's premises or a place of rest and to transport the coffin, bearers and mourners in two vehicles to the funeral;
- the necessary costs of one return journey from your home for you or your partner to arrange or attend the funeral if you are responsible for the funeral costs;
- up to £700 for other funeral expenses (or £120 if you have a pre-paid funeral plan that doesn't cover these expenses).

The following amounts are deducted from an award of a funeral payment (note that a funeral payment is recoverable from the deceased's estate):
- any of the deceased's assets that are available to you without probate or letters of administration, although if you have a joint account with the deceased the assets become yours at the point of death and cannot be deducted;
- any lump sum due to you or a member of your family on the death of the deceased from an insurance policy, occupational or war pension, burial club or similar scheme;
- any contribution towards the funeral costs from a charity or relative of yours or the deceased;
- any amount from a pre-paid funeral plan or similar scheme.

Payments from the Macfarlane, variant CJD or Eileen Trusts, the Fund or Skipton Fund, Caxton Foundation, MFET Ltd or London Bombings Relief Charitable Fund are ignored. Arrears of most benefits and tax credits are also ignored.

SFM&FE Regs, regs 9 & 10

How and when to claim – You must claim within three months of the date of the funeral using form SF200, available from a Jobcentre Plus office or the DWP Bereavement Service (0845 606 0265; textphone 0845 606 0285). If you are waiting for a decision on a qualifying benefit, the rules are the same as for Sure Start maternity grants (see 2 above).

C&P Regs, Sch 4, para 9

4. Cold weather payments

These are automatic payments (you do not need to claim) of £25 for each qualifying week made by the DWP if:
- the average temperature recorded or forecast over seven consecutive days at the designated weather station for your area is zero degrees Celsius (freezing) or less; *and*
- you have been awarded income support, income-based jobseeker's allowance (JSA) or income-related employment and support allowance (ESA) for at least one of those days and you are responsible for a child under the age of 5, or you are getting child tax credit that includes a disabled or severely disabled child element, or your income support, JSA or ESA includes one of the disability or pensioner premiums; *or*
- you have been awarded universal credit and have a child under the age of 5, or your award includes a disabled child element or an element for limited capability for work or work-related activity (or would do but for the fact that it includes a carer element), and you are not in employment or gainful self-employment during the qualifying week (although this does not apply if your award includes the disabled child element); *or*
- you have been awarded pension credit, or income-related

ESA that includes a work-related activity or support component, for at least one of those days; *and*
- you are not resident in a care home.

Social Fund Cold Weather Payments Regs

5. Winter fuel payments

This is a lump sum paid if you have reached pension credit qualifying age (see Chapter 42(2)) in the *'qualifying week'* (week beginning 16.9.13 for winter 2013/14).

You are not entitled to a payment if during that week you:
- are subject to immigration control or not ordinarily resident in Great Britain (see Chapter 49(2) and (3)), although you may be able to get one if you are residing in an EEA state or Switzerland; *or*
- have been receiving free inpatient treatment in hospital (or similar institution) for more than 52 weeks; *or*
- are in custody serving a sentence imposed by a court; *or*
- are getting pension credit, income-based jobseeker's allowance (JSA) or income-related employment and support allowance (ESA) and you have been living in a care home for 13 weeks or more at the end of the qualifying week (disregarding temporary absences).

Social Fund Winter Fuel Payment Regs

How much do you get? – If you or your partner do not receive pension credit, income-based JSA or income-related ESA and you are aged:
- under 80 (but over pension credit qualifying age), you will get £200 if you are the only person in the household entitled to a payment, or £100 if you share a household with one or more other people entitled to a payment;
- 80 or over, you will get £300 if you are the only person in the household aged 80 or over, or £150 each if there are more people aged 80 or over entitled to a payment. If one of you is 80 or over and the other aged under 80 (but over pension credit qualifying age) you will get £200 and £100 respectively.

If you are receiving pension credit, income-based JSA or income-related ESA, you will get £200 (or £300 if you or your partner are aged 80 or over) regardless of who else is in the household. If you are one of a couple and your partner receives pension credit, income-based JSA or income-related ESA, they will receive the payment instead.

If you have been living in a care home for 13 weeks or more at the end of the qualifying week and are not getting pension credit, income-based JSA or income-related ESA, you are entitled to £100 if you are aged under 80 (but over pension credit qualifying age), or £150 if you are aged 80 or over.

How do you claim? – You should automatically receive a payment without making a claim if you received a payment last year and your circumstances have not changed, or you are getting a state pension or other social security benefit (excluding child benefit or housing benefit) in the qualifying week. Otherwise, you must make a claim (ring 0845 915 1515 for a claim-form), which must be received by the Winter Fuel Payment Centre by 31.3.14.

24 Other loans and grants

1. What grants or loans are available?

Prior to April 2013, the DWP administered the discretionary social fund, which was made up of community care grants, crisis loans and budgeting loans (see *Disability Rights Handbook* 37th edition, page 124). From April 2013, the DWP only has responsibility for budgeting loans (see 2 below) and loans while you are waiting for a benefit claim to be processed (or *'short-term advances'* – see Chapter 57(6) for details). Community care grants and crisis loans for all other circumstances have been replaced by a new service delivered by local authorities. Each local authority will manage its own scheme, although the Welsh and Scottish governments are planning to operate national schemes (see below). Contact your town hall for details of the scheme where you live. In Northern Ireland, the service will be administered by the Social Security Agency.

Wales – The *'Discretionary Assistance Fund'* will be grant based and will provide two types of support:

■ *'individual assistance payments'* to enable independent living or continued independent living, preventing the need for institutional care;

■ *'emergency assistance payments'* to provide assistance in an emergency or when there is an immediate threat to health or wellbeing.

Scotland – The *'Scottish Welfare Fund'* will be grant based and will provide two types of support:

■ *'community care grants'* to help people on benefits who may have to go into care unless they get some support to stay at home, or if they are leaving any form of care and need help to set up their own home;

■ *'crisis grants'* to help people, typically on benefits, who are in crisis because of a disaster or an emergency.

Future changes – Budgeting loans will be replaced by *'budgeting advances'* within the new universal credit, but the rules of entitlement will not be exactly the same. Short-term advances will also be available within universal credit. See Box J.1 in Chapter 25 for more on universal credit.

2. Budgeting loans

To be eligible for a budgeting loan you must satisfy all the following conditions.

❏ You must be in receipt of (ie be the claimant of) one of the following *'qualifying benefits'* when your application for a budgeting loan is decided:
  – income-related employment and support allowance (ESA);
  – income support;
  – income-based jobseeker's allowance (JSA); *or*
  – pension credit,
  and you and/or your partner must have been receiving a qualifying benefit throughout the 26 weeks before the decision (ignoring breaks of 28 days or less). The three waiting days at the start of a JSA or ESA claim do not count. For joint-claim couples (see Chapter 15(2)), only the partner who is paid JSA is eligible for a budgeting loan.

❏ You or your partner must not be involved in a trade dispute.

❏ You must not have too much capital. The amount of any loan you get will be reduced on a pound-for-pound basis by any savings you or your partner have over £1,000 (or £2,000 if you or your partner are aged 61 or over). Capital is worked out in the same way as for the qualifying benefit depending on which benefit you are getting (except that Family Fund payments and refugee integration loans are disregarded).

❏ Your application must be for one of the following categories of expenses:
  – furniture and household equipment;
  – clothing and footwear;
  – maternity or baby items;
  – funeral expenses;
  – rent in advance and/or removal expenses to secure new accommodation;
  – improvement, maintenance and security of the home;
  – travelling expenses;
  – expenses associated with seeking or re-entering work;
  – HP and other debts for expenses associated with the above categories.

How is the amount of the loan calculated?

The maximum loan depends on whether you are single, a couple or have children. A baseline figure is set nationally, equating to the maximum loan for a single person. This amount may vary during the year according to the budgetary position. If you are not single, the maximum loan is calculated as follows:

■ a couple without children will get $1\frac{1}{3}$ times a single person amount;

■ someone with children will get $2\frac{1}{3}$ times a single person amount.

How much do you get? – The minimum award that can be made is £100 and the highest is the maximum available amount for your circumstances as calculated above (but can never be more than £1,500). The amount you are offered may be less than the maximum for the following reasons.

❏ The repayment rules may prevent full payment (see below).

❏ The amount of the award is reduced if you have capital or savings over the limit (see above).

❏ If you or your partner have another budgeting loan outstanding, the maximum amount you can get is reduced by the amount of your outstanding loan.

❏ If you asked for less than the maximum that you can be awarded, you will only get the amount you asked for.

Repayment of budgeting loans

A decision maker can only award an amount you are likely to be able to repay. The loan will be scheduled for repayment within 104 weeks at a standard rate. If you have asked for a loan (within your maximum amount) that cannot be repaid within 104 weeks at standard repayment rates, the decision maker may give you alternative options with higher repayment rates. However, they cannot ask you to pay more than 20% of your available income (ie your income-related ESA, income support or income-based JSA applicable amount or pension credit appropriate minimum guarantee plus any child tax credit or child benefit, but excluding housing costs).

Decisions about repayment terms are not subject to review, but if you have difficulty repaying the loan you can ask for the repayment rate to be reduced. Write to your Jobcentre Plus office giving details of your financial situation and how much you can afford to repay.

Loans are normally repaid by deductions from your or your partner's income-related ESA, income support, pension credit or income-based JSA. If you don't get enough benefit, or your benefit stops, deductions can be made from most other social security benefits, but not from disability living allowance, attendance allowance or child benefit.

The Social Fund (Recovery by Deductions from Benefits) Regs 1988

Applying for a budgeting loan

Apply on form SF500 (available from your local Jobcentre Plus office or www.gov.uk/budgeting-loans/overview), giving full details of your circumstances.

Reviews

You can ask for a review of a budgeting loan decision by a *'reviewing officer'* based in the office that made the decision. The reviewing officer will only look at your circumstances at the time of the original decision and is bound by the same rules as the original decision maker. You must request the review in writing within 28 days of the date the decision was issued to you. The time limit can be extended if there are *'special reasons'*; this is not defined in law, so each case should be considered on its merits. Your application must explain why you disagree with the decision. If a late review is not accepted or your circumstances have changed, it may be better to submit a new claim instead.

Means-tested benefits: common rules

25 Premiums

1. Introduction

This section covers the common rules for means-tested benefits, which provide a basic amount of money for you and your partner, if you have one, to live on. Support for children is now usually provided by child tax credit (see Chapter 19). This section covers the common rules for:

- income-related employment and support allowance (ESA);
- income support;
- income-based jobseeker's allowance (JSA);
- housing benefit; *and*
- pension credit.

Each of these benefits is calculated with reference to an *'applicable amount'*, which is the amount of money the law says you need to live on. The applicable amount is made up of a number of different elements, including flat-rate amounts known as *'premiums'*, which are covered in this chapter. Another element can cover certain housing costs; this is covered in Chapter 26. Your means-tested benefit could be affected by your earnings or other income; this is covered in Chapter 27. Finally, capital and savings can affect your benefit; we cover this in Chapter 28. Since income and savings are treated in a different manner for pension credit, we cover the separate rules for this benefit in Chapter 42.

Universal credit – The government is replacing those means-tested benefits and tax credits for people of working age with 'universal credit' (see Box J.1). This is being piloted from April 2013 in north-west England; nationwide roll-out starts in October 2013 on the basis of one district in each Jobcentre Plus region. A new claim for one of the current means-tested benefits or tax credits may be treated as a claim for universal credit instead, depending on where you live.

The premiums

There are seven types of premium:

- disability premium;
- severe disability premium;
- enhanced disability premium;
- pensioner premium;
- carer premium;
- family premium; *and*
- disabled child premium.

You are entitled to these premiums if you satisfy certain conditions, detailed in 2 to 8 below. The eligibility rules for these premiums are generally the same for each benefit; where there are differences, we will point this out. However, not all the premiums apply to each means-tested benefit.

The family premium, disabled child premium and enhanced disability premium (for a child) usually only apply to housing benefit. They can only apply to income support or income-based JSA if your claim for either of these benefits began before April 2004 and you continue to receive support for your children through that benefit rather than through child tax credit. The disability premium does not apply to income-related ESA (and has a limited application to housing benefit). Only the severe disability premium and carer premium apply to pension credit (and are named 'amounts' rather than premiums, although the eligibility rules are similar).

For the sake of simplicity, we generally confine the legal references to those applicable to income-related ESA and income support.

2. Disability premium

The disability premium does not apply to either income-related employment and support allowance (ESA) or pension credit. Nor does it apply to housing benefit if you have (or can be treated as having) a limited capability for work with respect to a claim for ESA (see Chapter 11(2)).

HB Regs, Sch 3, para 13(9)

For a single claimant aged 16 or over, the disability premium is £31. For a couple, the disability premium is £44.20, whether one or both of the couple count as disabled.

The disability premium can be awarded on top of any enhanced disability premium, carer premium or severe disability premium that is payable. The disability premium is payable only while the person who qualifies is under the qualifying age for pension credit (see Chapter 42(2)).

There are three ways of qualifying for the premium:

- you (or your partner) meet at least one of the disability conditions; *or*
- the person who is, or becomes, the claimant meets the incapacity condition; *or*
- for joint claims for jobseeker's allowance (JSA) only, you or your partner meet the limited capability for work condition.

IS Regs, Sch 2, paras 11-12; JSA Regs, Sch 1, paras 20G & 20H

The disability conditions (claimant or partner)

You (or your partner) must be:

- registered as blind, or taken off that register in the past 28 weeks; *or*
- receiving one of the following qualifying benefits:
  - attendance allowance;
  - disability living allowance (DLA);
  - personal independence payment (PIP);
  - long-term incapacity benefit;
  - severe disablement allowance (SDA);
  - the disability element or severe disability element of working tax credit;
  - war pensioner's mobility supplement;
  - constant attendance allowance;
  - armed forces independence payment;

(but you or your partner must satisfy the conditions for getting that benefit yourselves; it doesn't count if you are paid someone else's benefit as an appointee).

IS Regs, Sch 2, para 12(1)(a) & (2)

J.1 Universal credit

The *'universal credit'* is a single, integrated means-tested benefit payable to people of working age, whether in work or not. It replaces the following:

- child tax credit;
- housing benefit;
- income-related employment and support allowance;
- income-based jobseeker's allowance
- lincome support;
- working tax credit;

as well as parts of the social fund.

Do you qualify?

To qualify for universal credit, you (and your partner, if you are making a joint claim) must:

- be aged 18 or over (or aged 16 or 17 in certain cases);
- be under the qualifying age for pension credit (see Chapter 42(2));
- be in Great Britain (see Chapters 49(2) and 50(9));
- not be in education (see Chapter 40(2));
- have accepted a claimant commitment (see below);
- not have capital or savings of more than £16,000 (see below).

WRA 2012, Ss.3 & 4(1); UC Regs, reg 18

The claimant commitment

You must meet certain work-related requirements. These are recorded in a *'claimant commitment'* – which lists the requirements you are expected to meet in order to receive the benefit. There are four sets of requirements:

- no work-related requirements;
- work-focused interview requirement only;
- work-focused interview and work preparation requirements; *and*
- all work-related requirements.

The requirement that applies to you will depend on your circumstances. If you have a partner, you may have a different requirement to them (eg if one of you has responsibility for caring for a severely disabled person). Your universal credit may be reduced or stopped if you fail to meet a work-related requirement, although hardship payments may be available.

WRA 2012, Ss.13-28; UC Regs, regs 15-16 & 84-119

Capital or savings

The upper capital limit is £16,000 whether you are single or part of a couple; if your capital or savings are greater than this, you are not entitled to universal credit. Capital under £6,000 is disregarded. If you have capital or joint capital over the lower limit of £6,000, it is treated as yielding an income of £4.35 a month for each complete or incomplete £250 above the £6,000 limit. This income is added to other income you have (see below) in the universal credit calculation. Some kinds of capital are disregarded, eg the value of your home.

UC Regs, regs 45-50, 72 & Sch 10

How is universal credit worked out?

The amount of universal credit you are paid depends on your circumstances. Set amounts for different needs (called *'elements'*) are added together. Your earnings and other income are subtracted from this total. The resulting amount will be your universal credit. Not all your earnings are taken into account; some are disregarded, and then a *'taper'* is applied. See below for details.

Universal credit elements
Standard allowance

This is a basic amount to cover essential living costs for you (and your partner, in the case of a joint claim). Other elements can be added, which are:

Child elements

Elements are included for each child or *'qualifying young person'* (see Chapter 38(1)) for whom you are responsible.

An additional amount is included if you are responsible for a child/young person who is disabled. The amount is set at two different rates. The higher rate applies if they:

- receive disability living allowance (DLA) highest rate care component;
- receive personal independence payment (PIP) enhanced rate daily living component; *or*
- are registered blind.

The lower rate applies if they get any other rate of DLA or PIP. See Chapter 3 for details of DLA and Chapter 4 for PIP. An amount is included for each child/young person who qualifies.

UC Regs, regs 5 & 24

Capability for work elements

An element is included if you have a *'limited capability for work'* (LCW). A higher element is included if you have a *'limited capability for work and work-related activity'* (LCWRA). These are tested under the *'work capability assessment'* (see Chapter 11). If you move into full-time work, you can only retain either of these elements in limited circumstances (see Chapter 17(9)).

UC Regs, regs 27-28 & 38-44; Schs 6-9

Carer element

An element is included if you have *'regular and substantial caring responsibilities'* for a severely disabled person. You are considered to have such responsibilities if you would satisfy the eligibility conditions for carer's allowance (see Chapter 7(2)). However, you do not need to have made a claim for carer's allowance to have the element included.

If you are claiming jointly with your partner, and you both have caring responsibilities, two carer elements can be included (although not if you are caring for the same person). A carer element cannot be included at the same time as a LCW or LCWRA element; if you would otherwise be eligible for the carer element and either LCW or LCWRA, only the highest paid element is included.

UC Regs, regs 29-30

Childcare element

This can be included if you pay for registered childcare in order to stay in work. Generally, the childcare must be provided by a registered childcare provider or an equivalent. The childcare does not count if it is provided by a close relative of the child wholly or mainly in the child's home. Nor does it count if provided by a foster parent.

There is no set number of hours you need to work. 70% of your relevant childcare costs will be met each month (or 85% where lone parents or both earners in a couple pay income tax), up to the maximum amounts listed below. If you are a couple, you must both be in work, unless one of you is unable to look after the child because you:

- have a limited capability for work (see above);
- have regular and substantial caring responsibilities for a severely disabled person (see above); *or*
- are temporarily absent from your household (ie are in prison, hospital or a care home).

UC Regs, regs 31-35

Housing costs element

A housing costs element is included if you pay rent and may be included if you are an owner-occupier.

Renters – This element will cover your eligible rent. If you are a private tenant, your *'eligible rent'* will not be based on your actual rent but on a set amount based on the number of rooms your household is deemed to need. This is similar to the local housing allowance used for housing benefit (see Chapter 21(9)).

A room restriction will also apply if you rent social housing from a local authority or housing association. This is similar to the 'bedroom tax' (see Box H.4 in Chapter 21).

Deductions may also be made if you have any non-dependents living with you (see Chapter 21(21)).

You may be eligible for 'discretionary housing payments' if you have trouble meeting your rent due to these restrictions (see Chapter 21(16)).
UC Regs, regs 25-26 and Sch 4

If you are in certain types of supported accommodation, you will get help with your rent through universal credit as normal, but your housing support costs will still be met through housing benefit.

Owner occupiers – If you are an owner-occupier, you may get support for mortgage interest and certain service charges. There is a 3-month qualifying period before you can be paid this element. The rules are generally the same as for means-tested benefits (see Chapter 26). However, you cannot be paid the element if you or your partner have any earned income (irrespective of the number of hours you work or how much you are paid). Also, you will not be subject to deductions because you have non-dependants living with you.
UC Regs, regs 25-26 and Sch 5

Element		amount per month
Standard allowance		
■ Single claimant	aged under 25	£246.81
Single claimant	aged 25 or over	£311.55
■ Joint claimants	both aged under 25	£387.42
Joint claimants	either aged 25 or over	£489.06
Child elements		
■ First child or qualifying young person		£272.08
■ Second and each subsequent child or qualifying young person		£226.67
Additional amount for a disabled child or qualifying young person		
■ Lower rate		£123.62
■ Higher rate		£352.92
Capability for work elements		
■ Limited capability for work		£123.62
■ Limited capability for work and work-related activity		£303.66
Carer element		£144.70
Childcare element		
■ Maximum amount for one child		£532.29
■ Maximum amount for two or more children		£912.50

UC Regs, reg 36

Housing costs element	See above

Earnings

The earnings calculation is based on a net figure (ie after tax, national insurance contributions and contributions to an occupational or personal pension scheme). Statutory sick pay, statutory maternity pay, statutory paternity pay and statutory adoption pay are treated as earnings.
UC Regs, regs 51-64

From your earnings, deduct the appropriate earnings disregard. You are allowed only one, whichever is highest.

Earnings disregard	amount per month
Single claimant	
Your award contains a housing costs element and:	
■ you are not responsible for a child (or qualifying young person)	£111
■ you are responsible for one or more children/ young people	£263
■ you have a limited capability for work	£192
Your award does not contain a housing costs element and:	
■ you are not responsible for a child (or qualifying young person)	£111
■ you are responsible for one or more children/ young people	£734
■ you have a limited capability for work	£647
You have a partner	
Your award contains a housing costs element and:	
■ neither of you are responsible for a child/ young person	£111
■ you are responsible for one or more children/ young people	£222
■ one or both of you have a limited capability for work	£192
Your award does not contain a housing costs element and:	
■ neither of you are responsible for a child/ young person	£111
■ you are responsible for one or more children/ young people	£536
■ one or both of you have a limited capability for work	£647

The taper

Once the disregard has been applied, your remaining earnings are subject to a 65% taper. As your earnings rise, your universal credit is reduced at a constant rate of 65p for each £1 of net earnings. So for each extra £10 earned, you keep £3.50 and £6.50 will be taken off your universal credit.
UC Regs, reg 22

Income other than earnings

Income other than earnings, eg other benefits, will usually be taken into account in full, so that your universal credit is reduced pound for pound. Exceptions include disability living allowance and personal independence payment.
UC Regs, reg 22(1)(a) & 65-71

The benefit cap

Total universal credit is limited to £500 a week if you are a lone parent or part of a couple, or £350 a week if you are single. This 'cap' does not apply if you have earnings (or joint earnings) of at least £430 a month or if someone in your family is receiving certain benefits (eg personal independence payment). The childcare element of universal credit is excluded from the cap. See Box H.1 in Chapter 21 for details.
UC Regs, regs 78-83

If your attendance allowance, DLA or PIP stops when you are in hospital, you won't lose the disability premium – it can continue for up to 52 weeks of your hospital stay.
IS Regs, Sch 2, para 12(1)(d)

The premium will not be withdrawn if the overlapping benefit rules mean you cannot be paid long-term incapacity benefit or SDA (eg because you start to receive a bereavement allowance).
IS Regs, Sch 2, paras 7(1)(a)

As mentioned above, the disability premium does not apply to a claim you make for housing benefit if you have (or can be treated as having) a limited capability for work with respect to a claim for ESA. However, if you are the ESA claimant and you have a partner who claims housing benefit instead, and one of you gets a qualifying benefit (eg DLA), then the disability premium could be awarded.

Backdating the premium – If you get one of these qualifying benefits backdated, you should ask for the disability premium to be backdated to either the start of your means-tested benefit claim or the start of your award of the qualifying benefit, whichever is the later.

The incapacity condition (claimant only)
This route is limited in scope. It is only relevant to people who made claims on the basis of incapacity prior to 27.10.08. To qualify under this condition, you must have been (or treated as having been) incapable of work or entitled to statutory sick pay during the qualifying period of 52 weeks (or 28 weeks if you are terminally ill) and still be incapable of work.
IS Regs, Sch 2, para 12(1)(b)

The limited capability for work condition
This applies only to joint claims for JSA (see Chapter 16(2)). To qualify under this condition, you or your partner must:
■ have had (or been treated as having) a limited capability for work during the qualifying period of 52 weeks (or 28 weeks if you are terminally ill); *and*
■ still have a limited capability for work. See Chapter 11 for details of the limited capability for work assessment.
Gaps of up to 12 weeks in your periods of limited capability for work (for any reason) are ignored.
JSA Regs, Sch 1, para 20H(1)(ee)

3. Severe disability premium
The severe disability premium (SDP) can be awarded on top of any disability premium, enhanced disability premium or pensioner premium that may be payable. It is £59.50 for each person who qualifies. To qualify:
■ you must receive a *'qualifying benefit'*. These are:
  – attendance allowance (or constant attendance allowance paid with industrial injuries disablement benefit or war pension);
  – disability living allowance care component at the middle or highest rate;
  – personal independence payment daily living component; *or*
  – armed forces independence payment; *and*
■ no one gets carer's allowance for looking after you; *and*
■ you technically count as living alone (see below).
Couples – You can qualify for the SDP if:
■ both you and your partner get a qualifying benefit; *and*
■ you technically count as living alone (see below); *and* *either*
■ no one gets carer's allowance for looking after either of you; *or*
■ someone gets carer's allowance for looking after just one of you.
If your partner is registered blind or severely sight impaired (or has been taken off that register in the past 28 weeks), you can still qualify for the SDP even if they do not get a

qualifying benefit. You are treated as if you were a single person.

If you both get a qualifying benefit and no one gets carer's allowance for looking after either you or your partner, your SDP will be £119.

If you both get a qualifying benefit, and one person gets carer's allowance for looking after you (or your partner), your SDP will be £59.50.

If two people receive carer's allowance for looking after you and your partner, you won't qualify for any SDP.
ESA Regs, Sch 4, paras 6 & 11(2); IS Regs, Sch 2, para 13 & 15(5)

Is someone caring for you?
If someone gets carer's allowance for looking after you, you cannot qualify for the SDP. If carer's allowance is not actually payable to your carer, for whatever reason, you can qualify for the SDP. For example, if carer's allowance cannot be paid to your carer because they get another non-means-tested benefit that cancels out carer's allowance under the *'overlapping benefit'* rules (which restrict you to getting paid just one type of non-means-tested benefit when you may be entitled to more than one), you may be entitled to the SDP. In this example, your carer may also qualify for a carer premium (see 6 below).

If your carer stops being paid carer's allowance, but it is some time before the office administering your means-tested benefit becomes aware of that fact, arrears of the SDP can be paid from the date that the carer's allowance stopped.
D&A Regs, reg 7(2)(bc)

Your carer cannot be forced to claim carer's allowance. The DWP will ask if anyone is caring for you, and may send you the carer's allowance claim-form to give to your carer, but nothing should happen if a non-resident carer decides not to claim. If your carer does claim carer's allowance, they will need you to confirm on the claim-form that they are caring for you for at least 35 hours a week.

Note that the deprivation of income and notional income rules apply also to carer's allowance (see Chapter 27(20)). Seek advice if you or your carer fall foul of these rules (see also *Decision Makers Guide*, Vol 5, para 28608).

Couples – It is possible for you and your partner to each get carer's allowance for looking after each other. Normally, this would disqualify you both from getting the SDP. However, when carer's allowance cannot actually be paid because of the overlapping benefit rules, the SDP would not be affected. If you both have overlapping benefits, such that neither of you are paid carer's allowance, you could get the higher SDP of £119, and also get two carer premiums (see 6 below).

Arrears of carer's allowance – Your premium is only affected once carer's allowance is actually awarded. Arrears of carer's allowance for any period before the date of the award will not affect your SDP.
ESA Regs, Sch 4, para 6(6); IS Regs, Sch 2, para 13(3ZA)

Living alone?
You cannot qualify for the SDP if you have a partner who is not also getting a qualifying benefit (see above) unless your partner is registered blind or severely sight impaired, or if you have anyone living with you who is classed as a *'non-dependant'*, eg an adult son or daughter, friend or relative. The following are not classed as non-dependants and their presence in your home is ignored:
■ anyone aged under 18;
■ anyone aged 18 or 19 who is part of your family and counts as a 'qualifying young person' for child benefit purposes (see Chapter 38(1));
■ any person (and their partner) who is not a *'close relative'* of you (or your partner) and *'jointly occupies'* your dwelling as a co-owner or is sharing legal liability to make 'rent' payments – a joint occupier, eg a joint tenant, cannot

count as a non-dependant. If a co-owner or joint tenant is a close relative of you (or your partner), they will count as a non-dependant (and so exclude you from the SDP) unless the co-ownership or joint liability began:
– before 11.4.88;* *or*
– after 11.4.88 but began *'on or before the date upon which [you or your] partner first occupied the dwelling in question';**
■ any person (and member of their household) who is not a close relative of you (or your partner) and who is your resident landlord sharing living accommodation with you, to whom you or your partner are *'liable to make payments on a commercial basis in respect of [your] occupation of [his or her] dwelling'*;
■ any person (and member of their household) who is not a close relative of you (or your partner) and who shares living accommodation with you and is *'liable to make payments on a commercial basis to [you or your partner] in respect of [his or her] occupation of [your] dwelling'*. A licensee, tenant or sub-tenant cannot count as a non-dependant;
■ a live-in helper (and their partner*) who has been placed with you by a charitable or voluntary body (not by a public or local authority), where the organisation (not the helper) charges you for that help. The charge need only be nominal.
ESA Regs, reg 71, IS Regs, reg 3

The presence of the following are also ignored:
■ someone who gets a qualifying benefit (see above);
■ anyone who is registered blind or severely sight impaired (or been taken off that register in the past 28 weeks).
ESA Regs, Sch 4, para 6(4)(a)&(c); IS Regs, Sch 2, para 13(3)(a)&(d)

If someone does not *'normally'* reside with you because they normally live elsewhere, they cannot count as a non-dependant (there is no definition of 'normally resides' in terms of time, frequency or anything else – see CSIS/100/93 and CIS/14850/96).

If you are already getting the SDP and someone else joins your household *'for the first time in order to care for [you or your partner]'*, the SDP continues for up to 12 weeks after the date they join your household.* This is to give them time to claim carer's allowance. Once carer's allowance is awarded, the SDP stops.
ESA Regs, Sch 4, para 6(4)(b) & (7); IS Regs, Sch 2, para 13(3)(c) & (4)
* For income-related employment and support allowance, income support, income-based jobseeker's allowance and pension credit only.

Close relatives and living arrangements
A *'close relative'* is a parent, parent-in-law, son, daughter, son-in-law or daughter-in-law, step-parent, stepson or stepdaughter, brother, sister or the partner of any of those.
ESA Regs, reg 2; IS Regs, reg 2

If you have a licence or tenancy agreement with a relative who is not a close relative, you (or they) would only be excluded from the SDP while you were residing with them if your occupancy agreement was not on a commercial basis.
Living independently? – If you have entirely separate living accommodation, you cannot be said to *'normally reside'* with other people living under the same roof (eg if you live in a separate 'granny flat', your right to the SDP is not affected, even if a close relative lives under the same roof).

If you are living under the same roof as other people, with a separate bedroom, kitchen and living room, you won't count as residing with those other people so you can qualify for the SDP. It makes no difference if you share a bathroom, lavatory or communal area (which does not include any communal rooms, unless you are living in sheltered accommodation).
Separate liability – If you share a living room or kitchen with other people but are *'separately liable to make payments in respect of [your] occupation of the dwelling to the landlord'*, you won't count as residing with those other people even if

they are close relatives. This would typically cover someone in supported lodgings.
ESA Regs, reg 71(6); IS Regs, reg 3(4)

Protecting pre-21.10.91 SDP
If you are a co-owner or joint tenant with a close relative and had an award of income support, including an SDP, in the week before 21.10.91, your position is protected. Protection will survive changes in the type of agreement, in the parties to the agreement, and even a move of home. It cannot survive a carer getting carer's allowance or a non-dependant joining your home. If you have a break off income support, you can regain your protected SDP if:
■ the break is no more than eight weeks (for any reason); *or*
■ the break is no more than 12 weeks (covered by the work 'trial period' provisions); *or*
■ you have just finished employment training or an employment rehabilitation course and you reclaim income support immediately.
IS (General) Amdt No.6 Regs 1991, regs 4-6

Hospital
If you enter hospital, the SDP will be withdrawn once your qualifying benefit is withdrawn – usually once you've been in hospital for 28 days.

For couples, if each of you receives a qualifying benefit, and one or both of you enters hospital, you will still get the SDP even after the qualifying benefit is withdrawn, but the SDP will only be paid at the rate of £59.50.
ESA Regs, Sch 4, paras 6(5) & 11(2)(b)(i); IS Regs, Sch 2, paras 13(3A) & 15(5)(b)(i)

If your carer enters hospital and their carer's allowance is withdrawn, you may get the SDP while they are in hospital.

4. Enhanced disability premium
The enhanced disability premium does not apply to pension credit. It is £15.15 for a single person and £21.75 for a couple where one or both qualify. You or your partner qualify for this premium if you or they are paid:
■ disability living allowance (DLA) highest rate care component; *or*
■ personal independence payment (PIP) enhanced rate daily living component; *or*
■ armed forces independence payment; *or*
■ you are in the employment and support allowance support group (see Chapter 10(7)).
The enhanced disability premium can be awarded on top of any disability premium or severe disability premium that may be payable. It is payable only while the person who qualifies is under the qualifying age for pension credit (see Chapter 42(2)).

If your DLA or PIP is withdrawn when you are in hospital, you won't lose the enhanced disability premium. It can continue for up to 52 weeks of the hospital stay.
ESA Regs, Sch 4, para 7; IS Regs, Sch 2, para 13A
Enhanced disability premium (child) – This premium generally applies only to housing benefit. It can still be paid with income support or income-based jobseeker's allowance if your claim began before April 2004 and you continue to receive support for your children through one of those benefits rather than child tax credit. The enhanced disability premium is paid at the rate of £23.45 for each child who qualifies.

A child qualifies for the enhanced disability premium if they are paid DLA highest rate care component or PIP enhanced rate daily living component. It can be awarded on top of a disabled child premium. If a child is in hospital, you keep the enhanced disability premium for as long as the child is treated as a member of your family.
HB Regs, Sch 3, para 15

5. Pensioner premium

The pensioner premium does not apply to pension credit or housing benefit. It is paid if you or your partner have reached the qualifying age for pension credit (see Chapter 42(2)). It can be awarded in addition to any severe disability premium or carer premium that may be payable.

There are only limited circumstances in which the pensioner premium will be relevant to an income support claim. It is payable only when the income support claimant is under the qualifying age for pension credit and their partner reaches that age first and chooses not to claim pension credit instead. Since pension credit has a number of features that make it more attractive than income support (particularly with respect to the way in which capital and savings are treated), this is not likely to occur very often.

The pensioner premium is normally £73.70 for a single person and £109.50 for a couple. For income-related employment and support allowance, however, these figures are then reduced by any work-related activity component or support component that may be payable (this ensures that your applicable amount, before any other premiums are added on, is equivalent to the pension credit 'standard minimum guarantee' – see Chapter 42(3)).

ESA Regs, Sch 4, paras 5 & 11(1)

Enhanced and higher pensioner premiums – For income support and income-based jobseeker's allowance, the pensioner premium was originally paid at three different levels: the pensioner, enhanced and higher pensioner premiums. Although these separate premiums still technically exist, they are now all paid at the same rate. The difference occasionally becomes important (we point out elsewhere in this *Handbook* when it does).

❑ **Pensioner premium** – You qualify for this if you or your partner have reached the qualifying age for pension credit but are still aged under 75.

❑ **Enhanced pensioner premium** – You qualify for this if you or your partner are aged 75-79 (inclusive).

❑ **Higher pensioner premium** – You qualify for this if you or your partner:

■ are aged 80 or over; *or*

■ have reached the qualifying age for pension credit and also satisfy the 'disability condition' for a disability premium (see 2 above).

There are other ways to qualify. For details see *Disability Rights Handbook* 25th edition, page 20.

IS Regs, Sch 2, paras 9-10

6. Carer premium

The carer premium can be awarded in addition to any of the other premiums covered in this chapter. It is £33.30 a week for each person who qualifies.

You qualify for a carer premium if you or your partner:

■ are actually paid an amount of carer's allowance; *or*

■ have an underlying entitlement to carer's allowance: ie you are entitled to carer's allowance but it cannot be paid because of the overlapping benefit rules (see Chapter 7(6)).

Eight-week extension – The carer premium can continue for eight weeks after you stop getting carer's allowance or lose an underlying entitlement to it. Your caring role can have ended temporarily or permanently and for any reason, with one exception: if the person you are caring for dies. In that case, since carer's allowance can also be extended for eight weeks, the carer premium can continue during the same period and is limited to that period. Thus, it must stop being paid eight weeks after the death of the person being cared for.

ESA Regs, Sch 4, para 8; IS Regs, Sch 2, para 14ZA

7. The family premium

This premium generally applies only to housing benefit. It can still be paid with income support or income-based jobseeker's allowance (JSA) if your claim began before April 2004 and you continue to receive support for your children through one of those benefits rather than through child tax credit.

The family premium is awarded if you have a dependent child or 'qualifying young person' (see Chapter 38(1)) aged under 20. You only get one family premium, regardless of the number of children you have. The ordinary rate of £17.40 is awarded if you are one of a couple or a lone parent, unless you have transitional protection for the housing benefit higher lone parent rate of £22.20 (see below). The ordinary rate can be awarded in addition to any other premium.

Protected lone parent rate – The lone parent rate was abolished on 6.4.98 but existing housing benefit claimants can continue to get it. You must:

■ have been a lone parent entitled (or treated as entitled) to housing benefit on 5.4.98 and have continued to be entitled to it;

■ not cease to be or become entitled to income support, income-based JSA or income-related employment and support allowance, although you can switch between these three benefits;

■ not be entitled to a disability premium or employment and support allowance additional component (see Chapter 10(8)).

HB Regs, Sch 3, para 3

8. Disabled child premium

This premium generally applies only to housing benefit. It can still be paid with income support or income-based jobseeker's allowance if your claim began before April 2004 and you continue to receive support for your children through one of those benefits rather than through child tax credit. The disabled child premium can be awarded in addition to any of the other premiums. The disabled child premium is £57.89 for each child who lives with you and counts as disabled. Your child counts as disabled if they:

■ are registered blind or severely sight impaired, or were taken off that register within the past 28 weeks; *or*

■ get disability living allowance (DLA), personal independence payment (PIP) or armed forces independence payment; *or*

■ no longer get DLA or PIP because they are in hospital; as long as they are still treated as a member of your family.

HB Regs, Sch 3, para 16

26 Housing costs

1. Basic rules

Income-related employment and support allowance (ESA), income support, income-based jobseeker's allowance (JSA) and pension credit can all help with mortgage interest payments and certain other housing costs. If you pay rent, you may be able to get housing benefit instead (see Chapter 21). For help with the cost of a care home, see Chapter 33. When universal credit is introduced (see Box J.1 in Chapter 25), housing costs may also be met by that benefit for those who are not working, but in many circumstances the support will be limited to 104 weeks.

Housing costs can be included in your applicable amount if:

■ you or your partner are liable for housing costs at the home you normally live in (see 2 below); *and*

■ the type of housing cost is covered (see 2 and 3 below); *and*

■ your mortgage was not taken out while you or your partner were on income-related ESA, income support, income-based JSA or pension credit or, in some cases, between claims for one or more of these benefits (there are some exceptions) – see 3 below.

ESA Regs, Sch 6, para 1; IS Regs, Sch 3, para 1

The amount of housing costs met is worked out taking into account the following:

■ whether your housing costs are 'excessive' (see 3 below);
■ an upper limit or 'ceiling' on loans (there are some exceptions) – see 4 below;
■ a standard rate of interest applied to loans (see 4 below);
■ deductions for any 'non-dependants' living with you (eg adult son or daughter, friend or relative). It is assumed they contribute towards your housing costs, whether they do or not. Unless your or your non-dependant's circumstances exempt you from the deduction, an amount is deducted from your assessed housing costs. The rules are almost the same as for housing benefit (see Chapter 21(21)). No deduction is made, however, if a deduction for that non-dependant is already being made from your housing benefit;

ESA Regs, reg 71 & Sch 6, para 19; IS Regs, reg 3 & Sch 3, para 18

■ a waiting period (ie a number of weeks you must be entitled to the means-tested benefit before housing costs are included in your applicable amount) – see 5 below.

Jobseeker's allowance – If you are claiming JSA and your award began on or after 5.1.09, any help with interest on qualifying mortgages or loans will be limited to a period of 104 weeks. This limit will not apply if you (or your partner in the case of a joint claim) were claiming either income support or ESA in the 12 weeks prior to your JSA award. In calculating the 104-week period, any linked periods when you come off JSA (see Chapter 16(15)) are disregarded.

Statutory Instrument 2008/3195, para 11

Absence from home – Generally, you can get help on only one home at a time and this must be the home you occupy. In some situations you are treated as occupying your home when you are not actually there – eg during a temporary absence or when moving home; the rules are almost the same as for housing benefit (see Chapter 21(6) and (7)).

ESA Regs, Sch 6, para 5; IS Regs, Sch 3, para 3

2. Housing costs you can get help with
Liability for housing costs

You (or your partner) must be liable for housing costs for the home you live in. You will not get help with housing costs if the person you pay is a member of your household. If it is reasonable to do so, you can be treated as liable if the person normally liable for the costs is not paying them and you must pay them to carry on living in your home.

If someone living with you is liable for the housing costs and that person is not a close relative of you or your partner, you can be treated as sharing the costs if it is reasonable to do so. A 'close relative' is a parent, parent-in-law, son, daughter, son-in-law or daughter-in-law, step-parent, stepson or stepdaughter, brother, sister or the partner of any of those.

ESA Regs, reg 2 & Sch 6, para 4; IS Regs, reg 2 & Sch 3, para 2

Housing costs covered

The following housing costs can be included as part of your applicable amount:

■ mortgage interest payments and interest on other loans taken out to buy your home (see 3 and 4 below);
■ interest on loans for certain repairs and improvements (see below);
■ some service charges payable as a condition of your occupancy (eg under a lease) relating to the provision of adequate accommodation (CIS/1460/1995). House insurance can be included if payments are made under the terms of the lease, rather than as a condition of the mortgage

(R(IS)4/92). Service charges for repairs and improvements listed below are not met, although you can get help to pay interest on a loan taken out to pay these charges. Service charges are not met if they would be ineligible under the housing benefit rules (see Chapter 21(12));

■ ground rent or other rent payable under a long lease of over 21 years;
■ payments under a co-ownership scheme;
■ rent if you are a Crown tenant;
■ payments for a tent and site fees;
■ rentcharges (sometimes due as a condition of a freehold).

ESA Regs, Sch 6, paras 16-18; IS Regs, Sch 3, paras 15-17

Interest on mortgages, hire purchase agreements or other loans is covered only if those mortgages, agreements or loans were used:

■ to buy your home – including buying your home jointly with others, buying the freehold if you are a leaseholder (R(IS)7/93) or buying out a joint owner;
■ to pay off an earlier loan, but only to the extent that the earlier loan would have already been met. For example, if your outstanding mortgage was £10,000 and you borrow £12,000 to repay it, only the interest on £10,000 of the second loan is covered;
■ for certain repairs and improvements (see below).

If part of a loan is taken out for a different purpose (eg a business loan), that part of the loan will not be covered.

ESA Regs, Sch 6, paras 16 & 17; IS Regs, Sch 3, paras 15 & 16

If your loan is covered, an amount is added to your applicable amount, worked out according to the rules in 4 below. See 5 below for when entitlement to housing costs can begin. If your lender is part of the Mortgage Interest Direct scheme, this amount is not paid to you but is paid 4-weekly in arrears to your lender.

Loans for repairs and improvements

The interest on loans taken out and used within six months (or longer if reasonable) to pay for repairs and improvements to your home is covered. These must be 'undertaken with a view to maintaining the fitness of the dwelling for human habitation' and fall within the following categories:

■ adapting your home for 'the special needs of a disabled person'. See below for who counts as 'a disabled person' for this rule;
■ provision of a bath, shower, sink or lavatory (and associated plumbing);
■ provision of ventilation, natural lighting, insulation or electric lighting and sockets;
■ provision of facilities for preparing and cooking food, storing fuel or refuse, or for drainage;
■ provision of separate bedrooms for children (or young people under 20) of different sexes aged ten or over who live with you and for whom you are responsible;
■ repairs to existing heating systems (see CIS/781/2002) or of unsafe structural defects; or
■ damp proofing.

Loans to pay service charges for any of these works are covered, as are loans used to pay off an existing loan for repairs, but only to the extent that the existing loan would have qualified.

ESA Regs, Sch 6, para 17; IS Regs, Sch 3, para 16

Who counts as a 'disabled person'? – Someone is considered to be 'a disabled person' if, at the date the loan is taken out:

■ they satisfy the conditions for a disability premium, disabled child premium, enhanced or higher pensioner premium (for income support and income-based jobseeker's allowance (JSA), but they don't actually have to be getting any of these premiums or be entitled to income support or JSA); or
■ they are being paid main-phase employment and support allowance (ESA), or have been disqualified from receiving it in certain circumstances (see Chapter 10(18)), or are

receiving limited capability for work national insurance credits; *or*

■ had they been entitled to income support, they would have qualified for the disability premium (for ESA); *or*

■ they would qualify for the disabled or severely disabled child elements of child tax credit (for income support, JSA and ESA); *or*

■ they are aged 75 or over (for pension credit and ESA); *or*

■ had they been entitled to income support, they would have qualified for the higher pensioner or disability premium (for pension credit); *or*

■ they are under 20, you or your partner are responsible for them and they get disability living allowance or personal independence payment (or would get one of these were they not in hospital), armed forces independence payment or are registered as blind (for pension credit).

The disabled person can be you, a member of your family or someone else who lives with you or will be living with you.

ESA Regs, Sch 6, para 1(3)-(4); IS Regs, Sch 3, para 1(3); SPC Regs, Sch 2, para 1(2)(a)

3. Housing costs you cannot get help with
Housing costs not covered
Your personal allowances are intended to cover day-to-day living expenses, including the cost of water and fuel. For this reason, water and fuel charges cannot be included as housing costs. Other housing costs not covered include:

■ housing costs covered by housing benefit;

■ ineligible service charges; the rules are similar to those for housing benefit – see Chapter 21(12);

■ capital repayments, endowment premiums, or arrears payable on a loan or mortgage;

■ mortgage interest on a new or additional loan taken out while you were on income-related employment and support allowance (ESA), income support, income-based jobseeker's allowance (JSA) or pension credit, or in some cases between claims for one or more of these benefits – see below;

■ excessive housing costs – see below.

Following changes to the rules on 2.10.95, some housing costs previously covered by income support can no longer be met: arrears of mortgage interest payments; loans for certain repairs and improvements; and extra help to separated couples with loans secured on the home. If, in the benefit week including 1.10.95, your applicable amount included interest for such a loan, it will continue to be met as long as you or your partner remain entitled to income support or income-based JSA. If you separate from your partner, you keep this protection.

Income Support (Gen.) Amdt. and Transitional Regs 1995

Mortgages taken out while on benefits or between claims
The general rule is that mortgage interest is not met on a loan taken out to buy a home while you or your partner were on a *'specified benefit'* (income-related ESA, income support, income-based JSA, pension credit or on certain New Deal options); or within a break in entitlement to a specified benefit of 26 weeks or less.

ESA Regs, Sch 6, para 6(2)-(5); IS Regs, Sch 3, para 4(2)-(4A)

Even if you were on a specified benefit when you took on the mortgage, you may be entitled to a restricted amount of help towards the interest if you were already receiving some form of housing support such as housing benefit. The intention in the following three cases is to restrict your entitlement to the level of help which you were already receiving when you took on the mortgage.

❏ **Replacement or additional loans** – If you already had a mortgage and you increased it or took out an additional loan while on a specified benefit (or between claims), the additional amount is not met. You can replace one mortgage with another but if the new one is larger, you will only get help up to the level available on the old mortgage. If your

new mortgage is used to buy a home and you pay off all or part of the mortgage on your old home from the sale of that property, help for the new mortgage is restricted to the level of help that applied to the old mortgage. It has been argued that this could allow a separated couple who sell their home to each have mortgage interest covered on a new home at the full amount of the previous mortgage (CIS/11293/1995).

ESA Regs, Sch 6, para 6(8); IS Regs, Sch 3, para 4(6); AH v SSWP(IS)[2010]UKUT 353 (AAC)

❏ **Previously getting housing benefit** – If you took on a mortgage while on a specified benefit (or between claims), help with mortgage interest and other housing costs (such as service charges and ground rent) is restricted to the level of housing benefit payable in the week before the week you bought the home. If you were getting both housing benefit and housing costs in that week, perhaps because you were on a shared ownership scheme, the restriction is applied to the total of housing benefit payable plus the housing costs included in your applicable amount. The restricted amount can only then increase if the standard interest rate (see 4 below) goes up or if there is an increase in service charges or ground rent, etc.

ESA Regs, Sch 6, para 6(10); IS Regs, Sch 3, para 4(8)

❏ **Applicable amount previously included only housing costs other than loan interest** (eg service charges or ground rent) – If you took on a mortgage while on a specified benefit (or between claims), help with mortgage interest and other housing costs is restricted to the level of the housing costs payable in the week before the week you bought the home. The restricted amount can only then increase if the standard interest rate goes up or there is an increase in service charges or ground rent, etc.

ESA Regs, Sch 6, para 6(13); IS Regs, Sch 3, para 4(11)

Exemptions – If you were on a specified benefit when you took out the mortgage, you can get help towards mortgage interest without the above restrictions for:

■ a loan taken out before 3.5.94;

■ a loan taken out, or increased, to buy *'alternative accommodation more suited to the special needs of a disabled person'* (see 2 above for who counts as a disabled person). This could include moving home to be nearer a carer (CIS/14551/96) or moving to sheltered housing;

■ an additional or increased loan taken out because you've sold your home to buy another solely to provide separate bedrooms for children (or young people under 20) of different sexes aged ten or over for whom you are responsible.

ESA Regs, Sch 6, para 6(2), (11) & (12); IS Regs, Sch 3, paras 4(2), (9) & (10)

Even if a loan is exempt from these restrictions, a ceiling may still be applied to it (see 4 below).

Excessive housing costs
The amount of housing costs met may be restricted if they are regarded as *'excessive'*, eg your home is larger than you need for your household, the area is more expensive than other areas where there is suitable alternative accommodation, or your housing costs are higher than those for suitable alternative accommodation in the area.

No restriction is made if it is not reasonable to expect you to move, taking into account the availability of suitable alternative accommodation, the level of housing costs in the area, and the circumstances of you and your family. In particular, the age and health of you and your family must be considered, as well as your employment prospects and the effect of a move on a child or young person's education. Other factors may also be relevant – eg whether you provide care for, or rely on the care or support of, someone nearby.

No restriction is made for the first 26 weeks of your claim or after a decision is made to introduce a restriction if you could afford the costs when you took them on; nor for a further 26 weeks if you're doing your best to find cheaper accommodation. The 26 weeks continues to run during a break in the means-tested benefit of 12 weeks or less.

If a restriction is applied, the amount of loan to be met is restricted to the amount you need to obtain suitable alternative accommodation.

ESA Regs, Sch 6, para 14; IS Regs, Sch 3, para 13

4. Calculating your housing costs

The outstanding balance of your qualifying mortgage(s) and/or loan(s) is multiplied by a standard interest rate (see below) to give a qualifying amount of interest for the year. A weekly rate of qualifying interest is calculated by dividing the yearly figure by 52. Other qualifying housing costs (eg service charges) are calculated at a weekly rate and added to this figure. The result is added to your applicable amount.

ESA Regs, Sch 6, para 11; IS Regs, Sch 3, para 10

Deductions from your housing costs are made for any non-dependant contributions (see 1 above).

In most cases, there is a waiting period before the loan interest is included in your applicable amount (see 5 below).

Once loan interest is included, reductions to the amount of eligible capital owing (eg if you make capital repayments) are only taken into account one year from the date the costs were first included in your applicable amount and then annually thereafter. If you move between income-related employment and support allowance (ESA), income support, income-based jobseeker's allowance (JSA) or pension credit, reductions in the outstanding balance are taken into account on the anniversary of the housing costs first being included in any of these benefits.

ESA Regs, Sch 6, paras 8(2)&(3) & 9(2)&(3); IS Regs, Sch 3, paras 6(1A)&(1B) & 8(1A)&(1B)

The ceiling on mortgages and loans

If your loan (or the total of your loans) is above a certain set level or ceiling, the interest met is worked out only on the part of the loan up to the ceiling. The ceiling is currently set at £100,000. However, a higher ceiling of £200,000 applies to claims of income-related ESA, income support and income-based JSA made on or after 5.1.09 (and which do not link to a previous claim made before 5.1.09 – see 5 below). The higher ceiling also applies if you were already entitled to one of these benefits on 5.1.09, but were serving the waiting period (see 5 below). The higher ceiling continues to apply if you move onto pension credit if no more than 12 weeks separate the last day of your claim for ESA, income support or JSA and the first day of your entitlement to pension credit. The higher ceiling is a temporary measure and will be reviewed at some stage.

ESA Regs, Sch 6, para 12(3)-(4); IS Regs, Sch 3, para 11(4)-(5); Statutory Instruments 2008/3195 & 2009/3257

Any loan taken out to adapt your existing home *'for the special needs of a disabled person'* (see 2 above) is ignored when working out whether your loans exceed the ceiling.

ESA Regs, Sch 6, para 12(8); IS Regs, Sch 3, para 11(9)

If you are eligible for housing costs on two homes, the ceiling is applied separately to each home.

ESA Regs, Sch 6, para 12(5); IS Regs, Sch 3, para 11(6)

The £100,000 ceiling applies to claims made from 10.4.95. If you have been on a means-tested benefit continuously since before this, existing loans will be met up to the level of the ceiling that applied at the date of the claim. For claims made:
■ prior to 2.8.93, there was no ceiling;
■ between 2.8.93 and 10.4.94, the ceiling was £150,000;
■ between 11.4.94 and 9.4.95, the ceiling was £125,000.
Loans you took out or increased while on a means-tested benefit are subject to whichever ceiling applied at the time you took out or increased the loan. Generally, a break in your claim(s) of just one day is enough to end this protection.

However, if are a *'work or training beneficiary'*, you can keep the protection during a break in your claim(s) of up to 104-weeks (see 5 below).

ESA Regs, Sch 6, para 15(6)

See Chapter 27(13) for the way in which payments from a mortgage protection insurance policy to cover the interest on the part of a loan above the ceiling are treated when your income is assessed.

Standard interest rate

The DWP uses a standard interest rate to calculate the amount added to your applicable amount. From October 2010 this has been set at the Bank of England's published monthly average mortgage rate. It will change only when the published average rate differs from the standard rate by 0.5% or more, at which point the new Bank of England average mortgage rate becomes the new standard rate.

ESA Regs, Sch 6, para 13; IS Regs, Sch 3, para 12

Before 2.10.95, housing costs were worked out using actual interest rates. There is transitional protection (called 'add back') for those who have received housing costs with a means-tested benefit since this date and who would otherwise have lost out when the rules changed. See *Disability Rights Handbook* 24th edition, page 23.

ESA Regs, Sch 6, para 20(1)(b); IS Regs, Sch 3, para 7

5. Waiting periods

Generally, there is a 13-week waiting period at the start of your entitlement to a means-tested benefit before housing costs are included in your applicable amount. The 13-week waiting period was introduced on 5.1.09. Prior to this, longer waiting periods were in place; for details, see *Disability Rights Handbook* 33rd edition, page 22.

The 13-week waiting period can sometimes be put into effect if the means-tested benefit is not actually in payment. This would apply if, without the inclusion of housing costs, your income would exceed your applicable amount. Once you have claimed the benefit, you can be 'treated as entitled' to it and the waiting period will proceed. After 13 weeks, if you make a new claim for the benefit, the housing costs can be included in your applicable amount, and payment of the benefit may begin. See below for details of when you can be treated as entitled to means-tested benefits.

The waiting period begins at the start of your benefit entitlement even if you have no housing costs at the time. So, if you take out a loan while on benefit, having already served the waiting period, and you are eligible for help with the costs, housing costs can be included immediately.

ESA Regs, Sch 6, para 8(1) & 9(1); IS Regs, Sch 3, para 6(1) & 8(1); Statutory Instrument 2008/3195

No waiting period

The waiting period does not apply to claims for pension credit. For income-related employment and support allowance (ESA) and income support, if your partner has reached pension credit qualifying age, housing costs are included in your applicable amount from the start of your benefit entitlement, or from the day they reach the qualifying age if this happens when you are part-way through the waiting period. Similar rules apply to income-based jobseeker's allowance (JSA) when you or your partner reach pension credit qualifying age. There is no waiting period for help with payments under a co-ownership scheme, rent for a Crown tenant or tent payments.

ESA Regs, Sch 6, para 10; IS Regs, Sch 3, para 9

If you are not entitled to the means-tested benefit during the waiting period

Throughout the waiting period, you must usually be entitled to the means-tested benefit, although breaks in entitlement of up to 12 weeks are ignored.

During a break in claims, or a change of claimant – You are treated as entitled to the means-tested benefit:

- during a gap in entitlement of 12 weeks or less;
- during a gap between claims of up to 52 weeks if you are protected under the back-to-work linking rule, or up to 104 weeks if you are a *'work or training beneficiary'* (see below);
- for any period in which it is decided retrospectively that you were entitled to the benefit (eg following an appeal);
- during any time your partner was getting (or treated as getting) the benefit for both of you if you swap to become the claimant instead;
- during a gap between claims while you or your partner were on certain government training schemes;
- for any period in which your ex-partner was getting (or treated as getting) the benefit for both of you, if you claim within 12 weeks of separating;
- for any period in which someone was claiming the benefit for you as their dependent child, if you claim within 12 weeks of the end of the claim and your claim includes a child who was also their dependant; *or*
- for any period in which your new partner was getting (or treated as getting) the benefit as a single person or lone parent, if you claim within 12 weeks of becoming a couple.

In the last three cases, the 12-week linking period is extended to 52 weeks if the back-to-work linking rule applies, or to 104 weeks if you (or, in the last case, your partner) are a *'work or training beneficiary'* (see below).

ESA Regs, Sch 6, para 15; IS Regs, Sch 3, para 14

You are treated as receiving income-related ESA during any time you have received income support, income-based JSA or pension credit, or during any break in entitlement to those benefits (as listed above). You are treated as receiving income-based JSA during any time you have received income support or income-related ESA (including entitlement breaks listed above). You are treated as receiving income support during any time you have received income-based JSA or income-related ESA (including entitlement breaks listed above).

ESA Regs, Sch 6, para 20(1)(c); Stat. Instrument 1996/206, reg 32

If your income or capital is over the limit – If you cannot get the means-tested benefit only because your income is higher than your applicable amount (or, in the case of income-related ESA or income-based JSA, you have contributory ESA or contribution-based JSA equal to or higher than your applicable amount) and/or your capital is over £16,000, you are treated as entitled to the benefit for up to 39 weeks if you satisfy one of the following conditions on each day (but gaps of up to 12 weeks are allowed):

- you are entitled to contributory ESA, contribution-based JSA, statutory sick pay or incapacity benefit; *or*
- you are entitled to national insurance credits for incapacity for work, limited capability for work or unemployment; *or*
- you are treated as entitled to the benefit during a break in claims, or a change of claimant (see above); *or*
- you are a lone parent or eligible for income support as a carer (even though you do not claim it) – provided you are not working 16 hours or more a week, your partner (if you are a carer) is not working 24 hours or more a week, you are not a full-time student excluded from income support or JSA (or, in the case of income-related ESA, receiving disability living allowance, personal independence payment or armed forces independence payment) and are not absent from the UK other than in circumstances described in Chapter 50(5). The 39 weeks run from when your unsuccessful claim is made, so don't delay claiming.

If you have a mortgage protection policy, the 39 weeks is extended to cover the period that payments are made under the policy, provided your capital is within the limit of £16,000 throughout.

ESA Regs, Sch 6, para 15(8)-(12); IS Regs, Sch 3, para 14(4)-(6)

Once you have qualified for housing costs
You will not have to serve the waiting period again if you have a break in your claim of 12 weeks or less, or longer if you are still treated as entitled to benefit (see above).

Back-to-work linking rule – If your means-tested benefit stops because you or your partner start work (employed or self-employed) or your working hours or earnings increase, you do not have to serve the waiting period again on a new claim if the break in claims is no more than 52 weeks. Housing costs can be included from the start of your new claim. Similar protection will be afforded if your participation in certain government training schemes takes you off the benefit.

ESA Regs, Sch 6, para 15(16) & (17); IS Regs, Sch 3, para 14(11) & (12)

Work or training beneficiary – If you are moving into work or training from ESA, you may be covered by a more generous 104-week linking rule if you are a *'work or training beneficiary'*. This applies if you had a limited capability for work for more than 13 weeks in your previous ESA award and you started work or training within one month of ceasing to be entitled to ESA. This rule does not apply if the reason for your previous ESA award ending was that you were found not to have a limited capability for work.

ESA Regs, Sch 6, para 1(3A)-(3C)

Starting work – When you start work, you may continue to get housing costs, payable as income support, for the first four weeks (see Chapter 17(4)).

Insurance payments – If you have a break in your claim of 26 weeks or less and payments from an insurance policy for unemployment have run out, your two claims are linked and the period in between, when you were receiving the insurance payments, is ignored. Consequently, housing costs will resume from the start of your linked claim.

ESA Regs, Sch 6, paras 15(13) & (14); IS Regs, Sch 3, para 14(8) & (9)

27 Income

1. Introduction

In this chapter we look at how the income you receive is treated when means-tested benefits are being calculated. The rules in this chapter apply to the following benefits:

- income-related employment and support allowance;
- income support;
- income-based jobseeker's allowance; *and*
- housing benefit – as long as you (and your partner) are under the qualifying age for pension credit or you (or your partner) are claiming one of the three benefits above; if not, the rules are similar to pension credit – see Chapter 42(5).

Where there are significant differences in the way income is treated for different benefits, we say so. As income is treated in a substantially different way for pension credit, we describe this separately in Chapter 42(5).

For the sake of simplicity, we generally confine the legal references to those applicable to income-related employment and support allowance and income support.

Disregarded income – All income is considered, including earnings, benefits and pensions. However, some income may then be disregarded, partially or fully. In 3 to 5 below, we outline how earnings are assessed and how much is disregarded; in 6 to 16, we detail how other income is treated.

Income or capital? – Generally, it will be clear whether a particular resource is income or capital, although the distinction is not defined in the regulations. Where it is unclear, the general principle (developed in case law) is that payments of income recur periodically and do not include ad hoc payments, whereas capital payments are one-off and not linked to a particular period (although capital may be paid in instalments). In some cases, the rules treat capital as income (see 18 below) and vice versa (see Chapter 28(8)).

In some cases you can be treated as possessing income that you don't actually have (see 20 below).

2. Whose income is included?

If you are one of a couple (married or living together as husband and wife, or in a same-sex partnership whether registered or not), your partner's income is added to yours. Otherwise, only your own income is taken into account; income belonging to dependent children is disregarded (unless you have a claim for income support or income-based jobseeker's allowance that began before April 2004 and you still receive support for your children through one of those benefits rather than through child tax credit – see *Disability Rights Handbook* 28th edition, page 25).

ESA Regs, reg 83; IS Regs, reg 23

3. Earnings from employment
How earnings from employment are assessed

The income assessment is normally related to your actual earnings in respect of a particular week. If you are paid monthly, that month's pay is multiplied by 12 and then divided by 52 to provide a weekly amount. If your income varies from week to week, there is discretion to take a more representative period and work out your average earnings over that period. If you have a regular pattern of working some weeks on, some weeks off, your average weekly earnings may be worked out over your working cycle: that average is then also taken into account in your off weeks. Otherwise, earnings are averaged over a period of five weeks, or over such other period as may more accurately enable average earnings to be determined.

ESA Regs, reg 94(1) & (6); IS Regs, reg 32(1) & (6)

If you are not being paid, or are underpaid for a service, 'notional' earnings may be taken into account (see 20 below). **Final earnings** – If you have just retired, or your job has ended or been interrupted for some other reason (but not if you have been suspended), your last normal earnings as an employee will usually be disregarded. This includes pay in lieu of notice, holiday pay (payable within four weeks of the employment ending or being interrupted) and pay in lieu of remuneration (but not periodic redundancy payments). These disregards only apply when the job ends or is interrupted before the first day of entitlement to the means-tested benefit. Retainer payments and payments received under employment protection legislation will be taken into account.

ESA Regs, Sch 7, para 1; IS Regs, Sch 8, para 1

Housing benefit – Your average weekly earnings are estimated over the five weeks before your housing benefit claim if you are paid weekly, or the two months before your claim if you are paid monthly. Your local authority can average them over another period if that would give a more accurate estimate.

HB Regs, reg 29

Working out net earnings

Do not count any payment in kind (see 10 below) or *'any payment in respect of expenses wholly, exclusively and necessarily incurred in the performance of the duties of the employment'*. Occupational pensions are not treated as earnings, but are normally taken into account in full (as income) less tax payable (see 6 below).

ESA Regs, Sch 8, para 3; IS Regs, Sch 9, para 3

For income support, income-based jobseeker's allowance and income-related employment and support allowance, do not count as earnings any of the following payments from your employer: sick pay, maternity pay, paternity pay, adoption pay, statutory sick pay (SSP), statutory maternity pay (SMP), statutory paternity pay (SPP) or statutory adoption pay (SAP). Instead, these are counted in full (as income) less tax, national insurance contributions and half of any contributions you make towards an occupational or personal pension.

ESA Regs, regs 95(2)(b) & Sch 8, paras 1&4; IS Regs, reg 35(2)(b) & Sch 9, paras 1&4

For housing benefit, the following are counted as earnings: sick pay, maternity pay, paternity pay or adoption pay from your employer and SSP, SMP, SPP and SAP.

HB Regs, reg 35(1)(i)-(j)

An advance of earnings or a loan made by your employer counts as capital.

ESA Regs, reg 112(5) & IS Regs, reg 48(5)

Count any other payment from your employer as earnings: eg bonuses, commission, payments towards travel expenses between your home and workplace or towards childminding fees and retainers. Also count pay in lieu of notice and holiday pay, unless your job has ended or been interrupted for some other reason – see 'Final earnings' above. Most non-cash vouchers, but not childcare vouchers, count as earnings.

ESA Regs, reg 95(1) & (3); IS Regs, regs 35(1) & (2A)

Deduct from your earnings income tax, national insurance contributions and half of any contribution you make towards an occupational or personal pension scheme.

ESA Regs, reg 96; IS Regs, reg 36

4. Earnings from self-employment

There are specific rules for working out income from self-employment related to the net profit of your business or your share of the business. If you get royalties or copyright payments, seek advice from an organisation supporting artists in your field (eg The Writers' Guild).

Step 1: Take full gross receipts of the business

This is the money you receive in respect of and generated by the business over a specific trading period. This is normally one year, but if you have recently started self-employment or there has been a change that is likely to affect the normal pattern of business, Jobcentre Plus can pick a different period more representative of your average weekly earnings.

ESA Regs, reg 92; IS Regs, reg 30

For housing benefit, earnings are usually assessed over the period covered by your last year's trading accounts. A different period can be used if appropriate, as long as it is no longer than one year.

HB Regs, reg 30

Step 2: Deduct the following expenses:

■ *'any expenses wholly and exclusively defrayed* [ie actually paid] *in that period for the purposes of that employment'*: this is subject to some exceptions and extra rules, eg the expenses must be 'reasonably incurred', and business entertainment is specifically excluded. Expenses can be apportioned between business and personal use (see R(FC)1/91 and R(IS)13/91);

- a repayment of capital on any loan used for replacing equipment or machinery, or for repairing existing business assets (less any insurance payments);
- the excess of any VAT paid over VAT received;
- expenditure out of income to repair an existing business asset (less any insurance payment);
- interest (but not capital) payments on a loan taken out for the purposes of the employment.

However, if you work as a childminder, simply deduct two-thirds of those earnings.

ESA Regs, reg 98(3)(a) & (5)-(9); IS Regs, reg 38(3)(a) & (5)-(9)

Step 3: To calculate your net profit, deduct:

- income tax – this is related to your appropriate personal tax allowances, on a pro rata basis if necessary (see Chapter 51(3));
- Class 2 and Class 4 national insurance contributions;
- half of any contribution to a personal pension scheme (including annuity contracts or trust schemes approved under tax law).

ESA Regs, regs 98(3)(b)-(c) & 99; IS Regs, regs 38(3)(b)-(c) & 39

Step 4: See which earnings disregards apply

Check to see which, if any, earnings disregards apply (see below).

5. Earnings disregards

After working out your total earnings, as above, deduct the appropriate *'earnings disregard'*. This applies to the earnings of employed earners and the self-employed. The level of the disregard will depend on which benefit you are claiming.

Employment and support allowance (ESA)

If you are doing 'permitted work' (see Chapter 17(3)), earnings from this work up to the permitted work earnings limit that applies in your case will be disregarded.

Up to £20 can normally be disregarded if you are doing any other kind of work that is allowed (see Chapter 17(3)).

If your earnings from permitted work are less than the limit that applies in your case, and you are undertaking duties as the disability member of a First-tier Tribunal, up to £20 a week of earnings from that work can also be disregarded until the permitted work earnings limit is reached. If your earnings from permitted work are less than the limit and you have a partner who is doing other work, up to £20 of their earnings can be similarly disregarded to make up the shortfall.

ESA Regs, Sch 7, paras 5-7

Other means-tested benefits

For housing benefit, if you are claiming contributory ESA, incapacity benefit or severe disablement allowance and are doing permitted work (see Chapter 17(3)), all your earnings up to the permitted work earnings limit that applies in your case will be disregarded. If your earnings from permitted work are less than this limit, earnings from other work that is allowed can also be disregarded until the limit is reached. If your earnings from permitted work are less than the limit and you have a partner who is doing other work, up to £20 of their earnings can be similarly disregarded to make up the shortfall.

The same disregard will apply to housing benefit if you are only claiming national insurance credits (for incapacity or limited capability for work) and are doing permitted work.

For income support, income-based jobseeker's allowance (JSA) and, if a permitted work disregard does not apply, housing benefit, disregard £20 a week of your earnings or joint earnings with your partner if any of the following apply.

❑ You qualify for a disability premium or, for housing benefit, a severe disability premium, work-related activity component or support component.

❑ You qualify for a carer premium. The disregard applies to the earnings of the carer; if you are the carer and your earnings are less than £20, up to £5 (or £10 for housing

benefit) can be disregarded from your partner's earnings, subject to the overall £20 maximum.

❑ You are a lone parent. For housing benefit only, the disregard for lone parents is £25.

❑ For income support and income-based JSA only, you qualify for the higher pensioner premium – but only if you or your partner were working part time immediately before reaching the qualifying age for pension credit and were then entitled to the £20 disability premium earnings disregard. Since then, you or your partner must have continued in part-time employment, although breaks of up to eight weeks when you were not getting the means-tested benefit are ignored.

❑ For income support and income-based JSA only, you are one of a couple and the benefit would include a disability premium but for the fact that the higher pensioner premium is applicable. Either you or your partner must be under the qualifying age for pension credit with either one of you in part-time employment.

❑ If you are working as a part-time firefighter, auxiliary coastguard on coast rescue activities, part-time member of a lifeboat crew or member of any territorial or reserve force, up to £20 of those earnings are disregarded. If you are part of a couple and you are both doing one of those jobs, you are still restricted to the joint earnings disregard of £20. If you are doing one of those jobs, your earnings are less than £20 and either you or your partner are also doing an ordinary part-time job, up to £5 (or £10 for housing benefit) can be disregarded from the earnings of the ordinary job, subject to the overall £20 maximum.

If you do not qualify for the £20 earnings disregard, disregard £5 from earnings if you are single. Disregard £10 from joint earnings if you are in a couple, whether one or both of you are working.

IS Regs, Sch 8, paras 4-9; HB Regs, Sch 4, paras 3-10A

For housing benefit there are two extra disregards: the 'childcare costs' and the 'additional earnings' disregards.

Childcare costs earnings disregard in housing benefit

For housing benefit only, you may get an extra earnings disregard for childcare costs.

❑ You must be:

- a lone parent working at least 16 hours a week; *or*
- in a couple and you both work at least 16 hours a week; *or*
- in a couple and one of you works at least 16 hours a week and the other counts as incapacitated, is a hospital inpatient or is in prison. You count as *'incapacitated'* if:
  - you get main-phase ESA, long-term incapacity benefit or severe disablement allowance; *or*
  - you get attendance allowance, disability living allowance, personal independence payment, armed forces independence payment, constant attendance allowance or mobility supplement (or payment has stopped because you are an inpatient); *or*
  - your housing benefit includes a disability premium (on account of your incapacity) or an additional component (on account of your limited capability for work); *or*
  - you are the claimant and have been incapable of work for at least 28 weeks (ignoring gaps of eight weeks or less) or have had a limited capability for work for at least 28 weeks (ignoring gaps of 12 weeks or less).

In each of these three categories you are still treated as working for up to 28 weeks when you are off sick and claiming statutory sick pay, ESA or income support or national insurance credits on the grounds of incapacity or limited capability for work. You will also still be treated as working when you are on maternity, paternity or adoption leave, as long as you are entitled to statutory maternity, paternity or adoption pay, maternity allowance or income support while on paternity leave. In each case, you must have previously been working for at least 16 hours a week.

❑ Your child must be aged 15 or under, or aged 16 or under if they are eligible for a disabled child premium (see Chapter 25(8)). The disregard is available until the day before the first Monday in September after their 15th or 16th birthday.

❑ The childcare must meet certain requirements. You must be paying an approved or registered childcare provider, including out-of-school-hours schemes run on school premises or provided by local authorities. If a relative of the child is providing the care, it needs to be done away from your home.

Disregard from your earnings childcare payments up to a maximum of £175 weekly for one child, or £300 weekly for two or more children.

HB Regs, regs 27(1)(c) & 28

If you get working tax credit or child tax credit and your earnings, once other earnings disregards have been taken off, are less than the disregard for childcare costs, then the disregard is made from the total of your earnings and your tax credits added together.

HB Regs, reg 27(2)

Additional earnings disregard in housing benefit

There is an additional earnings disregard, only in housing benefit, for certain groups of people who work on average either 16 or 30 hours or more a week. Disregard an extra £17.10 from earnings if you (or your partner):

■ receive the 30-hour element within your working tax credit (WTC) – see Chapter 19(7); *or*

■ are aged at least 25 and work at least 30 hours a week; *or*

■ work at least 16 hours a week; *and*

 – your housing benefit includes a family premium (see Chapter 25(7)); *or*

 – are a lone parent; *or*

 – your housing benefit includes a disability premium, work-related activity component or support component. If you are the one eligible for the premium or component, then you must be the one who is working for at least 16 hours a week.

Only one such £17.10 disregard can be made from earnings or from a couple's joint earnings. If your earnings are less than the sum of all the relevant earnings and childcare costs disregards, then £17.10 can be disregarded from any WTC that is awarded instead.

HB Regs, Sch 4, para 17

Earnings from territorial or reserve force training

If you or your partner receive earnings from any annual continuous training as a member of a territorial or reserve force for a maximum of 15 days in any calendar year, an earnings disregard ensures that you are still entitled to at least 10p income support or income-based JSA after the earnings have been taken into account. This is to protect entitlement to passported benefits in cases where earnings are paid at a higher level than income support or income-based JSA and to ensure that a new benefit claim is not necessary after the training is completed. Similar rules apply to income-related ESA if your partner receives earnings for such training.

ESA Regs, Sch 7, para 11A; IS Regs, Sch 8, para 15A

6. Income from benefits, tax credits and pensions

Most benefits are taken into account in full (less income tax payable) but some are completely or partly disregarded.

Benefits that are completely disregarded

The following benefits are completely disregarded:

■ guardian's allowance;

■ child benefit (unless you have a claim for income support or income-based jobseeker's allowance (JSA) that began before April 2004 and you continue to receive support for your children through one of those benefits rather than through child tax credit);

■ child dependants' additions to non-means-tested benefits (for income-related employment and support allowance (ESA), income support and income-based JSA; but with the latter two benefits, only if child tax credit has been awarded);

ESA Regs, Sch 8, paras 6 & 7(2)-(3); IS Regs, Sch 9, paras 5A & 5B

■ disability living allowance (DLA) and personal independence payment (PIP) mobility component;

■ war pensioners' mobility supplement;

■ DLA care component, PIP daily living component, attendance allowance and constant attendance allowance, severe disablement occupational allowance, exceptionally severe disablement allowance (payable under the War Pensions or Industrial Disablement schemes);

■ ex-gratia payments made to compensate for non-payment of DLA, attendance allowance, income-related ESA, income support or income-based JSA;

ESA Regs, Sch 8, paras 8-11; IS Regs, Sch 9, paras 6-9

■ social fund or local welfare provision payments;

■ Christmas bonus;

■ payment or repayment of health benefits, and payment made instead of Healthy Start vouchers, milk tokens or vitamins;

ESA Regs, Sch 8, paras 35, 35A, 37 & 45-46; IS Regs, Sch 9, paras 31, 31A, 33 & 48-49

■ certain supplementary payments or pensions for war widows, widowers or surviving civil partners;

■ dependants' additions to non-means-tested benefits if the dependant is not a member of your family;

ESA Regs, Sch 8, paras 49-52; IS Regs, Sch 9, paras (54-56) & 53

■ housing benefit;

■ armed forces independence payment.

ESA Regs, Sch 8, paras 64 & 66; IS Regs, Sch 9, paras 5 & 76A

If you save your benefit – Although these benefits are disregarded as income in the assessment, if there is money left at the end of the period for which the benefit is paid, it will be regarded as capital and, in most cases, will count with other savings. For example, if you save your mobility component towards a wheelchair, the savings will count as capital. Benefit can be disregarded as capital in limited cases – see Chapter 28(6). This will only affect your benefit if it takes your capital above the lower limit for tariff income (see Chapter 28(4)).

Benefits that are partly disregarded

For income-related ESA, income support and income-based JSA, disregard up to £10 of:

■ widowed parent's or widowed mother's allowance;

■ a war disablement pension;

■ a guaranteed income payment made under the Armed Forces and Reserve Forces Compensation scheme (including payment abated by a pension from that scheme or by a payment under the Armed Forces Early Departure scheme);

■ war widow's, widower's or surviving civil partner's pension;

■ comparable pensions to the above paid under non-UK social security legislation;

■ payments made from Germany or Austria to victims of Nazi persecution.

ESA Regs, Sch 8, para 17, IS Regs, Sch 9, para 16

For housing benefit, the rule is the same except that £15 is disregarded from the widowed parent's or widowed mother's allowance. Local authorities can choose to run a local scheme under which they disregard more than £10 of a war pension (or Armed Forces and Reserve Forces Compensation scheme payment) in housing benefit. Your local authority can tell you if it runs a scheme and how much it disregards.

HB Regs, Sch 5, paras 15 & 16

Tax credits

Working tax credit (WTC) is taken into account in full for income-related ESA, income support and income-based JSA. Child tax credit (CTC) is disregarded.

ESA Regs, Sch 8, para 7(1); IS Regs, Sch 9, para 5B

For housing benefit, both WTC and CTC are taken into account in full. They will be reduced, however, by any deduction being made to recover an overpayment of tax credit that arose in a previous year.

HB Regs, reg 40(6)

Additionally, if your earnings are less than the sum of all the relevant earnings and childcare costs disregards, the WTC taken into account can be reduced by the £17.10 additional earnings disregard (see 5 above).

Employer-paid benefits

ESA/income support/JSA – Statutory sick pay (SSP), statutory maternity pay (SMP), statutory paternity pay (SPP) and statutory adoption pay (SAP) are taken into account in full for income-related ESA, income support and income-based JSA, less Class 1 national insurance contributions, tax and half of any contributions you make towards an occupational or personal pension scheme.

ESA Regs, reg 95(2)(b) & Sch 8, paras 1 & 4; IS Regs, reg 35(2)(b) & Sch 9, paras 1 & 4

Housing benefit – SSP, SMP, SPP and SAP are counted as earnings for housing benefit. So when you go on sick leave, maternity leave, paternity leave or adoption leave, your SSP, SMP, SPP or SAP are added to any actual earnings you continue to receive. All the rules on assessing earnings then apply. In particular, you get an 'earnings disregard' (see 5 above) even if you receive only SSP, SMP, SPP or SAP.

HB Regs, reg 35(1)(i)

Occupational and personal pensions

Occupational, personal and state pensions are normally taken into account in full, less any tax payable. If you have reached pension credit qualifying age (see Chapter 42(2)), income from an occupational or personal pension or the Pension Protection Fund that would be available to you on application, or from a pension fund that could be turned into an annuity, may be taken into account as 'notional income' (see 20 below). The same applies to your partner.

ESA Regs, reg 104(8); IS Regs, reg 40(4)

ESA reductions

For income support and income-based JSA, if your partner is receiving contributory ESA that has had a reduction imposed upon it (see Chapter 10(17)), then the contributory ESA will be taken into account in full as if it had not been reduced. The same rule will apply to housing benefit if either you or your partner receive such a reduction in contributory ESA.

IS Regs, reg 40(6)

7. Charitable, voluntary and personal injury payments

Regular payments – Regular charitable and voluntary payments are usually disregarded. Charitable payments are payments made by a charitable trust at the trustees' discretion. Voluntary payments are similar, but not usually made from charitable trusts; they are payments that have a benevolent purpose and are given without anything being given in return (R(IS)4/94). Regular payments are those paid or due to be paid at recurring intervals, such as weekly, monthly, annually or following some other pattern. For income support and income-based jobseeker's allowance, the disregard does not apply to such payments made to strikers.

For maintenance payments, see 8 below.

ESA Regs, Sch 8, para 16; IS Regs, Sch 9, para 15

Irregular payments – If charitable or voluntary payments are not made or not due to be made to you (rather than to a third party – see 9 below) at regular intervals, they will be treated as capital. Irregular gifts in kind from a charity are disregarded.

ESA Regs, reg 112(7); IS Regs, reg 48(9)

Payments from specific trusts

Payments in kind or cash made by the Macfarlane Trusts, the Fund, the Eileen Trust, MFET Ltd, the Skipton Fund, the Caxton Foundation or the Independent Living Fund are disregarded.

Payments made by or on behalf of a person with haemophilia, HIV or hepatitis C (or their partner) who received money from any of these trusts or funds are disregarded in full if they originate from that trust or fund. Payments deriving from the Skipton Fund or the London Bombings Relief Charitable Fund are treated in the same way. To qualify for the disregard, the payment must be made to (or for the benefit of) the partner or former partner of the person who is making the payment (unless you are estranged, divorced or had your civil partnership dissolved), or to dependent children or young people (if they are a member of the donor's family, or were, but are now a member of the claimant's family). If the person making the payment has no partner or dependent children, a payment (including a payment from their estate if they are now dead) to their parent, step-parent or guardian is disregarded for a period of two years after their death, as long as the payment originates from any of these trusts.

ESA Regs, Sch 8, para 41; IS Regs, Sch 9, para 39

Personal injury payments

Payments made or due to be made at regular intervals are disregarded as long as they are:

■ from a trust set up from an award made because of any personal injury to you;
■ under an annuity purchased from funds derived from an award made because of any personal injury to you; *or*
■ received under an agreement or court order to pay you because of any personal injury to you.

Personal injury payments include vaccine damage payments (Chapter 47) and criminal injuries compensation payments (Chapter 46), as well as payments from insurance companies and damages awards by the courts.

ESA Regs, Sch 8, para 16(3); IS Regs, Sch 9, para 15(5A)

8. Maintenance payments

Payments made towards the maintenance of children or young people who live with you (including those made voluntarily) by *'liable relatives'* are disregarded. A liable relative will normally be a former spouse or civil partner or a non-resident parent of the child or young person.

ESA Regs, Sch 8, para 60; IS Regs, Sch 9, para 73

Other maintenance payments (eg spousal maintenance) are taken fully into account, unless, for housing benefit, a family premium is included in the applicable amount, in which case £15 will be disregarded. If more than one payment is made in any week, they will be added together and treated as a single payment, so only one disregard can apply.

HB Regs, Sch 5, para 47

If you pay maintenance, there is no disregard for your payments.

9. Payments to third parties

A payment of income made to a third party in respect of you or your partner can be taken into account but only to the extent that it is used for everyday living expenses (see below). If it is used for something other than everyday living expenses (eg paying a garage for your car to be repaired or adapted) its value will be disregarded. If the payments are used to provide benefits in kind, see 10 below.

A payment made to a third party towards the cost of your care home is treated as your income. This may be partly disregarded under other rules (see 15 below).

A payment to a third party from an occupational or personal pension or the Pension Protection Fund is normally taken into account even if it is not used for everyday living expenses.

ESA Regs, reg 107(3); IS Regs, reg 42(4)

Everyday living expenses – These are defined as: food, ordinary clothing or footwear, household fuel, council tax, water charges, rent (for which housing benefit is payable) or any housing costs (which are met by employment and support allowance, income support or jobseeker's allowance). Ordinary clothing or footwear includes items for normal daily use, but does not include school uniforms, or clothing or footwear used solely for sporting activities.

ESA Regs, regs 2(1) & 107(3)(c); IS Regs, reg 42(9)

10. Payments in kind

Payments in kind, eg a bus pass, food, petrol, etc, are disregarded unless (for income support and income-based jobseeker's allowance) you are involved in a trade dispute. However, payments made to third parties that are used to provide benefits in kind to you are treated as your income.

ESA Regs, Sch 8, para 22; IS Regs, Sch 9, para 21

Non-cash vouchers from an employer that are liable for Class 1 national insurance contributions are not treated as payments in kind but as earnings. Vouchers not liable for contributions are treated as payments in kind (eg certain charitable vouchers) and are thus disregarded.

ESA Regs, reg 95(3); IS Regs, reg 35(2A)

11. Training and employment schemes

If you are on a government training programme or employment scheme (under either s.2 (but not s.2(3)) of the Employment & Training Act 1973 or s.2 (but not s.2(5)) of the Enterprise & New Towns (Scotland) Act 1990) any payment is disregarded unless it is:

- made as a substitute for employment and support allowance, incapacity benefit, income support, jobseeker's allowance or severe disablement allowance;
- intended to meet the cost of everyday living expenses (see 9 above) while you are participating in the programme or scheme; *or*
- intended to meet the cost of living away from home, if the payment is to cover rent charged for the accommodation where you are staying, for which housing benefit is payable.

ESA Regs, Sch 8, para 15: IS Regs, Sch 9, para 13

The following are also disregarded:

- payments to cover travel and other expenses while you are participating in the Mandatory Work Activity scheme or any of the jobseeker's allowance schemes for assisting people to obtain employment (eg the new enterprise allowance or the Work Programme) or undertaking work-related activity;
- return-to-work credit, in-work credit and work-search premium;
- payments to help a disabled person get or keep work, made under the Disabled Persons (Employment) Act 1944 – eg Access to Work payments – but not if it is a government training allowance.

ESA Regs, Sch 8, paras 1A, 15A, 15 & 48; IS Regs, Sch 9, paras 1A, 13 & 51

12. Payments towards education

The following are disregarded:

- education maintenance allowance and 16-19 bursary fund payments;
- repayments of student loans to certain newly qualified teachers;

- maintenance payments to the school or college for a dependent child or young person from someone outside your family (income-related employment and support allowance, income support and income-based jobseeker's allowance only);

ESA Regs, Sch 8, paras 13, 14 & 27; IS Regs, Sch 9, paras 11, 11A & 25A

- if you make assessed parental contributions to a student son or daughter, the amount you pay is disregarded from your income – unless the student is under 25, in advanced education and receives only a discretionary grant or gets no grant or loan, in which case the disregard is limited to £56.80 a week, less the amount of any discretionary grant payable (housing benefit only).

HB Regs, Sch 5, paras 19 & 20

Certain amounts of a student grant or loan, Access Fund payment or Career Development Loan can be disregarded (see Box N.3, Chapter 40).

13. Payments for your home

Employment and support allowance (ESA), income support, jobseeker's allowance (JSA) – For income-related ESA, income support and income-based JSA, the following payments related to your home are disregarded:

- payments under a mortgage protection policy used to meet repayments on a mortgage or on a loan for eligible repairs and improvements (see Chapter 26(2)) up to the amount of loan interest not met in your applicable amount, plus the amount due in capital repayments or endowment premiums, premiums on the mortgage protection policy and premiums on a buildings insurance policy;
- payments (from any source) made to you that are intended and used as a contribution towards:
  - payments due on a loan secured on your home that are not covered by income-related ESA, income support or income-based JSA – see Chapter 26(3);
  - housing costs covered by income-related ESA, income support or income-based JSA but not met in your applicable amount;
  - capital repayments or endowment premiums on loans covered by income-related ESA, income support or income-based JSA;
  - premiums on a policy taken out to meet any of the above costs or for buildings insurance;
  - any rent not met by housing benefit;
  (unless these are already covered by an insurance policy).

ESA Regs, Sch 8, paras 31 & 32; IS Regs, Sch 9, paras 29 & 30

Housing benefit – For housing benefit, disregard payments under an insurance policy taken out against the risk of being unable to maintain repayments on a loan secured on your home, and used to maintain repayments and premiums on that policy and any premiums for buildings insurance if this is a requirement of the loan.

HB Regs, Sch 5, para 29

14. Income from tenants and lodgers

Disregard the following income from tenants and lodgers:

- contributions towards living and accommodation costs made to you by someone living as a member of your household (but not if they are a commercial boarder or a sub-tenant);
- if you have sub-let part of your home (under a formal contract), a maximum of £20 from the weekly payment received from each sub-tenant;
- if you provide board and lodging in your own home, £20 and half of the remainder of the weekly charge paid by each person provided with such accommodation (even if that person lodges with you for just one night).

ESA Regs, Sch 8, paras 19-21; IS Regs, Sch 9, paras 18-20

15. Payments for care homes

Some payments towards the cost of your care are disregarded for income-related employment and support allowance, income support and income-based jobseeker's allowance. See also Chapter 33(4).

If the local authority arranged your care – Payments made by the local authority towards the cost of care home charges are fully disregarded.

ESA Regs, Sch 8, para 56; IS Regs, Sch 9, para 66

If the local authority did not arrange your care – Any payment intended for and used to meet the care home charge is partly disregarded (unless it is a regular charitable or voluntary payment, when it is fully disregarded – see 7 above). The amount disregarded is the weekly accommodation charge less your applicable amount.

ESA Regs, Sch 8, para 34; IS Regs, Sch 9, para 30A

16. Payments for children

The following payments for children or young people in your care are disregarded:

■ adoption and residence order allowances and special guardianship payments. However, for income support and income-based jobseeker's allowance, if your claim began before April 2004 and you continue to receive support for your children through one of those benefits rather than child tax credit, only the amount of allowance or payment that exceeds the child's personal allowance and disabled child premium is disregarded;

■ fostering allowances (for official arrangements only);

■ discretionary payments from social care or social work departments to help children in need or to provide help to young care leavers.

ESA Regs, Sch 8, paras 26, 28 & 30; IS Regs, Sch 9, paras 25, 26 & 28

17. Income generated from capital

Income derived from capital is generally not treated as income but is added to your capital from the date it is normally due to be credited to you. However, income derived from the following items of disregarded capital (see Chapter 28(6)) is treated as income:

■ your home;

■ premises you've acquired to live in, but have not yet been able to move in to;

■ premises occupied by a partner or relative who has reached the qualifying age for pension credit or is incapacitated, or a former partner (but not if you are estranged, divorced or had your civil partnership dissolved);

■ your former home if you are estranged, divorced or had your civil partnership dissolved;

■ premises you are taking reasonable steps to sell;

■ premises you intend to occupy and are taking legal steps to obtain possession of;

■ premises you intend to occupy but which need essential repairs or alterations;

■ business assets;

■ a trust fund from compensation for personal injury;

■ capital administered by the courts from damages awarded for personal injury or, for under-18s, compensation for the loss of a parent.

ESA Regs, reg 112(4); IS Regs, reg 48(4)

During the period in which you receive income from any of the premises listed above (other than the home you live in), any mortgage payments made, or council tax or water charges paid, in respect of the disregarded premises can be offset against that income. The amount above this is taken into account as income.

ESA Regs, Sch 8, para 23(2); IS Regs, Sch 9, para 22(2)

If you let out your property and it is not covered under one of the disregards above, rent is treated as capital not income. The full amount is taken into account as capital without any deductions for mortgage payments, etc.

18. Capital treated as income

If any capital is payable by instalments, each instalment outstanding when your claim is decided (or on the first day for which the means-tested benefit is paid if this is earlier), or at a later supersession, is treated as income if your total capital, including the outstanding instalments, adds up to more than £16,000. If your total capital is less than or equal to £16,000, each instalment is treated as a payment of capital.

The following are also treated as income:

■ periodic personal injury payments made to you under an agreement or court order (see 7 above for when these can be disregarded);

■ payments made under an annuity; *and*

ESA Regs, reg 105; IS Regs, reg 41

■ payments made to compensate you for past pay inequalities (single status payments).

CJSA/0475/2009 (CoA 'Minter')

Any capital treated as income is disregarded as capital.

ESA Regs, Sch 9, para 25; IS Regs, Sch 10, para 20

19. Miscellaneous income

The following types of income are disregarded:

■ expenses paid to a volunteer, including advance payments to cover expenses – but only if you are paid nothing else by the charity or organisation and are not treated as having 'notional' earnings (see 20 below);

■ expenses paid to public body service user group participants;

■ Victoria Cross/George Cross annuities and analogous payments;

■ income abroad while transfer to the UK is prohibited;

■ charges for currency conversion if income is not paid in sterling;

ESA Regs, Sch 8, paras 2, 2A, 12, 24 & 25; IS Regs, Sch 9, paras 2, 2A, 10, 23 & 24

■ payments in respect of a person not normally a member of your household but temporarily in your care, made by a health body, voluntary organisation or local authority (or by a person placed with you by the local authority). This covers respite care payments for overnight (or longer) stays or for just a few hours in the day. It does not cover any direct payments of housing benefit made to you;

ESA Regs, Sch 8, para 29; IS Regs, Sch 9, para 27

■ payments under an insurance policy taken out against the risk of being unable to maintain repayments under a credit agreement, hire purchase or conditional sale agreement, up to the amount used to maintain the repayments and pay premiums on that policy;

■ payments to a juror or witness in respect of attendance at court (but not if they are to compensate for loss of earnings or loss of benefit);

■ payments under the Assisted Prison Visits scheme;

ESA Regs, Sch 8, paras 33, 43 & 47; IS Regs, Sch 9, paras 30ZA, 43 & 50

■ community care or NHS direct payments (unless you use them to pay your partner for the care they give you, in which case the direct payment paid to your partner will be treated as their earnings and is taken into account – see 4 above for the way self-employed earnings are treated);

■ Sports Council National Lottery award, except for amounts awarded for everyday living expenses (see 9 above, although 'food' in this case does not include vitamins, minerals or other special dietary supplements intended to enhance performance);

■ discretionary housing payments from a local authority;

■ payments from a local authority under the Supporting People scheme.

ESA Regs, Sch 8, paras 53, 57, 62 & 63; IS Regs, Sch 9, paras 58, 69, 75 & 76

20. Notional income

Income that you do not actually possess may be taken into account in some circumstances.

❑ **Deprivation of income** – You are treated as possessing any income of which you have deprived yourself in order to get a means-tested benefit or increase it (the issue is similar to that of deprivation of capital – see Chapter 28(9)).

ESA Regs, reg 106(1), IS Regs, reg 42(1)

❑ **Income available if applied for** – You are treated as possessing income from the date that you could expect to receive it. This also applies to most social security benefits (but only up until the time you put in a claim). The rule does not apply to the following types of income:

■ jobseeker's allowance (for income support and income-related employment and support allowance (ESA) only);

■ working tax credit and child tax credit;

■ payments from a discretionary trust or a personal injury compensation trust;

■ compensation administered by the courts for personal injury;

■ employment rehabilitation allowances;

■ expenses paid to public body service user group participants;

■ income from a personal pension scheme (including an annuity contract or trust scheme approved under tax law), occupational pension scheme or the Pension Protection Fund (PPF), as long as you are under pension credit qualifying age (see Chapter 42(2)). For income-related ESA, income support and income-based jobseeker's allowance (JSA), once you reach pension credit qualifying age, if you fail to draw an income from the pension or PPF, you are assumed to have notional income. Income that could be obtained from money purchase benefits under an occupational or personal pension scheme is treated in the same way;

ESA Regs, reg 106(2)-(8); IS Regs, reg 42(2)-(2CA)

■ any Category A or B state pension, additional state pension or graduated retirement benefit that has been deferred – see Chapter 43(7) (for housing benefit only).

HB(SPC) Regs, reg 41(2)-(3)

❑ **Notional earnings** – If you are a volunteer, or engaged by a charitable or voluntary organisation, notional earnings cannot be assumed if it is reasonable for you to provide your services free of charge. (A carer may count as a 'volunteer' – see CIS/93/91, but see CIS/701/94 for exceptions.) If it is reasonable to expect you to charge for your services, or you are performing a service for someone else in some other capacity, you are treated as having *'such earnings (if any) as is reasonable for that employment unless* [you] *satisfy* [the decision maker] *that the means of that person are insufficient for him to pay, or to pay more, for the service'*. Decision makers are advised to assume earnings of at least the relevant national minimum wage. If notional earnings are assumed, seek advice.

ESA Regs, reg 108(3) & (4)(a); IS Regs, reg 42(6) & (6A)(a)

❑ **Income owed** – For income-related ESA, income support and income-based JSA, you are treated as possessing any income owing to you, but there are exceptions (eg income from a discretionary or personal injury trust, or delays in social security benefits).

ESA Regs, reg 107(1); IS Regs, reg 42(3)

❑ **Care homes** – Payments made towards the cost of your care home are treated as your income, but some of them may be disregarded (see 15 above).

28 Capital

1. Introduction

In this chapter we look at the way your capital is treated when means-tested benefits are being calculated. The rules in this chapter apply to the following benefits:

■ income-related employment and support allowance;

■ income support;

■ income-based jobseeker's allowance;

■ housing benefit – if you (and your partner) are under the qualifying age for pension credit or claiming one of the benefits listed above (otherwise the rules are similar to pension credit – see Chapter 42(6)).

Where there are significant differences in the way that capital is treated for different benefits, we say so. As capital is treated in a substantially different way for pension credit, we describe this separately in Chapter 42(6).

For the sake of simplicity, we generally confine the legal references to those applicable to income-related employment and support allowance and income support.

Your capital can affect your entitlement to means-tested benefits when it is above certain set limits (see 3 below). Capital includes savings, investments, some lump-sum payments and the value of property and land (but if you own the home you live in, the value of your home, garden, garage and outbuildings is not taken into account). Certain types of capital can be disregarded (see 6 below). Sometimes capital can be treated as income (see Chapter 27(18)) and vice versa (see 8 below).

2. Whose capital is included?

If you are one of a couple (married or living together as husband and wife, or in a same-sex partnership whether registered or not), your partner's capital is added to yours. Otherwise, only your capital is taken into account; capital belonging to dependent children is disregarded (see Chapter 27(2) for an exception; similar rules apply to capital).

ESA Regs, reg 83; IS Regs, reg 23

3. Capital limits

There is a *'lower capital limit'* and an *'upper capital limit'*. You cannot get any of the means-tested benefits listed in 1 above if your capital is above the upper limit of £16,000.

ESA Regs, reg 110; IS Regs, reg 45

If your capital is at or below the lower limit of £6,000, your means-tested benefit is unaffected. If you move permanently into a care home, an Abbeyfield Home or an independent hospital, this lower limit goes up to £10,000. If your stay is only temporary, the £6,000 limit still applies. For housing benefit, the lower limit is also set at £10,000 if you or your partner are over the qualifying age for pension credit (and not claiming income-related ESA, income support or income-based JSA).

If your capital is between the lower and upper limits, an amount of 'tariff income' is assumed (see 4 below).

Some types of capital are disregarded for these capital limits (see 6 below). You can also be treated as having capital that you may not actually possess: this is called 'notional capital' (see 9 below).

4. Tariff income

If your capital is between the lower and upper limits, a *'tariff income'* is assumed, ie your capital is treated as if it were generating income. Normally, £1 a week for every £250 (or part of £250) above the lower limit is included as income in this way (but see below for an exception). For instance, if you have capital of £6,300, £2 a week is included as income. Each time capital moves into the next block of £250 (even by as little as 1p) an additional £1 a week is included as income. This tariff income is then added to your other income when calculating entitlement to the means-tested benefit.

ESA Regs, reg 118; IS Regs, reg 53

For housing benefit, if you or your partner are over the qualifying age for pension credit (and not claiming income-related employment and support allowance, income support or income-based jobseeker's allowance), the assumed tariff income is £1 for every £500 (or part of £500) above the lower limit.

HB(SPC) Regs, reg 29(2)

If tariff income is included in your assessment, notify Jobcentre Plus if the amount of your capital changes. If your savings drop to the next lower tariff income band and you have not told Jobcentre Plus, you will be getting too little of the means-tested benefit. If your savings have increased to the next higher tariff income band and you have not told Jobcentre Plus, you will have been overpaid benefit. Watch out for the 'notional capital' rule (see 9 below). Keep records and all receipts to show how and why you spent your capital.

5. How is capital valued?

Capital is calculated at its current market or surrender value, less 10% if there would be costs involved in selling and less any mortgage or debt secured on the property.

ESA Regs, reg 113; IS Regs, reg 49

Joint capital – If you own property or other capital jointly with one or more others so that each person owns the whole asset jointly with no separate or distinct shares, then you are treated as though you own an equal share. Thus, if four people jointly own a capital asset, each will be treated as possessing 25% of that capital.

ESA Regs, reg 117; IS Regs, reg 52

However, if you share the property as tenants-in-common rather than as joint tenants, the share you are treated as owning should reflect the actual split.

R(IS)4/03

The decision maker must establish the market value or price that a willing buyer would pay to a willing seller for your share. The market value could be low or even nil if other joint owners would not be prepared to sell the property as a whole or to buy your share.

6. What capital is disregarded?

Benefits

Arrears (or an ex-gratia payment) of the following benefits are disregarded for 52 weeks after you get them: disability living allowance and attendance allowance (or equivalents under the Industrial Injuries or War Pensions schemes), housing benefit, discretionary housing payments, council tax benefit, income-related employment and support allowance (ESA), income support, income-based jobseeker's allowance, child tax credit and working tax credit.

If arrears made to rectify or compensate for an official error amount to £5,000 or more, and have been awarded in full since 14.10.01, they can be disregarded for 52 weeks from the date of receipt or for the remaining period of the award of the means-tested benefit, whichever is the longer period.

ESA Regs, Sch 9, para 11; IS Regs, Sch 10, para 7

Social fund and local welfare provision payments are disregarded. Payments or repayments of a health benefit in respect of NHS prescription charges, dental charges or hospital travelling expenses are disregarded for 52 weeks after you receive the money. Payments made instead of Healthy Start vouchers, milk tokens or free vitamins are disregarded for 52 weeks after receipt.

ESA Regs, Sch 9, paras 23, 23A, 37 & 38; IS Regs, Sch 10, paras 18, 18A, 38 & 39

Personal possessions

The value of personal possessions is disregarded, except those bought to reduce capital in order to get more benefit. A compensation payment for loss of or damage to personal possessions that is to be used for repair or replacements is disregarded for 26 weeks, or longer if that is reasonable.

ESA Regs, Sch 9, paras 14 & 12(a); IS Regs, Sch 10, paras 10 & 8(a)

Trust funds and personal injury payments

Personal injury payments – When a trust fund is created from payments for a personal or criminal injury to you or your partner, the value of the fund is disregarded indefinitely. 'Personal injury' includes a disease or an injury suffered as a result of a disease (R(SB)2/89). Trusts created from vaccine damage payments are covered, as may a trust of funds collected for a person because of their personal injuries. Actual payments from a trust fund for a personal or criminal injury can count in full as capital, but may be disregarded as income (see Chapter 27(7)).

If a lump-sum payment for a personal or criminal injury to you or your partner has not been put into a trust, it can be disregarded for up to 52 weeks from the date of receipt (to allow you time to set up a trust). However, this applies only to an initial payment; subsequent lump-sum payments made in consequence of the same injury count in full.

ESA Regs, Sch 9, paras 16 & 17; IS Regs, Sch 10, paras 12 & 12A

If capital is administered by the courts, damages awarded for personal injury and, for under-18s, compensation for the loss of a parent are disregarded.

ESA Regs, Sch 9, paras 43 & 44; IS Regs, Sch 10, paras 44 & 45

Life interest – The value of the right to receive any income under a life interest or from a life rent (this is a type of trust in Scotland) is disregarded. Actual income received counts in full as income.

ESA Regs, Sch 9, para 18; IS Regs, Sch 10, para 13

Specific trusts – Payments made under or by the Macfarlane Trusts, the Fund, the Eileen Trust, the Skipton Fund, the Caxton Foundation, the London Bombings Relief Charitable Fund, MFET Ltd or the Independent Living Fund are disregarded. Payments made by or on behalf of a person with haemophilia, HIV or hepatitis C may be disregarded under the same rules as income (see Chapter 27(7)).

ESA Regs, Sch 9, para 27; IS Regs, Sch 10, para 22

A payment from the government-funded trust for people with variant Creutzfeldt-Jakob disease (vCJD) paid to a person with vCJD or their partner is disregarded for life. If the trust payment is made to a parent or child of a person with vCJD (including payment from the estate if they have died), it is disregarded for two years from the date it is paid or until the child reaches age 20 or leaves full-time education, whichever is the latest.

ESA Regs, Sch 9, para 53; IS Regs, Sch 10, para 64

Training and employment

Disregard the following:

■ business assets while you are *'engaged as a self-employed earner'*. If you've ceased that self-employment, the assets will be disregarded for as long as is reasonable in the circumstances to allow you to dispose of them. However, if sickness or disability means you cannot work as a self-employed earner, your business assets will be disregarded for 26 weeks from your date of claim, or longer if that is reasonable in the circumstances. You must intend to start or resume work in that business as soon as you are able to or as soon as you recover;

ESA Regs, Sch 9, para 10; IS Regs, Sch 10, para 6

■ payments (but not a government training allowance) made under the Disabled Persons (Employment) Act 1944 to help a disabled person get or keep work;

■ start-up capital under the Blind Homeworkers' scheme.

ESA Regs, Sch 9, paras 41 & 42; IS Regs, Sch 10, paras 42 & 43

Disregard for 52 weeks from the date of receipt:

■ payments to cover travel and other expenses while you are participating in the Mandatory Work Activity scheme or any of the jobseeker's allowance schemes for assisting people to obtain employment (eg new enterprise allowance or the Work Programme) or undertaking work-related activity;

■ any payment from a government training programme or employment scheme (under either s.2 of the Employment and Training Act 1973 or s.2 of the Enterprise and New Towns (Scotland) Act 1990);

■ any discretionary payment or arrears of subsistence allowance from an Employment Zone contractor.

ESA Regs, Sch 9, paras 1A, 32A, 32 & (48 & 49); IS Regs, Sch 10, paras 1A, 30 & (58 & 59)

Your home

The following items are disregarded:

■ the value of your own home;

■ the value of premises you've acquired, if you intend to move in within 26 weeks of the date of purchase;*

■ any sum directly attributable to the proceeds of the sale of your former home that you intend to use to buy another home within 26 weeks of that sale;*

ESA Regs, Sch 9, paras 1, 2 & 3; IS Regs, Sch 10, paras 1, 2 & 3

■ the value of premises occupied wholly or partly by your partner or by a relative, if they have reached pension credit qualifying age or are incapacitated; or former partner if you are not estranged, divorced or had your civil partnership dissolved;

■ the value of your former home for 26 weeks after you left it because of divorce, civil partnership dissolution or estrangement from your former partner. If the former partner is a lone parent, the value is disregarded for as long as they occupy your former home;

■ the value of premises that you are taking reasonable steps to dispose of, for 26 weeks from the date on which you first took such steps;*

ESA Regs, Sch 9, paras 4, 5 & 6; IS Regs, Sch 10, paras 4, 25 & 26

■ the value of premises you intend to occupy as your home if you are taking steps to obtain possession and have either sought legal advice or commenced legal proceedings in order to obtain possession. The value is disregarded for 26 weeks from the date on which you first sought such advice or started proceedings (whichever is earlier);*

■ the value of premises you intend to occupy as your home once 'essential repairs or alterations' make the premises 'fit for such occupation', for 26 weeks from the date on which you first took steps to get the premises repaired or altered.* This can help if you are adapting your property using a disabled facilities grant;

ESA Regs, Sch 9, paras 7 & 8; IS Regs, Sch 10, paras 27 & 28

■ any sum paid to you because of damage to, or loss of, the home or any personal possession and intended for its repair or replacement, or any sum given or loaned to you expressly for essential repairs or improvements to the home, will be disregarded for 26 weeks if you are going to use that sum for its intended purpose;*

■ any sum deposited with a housing association as a condition of occupying the home. If you've removed that deposit and intend to use it to buy another home it can be disregarded for 26 weeks;*

ESA Regs, Sch 9, paras 12 & 13; IS Regs, Sch 10, paras 8 & 9

■ any grant made by a local authority (if you are one of its tenants) to buy premises you intend to live in as your home, or to do repairs or alterations needed to make the premises fit for you to live in. The grant is disregarded for 26 weeks;*

■ arrears of discretionary housing payments from a local authority for 52 weeks from the date received.

ESA Regs, Sch 9, paras 36 & 11(1)(c) ; IS Regs, Sch 10, paras 37 & 7(d)

* In each case more time is allowed if reasonable in the circumstances to enable you to conclude the matter.

Right to receive income or payment in future

Certain forms of capital can be released at some stage to provide you with income or payment in the future. The following types are disregarded:

■ any future interest in property other than land or premises that have been let by you;

■ the capital value of the right to receive any income under an annuity, and the surrender value of an annuity;

■ the capital value of the right to receive income that is disregarded because it is frozen abroad;

ESA Regs, Sch 9, paras 9, 15 & 19; IS Regs, Sch 10, paras 5, 11 & 14

■ the full surrender value of a life insurance policy;

■ the value of the right to receive an occupational or personal pension, and the value of funds held under a personal pension scheme (including annuity contracts and trust schemes approved under tax law);

■ the value of the right to receive any rent, except where you have a future interest in the property.

ESA Regs, Sch 9, paras 20, (28 & 29) & 30; IS Regs, Sch 10, paras 15, (23 & 23A) & 24

Other capital

The following types of capital are disregarded:

■ where any payment of capital 'falls to be made by instalments, the value of the right to receive any outstanding instalments' (see also Chapter 27(18));

■ discretionary payments from social care or social work departments to help children in need or to provide help to young care leavers;

■ a refund of tax deducted on loan interest if that loan was taken out in order to buy the home or to carry out repairs or improvements to the home;

ESA Regs, Sch 9, paras 21, 22 & 24; IS Regs, Sch 10, paras 16, 17 & 19

■ any charge for currency conversion if your capital is not held in sterling;

■ payments in kind made by a charity, the Macfarlane Trusts, the Fund, the Eileen Trust (for income-related ESA), MFET Ltd, the Skipton Fund, the Caxton Foundation or the Independent Living Fund;

■ payments made to a juror or witness in respect of attendance at a court (but not if it was to compensate for loss of earnings or loss of benefit);

ESA Regs, Sch 9, paras 26, 31 & 34; IS Regs, Sch 10, paras 21, 29 & 34

■ Victoria Cross/George Cross payments;

■ a Sports Council National Lottery award, less everyday living expenses (see Chapter 27(9)), although 'food' in this case does not include vitamins, minerals or other special dietary supplements intended to enhance performance, for 26 weeks after you receive payment of the award;

■ £10,000 special payment made to you or your partner (or for a deceased spouse/civil partner or partner's deceased spouse/civil partner) because of internment by the Japanese during the Second World War;

ESA Regs, Sch 9, paras 45, 47 & 50; IS Regs, Sch 10, paras 46, 56 & 61

■ education maintenance allowance and 16-19 bursary fund payments;

■ payments made to you or your partner (or for a deceased spouse/civil partner or partner's deceased spouse/civil partner) to compensate for being a slave labourer or a

forced labourer, suffering property loss or personal injury or being the parent of a child who had died, during the Second World War;
- payments from local authorities under the Supporting People scheme;

ESA Regs, Sch 9, paras 52, 54 & 55; IS Regs, Sch 10, paras 63, 65 & 66

- community care or NHS direct payments;
- a payment made under s.2(6)(b), 3 or 4 of the Adoption and Children Act 2002;
- a special guardianship payment.

ESA Regs, Sch 9, paras 56, 57 & 58; IS Regs, Sch 10, paras 67, 68 & 68A

Disregard the following for 52 weeks after you receive them:
- payments made under the Assisted Prison Visits scheme;
- arrears of supplementary pensions to war widows, widowers and surviving civil partners.

ESA Regs, Sch 9, paras 39 & 40; IS Regs, Sch 10, paras 40 & 41

7. Loans

If you borrow money, it will almost always count as money you possess (generally as capital if it is a one-off loan or, in some cases, as income if it is part of a series of payments). You may be able to argue that a loan should not count as capital if the money was given to you for a specific purpose and on condition that it be repaid if it is not used in that particular way.

8. Income treated as capital

The following payments of income are treated as capital:
- income derived from capital (but see Chapter 27(17));
- income tax refunds;*
- irregular charitable or voluntary payments (other than payments made under or by the Macfarlane Trusts, the Fund, the Eileen Trust, MFET Ltd, the Skipton Fund, the Caxton Foundation or the Independent Living Fund);*
- holiday pay payable more than four weeks after the employment ends or is interrupted;*
- advance of earnings or a loan from an employer;*
- payment for a discharged prisoner (for income-related employment and support allowance, income support and income-based jobseeker's allowance (JSA));
- lump-sum payment of arrears of Employment Zone subsistence allowance;
- a bounty paid no more than once a year to a part-time firefighter, for coast rescue duties or running a lifeboat, or to a member of the Territorial Army or reserves.

* except for those involved in a trade dispute (for income support/JSA)

ESA Regs, reg 112; IS Regs, reg 48

In addition to the above, arrears of child tax credit and working tax credit are treated as capital for housing benefit.

HB Regs, reg 46

9. Notional capital

If you are held to have deprived yourself of some capital in order to get or increase a means-tested benefit, the law says the capital must be treated as if you still had it. This is called *'notional'* capital. In some cases, the amount of notional capital along with actual capital will exclude you from the benefit. Or, you may be entitled to the benefit, but because of your notional capital the assessment is related to a higher tariff income than your actual capital warrants (see 4 above).

If there were good reasons for spending your capital, and getting the means-tested benefit (or more of it) wasn't a significant motive for spending part of your savings, you should not be affected. It is worth appealing if capital you no longer have is taken into account, but seek expert advice and check Commissioners' decisions R(IS)1/91, R(SB)38/85, R(SB)40/85, R(SB)9/91 and CIS/242/93.

If you are held to have notional capital on this basis, you won't be excluded from the means-tested benefit permanently,

nor will a tariff income be related permanently to the higher amount of notional capital. Jobcentre Plus will apply the *'diminishing notional capital rule'*, which reduces the amount of notional capital over time (see below).

ESA Regs, reg 115; IS Regs, reg 51

Diminishing notional capital rule

Your notional capital is treated as having been reduced by the amount of the means-tested benefit 'lost' over a set period. If you are held to have deprived yourself of an amount of capital, Jobcentre Plus will work out:
- how much benefit you would have been entitled to in the normal way if you had no notional capital – (A);
- how much benefit, if any, you are entitled to on the basis of your notional capital (as well as actual capital) – (B);
- (A) minus (B) = the benefit you have lost – (LB).

If you have also lost any of the other means-tested benefits, Jobcentre Plus (or the local authority) will add on those amounts of lost benefit, eg LB 1 (income support) + LB 2 (housing benefit) = total lost benefit (TLB).

Your notional capital is treated as being reduced each week by your total lost benefit.

The decision on your claim for a means-tested benefit will include the amount of that benefit you have lost because of notional capital. Keep that decision letter. You may need to produce it if you claim another means-tested benefit and you are held to have deprived yourself of some capital in order to get that benefit as well. For example, if you are excluded from income support because of notional capital and you are also held to have deprived yourself of some capital to get housing benefit, you will need to show the income support decision letter to the local authority department dealing with your housing benefit claim. It is possible to receive different decisions on deprivation of capital, and different amounts of notional capital, for each benefit.

If the notional capital rule reduces your entitlement to the means-tested benefit – Each time your notional capital goes below another tariff income step, you will be entitled to more benefit. A change of circumstances may also increase or reduce your benefit. Both (A) and (B) will be re-calculated, giving you a new amount of lost benefit (LB(2)). For other means-tested benefits, the amount of lost benefit may also change, so you will add these on (LB 1(2) + LB 2(2), etc). Your notional capital will now be treated as being reduced by your current total lost benefit (TLB(2)).

If the notional capital rule means you are no longer entitled to the means-tested benefit – Once your total lost benefit is worked out, it cannot be reduced. It can only be increased to enable your notional capital to diminish faster, eg if there is a change of circumstances that would increase the amount of benefit to which you would be entitled. However, whenever the amount of notional capital you are deemed to have changes, the new amount is fixed for a period of 26 weeks. The onus is on you to make a fresh claim for each benefit affected by the deprivation of capital rule and to produce the decision letters showing the amount(s) of the other lost benefit(s).

More deprivation? – If you have actual capital as well as notional capital, you should still be careful about how you spend your actual capital. Obviously, you will have to draw on actual capital to help supplement your income and cover expenses not met by benefit. But the deprivation of capital rule can be re-applied to the actual capital spent.

ESA Regs, reg 116; IS Regs, reg 51A

This section of the Handbook looks at:

Practical help at home

29 Care services

1. What is community care?
Community care is defined as *'providing the right level of intervention and support to enable people to achieve maximum independence and control over their own lives'*.
NHS and Community Care Act 1990

Adult social care (England) – The *Vision for Adult Social Care: Capable Communities and Active Citizens* (November 2010) moves forward the transformation of 'adult social care' (previously adult social services) initiated by *Putting People First* (2007). It lays the ground for local authorities to provide 'personal budgets', preferably as direct payments, to everyone eligible (see 4 below).
LAC(DH)(2009)1; LAC(DH)(2010)7

Future plans for adult social care were set out in the White Paper *Caring for our future* and the draft Care and Support Bill (published in July 2012). The proposed legislation creates a single law for adult care and support to replace existing legislation. As part of its pre-legislative scrutiny process, the Department of Health is considering views submitted in the consultation process.

Healthcare and social care
There is no obvious dividing line between a social care need and a healthcare need. Legislation allows adult social care and health bodies to work together using pooled budgets and joint commissioning of services. Health bodies might not provide services they consider are not reasonably required, taking into account their own resources.
England and Wales – It is important to know if your care needs are considered to be healthcare needs under the NHS, as most healthcare is free at the point of delivery but there are charges for most social care.

Local authorities in England and Wales can only provide or arrange social care packages. The NHS is responsible for meeting the cost of registered nursing care in care homes that provide it, as well as all other reasonably required healthcare (see Chapter 32(3)).

In England, the *National Framework for NHS Continuing Healthcare and NHS-funded Nursing Care,* and in Wales, *Continuing NHS Health Care: The National Framework for Implementation in Wales* (see Box L.1), outline the criteria under which the NHS should fully fund care, including social care (and in care homes, including the accommodation costs). The criteria were developed as a result of the *Coughlan* and *Grogan* cases, which established that where a person's primary need is a health need, the

NHS should fully fund the care.
Coughlan [1999] Civ 1871 (EWCA); Grogan v Bexley NHS care trust [2006] 44 (Admin) (EWHC)

Scotland – Local authority social work departments have duties to provide help to *'persons in need'* and are responsible for the provision of a range of care services. Social work departments and health boards have set up pooled budget arrangements and community healthcare partnerships with single shared assessments. There is free nursing and personal care for people over 65.
Northern Ireland – Health and social care are provided by health and social care trusts, commissioned by a Health and Social Care Board.

2. Intermediate care services
England – *'Intermediate care services'* promote independence by helping people to either leave hospital earlier or avoid admission (to hospital or a care home). One or several services may be offered as part of your intermediate care plan and are usually provided by teams aimed at your *'re-ablement'*. Intermediate care is an intensive service normally lasting no longer than six weeks and often arranged very quickly. Although it covers both health and social care, it should be free. Support can be provided in your home, housing schemes, day centres, hospitals or rehabilitation centres.

When intermediate care services end, you should be assessed to see if you require ongoing health services and/ or social care.
Intermediate Care – Halfway Home (Dept of Health: 2009)

Wales – The short-term support system, referred to as *'6-weeks support at home for vulnerable people'*, helps people being discharged from hospital and helps prevent those at risk from having to enter hospital. This is defined by the *National Framework for Older People* (2006) .
NAfWC 43/02

Scotland – People aged 65 or over can have free home care for up to four weeks following some types of hospital treatment, including surgery as a day patient and overnight stays. Home care is wider in definition than 'personal care' and includes aids and equipment, Meals on Wheels, laundry and shopping needed during a period of recovery. The *Intermediate Care Framework* aims to encourage the development of re-habitation and other services to stop unnecessary hospital admissions and promote timely hospital discharges.
CCD 2/2001; CCD 5/2003

Northern Ireland – The intermediate care system is similar to England.
HSS(ECCU) 2/2005

Delayed discharges
Discharge from hospital should not be delayed if you are fit for discharge.
England – If the delay is due to community care services not being in place, the local authority must reimburse the health trust financially. Health trusts must inform adult social care of patients likely to require services. You should not be pressured into leaving hospital until suitable care

arrangements are in place. If you are returning home, adult social care must review your case within two weeks to ensure the care package is adequate.

Community Care (Delayed Discharges etc) Act 2003; LAC(2003)21

Wales – Delayed transfers of care are recorded and monitored and action taken to address the causes, but there is no system of reimbursement.

Scotland – Community Health Partnerships aim to reduce to zero the number of delayed discharges over 14 days by April 2015.

Expert Group Report, Scottish Government 2011

3. Getting an assessment of your needs

If you have difficulty managing at home because of age, illness or disability, you can ask for an assessment of your needs. If it is apparent to your local authority that you might have a need for services, you should not have to ask for an assessment. See Box K.1 for the law on assessments. Even if the authority is unlikely to provide a service because of its resource constraints, you should not be denied an assessment.

LAC (2004)24; R v Bristol CC ex p Penfold [1998] (1CCLR 315)

If you need assistance urgently, your local authority can temporarily provide or arrange community care services

---

K.1 The law and community care

The law on assessments set out in this box also applies if you want an assessment of your need for care in a care home. The duties and powers of statutory authorities come from Acts, Regulations and Orders, as interpreted by case law. In following the law, authorities must act in accordance with Directions and mandatory/statutory guidance, and take account of other guidance (see Box L.1, Chapter 32).

Most of the provisions in Scotland come under different legislation. Although broadly equivalent to the law in the rest of the UK, there are some important differences. Guidance in the different nations may indicate differing application or interpretation of principles.

Assessments legislation

NHS & Community Care Act 1990 – S.47(1) states: *'... where it appears to a local authority that any person for whom they may provide or arrange for the provision of community care services may be in need of any such services, the authority (a) shall carry out an assessment of his needs for those services, and (b) having regard to the results of that assessment, shall then decide whether his needs call for the provision by them of any such services.'*

Disabled Persons (Services, Consultation & Representation) Act 1986 – S.4 states: *'When requested to do so by – (a) a disabled person [...] or (c) any person who provides care for him [...] a local authority shall decide whether the needs of the disabled person call for the provision by the authority of any services in accordance with s.2(1) of the [Chronically Sick & Disabled Persons Act 1970 (CSDPA)] (provision of welfare services).'*

Carers (Recognition & Services) Act 1995 – S.1(1) states: *'...in any case where – (a) a local authority carry out an assessment under s.47(1)(a) of the NHS & Community Care Act 1990 of the needs of a person for community care services, and (b) an individual (carer) provides or intends to provide a substantial amount of care on a regular basis for the [...] person, the carer may request the local authority, before they make their decision as to whether the needs of the [...] person call for the provision of any services, to carry out an assessment of his ability to provide and to continue to provide care for the [...] person; and if he makes such a request, the local authority shall carry out such an assessment and shall take into account the results of that assessment in making that decision.'*

Carers & Disabled Children Act 2000 (not applicable in Scotland) – S.1(1) states: *'If an individual aged 16 or over ('the carer') – (a) provides or intends to provide a substantial amount of care on a regular basis for another individual aged 18 or over ('the person cared for'), and (b) asks a local authority to carry out an assessment of his ability to provide and to continue to provide care for the person cared for, the local authority must carry out such an assessment if it is satisfied that the person cared for is someone for whom*

it may provide or arrange for the provision of community care services.'

S.2(1) states: *'The local authority must consider the assessment and decide: (a) whether the carer has needs in relation to the care which he provides or intends to provide; (b) if so, whether they could be satisfied (wholly or partly) by services which the local authority may provide; and (c) if they could be so satisfied, whether or not to provide services to the carer.'*

The services must *'help the carer care for the person cared for, and may take the form of physical help or other forms of support'*. Although provided to the carer it may take the form of a service delivered to the cared-for person if both agree and it does not include anything of an intimate nature.

Scotland

S.12 of the **Social Work (Scotland) Act 1968** sets out local authorities' *'general duty'* to promote social welfare by making available advice, guidance and assistance to *'persons in need'*. Local authorities have a duty to undertake an assessment of need under s.12A of the 1968 Act. S.2 of the **Chronically Sick & Disabled Persons (Scotland) Act 1970** sets out local authorities' duty to provide disabled people with the services they have been assessed as needing. Ss.8-11 of the **Community Care & Health (Scotland) Act 2002** provide a framework for carers' assessments.

Northern Ireland

In addition to the above, the CSDPA(NI) 1978, Health & Personal Social Services (NI) Act 1972, Disabled Person's (NI) Act 1989, Carers & Direct Payments (NI) Act 2002 and Health & Social Services (NI) Act 2002 contain the relevant legislation.

Children

The assessment of, and provision of services to, children, including disabled children, usually come under the **Children Act 1989** (in Scotland, the **Children (Scotland) Act 1995**). Assessment of need is undertaken under s.17(2) and Schedule 2, para. 3 (s.23 in Scotland) using the *Framework for the Assessment of Children in Need and their Families* issued in 2000 (2001 Wales). S.17 (s.22 in Scotland) places on local authorities a general duty to safeguard and promote the welfare of children in need.

Disabled children are also entitled to all services available under s.2 CSDPA.

Providing community care services

Following an assessment, the local authority must decide how it will meet the identified needs of the following people:
- provision of residential accommodation to *'persons aged 18 or over who by reason of age, illness, disability or any other circumstances are in need of care and attention which is not otherwise available to them'* – s.21(1)(a) **National Assistance Act 1948** (NAA) (see Chapter 32(4));
- *'persons aged 18 or over who are blind, deaf or dumb or*

before an assessment is carried out. Once temporary services are in place, the authority is required to assess you as soon as practicable.

Self-assessment (England) – A process of *'self-directed support'* has been developed under the *'Personalisation Agenda'*. The Personalisation Agenda aims to give you choice and control over how your needs are met. You (together with any family member or advocate) will assess your needs, with support from social care staff, and will be involved in producing a *'support plan'*. As well as covering care issues, the support plan can include quality-of-life issues, eg work, leisure, domestic and family tasks. Adult social care will then allocate funding, called a *'personal budget'* (see 4 below).

Putting People First (2007)

Delays – There are no national rules about how quickly assessments must take place, although the government has set targets for local authorities, many of which have their own targets. If you experience unreasonable delay, use the complaints procedure first and then the appropriate Ombudsman (see 6 below under 'Further steps').

Eligibility criteria guidance

In deciding whether you will be provided with services, the

---

who suffer from mental disorder of any description, and other persons aged 18 or over who are substantially and permanently handicapped by illness, injury, or congenital deformity or such other disabilities as may be prescribed'. S.29 NAA gives a general provision to promote the welfare of the above people including workshops, suitable work in their own homes or elsewhere, recreational facilities, information on services and keeping a register;

■ those above (to whom s.29 NAA applies) who are *'ordinarily resident in their area'.* The local authority has a duty under s.2 CSDPA to make arrangements for the provision of a range of services. Chapter 29(4) lists these services;

■ old people – a general power, under s.45 **Health Services & Public Health Act 1968**, to promote welfare by providing services;

■ *'any person who is suffering from illness, is pregnant or has recently given birth, is aged, or handicapped as a result of having suffered from illness or by congenital deformity'.* Local authorities have a duty, under para. 3 of Schedule 20 of the **NHS Act 2006**, to provide adequate home help, day care and training centres and may provide laundry services for households when such help is required owing to the presence of the above;

■ persons who were detained or admitted to hospital under ss.3, 37, 47 or 48 of the **Mental Health Act 1983**. S.117 of the 1983 Act also places a duty to provide aftercare services. In Scotland, under ss.25-27 of the **Mental Health (Care & Treatment) (Scotland) Act 2003**, local authorities have a duty to provide services for people with a mental disorder regardless of whether they have been in hospital.

Providing direct payments

Local authorities have the power to make direct payments (cash in lieu of directly provided services) to meet assessed eligible needs under the **Health & Social Care Act 2001** and the **Community Care (Direct Payments) Act 1996**. S.7 of the **Community Care & Health (Scotland) Act 2002** gives authorities wider powers to make direct payments to people to arrange and purchase community care.

Registered nursing care
(not applicable in Scotland)

Health & Social Care Act 2001 – S.49 removes the power of local authorities to provide nursing care by a registered nurse.

Free personal and nursing care
(only applicable in Scotland)

Community Care & Health (Scotland) Act 2002 – defines the care for which local authorities should not charge as personal care and support as defined in s.2(28) of the Regulation of Care (Scotland) Act 2001, whether or not from a registered nurse.

Charges

Local authorities can charge for non-residential services (eg domiciliary and day care services) under s.17 of the **Health & Social Services & Social Security Adjudications Act 1983** (or under ss.12 and 87 of the **Social Work (Scotland) Act 1968**). In Wales such charges are determined in accordance with the Social Care Charges (Wales) Measure 2010. There are different rules for charges for services to children provided under the Children Act 1989 or Children (Scotland) Act 1995.

Those whose domiciliary or residential services are provided under s.117 of the Mental Health Act 1983 cannot be charged. In Scotland, charges can be made for such aftercare services, but this should not be for personal care provided to a person aged 65 or over (**Community Care & Health (Scotland) Act 2002**).

Information

Legislation requires authorities to publish information.
NHS & Community Care Act 1990 – S.46(1)(a) and s.5A of the Social Work Scotland Act (1968) state: *'Each local authority (a) shall [...] prepare and publish a plan for the provision of community care services in their area.'*
Chronically Sick & Disabled Persons Act 1970 – S.1 states: *'(2) Every [local] authority (a) shall cause to be published from time to time [...] general information as to the services provided... under s.29, which are for the time being available in their area; and (b) shall ensure that any [...] person [...] who uses any of those services is informed of any other [relevant] service provided by the authority.'*
Carers (Equal Opportunities) Act 2004 – S.1 requires local authorities to inform carers of their right to an assessment.

Publications

If you are challenging a decision about the help you get or need at home or about care in a care home, the following may be useful:

❏ *Paying for Care Handbook* (2009, Child Poverty Action Group)

❏ *Community Care and the Law* by Luke Clements and Pauline Thompson (2011, Legal Action Group)

❏ *Community Care Law Reports* (Legal Action Group) – a quarterly digest of case law

❏ *Encyclopaedia of Social Services and Child Care Law (Volume 3)* (Sweet and Maxwell) – community care legislation including amendments to Acts and regulations

❏ *Social Work Law in Scotland* by Thomas Guthrie (2011, Bloomsbury)

❏ *Community Care Practice and the Law* by Michael Mandelstam (2009, Jessica Kingsley)

local authority will compare your assessed needs with the eligibility criteria it has set for community care services. Eligibility criteria set out the circumstances that must be present before you are considered eligible for services. In setting the criteria, authorities must gauge whether, if needs are not addressed, the risks to independence and well-being (or other consequences) are critical, substantial, moderate or low. They will often only provide services for critical and substantial needs and will offer advice if you are in the lower-need groups. Authorities publish information about their assessment procedures and eligibility criteria.

England – *Prioritising Need in the Context of Putting People First*, although not accompanied by any circular, is policy guidance and must be followed unless there is a very good reason not to.
Gateway Reference 13729 (2010)

Wales – Guidance is contained within *Creating a Unified and Fair System for Assessing and Managing Care 2002*.
NAfWC 09/02

Scotland – The Single Shared Assessment IoRN (Indicator of Relative Need) is a national tool to support professionals and managers in decisions about the use of resources and the planning of services. Further developments of IoRN are currently being explored.
CCD 10/2004; CCD 5/2004

Northern Ireland – *Fair Access to Care Services* is applied.

Assessments for carers

Carers can request that an assessment of their own needs be carried out when the person for whom they are caring is assessed for services. The assessment of the carer should be taken into consideration in the decisions made as a result of the disabled person's assessment. See Box K.1 for more information on carer's rights.

England – Carers have the right to be assessed independently even if the person they care for is not being assessed. A carer's assessment may result in services or a personal budget (see 4 below) being provided to the person cared for, or, additionally, the carer may receive services in their own right. Local authorities should have a voucher scheme to help carers access short-term breaks. Authorities can charge carers for services provided directly to them, but some provide them free.

Local authorities are required to inform carers of their right to an assessment and to promote equality of opportunity for carers. A carer's employment, educational and recreational intentions must be taken into account by adult social care. Authorities should co-ordinate a multi-agency approach if they believe a carer's ability to provide care might be enhanced by health, housing or education services.
Carers (Equal Opportunities) Act 2004

Wales – Similar provisions exist in Wales. In addition, local health boards must work with local partners to publish and implement local information and consultation strategies setting out arrangements for:

■ providing information and guidance for carers to enable them to carry out their caring role effectively; *and*
■ the full involvement of carers in decisions regarding the provision of services to them and the person(s) they care for.

These strategies also promote better referral and signposting of carers to sources of advice and support, including carers' needs assessments.
Carers Strategies (Wales) Regs 2011

Scotland – A carer may receive support (ie information, advice or access to other resources) from a local authority to assist them in their caring role. Guidance states that authorities should not charge carers for support provided to them. Authorities have a duty to inform carers (but not paid carers) of their right to an assessment. Although carers have no automatic

right to services, such an assessment can result in additional help being provided to the person cared for. Authorities are also required to take into account the contribution and views of carers, together with the views of the person being cared for, before deciding on services to be provided.
CCH(S)A

Northern Ireland – There are similar provisions.
Carers and Direct Payments (Northern Ireland) Act 2002

The assessment result

You should be informed in writing of the assessment result. You may be involved in the drawing up of the support plan (see above), a copy of which should be given to you.

If you are offered a personal budget (see 4 below), you should be given an *'indicative budget'*, which is the amount that adult social care considers is sufficient to meet the needs identified in your support plan. It is important that your support plan and the indicative budget are detailed so you can see which of your needs have been taken into account, how much they are likely to cost, what services, if any, will be provided and who will provide them. So if your indicative budget doesn't meet all the needs to be paid for in your support plan, it should be adjusted to ensure that it does.

Unhappy with the result? – If you're refused an assessment or feel it has not taken account of your needs, or there is a delay in carrying it out, you can use the complaints procedure (or seek legal advice if it is urgent) – see 6 below.

In England, the policy guidance *Prioritising Need* (see above) makes it clear that the carrying out and completion of a community care assessment should not be contingent on whether or not you can pay for care services, be they provided in a care home or in your own home. The situation is similar in Scotland. With respect to services in your own home, a local authority should arrange those services irrespective of resources or capacity, if they are what you are assessed as needing.

Review of services

Local authorities should review service users' needs annually. A review can be requested if you feel your needs warrant it, eg if your circumstances have changed.

4. What help can be provided?

Local authorities have a legal duty to meet eligible needs. While other needs may be provided for, there is no requirement to do so. See Box K.2 for types of services that may be available. The Personalisation Agenda in England allows for more flexibility in what adult social care can fund through your personal budget.

The personal budget (England) – This will be met either by *'direct payments'* (see below) or by adult social care holding the budget themselves or with a support broker and arranging services as directed by you (or by a combination of the two). The level of personal budget you are allocated may be determined by the local authority using a *'resource allocation scheme'*.

Resource allocation schemes – These have no statutory basis but are used widely in calculating personal budgets. Courts have been critical of the lack of transparency in these schemes, holding that a scheme should only be a starting point, there remains an absolute duty to meet eligible needs, and local authorities have a duty to explain how an individual's personal budget has been arrived at.
R(Savva) v Kensington and Chelsea [2010] 414 (Admin) (EWCH) (13 CCLR 227);
R(KM) v Cambridge CC [2012] (SC)

Scotland – A similar system, *'Individual Budgets'*, operates.

Direct payments

Direct payments as part of a personal budget allow a person who has been assessed as having eligible needs to receive cash to arrange and pay for services. You can have a combination of some services provided directly by adult social care (a managed personal budget) and others arranged by yourself with direct payments. Direct payments may give you more control over the way your care needs are met.

Health & Social Care Act 2001; Health & Social Care Act 2008; Social Care (Self-directed Support) (Scotland) Act 2013; Community Care, Services for Carers & Children's Services (Direct Payments) (England) Regs 2009/(Wales) Regs 2011

Who can have a direct payment?
Local authorities have a duty to offer direct payments to people who fall within the following rules.

England and Wales – To get a direct payment, you must be at least 16 and be a disabled person, carer or someone with parental responsibility for a disabled child. You must have been assessed as having eligible community care needs or eligible carer needs. Direct payments can be available to people who lack the mental capacity to agree to and manage the payments themselves; payments can be made to a willing and appropriate person (a *'suitable person'*) on the disabled person's behalf. Local authorities also have the power to offer direct payments to people subject to certain mental health legislation but not to most people subject to criminal justice legislation.

Scotland – With a small number of exceptions, anyone, regardless of age, who is assessed as needing an eligible care service will be eligible for direct payments (as part of 'self-directed support').

Northern Ireland – You are eligible to receive direct payments if you are over 16 and have been assessed as needing personal care. This includes carers.

What can direct payments be used for: England, Wales and Northern Ireland
Direct payments can be used to arrange services (including equipment) to meet your assessed needs. Local authorities should allow you to choose how best to meet your assessed needs. Direct payments cannot be used, however, to purchase care in a care home, apart from periods of up to four weeks respite care (120 days for children) in any one year. Separate periods in a care home of less than four weeks are added together towards the maximum only if you are at home for 28 days or less in between.

Direct payments cannot normally be used to pay for services from your spouse, partner or a close relative (or their spouse or partner) living in your household unless, in exceptional circumstances, *'the local authority is satisfied that securing a service from such a person is necessary to meet satisfactorily the prescribed person's needs for that service'*. You can use your direct payment to employ a relative if they are not living with you. You cannot use a direct payment to purchase services from the local authority.

Guidance to local authorities encourages them to ensure that support is available for users of direct payments. Authorities must check that the money you have been given is spent on the care you have been assessed as needing. If not, they could ask for it to be paid back.

The Disability Rights UK Independent Living Advice Line (0845 026 4748) gives advice on direct payments as well as general advice and information about independent living organisations.

What can direct payments be used for: Scotland
You have the option to manage your individual budget as a direct payment. This means that if you are assessed as requiring certain services, you receive funding to cover the costs and you decide how the money should be spent. The amount of funding being made available should be made clear to you and the transfers of funding by you will be monitored by the local authority.

You can use direct payments to purchase a wide range of services (including equipment) from the local authority, eg help with shopping or accessing community psychiatric nursing. You can employ a close relative provided the authority is *'satisfied that securing the service from such a person is necessary to meet the beneficiary's need for that service or, subject to an exception, is necessary to safeguard or promote the welfare of a child in need'*.

Local direct payment support organisations can give advice and practical assistance. For details, ring your local authority or Update (0131 669 1600), or go to www.selfdirectedsupportscotland.org.uk.

How much are you paid?
Local authorities determine the direct payment rate. They must make direct payments equal to their estimate of the reasonable cost of the service to meet your assessed needs and fulfil your legal obligations (eg training, national insurance payments, employers' liability insurance, holiday and sick pay) if you employ your carer/s as *'personal assistant/s'*. If you choose a more expensive way to meet your assessed needs than is *'reasonable'*, you will have to pay the extra cost yourself. Payments made will not affect your benefits but may affect benefits received by the person you pay. If you claim benefit as a couple, any direct payment you pay to your partner for care you receive will be taken into account as income in your couple benefit calculation.

You may be asked to contribute towards the cost of your care. The amount of your contribution will be calculated using the same charging rules as for care arranged by the local authority (see 5 below). You will be paid your direct payment either net (with the charge taken off) or gross (where you pay the amount you are assessed to pay in the same way as if you were getting a service).

If you are unhappy with the amount you are offered or any other aspect of the direct payment, you should use the complaints procedure (see 6 below).

What are your rights to services?
If you are disabled and assessed as needing care services, your local authority has a duty to make arrangements for their provision. Examples of the types of care services which may be provided include:
- practical help at home (eg a home help);
- providing, or help in getting, a radio or television or access to a library or similar recreational facilities;
- lectures, games, outings or other recreational facilities outside your home and any help you need to take advantage of educational facilities;
- help with travelling to any of these or similar activities;
- any adaptations (eg a ramp or lift or special equipment) you need in your home *'for greater safety, comfort or convenience'*; this can even include building an extra room on the ground floor;
- holidays;
- meals, either at home or a local centre;
- a telephone, and any special equipment necessary to use the phone (eg Minicom).

CSDPA, S.2; CSDPA (Scotland) Act 1972; CSDPA (Northern Ireland) Act 1978

See Box K.1 for the definition of disability and legal entitlement to care services.

Although the provision of these services is determined on the basis of your assessed needs, local authorities cannot have blanket policies to not provide these services.

Supporting People services
The Supporting People programme provides housing-related support to prevent problems that can lead to

hospitalisation, institutional care or homelessness and to support people leaving an institutional environment.

In England and Scotland, there is no longer ring-fenced funding for Supporting People and in some local authorities assistance is extremely limited.

In Wales, a statutory scheme still operates.

Local Government Act 2000, S.93(8); The new Supporting People Programme Grant (SPPG) Guidance (Wales)

Your needs and local authority resources

Local authorities may wish to refuse or withdraw services or not award a personal budget because of a shortage of resources. They may tighten eligibility criteria defining needs they will meet and services they will provide.

Although a local authority can take its resources into account when setting its eligibility criteria (so the criteria might be tightened when resources are short), if you come within the criteria, and a decision is made that you have eligible needs, it cannot use lack of resources as a reason not to meet your needs or provide the services to meet them. However, when meeting your eligible needs, the authority is entitled to exercise flexibility and can take resources into account when deciding how your needs are met, eg it may provide the cheaper option. It cannot take its resources into consideration if you would be left at severe physical risk if services were not provided.

R v Kirkless MBC ex p Daykin [1997-98] (1CCLR 512)

Once services are provided or a personal budget awarded, an authority may not withdraw or reduce them (whether or not as a result of introducing stricter eligibility criteria) without conducting a review of your community care assessment.

Seek advice (see 6 below) if you are not getting the services or personal budget you need because of local authority resources problems. Courts have been consistent in finding that authorities cannot take resources into account once you have been assessed as having an eligible need.

5. Do you have to pay for your care?

A local authority may charge for non-residential care and support, including domiciliary services (ie services provided at home) and other services in the community (eg day care and outreach), that it either provides or arranges. If you have a personal budget for non-residential care and support that is taken as a direct payment (see 4 above), the authority may make a payment that deducts the amount you are required to pay as a contribution to the total personal budget. Carers may also be charged for direct services they receive.

When can charges not be made?

Local authorities cannot charge or require a contribution from:

K.2 Checklist of care services

Where to get help

To find out what help is available, first contact your area adult social care department. If you are not eligible for a local authority service, they should be able to put you in touch with the right organisation. Listed below are some services that may be available in your area. Local authorities have a legal duty to provide information about services available (see Box K.1).

How can you register as disabled?

England and Wales – If your disability is *substantial and permanent* you can register with your local authority by contacting the area office of the adult social care department. Registering may not have any immediate benefit, but the more accurately the register reflects the number of disabled people in the community, the better services can be tailored to meet needs. You do not have to register to qualify for an assessment or obtain services.

Scotland – There is no requirement to register as disabled to qualify for services.

Sight impairment – If you have a sight impairment, your ophthalmologist or hospital eye specialist will advise if you are able to register as sight impaired. There are two levels of registration: blind/severely sight impaired and partially sighted/sight impaired. Every local authority in the UK has a duty to keep a register of sight-impaired people in their area. There are a number of concessions available to people who are registered; contact RNIB for details (helpline 030 3123 9999; www.rnib.org.uk).

Services at home

Adaptations – see Chapter 31.

Alarm system – emergency help via an alarm button. Contact adult social care.

Benefits – see Benefits Checklist (pages 4 and 5).

Care Attendant scheme – voluntary schemes to help give carers a break. Contact the Carers Trust (www.carers.org; 0844 800 4361) or adult social care.

Direct payments – made by adult social care departments (or health and social service boards or trusts in Northern Ireland) for you to purchase care to meet your care needs – see Chapter 29(4).

District/community nurses – provide nursing care at home or in a care home, or arrange to supply nursing equipment, as well as incontinence aids. Contact through your GP or health centre.

Energy efficiency schemes – see Chapter 31(4).

Equipment – see Chapter 30.

Good neighbour scheme – volunteers who will socially visit older people or people with a disability.

GPs – your general practitioner is the key person in ensuring you get, or are referred to, the services you need. If you are dissatisfied with your GP you should consider changing.

Health visitors – can provide information and advice on local services and act as a liaison or referral point between disabled people and adult social care departments. Health visitors visit all families with children under 5. Contact through your GP, health centre or child health clinic.

Home carers – can provide personal care assistance in the home such as help with getting up, washing and getting dressed.

Home helps or domestic help workers – can provide practical help in the home – eg shopping or housework. May be provided by a private agency rather than adult social care. There is a home help service in Northern Ireland.

Home visits – you can arrange a home visit from a chiropodist, dentist, doctor, hairdresser, occupational therapist, optician or a physiotherapist. An advice worker may be able to visit you at home.

Hospital after-care schemes – see 'Intermediate care' below.

Incontinence – for continence services from continence advisers or district/community nurses, see Chapter 30(3).

Intermediate care – intensive therapeutic care to prevent hospital admission or enable you to leave hospital earlier. It usually lasts for up to six weeks and may be free – see Chapter 29(2).

Laundry service – see Chapter 30(3).

- anyone (family, carer or friend) other than the person using the service (but see below for how the income and capital of couples is treated);
- the parent or guardian, for children's services* if the child is under 16 and the parent or guardian is on income support or receiving any element of child tax credit other than the family element;
- a young person, for services* if the young person is aged 16-18 and on income support, income-based jobseeker's allowance or income-related employment and support allowance;
- you, if you have any form of Creutzfeldt-Jakob disease (CJD), as you should be exempt from charges.

* provided under the Children Act 1989 (or Children (Scotland) Act 1995)

Neither can authorities charge for:

- intermediate care services in England, or in Scotland if you are aged 65 or over (see 2 above);
- equipment (in England). Minor adaptations costing less than £1,000 are also free (see Chapter 30(1));
- advice about the availability of services or for the assessment, including assessment of community care needs.

Fairer Charging Policies for Home Care & other non-residential Social Services (October 2012 - England)

Local authorities in England and Wales cannot charge for services provided under s.117 of the Mental Health Act 1983. In Scotland, local authorities have a duty to provide services to those who have, or who have had, a 'mental disorder'. Authorities can charge for aftercare services. However, guidance states that authorities cannot charge for aftercare if it is provided under a supervision or community care order.

Mental Health (Care & Treatment) (Scotland) Act 2003, S.28; SWSG1/1997

Northern Ireland – If you are 75 or over, you are not charged for your home help service. Charges for people under 75 are explained in circular HSS(SS)1/80, which has been regularly amended.

Health and Personal Social Services (Assessment of Resources) Regs 1993; HSS(SS)1/80

Free personal care: Scotland

People aged 65 or over are not charged for personal care. If you live at home, the amount of such care you will receive is determined by local authority assessment, with no limit set to the amount authorities can provide. Limits apply if you live in a care home (see Chapter 32(4)). Free personal care services may be arranged by the authority, or you can ask for a direct payment (see 4 above). Receipt of free personal care while you live at home will not adversely affect entitlement to attendance allowance, disability living allowance (DLA), personal independence payment (PIP) or any other state benefit. *'Free personal care'* includes:

- help with personal assistance;

Library – you can get home visits from the library service. Organisations such as Listening Books might also be helpful (www.listening-books.org.uk; 020 7407 9417).

Meals on Wheels – meals delivered to your house, run by adult social care or by local voluntary or commercial agencies. Contact adult social care for details.

Occupational therapists – can help you learn or relearn the skills of independent self-care and personal management in all aspects of everyday life. They can also offer advice on, or arrange provision of, necessary equipment or adaptations to your home. Contact them through adult social care or the health authority.

Odd job schemes – sometimes called Handy Person schemes, give practical help with tasks you cannot manage (eg decorating, gardening, etc) and are usually run by a voluntary group.

Personal budget – an allocation of funding given to users to meet their assessed needs. Can be taken as a direct payment or left to local authorities to commission the services (or a combination of the two). See Chapter 29(4).

Physiotherapists – provide treatment and advice to relieve pain and help restore and maintain mobility. This includes advice about equipment. Contact your GP for a referral.

Re-ablement – see 'Intermediate care' above.

Rehabilitation – some hospitals have rehabilitation departments that provide services and therapies to help patients develop their maximum ability. May also be provided at health centres, at home or at other suitable centres.

Self-help and socialising – PHAB organises clubs and holidays that bring disabled and able-bodied people together (www.phab.org.uk; 020 8667 9443).

Sheltered or supported housing – housing schemes with some support or warden services.

Sitting-in service – see 'Care Attendant scheme'.

Sleeping-in service – allows your carer a night or weekend away.

Social workers or care managers, community care practitioners – play a key role in getting services into your home and offering advice.

Speech and language therapists – for all forms of communication and swallowing disorders.

Support for a carer – contact Carers UK (www.carersuk. org; 0808 808 7777) or the Carers Trust (www.carers.org; 0844 800 4361).

Supporting people services – see Chapter 29(4).

Telecare – passive sensors around your home can alert someone if you need urgent help. See Chapter 30(6).

Telephone – if you can't handle and/or read a printed phone book, register for free use of Directory Enquiries (ring 195 for details).

Services away from home

Adult education – contact your local authority or library.

Advice – contact your local authority for a list of local advice centres. See also Chapter 59.

Care homes – can be provided by local authorities, the NHS, private and voluntary organisations (see Chapters 32, 33 and 34).

Day centres – provided by the local authority or by voluntary organisations as places where older people or those with disabilities can meet. Meals, therapies and activities are usually available.

Day hospital care – some hospitals offer hospital stays during the day but you return home at night.

Employment schemes – contact adult social care and/or the disability employment adviser (see Chapter 18(1)).

Holiday/short-term care – a 'foster' scheme with volunteer families.

Respite or short-stay care – can be in a hospital or a care home and allows carers a break or holiday (see Box B.13 in Chapter 5 and Chapters 33 and 35 for the benefit implications).

Transport – many adult social care departments arrange transport to day centres and workshops for people with disabilities. The British Red Cross offers a transport and escort service for people unable to use public transport or travel alone. In some areas there are other schemes, such as Dial-a-Ride. For information on free local bus travel for older and disabled people, see Box B.16 in Chapter 6.

- personal hygiene;
- continence management;
- dealing with problems arising from immobility;
- simple treatments;
- counselling and psychological support, including behaviour management;

- the provision of reminding and safety devices; *and*
- broad provision for food and diet.

The definition of free personal care covers physical assistance with care and help with the mental processes related to that care – eg helping someone to remember to wash.
CCH(S)A

K.3 Independent Living Fund

The Independent Living Fund (ILF) provides financial support for disabled people to live independently. It is a government-funded but independent and discretionary trust fund. A legally binding *'trust deed'* sets out the powers and procedures of the trustees and the eligibility criteria for help from the Fund. Money from the ILF is ignored when means-tested benefits are being calculated.

The ILF is closed to new applicants. Current users will be supported until 31.3.15, although restrictions have been placed on increases (see below). The ILF will close on 31.3.15 and local authorities in England (and the devolved administrations in Scotland, Wales and Northern Ireland) will then have sole responsibility for meeting the eligible care and support needs of current ILF users.
'Independent Living Support', Written Ministerial Statement, 18.12.12

Existing ILF recipient awards

Awards are discretionary, but there are basic guidelines that the trustees must consider. To continue to qualify for help from the ILF, you should normally fulfil all of the following conditions. You must:

- be severely disabled to the extent that extensive help with personal care or household duties is needed to maintain an independent life in the community; *and*
- be receiving disability living allowance (DLA) highest rate care component; *and*
- be receiving qualifying services or cash to a value of at least the relevant weekly *'threshold sum'* from your local authority; *and*
- have less than £23,250 savings; *and*
- be living alone or with people who are unable to fully meet your care needs.

How much must existing ILF recipients contribute?

You are expected to put at least half of your DLA care component towards the cost of your care. The exact amount will depend on a financial assessment, based on income support rules (see Chapter 15(7)). If you are one of a couple, your capital and income will be counted jointly, except that earnings are always disregarded. If you lose your DLA highest rate care component, ILF payments can continue if you are asking for a review of the decision or are in the process of appealing to a First-tier Tribunal. Payments will be suspended for the duration of any subsequent appeals.

If you get a means-tested benefit – If you get a means-tested benefit (income support, income-based jobseeker's allowance, income-related employment or support allowance or pension credit guarantee credit), you are expected to contribute any severe disability premium (or pension credit equivalent).

If you do not get a means-tested benefit – The extra amount you are expected to contribute is calculated by working out your income (excluding earnings), and deducting from this any allowances (see below) and the amount you would get if you were on income support (excluding the severe disability premium).

The allowances deducted from your income are based on those for income support but some are more generous. All mortgage payments and endowments are taken into account.

Earnings are disregarded. Tariff income is assumed from £14,250.

If you are charged by your local authority at the time of application for the care it is providing, the charge will be deducted from the amount the ILF will expect you to contribute. However, restrictions introduced on 20.8.10 mean that any increase in charges made by the authority after that date will not be taken into account and the amount of your contribution will remain the same. The authority should take into account any contribution you make to your ILF award when assessing your resources for any contribution or charge you are required to make towards your personal budget. If you are moving from an authority that does not charge for the services you receive from adult social care, to an authority that does charge, your new charge will be taken into account by the ILF when assessing your contribution.

The ILF contribution rules cover the UK, so in Scotland you may be charged by the ILF for personal care if you are under 65. People 65 or over who receive ILF payments can seek advice about whether their local authority would provide an equivalent amount of free personal care.

Increases to individual awards – Limited inflationary increases may be considered when payments are reviewed every two years. ILF payments may be increased to allow users to meet statutory employment obligations (as well as employment support such as advertising and payroll support). Increases may also be considered if a change in someone's living arrangements affects their support needs.
ILF Policy Circular Document No 01/11

Going into hospital or a care home

If you are admitted to hospital or other type of residential or institutional care, ILF payments will continue for four weeks, after which they will be suspended. Your case can be kept open for up to 52 weeks (or longer at the discretion of the ILF) and your payments reinstated if you return to live independently in the community within that time.

Employment issues

It is important to check the status of the care/personal assistants who work with you. Each case is different and is judged on its merits by HMRC. If you employ a worker directly, you should assume you are the employer unless you are sure the assistant is self-employed. You have all the responsibilities of an employer – eg paying employer's national insurance contributions, etc. HMRC has a simplified way of collecting tax in these situations. If the decision causes any difficulty, ring the HMRC Taxes Helpline (0845 300 0627; textphone 0845 302 1408) or contact the ILF for general advice (0845 601 8815).

The Disability Rights UK Independent Living Advice Line (0845 026 4748: Mon and Thurs 9am-1pm) has details of books and pamphlets to help people who employ their own care workers.

Appeals

If you are dissatisfied with any aspect of how the ILF has dealt with your case, contact the: ILF Complaints and Decision Review Manager, Equinox House, Island Business Quarter, City Link, Nottingham NG2 4LA. (0845 601 8815; complaints.review@ilf.org.uk).

Free personal care payments start from the date the assessed service is provided and cannot be backdated (eg to the date of referral or date of assessment). If you are assessed as requiring free personal care but told you will have to wait before it can be provided, seek advice. You may be charged for shopping, domestic chores or other forms of non-personal care.

A Court of Session judgment has ruled that a local authority is only obliged to provide free personal care if it is the provider of the service; it is at the authority's discretion whether to provide the payment to a private care provider.

CCD 1/2008; Argyll & Bute Council – Judicial review of Decision of Scottish Public Services Ombudsman [2007] CSOH 168

How much can you be charged in England?
Local authorities have the power to charge for non-residential services or to require contributions to direct payments. Charging/contribution policies for non-residential care vary considerably. Department of Health guidance, *Fairer Charging* (and associated practice guidance), lays down a framework as to how authorities should charge for services.

Fairer Charging Policies for Home Care & other non-residential Social Services (October 2012); LAC(DH)(2012)3

Fairer Contributions Guidance 2010 gives Department of Health guidance in relation to personal budgets. It states that a financial assessment is not required for the first eight weeks of a personal budget-holder going into residential care (or for up to four weeks if they receive a direct payment).

Fairer Contributions Guidance 2010: Calculating an individual's contribution to their personal budget, para 7(2)

Fairer Charging instructs local authorities on minimum levels that individuals should be left with following charging. Authorities can decide not to charge at all or can have policies that are more generous than the guidance. If there are charges (which is the case in nearly all authorities), each person's circumstances must be considered individually. The authority should give you written details of how much you will be charged, a breakdown of how this has been worked out and details of what to do if you think you cannot afford the charge.
Calculating the charge – After paying the required charge, your income should not be reduced below the basic level of income support (ie the personal allowance and appropriate premium(s) – excluding the severe disability premium) or pension credit, plus a buffer of 25%.

Importantly, earnings are disregarded. If the local authority takes your capital into account, the minimum limit above which you can be charged the full cost of the service should be the same as for care in a care home (see Box L.2, Chapter 34), and the authority can use the same tariff income. Authorities can be more generous if they wish.

Usually only your own income and capital are taken into account. However, for couples, *Fairer Charging* indicates that a partner's income and capital can be taken into account if the user has a legal entitlement to it or if benefit is paid to one of a couple for both. The expenditure needs of both partners may need to be taken into account: *'Where an assessed charge for the individual user would reduce a couple or a household below basic levels of Income Support, plus a 25% buffer, taking account of the resources and expenditure of the couple or the household, as appropriate, then an assessment should be applied on the basis of the household.'*

Fairer Charging Policies for Home Care & other non-residential Social Services (October 2012), paras 63 & 64

Disability benefits and disability-related expenditure – The guidance states that disability-related benefits (defined as the severe disability premium, DLA care component, attendance allowance, constant attendance allowance and exceptionally severe disablement allowance) may be taken into account as income. It is likely the PIP daily living component will also be treated in this way, but to date *Fairer Charging* has

not been amended to reflect the introduction of PIP. DLA mobility component is disregarded as income (this is also likely to apply to PIP mobility component). Local authorities were recently reminded that DLA mobility component was excluded by law from being taken into account for charges except where prescribed and that the duty to meet a person's assessed needs does not change because that person is receiving DLA mobility component.

LAC(DH)(2012)3, Part IV; SSCBA, S.73(14)

If disability-related benefits are taken into account, the local authority should assess your disability-related expenditure (DRE); guidance gives examples of the main types, including expenditure on additional clothing or heating, private care or complementary therapies.

The High Court has held that a local authority should have carried out a home visit to gather the information required to assess the amount of DRE. It also found that the authority was wrong to deny that costs related to a service user's holiday, eg paying a carer to accompany them, could be DRE. The court held that such costs are capable of being DRE if they can be considered *'reasonable expenditure needed for independent living'*.

R(B) v Cornwall CC [2009] 491 (Admin) (EWHC)

Some local authorities have decided to allow a set amount for normal disability-related costs in order to avoid intrusive questions; it varies from authority to authority. Authorities have their own lists of DRE but these might not be comprehensive and you can ask for a review for other expenditure to be taken into account. Payments to relatives might be disallowed as DRE, but authorities should look at each case on its merits.

R on the application of Stephenson v Stockton on Tees BC [2005] Civ 960 (CoA) (7CCLR 459)

If you get higher rate attendance allowance or highest rate DLA care component (ie for both daytime and night-time care needs) but you receive only day services, the local authority should not take all of your benefit into account, just the part for daytime care.

R v Coventry City Council ex p Carton [2001] (4CCLR 41)

How much can you be charged in Wales?
Local authorities have the discretion to charge and can be more generous than the legislation requires. They are required (if they decide to charge) to include certain financial safeguards so that service users keep a minimum amount of their income. This includes a financial buffer of 35% (and a further 10% flat-rate DRE disregard) above basic levels of income support, employment and support allowance or pension credit. There is a weekly maximum charge of £50 for non-residential social services.

The Social Care Charges (Wales) Measure 2010

How much can you be charged in Scotland?
The charge will be determined by your local authority, subject to an assessment of your needs and means to pay. Guidance on charging for non-personal care services provides minimum charging thresholds, which are uprated annually: the rates for 2013/14 are £120 per week for a single person (£183 for a couple) under 60, and £170 per week for single person (£259 for a couple) over 60.

CoSLA: National Strategy and Guidance for Charges Applying to Non-residential Social Care Services (2013/14)

If you cannot afford to pay the charge
If it charges for services, the local authority has a duty to decide how much you can afford to pay and reduce the charge, or not charge you, if it is not reasonable for you to pay the charge. It may not withdraw a service or a personal budget because you fail to pay the charge. This is because the decision to meet a need is separate from, and comes before, any decision to charge for the service.

Complaints – You can complain about the amount you are being charged using the procedure described in 6 below. Some authorities have a charges complaints or appeals procedure that is shorter than the standard complaints procedure, but you can insist on using the standard complaints procedure.

In Wales, under the *First Steps Improvement Package*, local authorities must have a review process that allows service users to seek a review of their notified charge. This review does not replace or restrict use of an authority's complaints procedure (see 6 below), but is intended to complement it by way of resolving basic issues quickly.

6. If you are not satisfied with your care services
Complaints
England – There is a two-stage combined health and adult social care complaints procedure. Complaints should normally be made within 12 months of the incident/issue, unless there are special circumstances. You can complain in writing, orally or by email, and your complaint should be acknowledged within three working days. The local authority should then contact you and offer to discuss the complaint and the way it will be handled and explain the possible results. The complaint should then be investigated speedily and efficiently. When the investigation is finished (which should be in a maximum of six months), you should be given a written explanation of how it was considered and the conclusion. If you are not happy with the resolution, you can take the matter to the Local Government Ombudsman (see Chapter 60).

Local Authority Social Services Complaints (England) Regs 2006; Local Authority Social Services & NHS Complaints (England) Regs 2009

Wales – The complaints procedure has three stages: local resolution, formal consideration and independent panel. It is hoped that most complaints will be resolved at the local resolution stage. This should happen within ten days, although it can be extended by another ten days if you request or agree to it. If the matter is not resolved, it should move to the next stage, formal consideration; this can be a formal investigation or resolved in another way such as mediation. This should be completed in 25 days. If you are still not happy, or there is no response to your complaint after three months, you can ask for an independent panel. A panel should be arranged within 20 days of your request, a report of the finding produced within five days and a decision by the authority within 15 working days. The panel is independent of the authority and consists of people selected and trained by the Welsh government. If you are still not happy, you can take your case to the Public Services Ombudsman for Wales. The Ombudsman can also consider complaints directly after local authority consideration.

The Social Services Complaints Procedures (Wales) Regs 2005

Scotland – The procedure is similar to Wales but with different time limits. A third-stage review panel has 56 days to provide written recommendations and the local authority has 42 days to decide on action. The right to complain extends to carers. The authority should provide information on the procedural steps of the assessment and care plan and, if relevant, on how an independent advocate can be made available.

Social Work Representations Procedure (Scotland) Order 1990; Social Work Representation Procedure (Scotland) Directions 1996

Further steps
You may wish to take your complaint to local councillors or your MP (MSP in Scotland or Assembly Member in Wales) if you feel it would be helpful for them to know the system is not working for you. If you have exhausted the complaints procedure, you can contact the relevant Ombudsman: Local Government Ombudsman in England, Northern Ireland Ombudsman in Northern Ireland, Scottish Public Services Ombudsman in Scotland and Public Services Ombudsman

for Wales in Wales (see Chapter 60(5)). The Ombudsman can investigate complaints against local authorities if there has been maladministration.

Local Authority Social Services Act 1970

If it is not possible to resolve your dispute via the complaints procedure, you may wish to consider a legal remedy such as judicial review. You can also complain to the local authority's Monitoring Officer (usually the Chief Executive or Chief Legal Officer) who is responsible for ensuring that decisions are lawful and procedures correctly followed. It is also possible to ask the Secretary of State to use her/his default powers, but these extend only to statutory duties, not to discretionary powers – ie if you feel the authority has withdrawn or failed to provide a service that it has a duty under law to provide.

It may be useful to contact a national organisation or seek legal advice to discuss ways of pursuing your case. You must act quickly. Contact a law centre (see Chapter 59(2)) or the Disability Law Service (020 7791 9800; www.dls.org.uk).

Scotland – The rules applicable to judicial review and involvement of the Monitoring Officer apply as above. If you need community care help because of mental health problems, learning disability or dementia, contact the Mental Welfare Commission (Freephone 0800 389 6809; www.mwcscot.org.uk). The Commission cannot force changes, but it can make recommendations and carry out enquiries.

30 Help with equipment

1. Items for daily living
Under section 2 of the Chronically Sick & Disabled Persons Act (CSDPA), local authorities have a duty in some circumstances to arrange for the provision of equipment and/or to assist with home adaptations for disabled people. This duty arises when the authority has assessed you and decided your needs are sufficiently high to qualify for assistance – an *'eligible need'* (see Chapter 29(3) for details of the assessment).

CSDPA, S.2 (England, Scotland & Wales); Chronically Sick & Disabled Persons (N. Ireland) Act 1978

Equipment
The CSDPA refers to additional facilities concerned with your safety, comfort and convenience, including communication facilities. It also refers to practical assistance in the home, outings, educational opportunities, holidays, etc – all of which could involve a need for equipment.

Home adaptations
The CSDPA contains a duty to arrange for assistance with carrying out home adaptations. Typically, this duty will apply to so-called minor adaptations, but may also cover expensive major adaptations that are not (easily) removable. The local authority must decide whether the cost of major adaptations (eg provision of an extra bathroom or toilet) falls within the criteria for provision of a housing grant under housing legislation (see Chapter 31), whether it comes within social care criteria under the CSDPA, or whether a housing grant may be topped up to meet eligible needs. Not all authorities are fully aware of their duties in this respect.

Landlords and the Equality Act
Public and private landlords must make reasonable adjustments for disabled tenants. This could include provision of auxiliary aids and adaptations (eg signs, notices, taps, door handles, doorbells and door entry systems) but not involving removal or alteration of a building feature or fixtures.

Equality Act, Part 4 & the Disability Discrimination (Premises) Regs 2006 (SI 2006/887)

Restrictive policies
Local authorities often operate restrictive policies, eg some say as a matter of policy they do not provide certain types of equipment. Such blanket policies may be unlawful if they are applied without taking individual needs into account. Some authorities may refuse to provide equipment on the grounds that they lack the resources. This, too, is unlawful if you have been assessed as having an eligible need.

Carers
In England and Wales, local authorities have a duty to assess informal carers and provide services for them (see Chapter 29(3)). These services are not defined but could in principle cover equipment used by the carer (rather than the cared for person).

Charges
In England, legislation prevents local authorities from charging for equipment provided under the CSDPA or under section 2 of the Carers & Disabled Children Act 2000, or for minor adaptations costing less than £1,000 provided under either of those Acts. Guidance says the cost of a minor adaptation is to be calculated in terms of both its purchase and installation expenses. Some authorities try to charge people for maintaining or insuring the equipment; it is unclear whether this is lawful.

In Wales, local authorities have a legal power to make charges for equipment but in practice might not exercise it.

In Scotland, under the Community Care & Health (Scotland) Act 2002 certain personal care equipment must be free for people aged 65 or over, although what is covered is limited. Personal care would include such things as memory and safety devices, eg sound/movement alarms linked to light controls to guide people with dementia to the toilet and minimise risks related to wandering at night. It does not include community alarms and other associated devices. Scottish guidance states that *'frail older people'* should not be charged for equipment and minor adaptations provided by local authorities if these are supplied and fitted either immediately prior to hospital discharge or within the following four weeks.

For the charging rules generally, see Chapter 29(5).

Transforming Community Equipment Services
In England, under the initiative *Transforming Community Equipment Services* local authorities and the NHS often work together to enable people to choose some items of equipment themselves. Following a needs assessment, an equipment 'prescription' is issued. This prescription may be taken to a retail outlet and the equipment will be supplied up to a specified cost; you may choose a more expensive variation of the prescribed equipment if you pay the difference.

Direct payments
If certain conditions are met, local authorities have a duty to make direct payments (see Chapter 29(4)) for equipment as well as for other community care services. Direct payments are not currently available through the NHS for healthcare equipment but may be in the near future.

Buying your own equipment
Specially designed equipment (sometimes called assistive technology or AT) can be a key factor in enabling people to live as independently as possible. Before buying, check whether the equipment you need could be available on long-term loan through adult social care or the NHS, following a needs assessment.

If you are unsure about what to buy, ask to use the equipment on a trial basis. Many items are small, relatively inexpensive and can make an enormous difference. Consider carefully more expensive items, eg electric scooters, riser/recliner chairs, electric wheelchairs, walk-in baths or special beds. These can cost thousands of pounds and may not be what you require, so you will need expert objective advice. Look for supply companies who are recommended or members of a recognised and regulated organisation, eg the British Healthcare Trades Association.

Occupational therapists, employed by statutory authorities or working independently, may be able to give you advice, as may other health and social care professionals such as physiotherapists, district nurses, health visitors and social workers.

For information about VAT relief on equipment, see Chapter 52. If an occupational therapist recommends an item of equipment ask if there is a centre where you can see it (see Box K.4) or look at a website that displays alternatives (eg www.livingmadeeasy.org.uk).

2. Healthcare equipment
The NHS may provide equipment for particular health conditions, eg beds, hoists, wheelchairs, commodes, urinals and continence pads. However, as some of these are also aids to daily living, NHS and local authority providers would need to agree who is responsible for providing equipment.

Legally, it is not easy to challenge non-provision of equipment by the NHS if it argues it is short of money; however, blanket policies on provision are unlawful. Every equipment package should be provided on the basis of individual need and assessment.

In the first instance, apply for items via your doctor, district nurse/health visitor, continence adviser, occupational therapist, physiotherapist or social worker. GPs can prescribe appliances on an approved list (the *Drug Tariff*), including catheters, elastic hosiery, supports, etc, which have standard prescription charges in England and are free in Northern Ireland, Scotland and Wales (see Chapter 54(2)).

An NHS consultant may prescribe equipment necessary for a patient's treatment – eg walking aids, orthotics, supports and prosthetics. Depending on the patient's condition, these may be free or there may be special prescription charges. Standard prescription charges apply to Drug Tariff items for outpatients in England (and are free in Northern Ireland, Scotland and Wales).

Consultants can prescribe hearing aids, or patients can be referred by their GP to the audiology department. NHS hearing aids and new batteries are free. However, if you lose or damage your hearing aid, you may be asked to pay towards the cost of replacing or repairing it.

Hospital ophthalmologists can prescribe items varying from low-vision aids to more complex items like eye prostheses. Visual assessments and the provision of aids are also available from accredited optometrists, although there may be a charge for consultation.

3. Services to help with incontinence
Incontinence has physical, emotional and social consequences. It is important to get advice from an NHS continence adviser, GP, practice nurse or physiotherapist to see if there is treatment that might help. Your need for assistance should be taken into account during a local authority community

care needs assessment. There are several types of provision: advice about management of incontinence, treatment (eg drugs, physiotherapy and surgery), supplies and equipment, laundry services and disposal of waste. However, these provisions may vary between authorities.

How to get help

The NHS may supply, free of charge, continence aids and equipment – including commodes, bed linen, continence pads, protective pants, inter-liners, disposable draw sheets, bedpans, etc. For an individual, the NHS decides on the quantity and quality of items, and sometimes decides not to supply any. Although this may seem unfair, it is not normally easy to challenge this legally. However, the NHS should provide incontinence aids free of charge (in England and Wales) for residents in nursing homes (ie those that provide registered nursing care). Protective pants and pads are not available on GP prescription (except in Scotland).

If you cannot get an item through the NHS, you can buy it from chemists (although the range may be limited) or from specialist mail-order firms. Body-worn urinary appliances can be prescribed by GPs, but you need to take the prescription to a chemist or surgical supplier that has a skilled fitting service. For more information ring PromoCon (0161 607 8219) or the Bladder and Bowel Foundation (01536 533 255).

K.4 For more information

Equipment
Contact the Disabled Living Foundation, 380-384 Harrow Road, London W9 2HU (helpline 0845 130 9177) for general information, advice and factsheets on equipment. Visit their comprehensive equipment website (www.livingmadeeasy.org.uk) or use their online self-assessment tool, 'AskSARA' (www.asksara.org.uk).
Disabled Living Centres and Communication Aids Centres – display a range of equipment, and some sell equipment. You can often try equipment and get advice about what might help you best. Contact Assist UK for a list of local centres (0161 832 9757; www.assist-uk.org).

Social care and NHS
Ask your GP, social worker or health visitor for advice. See also Age UK factsheets FS6 *Finding help at home*, FS24 *Self-directed support* and FS42 *Disability equipment and how to get it*.

Specialist information and advice
You can get specialist information on all aspects of community care from organisations such as:
- Carers UK – 0808 808 7777; www.carersuk.org
- Independent Age – 0845 262 1863; www.independentage.org
- Age UK – 0800 169 6565; www.ageuk.org.uk
- Mind – 0300 123 3393; www.mind.org.uk
They can offer practical suggestions if you haven't been able to resolve the problem locally (see Chapter 29(6) 'Further steps' for some suggestions). In Scotland, the Age Scotland helpline is useful (0845 125 9732). For information and links regarding provision of equipment, go to www.gov.uk/browse/disabilities/equipment
Going For Independence – is a social enterprise providing information and advice on equipment (including Telecare and electronic technology) and adaptations, including how to access independent occupational therapists and other therapists (01287 204 204; www.goingforindependence.org).

How to obtain a laundry service
If a laundry service is available in your area, it will normally be run by adult social care (probably attached to the home help service) or by the NHS. Some areas do not have a laundry service, but extra help may be given through the home help service. For families with very severely disabled children, the Family Fund may be able to provide washing machines and/or dryers (see Chapter 37(8)). If you cannot cope with the practical problems arising from incontinence, you may qualify for the daily living component of personal independence payment or attendance allowance (see Chapters 4 and 5).

4. Environmental control systems and communication aids

Environmental controls enable people with severe disabilities to operate electrical appliances and equipment from a central control, with switching mechanisms adapted to meet their needs; contact an occupational therapist or your GP. For more sophisticated equipment, an NHS specialist will assess your needs and arrange for installation. The equipment is provided on loan and serviced free of charge. Simpler environmental control systems can be provided by local authorities, although they are not always aware of their potential obligations under the Chronically Sick & Disabled Persons Act (see 1 above).

People with severe difficulties in speaking or writing can be helped by a range of communication aids – from charts with pictures to specially adapted computers and electronic voice output devices. These can be provided by local authorities or schools, or through the Access to Work scheme run through your local Jobcentre Plus office (see Chapter 18(5)). NHS speech and language therapists can refer you to a communication aids centre for advice and assessment. However, communication aids are subject to significant rationing and may not be easy to get.

5. Wheelchairs

Under the NHS, wheelchairs (manual or electrically powered) are supplied and maintained free of charge for a disabled person whose need for such a chair is permanent.

If you are severely disabled, electrically powered indoor/outdoor wheelchairs can be provided if you are unable to walk or propel an ordinary wheelchair. The NHS locally applies eligibility criteria, along the lines that you are unable to propel a manual wheelchair and are able to benefit from an improved quality of life and handle the chair safely. In Scotland, similar criteria are set nationally for powered wheelchairs.

Attendant-controlled powered wheelchairs are issued when it is difficult for the disabled person to be pushed out of doors – eg when the attendant is aged, the district is hilly, or the person cannot operate a powered indoor/outdoor wheelchair by themselves.

NHS trusts in England have a voucher scheme. Users can top up an NHS voucher with their own financial contribution towards a more expensive or sophisticated wheelchair. You may be unable to use the voucher scheme to get a powered wheelchair, but you could use the Motability scheme to hire-purchase an electric wheelchair (see Box B.16, Chapter 6).

If you think you might need a wheelchair you should be referred to your local wheelchair centre for assessment. Your GP, health centre, physiotherapist or occupational therapy department can tell you where your local wheelchair centre is, or you can ring NHS Direct (0845 4647). In principle, any wheelchair available may be supplied by the NHS to meet assessed individual need. However, NHS wheelchair services are significantly under-resourced and operate restrictive eligibility criteria as well as waiting times. This means you may not get the wheelchair you need, or you may have to wait an undue length of time to get it. If you need a wheelchair urgently and face a long waiting period, your local Red Cross may be able to lend you one for a small weekly charge.

6. Community alarms and Telecare

Community alarms are used to call for help and are particularly useful to people who live alone or who are on their own for substantial periods of the day or night, or if both partners are frail. Some local authorities provide community alarms through their housing or adult social care departments, or they can be supplied by private companies. There is usually a charge for this service.

Telecare – This is an extension of the community alarm system and provides a way of discreetly monitoring the home environment and managing personal risk, for example by means of sensors (eg for gas, smoke or movement). Should an emergency occur, a signal is sent automatically to a call centre, which will take appropriate action in accordance with agreed protocols. Telecare is particularly appropriate for people who have a tendency to fall, have health problems that require monitoring or are at significant risk through forgetfulness. There is usually a charge for this service.

7. Other sources of equipment

Although local authorities and the NHS are the main statutory providers of equipment, you can obtain equipment through other channels.

The Access to Work scheme, run via Jobcentre Plus, may fund equipment needed for work (see Chapter 18(5)).

Schools or local authorities can provide equipment needed for education, and authorities sometimes have an absolute duty to do so if the need is specified in the educational section of a child's statement of special needs.

Local and national voluntary organisations (including the Family Fund (Chapter 37(8)) can help by lending or hiring equipment or providing a grant to buy it (see Box K.4).

Charities for specific medical conditions often provide help and advice on equipment, as do other general charities (see Box K.4).

31 Housing grants

1. Housing renewal grants system

Mandatory disabled facilities grants are available from local authorities in England and Wales (see 2 below). Local authorities in these two countries also have a discretionary power to help with adaptation or improvement of living conditions by providing grants, loans, materials or other forms of assistance (see 3 below).

Community equipment, aids and minor adaptations that assist with living at home or aid daily living and cost less than £1,000 should be provided free of charge in England. In Wales, the Rapid Response Adaptations Programme aims to provide adaptations costing up to £350 within 15 days of a referral by your local authority or health worker.

In Scotland, the housing grants system is different (see Box K.5).

2. Disabled facilities grants

A mandatory disabled facilities grant can help with the cost of adapting a property for the needs of a disabled person.

To be eligible for a disabled facilities grant, you must be:
■ an owner occupier; *or*

■ a private tenant; *or*
■ a landlord with a disabled tenant; *or*
■ a local authority tenant; *or*
■ a housing association tenant.

Occupiers of caravans and some houseboats are also eligible.
HGCRA, S.19

You are treated as disabled if:
■ your sight, hearing or speech is substantially impaired; *or*
■ you have a mental disorder or impairment of any kind; *or*
■ you are physically substantially disabled by an illness, injury, impairment present since birth, or otherwise; *or*
■ you are registered (or could be registered) disabled with the social care department.
HGCRA, S.100

A grant can be awarded for:
■ facilitating a disabled occupant's access to and from the dwelling;
■ making the dwelling safe for the disabled occupant and others residing with them;
■ facilitating a disabled occupant's access to a room used or usable as the principal family room;
■ facilitating a disabled occupant's access to, or providing, a room used or usable for sleeping in;
■ facilitating a disabled occupant's access to, or providing, a room in which there is a lavatory, bath or shower and wash-hand basin, or facilitating the use of any of these;
■ facilitating the preparation and cooking of food by the disabled occupant;
■ improving the heating system to meet the disabled occupant's needs, or providing a suitable heating system;
■ facilitating a disabled occupant's use of a source of power, light or heat;
■ facilitating access and movement around the home to enable the disabled occupant to care for someone dependent on them, who also lives there;
■ facilitating access to and from a garden by a disabled occupant; *or*
■ making access to a garden safe for a disabled occupant.
HGCRA, S.23(1)

The test of resources

Disabled facilities grants for adults are means tested, but there is no means test if an application is made for the benefit of a disabled child or qualifying young person.

The relevant person – A test of resources is applied to the person with disabilities and their partner, if they have one. This is so even if the disabled person is not the grant applicant. For example, a disabled person lives with his brother, who has sole ownership of the property. The brother can apply for a disabled facilities grant to carry out adaptations for the benefit of his disabled brother. The test of resources applies only to the disabled brother (known as the *'relevant person'*) not to the brother who made the application.
HRG Regs, reg 5

The test of resources – The test is similar, but not identical, to the housing benefit calculation (see Chapter 21(20)), but there are a number of important differences.
❏ There are no non-dependant deductions.
❏ There is an extra premium (the *'housing allowance'*, sometimes called the 'grant premium') designed to reflect housing costs, currently £61.30. This is added to the total applicable amount for every grant application.
❏ If the relevant person receives income-related employment and support allowance (ESA), income support, income-based jobseeker's allowance, the guarantee credit of pension credit, housing benefit, council tax benefit (for applications approved before 1.4.13), or working tax credit or child tax credit (where annual income for the purposes of assessing tax credit entitlement is less than

£15,050), the applicable amount is automatically £1 and all their income and capital are disregarded, giving a zero contribution (see below).

❏ There is no capital cut-off point. The first £6,000 of capital is disregarded. Weekly tariff income is assumed on capital over £6,000, at £1 for each £250 or part thereof for those under 60, and at £1 for each £500 or part thereof where the disabled person or their partner is 60 or over.

❏ Some regulations, including provisions relating to the disability premium and the rate of tariff income from savings, refer specifically to being 60 years old rather than pension credit qualifying age.

❏ A relevant person aged 60 or over but not yet of pension credit qualifying age can qualify for a pensioner premium of £63.55 for a single person or £94.40 for a couple.

❏ There is a system of stepped tapers on 'excess income'.

❏ Personal allowances and premiums are often not uprated at the same time as those for housing benefit, and for a number of years have been frozen. The personal allowance for single people/lone parents entitled to main-phase ESA is £64.30.

❏ Working tax credit and child tax credit are disregarded as income.

❏ There are no ESA additional components as part of the applicable amount, but receipt of main-phase contributory ESA is a qualifying route for the disability premium.

❏ War Pensions Scheme payments for those with a disablement of 80% or higher and in receipt of constant attendance allowance and Armed Forces Compensation Scheme payments (tariff 1-6) are disregarded.

❏ The government has not yet stated how the test of resources will be amended to take account of universal credit.

Working out your contribution

The test of resources is designed to calculate how much, if anything, you can afford to contribute towards the cost of the works. It is done by calculating the value of a notional standard repayment loan you could afford to take out using a proportion of your 'excess income' (see below) to repay the loan. If you have no excess income, your contribution will be zero. The higher the amount of excess income, the higher the proportion expected to be used towards repaying the notional loan. The calculation is as follows:

Step 1: Work out your capital

Your capital, together with your partner's, is taken into account. Certain types of capital are disregarded. The rules are similar to those for means-tested benefits (see Chapter 28). However, the capital value of the dwelling to which your application relates is disregarded whether or not you live there. The first £6,000 of your capital is ignored. Tariff income of £1 per £250 (or part thereof) over £6,000 is assumed if the relevant person is aged under 60, and £1 per £500 (or part thereof) if the relevant person is 60 or over.
HRG Regs, reg 40

Step 2: Work out your income

Your average earnings and other income are based on your income over the 12 months before your application or a shorter period if that gives a more accurate figure. The earnings and income disregards are similar to those for housing benefit (see Chapter 27).
HRG Regs, regs 20, 21 & 22

Step 3: Work out your applicable amount

This represents your weekly living needs and those of your family (see Chapter 21(24) and (25)). Add the housing allowance (see above).
HRG Regs, reg 14

Step 4: Work out your excess income

If your income is less than or equal to your applicable amount, you have no excess income. Your contribution is zero. If your

income is greater than your applicable amount, the excess income is the difference between the two figures.

Step 5: Work out your contribution

Excess income is apportioned into a maximum of four bands and multiplied by the relevant 'loan generation factor(s)'. The bands and multipliers are shown below.
HRG Regs, reg 12

Loan generation factors	owner occupiers	tenants
Band 1: First £47.95	18.85	11.04
Band 2: £47.96 to £95.90	37.69	22.09
Band 3: £95.91 to £191.80	150.77	88.34
Band 4: £191.81 or more	376.93	220.86

The aggregate of Bands 1-4 is the value of the notional loan the relevant person is expected to contribute towards the cost of the works.

Example: An applicant who is an owner occupier with an excess income of £100 would calculate their contribution as follows:

Band 1: £47.95	x 18.85 =	£903.86
Band 2: £47.95	x 37.69 =	£1,807.24
Band 3: £4.10	x 150.77 =	£618.16
Applicant's contribution		*£3,329.26*

The applicant's contribution would therefore be £3,329.26. If the total cost of the works were £11,000 the grant would be calculated as follows:

Total cost of works	£11,000.00
Less applicant's contribution	£3,329.26
Grant amount	*£7,670.74*

Subsequent grants

If a relevant person has had to make a contribution to a previous grant on the same dwelling (in the last ten years for owner occupiers or five years for tenants), the value of that contribution is deducted from the assessed contribution on a subsequent grant application. The works under the first grant must have been carried out to the local authority's satisfaction for this offsetting to apply. If the contribution on the earlier grant was more than the cost of the works, leading to a 'nil-grant approval', the value of the works properly carried out can be offset against a subsequent grant contribution.
HRG Regs, reg 13

Applying for a disabled facilities grant

Disabled facilities grants are administered by the local housing authority rather than the social care department (if these are different). An application form should be available from the housing authority. It must be supported by a certificate stating that the disabled occupant intends to live in the property for at least five years after the works are completed, or for a shorter period if there are health or other special reasons.
HGCRA, Ss.21 & 22

Approval of a disabled facilities grant

The maximum grant payable under a mandatory disabled facilities grant is £30,000 in England, £25,000 in Northern Ireland and £36,000 in Wales. Local authorities could provide further assistance for extra costs under their discretionary power (see 3 below).
The Disabled Facilities Grants (Maximum Amounts & Additional Purposes) (England) Order 2008, Reg 2

In order to approve an application for a disabled facilities grant, the housing authority must be satisfied that the works are both necessary and appropriate for the needs of the disabled person, and reasonable and practicable in relation to

the property. In determining whether the works are necessary and appropriate, the housing authority must consult with social care. This is why housing authorities often direct people to the social care department first for an assessment (normally by an occupational therapist).
HGCRA, S.24

It is important to make a formal application for a grant because the 6-month time limit for the local authority to make a decision only begins from the date of the formal application.

The authority cannot refuse to allow you to make a formal application or refuse to give you an application form.
HGCRA, S.34

If you do not get a decision within six months of submitting a formal application, write and ask why and request that a decision be made. Seek legal advice if you still do not get a decision or if you have been prevented from applying. Alternatively, you can make a complaint of maladministration to the relevant Ombudsman (see Chapter 60(5)).

K.5 Grant system in Scotland

In Scotland local authorities are allowed to provide grants, loans, subsidised loans, practical assistance and information or advice to home owners for repairs, improvements, adaptations and the acquisition or sale of a house.
HSA, S.71

Grants and loans
Assistance *must* be by way of a grant if the adaptations are essential to the disabled person's assessed needs and the work is structural or involves permanent changes to the house (except extensions for living accommodation in the existing structure or any other structure). A grant must also be given for work to provide a standard amenity to meet the needs of a disabled person, ie a fixed bath or shower, wash-hand basin or sink (in each case with a hot and cold water supply) or a toilet.

The grant will be 100% of approved costs if the applicant or a member of their household receives income-related employment and support allowance, income-based jobseeker's allowance, income support or the guarantee credit of pension credit. In other cases, the minimum grant will be 80%.
Housing (Scotland) Act 2006 (Scheme of Assistance) Regs 3 & 4

Guidance
A guide for disabled people in private housing is available at www.scotland.gov.uk/Resource/Doc/266465/0079748.pdf. Statutory guidance provided to local authorities is available at www.sehd.scot.nhs.uk/publications/CC2009_05.pdf.

Tenants
Tenants are eligible for a grant or loan where the work to which the grant or loan relates:
■ has, for a period of two years preceding the tenant's application, been the tenant's responsibility under the tenancy;
■ is for the adaptation of a disabled person's house to make it suitable for their accommodation, welfare or employment, or for the reinstatement of any house adapted; *or*
■ is required as a matter of urgency for the health, safety or security of the occupants of a house, including, in particular, work to repair it or to provide a means of escape from fire or other fire precautions.
For further information go to www.scotland.gov.uk/Resource/Doc/348026/0115913.pdf.
HSA, S.92

Applications
A grant or loan application must include full details of the proposed work, including plans, specifications, location of the work, an estimate of the cost and other information the authority may reasonably require. An authority may require information to support the accuracy of such details.
HSA, S.74

Decisions on applications
The local authority has discretion to approve or refuse an application for a grant or loan. If one is approved, the authority must work out the approved expense and, where the application is made for a grant or subsidised loan, the applicant's contribution. The authority may only approve a grant or loan application if it considers that:
■ the owners of all the land on which the work is to be carried out have given written consent to the application and to being bound by the conditions of the grant or loan (if the premises to which adaptations are to be made are in a tenement and the adaptations are to the common area, then the consent of all co-owners is required);
■ the house will provide satisfactory accommodation for a reasonable time and meet reasonable standards of physical condition and amenities; *and*
■ the work will not prevent the improvement of any other house in the same building. The authority must not approve an application if the work has already begun, unless there were good reasons for starting the work early.
HSA, S.75

Energy Assistance Package
The Energy Assistance Package aims to help maximise incomes, reduce fuel bills and improve energy efficiency in homes. It has four stages:
■ an initial energy audit: anyone can get free energy advice by ringing the Home Energy Scotland Hotline (0800 512 012);
■ help with improving incomes and reducing energy bills for people vulnerable to fuel poverty;
■ a package of standard insulation measures (cavity wall and loft insulation) available to people in private sector housing who: are aged 70 or over and have no central heating; or are aged 75 or over; or receive a qualifying benefit;
■ more enhanced energy efficiency measures available to people in private sector housing (either as owner or tenant) who:
 – are aged 60 or over and have no central heating present; *or*
 – live in energy-inefficient homes and are aged 75 or over, or receive a qualifying benefit *and* are aged 60 or over, or have a child under 16, or are pregnant.
The Boiler Scrappage scheme can give £400 vouchers to owner occupiers towards the cost of replacing energy inefficient boilers (contact 0800 512 012 for details).

The Green Homes Cashback Scheme offers up to £500 towards energy efficiency measures recommended in an Energy Performance Certificate (EPC) or Green Deal assessment. You can also claim up to £100 towards the cost of an EPC (0800 512 012; www.energysavingtrust.org.uk/scotland/Take-action/Find-a-grant/Green-Homes-Cashback-Scheme).

If approved, the adaptations should usually be completed within one year by one of the contractors who supplied an estimate for the application. The housing authority has the discretion to approve a mandatory grant but to stipulate that it will not be paid for up to 12 months from the date of application.

HGCRA, Ss.36, 37 & 38

If, after the application has been approved, the disabled person's circumstances change before the works are completed, the local housing authority has a discretion as to whether to proceed with paying for all, part or none of the works. It must take into account all the circumstances of the case before deciding how to proceed.

HGCRA, S.41

Local authorities may place a charge against a property if a disabled facilities grant exceeds £5,000 and the application is from an owner. In deciding whether to place a charge on a property, authorities should consider the circumstances of the applicant. The charge would apply for ten years, which means the value of the charge could be repayable if the adapted property is sold within ten years. In England, the maximum charge is £10,000. In Wales, the size of the charge is determined by the local authority. If an authority has imposed a charge, and the property is sold within ten years, the authority must consider in each case whether it is reasonable to collect the charge, having regard to the financial and other circumstances of the grant recipient and the reasons for the sale of the property.

Disabled Facilities Grant (Conditions relating to approval for payment of Grant) General Consent 2008 (England)
Disabled Facilities Grant (Conditions relating to approval for payment of Grant) General Consent 2008 (Wales)

3. Discretionary power to assist with housing repairs, adaptations and improvements

Local housing authorities in England and Wales have a discretionary power to provide financial and other assistance for repairs, improvements and adaptations. Local authorities can set their own conditions for assistance, such as whether

---

K.6 For more information

Guidance on assistance with repairs, improvements and adaptations is in Circular 05/2003, *Housing Renewal* (Office of the Deputy Prime Minister, 17.06.03) and *Delivering Housing Adaptations for Disabled People: A Good Practice Guide* (Communities and Local Government, June 2006) available at www.gov.uk/government/publications/delivering-housing-adaptations-for-disabled-people. Equivalent guidance for Wales is in National Assembly for Wales Circular 20/02; Annex D, on disabled facilities grants, and was revised in April 2007.

For where to get copies of law and guidance, see page 6.

A leaflet on disabled facilities grants is available at www.gov.uk/government/publications/disabled-facilities-grant and can be ordered in alternative formats.

Independent home improvement agencies offer advice about grants and help people apply for grants, obtain other sources of finance to help pay for works, find good builders and ensure works are properly carried out. Ask your local authority if there is one in your area, or contact: Foundations (0845 864 5210; www.foundations.uk.com), Care & Repair Scotland (0141 221 9879; www.careandrepairscotland.co.uk) or Care & Repair Cymru (029 2067 4830; www.careandrepair.org.uk).

For information about VAT relief on building works, see leaflet 701/7, *VAT reliefs for people with disabilities*, available from HMRC (0845 010 9000).

---

to carry out a means test and the circumstances under which financial assistance should be repaid. Assistance may be in the form of grants, loans, labour, materials, advice or in any combination of these. Accommodation may be acquired, adapted, improved or repaired, demolished or replaced (if it has been demolished). Authorities may take security, including a charge on a person's home. People in all tenures may be helped, including owner occupiers, tenants and landlords (including companies and registered social landlords). To find out what is available in your area, contact your local housing authority, which must make available a summary of its scheme.

Regulatory Reform (Housing Assistance)(England & Wales) Order 2002, art 3

When providing assistance, the local authority must set out in writing the terms and conditions that apply and must take into account your ability to afford any repayment or contribution towards the costs. If you are refused assistance, ask for a written decision and ask what system of review or appeal the authority operates. If you are still not happy with the decision, you should seek advice and/or consider making a complaint to the relevant Ombudsman (see Chapter 60(5)).

Northern Ireland – In Northern Ireland, discretionary grants are different. For details, contact the Northern Ireland Housing Executive, The Housing Centre, 2 Adelaide Street, Belfast BT2 8PB (028 9024 0588; www.nihe.gov.uk).

4. Energy efficiency grants

The *Green Deal* is a new way of paying for energy-efficiency improvements through future savings on your energy bills in England, Scotland and Wales. There are 45 measures or areas of home improvement approved to receive funding under the Green Deal, covering:

■ insulation;
■ heating and hot water;
■ glazing;
■ microgeneration (generating your own energy).

There is a 4-stage process to the Green Deal:

■ assessment to identify the most cost-effective improvements;
■ finance from a provider;
■ installation;
■ repayment through your future electricity bill.

For impartial advice on energy saving and the Green Deal:

■ in England and Wales, ring the Energy Saving Advice Service on 0300 123 1234;
■ in Scotland, ring 0800 512 012 to be directed to your local Energy Saving Scotland advice centre.

Northern Ireland – The Warm Homes scheme provides insulation grants to owner occupiers and private tenants who are in receipt of a qualifying benefit. Warm Homes Plus provides grants for insulation and repair or installation of central heating for householders in receipt of a qualifying benefit. For enquiries and applications, ring 0800 988 0559 or see www.warm-homes.com.

Scotland – See Box K.5.

5. Alternative housing

Many people prefer to move to a property designed to be accessible for a disabled person rather than undertaking major adaptations to their present home. However, even an accessible property may require some adaptations to suit your particular needs.

If you are seeking social housing (ie council or housing association properties), contact your local authority and make sure you go on the housing register. It is important to stress your housing requirements. Most housing association properties are allocated via local authorities but some associations operate their own waiting lists, particularly for wheelchair users, so it is worthwhile contacting housing associations directly.

This section of the Handbook looks at:

Care homes

32 Help with care home fees

1. Who can get help with care home fees?

If you need help with care home accommodation and fees you need to approach your local authority adult social care department. Help will be provided only if you have assessed eligible needs (see Chapter 29(3) and Box K.1). If your primary need is for healthcare rather than social care, you will be entitled to fully funded NHS continuing healthcare (see 3 below).

❏ **England and Wales** – Local authorities are responsible for funding social care needs (subject to a financial assessment of your ability to contribute towards the cost – see Chapter 34). Even if it is decided that the NHS is not responsible for the full fees of the care home under NHS continuing healthcare, it is still responsible for your registered nursing costs in a home providing nursing care (see 3 below).

❏ **Scotland** – Local authority social work departments will pay a set amount (£241 a week in 2013/14) for both nursing and personal care if you are 65 or over; you should only be asked to contribute towards accommodation and living costs (see 4 below). If you are under 65, the authority will pay a fixed amount towards nursing care only (£75 a week in 2013/14).

❏ **Northern Ireland** – Payments for nursing costs are made by health and social care trusts.

If you get help from adult social care, the amount you pay normally depends on an assessment of your means. Chapter 33 covers the benefits you can receive in a care home and Chapter 34 covers the way local authorities assess how much you should pay if they are helping with funding your place.

The system of assessing needs and charging is the same whether your accommodation is provided in a home managed or owned by a local authority, or in a home managed or owned by a voluntary or private organisation (sometimes described as the 'independent sector').

NAA, ss.21, 22 & 26

If you enter a care home and don't want or need help with the fees, you should still ask for an assessment of your needs, as the local authority may suggest other options to meet your care needs and could advise whether the type of home you plan to go into is suitable for your needs, and whether, once your capital is below the capital limit for your country (see Box L.2, Chapter 34), it will agree to help with the funding.

It is useful to find out what fee the local authority is prepared to pay for someone with your needs. You can then compare it to prices quoted by homes you visit. Many homes charge people who pay for themselves more than they charge local authority-funded residents, although some are prepared to reduce this charge if you later need help from the authority. This is important if you think you might need local authority funding in the future.

Hospices – Care in hospices is free at the point of use.

Aftercare services – In England and Wales, care in care homes must be free of charge for people who have previously been detained in hospital for treatment under the Mental Health Act 1983 and are entitled to aftercare services under s.117 of that Act.

Mental Health Act 1983, S.117; R v Manchester CC ex p Stennett HoL [2002] (5 CCLR 500); LAC 2000/11

In Scotland, local authorities can charge for aftercare and other services provided under sections 25-27 of the Mental Health (Care and Treatment) (Scotland) Act 2003 although not for those who have been subject to a supervision or community care order. Any charge should be means tested and offset against entitlement to free personal or nursing care if you are 65 or over, or for just nursing care if you are under 65.

In Northern Ireland aftercare services, which can include care homes, are provided free.

Mental Health Order (NI) 1986

2. Different types of care homes

Care homes are run by a range of providers. Health bodies as well as local authorities can arrange care in homes that provide nursing. We use the term '*care home*' when talking about any of the types of homes listed below. All homes must be registered and have evidence that they meet outcomes specified in regulations.

❏ In England, the Care Quality Commission registers and inspects homes and reports are available on its website (www.cqc.org.uk).

❏ In Scotland, homes are registered and regulated by the Care Inspectorate (www.scswis.com).

❏ Care homes in Wales are registered and regulated by the Care and Social Services Inspectorate Wales (www.cssiw.org.uk).

❏ Homes in Northern Ireland are registered and inspected by the Regulation and Quality Improvement Authority (www.rqia.org.uk).

Care homes are required to provide service users with appropriate information and support in relation to their care or treatment.

Homes providing personal care – These can be run by private or voluntary organisations or private individuals. Personal care means: physical assistance given to a person in connection with bodily functions such as feeding, bathing, toileting, etc and '*the prompting, together with supervision, of a person, in relation to the performance of any of the activities of physical assistance, where that person is unable to make a decision for themselves in relation to performing such an activity without such prompting and supervision*'. The need for personal care triggers the requirement for care home registration.

Health & Social Care Act 2008 (Regulated Activities) Regs 2010, reg 2

There is no longer a requirement for homes to provide board as well as personal care, although most do. Some local authorities provide care homes, mostly for older people, but also hostels for people with learning disabilities and for those with, or recovering from, a mental illness. Some local authority and independent hostels, which tend to be for younger people, do not provide board as they want to encourage independence. In this case you may count as a 'less dependent resident' (see Chapter 34(5)).

If healthcare is needed it should be provided by community health services in the same way as for a person in their own home.

Homes providing nursing care – These may be run by NHS bodies or independent organisations. They provide nursing care as well as personal care, and as part of their registration criteria must have a suitably qualified registered nurse working at the home at all times. Health services such as continence advice, stoma care, physiotherapy, chiropody, specialist feeding equipment, etc, as well as free continence products, should be provided to residents by the NHS.

3. Healthcare and nursing care

Most people who need help to pay for their care get it from the local authority. However, for people with many or complex healthcare needs and who have a primary healthcare need, the NHS will be responsible for the full cost of their fees in a care home (most often in a nursing home but sometimes in a residential care home). Even if you get help from the local authority to pay for your care in a home providing nursing care, the NHS is responsible (in England and Wales) for paying for any care you receive from a registered nurse (see below).

In Scotland, the local authority remains responsible for nursing costs but cannot charge you the £75 (2013/14) considered to be the cost of nursing care (see 4 below).

NHS continuing healthcare

'*NHS continuing healthcare*' means a package of care arranged and funded solely by the NHS for a person aged 18 or over to meet physical or mental health needs that have arisen as the result of illness. From 1.4.13, Clinical Commissioning Groups and the NHS Commissioning Board have assumed responsibilities for NHS continuing healthcare.

Individuals with complex, intense or unpredictable healthcare needs, and whose primary need for accommodation arises from their health needs and who are assessed as meeting the eligibility criteria for NHS continuing healthcare should be funded by the NHS. Care home residents fully funded by the NHS do not contribute towards their care home fees but are usually treated as hospital inpatients for benefits purposes (see Chapter 33(1)). The overriding test for NHS continuing healthcare is whether a person's primary need is for healthcare. You can request an assessment for NHS continuing healthcare wherever you are – whether at home, in hospital or in a care home.

England – Eligibility for NHS continuing healthcare is established using the directions (see Box L.1) and guidance: *The National Framework for NHS Continuing Healthcare and NHS-funded Nursing Care* (November 2012). The guidance lays out the principles and processes that should be followed when deciding whether someone has a 'primary health need' and is therefore eligible for NHS continuing healthcare funding. The guidance states that the assessment should be person-centred and understandable, and that your

---

L.1 Directions, guidance and circulars

Local authorities and health bodies should follow directions, guidance and circulars, which are usually available on the internet. Guidance should be read in conjunction with the relevant legislation (see Box K.1).

England: Health Service Directions, Guidance and Circulars (HSGs and HSCs); Local Authority Circulars (LACs and LAC(DH)s) (www.dh.gov.uk).

Scotland: Community Care Circulars (CCDs); Chief Executive Letters (CELs) (www.scotland.gov.uk).

Wales: Welsh Government Circulars (WGCs), previously Welsh Assembly Government Circulars (WAGCs); National Assembly for Wales Circulars (NAfWCs) and Welsh Office Circulars (WOCs); Welsh Health Circulars (WHCs) (www. new.wales.gov.uk).

Northern Ireland: Bills and statutory rules plus Office of Social Services Circulars/Guidance; Health Service Circulars (HSS); Letters and Urgent Communications (www.dhsspsni. gov.uk).

Challenging decisions

Useful directions/guidance/circulars:

❏ **CRAG** – *Charging for Residential Accommodation Guide:* a new version is issued each April and updates when required. England: CRAG amendment 32 (October 2012). Scotland: CCD 2/2013. Wales: WGC 006/2013. In Northern Ireland guidance is available at: www.dhsspsni. gov.uk/ec-residential-accommodation

❏ **Ordinary residence** – England: *Guidance on the identification of the ordinary residence of people in need of community care services* (revised July 2011). Scotland: CCD 3/2010. Wales: WOC 41/93 (due for revision). See also: *Cross-border arrangements between England and Wales* (March 2010).

❏ **Choice of Accommodation Directions** – England: LAC (2004)20. Scotland: CCD 8/2003. Wales: WHC (2004)066.

❏ **NHS continuing healthcare** – England: *The NHS Continuing Healthcare (Responsibilities) Directions* (2009); *The National Framework for NHS Continuing Healthcare and NHS-funded Nursing Care* (revised November 2012). Scotland: *NHS Scotland Continuing Health Care* CEL 6 (2008). Wales: *Continuing NHS Healthcare: The National Framework for Implementation in Wales* (August 2010).

❏ **Deferred payments** – England: LAC (2001)25; LAC (2002)15. Scotland: CCD 13/2004. Wales: NAfWC 21/03.

❏ **NHS-funded nursing care** – England: guidance is contained in the National Framework (see 'NHS continuing healthcare' above). Wales: NAfWC 25/2004.

❏ **Free personal care** – Scotland: CCD 5/2003.

❏ **Intermediate care** – England: LAC (2001)1; LAC (2003)14; LAC(DH)(2010)6. Wales: NAfWC 43/02.

❏ **Fairer charging for non-residential services** – England: LAC(DH)(2012)3; *Fairer Charging Policies for Home Care & other non-residential Social Services* (October 2012); *Fairer Contributions Guidance 2010 (Calculating an Individual's Contribution to their Personal Budget)*. Wales: *Introducing More Consistency in Local Authorities' Charging for Non-Residential Social Services – Guidance for Local Authorities*. Scotland: *COSLA National Strategy and Guidance for Charges Applying to Non-residential Social Care Services 2013/14*.

❏ **Charging for re-ablement** – England: LAC(DH)(2010)6

❏ **Fair Access to Care** – England: *Prioritising need in the context of Putting People First: A whole system approach to eligibility for social care – guidance on eligibility criteria for adult social care* (2010).

carers and other agencies should be involved. The guidance advises that the following factors should be considered when making a decision as to whether your primary need is for healthcare:

- the nature of the needs, including the type of interventions and help required;
- intensity – the extent and severity of needs, including the need for sustained care;
- complexity – how the needs arise, whether they are stable or require monitoring;
- unpredictability – the degree to which needs fluctuate and the level of risk if adequate and timely care is not provided.

If it is decided that you have a primary need for healthcare, the NHS will be responsible for providing for your health *and* social care needs. The guidance advises that the decision should generally be made within 28 days.

If you think you are eligible for NHS continuing healthcare, ask your GP for the contact point for your area.

Wales – *Continuing NHS healthcare: the national framework for implementation in Wales* (May 2010) sets out the principles and processes that should be followed when deciding whether someone has a 'primary health need' and is therefore eligible for continuing NHS healthcare. It also states that if someone has health needs that are beyond the powers of a local authority, that does not of itself mean the individual is eligible for continuing NHS healthcare; in these circumstances joint packages of health and social care are appropriate.

WAGC 015/2010

Scotland – Guidance on continuing care aims to improve transparency in decision making. Eligibility is based on evidence of need following a comprehensive assessment.

NHS Scotland Continuing Health Care CEL6 (2008)

Problems with NHS continuing healthcare

If you feel your need for nursing home care is primarily due to health needs, but you have been refused NHS continuing healthcare, there are a number of steps you can take.

England – A decision notice should be sent to you setting out the basis on which the decision was made and explaining the arrangements and timescales for dealing with a review of the eligibility decision in the event that you or someone acting on your behalf disagrees with it. There are two stages involved in dealing with a request for a review:

- a local review process at Clinical Commissioning Group (CCG) level; *and*
- a request to the NHS Commissioning Board (the 'Board'), which may then refer the matter to an independent review panel (IRP), which will consider the case and make a recommendation to the CCG.

If using the local review process would cause undue delay, the Board has the discretion to agree that the matter should proceed direct to an IRP, without completion of the local process. At this stage, you should consider getting advice or an advocate from a voluntary agency or your local Patient Advocacy and Liaison Service (www.pals.nhs.uk). The role of the IRP is advisory, but its recommendations should be accepted by the Board (and subsequently by the CCG) in all but exceptional circumstances.

If, after this, you still disagree with a decision, you can ask for the case to be considered by the Parliamentary and Health Service Ombudsman (see Chapter 60(5)).

National Framework for NHS Continuing Healthcare & NHS-funded Nursing Care, part 1, paras 145– 57

If you are already receiving NHS continuing healthcare, your case should be reviewed after three months and each year following that. If a decision is made that you no longer satisfy the criteria for NHS continuing healthcare, you have the right of review as above.

If you disagree with the type and location of the NHS care offered or the treatment received, you should complain using the normal adult social care and NHS complaints procedure (see Chapter 29(6)).

Wales – You or your representative have the right to ask the local health board to review the decision about your eligibility for continuing NHS healthcare or NHS-funded nursing care; this should happen before you are discharged from hospital or a care package finalised. The local health board should deal with your request for a review quickly and informally (normally within 14 days) and if you are in hospital you can remain there while it is considered. If, after this, you are still dissatisfied, the local health board can convene an independent review panel (IRP). If you disagree with the IRP decision you can use the NHS complaints procedure (see Chapter 60(4)) or you can contact the Public Services Ombudsman for Wales (0845 601 0987). At any time, you can contact your Community Health Council for advice.

Scotland – First, request a review by your health board. This will seek a second assessment/review by another medical practitioner. Such reviews should normally be heard within two weeks. If you remain dissatisfied, you can follow the NHS Scotland complaints procedure; this should normally be done within six months of the initial decision. If you still disagree with the health board's decision, you can ask to have your case considered by the Scottish Public Services Ombudsman (0800 377 7330). Full details are contained in the guidance (CEL6 (2008)).

NHS-funded nursing care

In England and Wales, even if you do not qualify for fully funded NHS continuing healthcare, the NHS is responsible for funding the cost of nursing provided by a registered nurse: *'NHS-funded nursing care'* (FNC). This is determined by a framework that is part of the NHS continuing healthcare assessment.

In England, the standard FNC rate is £109.79 (for people on the earlier 'high band' rate, there is a transitional rate of £151.10). In Wales, nursing rates are set by local health boards. The standard weekly rate agreed from April 2012 was £120.56 a week. This is due for review in 2013/14. In Scotland, your local authority pays £75 towards nursing care (see 4 below). In Northern Ireland, the nursing care rate from April 2013 remains at £100 a week.

Payment is made either to the care home (which must pass it on to you or reduce your fees by that amount or explain how the amount has been taken into account in calculating your fees) or to the local authority if it is arranging for your care and accommodation. If you are paying the care home fees yourself, you should be given a statement specifying the fees payable for your nursing, personal care and accommodation. If you are being charged for nursing costs covered by the NHS FNC payment, take this up with the care home manager. If you are not satisfied with the explanation, you could raise the matter with the CCG or local health board responsible for the FNC payment. You can also request an independent review (see above).

If you are funded by the local authority, you also have your nursing costs met by the NHS FNC, but this does not affect the level of charges unless your income is such that the authority charges meant you were paying for part of your nursing costs.

4. Local authority responsibilities

England and Wales – Local authorities have a duty to provide residential care for all those who *'by reason of age, illness, disability, or any other circumstances are in need of care and attention which is not otherwise available to them'*. Authorities can meet this duty by providing it (subject to a charge – see Chapter 34) in one of their homes or arranging it in an independent sector care home.

NAA, Part III, Ss.21(1)(a) & 22

Scotland – There is a similar duty for local authorities to provide care home placements.

Social Work (Scotland) Act 1968, s.59

If you are 65 or over and assessed as requiring personal care (see Chapter 29(5)) in a care home, you can receive a fixed payment of £166 a week, with a further payment of £75 if you require nursing care (£241 in total), from your local authority. Care home residents who are under 65 can only be considered for the nursing care payment. These payments are made regardless of your income and capital and are issued by the authority direct to the care home.

CCH(S)A; CCD 5/2003

You can choose whether or not to take the payments for your care. If you take payments, you can decide whether you want the local authority to contract with the home for just the payments it is making (with you contracting separately with the home for your accommodation and living expenses) or to make the contract with the home on your behalf for all of the costs. There may be advantages in this arrangement, since the authority's standard contract may restrict increases in the care home fees and may also include provisions for monitoring the quality of care. If you choose not to take care payments, you can continue to make your own arrangements direct with the home. A Court of Session judgment stated that a local authority is only obliged to provide free personal care if it is providing the service; it is at the authority's discretion whether or not to provide the payment to a private care provider.

Argyll & Bute Council – Judicial review of Decision of Scottish Public Services Ombudsman [2007] CSOH 168

If you are admitted to hospital, your local authority will continue to make payments (including direct payments) at the full flat rate for two weeks after your admission and at 80% for a subsequent month, or until your future placement arrangements are confirmed. You will still need to pay for accommodation and living costs. You may get help with these costs, but that will depend on a financial assessment carried out by the local authority (see Chapter 34).

CCD 5/2003

Northern Ireland – The duty is contained within Article 15 of the Health and Social Services (NI) Order 1972.

5. How to apply for help

If you think you might need care in a care home, either on a temporary or permanent basis, ask your local authority for a needs assessment (see Chapter 29(3)). Funding will only be given if the authority thinks your needs can best be met in a care home. Guidance advises that *'the law does not allow authorities to refuse to undertake an assessment of care needs for anyone on the grounds of the person's financial resources'* – eg because you have capital above the capital limit. They should advise you about the type of care you require and what services are available.

LAC (98)19

Local authorities have been reluctant, in some cases, to provide very expensive packages of care for people to remain in their own homes. It is often cheaper to arrange for people to go into a care home. Case law has established that it may be lawful to provide care in a care home rather than meet 24-hour needs at home. However, the Local Government Ombudsman found maladministration causing injustice when a local authority failed to consider a man's wishes when placing him in a residential home, and said, *'Councils have no right to disregard a client's wishes in this manner.'*

London Borough of Hillingdon (07A01436) September 2008

In relation to healthcare, a Health Service Ombudsman ruling agreed that a person with dementia should be entitled to constant care at home and that their psychological needs should have been taken into account in NHS and social services assessments.

Pointon, E22/02-03

It was noted in a High Court judgment that assessors should also consider aspects under Article 8 of the Human Rights Act (concerning the right to a home life).

Gunter v SW Staffs PCT [2005] 1894 (Admin) (EWHC)

Some local authorities have a lower ceiling on the amount of care they will provide for older people in their own homes or in care homes than they will for younger disabled people. The Public Sector Equality Duty, which came into force on 1.10.12, means that organisations responsible for planning, commissioning or delivering health or social care services can only differentiate in the treatment of service users in different age groups if this can be objectively justified. See Chapter 29(6) for details of what to do if you disagree with the local authority decision.

Equality Act 2010

If it is agreed you need care in a care home and you need help with the funding because you cannot afford the fees, the local authority enters into a contract with the home and is liable for the full cost of your care home. It will usually recover from you any contribution you are assessed as having to pay, according to national rules (see Chapter 34). Even if you agree to pay an assessed contribution directly to the care home, the local authority remains liable for the full cost. Nursing care costs are the responsibility of the NHS, as described in 3 above.

Even if you can pay the fees yourself, this does not necessarily mean the authority should not arrange your care. If your capital is over the capital limits and you are liable to pay for yourself, a local authority *'must satisfy itself that [you are] able to make [your] own arrangements, or have others who are willing and able to make the arrangements for [you]'*. If you are too frail physically or mentally to make your own contract with the home, and others are not willing or able, the authority must make the arrangements and charge the full cost. If you are managing someone's affairs it may be advisable to consider refusing to make the arrangements if the person would get the same care home cheaper through a local authority contract.

LAC (98)19

Urgent cases

If your need is urgent, the local authority can arrange for care in a care home without carrying out a formal needs assessment. The assessment should then be done as soon as possible following admission.

6. Capital and property

The local authority must ignore capital within the upper capital limit when deciding if it needs to make arrangements for care in a care home. The value of your own home should not be included in the decision about whether the authority needs to make the arrangements for you if you are going to enter into a 'deferred payment agreement' (see Chapter 34(9)). It must disregard the property for the first 12 weeks of a permanent stay.

Guidance states that once the authority has decided you need care and attention that is not otherwise available, it should make arrangements for you *'without undue delay'*. If it is unable to do so, the authority should *'ensure that suitable arrangements are in place to meet the needs of [you and your] carer'*.

If you are already in a care home, the authority should take over the arrangements to ensure you are not forced to use up capital below the upper capital limit for your country (see Box L.2, Chapter 34). Guidance in England has strengthened this and local authorities are reminded that they *'need to ensure that they are in a position to provide Part III accommodation as soon as they are aware that the resident needs it. Once the council is aware of the resident's circumstances, any undue delay in undertaking an assessment and providing accommodation if necessary would mean that the council has not met its statutory obligations. Consequently, the council could be liable to reimburse the resident for any payment he has made for the accommodation which should have been met by the council pursuant to its statutory duties.'*

LAC (98)19; SWSG 2/99; LAC (2001)25

In a care home and capital reaching the capital limit

If you're already in a care home but have not needed help because your capital was above the capital limit, you'll need to contact the adult social care department where the care home is situated when your capital nears the figure set for that year. This applies even if you moved to a care home in a new local authority area from that which you were in when you lived in your home in the community. The local authority will then assess whether you actually need care in a care home and whether it will meet the cost in that particular home. The help you receive should start from the time your capital reaches the upper capital limit.

Ordinary Residence Guidance (revised December 2011) para 72

Couples with joint capital – If you have a joint account in excess of £46,500, it may be worth splitting your account so that you don't have to wait until your joint account is down to this figure. For example, if you have £55,000 in a joint account, your partner will only get help after £8,500 has been paid in fees and your account is down to £46,500. If you split the account so you each have £27,500, help will be available after spending only £4,250 in fees. This example uses the capital limits for England and Northern Ireland; in Scotland and Wales different amounts will apply.

7. Choice of home

If the local authority decides, after the needs assessment, to offer you a place in a care home, it may suggest a particular home or give you advice on homes to choose from. In all cases where a local authority is making the arrangements, you have the right to choose your own care home: 'preferred accommodation'(see 8 below).

However, if a health body places you in a home providing nursing care and pays the full fee, you do not have the same right to choose a particular home, although Department of Health guidance states that *'[health trusts] should commission services using models that maximise personalisation and individual control and that reflect the individual's preferences as far as possible.'*

The National Framework for NHS Continuing Healthcare & NHS-funded Nursing Care, para 169

8. Preferred accommodation
England and Wales

If you tell your local authority you want to enter a particular care home, that home is called *'preferred accommodation'*. There are legally binding directions and regulations intended to ensure you have a genuine choice over where you live. In reality, this choice may be restricted, as described below. Guidance states that there should be a presumption in favour of individuals being able to exercise reasonable choice in the care they receive. It states that if a local authority cannot provide a place in your preferred home, it must give clear and reasonable justification (in writing) that relates to the directions on choice. It also states that if you need to be placed in another area that is more expensive than the normal costs, the authority should pay more.

If you have preferred accommodation, the local authority must arrange for care in that accommodation, as long as:

- it is suitable in relation to your assessed needs. The assessment should be individual and a home should not be deemed suitable for a person just because it satisfies registration for that type of person;
- it is available. If a place is not available in your preferred home, you may have to wait. The authority should ensure that adequate and suitable care is available while you wait, taking account of your needs and wishes. If you unreasonably refuse to move to a suitable interim arrangement, the authority can decide it has reasonably met its statutory duties and may ask you to make your own arrangements. Seek advice if this happens;
- the home is willing to provide a place subject to the authority's usual terms and conditions for such accommodation;
- the accommodation would not cost the authority more than it would usually expect to pay for accommodation for someone with your assessed needs; *and*
- it has legal power to make such a placement.

Protocols have been developed regarding placements and funding structures in homes providing nursing care across the UK. Seek advice if you plan to move between countries.

NAA (Choice of Accommodation) Directions 1992; LAC (2004)20

In Wales: NAfWC 46/2004 & WHC (2004) 066

Scotland

You can choose to move into a preferred home if:

- there is a place available;
- the social work department has decided the home is suitable for your needs;
- the social work department and the owner of the home can agree a contract;
- the home you have chosen will not cost the social work department more than it usually expects to pay for a home providing the sort of care you need; *and*
- the home is willing to accept you.

If there is no place available in the home you have chosen, you can ask social work staff to provide you with help to stay in your own home until there is a suitable vacancy.

Social Work (Scotland) Act 1968, Ss.12 & 59; SWSG5/93; CCD 8/2003

9. More expensive homes
Top-up or third-party payments

If you have chosen a home that costs more than your local authority would usually expect to pay for someone with your needs, the authority can make arrangements for your preferred home (given that it satisfies the other conditions in 8 above) if you (in certain defined circumstances – see below) or a third party will meet the shortfall and continue doing so for as long as you are likely to be in that care. This is usually known as a top-up or third-party payment. You should not be asked for a top-up if you moved into a more expensive home for necessity, eg it was the only home available that met your care needs (see below).

Local authorities must ensure that a third party is reasonably able to pay top-up fees for the time you are in the home. If the third party is unable to keep up payments, you may have to move to a cheaper home; seek advice if this is likely to happen.

The local authority cannot set arbitrary ceilings on the amount it will contribute towards care in a care home and to routinely require third parties to make up the difference. Only when a person has expressed a choice of preferred accommodation should the authority consider a third-party top-up arrangement.

The local authority must be able to justify its usual cost and show it is enough to buy a reasonable level of service without contributions from third parties. A series of challenges have been brought by care home providers to local authority decisions on the usual rates to be paid for placements. All except one have been successful, with the common grounds of challenge being a failure by the authority to undertake lawful consultation with the care providers and/or a failure to have due regard to the actual costs of care in accordance with statutory guidance. If your choice of accommodation is refused (or you are asked to pay a top-up) on the grounds that the rate payable is greater than the usual cost adopted by the authority, then the decision may be challengeable if the figure was set unlawfully in the first place.

NAA (Choice of Accommodation) Directions 1992; LAC (2004)20; 2011 Judgments: EWHC 2676 (Admin); EWHC 3096 (Admin), EWHC 3371 (Admin); 2012 Judgments: EWHC 1867 (Admin); EWHC 236 (Admin) (unsuccessful); EWHC 2655 (Admin)

If the local authority places you in more expensive accommodation because there are no vacancies in 'usual cost' homes, the authority, not a third party, should meet the additional cost. Nor should the authority seek a top-up payment if an individual's physical, psychological or other needs are such that they can only be met in a more expensive home. This could be because of language, culture, religion or the need to be near family so that regular visits can be made. In some areas it is difficult to find a home that will accept you at the price the authority is prepared to pay. You should complain if there are too few homes in the area with vacancies at the authority's usual rate, as your choice is therefore restricted. See Chapter 29(6).

England and Wales – In England and Wales, guidance is clear that the local authority remains responsible for the care home's full fees even if a third party is making a contribution. Authorities should not encourage homes to make separate arrangements with relatives for top-up payments that are not included in the authority's contract with the home. If your relatives are asked to make a separate payment, you should refer the home owner to the local authority. Third parties may have to meet the greater share of any subsequent fee increases.

LAC (2004)20; NAfWC 46/2004

Scotland – Scottish guidance states that the local authority has discretion to collect top-up payments and contract with the care home, or to leave the third party to make top-up payments direct to the home. If a home's fees rise above the level of the third-party agreement, the authority should consider the impact of moving the person to a cheaper room or home and take steps, where possible, to enable the resident to remain in their current home.

CCD 6/2002 and CCD 5/2003, CCD 1/2012 (contains CRAG)

Self top-ups
As a resident, you are not usually allowed to make your own top-up payment, eg by using your personal allowance, disregarded income or capital.

R v E Sussex ex p Ward [2000] (3 CCLR 132)

It is permissible, according to the Department of Health, for you to pay for 'extras' that are outside of the care package. As long as you do not feel pressured by the home owner or the local authority, there is no reason why you should not enter into a contract with the home owner for extra services.

People who are either within the period of the 12-week disregard of their property or using the provisions for a 'deferred payment agreement' (see Chapter 34(9)) can use their own money to pay a top-up (known as a 'self top-up') for a more expensive home. This is to cover people who will only receive temporary funding until they sell their home.

LAC (2004)20; LAC(DH)(2011)1

People in Scotland who are better off as a result of receiving free personal or nursing care can use some of their money to pay for a more expensive care home.

Additional Payments (Scotland) Regs 2002; CCD 7/2002 & CCD 2/2005

Top-ups and healthcare
If you are receiving NHS continuing healthcare (see 3 above) in a care home, the full cost of care to meet your need will be provided. However, there may be other charges levied by the care home for non-care services which you may wish to buy. Unless it is possible to separately identify and deliver the NHS-funded elements of the service, it will not usually be permissible for individuals to pay for higher-cost services and/or accommodation (as distinct from purchasing additional services). There may be circumstances where the Clinical Commissioning Group should consider the case for paying a higher-than-usual cost, for example if an individual with challenging behaviour wants a larger room and the behaviour is linked to feeling confined.

The National Framework for NHS Continuing Healthcare & NHS-funded Nursing Care, part 2, para 99.2

In the High Court a patient challenged the legality of having to pay a top-up when the primary care trust had entered into a contract with a care home for the standard rate for basic accommodation to meet their assessed needs. The court found that the trust's refusal to pay in full for the claimant's NHS continuing healthcare package at the more expensive home was reasonable, and that the arrangement was lawful.

R (Southall) v Dudley PCT [2009] 1780 (Admin) (EWHC)

10. Complaints
All care homes must have a complaints procedure that is accessible and explained to you. Initially, you should complain to the manager of the home. The complaints procedure for the home should also make it clear how to complain to the appropriate registration body (see 2 above). People who make their own arrangements and fund their own care can complain to the Local Government Ombudsman if their complaint has not been resolved by the care home provider.

Local Government Act 1974, Part IIIA (as amended by the Health Act 2009)

If the NHS or local authority is involved in any way with your care, you can use the adult social care and NHS complaints procedures (see Chapters 29(6) and 60(4)). If you are not satisfied with the outcome of your complaint, you have the right to request that the Local Government Ombudsman or the Parliamentary and Health Ombudsman considers your complaint (see Chapter 60(5)).

33 Benefits in care

1. What benefits are you entitled to?
If you have moved into a care home (either temporarily or permanently), with or without help from the local authority, the only social security benefits that may be affected are:
- attendance allowance;
- disability living allowance care component;
- personal independence payment daily living component;
- constant attendance allowance and exceptionally severe disablement allowance;
- income-related employment and support allowance, income-based jobseeker's allowance, income support and universal credit;
- pension credit;
- housing benefit.

All other social security benefits can be claimed and paid in the normal way, subject to the standard rules outlined in the rest of this Handbook. It normally makes no difference whether the care home you are in is owned or managed by a local authority or by a private or voluntary organisation.

NHS-funded healthcare in a care home

If you have moved into a care home (usually a nursing home) you may be eligible for fully-funded NHS continuing healthcare to meet the costs of your accommodation and care if your primary need is for healthcare (see Chapter 32(3)). You will normally be treated as if you are in hospital for benefit purposes (see Chapter 35).

Any retrospective continuing healthcare funding paid by the NHS will not mean you have to repay any social security benefits you've received, even though any charges you have paid to the local authority or the care home should be refunded to you.

Decision Makers Guide, paras 18067-18069

If you are not eligible for NHS continuing healthcare in a care home, you may be entitled to NHS funding for care provided by a registered nurse (see Chapter 32(3)). If you cannot meet the remaining costs of your accommodation and care, the local authority can provide the additional funding, subject to a charging assessment (see Chapter 34).

It is not always clear which body, under which power, is or should be funding your stay in a care home and which benefits are payable as a result. A Tribunal of Commissioners held that funding responsibility for residents living in a nursing home lies with the local authority if the nursing needs are *'incidental and ancillary to other care needs'* and with the appropriate health body if they are not.

R(DLA)2/06

2. Disability benefits

Normally, you cannot be paid the following benefits after the first 28 days in a care home:

■ attendance allowance – see Chapter 5(7);
■ disability living allowance (DLA) care component – see Chapter 3(8); *or*
■ personal independence payment (PIP) daily living component – see Chapter 4(8).

However, if you pay the fees for the care home without funding (or only with interim funding) from the local authority, you will be able to keep your attendance allowance, DLA care component or PIP daily living component (see below).

The armed forces independence payment can continue to be paid indefinitely if you are in a care home.

Resident in a care home

You will be considered to be *'resident'* in a care home, and therefore not entitled to payment of attendance allowance, DLA care component or PIP daily living component, if the costs of any *'qualifying services'* (accommodation, board and personal care) provided for you are paid for out of public or local funds under specified legislation (see Chapters 4(8) and 5(7) under 'What is a care home'). For attendance allowance and DLA, qualifying services do not include services such as domiciliary services, including personal care, provided to you in your own home. If you go into a care home from the community, the days you enter and leave are counted as days in the community.

AA Regs, reg 7; DLA Regs reg 9; PIP Regs regs 28 & 32(2)

Prior to April 2011, you could keep your attendance allowance or DLA care component if you were in a care home that received certain NHS funding for people with learning disabilities. As responsibility for this has now been transferred to local authorities, you will no longer be entitled to attendance allowance or DLA care component (unless you are self-funding, see below).

Mobility component

DLA and PIP mobility component are not affected by stays in a care home. They are only affected if your stay is in hospital or a similar institution (but see below).

NHS continuing healthcare

A Court of Appeal judgment held that a person receiving fully-funded NHS continuing healthcare in a residential care home (see Chapter 32(3)) should continue to receive the DLA mobility component as they cannot be considered to be an inpatient. (This does not apply, however, to people in nursing homes as these are considered to be 'hospitals or similar institutions'.)

DLA care component is not payable if a person is receiving NHS continuing healthcare in a nursing home or a residential care home. However, a Court of Appeal judgment meant that until April 2013 (when the legislation was amended to restore the pre-Court of Appeal position) DLA care component was payable if someone was receiving NHS continuing healthcare in a residential care home as long as there were no qualified health professionals employed at the care home and the person did not receive medical or other treatment at the care home.

Sec. of State for Work & Pensions v Alexander Slavin [2011] Civ 1515 (EWCA); DMG Memo 4/12; SSCBA, Ss.67(4) & 72(8)

Paying your own fees

If you are paying your own fees, you are a *'self-funder'* and can receive attendance allowance, DLA care component or PIP daily living component as long as you:

■ do not get any funding from the local authority; *or*
■ are only getting funding on an interim basis from the local authority and will be paying it back in full; ie you are a *'retrospective self-funder'*. This is most likely to apply if you are in the process of selling your home and/or you have a 'deferred payment agreement' with the authority (see Chapter 34(9)).

AA Regs, reg 8(6); DLA Regs, reg 10(8); PIP Regs, reg 30(5); R(A)1/02 & Decision Makers Guide, para 61735

An Upper Tribunal decision examined the issue of DLA care component stopping when a person becomes a funded care home resident. It was held that payment should be suspended rather than superseded if there is a possibility the resident will become a retrospective self-funder (thus making it easier to backdate payment of DLA care component where appropriate).

2010 UKUT 231 AAC (CA/2364/2009)

Another Upper Tribunal decision held there was no need for a prior agreement with the local authority for care home fees to be repaid in order for DLA care component to be paid.

2011 UKUT 293 AAC (CDLA/1340/2009)

As *'qualifying services borne out of public or local funds'* do not include NHS-funded nursing care, you can receive attendance allowance, DLA care component or PIP daily living component if you are in a nursing home receiving NHS-funded nursing care only (and not NHS continuing healthcare; see Chapter 32(3)) and the above two bullet points apply.

SSCBA, Ss.67(4) & 72(8); PIP Regs, reg 28

Scotland – If you are 65 or over you will not be entitled to attendance allowance, DLA care component or PIP daily living component (after 28 days in the care home) if you are receiving local authority help with the cost of your care under the 'free personal care' arrangements (see Chapter 29(5)). If you are under 65, you will continue to be paid DLA care component or PIP daily living component if the only help you get is for 'free nursing care'.

Direct payments

Local authorities can give you direct payments (or 'self-directed support' in Scotland), as part of a personal budget, so that you can arrange your own care at home or buy up to four weeks respite care in any one year (see Chapter 29(4)). Although attendance allowance, DLA care component and PIP daily living component will not normally be affected in these circumstances, they could be affected if you need another period of care or hospital treatment within the linking period (see Chapters 3(8), 4(8) and 5(7)).

Example: You receive the PIP daily living component. You use your direct payment to buy four weeks in a care home, then two weeks later your carer falls ill, so you return to the care home. This time your stay is funded by the local authority under a contract with the home. Your PIP daily living component is affected immediately as it links with a period when your care was funded by local authority money because you were using the payment from the authority to buy your respite care.

3. Housing benefit
Registered care homes
You cannot usually get housing benefit for the costs of a registered care home (see below for help with meeting the costs of your own home). For housing benefit purposes, *'residential accommodation'* is defined as accommodation provided in a care home or an independent hospital. Care homes, including local authority care homes, are required to be registered with the appropriate body (see Chapter 32(2)).
HB Regs, reg 9(4)

Some care homes have de-registered and become 'Supported Living' accommodation. In this situation you will usually be able to claim housing benefit.

Shared Lives – If you live in a 'Shared Lives' household, you are eligible to claim housing benefit as this is not defined as 'residential accommodation'.
HB/CTB Circular A20/2005, para 12

Help with meeting the costs of your own home
If you go into a care home for a temporary stay or for respite care, you can continue to receive housing benefit – or help to cover mortgage interest payments with income support, income-based jobseeker's allowance (JSA), income-related employment and support allowance (ESA) or the guarantee credit of pension credit – for up to 52 weeks, as long as:
■ your stay is not likely to last longer, or in exceptional circumstances substantially longer, than this;
■ you intend to return to your own home; *and*
■ you have not rented your normal home to someone else.
HB Regs, reg 7(16)

However, if you go into a care home for a trial period with a view to a permanent admission but you intend to return to your home if the care home does not suit you, then housing benefit (or mortgage interest payment in income support, income-based JSA, income-related ESA or pension credit) is paid only for up to 13 weeks (see Chapter 21(6)). If the care home suits you and you are not going to return home, then, if the other conditions continue to be satisfied, you will continue to be eligible for housing benefit for the whole 13-week period.
HB Regs, reg 7(11) & (12); R(H)4/06

If you become a permanent resident at the end of the 13-week trial period or if you move directly to a care home on a permanent basis from your former home, and you remain liable for the rent on your former home (because a notice period for the termination of the tenancy is being served), you can be treated as occupying your former home for up to four weeks, as long as that liability could not reasonably have been avoided. Hence, housing benefit can be paid on your former home for that period.
HB Regs, reg 7(7)

4. Means-tested benefits (under pension credit qualifying age)
Capital limits in care homes
If you are a resident under pension credit qualifying age (see Chapter 42(2)) in any type of registered care home mentioned in this section of the Handbook, you may be able to claim income support, income-based jobseeker's allowance (JSA) or income-related employment and support allowance (ESA) if your capital is £16,000 or less.

Tariff income of £1 for every £250 or part thereof starts at £10,000 for permanent residents and £6,000 for temporary residents (see Chapter 28(4)). If you have reached pension credit qualifying age, see 5 below.

If you know you want to stay in a care home, your admission can be permanent from the start. Most local authorities, however, prefer you to have a trial period to see if you like it. During a trial period (and for temporary stays), the lower capital limit for income support, income-based JSA and income-related ESA is £6,000. This only goes up to £10,000 when your stay is permanent. The upper capital limit is £16,000 for both temporary and permanent residents. You are still considered to be a permanent resident if you are temporarily absent from the care home.

Calculation of means-tested benefits in care homes
If you are resident in a care home, over 16 and under pension credit qualifying age, your income support, income-based JSA or income-related ESA is worked out in the standard way (see Chapters 13(6), 15(8) and 16(23)) by adding:
■ your personal allowance/prescribed amount; *and*
■ any premiums to which you are entitled (which can include the severe disability premium (SDP) while disability living allowance (DLA) care component or personal independence payment (PIP) daily living component is payable). There is no disability premium for income-related ESA. See Chapter 25; *and*
■ for income-related ESA, any additional component (see Chapter 13(7)).
Even if you are not entitled to income support, income-based JSA or income-related ESA in your own home, you may be entitled when you go into a care home.

Temporary admission (single person) – If you go into a care home for a temporary period, the amount of income support, income-based JSA or income-related ESA you receive will usually not change because you will be treated as normally residing in your own home (but see note below).

Temporary admission (couple) – If one of you goes into a care home or if you go into different rooms in the same care home or into different care homes for a temporary period, for income support, income-based JSA or income-related ESA purposes you will still be assessed as a couple, but you will each get the appropriate single person rate in your applicable amount if this amount is more than the couple rate. If the appropriate single person rate is the greater amount, the person at home (or in a different room in the same care home or in a different care home) will get a single rate personal allowance/prescribed amount plus any appropriate premiums and any housing costs (and any additional component for income-related ESA), and the person in care will get a single rate personal allowance/prescribed amount plus appropriate premiums (and any additional component for income-related ESA). These are then added together, and your combined income is taken from this figure to give the amount of income support, income-based JSA or income-related ESA to be paid to the claimant.

If you go into the same room in the care home, you will receive the couple rate of income support, income-based JSA or income-related ESA plus appropriate premiums (and any additional component for income-related ESA). Housing benefit will continue to be paid for your rent at home.
IS Regs, Sch 7, para 9; JSA Regs, Sch 5, para 5; ESA Regs Sch 5, para 4

Note: If the SDP and, for income support and income-based JSA only, the enhanced disability premium, are included in the calculation, they will no longer be included if payment of DLA care component or PIP daily living component ceases.

The enhanced disability premium will continue to be included in the applicable amount for income-related ESA if you are in receipt of the support component.

SDP and temporary admissions – There is often confusion about the payment of the SDP if one of a couple goes into a care home for a temporary period. If carer's allowance is paid to a carer, SDP will not be paid. However, in other circumstances, a Commissioner's Decision held that the SDP should be included in the calculation of income support, income-based JSA or income-related ESA for each qualifying person, even where a partner in the community may have prevented its inclusion previously.

R(IS)9/02 & Decision Makers Guide, Vol 4, paras 23231-33

In practice, SDP is often left out of the calculation for both temporary and permanent admissions, and if you are being assessed by the local authority you do not see any benefit from the extra money anyway. In this case, you should check that the authority is not assuming you are getting SDP and therefore including it in the calculation of your charge, even if you are not being paid it.

Some local authorities do not assess the charge for temporary stays and charge a flat rate instead for the first eight weeks. Where this is the case, if no one receives carer's allowance for caring for you and the DWP has not included SDP as part of their calculation, seek advice, since any additional benefit you receive will not be taken away in local authority charges.

Permanent admission (single person) – If you go into a care home on a permanent basis, the amount of any income support, income-based JSA or income-related ESA will usually only change in the following circumstances (but see note below):

❑ If you have capital between £6,000 and £10,000, an increase in the amount of income support, income-based JSA or income-related ESA will be payable, as there will no longer be a tariff income applied because of the increased lower capital limit from £6,000 to £10,000 (see above).

❑ If you have capital between £10,000 and £16,000, a reduction in the amount of tariff income will be applied (and therefore an increase in income support, income-based JSA or income-related ESA), due to the increased lower capital limit.

❑ If you are a single person and have a carer receiving carer's allowance, or you are living with a non-dependant in the community, you may become entitled to, or there may be an increase in the amount of, income support, income-based JSA or income-related ESA payable when you enter a care home permanently. This is because carer's allowance will no longer be payable to your carer and your non-dependant will no longer count as a non-dependant. Therefore, the SDP will be included in the income support, income-based JSA or income-related ESA calculation for any period in which attendance allowance/DLA care component/PIP daily living component remains in payment.

IS Regs, Sch 2, para 13(2)(a); JSA Regs, Sch 1, para 15(1); ESA Regs, Sch 4, para 6(2)(a)

If you are retrospectively self-funding (see 2 above) you will still be entitled to income support, income-based JSA or income-related ESA if you are selling your property.

Permanent admission (couple) – If you are permanently in a care home, each of you will be treated as separate single claimants.

IS Regs, reg 16(1) & (3)(e); JSA Regs, reg 78(1) & 3(d); ESA Regs, reg 156(1) & 4(d)

Jointly owned capital will be split and the income support, income-based JSA or income-related ESA calculation should be based solely on each of your individual capital and income. See Chapter 32(6) for information about joint capital. If you both enter the same care home you may still be assessed by the DWP as a couple, although case law (R(IS)1/99) has established that most people should be assessed as separate individuals even if they share a room. Seek advice if you are treated as a couple in this situation.

Note: If the SDP and, for income support and income-based JSA only, the enhanced disability premium, are included in the calculation, they will no longer be included if payment of DLA care component/PIP daily living component ceases. The enhanced disability premium will continue to be included in the applicable amount for income-related ESA if you are in receipt of the support component.

Maintenance and liable relatives

The income and capital of the non-resident spouse or civil partner cannot be taken into account in determining a permanent resident's claim to income support, income-based JSA or income-related ESA. However, spouses or civil partners are each liable to maintain the other and the non-resident spouse/civil partner can be asked to make a contribution. The non-resident should not feel pressured into paying more than they can reasonably afford given their actual resources and expenses. Unless the DWP obtains a court order, payment is voluntary. In practice, legal proceedings are rarely undertaken, although the DWP may put pressure on the non-resident spouse/civil partner to make 'voluntary' payments. Normally, payments made by the non-resident spouse/civil partner are taken into account as the resident spouse's/civil partner's income. But if you are receiving payments to help meet the costs of more expensive 'preferred' accommodation (see Chapter 32(8)), they are ignored for income support, income-based JSA and income-related ESA.

Note: Liable relative rules do not apply to pension credit.

5. Pension credit

Capital limits in care homes

Capital under £10,000 for temporary (or trial period) and permanent residents, does not attract any 'deemed' income (see Chapter 42(6)). Deemed income from capital above £10,000 is £1 a week for every £500 or part thereof. (Deemed income is calculated differently by local authorities when assessing your charges – see Box L.2.) There is no upper capital limit.

Calculation of pension credit in care homes

If you are a resident in a care home and have reached pension credit qualifying age (see Chapter 42(2)), your pension credit guarantee credit element is worked out in the usual way by adding together your 'standard minimum guarantee' and any additional amounts to which you are entitled, which can include the *'additional amount for severe disability'* while a qualifying benefit is payable (the *'qualifying benefits'* are: attendance allowance, disability living allowance (DLA) care component at the middle or highest rate and personal independence payment (PIP) daily living component). See Chapter 42(3). The pension credit savings credit element is also worked out in the usual way (see Chapter 42(4)).

If you are 65 or over, both elements will normally have an *'assessed income period'* of up to five years (this can be indefinite if you are aged 75 or over). During a typical 5-year award period, certain elements of your income are treated as constant with deemed annual increases built in. It is not a fixed award, as the deemed increases will alter the amount of the award from year to year. This will usually mean that if you are going temporarily into a care home there will be no need to notify the DWP. However, if you receive a qualifying benefit, you will still need to inform the Blackpool Benefits Centre (see inside back cover) if your temporary stay will be for more than 28 days (or less if you have been in hospital or a care home within the previous 29 days, as this period will be linked – see Chapter 5(7) and Box B.13). If you are going into a care home on a permanent basis, any assessed income period will end and therefore you will need to inform the DWP.

SPCA, S.9(4)(b); SPC Regs, reg 12(c)

Temporary admission (single person) – There will usually be no change in the amount of pension credit you receive because you will be treated as normally residing in your own home (but see note below).

Temporary admission (couple) – There is no provision for the treatment of couples as two single people in terms of the 'appropriate minimum guarantee' (see Chapter 42(3)) if one is going into a care home on a temporary basis. This means the amount of pension credit payable will usually be the same as the amount payable when you were both living at home. However, if the 'additional amount for severe disability' (see above) is included in the calculation at the single or couple rate, it will no longer be included if the qualifying benefit (see above) in payment to the resident has been suspended. This is the case even if your partner is living at home in the community and receiving a qualifying benefit themselves. This is because you, as the resident, are treated as still being in the household and not disregarded for the purposes of qualifying for the additional amount for severe disability. A similar situation occurs when one of a couple is temporarily in hospital, but the pension credit regulations provide for this by allowing a single additional amount for severe disability to continue in payment for the partner at home. In practice, however, the DWP also appears to apply this hospital provision to a care home situation.

SPC Regs, reg 6(5) & Sch 1, para 1(2)(b)

The treatment of couples as couples for pension credit appropriate minimum guarantee purposes in these circumstances instead of as single people also has problematic knock-on effects for local authority charging (see Chapter 34(6)).

Permanent admission (single person) – If you go into a care home on a permanent basis, the pension credit amount will usually change only if you are living with a non-dependant in the community or you had a carer in receipt of carer's allowance. This is because you may become entitled to pension credit (or there may be an increase in the amount of pension credit) due to the additional amount for severe disability being included in the appropriate minimum guarantee for any period that a qualifying benefit (see above) remains in payment.

SPC Regs, reg 5(1)(b) & Sch 1, para 1(1)(a)

As there is no upper capital limit for pension credit you may be entitled to it while living in a care home even if your capital is more than the local authority charging capital limit and you are therefore self-funding.

You will also be entitled to pension credit if you are retrospectively self-funding (see 2 above) because you are selling your property.

Permanent admission (couple) – If you are permanently in a care home, each of you will be treated as separate single claimants. Joint capital will be split, and the pension credit calculation should be based solely on each of your individual capital and income (see Chapter 32(6) for information about joint capital). If you both enter the same care home you may still be assessed by the DWP as a couple, although case law has established that most people should be assessed as individuals even if they share a room. Seek advice if you are treated as a couple in this situation.

SPC Regs, reg 5(1)(b); R(IS)1/99

Note: If the additional amount for severe disability was included in the calculation sof pension credit when you were in the community, it will no longer be included if payment of the qualifying benefit (see above) has ceased.

6. Special help for war pensioners

If you get a war disablement pension or have had a gratuity for your disability, you may qualify for help with your care home fees from the Service Personnel and Veterans Agency. It can cover medical treatment, nursing home fees and respite breaks that you need wholly or mainly because of that disability. You are not means tested for these services but you must apply before arranging them. Contact the Veterans Helpline for details (0800 169 2277).

34 Charging for care

1. Legal basis of the financial assessment

Section 22(1) of the National Assistance Act 1948 (as amended) and subsequent regulations confer a duty on local authorities to charge for accommodation, whether in a care home owned by a local authority or in an independent care home.

The National Assistance (Assessment of Resources) Regulations 1992 (as amended) specifies the calculation of charges. These rules are explained in the *Charging for Residential Accommodation Guide* (CRAG). Local authorities must take account of the CRAG because it is statutory guidance. It is updated and circulars are issued with each amendment. This chapter largely reflects English guidance; see Box L.1 for details of the guidance for Scotland and Wales.

2. Standard rate

The local authority must fix a standard rate for the accommodation. The standard rate for local authority care homes is the full cost to the authority of providing your place in that accommodation. The standard rate for independent care homes is the gross cost to the authority of providing or paying for your place in that accommodation under a contract with the independent care home.

NAA, Ss.22(2) & 26(2)

Even if you have sufficient income or capital to pay the standard rate, you can, in some circumstances, have the authority make the arrangements for you but you will be assessed to pay the full cost (less any NHS-funded nursing care if you are in a nursing home; see Chapter 32(3)).

If you cannot pay the standard rate, the local authority must assess your ability to pay under national rules and calculate what lower amount to charge you.

NAA, S.22(3)

The financial assessment is based on your income and capital.

3. Income and capital

Income – In general, assume all income counts unless all or part of it is specifically disregarded. The 'income disregards' are similar to those for income support (see Chapter 27). However, income support, income-based jobseeker's allowance, income-related employment and support allowance and pension credit are taken into account as income by local authorities (except for payments towards housing costs and the savings disregard applied to the savings credit element of pension credit). See Box L.2 for details.

Capital – If you are in a care home (on either a permanent or temporary basis) and your savings are above the upper capital limit for your country, you will have to pay the standard rate for your accommodation until your capital drops to this limit. Some capital is ignored or disregarded in the assessment. If you have capital above the lower capital limit for your country, a tariff income is assumed. Capital is either *'actual'*, ie you own it and it is available to you, or *'notional'*, ie you are treated as owning the asset even if it is unclaimed or transferred to another person in an effort to avoid care home charges. See Box L.2 and 8 to 10 below for details (including about how your property is treated).

Local authorities must provide care in care homes for those who need it unless it is *'otherwise available to them'*. The Health and Social Care Act 2001 and its subsequent regulations reaffirm that authorities cannot say that accommodation is *'otherwise available'* if your capital is less than the upper capital limit. In Scotland, the House of Lords ruled that it would be unlawful to cease funding a care home placement on the grounds that a person had the capital to make their own arrangements if the capital at the time of needs assessment was only notional.

Robertson v Fife Council [2002] UKHL 35 (HoL) (5 CCLR 543)

If you enter into a deferred payments agreement (see 9 below), your former home is not included by the authority in deciding whether accommodation is otherwise available.

Health & Social Care Act 2001, S.55; CCH(S)A

4. Key points of the assessment

❏ The local authority does not have to carry out a charging assessment for the first eight weeks of a stay in care; it can charge what is reasonable. Most authorities use this rule for respite care to avoid multiple assessments.

NAA, S.22(5A)

❏ If you count as a 'less dependent resident', the local authority can ignore the whole of the charging assessment if reasonable in your situation (see 5 below).

❏ If you are a temporary resident in the care home, the charging assessment is slightly different in order to allow for your costs at home (see 11 below).

❏ If you are one of a couple, the law does not allow a joint charging assessment; only the resident's own income and capital affects the assessment. However, see 6 below for when the non-resident partner is the claimant of benefit paid in respect of both members of the couple.

CRAG, para 4.001

❏ Whatever your source(s) of income, you will generally be left with no less than the personal expenses allowance (PEA) of £23.90 a week (£24.50 in Wales). Except for any income ignored in the assessment (see Box L.2), the rest of your income goes towards meeting the standard rate for your accommodation (see 2 above).

❏ Any difference between what you pay and the standard rate is met by the local authority, which is liable for the full cost of the fees (but see Chapter 32(9) if you have chosen more expensive accommodation than the authority thinks you need).

❏ If the application of the law affects you unfairly, urge the local authority to use its discretion to correct that unfairness by letting you keep more of your income than your weekly PEA (see 7 below).

NAA, S.22(4)

❏ The assessment is based largely on income support rules but there are some important differences, and the local authority has some discretion (see Box L.2).

❏ In England and Wales, if your accommodation is provided as part of your aftercare package under section 117 of the Mental Health Act 1983, you should not be charged for your accommodation. (In Scotland, such accommodation and other services are normally chargeable.) See Chapter 32(1) for details.

LAC 2000/3; R v Manchester CC ex p Stennet [2002] (HoL) (5 CCLR 500)

You should seek advice if you are being charged or have been charged in the past and have not received a refund. If you receive aftercare under s.117 you will be entitled to benefits (including income support, income-based jobseeker's allowance, income-related employment and support allowance and pension credit) in the normal way. Disability living allowance (DLA) care component and attendance allowance, however, will not be payable, as case law suggests that s.117 is an *'enactment relating to persons under disability'* for the purposes of defining those people 'resident in a care home' for whom DLA care component or attendance allowance is not payable.

CDLA/870/04; Decision Makers Guide, Chapter 61, Appendix 1

5. Less dependent residents

You are a *'less dependent resident'* if you live in an establishment not registered with the appropriate body (see Chapter 32(2)) or you live in local authority accommodation where no board (ie meals) is provided. In such cases, the authority has complete discretion to ignore the whole of the charging assessment if *'reasonable in the circumstances'*. This is because it has been recognised that to live as independently as possible you will need to be left with more than the personal expenses allowance.

AOR Regs, reg 5; CRAG, paras 2.007 & 2.008

If you live in registered accommodation and do not qualify as a 'less dependent resident', a similar effect can be achieved by a variation of the personal expenses allowance in the charging assessment (see 7 below).

CRAG, para 5.008

6. Couples

Couples and maintenance

The local authority has no power under the National Assistance Act to assess couples jointly. The financial assessment should be of the income and assets of the resident only, including entitlements to income support, income-based jobseeker's allowance (JSA), income-related employment and support allowance (ESA) or pension credit.

CRAG, para 4.001

The spouse remaining at home has no obligation to fill in any sections of the assessment form asking about their income and assets. Indeed, guidance underlines this, stating that *'local authorities should not use assessment forms for the resident which require information about the means of the spouse'*.

Liable relatives – The liable relative provision has been abolished. This means a local authority no longer has the power to approach your spouse for any contribution to the cost of care and accommodation unless they are receiving a benefit that is paid to them in respect of both of you as a couple (see below).

Benefit paid to non-resident partners in respect of couples

If you are one of a couple (including same-sex couples) going temporarily into a care home and your partner is the claimant of income support or pension credit in respect of both of you, guidance states that *'it would be reasonable to expect the partner receiving the income support/pension credit to contribute to the charge for accommodation for the other partner a sum equivalent to the income support/pension credit payable for that partner'*.

CRAG, para 4.006

The issue for local authorities is what constitutes a reasonable amount. For couples in receipt of income support, income-based JSA or income-related ESA, the situation is quite straightforward, as, in most cases, the applicable amount in these circumstances is usually calculated using two single people's applicable amounts added together (see Chapter 33(4)), which can be apportioned to find out the amount paid in respect of the resident. However, for couples in receipt of pension credit, the situation is complicated by the fact that pension credit is calculated using the couple 'appropriate minimum guarantee' (see Chapter 33(5)).

The same apportionment issue arises for local authorities when they are deciding how much to increase the personal expenses allowance by to allow an amount for the partner in the community when the resident is the claimant of pension credit for both members of the couple. See 7 below for a common approach to this issue taken by authorities.

7. Personal expenses allowance

You receive the same personal expenses allowance (PEA) (£23.90; £24.50 in Wales) whether you are in a local authority or an independent care home and whether it is on a temporary or permanent basis. Your PEA can be spent as you wish on personal items. Neither the care home nor the local authority can require you to spend your PEA in any particular way.

If you are unable to manage your PEA because of ill health, the local authority may (subject to your agreement, or that of your personal representative) deposit it in a bank account on your behalf and use it to provide for your extra needs. Money unspent at the time of your death will form part of your estate.

Guidance reminds local authorities that the PEA should not be used for care that has been contracted for by the authority and/or assessed as necessary by the authority or the NHS. Needs for continence supplies or chiropody should be reflected in the care plan and there should be no pressure from local authorities or care home providers to spend the PEA on these. The PEA can be used to buy extra services from the care home if they are genuinely additional to services that have been contracted for by the authority and/or assessed as necessary by the authority or NHS.

CRAG, paras 5.005 & 5.006; LAC(DH)(2010)2, Annex, para 4; LAC(DH)(2011)1

Increasing the PEA

Local authorities have discretion to allow more PEA in 'special circumstances' – eg if you need to keep more of your income to lead a more independent life or pursue an activity that is important to you. Guidance makes it clear that certain activities or services, although not specifically included in the resident's care plan, can contribute significantly to optimum independence and well-being. Guidance also reminds authorities that if a resident is temporarily absent, there is discretion to vary the PEA to enable the resident to have more money while staying with family or friends.

NAA, S.22(4); LAC 97/5; CRAG, para 5.006

If you are one of a couple, the PEA may be increased so that you can help support your partner at home, perhaps because you are not married or registered as civil partners and so cannot have half of your personal or occupational pension disregarded (see Box L.2), or because, as the resident, you are in receipt of a means-tested benefit (income support, income-based jobseeker's allowance (JSA), income-related employment and support allowance (ESA) or pension credit) paid in respect of both of you.

CRAG, para 5.008

Basically, the local authority should not require a charge that would leave your partner without enough money to live on. However, the authority could consider being on a means-tested benefit as 'having enough to live on'.

CRAG, para 4.002

Couples and varying the PEA – If you are one of a couple going temporarily into a care home and you are the claimant of income support, income-based JSA or income-related ESA in respect of both of you, the local authority usually apportions the benefit according to your individual incomes because it is usually calculated using two single people's applicable amounts added together (see Chapter 33(4)). However, if you are one of a couple going temporarily into a care home and you are the claimant of pension credit in respect of both of you, the position is less straightforward because pension credit is calculated using the couple 'appropriate minimum guarantee' rather than two single people's appropriate minimum guarantees added together (see Chapter 33(5)). This means local authorities must decide how to carry out an apportionment. In most cases, it seems that as a starting point authorities either:

■ divide the couple rate 'standard minimum guarantee' equally (ie £222.05 divided by 2 = £111.03) and add any additional amounts included in the appropriate minimum guarantee to the amount for the person for whom it is paid. Then they deduct assessable income received by the partner to reach an amount by which to vary the PEA; or
■ allow the amount that would be paid by way of the pension credit guarantee element to the partner as if they were a single person and vary the PEA by this amount.

These different approaches produce significant variations across the country in the amounts allowed in charging assessments for partners in the community. If the amount allowed for your partner leaves them without enough money to live on, you should seek advice with a view to using the complaints procedure (see Chapter 29(6)).

Guidance states that local authorities should ensure that the partner remaining at home receives at least the basic level of income support/pension credit for a single person and any premiums/additions to which they may be entitled in their own right and that a voluntary agreement by the partner to disclose information may be needed to achieve this.

CRAG, para 4.007

8. Treating your home as capital

The value of your previous home will be ignored when the local authority assesses your resources:

■ if you are temporarily resident in a care home; or
■ for the first 12 weeks of being a permanent resident in a care home provided by the authority under Part III of the National Assistance Act 1948, irrespective of whether you were already in a care home as a self-funder. (Seek advice if your local authority does not apply the disregard because you have been self-funding in a care home prior to applying for local authority help.) Many authorities have arrangements to allow residents to use the value of their property (which may be their only capital resource) during the 12-week disregard to defer a self top-up, especially if the resident has no third party willing to top up their more expensive care home fees (see Chapter 32(9));
■ if the home is occupied by your partner/former partner (unless you are estranged or divorced from them); or
■ if the home is occupied by your estranged or divorced partner and they are a lone parent with a dependent child; or
■ if the home is occupied by a relative of yours or a relative of a member of your family who is:
  – aged 60 or over; or
  – incapacitated; or
  – aged under 16 and a child for whom you are liable to maintain.

A 'relative' is your parent, parent-in-law, son, daughter, son/daughter-in-law, step-parent, stepson/daughter, brother, sister, or the partner (including civil partner) of any of the above, grandparent, grandchild, uncle, aunt, nephew or niece.

'Incapacitated' is not defined but guidance says you count as incapacitated if you get incapacity benefit, severe disablement allowance, disability living allowance, personal independence payment, attendance allowance or constant attendance allowance, or you would satisfy the incapacity conditions for any of these.

Local authorities have discretion to ignore the value of the property if anyone else lives there (see Box L.2).
AOR Regs, Sch 4

If your home is taken into account, its value will be based on the current selling price, less any debts (such as a mortgage) charged on it, and less 10% in recognition of the expenses that would be incurred in selling it. Its value should be reassessed periodically. The capital value of your home is assessed in this way until it is sold and added to other capital you have; the local authority may help towards your fees while your home is being sold. Seek advice if you are refused help with funding pending the sale of your home if the authority has assessed you as needing care in a care home. Once your home is sold, the capital realised from the sale, less any debts and the expenses involved in the sale, is taken into account.
AOR Regs, reg 23; CRAG, paras 6.014(a) & 6.018

The local authority cannot make you sell your home to pay the assessed charge for your accommodation, other than through the courts. However, the authority can place a legal charge on the property so that it can recover outstanding debts when the property is eventually sold. If the property is jointly owned, the authority is advised to put a caution (or security) on it, which has a similar effect.
HASSASSA, S.22 (S.23 in Scotland); CRAG, Annex D(3.5) – similar provisions apply in Scotland

The method of valuing your interest or share in joint property is outlined in Box L.2.

The value of any other property you own will usually be taken into account as capital.

9. Deferred payment agreements

'Deferred payment agreements' are available to people in care homes who do not wish to sell their home (for whatever reason) or face a delay in selling it, and have:
- less than the upper capital limit in England, the capital limit in Wales and the lower capital limit in Scotland (disregarding the value of their home); *and*
- insufficient income to meet the cost of their placement.

Health & Social Care Act 2001, S.55; CCH(S)A 2002, S.6

The scheme allows the local authority to enter into a written agreement with the resident whereby:
- the authority places a legal charge or charging order on the resident's property;
- the authority contracts to pay the full fees of the placement to the home;
- the resident is assessed to pay a weekly charge to the authority based on their weekly income (less the personal expenses allowance); *and*
- payment by the resident of the balance of the weekly cost of the placement is deferred until the resident dies or the property is sold.

Local authorities have discretion as to whether to enter into an agreement in individual cases.

Guidance states that caution should be exercised if there is a mortgage on the property or the amount of the deferred payment is very high. If an authority refuses to enter into an agreement, it should put that decision in writing. Authorities are expected to have deferred payment schemes and could be challenged if they do not consider exercising their discretion to offer deferred payments. Use the complaints procedure if you wish to challenge the decision (see Chapter 29(6)).
LAC (2001)25; LAC (2002)15; LAC(DH) (2009)3

Points to note:
- Deferred payments should not be used if the value of your home should be disregarded (see Box L.2).
- Residents should be given full information about the scheme and advised to seek independent financial advice before entering an agreement.
- If you enter into an agreement, you may have to pay for land registry searches and other legal expenses relating to placing a legal charge on your property.
- Deferred payments are interest free, although local authorities can charge interest, at a reasonable rate, on the debt from 56 days after your death or after you terminate the agreement. (However, the draft Care and Support Bill (see Chapter 29(1)) proposes that regulations are laid to enable administrative costs and interest to be charged on deferred sums.)
- Local authorities can place a 'legal charge', a type of secured loan, on your property under alternative legal provisions. However, this provision should be used only if you are unwilling to pay your assessed contribution and a debt arises. Your consent is not required. If the authority puts a charge on your property, it has a duty to charge reasonable interest on any sum owed after the day of death. Before then, the authority cannot charge you interest. In certain situations, you can change from being subject to such a legal charge to having a deferred payment agreement.
HASSSASSA, Ss.22 & 24; CRAG, para 7.025; LAC (2002)15
- Local authorities can make allowances for ongoing expenses relating to the property, but this may increase the debt repayable when the property is sold.

Deferred payment agreements and benefits
If you enter a deferred payment agreement you should note the following effects on your benefit entitlement.
- If you are under pension credit qualifying age, you will not be entitled to income support or income-related employment and support allowance (ESA) while the property is not up for sale if your interest in the property is worth more than £16,000. If you have reached pension credit qualifying age, it is also unlikely that you will be entitled to pension credit if your house is not up for sale, as the tariff income applied on capital above £10,000 is likely to mean your income will exceed your 'appropriate minimum guarantee'. This means the total debt repayable to the local authority at the end will be greater. If your property is at the lower end of the market it is worth checking to see if you could still get the guarantee credit of pension credit or if it affects your savings credit.
- You will retain your entitlement to attendance allowance, disability living allowance care component or personal independence payment daily living component during a deferred payment agreement because you will be treated as a 'self-funder', if it is clear you will eventually pay back the local authority in full. This is the case even if you get income support, income-related ESA or pension credit with the severe disability premium (or pension credit equivalent) during this period. In Scotland this will not apply if you are 65 or over and receiving free personal care (see Chapter 33(2)).

L.2 Capital and income

Local authority assessments of capital and income are similar to those for income support. In this box we outline how local authority assessments of capital and income differ from those of means-tested benefits (including income support, income-related employment and support allowance (ESA), income-based jobseeker's allowance (JSA) and pension credit – see Chapters 27, 28 and 42(5)-(6)).

Capital limits

For local authority charging purposes these are:
- in England and Northern Ireland, £23,250 upper limit and £14,250 lower limit for tariff income purposes; in Scotland, £25,250 upper limit and £15,500 lower limit; in Wales, one capital limit of £23,750 (and therefore no tariff income assessment required); for both temporary and permanent residents.

For ESA/income support/JSA, the capital limits are:
- £16,000 upper limit and £6,000 lower limit (for tariff income) for temporary residents;
- £16,000 upper limit and £10,000 lower limit (for tariff income) for permanent residents.

For pension credit, there is no capital upper limit. A £10,000 limit for tariff income purposes applies to both temporary and permanent residents.

Note: The tariff income for all local authority charging purposes and ESA/income support/JSA purposes is calculated using £1 a week for every £250 or part thereof in excess of the lower limits. For pension credit purposes only, tariff income (or 'deemed income') is £1 a week for every £500 or part thereof in excess of the limit.

Arrears of benefits

There is a 52-week limit on the disregard of arrears of some benefits for charging assessments. For means-tested benefits, this period is extended in certain circumstances (see Chapters 28(6) and 42(6)).

Your home

See also Chapter 34(8). If you are a temporary resident, the value of 'one dwelling' is ignored if:
- you intend to return to live in it as your home; *and*
- it is still available to you; *or*
- your property is up for sale and you intend to use the proceeds to buy a more suitable property to return to.

AOR Regs, Sch 4, para 1

Temporary resident – You count as a *'temporary resident'* if your stay is unlikely to last more than 52 weeks or *'in exceptional circumstances (is) unlikely substantially to exceed that period'*.

AOR Regs, reg 2(1)

If you are unsure of your long-term plans, it is usually best to say you intend to return to your own home. However, if you are one of a couple going into a care home on a trial basis with a view to a permanent stay, you will still be treated as a couple for pension credit purposes, whereas if you are one of a couple going permanently into a care home you will be treated as two single people and any pension credit entitlement will be paid to each of you based on your individual resources. Therefore, it may be financially beneficial in these circumstances to be permanent from the day of entering the care home (see Chapter 34(6) and (7)).

Permanent resident – You count as a *'permanent resident'* if you are not a temporary resident and the agreed intention is for you to remain in a care home.

LAC (2002)11, para 25; CRAG, para 3.002

The local authority must disregard the value of your property for the first 12 weeks that you are a permanent resident in a care home (see Chapter 34(8)). In addition to the statutory property disregards listed in Chapter 34(8), the local authority has discretion, not found in means-tested benefits, to disregard the value *'of any premises occupied in whole or in part by a third party where the local authority considers it would be reasonable to disregard the value of those premises'*. Examples are given where a carer has given up their own home in order to care, or the person remaining is an elderly companion of the resident, particularly if they have given up their own home. These examples are not exhaustive. If you think a disregard should apply to your property, and it has not been, use the complaints procedure (see Chapter 29(6)).

AOR, Sch 4, para 18; CRAG, para 7.011

While your home is up for sale

Unlike for means-tested benefits, if you are a permanent resident when your old home is up for sale, the local authority does not ignore the value for 26 weeks or longer where reasonable. It counts as capital from the 13th week after you have become a permanent resident. See also Chapter 34(8).

AOR Regs, Sch 4, para 1A

Although the local authority may help towards your care home fees while your home is up for sale, you will have to pay back the full amount once the home is sold. See also Chapter 34(9) for information about deferred payment agreements.

If you jointly own property

Only your actual interest should be valued and it is recognised that it might be hard to find a willing buyer for a part-share in a property. Seek advice if you disagree with how your share is valued.

CRAG, para 7.017

ESA/income support/JSA use a 'deemed' share based on the number of owners rather than the actual share in the property (see Chapter 28(5)).

If you jointly own a property with your spouse or civil partner who decides to sell in order to move (eg to a smaller house), you can give them some of your share of the proceeds to help buy the new home. The local authority should not consider this as deprivation of capital.

CRAG, para 6.069

Joint capital

If you jointly own capital (other than property) with your partner (or any other person), the local authority, to avoid administrative difficulties, will divide it into equal shares in the charging assessment regardless of what your actual share is. Once you are in sole possession of your actual share, you will be treated as owning that actual amount.

AOR Regs, reg 27(1); CRAG, para 6.013

This applies whether you are a temporary or permanent resident, unlike the means-tested benefit rules for couples, which count your capital together until you become a permanent resident, when the local authority divides your capital.

Personal possessions

The value of these is ignored unless you acquired them with the intention of reducing your capital in order to satisfy a local authority that you are unable to pay for your accommodation at the standard rate or to reduce the rate at which you would otherwise be liable to pay for your accommodation.

AOR Regs, Sch 4, para 8

Deprivation of capital

Local authorities have powers that may be used to treat you as having notional capital, ie as possessing capital that you have given away. Chapter 34(10) explains the deprivation of capital rule. However, there is also an additional power, the '6-month rule', which has different conditions.

The 6-month rule
The 6-month rule may be applied if you:

- transferred cash or any other asset, which would have affected the charging assessment, to someone else; *and*
- did this *'knowingly and with the intention of avoiding charges for the accommodation'; and either*
- transferred the asset six months or less before the day the local authority had arranged a placement in a care home; *or*
- transferred the asset while you were being funded by the local authority in a care home; *and either*
- were not paid anything, or given anything, in return for the transfer; *or*
- were paid, or given something, less than the value of the asset in return for the transfer.

If a resident is self-funding in an independent sector home, and has not been assessed or had their placement arranged by a local authority, the 6-month rule applies only if the authority takes over the arrangements within that time.
HASSASSA, S.21(1); CRAG, Annex D(2.1)

If the 6-month rule applies, the person to whom you transferred the asset is *'liable to pay ... the difference between the amount assessed as due to be paid for the (residential) accommodation ... and the amount (which you are paying)'*. The local authority may:

- use the deprivation of capital rule (see Chapter 34(10)) to base the charging assessment on the amount of 'notional capital' you gave away, as well as on your actual capital and income; *or*
- if you cannot pay the assessed charge, use the 6-month rule to transfer the liability for the part of the charges assessed as a result of the notional capital from you to the person(s) to whom you transferred the asset, up to the value of the transferred asset.

CRAG, para 6.073
Some people mistakenly think that if they have given away assets more than six months before entering a care home, it cannot affect the amount they would have to pay for a care home. However, if a significant purpose of giving away an asset was to get help, or more help, from the local authority with the cost of a care home, the deprivation of capital rule may be applied – even if the transfer took place more than six months before (see Chapter 34(10)).
AOR Regs, reg 25(1); CRAG, paras 6.062 to 6.072

Obviously, if you have given away something that would not have affected the charging assessment at all, the deprivation of capital rule cannot apply, nor can the 6-month rule. If the local authority refuses to arrange a place for you in a care home because the asset you gave away, together with other savings, was worth more than the capital limit in your country (see above), seek urgent advice.
See also Robertson v Fife Council [2002] UKHL 35 (HoL)

Charitable and third party payments
The way charitable, voluntary and personal injury payments are treated in a local authority charging assessment has been changed to reflect the way they are treated for means-tested benefits. See Chapters 27(7) and 28(6). In 2010 the Department of Health consulted on proposals to enable local authorities to take account of the care element of personal injury compensation awards in all circumstances. A response is expected after scrutiny of the Care and Support Bill 2012.

Third-party payments to meet a shortfall for more expensive accommodation are always taken fully into account as your income by the local authority. This is not the case for means-tested benefits.

Income
- Attendance allowance, disability living allowance (DLA) care component and personal independence payment (PIP) daily living component are only disregarded if you are a 'temporary resident' (see above). Different rules apply in Scotland (see Chapter 33(2)).
- DLA and PIP mobility component are disregarded.
- Income support, income-related ESA, pension credit and income-based JSA are taken fully into account but payments in these benefits made towards housing costs (eg payments toward mortgage interest) are disregarded. See below for the savings disregard applied to the savings credit element of pension credit.
- Housing benefit being paid in relation to your usual home is disregarded (regulations including council tax reduction are being awaited at time of writing).
- The local authority can disregard any payments you are making towards your housing costs as a temporary resident (see Chapter 34(11)).
- If you receive a child or adult dependant's addition to a contributory benefit (eg as part of your incapacity benefit or state pension), it is disregarded if it is paid to the person for whom it is intended.
- Working tax credit is taken fully into account.
- Child tax credit is disregarded.
- Child support maintenance payments, child benefit and guardian's allowance are disregarded (unless the child is in the accommodation with you).
AOR Regs, Sch 3
- Earnings from employment as an employed earner or a self-employed earner are disregarded (from 8.4.13).
AOR Regs, reg 9A
- If you do not live with your spouse/civil partner, half your personal or occupational pension or payment from a retirement annuity contract will be disregarded if you pass at least this amount to your spouse/civil partner. If you pass nothing or less than half, there is no disregard. The disregard is for both temporary and permanent residents. (The means-tested benefit rules do not have a similar disregard.)
AOR Regs, reg 10A

Savings disregard
The Department of Health and devolved governments apply a savings disregard for residents aged 65 or over. The amounts below are for 2013/14.

- If you are a resident in receipt of pension credit savings credit with pre-pension credit qualifying income of between £115.30 (savings credit threshold) and £145.40 (standard minimum guarantee) a week (or between £183.90 and £222.05 for couples) you will have a disregard of an amount equal to the savings credit award or £5.75 (£5.90 in Scotland) a week (£8.60 (£8.85 in Scotland) for couples), whichever is less.
- If you are a resident in receipt of pension credit savings credit with pre-pension credit qualifying income in excess of £145.40 a week (£222.05 for couples) you will have a disregard of £5.75 (£5.90 in Scotland) a week (£8.60 (£8.85 in Scotland) for couples).
- If you are a resident who is not in receipt of pension credit savings credit because, although you have qualifying income, your total income is in excess of £190.55 a week (£279.27 for couples), you will have a disregard of £5.75 (£5.90 in Scotland) a week (£8.60 (£8.85 in Scotland) for couples).
AOR Regs, Sch 3, para 28H

It is important to ensure you receive all the benefits you are entitled to during the period of the deferred payment agreement to help reduce the debt to the local authority. Authorities may also consider allowing a deferred self top-up if you have chosen more expensive accommodation than the authority thinks you need (see Chapter 32(9)).

10. Deprivation of capital

If you have given away assets, eg your former home, or sold them for less than they are worth to avoid or lessen the charge, or converted them into a form that is disregarded to take advantage of the disregard, the local authority may take their value into account in the charging assessment. These *'notional capital'* rules are not mandatory and local authorities have discretion not to apply them. If they do apply them, they are similar to the notional capital rules for means-tested benefits (see Chapter 28(9)).

AOR Regs, reg 25(1); CRAG, paras 6.062 to 6.072

The local authority can, however, decide that property has been disposed of in order to reduce the residential charge without having to decide that the resident knew of the capital limit or anticipated the need to enter a care home.

Yule v South Lanarkshire Council [2000] (SLT1249)

Additionally, a local authority must take account of the resident's 'subjective purpose' in disposing of the property and give reasons for accepting or rejecting any evidence provided by the resident.

R (on the application of Beeson) & Dorset CC & SoS for Health [2002] HRLR15 (EWCA)

The local authority *'diminishing notional capital'* rule reduces any notional capital on a weekly basis. It is reduced by the difference between the charge you are currently paying and the charge you would have paid if the authority had not taken notional capital into account.

AOR Regs, reg 26

The 6-month rule – If capital is transferred to another person not more than six months before the date of the local authority arranging the placement in a care home or if it is transferred while the person is residing in the care home arranged by the authority, there is an additional local authority power, not available in the rules for means-tested benefits, which may mean that the person to whom the asset is transferred is liable to pay the difference between the amount assessed as due to be paid for the care home and the amount that you are paying (see Box L.2).

HASSASSA, S.21(1)

11. Meeting the costs of your own home

If you are a *'temporary resident'* (see Box L.2), the local authority can disregard payments you are making towards *'any housing costs... including any fuel charges, which are included in the rent of a dwelling to which (you) intend to return... to the extent that the local authority considers it reasonable in the circumstances to do so'.*

AOR Regs, Sch 3, para 27

Housing costs can include service charges, insurance premiums, water rates, standard charges for fuel and any rent or mortgage payments not covered by means-tested benefits or Supporting People payments.

CRAG, paras 3.018 & 3.019

If no one is living in your home and you have entered a care home for a short period, see Chapters 21(6) and 33(3) for information about housing benefit.

After 52 weeks, or 13 weeks in the case of a trial period, you will be excluded from housing benefit or means-tested benefit housing costs. However, your liability to pay rent and/ or a mortgage in respect of your former home continues until you have terminated your tenancy or sold your home. If you have given notice on your tenancy in the community, you will be able to continue to claim housing benefit for up to four weeks (see Chapter 33(3)).

If your former home is vacant and you are a permanent resident you should not have to pay council tax.

If your partner, children or relatives continue to live in your home, the help they can receive for housing costs depends on their circumstances. If they are paying the housing costs, even though you are the person liable for them, they can claim housing benefit or means-tested benefit housing costs instead of you.

12. What happens if you move out?

When you move out of a care home, you will be entitled to benefits in the usual way. Your local adult social care department will be able to advise you on local authority benefits and services available in your area (see Chapters 29 and 30 for details).

If you leave the care home on a temporary basis, the local authority can use its discretion to vary the personal expenses allowance to enable you to have more money while away.

NAA, S.22(4); LAC 97/5, para 8

You may be able to claim personal independence payment daily living component or attendance allowance for periods away from the care home. Chapter 33 covers the effect on benefits of stays in, and absences from, care homes.

This section of the Handbook looks at:

Hospital

35 Benefits in hospital

1. What should you do beforehand?

Stays in hospital (or a similar institution – see below) as an inpatient can affect benefits. Four of the principal disability benefits – attendance allowance, disability living allowance (DLA), personal independence payment (PIP) and carer's allowance – can be stopped after just a few weeks in hospital, as can child benefit (see 4 below). In turn, this can affect your entitlement to income-related employment and support allowance, income support, housing benefit and pension credit (see Box M.1). Consequently, you should let the DWP know if you or a dependant are admitted to hospital. If you get carer's allowance, you must tell the DWP if the person you are caring for is admitted. If you get housing benefit and a spell in hospital results in attendance allowance, DLA, PIP, carer's allowance or child benefit being stopped, you also need to tell the local authority.

Write to the office(s) dealing with your benefits to let them know the date you expect to be admitted to hospital and how long you are likely to stay. You should still report your actual admission or tell the office(s) if it is cancelled or postponed. If you can, do this beforehand; otherwise, do it as soon as possible.

Fit notes – If you need fit notes to get benefit when in hospital, ask the ward sister or charge nurse for one.

Hospital or similar institution – Benefits are affected by a stay in a *'similar institution'* in the same way as a stay in hospital. This is not defined in legislation, although you must receive inpatient medical treatment or professional nursing care in the home under specified NHS legislation. What matters is not so much the nature of the accommodation, but whether your assessed needs for care are such that the NHS is under a duty to fund the accommodation free of charge, in which case you will still be treated as an inpatient.

HIP Regs, reg 2(4); R(DLA)2/06

Private patients – If you are a private patient paying the whole cost of accommodation and non-medical services in hospital, you are not deemed to be an inpatient and therefore the normal rules of benefit entitlement apply, not those described in this chapter.

2. Hospital fares

You may be able to get help with fares or other travel expenses for yourself (and for someone who has to go with you, where it is deemed medically necessary) if you are either exempt from NHS charges or qualify for full help with them (see Chapter 54(1)). Help is also available if you are covered by the low income scheme (see Chapter 54(5)). If your income is above the low-income level but would fall below it if you paid the fares, you may still be eligible for help with part of the cost. Help with fares or other travel expenses is also available if you:

■ live in the Isles of Scilly and need to travel to a mainland hospital; *or*

■ live in the Scottish Islands or Highlands and need to travel more than five miles by sea or 30 miles by land to get to hospital; *or*

■ are getting NHS treatment abroad. Costs can be met up to the embarkation point; the overseas travel is part of the treatment costs and must be agreed beforehand by the health authority.

NHS(TERC) Regs, regs 3, 5, 5B, 6 & 9

Parents – If your child (under 16) has to go into hospital or attend on a regular basis, you may claim help with travel expenses to accompany your child to and from the hospital.

NHS(TERC) Regs, regs 3(3)(a)

Inpatients sent home on short leave – If you are sent home temporarily as part of your treatment or for the hospital's convenience, your fares are regarded as part of your treatment costs and should be met by the hospital and not under the hospital travel expenses means-tested scheme.

What travel expenses can be covered?

The law allows help with *'the cost of travelling by the cheapest means of transport which is reasonable having regard to [your] age, medical condition and any other relevant circumstances'*, which normally means the cost of standard-class public transport. If public transport is available but you choose to go by car, your fuel costs would normally only be covered up to the amount of the standard-class fare. However, if there is a valid reason why you cannot use public transport (eg you are unable to use it because of a physical disability or it is not available) and you go by car or taxi, your fuel costs or fares will be covered. You must get agreement from the hospital first for the use of taxis. The travel costs of an escort can also be met if you need to be accompanied for medical reasons.

If you are travelling overseas for NHS treatment you are covered under the same rules, subject to the health authority's agreement to the mode of transport.

NHS(TERC) Regs, regs 3(5) & (6)

How to claim the cost of fares

The hospital will refund your fares if you produce proof of your entitlement (eg your benefit award letter or tax credit exemption certificate) and your travel receipts. If you have already claimed on low-income grounds, show your HC2 certificate (full entitlement) or your HC3 certificate (partial entitlement).

If you haven't yet claimed on low-income grounds, use form HC5 to claim a refund, and form HC1 to establish your entitlement to full or partial help. The forms can be obtained by ringing the NHS Helpline (0845 850 1166). The HC5 must be returned within three months of paying your fares.

Partial help with fares – The amount shown on an HC3 certificate for partial help is the amount you are expected to be able to pay for travel expenses in any one week (from Sunday to the following Saturday). If your actual hospital travel expenses in any particular week covered by that HC3 certificate are higher, the excess is refunded. This helps if you have to travel long distances to hospital or if you have to make several visits to the same, or to different, hospitals within the same week.

Other sources of help
Other possible sources of help with travel expenses for patients and visitors include hospital endowment funds, education departments, adult social care departments, the Family Fund (see Chapter 37(8)) and various charities. For advice about these, contact a hospital social worker or an advice centre. Further information is available on the Department of Health website (www.dh.gov.uk).

M.1 What happens to means-tested benefits?

This box relates to:
■ income-related employment and support allowance (ESA);
■ income support;
■ housing benefit; *and*
■ pension credit.

These benefits can continue to be paid throughout your stay in hospital, but may be reduced depending on your circumstances.

Stage 1 – from day one
There is normally no cut in your benefit during your first 28 days in hospital, unless you had been in hospital or a care home in the 28 days before the current hospital stay and your attendance allowance, disability living allowance (DLA) or personal independence payment (PIP) is withdrawn as a result, in which case, see Stage 2 below.

Extra benefit – Income-related ESA, income support or pension credit do not increase if either you or your partner go into lodgings to be near a member of your family who is in hospital. You may qualify for the severe disability premium (or equivalent pension credit addition) temporarily while your carer or another non-dependant is in hospital. See Chapter 25(3).

Stage 2 – after 28 days
After 28 days in hospital, attendance allowance, DLA for an adult and PIP are withdrawn (they may be withdrawn earlier if you had been in hospital or a care home in the 28 days before the current hospital stay; see 4 in this chapter). Once one of these qualifying benefits is withdrawn, any severe disability premium (or equivalent pension credit additional amount) payable is also withdrawn. However, if you have a partner and both of you had been getting attendance allowance, DLA care component (at the middle or highest rate) or PIP daily living component, you keep the premium even after the qualifying benefit is withdrawn, but at the single rate of £59.50.
ESA Regs, Sch 4, paras 6(5) & 11(2)(b)(i); IS Regs, Sch 2, paras 13(3A) & 15(5) (b)(i); PC Regs, reg 6(5) & Sch 1, para 1(2)(b)

A carer premium (or equivalent pension credit additional amount) may be withdrawn at stages 2, 3 or 4 depending on your situation. In general, it is withdrawn eight weeks after carer's allowance stops or, if your carer's allowance is overlapped by another benefit, after attendance allowance, DLA care component or PIP daily living component stops (see Chapter 25(6)).

If you are entitled to an amount of income-related ESA or income support only because of the inclusion of a severe disability premium in your applicable amount, the withdrawal of this premium at the 28-day stage means the loss of income-related ESA or income support. The same applies in the case of the withdrawal of an additional amount for severe disability in the guarantee credit of pension credit. If you are getting housing benefit, you should tell your local authority about the loss of income-

related ESA, income support or pension credit so they can reassess your award.

Stage 3 – after 12 weeks
After 12 weeks in hospital, there is a change if the patient is a dependent child. DLA for the child is withdrawn. A disabled child premium or enhanced disability premium based on the DLA is not withdrawn until the child ceases to count as a dependant.
HB Regs, Sch 3, paras 15(1)(b) & 16(a)

Stage 4 – after 52 weeks
You can continue to receive income-related ESA, income support and pension credit for the entire duration of your stay in hospital. However, for income support any disability premium, enhanced disability premium or higher pensioner premium will stop after you have been a hospital inpatient for 52 weeks (unless you have a partner who remains at home and satisfies the condition for the premium themselves).
IS Regs, reg 2(1) & Sch 2, paras 10(6), 11(2) & 13A(2)(b)-(d)

Similarly, any premiums and the work-related activity or support components in income-related ESA are removed after you have been in hospital for 52 weeks if you are single or, if you are part of a couple, if your partner has been in hospital for 52 weeks (in which case you would be better off if you were assessed as a single person and could thus retain the relevant premiums and components).
ESA Regs, Sch 5, para 13

If non-dependant deductions are being made from your income-related ESA, income support, pension credit or housing benefit, they will stop after your non-dependant has been a hospital inpatient for 52 weeks (ignoring absences from hospital of up to 28 days).
ESA Regs, Sch 6, para 19(7)(g); IS Regs, Sch 3, para 18(7)(g)

Housing costs – Once you have been away from your own home continuously for 52 weeks, you can no longer be treated as occupying it as your home. You would therefore no longer be entitled to income-related ESA, income support or pension credit housing costs or housing benefit, though someone still living in your home could possibly claim these benefits if they were treated as liable to pay the rent or housing costs themselves.

Child – Once a child has been in hospital for 52 weeks you continue to have an allowance for them included in your income support assessment (if it is still included) for as long as you keep visiting the child.

Treatment abroad – Special rules apply for patients receiving NHS hospital treatment abroad (see Chapter 50(3) and (5)-(6)).

Pension credit
The guarantee credit of pension credit is reduced in a similar fashion to income-related ESA and income support. The savings credit element is not reduced directly, but the amount may still change once the additional amounts in the 'appropriate minimum guarantee' of the guarantee credit are withdrawn or when you are no longer treated as a couple.

War pensioners – If you attend hospital for treatment for a war disablement, you can claim for expenses regardless of your income. Write to the Service Personnel and Veterans Agency, Norcoss, Thornton-Cleveleys FY5 3WP.

3. What happens to means-tested benefits?
If you go into hospital, income-related employment and support allowance, income support and pension credit can sometimes continue to be paid indefinitely without being reduced. However, the disability, enhanced disability and higher pension premiums in income support (and any premiums and additional components in income-related employment and support allowance) are removed after 52 weeks. Also, if benefits such as disability living allowance, attendance allowance, personal independence payment or carer's allowance are withdrawn, this will affect the amount of benefit you receive. See Box M.1 for details.

Income-related employment and support allowance, income support and pension credit can continue to be paid during a temporary absence abroad for the purpose of receiving NHS hospital treatment (see Chapter 50(3) and (5)-(6)).

Jobseeker's allowance
You cannot normally claim jobseeker's allowance (JSA) while you are in hospital because you will not be deemed capable of work or able to satisfy the labour market conditions. However, if you are already receiving JSA when you go into hospital, you can be treated as being capable of, available for and actively seeking work for up to two weeks using the short-term illness rules (see Chapter 16(8)). You can do this twice within any 12 months of the same jobseeking period.

When your JSA stops, you should claim employment and support allowance.

JSA can continue to be paid during a temporary absence abroad for the purpose of receiving NHS hospital treatment (see Chapter 50(7)).

Housing benefit
If you get housing benefit, the applicable amount may change during a spell in hospital as a consequence of the withdrawal of benefits such as attendance allowance, disability living allowance, personal independence payment or carer's allowance. See Box M.1 for details.

Tax credits
Child tax credit and working tax credit are not automatically affected by a stay in hospital. However, if you cease to be treated as employed because of a stay in hospital you would no longer qualify for working tax credit (see Chapter 19(6)).

4. What happens to non-means-tested benefits?
Most non-means-tested benefits continue to be paid indefinitely. The exceptions are attendance allowance, disability living allowance (DLA), personal independence payment (PIP) and carer's allowance, as well as child benefit, guardian's allowance and any child dependant's addition that may still be payable with other benefits. They are treated in the following way.

During the first 28 days
Generally, attendance allowance, DLA for adults and PIP can be paid for the first 28 days of a hospital stay. Once you have been in hospital for more than 28 days, these benefits stop.
AA Regs, regs 6 & 8(1); DLA Regs, regs 8, 10(1) & 12A-12B(1)(a); PIP Regs, regs 29 & 30(1)

Attendance allowance, DLA care component and PIP daily living component will stop before the 28 days is up if you had been in hospital or a care home in the 28 days before

the current hospital stay. The number of days during each hospital (or care home) stay are added together and payment of the benefit will stop after a total of 28 days.
AA Regs, regs 8(2); DLA Regs, reg 10(5); PIP Regs, reg 32(4)

The mobility component of both DLA and PIP will stop before the 28 days is up only if you had been in hospital in the 28 days before the current hospital stay.
DLA Regs, reg 12B(3); PIP Regs, reg 32(4)

You count days in hospital from the day after you are admitted to the day before you go home. Neither the day you go in nor the day that you leave count as days in hospital.
AA Regs, reg 6(2A); DLA Regs, reg 8(2A) & 12A(2A); PIP Regs, reg 32(2)

After 28 days
Attendance allowance, DLA for adults and PIP stop. Your carer's allowance will stop if the person you are caring for has been in hospital for more than 28 days and their attendance allowance, DLA care component or PIP daily living component has stopped.

If you claim attendance allowance, DLA or PIP when you are already in hospital, it cannot be paid until you leave.

Constant attendance allowance (payable in the War Pensions and Industrial Injuries schemes) and war pensioners' severe disablement occupational allowance stop.
NMAF(DD)SP Order, art 53

Motability – If you have a Motability agreement in force when you go into hospital, DLA mobility component can no longer be extended beyond the first 28 days of a hospital stay. An exception will apply if you were a hospital inpatient on or before 8.4.13 and had a Motability agreement in force at that time. In this case, the mobility component can continue to be paid to Motability for the full term of the agreement. Such an arrangement cannot be extended beyond 8.4.16.
DLA Regs, reg 12B(7)-(8A)

After 12 weeks
Child in hospital – Child benefit or guardian's allowance is paid for the first 12 weeks if your child or a child you care for goes into hospital. After 12 weeks, you can continue to get these benefits for a child in hospital only if you are regularly spending money on the child's behalf (eg on clothing, pocket money, magazines). If you continue to get child benefit you will continue to get any child dependant's addition that may still be payable with other benefits (such as incapacity benefit), but otherwise this will also end.
SSCBA, S.143(4) & CB Regs, reg 10

DLA care component and mobility component for a child under 16 stop after 12 weeks in hospital. DLA care component may stop before the 12 weeks are up if your child had been in hospital or a care home in the 28 days before the current hospital stay. DLA mobility component will stop before the end of 12 weeks only if your child had been in hospital in the 28 days before the current hospital stay. See Chapter 3(7) and (8) for more details.
DLA Regs, regs 10(2) & 12B(1)(b)

M.2 For more information

- DWP1029 *Going into hospital?*, free from local Jobcentre Plus offices or www.dwp.gov.uk/docs/dwp1029.pdf.
- HC 11 *Help with health costs*, free from the NHS Helpline: 0845 850 1166.
- Leaflet 2 *Notes for people getting a war pension living in the United Kingdom*, free from your local Veterans' Welfare Office (contact details from Veterans Helpline: 0800 169 2277, textphone 0800 169 3458 or www.veterans-uk.info).

If you or your partner are in hospital – Child benefit normally continues to be paid.

Carer's allowance stops after the carer has been in hospital for 12 weeks (but it may stop sooner – see Chapter 7(10)).

Employer-paid benefits

Going into hospital does not affect entitlement to statutory sick pay, statutory maternity pay, statutory adoption pay or statutory paternity pay.

5. Long-term stays

If you have to stay in hospital for a long-term period, you will continue to receive your full entitlement to state pension, incapacity benefit or severe disablement allowance for an indefinite period (as long as you continue to satisfy the other conditions of entitlement to these benefits). If you have been placed in the support group (see Chapter 10(7)), you may continue to receive contributory employment and support allowance (ESA) for an indefinite period, although the support component is removed after you have been in hospital for 52 weeks.

Income-related ESA, income support and pension credit can also be paid for an indefinite period (again, as long as the other conditions of entitlement are met), although the rate may be affected by the withdrawal of benefits such as disability living allowance (see Box M.1). Also, the disability, enhanced disability and higher pension premiums in income support are removed after 52 weeks (unless you have a partner at home who satisfies the conditions for the premium themselves). Similarly, any premiums and the work-related activity or support components in income-related ESA are removed after you have been in hospital for 52 weeks if you are single; if you are part of a couple, these are removed after your partner has been in hospital for 52 weeks.

Housing costs – Once you have been in hospital for a continuous period of 52 weeks, if you have no dependants living in your home, you can no longer receive income-related ESA, income support or pension credit housing costs, nor can you normally get housing benefit. The maximum period of absence in one stretch during which income-related ESA, income support or pension credit housing costs and housing benefit can be paid is 52 weeks (see Chapter 21(6) for the housing benefit rules; those for the other three benefits are similar). If you have dependants or other people living in your home, their right to benefit depends on their own circumstances. If you are one of a couple and have been in hospital for 52 weeks, you and your partner are treated as separate claimants.

6. What about when you leave hospital?

Whether or not any benefit has been changed or stopped while you or a dependant have been in hospital, make sure you inform the office that administers each benefit as soon as you know the date you or your dependant are coming home.

You should still report your actual date of discharge, or tell the appropriate office if it is cancelled or postponed.

Temporary absence from hospital

If you, or a dependant, spend a few days at home – perhaps for a trial run, or if you are in and out of hospital on a regular pattern – tell the office that administers each benefit and ask them to pay the full amount of benefit for the days at home. Get a note from the hospital to say how many days you have at home. For all benefits except attendance allowance, disability living allowance (DLA) and personal independence payment (PIP), the day you are admitted is treated as a day *out* of hospital and the day you are discharged is treated as a day *in* hospital. For attendance allowance, DLA and PIP, see below.
HIP Regs, reg 2(5)

Can your carer get carer's allowance? – If you go home regularly each weekend and receive attendance allowance, DLA care component (at the middle or highest rate) or PIP daily living component, your carer might qualify for the full rate of carer's allowance. This is because carer's allowance is a weekly benefit and is never paid on a daily basis. See Chapter 7(2) to check whether your carer can meet the 35 hours a week caring test.

Attendance allowance, DLA and PIP – These are adjusted to be paid at a daily rate where you are expected to return to hospital within 28 days. Attendance allowance, DLA care component and PIP daily living component are also paid at a daily rate where you are expected to return to a care home within 28 days. The daily rate provisions cease to apply once you have been out of hospital for 28 days.

The daily rate provisions do not apply if, on the day of discharge, you are not expected to return to hospital within 28 days, even if you do return to hospital within that period. If you are not expected to return to hospital within 28 days (and when you are finally discharged from hospital) full benefit resumes from the first pay day.
C&P Regs, reg 25; UCPIP(C&P) Regs, reg 50

Both the day you are admitted or return to hospital and the day you are discharged or leave hospital count as days out of hospital. You can be paid for both of those days as well as whole days out of hospital.
AA Regs, reg 6(2A); DLA Regs, regs 8(2A) & 12A(2A); PIP Regs, reg 32(2)

Permanently out of hospital

In general, you should get the benefit you were getting before you went into hospital at the normal rate. If you go from hospital into a care home, see Chapter 33.

If you did not draw any benefit before you went into hospital, see Chapter 10 on employment and support allowance or, if you have reached pension credit qualifying age, Chapter 42. Once you leave hospital, all the normal rules for these benefits will apply to you.

7. Discharged before you're ready?

If acute nursing care in hospital is no longer essential for you, the hospital will clearly wish to discharge you. It may be impossible for you to return home without support services in place. Before being discharged, your care needs should have been assessed. Don't agree to a discharge unless you are happy with the arrangements for continuing care and support as set out in your care plan (see Chapter 29(3)). Don't agree to move to a care home unless you are absolutely clear about how, and for how long, the full cost will be met. See Chapters 29 to 34 for more details about care at home and in care homes.

Children and young people

36 Maternity and parental rights

1. Help with health costs

You are entitled to free prescriptions and dental treatment if you are pregnant or have had a baby in the past 12 months and have a valid maternity exemption certificate. Ask your doctor, midwife or health visitor for form FW8.

Vouchers to buy milk (including infant formula milk) fruit and vegetables are available under the Healthy Start scheme. This is for pregnant women and families on certain means-tested benefits who have children under the age of 4. For details see Chapter 54(6).

2. Maternity and parental leave

Maternity leave – Employed women are entitled to 52 weeks' statutory maternity leave. You must fulfil strict notice conditions, including letting your employer know you are pregnant and telling them, by the end of the 15th week before your baby is due, when you want to take your maternity leave.
MPL Regs, regs 4-12A

Parental leave – Parents who have worked for the same employer for at least one year are entitled to 18 weeks' unpaid parental leave, which can be taken up until the child's 18th birthday. You cannot take more than four weeks' parental leave for any one child in a year, unless otherwise agreed with your employer.
MPL Regs, regs 13-16

Time off for antenatal care – Every pregnant employee is entitled to time off with pay to keep antenatal appointments made on the advice of a doctor, midwife or health visitor.

3. Statutory maternity pay

If you are an employee, you may be able to get statutory maternity pay (SMP) from your employer when you stop work to have your baby. You will not have to repay it if you do not return to work. If you have more than one employer, you may be eligible for SMP from each employer. You qualify if:

■ you have been employed by the same employer continuously for at least 26 weeks into the 15th week (the *'qualifying week'*) before the week the baby is due (a 'week' starts on Sunday and runs to the end of the following Saturday); *and*

■ you are employed in the qualifying week (it doesn't matter if you are off work sick or on holiday); *and*

■ your average gross weekly earnings are at least £109; *and*

■ you give your employer the right notice (see below).
SSCBA, Ss.164 & SMP Regs, reg 11(1)

How much do you get? – SMP is paid by your employer for up to 39 weeks. For the first six weeks you get 90% of your average weekly earnings (with no upper limit). The average is calculated from your gross earnings in the eight weeks, if paid weekly, or two months, if paid monthly, before the end of the 15th week before the week the baby is due. The remaining 33 weeks are paid at the standard rate of £136.78, or 90% of your average weekly earnings if this calculation results in a figure that is less than £136.78.
SSCBA, S.166 & SMP Regs, reg 21

SMP is treated as earnings, so deductions such as income tax and national insurance contributions will be made.

When is it paid? – SMP can start from the 11th week before the week in which the baby is due. You decide when you stop work and start your maternity pay period; you can work up until the baby's birth. If your baby is born early (ie prior to the 11th week before the week it is due), SMP will start the day after the birth. See 8 below if you are off work with a pregnancy-related illness.
SSCBA, S.165 & SMP Regs, reg 2

You can work during your maternity pay period for the employer paying you SMP for up to ten days ('keeping in touch' days) without losing any SMP.
SMP Regs, reg 9A

How do you claim? – You must tell your employer at least 28 days before the date you want to start your SMP, or if this is not possible, as soon as is reasonably practicable. Your employer may ask you to inform them in writing. You must also give them your maternity certificate (form MAT B1), which your doctor or midwife will normally give you at the next antenatal appointment following your 21st week of pregnancy. Tell your employer as soon as is reasonably practicable if your baby is born early.
SSCBA, S.164(4)&(5)

If you can't get SMP – If you are not eligible for SMP, your employer must give you form SMP1 within seven days of their decision and must also return your maternity certificate. You may be eligible for maternity allowance (see 4 below).

Challenging a decision – You can ask your employer for a written statement about your SMP position. If you disagree, you can refer your case to HMRC Statutory Payments Disputes Team (0191 225 5221) for a formal decision. If HMRC decides against you, you can appeal to a First-tier Tribunal (Tax Chamber). Your employer can also appeal.

4. Maternity allowance

If you cannot get statutory maternity pay, you may qualify for tax-free maternity allowance (MA). To qualify, you must have been employed or self-employed for at least 26 weeks in the 66 weeks before the week in which the baby is due (the *'test period'*), and earned an average of at least £30 a week for any 13 weeks in this test period.
SSCBA, S.35

How much do you get? – MA is £136.78 a week, or 90% of your average weekly earnings (whichever is less). Jobcentre Plus will add up your gross earnings in the 13 weeks during the 66-week test period in which you earned the most, then

divide by 13 to work out your average weekly earnings. Earnings in different jobs and from a mixture of employed and self-employed work can be added together. If you are self-employed and have paid 13 Class 2 national insurance contributions in the test period, you will be treated as having earnings sufficient to result in the full rate of MA. You will be treated as having earnings of £30 for any week in which you are covered by a small earnings certificate of exception.
SSCBA, S.35A

When is it paid? – MA is paid for up to 39 weeks and can start from 11 weeks before the expected week of childbirth. If you are employed or self-employed you may delay the start of your MA until the baby's birth (but see 8 below if you are off work with a pregnancy-related illness). If you are not employed, your MA will start from the 11th week before the expected week of childbirth.

Once you are on MA you can work for your employer (or as a self-employed person) for up to ten 'keeping in touch' days and continue to receive it.
SSCBA, S.35(2)

How do you claim? – Fill in claim-form MA1 and send it to Jobcentre Plus together with your maternity certificate (MAT B1) and form SMP1 (if you did not qualify for SMP from your employer). If you have more than one employer, you must get an SMP1 from each employer. MA1 forms are available from the Jobcentre Plus claim-line (0845 608 8610, textphone 0845 608 8553), your antenatal clinic or the website (www.gov.uk/maternity-allowance/how-to-claim). Send in form MA1 as soon as you can after you are 26 weeks pregnant. Don't delay claiming because you are still working or waiting for the MAT B1 or SMP1 – you can send them later; MA can only be backdated for up to three months. If you are not entitled to MA, Jobcentre Plus should check if you can get employment and support allowance instead (see 8 below).

N.1 For more information

Pregnancy and parenthood
Useful guides include:
■ *A guide to Maternity Benefits* (NI17A) from the DWP (www.dwp.gov.uk/advisers/ni17a)
■ *Employer Helpbook for Statutory Maternity Pay* (E15) and *Employer Helpbook for Statutory Paternity Pay* (E19) from HMRC (www.hmrc.gov.uk/helpsheets/e15. pdf and www.hmrc.gov.uk/helpsheets/e19.pdf)
Disabled parents can get information from Disability, Pregnancy and Parenthood International (Helpline 0800 018 4730; www.dppi.org.uk) and the Disabled Parents Network (0300 330 0639; www.disabledparentsnetwork. org.uk). Advice on maternity and parental leave is available from Working Families (Helpline 0800 013 0313; www.workingfamilies.org.uk), whose free guide *From Child to Adult*, on disability, transition and family finances, can be downloaded from the website.

Education
■ Contact a Family can offer advice on special educational needs (Helpline 0808 808 or www. cafamily.org.uk/advice-and-support/sen-national-advice-service/).
■ The Advisory Centre for Education Adviceline, for independent advice on a wide range of education issues: 0300 011 5142 (Monday to Wednesday 10am to 1pm); www.ace-ed.org.uk.
Scotland – For advice and the *Parent's guide to additional support for learning*, contact Enquire (0845 123 2303; www.enquire.org.uk/publications/parents-guide).

The benefit cap – Maternity allowance is included in the list of benefits to which the 'benefit cap' applies. The cap limits the total weekly benefits that can be claimed to £500 for lone parents and couples, and £350 for single claimants. See Box H.1 in Chapter 21 for details (including exemptions).

5. Paternity leave
There are two types of paternity leave: ordinary and additional. To qualify for either type you must be the:
■ father of the child;
■ mother's husband or partner;*
■ child's adopter; *or*
■ husband or partner* of the child's adopter.
* Including same-sex partners
You must also have worked for the same employer for at least 26 weeks by the 15th week before the baby is due or the week in which you are notified of being matched with a child for adoption. You must still be employed with the employer in the week before you want to start your leave. You must fulfil strict notice conditions.

Ordinary paternity leave – This is one or two consecutive weeks' leave to support the mother or care for the child. Ordinary paternity leave must be taken within 56 days of the birth or adoption placement. Use form SC3 to notify your employer (available from: www.gov.uk/paternityleave/how-to-claim).
The Paternity & Adoption Leave Regs 2002

Additional paternity leave – This is set at a maximum of 26 weeks. You must be taking time off from work to care for the child. The child's mother or adopter must have previously been entitled to statutory maternity leave or pay, statutory adoption leave or pay, or maternity allowance, and has now returned to work. Additional paternity leave can be taken between 20 weeks and one year after your child is born or placed for adoption. Use the following forms to notify your employer: SC7 for births, SC8 for UK adoptions and SC9 for overseas adoptions (all available from www.gov.uk/paternityleave/how-to-claim).
The Additional Paternity Leave Regs 2010

6. Statutory paternity pay
If you are taking time off work to care for a child, you may be entitled to statutory paternity pay (SPP). There are two types, ordinary and additional, reflecting the two types of leave available (see 5 above). In either case, to be eligible, you must have worked for the same employer for at least 26 weeks by the 15th week before the baby is due or by the week in which you are notified of being matched with a child for adoption. You must have average gross weekly earnings of at least £109. SPP is £136.78 a week or 90% of your average earnings (whichever is less). You must fulfil strict notice conditions; if you have already given your employer notice that you plan to take paternity leave, this can serve for SPP as well.

Ordinary SPP – This is payable for one or two consecutive weeks. It must be taken within eight weeks of the birth or adoption placement.
SSCBA, S.171ZA-E

Additional SPP – This may be paid if the child's mother or adopter was entitled to statutory maternity leave or pay, statutory adoption leave or pay, or maternity allowance, and has now returned to work and any relevant pay has stopped. Additional SPP is only payable during the remainder of your partner's 39-week maternity pay or adoption pay period.
The Additional Statutory Paternity Pay (Gen.) Regs 2010

If you can't get SPP – If you are not eligible for SPP, your employer must give you form OSPP1 (or form ASSP1 for additional paternity pay) explaining why you don't qualify. You may be able to claim income support during paternity leave (see Box E.1, Chapter 15).

7. Rights for adoptive parents

You have a right to 52 weeks' adoption leave if you have worked for the same employer for at least 26 weeks by the week in which you are notified of being matched with a child for adoption. A couple adopting jointly can choose who takes adoption leave and who takes paternity leave.

The Paternity & Adoption Leave Regs 2002, regs 15-27

Statutory adoption pay (SAP) is £136.78 a week or 90% of your average earnings (whichever is less). It can be paid for up to 39 weeks. To qualify for SAP, you must have worked for the same employer for at least 26 weeks by the end of the week in which you are notified of being matched with a child for adoption and have average gross weekly earnings of at least £109. You can continue to be paid SAP if you work for your employer for up to ten days during your adoption pay period.

Adoptive parents can also get parental leave (see 2 above).

SSCBA, S.171ZL-N

8. Unable to work due to sickness or disability?

If you are employed, you may be able to get statutory sick pay (SSP) – see Chapter 9. If you can't get SSP, you may be able to get employment and support allowance (ESA) – see Chapter 10.

If you are entitled to SMP or maternity allowance

You can stay on SSP up until the date of the baby's birth, or the date you are due to start your maternity leave. But if you are off work with a pregnancy-related illness in the last four weeks before the week the baby is due, your statutory maternity pay (SMP) or maternity allowance starts automatically.

SMP Regs, reg 2(4)

SMP – Once your SMP begins, any SSP stops. You can continue to receive ESA while you are on SMP if you continue to satisfy the basic conditions for it (see Chapter 10(9)). Contributory ESA and SMP overlap, so you are paid whichever is higher. SMP is treated as income with respect to income-related ESA, less Class 1 national insurance contributions, tax and half of any contributions you make towards an occupational or personal pension scheme.

ESA Regs, regs 80 & 95(2)(b) & Sch 8, paras 1 & 4

Maternity allowance – You can claim or continue to receive ESA while receiving maternity allowance if you continue to satisfy the basic conditions for it. Contributory ESA and maternity allowance overlap, so you are paid whichever is higher. Maternity allowance is treated in full as income with respect to income-related ESA. You are automatically treated as having a limited capability for work while you are entitled to maternity allowance.

ESA Regs, reg 20(e)

If you are not entitled to SMP or maternity allowance

You may be entitled to ESA from six weeks before the week the baby is due and up to two weeks after the birth if you satisfy the basic conditions (see Chapter 10(9)). You need your maternity certificate, but not medical certificates, and will be treated as having a limited capability for work (see Chapter 11(2)).

You may be able to get ESA outside of these weeks, but must usually pass the limited capability for work assessment and satisfy the basic conditions. You will be treated as having a limited capability for work during your pregnancy if there would be a serious risk to the health of you or your unborn child if you did not refrain from work (see Chapter 11(2)).

ESA Regs, reg 20(d) & (f)

9. When the baby is born

Claim child benefit (see Chapter 38).

A new baby may entitle you to child tax credit for the first time. If you already get this, your entitlement will increase from the date of birth if you notify HMRC within one month. See Chapter 19.

A new baby may mean you can get more help or qualify for the first time for housing benefit (see Chapter 21). Tell your local authority housing benefit section.

Your baby automatically qualifies for free prescriptions.

You have six weeks (21 days in Scotland) to register your baby's birth. When you register the birth, the registrar will give you form GMS1 (EC58 in Scotland). You need to complete this and send it to your GP so your baby can get an NHS card.

See Chapter 23(2) for details of the Sure Start maternity grant.

37 Disabled children

1. What help can you claim?

If your child is disabled, you may be entitled to benefits or services described elsewhere in this Handbook. Your right to some benefits or services will depend only on the effect of your child's disability. Your right to others will depend on your own financial or other circumstances. The benefits checklist on pages 4-5 is a quick guide to the help available. In this chapter we highlight some of the specific help for disabled children. For further information, ring the Contact a Family Helpline (Freephone 0808 808 3555).

From birth

You can register your child with the local authority social care department. You can also apply to the authority for an assessment of your child's special needs.

If your child is registered as blind you may get:
- a disabled child premium in the assessment of your housing benefit and health benefits and a disabled child element with your child tax credit;
- a 50% reduction on your TV licence if you transfer the licence into the child's name.

There is no lower age limit in law for registering a child as blind. Apply in writing to your social care (or social work) department for registration as soon as you are given a diagnosis, or you think one likely. If you experience any difficulty, contact the RNIB (Helpline 0303 123 9999; www.rnib.org.uk).

You may get help from the Family Fund with some of the extra costs arising from a child's disability (see 8 below).

If you have been getting income support, income-related employment and support allowance (ESA), income-based jobseeker's allowance (JSA) or pension credit for at least 26 weeks, you may be eligible for a budgeting loan to help meet one-off costs (see Chapter 24(2). Grants to meet one-off costs are now administered by local authorities; contact your town hall for details.

You may get help with adaptations in the home (see Chapter 31).

You can get vouchers towards milk, fruit and vegetables if you are pregnant or have a child under 4 and get certain means-tested benefits. Pregnant women aged under 18 qualify regardless of whether they get one of these benefits. See Chapter 54(6) for details.

From age 13 weeks

You can be paid the care component of disability living allowance (DLA) for your baby from when they are 3 months old; claim any time beforehand. See 2 below and Chapter 3(14). If your baby is terminally ill (Box B.8, Chapter 4 explains the legal definition), they qualify automatically for the highest rate care component and payment can begin as soon as you claim DLA after the birth.

If your baby is awarded DLA, you may get a disabled child premium included in the assessment of your housing benefit and health benefits, or a disabled child element included in the assessment of your child tax credit. If DLA highest rate care component is awarded, an enhanced disability premium (or for child tax credit, a severely disabled child element) will also be included in the assessment.

If your baby is awarded DLA middle or highest rate care component, you may be eligible for carer's allowance (see Chapter 7).

The new benefit cap (which limits the total weekly benefits that can be claimed; see Box H.1 in Chapter 21) will not apply to your household if your child is awarded DLA.

From 2 years

You can claim a vaccine damage payment (see Chapter 47).

Your child will be eligible for a special educational needs assessment. Local authorities in England and Wales have a duty to identify any child who may have special educational needs. You can ask them to assess your child. If the authority gives you a statement of your child's special educational needs, it should be reviewed at least annually. However, if your child is under 5 the authority should consider reviewing the statement every six months. You can ask for an assessment for a child aged under 2, but the authority is not bound by the legal provisions that apply to older children. In Scotland, there are similar provisions. See Box N.1 for more information.

Education Act 1996, Part IV

You may be able to apply for a Blue Badge for parking concessions once your child is 2 years old. It is possible to apply for a child under 2 if they have a condition that means they must always have bulky equipment out of doors or be near a vehicle in case they need treatment (see Chapter 6(1)).

From 3 years

A disabled child can be paid DLA higher rate mobility component (see 2 below and Chapter 3(9)). Claim from three months beforehand. The higher rate mobility component can give access to leasing or purchasing a car through the Motability scheme (see Box B.16, Chapter 6) and lead to automatic entitlement to a Blue Badge for parking (see Chapter 6(1)).

You can apply for road tax exemption if your child gets higher rate mobility component (see Chapter 6(2)).

From 5 years

A disabled child can be awarded DLA lower rate mobility component. Claim from three months beforehand. It is often awarded to children with a learning disability or sensory impairment, but any disabled child who needs extra supervision or guidance outdoors on unfamiliar routes may qualify (see Chapter 3(13)).

If you get income support, income-related ESA, income-based JSA, pension credit guarantee credit or support under the Immigration and Asylum Act 1999, you are entitled to free school meals for each child attending school. You also qualify if you get child tax credit (but are not eligible for working tax credit) and your taxable income is below £16,190 (£15,910 in Scotland). In Scotland and Northern Ireland, there are also certain circumstances where you can qualify if you get working tax credit alongside child tax credit (in Scotland this applies if your taxable income is less than £6,420; in Northern Ireland it applies if your child attends a nursery, primary or special school and your taxable income is below £16,190).

In some cases you can get a discretionary school clothing grant from the local authority.

If your child has to travel more than two miles to school, the travel is free. For a disabled child, you may get help even if travel to school is less than two miles. Local authorities also have discretion to help meet a parent's travel costs if a child boards in a grant-maintained special school that is some distance from the family home.

From 8 years

If your child has to travel more than three miles to school, travel is free. For a disabled child, you may get help even if travel to school is less than three miles.

From 16 years

At 16, a disabled child has the option of claiming social security benefits in their own right (see Chapter 39).

From June 2013, young people aged 16 or over will no longer be able to make a new claim for DLA and will need to apply for personal independence payment instead. See Chapter 39(2) for details.

2. Disability living allowance

Disability living allowance (DLA) provides help towards the extra costs of bringing up a disabled child. It is paid on top of almost any other income you may have and gives you access to other kinds of help. DLA has two parts:

- **a care component** – for children needing a lot of extra personal care, supervision or watching over because of their disability. This is paid at three different rates. It can be paid from the age of 3 months, or from birth for a terminally ill baby;
- **a mobility component** – a higher rate for children aged 3 years or over who cannot walk or have severe walking difficulties and a lower rate for children aged 5 or over who can walk but who need extra guidance or supervision on unfamiliar routes outdoors. The higher rate may also be paid to children getting the highest rate care component who are severely mentally impaired with extremely disruptive behaviour, and to children who are deaf-blind or who have a severe visual impairment.

See Chapter 3 for details.

3. Carer's allowance

If your child gets the middle or highest rate of disability living allowance care component or the daily living component of personal independence payment at any rate, you may get carer's allowance for looking after them (see Chapter 7). Carer's allowance is not means tested, but if you are working you cannot earn more than £100 a week (after deductions for certain allowable expenses) – see Chapter 7(5).

If you are on a low income and entitled to carer's allowance (even if it cannot be paid because you receive another benefit), you may get a carer premium included in the assessment of your income support, income-related employment and support allowance, income-based jobseeker's allowance or housing benefit (see 4 below and Chapter 25(6)) or an additional amount for carers in your pension credit assessment.

4. Low income benefits

You may be entitled to income support if your income is less than your 'applicable amount' (a set amount representing your weekly living needs) and your savings are no more than £16,000. See Chapter 15.

You may be eligible for income support if you are under pension credit qualifying age (see Chapter 42(2)) and care for a child (regardless of their age) who gets the middle or highest rate disability living allowance (DLA) care component or any rate of the daily living component of personal independence payment (PIP). If your child does not get DLA/PIP at one of these rates, you may still get income support on some other basis (see Box E.1, Chapter 15). For instance, you may be able to claim income support as a lone parent if you are responsible for a child under the age of 5. Normally, you cannot claim income support if you work 16 hours or more a week, but this restriction does not apply if you are eligible for income support as a carer. However, your partner must not be working 24 hours a week or more (unless they too can be treated as a carer for income support).

If you are not eligible for income support, you may get income-based jobseeker's allowance (see Chapter 16). Alternatively, if you have a limited capability for work because of ill health or disability, you may get income-related employment and support allowance (see Chapter 13). If you have reached pension credit qualifying age, you will need to claim pension credit instead (see Chapter 42).

Carer premium – If you or your partner are entitled to carer's allowance, a carer premium (or pension credit equivalent) is included in the assessment (see Chapter 25(6)).

5. Tax credits

Child tax credit (CTC) – This is an income-related payment for people (whether in or out of work) who are responsible for children. A disabled child element is included in the CTC assessment for each child who is registered as blind or gets either disability living allowance (DLA) or personal independence payment (PIP). A further payment, the severely disabled child element, is included for each child who gets DLA highest rate care component or the daily living component of PIP at the enhanced rate. See Chapter 19(10).

Working tax credit (WTC) – This provides financial support for people in (relatively) low-paid work. Only certain groups of people can claim, including lone parents working 16 hours or more a week who have a dependent child. Couples with a dependent child normally need to work at least 24 hours a week, although there are some exceptions (including where one partner works at least 16 hours and their partner is entitled to carer's allowance). These hours can be worked by one parent or shared between the couple, so long as one partner works at least 16 hours. See Chapter 19(5) for more details.

6. Help with housing costs

If you rent your home, you may get housing benefit, whether or not you are working. Your savings must be no more than £16,000 (unless you or your partner receive the guarantee credit of pension credit). See Chapter 21 for details.

The assessment for housing benefit will include:
- a disabled child premium for each child who is registered as blind or who gets disability living allowance (DLA) or personal independence payment (PIP) at any rate;
- an enhanced disability premium for each child who gets DLA highest rate care component or PIP daily living component at the enhanced rate;
- a carer premium if you or your partner are entitled to carer's allowance.

For details of the help available towards council tax, see Chapter 22. You may also get a reduction in your council tax through the Disability Reduction scheme if your child uses a wheelchair indoors or needs an extra room because of their disability (see Chapter 22(8).

Income support, income-based jobseeker's allowance, income-related employment and support allowance and the guarantee credit of pension credit can all include help with mortgage interest payments and interest on a loan used to adapt your home for the special needs of your disabled child (see Chapter 26). If you need adaptations in the home, check first to see if you can get help from social care (Chapter 29) or a disabled facilities grant from your local housing authority

(Chapter 31) or a housing grant in Scotland (see Box K.5, Chapter 31). A disabled facilities grant to meet the needs of a disabled child in England, Wales or Northern Ireland is not means tested.

7. Child support

Most forms of child support maintenance from an ex-partner are fully disregarded as income for all means-tested benefits and tax credits. For details, see Chapter 27(8).

8. Family Fund

The purpose of the Family Fund is to ease the stress on families arising from the day-to-day care of a severely disabled child by providing grants and information. It is an independent charity financed by the government.

Do you qualify? – You can apply for help from the Fund if you are caring at home for a severely disabled child under the age of 18 and you are entitled to tax credits or certain benefits. The Fund is discretionary but works within general guidelines agreed with the government. You cannot get help for a child who is in local authority care.

What kind of help is there? – The Family Fund cannot help with items that should be available from your health or local authority but can complement that support. It can help with:
- holidays or leisure activities for the whole family;
- a washing machine or tumble dryer if you need to do extra washing because of your child's disability;
- bedding and clothing if there is extra wear and tear;
- transport expenses if your child does not get higher rate disability living allowance mobility component but has difficulty getting around;
- driving lessons for your child's main carer;
- play equipment related to your child's special needs.

The Fund will also consider other items related to the care of your child.

Applying to the Family Fund – You can get an application form from the Family Fund, 4 Alpha Court, Monks Cross Drive, York YO32 9WN (0844 974 4099), or apply online (www.familyfund.org.uk). The Fund may ask one of their visitors to arrange to see you if it is the first time you've applied. If you wish to appeal against a decision or make a complaint, you can write to the Chief Executive.

38 Child benefit

1. Do you qualify?

You can get child benefit if you are responsible for a dependent child or qualifying young person, you pass the residence and presence tests and are not subject to immigration control (see Chapter 49(2) and (3)). There is no lower age limit for the child. You do not have to be the parent or stay at home with the child. Child benefit is administered by HMRC.

Dependent child – This is a child under the age of 16.

Qualifying young person – This is a young person under the age of 20 and in full-time, non-advanced education (ie more than 12 hours a week at school or college) or approved, unwaged training. The training must not be provided under a contract of employment. Nineteen-year-olds can only be included if they started such education or approved training before their 19th birthday (or were accepted or enrolled to undertake it). You cannot count homework, private study, unsupervised study or meal breaks towards the 12 hours and the education can only be up to and including A-level, NVQ Level 3 or equivalent. If the young person becomes entitled to employment and support allowance, income support, income-based jobseeker's allowance or any tax credit, you cannot get child benefit for them.

SSCBA, S.142 & CB Regs, regs 1, 2, 3 & 8

What happens when the young person leaves school?
If the young person has left school, college or approved unwaged training you can continue to be entitled to child benefit for them until the first Sunday after the 'terminal date', which is the first of the following dates after the young person's education or approved training ceases: the last day in February, May, August or November.

CB Regs, reg 7(2)

Child benefit extension period – When a 16/17-year-old ceases education or approved training, you may continue to be entitled to child benefit during the *'child benefit extension period'*, which lasts for 20 weeks starting from the Monday following the week in which the young person ceased to be in education or training. To be entitled to child benefit during the extension period you:

■ must write and ask for benefit to continue within three months of the education or training finishing; *and*
■ must have been entitled to child benefit immediately before the extension period began.

The young person must be:

■ under 18 and not in education or training; *and*
■ registered for work, education or training, as directed by Jobcentre Plus; *and*
■ not working for 24 hours or more a week.

CB Regs, reg 5

Other conditions
You cannot get child benefit if:

■ the child or young person is in local authority care or in detention for more than eight weeks unless they regularly stay with you for at least one day each week (midnight to midnight). But you can get child benefit if the child or young person is home for seven consecutive days plus an extra one week's benefit if they are at home for at least one day at the end of that seven days;
■ you get an allowance as the foster carer or prospective adopter of a child or young person placed with you by a local authority;
■ the young person is married, in a civil partnership or cohabiting.

SSCBA, Sch 9, paras 1 & 3; CB Regs, regs 12, 13 & 16

2. How much do you get?
For an only or eldest child (or qualifying young person), you will receive £20.30 a week. For each other child or qualifying young person, you will receive £13.40 a week. These rates were frozen for three years from April 2011.

Does child benefit affect means-tested benefits? – Child benefit is ignored when calculating entitlement to working tax credit, child tax credit, income-related employment and support allowance, housing benefit, income support and income-based jobseeker's allowance (unless your claim for one of the latter two benefits began before April 2004 and you continue to receive support for your children through it).

Child dependants' additions – If you are still entitled to a child dependant's addition with another benefit, the addition is reduced to £8.10 if you get the higher £20.30 rate of child benefit for that child or young person.

The income tax charge
From January 2013, the value of your child benefit will be reduced through a tapered income tax charge if you, or your partner, have an *'adjusted net income'* (ie your income less things like pension contributions) of over £50,000 for the tax year. If both you and your partner have adjusted net income of over £50,000, the one with the higher income is liable for the charge (regardless of who receives the child benefit).

The charge is equal to 100% of child benefit received if your income is £60,000 or more, or a sliding scale from 0% to 99% of child benefit received if your income is between £50,000 and £60,000.

You can elect not to receive child benefit if you or your partner do not wish to pay the new charge. You may subsequently decide to withdraw that election if you or your partner are no longer liable to pay the charge.

More information is available on the independent revenue benefits website (www.revenuebenefits.org.uk/child-benefit/policy/policy-changes/).

3. Who should claim it?
The person responsible for the child or young person must make the claim and must be living with them or be contributing at least the rate of child benefit for their support.

SSCBA, S.143(1)

People who get child benefit for a child under 12 are entitled to 'credits for parents and carers' (see Box D.7, Chapter 12). These can protect the amount of state pension you may get. So if your national insurance contribution record is affected because you are bringing up children, it is important to claim child benefit.

More than one person can be eligible for child benefit for the same child, but only one person can be paid.

4. How do you claim?
Just after your baby is born you should receive an information pack containing a child benefit claim-pack. If you don't receive one, you can get a CH2 claim-form by ringing the Child Benefit Helpline (see below) or downloading one from www.hmrc.gov.uk/childbenefit.

You will be asked to send the birth or adoption certificate with the form, but do not wait. You can send certificates later. Send everything to the Child Benefit Office (see inside back cover).

Don't delay making your claim. It can only be backdated for three months from the date HMRC receives it.

For more information contact the Child Benefit Helpline (0845 302 1444; textphone 0845 302 1474).

5. What happens after you claim?
The birth or adoption certificate will be returned to you and you will be sent a written decision. Benefit is normally paid 4-weekly in arrears unless this would cause 'hardship'; in that case you must write to HMRC saying why you want weekly payments. You have the choice of payment into a bank, building society or Post Office card account (see Chapter 57(5)). If your claim is not successful or is stopped later, you can appeal against the decision (see Chapter 58).

The benefit cap – Child benefit is included in the list of benefits to which the 'benefit cap' applies. The cap limits the total weekly benefits that can be claimed to £500 for lone parents and couples, and £350 for single claimants. See Box H.1 in Chapter 21 for details (including exemptions).

6. Guardian's allowance
This is a tax-free benefit for anyone looking after children who are effectively orphans. You can get guardian's allowance if you are responsible for a child who is not your birth or adopted child and both parents of the child are dead, or one is dead and the other is:

■ missing; *or*
■ divorced or had their civil partnership dissolved and liable for neither custody or maintenance of the child; *or*

■ serving a prison sentence of more than two years from the date the other parent dies; *or*
■ detained in a hospital under certain sections of the Mental Health Act 1983 (or equivalents).

SSCBA, S.77(2) & Guardian's Allowance (Gen.) Regs, regs 6 & 7

Guardian's allowance is £15.90 a week and does not depend on your income or savings or whether you have paid national insurance contributions. It can be paid in addition to child benefit. Guardian's allowance is included in the list of benefits to which the 'benefit cap' applies (see 5 above). Claim on form BG1 and send it to the Guardian's Allowance Unit at the Child Benefit Office.

39 Young disabled people

1. Becoming a claimant
At 16 you can claim benefits in your own right, even if you are still at school. If your parents are still entitled to child benefit and child tax credit for you as a 'qualifying young person' (see Chapter 38(1)) these payments will stop if you claim employment and support allowance, jobseeker's allowance, income support or tax credits. It is important to get a 'better-off' calculation, as you and your family may be worse off if you do claim in your own right.

Appointeeship – If you were entitled to disability living allowance as a child, the DWP will have authorised your parents or someone else responsible for you to claim on your behalf. When you are 16, the DWP will review the arrangement by conducting a home visit. If you are mentally capable of managing your money yourself or with support, the authorisation should end. If you are unable to act for yourself, the DWP can change the authorisation into an 'appointeeship', which will be extended to all the social security benefits you receive. See Chapter 57(4).

2. From disability living allowance to personal independence payment
From 8.4.13, personal independence payment (PIP) is replacing disability living allowance (DLA) for people aged 16 to 64 inclusive. DLA remains in place for children until their 16th birthday. If you turn 16 on or after 8.4.13, whether you can renew your DLA or claim PIP will depend on the date of your birthday.

If you turn 16 before 7.10.13, you will be able to renew your claim for DLA; if you are awarded DLA on renewal, you will re-assessed under PIP at a later date. See Chapter 3(27) for details of DLA for people aged 16 and over.

If you turn 16 on or after 7.10.13, you will be re-assessed under PIP (unless your existing DLA award was made under the special rules – see Box B.8 in Chapter 4). Your parent or guardian will be sent a letter about this process when you reach the age of 15 years and 7 months (which could be from May 2013). They will be asked if you need an appointee and about your preferred methods of communication. Your DLA will continue to be paid until a decision on your PIP entitlement is made. See Chapter 4 for more on PIP, and Box B.6 in that chapter for more on the re-assessment process.

3. Employment and support allowance
Employment and support allowance (ESA) can be paid from your 16th birthday. Entitlement depends on getting through the work capability assessment (see Chapter 11). ESA has two separate elements: contributory ESA and income-related ESA. You may be entitled to either one or both (see Chapter 13(5)).

Contributory ESA – To be entitled to contributory ESA, you must normally satisfy the national insurance contribution conditions (see Chapter 12(6)). Prior to 1.5.12, the requirement to satisfy the contribution conditions could be waived if your limited capability for work began before the age of 20 (or 25 in some cases). This would enable you to receive *'contributory ESA in youth'* (CESA(Y)).

If you were already receiving CESA(Y) by 1.5.12 and are in the work-related activity group (see Chapter 10(6)) it can only be paid for a maximum of 12 months. This period will include any time already spent on CESA(Y) prior to 1.5.12. If you are in the support group (see Chapter 10(7)), the 12-month time limit for existing CESA(Y) awards will not apply.

For details on CESA(Y), see the *Disability Rights Handbook* 36th edition, page 63.

Income-related ESA – You can be paid this from the start of the claim if you satisfy all the usual conditions of entitlement, including the rules on income and capital (see Chapter 13).

Late claims – If you miss claiming ESA from your 16th birthday, your award can be backdated for up to three months (see Chapter 10(12)).

ESA rates – ESA basic allowances and components are generally paid at rates unconnected to age (see Chapter 10(8)). However, in the 13-week assessment phase, the basic allowance of ESA for 16-24-year-olds is paid at the lower rate of £56.80. In the main phase, basic allowances and additional components are paid at the same rate regardless of age.

4. ESA and full-time education
CESA(Y) and income-related ESA have different rules about the hours and type of education you can undertake without affecting your entitlement.

CESA(Y) – If you are aged 16, 17 or 18, you are normally excluded from CESA(Y) if you are in school or full-time education of 21 hours or more a week. Lunch breaks, breaks between lessons, free periods and periods of private (unsupervised) study or homework do not count. From age 19, there are no rules limiting the hours and type of study you can do. When adding up the number of hours you study each week, you should ignore *'any instruction or tuition which is not suitable for persons of the same age who do not have a disability'*.

ESA Regs, reg 12; R(S)/87

Income-related ESA – If you don't qualify for contributory ESA, you may qualify for income-related ESA. If you are in full-time education, you must be entitled to disability living allowance or personal independence payment to qualify. You will be then be treated as having a limited capability for work without having to pass the work capability assessment. You may be sent an ESA50 form to assess whether you meet the criteria for the work-related activity group (see Chapter 10(6)) or the support group (see Chapter 10(7)). If you are in the work-related activity group, you will still have to attend work-focused interviews and take part in work-related activity. For details, see Chapter 13(4).

ESA Regs, reg 18

5. Income support
You can claim income support instead of employment and support allowance if you fit into one of the categories listed in Box E.1, Chapter 15.

In education – If you have no parents or are living away from your parents for one of the reasons listed in Chapter 15(5), you can claim income support if you are under 21 and have enrolled on, been accepted for or are undertaking a course of full-time non-advanced education. You can still claim if you are aged 21, if you were already on the course when you reached that age.

6. Universal credit
The government is replacing means-tested benefits (including income-related employment and support allowance and income support) with universal credit. This is being piloted from April in north-west England; nationwide roll-out starts in October 2013 on the basis of one district in each Jobcentre Plus region. You cannot get universal credit if you are age 16 or 17 unless you:
- have a limited capability for work under the work capability assessment (see Chapter 11(2)) or are still waiting to be assessed;
- have regular and substantial caring responsibilities for a severely disabled person;
- are responsible for a child;
- are a member of a couple and your partner is responsible for a child or qualifying young person (see Chapter 38(1));
- are pregnant, between 11 weeks before and 15 weeks after the expected date of the birth of your baby; *or*
- are without parental support.

UC Regs, reg 8
For more on universal credit, see Box J.1 in Chapter 25.

40 Financing studies

1. Loans, grants and bursaries
Financial support for new students in higher education comes in the form of tuition fee loans, means-tested loans for living expenses, and supplementary grants and institutional bursaries and scholarships for students in particular circumstances (see Box N.4).

Entitlement to student support depends on where you are studying and where you are from. Contact:
- Student Finance England, if you live in England;
- Student Finance Northern Ireland, if you live in Northern Ireland;
- the Student Awards Agency for Scotland (SAAS), if you live in Scotland;
- Student Finance Wales, if you live in Wales.

See Box N.4 for contact details.

Fees – Universities and colleges across the UK can charge up to £9,000 a year for full-time undergraduate courses. Institutions in Northern Ireland charge up to £3,465 a year for students from Northern Ireland. Students from Scotland studying in Scotland on their first higher education course are exempt from tuition fees. Students from Scotland studying elsewhere in the UK follow the same rules as students from England, Northern Ireland and Wales regarding fees, but support will be different. Students in Wales can get a grant towards the cost of any fees above £3,575.

Full-time loan
Eligible students can apply for student loans for living costs and tuition fees. You begin to pay back the loan once you reach a certain salary level. If you receive a maintenance grant (see below), the maximum loan for living costs you can receive will be reduced. For further information, go to

www.gov.uk/browse/education/student-finance or the website of the equivalent funding body in Northern Ireland, Scotland or Wales (see Box N.4).

Grants and bursaries
Maintenance grant – In England, grants of up to £3,354 are available, depending on household income. An income-assessed 'special support grant' of up to £3,354 is payable, instead of the maintenance grant, to students eligible for means-tested benefits. It will be disregarded in the assessment of entitlement to those benefits. Welsh students from lower-income households may be eligible for an Assembly Learning Grant of up to £5,131. In Northern Ireland a maximum grant of £3,475 is payable.

Institutional bursaries and scholarships – Universities and colleges in England charging more than £6,000 must have measures in place to recruit students from poorer backgrounds and support them when they are studying. Each university has its own scheme, but they generally include means-tested bursaries and scholarships. Some students whose household income is less than £25,000 a year may get help through the National Scholarship Programme (NSP). NSP funding can be worth £3,000 or more, made up of partial fee-waivers, a free foundation year, cash and accommodation bursaries. Students in Northern Ireland and Wales should ask universities and colleges directly about extra bursaries to students receiving the full maintenance grant.

Part-time students
Part-time students from England starting courses from September 2012 and studying at least 25% of the intensity of the equivalent full-time course can apply for tuition fee loans on the same basis as full-time students. Part-time students in England are not eligible for living cost loans or grants. Part-time students from Northern Ireland and Wales on courses involving at least half the hours of a full-time course and who are on low incomes can apply for a means-tested fee grant and course grant to help with course expenses, books and travel. Part-time students from Scotland studying in Scotland can apply for a grant from SAAS towards fees and other study costs.

N.2 Rates of grants and loans (2013/14)

Student grants (England)
Maintenance grant
English students enrolled September 2012 onwards – Up to £3,354 payable with full grant below £25,000 income, reducing to nil above £42,600.
English students enrolled 2009/10 to 2011/12 – Up to £3,080 payable with full grant below £25,000 income, reducing to nil above £50,706. (There is a higher upper threshold for 2008 entry students and lower thresholds for pre-2008 entry students.)

Part-time grants
English students who started before September 2012 can receive a variable tuition fee grant, depending on income and payable at one of three rates: for a course studied at between 50-59% of the intensity of a full-time course, the maximum is £845; for 60-74%, £1,015; for 75% plus, £1,270. An additional non-repayable grant of up to £275 can help meet the costs of books, travel and course expenditure.

Note: For the grants elsewhere in the UK, contact the relevant funding body.

Supplementary grants

If you are on a designated course and funded by Student Finance in England, Northern Ireland or Wales, and meet the residency criteria, you may be eligible for supplementary grants including:

- disabled students' allowances (DSAs) – see below;
- parents' learning allowance and childcare grant – for full-time students with dependent children;
- adult dependants' grant;
- travel costs, if you attend a clinical placement in the UK as part of your full-time course in medicine or dentistry or a college or university outside the UK.

Dependants' grants and grants for students with child dependants and travel costs are means tested. Previous study may prevent you getting maintenance grants and help with tuition fees but does not affect entitlement to supplementary grants. In Scotland similar grants are available for single parents and students with adult dependants; contact the SAAS for details.

Disabled students' allowances – DSAs are not means tested. They are for additional disability-related costs of study, covering specialist equipment, non-medical helpers and general or other expenditure. Full- or part-time postgraduates in the UK can get DSAs if they do not receive an equivalent award from their Research Council (or similar organisation). For rates, see Box N.2. To receive a DSA, you will require a needs assessment to identify your extra study-related needs. Your awarding authority will advise on the process. For more information see Box N.4 and ask the Student Finance body for the leaflet *Bridging the gap*.

Other financial support

Other sources of financial support include:

Access to Learning Fund, Discretionary and Support Funds – Funds available to students experiencing financial hardship are known as the Access to Learning Fund (England), Support Fund (Northern Ireland), Discretionary Fund (Scotland) and Financial Contingency Funds scheme (Wales). Contact the student support officer responsible for financial advice at your educational institution.

Education maintenance allowance (EMA) – This is a term-time payment of £30 a week for eligible students, depending on household income. Students must attend school or college from Year 12 and follow a course up to level 3. EMA is not available to students in England.

16-19 Bursary Fund (England) – This scheme is made up of two elements. The first element is a bursary of £1,200 a year payable to students who are:

- in care or have left care;
- getting income support; *or*
- getting employment and support allowance and either disability living allowance or personal independence payment.

The second element is a Discretionary Fund for students who need help with the costs of transport, food or equipment. The school or college decides how much to pay and when to pay it. Payments may be in kind, eg a transport pass, and can be linked to behaviour or attendance.

NHS bursaries – These are for NHS-funded places on health professional courses.

Postgraduate courses – Financial support may be available from a range of sources (eg from the Research Councils, your university or charitable trusts), depending on your subject.

Professional and Career Development Loans – These are for vocational courses, sponsored by the government and offered by banks. You can borrow £300 to £10,000, but if you have a poor credit rating you may not receive this support.

Charities and trusts – Trusts will not usually provide your main source of finance, but may give top-ups or pay for a special need. Some trusts give small grants or loans to students with disabilities who are in particular difficulty. See Box N.4.

2. Students and means-tested benefits

This section covers the position of disabled students under 20 on advanced courses, and 20 or over in full-time advanced or non-advanced education. See Chapter 39 for the position of disabled students under 20 on non-advanced courses.

When claiming means-tested benefits, you are treated as a full-time student from the date your course starts through to the last day of the course, or earlier if you completely abandon or are dismissed from the course.

Disabled students' allowances (DSAs)

The figures shown are English rates and are the maximum in each case for disability-related costs of study. For rates elsewhere in the UK, contact the relevant funding body (see Box N.4).

Major items

Specialist equipment	£5,161 per course

Non-medical helper

Full-time course	£20,520 a year
Part-time course up to 75%	£15,390 a year

General/other expenditure

Full-time course	£1,724 a year
Part-time course up to 75%	£1,293 a year

Postgraduate (maximum DSA) £10,260 a year
For postgraduate courses in England and Wales there is one allowance for all costs. PGCE/ITT courses are eligible for DSAs at undergraduate rates. DSAs for postgraduate study in Scotland and most Research Council-funded study are the same as undergraduate rates.

Travel: Extra travel costs incurred because of disability, not normally for everyday travel costs: no maximum amount.

Student loans
Tuition fees

Tuition fees vary according to the country in which students study. Universities and colleges can charge up to £9,000 a year for full-time undergraduate courses. Tuition fee loans are available to cover the costs; they are paid direct to the institution. You must start repaying the loan in instalments after you finish the course and are earning over a certain amount. Institutions in Northern Ireland charge a maximum of £3,575 a year to students from Northern Ireland. Most Scottish students studying in Scotland do not pay tuition fees for full-time courses.

Living costs

Place of residence	Full year	Final year
Parental home	£4,375	£4,020
London	£7,675	£6,990
Elsewhere	£5,500	£5,115

These rates are for English students who started higher education in September 2012 or later. Rates for students who started their course before September 2012 are different; contact Student Finance England for details (see Box N.4). For the rates elsewhere in the UK, contact the relevant funding body.

Whether your course is full time or part time usually depends on how it is classed by the institution. However, a course of government-funded further education in England or Wales is full time if it involves more than 16 guided learning hours a week. In Scotland, it is full time if structured learning packages make up the hours to over 16 and up to 21 a week.
ESA regs, reg 131; IS Regs, reg 61

Part-time students – If you are eligible for income-related employment and support allowance (ESA) or income support under the usual rules you can study part time.

Couples – If your partner is not a student they may be able to claim means-tested benefits in the normal way.

Income-related ESA
Chapter 13 deals with the rules for claiming income-related ESA. Full-time students can claim only if they are entitled to disability living allowance or personal independence payment.
ESA regs, reg 18

If you qualify for income-related ESA as a full-time student and are not a qualifying young person for child benefit purposes (see Chapter 38(1)), you will be treated as having a limited capability for work (see Chapter 11(2)) without having to pass the work capability assessment.
ESA regs, reg 33(2)

Income support
Chapter 15 deals with the main rules for income support. You are eligible for income support during term time and all the vacations if you fit into one of the following categories:
- you have been receiving income support on the grounds of disability or incapacity since before 27.10.08 and have not yet been transferred to ESA (See Chapter 14(1)); *and*
  - your applicable amount includes a disability or severe disability premium; *or*
  - you have been incapable of work (or entitled to statutory sick pay) for 28 weeks; *or*
  - you are claiming disabled students' allowance (DSA) because of deafness;
- you are a lone parent with a child under 5. If your child was aged over 5 years on 21.5.12, transitional rules can protect your claim as long as your income support does not stop for any reason during your course. If you started a full-time course between 25.10.10 and 20.5.12, you can continue to claim income support until your course ends or until your youngest child reaches 7, whichever comes first. If you started your course between 26.10.09 and 24.10.10, your claim can be protected until your youngest child reaches 10. If you started before 25.10.09, your claim can be protected until your youngest child reaches 12;
- you are a refugee on a course learning English;
- you have limited leave in the UK subject to 'no recourse to public funds' and have a temporary problem getting funds from your usual source.

If you are single or a student couple (ie both of you are full-time students) and you have responsibility for a child or young person, you can claim income support during the summer vacation if you are eligible under the usual rules (see Box E.1, Chapter 15). Alternatively, you could claim jobseeker's allowance (JSA) if you are available for work (see 4 below).
IS Regs reg 4ZA & Sch 1B

Pension credit
Pension credit is not affected by any type of study you do. Student loans and grants are completely ignored as income.

Housing benefit
Most students on full-time courses are excluded from housing benefit until their course ends. However, you can claim housing benefit if you:

- get income-related ESA, income support or income-based JSA as a full-time student;
- have or are treated as having a limited capability for work under ESA rules for a continuous period of 28 weeks (two or more periods of limited capability can be added together if they are no more than 12 weeks apart);
- qualify for a disability premium or severe disability premium, or you have been incapable of work for 28 weeks or you qualify for a DSA because of deafness;
- are a lone parent with a dependent child under 16 or qualifying young person under 20;
- are one of a couple and your partner is not a student. Your partner can claim housing benefit (the student rules will apply to your income);
- are one of a couple, your partner is also a student and you have a dependent child. You will be eligible for housing benefit throughout the course (not just in the summer vacation as for JSA and income support);
- or your partner have reached the qualifying age for pension credit (see Chapter 42(2));
- can get housing benefit temporarily while waiting to return to your course after an agreed break because you were ill or had to care for someone. You can get housing benefit once you have recovered or your caring responsibilities have ended until either the date you return to your course or the date your education establishment has agreed you can return to your course, whichever is earlier, but only for a maximum period of one year and providing you are not eligible for a student loan or grant during this time;
- you are under 21 and a full-time student on a non-advanced course (the age limit can be extended to under 22, if you turned 21 while on the course), or you are a 'qualifying young person' for child benefit purposes (see Chapter 38(1)).
HB Regs, reg 56

Living in student accommodation – If you are eligible for housing benefit you can claim if you are renting accommodation provided by the educational establishment.
HB Regs, reg 57

Two homes – If you have a partner and have to live in two separate homes while you are on the course, you can get housing benefit for both homes only if you are eligible for housing benefit as a student.
HB Regs, regs 7(6)(b)

Non-dependant deductions – If you are a full-time student living in someone else's home as a non-dependant, no deduction is made from the householder's housing benefit during your period of study, including summer vacations. If you get a job (for 16 or more hours a week) during the summer vacation, a non-dependant deduction will be applied.
HB Regs, reg 74(7)(c)-(e)

Size criteria restriction – If you are a full-time student living away from your normal home, for the purpose of calculating the householder's housing benefit you will still count as occupying a room for up to 52 weeks' absence.

Universal credit
Once universal credit has been introduced (see Chapter 1(2) and Box J.1 in Chapter 25), you will not normally be able to claim the benefit if you are undertaking:
- a course of full-time advanced education (ie a course leading to a first degree or postgraduate degree, a higher education or higher national diploma or any other course of a standard above advanced GNVQ or equivalent);
- any other full-time course of study or training and are supported by a loan, grant or bursary; *or*
- any other course of study or training that is not compatible with any work-related requirements that have been placed on you by a DWP personal adviser.
WRA 2012, S.4(1)(d); UC Regs, reg 12

You will be able to claim universal credit as a student (and not be ignored for the purposes of calculating the universal credit maximum amount) if you:

■ are in non-advanced education, are under the age of 21 (or are 21 and reached that age whilst undertaking the course) and have no parental support;

■ are entitled to attendance allowance, disability living allowance or personal independence payment *and* you have a limited capability for work (see Chapter 11(2));

■ are responsible for a child or 'qualifying young person' (see Chapter 38(1));

■ are a single foster parent;

■ are one of a couple, your partner is also a student and they are responsible for a child or qualifying young person (including as a foster parent); *or*

■ are over the qualifying age for pension credit (see Chapter 42(2)) and you have a partner who has not reached that age.

UC Regs; reg 14

3. Effect of a loan, grant or bursary

The way in which loans, grants or bursaries affect income-related employment and support allowance (ESA), income support, income-based jobseeker's allowance (JSA) and housing benefit depends on whether the income is intended for living costs or course costs, and on the period of time it is intended to cover. In general, loans, grants or bursaries specifically intended to cover course costs are disregarded. Course costs include tuition fees, examination fees, travel, books and equipment. Amounts intended to cover maintenance of a dependent child or childcare costs are disregarded.

If you are entitled to a student loan, it is treated as income regardless of whether you actually take it or not. This rule will not apply to any income-related ESA you claim if you have to suspend your course because of illness.

Period of study – In general, loans, grants and bursaries that cannot be disregarded are taken into account over the period for which they are payable. How your loan counts as income depends on what year of the course you are on.

❑ In your first year, the loan income will be disregarded until the first day of the first term.

❑ Between your first and final year, the loan is usually taken into account from the start of the first benefit week in September until the end of the last benefit week in June (42 or 43 weeks).

❑ In your final year, the loan is divided by the number of weeks from the start of the first benefit week in September until the benefit week that coincides with the last day of your course.

ESA Regs, reg 137; IS Regs, reg 66A

Box N.3 lists different types of student support and how they count as income for assessing income-related ESA, income support, income-based JSA and housing benefit.

Other payments

Access to Learning and other hardship funds – Rules differ according to how the funds will be used.

❑ A payment intended to cover one-off costs counts as capital. This will be disregarded for 52 weeks unless it is intended for daily living expenses, in which case it will be taken into account immediately. *'Daily living expenses'* can include food, ordinary clothing, rent eligible for housing benefit, fuel and water charges.

❑ Payments made in instalments count as income. This income will be disregarded in full unless the payment is for daily living expenses, in which case £20 a week will be disregarded.

❑ Payments intended to bridge the gap before starting a course or receiving the student loan are disregarded even if they are intended to cover daily living expenses.

ESA regs, reg 138, IS Regs, reg 66B

N.3 Student support and means-tested benefits

Type of student support	Counted as income
Full-time student maintenance loan The maximum loan you are entitled to is treated as income, whatever amount you actually borrow.	Yes

If you don't apply for a loan, the decision maker will still take into account the maximum loan you could have got if you had applied.

Where the parents or partner of a disabled student are unable or unwilling to meet their assessed contribution to a loan or grant in full, only the actual contribution is taken into account.

Loan disregards
When your benefit is worked out, £10 a week of your loan is disregarded. In addition, disregard the following:
a) £303 a year for travel costs from a loan (academic year 2012/13); *and*
b) £390 a year for books and equipment from a loan (academic year 2012/13).

Tuition fees loan The loan is paid direct to the university.	No
Disabled students' allowance and travel expenses grant	No
Childcare grant and parents' learning allowance	No
Special support grant	No
Maintenance grant This counts in full as income and is divided over the same period as the student loan.	Yes

If you are not eligible for a student loan, the equivalent disregard for travel and books applies.

Adult dependants' grant This counts in full as income and is divided over the same period as the student loan.	Yes
Institutional bursaries and scholarships If the bursary is to help with course costs	No
If the payments are for living costs	Yes
NHS and social work bursaries and grants Amounts for travel expenses, course costs and childcare are disregarded. The bursary is divided over 52 weeks.	Yes
Social work incentive bursary (studying in Northern Ireland) Amounts intended to cover course and travel costs	No
Postgraduate awards	Yes
Professional and Career Development Loans The part intended to cover fees/examination costs	No
Amounts intended for everyday living expenses	Yes

These parts of the loan are divided over the number of weeks of study for which the loan was paid.

Voluntary or charitable payments – One-off or irregular payments are treated as capital. Regular payments are disregarded as income (see Chapter 27(7)).

Leaving early? – If you stop being a full-time student before the end of your course, a loan may continue to be taken into account but without any disregard, whether or not you repay all or part of it. Grants that must be repaid continue to be taken into account as income until you've repaid them or until the end of the term or vacation when you left the course.

ESA regs, reg 91(4) & 104(4)-(7), IS Regs, reg 29(2B) & 40(3A)-(3AB)

N.4 For more information

Careers help

In England, schools currently provide careers advice to 14-16-year-olds. Face-to-face guidance is very limited and schools instead provide web, email and phone support. Local authorities have a duty to focus on supporting disadvantaged groups. Disabled young people should be able to get careers advice up to the age of 25 if they have an S.139A learning difficulty assessment.

The National Careers Services provides advice online and through a helpline and webchat to those aged 13 or over. A face-to-face service is available to those aged 19 or over. Adults with a disability, learning difficulty or health condition should get at least three face-to-face sessions. Contact: 0800 100 900; nationalcareersservice. direct.gov.uk.

For advice in Scotland and Wales, contact Skills Development Scotland (www.skillsdevelopmentscotland. co.uk/) and Careers Wales (www.careerswales.com)

If you have left higher education, you can use the careers service where you studied or at your nearest university. You should be able to visit for up to three years after graduation. Prospects has an extensive graduate careers website (www.prospects.ac.uk).

Contact a disability employment adviser at Jobcentre Plus about further education and training (see Chapter 18(1)).

Student grants and loans

For information on student grants, loans and entitlement, contact the relevant funding body:

- **England**: Student Finance England (0845 300 5090; www.studentfinanceengland.co.uk/)
- **Northern Ireland**: Student Finance Northern Ireland (0845 600 0662; www.studentfinanceni.co.uk)
- **Scotland**: Student Awards Agency for Scotland (0300 555 0505; www.saas.gov.uk)
- **Wales**: Student Finance Wales (0845 602 8845; www.studentfinancewales.co.uk)

For information on:

- repayment of student loans, contact: The Student Loans Company, 100 Bothwell Street, Glasgow G2 7JD (0845 026 2019; www.slc.co.uk)
- Professional and Career Development Loans, contact: the National Careers Service (0800 100 900; www. gov.uk/career-development-loans)
- Access to Learning Fund: ask your student union, personal tutor or welfare office

Charities and trusts

An information booklet for disabled students, *Funding from charitable trusts*, is available to download free at www.disabilityrightsuk.org/funding-charitable-trusts

4. Other benefits

Jobseeker's allowance (JSA)

Students on full-time courses are normally excluded from JSA until the end of their course, or until they abandon it or are dismissed from it. However, if you are single or have a partner who is also a student and you are responsible for a child or young person, you can get JSA during the summer vacation if you are available for work.

You can get JSA temporarily while waiting to return to your course after an agreed break because you were ill or had to care for someone. The rules are the same as for housing benefit (see 2 above). For details on JSA, see Chapter 16.

JSA Regs, reg 1(3D)

Contributory employment and support allowance (ESA)

In general, contributory ESA is payable during vacations and term time and is not paid at a reduced rate because of any grant or loan you get. However, if you are under 19 you may be caught by the full-time education exclusion (see Chapter 39(4)). If your contributory ESA ends after 12 months of claiming, you may become eligible to claim income-related ESA (see Chapter 13) if you are entitled to disability living allowance (DLA) or personal independence payment (PIP). *Note:* To be entitled to ESA you must go through the work capability assessment (see Chapter 11). In considering your ability to carry out the activities in this assessment, Jobcentre Plus will look at how you manage in your daily life, including the time you attend your course. When starting a course you must declare this as a change of circumstances. This may trigger a reconsideration of your benefit, but does not necessarily mean you will lose it.

DLA and PIP

DLA (see Chapter 3) and PIP (see Chapter 4) are not means tested, so grant or loan income will not affect the amount of your benefit. There are no rules that restrict the hours or type of study you can do. However, starting an education course may suggest that your care or mobility needs have changed, so your benefit entitlement could be reconsidered. From October 2013, if you get DLA and report a change in your care or mobility needs, you will be re-assessed under PIP (see Box B.6 in Chapter 4).

DLA, PIP and student support – If your college or university provides you with care and assistance, it may claim some, or all, of your DLA care component or PIP daily living component towards their costs. The care component or daily living component will stop if you are living in a residential college that counts as a 'care home' (see Chapter 4(8) for the definition; the rules are the same for DLA).

Students in higher education requiring help with personal care to follow a course can claim disabled students' allowances to cover the cost of academic non-medical helpers (see 1 above and Box N.2). For basic personal care you should apply for assistance from your adult social care department (see Chapter 29).

Disability Rights UK publications

Into Higher Education

For disabled students thinking about studying in higher education:

- how to choose a course
- how to apply
- what support will be available
- accessibility and personal care

Free download available from
www.disabilityrightsuk.org

This section of the Handbook looks at:

Retirement

41 Benefits in retirement

1. What benefits can you get?

You can claim state pension once you reach *'state pension age'*, currently 65 for men and 60 for women born before 6.4.50. Changes to state pension age are underway; see Chapter 43(2) for details. Pension credit is a means-tested benefit for people who have reached the qualifying age. See Chapter 42 for details.

This chapter looks at other benefits you may be able to get at state pension age. Sometimes you need to decide whether to draw state pension or receive another benefit instead. Some benefits, such as attendance allowance, can be paid in addition to state pension.

2. What if you go on working?

You can claim state pension at state pension age whether or not you go on working. If you put off claiming state pension, you may be able to earn extra state pension or receive a one-off taxable lump-sum payment (see Chapter 43(7)).

If you work after state pension age you will not have to pay national insurance contributions. You will need to give your employer an 'age exception certificate'; if you make a claim for state pension shortly before state pension age, there will be information about this in the pack you are sent. Alternatively, you can get the certificate by calling the HMRC national insurance helpline (0845 302 1479).

SSCBA, Ss.6(2) & 11(2)

Statutory sick pay – If you are employed, are earning £107 a week or more, and have been sick for four or more days in a row, claim statutory sick pay from your employer. There is no age limit.

3. Employment and support allowance and incapacity benefit

If you receive long-term incapacity benefit or employment and support allowance, it will stop when you reach state pension age. You should claim state pension instead.

SSCBA, S.30A(5); WRA, S.1(3)(c)

4. Carer's allowance

There is no upper age limit for claiming carer's allowance but you must satisfy the usual conditions of entitlement (see Chapter 7(2)).

If you are entitled to carer's allowance after state pension age you may not appear to be better off due to the overlapping benefit rules. Carer's allowance overlaps with state pension, so once you reach state pension age and draw your pension,

carer's allowance can only continue to be paid if your state pension is less than £58.45 a week (the rate of carer's allowance). However, even if your carer's allowance is overlapped, it is often still worth claiming because it can increase your income from pension credit or housing benefit through the carer addition or carer premium (see below).

OB Regs, reg 4(1)&(5)

If you were 65 or over and entitled to invalid care allowance on 27.10.02, your carer's allowance continues even if you no longer care for a disabled person or you start earning over £100 a week. Otherwise, you must continue to satisfy the conditions of entitlement for carer's allowance in order to receive it after the age of 65.

Carer addition and carer premium – While you receive carer's allowance, or would receive it but for the overlapping benefit rules, your *'appropriate minimum guarantee'* for pension credit includes a carer addition of £32.60, or your *'applicable amount'* for housing benefit includes a carer premium of the same amount. This means you may start receiving higher levels of these benefits when you are awarded carer's allowance, or you may become entitled to benefit for the first time.

As explained above, if you were aged 65 or over and entitled to invalid care allowance on 27.10.02, you can continue to be entitled to carer's allowance – and thus the carer addition or premium – even if you are no longer caring for the disabled person.

The carer addition or premium continues for up to eight weeks after your entitlement to carer's allowance ceases – eg if the disabled person's qualifying benefit (see Chapter 7(2)) is withdrawn after 28 days in hospital. If the disabled person regains the qualifying benefit, your carer addition or premium should resume.

SPC Regs, Sch 1, para 4

5. Severe disablement allowance

Severe disablement allowance (SDA) was abolished for new claimants from 6.4.01 onwards, so the information here applies only to people entitled to it before that date. For more information about SDA, see Box D.9 in Chapter 14.

SDA overlaps with state pension. If your state pension is lower than SDA, your state pension can be topped up to your full SDA entitlement, including any age-related addition. On the other hand, you can put off claiming state pension and keep your tax-free SDA. If you would be due to pay tax on your state pension, you may be better off doing this in some situations even if your pension is a bit higher than your SDA. However, state pension, but not SDA, counts as qualifying income for the savings credit element of pension credit (see Chapter 42(4)).

OB Regs, reg 4(1)&(5)

Once you reach 65 you continue to get SDA even if you are no longer incapable of work or 80% disabled, provided you were entitled to SDA immediately before your 65th birthday. You no longer need to send in medical certificates.

SDA Regs, reg 5

6. Care and mobility

Attendance allowance – This is a benefit for ill or disabled people aged 65 or over. There is no upper age limit. Many older people fail to claim attendance allowance. Some people do not realise that it is tax free, not means tested, and can be paid on top of state pension or pension credit. Others put their problems down to old age rather than disability. See Chapter 5 for full details.

Personal independence payment – If you are 65 or over you cannot start to receive personal independence payment. However, if you were getting personal independence payment before you reached 65, you continue to be eligible if you continue to satisfy the other conditions. See Chapter 4.

7. Housing benefit

You may be entitled to help with all or part of your rent through housing benefit. If you apply for pension credit you will be asked if you want to claim housing benefit. If you are not entitled to pension credit, you may still be eligible; in this case, claim directly from the local authority, not the DWP. See Chapter 21 for details.

8. Other benefits

For information on help towards your council tax, see Chapter 22. Chapter 23(5) covers winter fuel payments. For information on grants from local authorities for other one-off expenses, see Chapter 24. For help towards NHS health costs, see Chapter 54.

42 Pension credit

1. What is pension credit?

Pension credit is the commonly used name for state pension credit, a means-tested benefit for people who have reached the qualifying age. Pension credit has two elements:

❏ **Guarantee credit** – If your income is below a certain level, known as the 'appropriate minimum guarantee', the guarantee credit makes up the difference (see 3 below).

❏ **Savings credit** – This can be paid if you or your partner are aged 65 or over. It is intended to provide extra money for people who have made modest provision for their retirement (see 4 below).

Pension credit can help meet mortgage interest payments and other housing costs. You may get housing benefit to help with rent (see Chapter 21) and help from your local authority towards your council tax (see Chapter 22). If you get the guarantee credit, you will be passported to full housing benefit and council tax support, and may be entitled to help with health costs, such as free dental treatment (see Chapter 54), and with hospital fares (see Chapter 35(2)). If you receive either element, you may get help from the social fund (see Chapter 23), budgeting loans (Chapter 24(2)) and energy efficiency grants (see Chapter 31(4)).

Future changes – As universal credit replaces means-tested benefits for people of working age (see Box J.1 in Chapter 25), the support currently available for rent and dependent children through two of those benefits, housing benefit and child tax credit, will no longer be available. To replace these benefits for claimants who have reached pension credit qualifying age, two new elements will be introduced for pension credit: a 'housing credit' (to cover eligible rent) and additional amounts for children (which will be similar to those available under universal credit). These changes will take place for new pension credit claims from October 2014.

2. Who can claim pension credit?

To claim pension credit, you must have reached the 'qualifying age', which is being raised from 60 to 66 between April 2010 and October 2020, alongside the rise in women's state pension age. To check the qualifying age at the time you want to claim, contact The Pension Service (0800 991 234) or use the state pension age calculator at www.gov.uk/calculate-state-pension.

Only one member of a couple can claim. You are considered to be one of a couple if you are married, in a civil partnership, or cohabiting (whether with someone of the opposite or the same sex). Your partner can currently be younger, but, if you are entitled to universal credit once it has been introduced (see Chapter 1(2)), you will only be able to claim pension credit once you have both reached the qualifying age.

You must be present in Great Britain (GB), habitually resident and not subject to immigration control (see Chapter 49(2) and (3)). Pension credit can be paid for the first 13 weeks of a temporary absence from GB (see Chapter 50(6)). There is no limit on the number of hours you can work, but most earnings are taken into account (see 5 below). There is no capital limit for pension credit, but capital over £10,000 will be counted as generating income (see 6 below).

SPCA, Ss.1 & 4(1); SPC Regs 1(2)

3. Calculating your guarantee credit

Guarantee credit is calculated by comparing your 'appropriate minimum guarantee' with your income (see 5 below for how income is calculated). Your appropriate minimum guarantee always includes a 'standard minimum guarantee', which is:

■ for a single claimant: £145.40 a week;

■ for couples: £222.05 a week.

Your appropriate minimum guarantee can also include:

■ an additional amount for severe disability of £59.50 a week for a single person or couple if one partner qualifies (or £119 for a couple if both qualify), worked out in the same way as the severe disability premium (see Chapter 25(3));

■ an additional amount for carers of £33.30, worked out in the same way as the carer premium (see Chapter 25(6));

■ an amount for any eligible housing costs such as mortgage interest (see Chapter 26);

■ a 'transitional' extra amount if you were getting income support, income-based jobseeker's allowance or income-related employment and support allowance immediately before you started to get pension credit that was payable at a higher rate than the pension credit.

SPC Regs, reg 6 & Sch 1

Pension credit does not include any amounts for children. If you have children, claim child tax credit (see Chapter 19).

Your income, as calculated in 5 below, is compared to your appropriate minimum guarantee. If your income is less, the difference is paid as your guarantee credit.

SPCA, S.2(2)

Example: Rashida is single and her only income is state pension of £110.15 a week. Her guarantee credit is worked out as follows:

Appropriate minimum guarantee	£145.40
Less income	£110.15
Guarantee credit	*£35.25*

4. Calculating your savings credit

Savings credit may be paid if you or your partner are 65 or over and have *'qualifying income'* above your *'savings credit threshold'*.

Savings credit thresholds	per week
Single person	£115.30
Couple	£183.90

Some people will receive savings credit and guarantee credit; others will receive only savings credit. The maximum amount of savings credit payable is £18.06 a week for a single person and £22.89 for a couple (the government is reducing these amounts each year). The calculation is as follows:

Step 1: Work out your total income
This is the same figure used in the guarantee credit calculation (see 5 below for how income is calculated).

Step 2: Work out your appropriate minimum guarantee
Again, this is the figure used for guarantee credit (see 3 above).

Step 3: Work out your qualifying income
This is your total income used to calculate guarantee credit but excluding working tax credit, incapacity benefit, contributory employment and support allowance, contribution-based jobseeker's allowance, severe disablement allowance, maternity allowance or maintenance payments made by a spouse/civil partner or former spouse/civil partner.

Step 4: Compare the savings credit threshold with your qualifying income
If your qualifying income is the same as or less than the savings credit threshold (see above) you will not be entitled to savings credit. If your qualifying income is more than the threshold, make a note of the difference and go to Step 5.

Step 5: Calculate 60% of the difference from Step 4
Work out 60% of the difference between the savings credit threshold and your qualifying income. If the result is more than the maximum savings credit figure of £18.06 for a single person (or £22.89 for a couple), use the relevant maximum savings credit figure instead.

Step 6: Calculate the savings credit
❏ If your total income is the same as or less than your appropriate minimum guarantee, your savings credit will be the figure you arrived at in Step 5.
❏ If your total income is more than your appropriate minimum guarantee, you must work out 40% of the difference between your total income and your appropriate minimum guarantee. You then deduct this 40% figure from the amount you arrived at in Step 5.

SPCA, S.3 & SPC Regs, regs 7 & 9

Example: Paul is a single claimant with a state pension (basic and additional) of £130 a week and an occupational pension of £52.20 a week. Using the steps above, the calculation is as follows:
Step 1: Paul's total income is:

State pension	£130.00
Plus occupational pension	£52.20
Total income	*£182.20*

Step 2: His appropriate minimum guarantee is £145.40 – he does not qualify for any of the additional amounts. His income is above this amount so he does not qualify for guarantee credit.
Step 3: All his income is qualifying income so his qualifying income is also £182.20.
Step 4: He compares his qualifying income with the savings credit threshold (£115.30 for a single person). It is higher, so he works out the amount by which his qualifying income is above the threshold:

Qualifying income	£182.20
Less Paul's savings credit threshold	£115.30
Difference equals	*£66.90*

Step 5: He works out 60% of the difference:

£66.90 x 60% =	£40.14

This is more than the maximum savings credit of £18.06 for a single claimant, so for the next step he uses that figure of £18.06.
Step 6: His total income is more than his appropriate minimum guarantee – the difference is:

Paul's total income	£182.20
Less appropriate minimum guarantee	£145.40
Difference equals	*£36.80*

He works out 40% of this difference, which comes to £14.72. He takes this figure from the maximum savings credit (the result of Step 5):

Maximum savings credit	£18.06
Less	£14.72
Savings credit	*£3.34*

Not sure if you are entitled to savings credit?

The calculation for savings credit is complicated. If you are not sure whether you qualify, you should apply anyway. For more information about your likely entitlement, see www.gov.uk/pension-credit-calculator or contact a local advice agency.

5. Income

You need to add up your income to work out any entitlement to pension credit. Some types of income, including state and private pensions are counted in full; some types of income are fully disregarded, others are partially disregarded. If you have a source of income not covered below, check with The Pension Service to see how it is treated.

In general, income is calculated in a similar way to means-tested benefits for younger people, but there are differences. Income is assessed after deduction of income tax and, in the case of people with earnings, after deduction of national insurance contributions and half of any contribution made to a private pension. Income is assessed on a weekly basis, so if you have income paid for other periods it is divided into weekly amounts. For a couple, the income of both partners is added together.

SPC Regs, regs 14, 17 & 17A(4A)

Income generally counted in full – The following types of income are counted in full:
- earnings (which can include any statutory sick/maternity/paternity/adoption pay) but see below for partial disregards;
- working tax credit;
- state, occupational and private pensions;
- annuities and retirement annuity contracts;
- most social security benefits (except those listed below);
- war disablement or war widow's/widower's pension (but see below for disregards);
- regular payments from an equity release scheme;
- income from the Financial Assistance Scheme;

SPCA, S. 15(1) & 16(1); SPC Regs, reg 17A(2)(h)-(j)

- guaranteed income payment made under the Armed Forces and Reserve Forces Compensation scheme (but see below for disregards);
- pension paid to victims of Nazi persecution (but see below for partial disregards);
- maintenance payments from a spouse/civil partner or former spouse/civil partner;
- payments from boarders, lodgers or sub-tenants (but see below for partial disregards);
- income from the Pension Protection Fund;
- 'deemed income' from capital over £10,000 (see 6 below).

SPC Regs, regs 15(5)-(6)

Disregarded income – Forms of income that are completely disregarded include:

- attendance allowance, disability living allowance, personal independence payment, constant attendance allowance, armed forces independence payment and war pensioner's mobility supplement;
- housing benefit;
- Christmas bonus;
- social fund payments including the winter fuel payment;
- bereavement payment;
- child benefit, child tax credit, guardian's allowance and child special allowance;
- increases for dependent children paid with certain other benefits;
- exceptionally severe disablement allowance (paid in the War Pensions and Industrial Injuries schemes) and war pensions' severe disablement occupational allowance;

SPC Regs, reg 15(1) & Sch 4, para 3

- war widow's, widower's or surviving civil partner's supplementary pension;
- payments, other than social security benefits or war pensions, paid as a result of a personal injury that you or your partner receive;
- income abroad while transfer to the UK is prohibited;
- charges for currency conversion if income is not paid in sterling;
- actual income from capital;

SPC Regs, Sch 4, paras 4-6, 13-14, 15, 16 & 18

- payments from your local authority social services department for personal care;
- charitable and voluntary payments (except for voluntary payments from a spouse/civil partner or former spouse/civil partner, which are counted in full); *and*
- any other type of income not specified in the legislation as being counted.

Partially disregarded income – Forms of weekly income that are partially disregarded include:

- £5 of your earnings from work if you are single or £10 if you are a couple. A higher £20 disregard applies in some situations, eg for some disabled people or carers. The rules are similar to those for other means-tested benefits (see Chapter 27(5)), but there are minor differences; for details contact an advice centre or The Pension Service;

SPC Regs, Sch 6

- £10 of the total of any income from a war widow's, widower's or surviving civil partner's pension, war disablement pension, a guaranteed income payment made under the Armed Forces and Reserve Forces Compensation scheme (including payment abated by a pension paid under the scheme), or pension paid for victims of Nazi persecution or widowed parent's/mother's allowance;
- £20 payment from a tenant, sub-tenant or boarder. In the case of a boarder, half of any payment above £20 is also disregarded. The disregard applies to each tenant and/or boarder making payments;
- if you have used the equity in your home to buy an annuity, any part of the income that is being used to pay the interest on the loan is disregarded.

SPC Regs, Sch 4, paras 1, 7-7A, 8-9 & 10

Income from trust funds

This will be ignored if the trust fund was set up from a lump sum received for a personal injury. In other situations, trust fund income is generally taken into account. Discretionary payments made by trustees are disregarded, unless they are for everyday living expenses (see Chapter 27(9)), in which case up to £20 can be disregarded.

SPC Regs, Sch 4, paras 11 & 13

Notional income

In some cases you can be treated as having 'notional' income that you are not actually receiving. This will apply if there is income available that you have chosen not to take – eg if you have not claimed your state pension or not drawn a personal or occupational pension that you are entitled to. You may also be assessed as having notional income if you have given up the right to an income you could have received.

SPC Regs, reg 18

6. Capital

Capital includes any savings, investments, land and property you own. If you have capital of £10,000 or less, this will not affect your pension credit. There is currently no upper capital limit for pension credit* but if you have capital of more than £10,000 you will be counted as having an extra £1 a week income for every £500 (or part of £500) over this limit. In pension credit this is officially called *'deemed income'*, while for other benefits the term is 'tariff income'. For example, if you have savings of £11,050 you will be deemed to have an income of £3 a week from that capital; if you have savings of £19,300 you will have a deemed income of £19 a week. If you have a partner, your capital is assessed together, but the amount that is disregarded (see below) is still the same.

SPCA, Ss.5 & 15(2) & SPC Regs, regs 14 & 15(6)

Most forms of capital are taken into account including: cash, bank and building society savings, National Savings accounts and certificates, stocks and shares, premium bonds, income bonds and property (other than your home). However, some types of capital are disregarded (see below).

* An upper capital limit will be introduced from October 2014 when the 'housing credit' is introduced (see 1 above). At the time of writing, further details are not known.

How capital is valued – Your capital is generally valued at its current market or surrender value, less 10% if there would be costs involved in selling and less any debt secured on the property.

SPC Regs, reg 19

Joint capital – If you own capital jointly with other people you would normally all be assessed as having an equal share. See Chapter 28(5) for more about valuation of joint property for other means-tested benefits; the position is similar for pension credit.

Disregarded capital

In working out your deemed income from capital, the following types of capital are disregarded indefinitely or for a certain period of time.

❏ **Your home and property**

- the value of your home;
- the value of any property occupied by someone who is a 'close relative' (see Chapter 25(3) for the definition of 'close relative'), grandparent, grandchild, uncle, aunt, nephew or niece of yourself or your partner, if they have reached pension credit qualifying age or are *'incapacitated'*. The value will be disregarded if your partner or former partner lives there and you are not estranged or divorced or had your civil partnership dissolved (eg if you have moved to a care home);
- the value of a property for up to 26 weeks if: you have acquired it and plan to live there; you are trying to sell it; you are carrying out essential repairs or alterations in order to live there; or you are taking legal action so you can live there. In each case, more time is allowed if that is reasonable in the circumstances to enable you to conclude the matter;
- the value of your former home if you left because of a breakdown in the relationship with your partner for up to 26 weeks (or indefinitely if your former partner lives there and is a lone parent);
- any future interest in property other than land or premises that have been let by you;

SPC Regs, Sch 5, paras 1-7

- the following types of capital received for specific purposes are ignored for up to a year (or until an assessed income period ends if that is longer – see 9 below): money received, eg from the sale of a property, that is earmarked to buy a new home; money from an insurance policy that is to be used for repair or replacement; or money such as a loan or grant to pay for essential repairs or improvements.

SPC Regs, Sch 5, paras 17-19

❏ **Other disregards**
- personal possessions;
- business assets while you are *'engaged as a self-employed earner'*. If you've ceased that self-employment, the assets will be disregarded for as long as is reasonable in the circumstances to allow you to dispose of them. If sickness or disability means you cannot work as a self-employed earner, your business assets will be disregarded as long as you intend to start or resume work in that business as soon as you are able to or as soon as you recover;
- the surrender value of a life insurance policy (although if this matures or is cashed in, the money you receive will count as part of your capital);
- the value of a pre-paid funeral;

SPC Regs, Sch 5, paras 8, 9, 9A, 10 & 11

- the £10,000 ex-gratia payment made to Far Eastern Prisoners of War or their widows, widowers or surviving civil partners;
- Second World War Compensation Payments – eg for forced labour or lost property;
- any charge for currency conversion if your capital is not held in sterling;
- the value of the right to receive income from an occupational pension, personal pension or retirement annuity contract (although you may still be treated as possessing notional income – see 5 above);
- a lump-sum payment received because you deferred drawing your state pension for 52 weeks or more (see Chapter 43(7));
- any community care or NHS direct payments.

SPC Regs, Sch 5, paras 12, 14, 21, 22-23, 23A, 23C

Personal injury payments and trust funds
If you or your partner received a lump-sum payment due to a personal injury, an amount of capital equal to the money you received will be disregarded. If you used the money to set up a trust fund, the value of this trust will be ignored. Payments from special trusts, eg the Macfarlane or Eileen Trusts are also disregarded indefinitely or for a certain period. The rules are the same as for other means-tested benefits (see Chapter 28(6)).

SPC Regs, Sch 5, paras 13, 15, 16 & 28

Arrears of benefits
Arrears (or ex-gratia payments) of the following benefits are ignored for 52 weeks after you get them or until the end of your assessed income period (if you have one and it is longer): attendance allowance, disability living allowance, housing benefit, personal independence payment, armed forces independence payment, council tax benefit, income support, income-related employment and support allowance, income-based jobseeker's allowance, pension credit, supplementary pensions (paid to war widows, widowers or surviving civil partners), constant attendance allowance and exceptionally severe disablement allowance (paid under the War Pensions or Industrial Injuries schemes), child tax credit, child benefit and social fund payments. If the amount of arrears or compensation is £5,000 or more and it is paid because of official error, and you receive the payments while you are getting pension credit, it will be ignored for as long as you continue to receive pension credit. Payments under Supporting People services are treated in the same way as arrears of benefits.

SPC Regs, Sch 5, paras 17, 20, 20A & 20B

Notional capital
If you have 'deprived' yourself of capital in order to get pension credit or to increase the amount you receive, you will be treated as still having that capital; this is known as *'notional capital'*. This might occur if you gave money to a relative in order to get more pension credit. However, you will not be assessed as having notional capital if you used your savings to repay or reduce a debt or to buy goods or services that are 'reasonable' given your circumstances – eg a decision maker might consider replacing a car to be reasonable but not buying a Rolls Royce. Notional capital you are treated as having will reduce over time in line with the rules for other means-tested benefits (see Chapter 28(9)).

SPC Regs, regs 21-22; DWP guide to Pension Credit: PC10S

7. How to claim
Ring The Pension Credit application line (Freephone 0800 991 234) to make a claim over the phone or get a form sent to you. You can download a PC1 claim-form from www.gov.uk/pension-credit/how-to-claim. Alternatively, an advice agency or local Pension Service staff can help you fill in the form, either at an advice session or through a home visit.

8. Backdating and advance claims
Normally, your pension credit will run from the date on which your written claim is received at the relevant office, or the date of a claim by phone or in person (including someone acting on your behalf) that is subsequently confirmed by a signed statement. Your claim can be backdated for up to three months if you met the qualifying conditions throughout that period.

C&P Regs, reg 19(2)-(3)

If you will become eligible for pension credit in the future, for instance because you are coming up to state pension age or you are about to have a drop in income, you can make a claim up to four months in advance of this change.

C&P Regs, reg 4E

9. Assessed income period and change of circumstances
When you claim pension credit, The Pension Service will decide whether you are entitled to guarantee credit, savings credit or both. If you or your partner are aged 65 or over and the other is at least 60, the decision maker may also set an *'assessed income period'* (AIP), which is generally up to five years. During the AIP you do not have to inform The Pension Service of any changes in your *'retirement provision'* (see below). Unless there are likely to be changes in the next 12 months that will affect your retirement provision, the AIP will normally be the maximum allowed.

If you are aged 75 or over, the AIP will normally be set for an indefinite period. If your AIP runs out after you reach 80, you will not normally need to be reassessed. Even if your AIP has been set for an indefinite period, there are still changes that will bring it to an end, as set out below.

SPCA, Ss. 6-10 & SPC Regs, reg 10

Retirement provision – Your retirement provision refers to any of the following that either you or your partner may possess or receive:
- income from capital;
- other pensions including an occupational, personal, private or stakeholder pension scheme, an overseas pension arrangement;
- regular payments from an equity release scheme;
- income from retirement annuity contracts or other annuities;
- payments made from the Financial Assistance Scheme and Pension Protection Fund.

SPCA, Ss. 7(6) & 16; SPC Regs, reg 11(2)

Changes of circumstances during the AIP – Changes in your state pension will automatically be taken into account during the AIP. So when your state pension is uprated, your pension credit will be amended accordingly. Adjustments will also be made automatically, where appropriate, to other pensions or annuity income. For example, if your occupational pension increases each April in line with inflation, this will be taken into account. In order for this to happen, you may be asked about any regular changes to your pensions when you apply for pension credit.

SPCA, S.10 & SPC Regs, regs 10(4)-(7)

Other changes to your retirement provision will be ignored for the rest of the AIP. For example, if you inherit some capital or win money from Premium Bonds you will not need to inform The Pension Service. Any increase in capital or other retirement provision will only be taken into account when your AIP ends. On the other hand, if your retirement provision falls (eg your capital goes down) so that you are entitled to more pension credit, you can ask for your award to be superseded. The Pension Service will then reassess your retirement provision and if this is less than the figure they have been using, your pension credit may increase.

SPCA, S. 8

During an AIP, you must still report other changes in circumstances that may affect your benefit, including a change in earnings, moving home, a change in family circumstances or a period in hospital (see Chapter 35(3)).

When the AIP will end – Your AIP will end if:
- you marry, form a civil partnership or get a new partner;
- you stop being treated as a couple – eg because your partner dies or moves permanently into a care home;
- you or your partner become 65;
- you no longer satisfy the entitlement conditions for pension credit;
- part of your retirement provision stops being paid temporarily or the amount being paid is less than the amount due and you ask for your pension credit to be recalculated;
- you have no partner and move into a care home permanently.

If a supersession results in the end of your AIP, pension credit changes from the day following the end of the period.

SPCA, S. 9(4) & SPC Regs, reg 12

What if you are not given an AIP? – If you are not given an AIP, you will need to report all changes of circumstances that could affect your benefits entitlement, including changes in pensions and savings. When you receive an award of pension credit you will be advised which changes must be reported.

10. How pension credit is paid

For people who started claiming pension credit prior to 6.4.10, it is normally paid weekly in advance on a Monday. If you reach the qualifying age from 6.4.10 onwards, it is normally paid weekly, fortnightly or four weekly in arrears with the pay day determined by your national insurance number.

If the weekly amount of pension credit due is less than £1, payments may be made at intervals of up to 13 weeks in arrears. If the weekly amount is less than 10p, no pension credit will be paid unless it can be paid with another benefit. See Chapter 57(5) for more about benefit payments.

C&P Regs, regs 26B & 26BA; SPC Regs, reg 13

11. Decisions and appeals

Decisions on your pension credit claim are made by DWP decision makers based at The Pension Service (see Chapter 2(2)). The rules for decisions and appeals are the same as for other DWP benefits (see Chapter 58).

43 Retirement pensions

1. State pension

The two main categories of state pension are contributory and are known as Category A and Category B pensions. Category A pensions are normally based on your own national insurance contribution record. Category B pensions are based on a spouse or civil partner's contribution record. Category D pensions are non-contributory and payable only to people aged 80 or over.

All categories of state pension are taxable.

2. When can you get a state pension?

You can get a state pension if you have reached state pension age, you meet the contribution conditions (see Box O.1) and, where necessary, have made a claim. If you do not draw your state pension at state pension age, you may get extra state pension or a one-off taxable lump-sum payment when you do start to claim (see 7 below).

Changes to state pensions were introduced on 6.4.10. These include a gradual rise in women's state pension age (see below), changes to the contribution conditions and changes to who can receive Category B pensions. The rules that apply to you will depend on whether you reached state pension age before 6.4.10 or on or after that date.

State pension age – For men, state pension age is currently 65 and for women born on or before 5.4.50 it is 60. The Pensions Act 1995 introduced an equal state pension age of 65 for both men and women; this is being phased in over a number of years. Once that phase is complete in November 2018, retirement ages for both men and women who have not yet reached state pension age will rise to 66 by October 2020. For women born on or after 6.4.50, state pension age will depend on their date of birth. Contact The Pension Service or check the state pension profiler at www.gov.uk/calculate-state-pension. The state pension age will gradually rise to 68 for both men and women from 2026.

3. Working and the state pension

Earnings you receive after reaching state pension age do not affect your state pension and you do not have to pay national insurance contributions on them. If you carry on working and do not draw your pension you may earn extra state pension or a one-off lump sum (see 7 below). If you have already claimed your state pension, you can give up your claim in order to earn extra state pension or receive a lump sum. You can only give up a state pension once, and cannot backdate that choice.

WBRP Regs, reg 2(1) & (2)

There is an earnings limit for an increase for an adult dependant (see 4 below).

4. Category A state pension

This is normally based on your own national insurance (NI) contribution record. However, widows, widowers, surviving civil partners, divorced people and those whose civil partnership has been dissolved may be able to use the contribution record of their former spouse/civil partner to help them qualify.

SSCBA, S.44(1) & 48 and WBRP Regs, reg 8

If you have met the contribution conditions in full, you can receive a basic state pension of £110.15 a week. You may receive less if you do not have a full contribution record. It is no longer possible to make a new claim for an increase for a dependent adult or child. However, if you are already receiving an increase, then the weekly amounts are:

Dependant's increase	per week
For an adult dependant	£63.20
For the first dependent child (tax free)	£8.10
For each other dependent child (tax free)	£11.35

SSCBA, S.44(4) & Sch 4(Part IV)

Adult dependant's increase

Since 6.4.10 it has not been possible to claim this. However, if you are already receiving it, you can continue to receive it until you no longer meet the conditions or until 5.4.20, whichever is earlier.

PA, S.4

Before 6.4.10, claims could be made for a dependent wife or someone looking after your dependent child, or in limited circumstances, a husband.

SSCBA, Ss.83-85

If the dependant is working, the increase will not be paid if they earn more in any week than their earnings limit (occupational and personal pensions count as earnings here). The earnings limit for an adult dependant is £71.70 if the dependant lives with you, and £63.20 if you do not live together (except in the case of a person who looks after your children but does not live with you, where there is no earnings limit).

Social Security Benefit (Dependency) Regs, reg 8

If your adult dependant receives an income maintenance benefit (eg contributory employment and support allowance) that benefit will reduce or cancel out a dependant's increase to your state pension.

OB Regs, reg 10

Child dependant's increase

This is not payable on new claims for state pension from 6.4.03. If you have dependent children, you should claim child tax credit at the same time that you claim state pension (see Chapter 19).

5. Category B state pension

This is a pension based on the contribution record of your spouse/civil partner or late spouse/civil partner. If they had not fully met the contribution conditions, you will receive a reduced-rate state pension.

Married women

If you have no basic state pension, or a basic state pension of less than £66 based on your own contributions, you can claim a Category B pension of up to this amount based on your husband's contribution record once both of you have reached state pension age. Before 6.4.10, your husband had to have claimed his own state pension before you could claim a Category B pension based on his contributions. However, the rules have changed so you can now claim this even if your husband is deferring his pension. If he has a reduced contribution record, you will receive a proportionally reduced state pension. Any earnings you receive after you reach state pension age do not affect your state pension.

SSCBA, S.48A; PA, S.2

Married men and civil partners

If you are entitled to a basic state pension of less than £66 a week, you may be able to claim a Category B pension based on your wife's or civil partner's contribution record as long as they were born on or after 6.4.50 and you have both reached state pension age. In practice, this means that husbands and female civil partners could start to qualify from May 2010 and male civil partners from April 2015.

Widows, widowers and surviving civil partners

If you qualify for a full Category B pension, you could get £110.15 a week basic state pension, and, if applicable, a proportion of the additional state pension built up by your late spouse or civil partner.

SSCBA, S.48B

Category A and Category B pensions overlap. So if, for example, you are a married woman with a basic state pension of £30 based on your own contributions, you cannot receive this in addition to a £66 Category B pension based on your husband's contributions. Instead, your state pension will be topped up to £66 using your husband's contributions.

SSCBA, Ss.51A and 52

6. Additional state pension

Your Category A or B pension may include an additional state pension. From 1978 to April 2002 this was built up under the *'state earnings-related pension scheme'* (SERPS). In April 2002 the *'state second pension'* (S2P) replaced SERPS. If you are an employee with annual earnings above the level needed to qualify for the basic state pension, you will be contributing to the additional state pension unless you are contracted out and paying into your employer's contracted-out salary-related pension scheme (see Box O.3). From 2002, some people who do not have earnings will be credited with earnings for S2P purposes (see below).

Note that an additional state pension can be paid on its own if you aren't entitled to any basic state pension. In some situations it is also payable with incapacity benefit (but only for people who previously received invalidity benefit and are covered by the transitional rules) and with the widowed parent's allowance or widow's pension.

Widows, widowers and surviving civil partners may be able to inherit part or all of their spouse/civil partner's SERPS and half of their S2P as part of their state pensions. For more information, contact The Pension Service.

Calculating your additional state pension

To calculate this, your earnings each year are added together (up to the upper-accruals point, currently £770 a week) from April 1978 (or the tax year in which you reach age 16, if later) up to the April before you reach state pension age. The DWP then takes away the qualifying level of earnings for the basic state pension in each year (£109 a week in 2013/14). This leaves a surplus of earnings for each year, which are then re-valued in line with increases in average earnings.

The original formula provided a state pension based on 25% of earnings between the specified levels. However, changes were introduced to phase in, between 1999 and 2009, a reduction in the amount of additional state pension people receive. The main aim of these changes was to reduce the maximum level of SERPS from 25% of earnings to 20% for people reaching state pension age from 2009 onwards (with some protection for years up to 1987/88).

Under S2P the amount of additional state pension someone earns is calculated in a different way. Currently, part of S2P builds up at a flat rate of £1.70 a week; the rest builds up at 10% of earnings between specified levels. In the future, none of your S2P will build up based on the amount you earn; instead it will all build up at a flat rate.

SSCBA, Ss.44(3)(b) & (5)-(8) and 45

O.1 State pension – the qualifying conditions

This box explains the contribution conditions for the basic state pension. Your contribution record is built up through paid national insurance contributions and national insurance credits. The rules that apply will depend on whether you reached state pension age on or after 6.4.10 or before that date. Your contribution record may be protected by *'home responsibilities protection'* (HRP) for years from 1978/79 to 2009/10 if you were looking after a child or caring for someone and do not have sufficient contributions or credits to count towards your basic state pension (see Box O.2).

If you reached state pension age before 6.4.10

If you reached state pension age before 6.4.10, you must meet two conditions to qualify for the basic state pension.

The first condition – In at least one tax year since 6.4.75 you paid sufficient contributions for this to be a 'qualifying year' (see below for what is meant by a qualifying year) or you paid 50 flat-rate contributions at any time before 6.4.75. You are treated as satisfying this condition if you are entitled to long-term incapacity benefit or main-phase employment and support allowance in the year you reach state pension age, or the preceding year.

The second condition – To receive a full basic state pension, about nine out of every ten years of your 'working life' need to be qualifying years. If you do not have sufficient qualifying years for a full basic state pension, you may get a partial pension, but at least a quarter of the years in your 'working life' must count as qualifying years, otherwise no pension is payable.

SSCBA, Sch 3, para 5(2),(3),(6)&(6A); WBRP Regs, reg 6

Working life – Your *'working life'* is the period on which your contribution record is based. This is normally from the start of the tax year in which you became 16 to the last full tax year before you reach state pension age.

Women who reached state pension age before 6.4.10 normally have a working life of 44 years so will need to have 39 qualifying years for a full basic state pension and at least ten qualifying years to receive any basic state pension.

Men who reached state pension age before 6.4.10 normally have a working life of 49 years so will need at least 44 qualifying years for a full basic state pension and at least 11 qualifying years to receive any basic state pension.

SSCBA, Sch 3, paras 5(5)&(8)

If you reach state pension age on or after 6.4.10

If you reach state pension age on or after 6.4.10, you can receive a basic state pension as long as you have at least one qualifying year during your working life (which runs from the year you reached 16 to the last full tax year before you reached state pension age).

To receive a full basic state pension you will need at least 30 qualifying years. If you have at least one qualifying year, but less than 30, you will receive a partial basic state pension.

The qualifying years can be based on paid contributions, credits or a combination of the two. As explained in Box O.2, any years of HRP you have built up will be converted into qualifying years of credits.

National insurance contributions and credits

Contributions – From 1948 until 1975 contributions were paid at a flat rate. Between 1961 and 1975 there was also a system of graduated contributions, which give entitlement to graduated retirement benefit.

Since 1975, employees pay Class 1 contributions as a percentage of gross earnings, collected with income tax. Class 2 contributions (self-employed) also count towards the basic state pension (but not state second pension) and it is sometimes possible to pay Class 3 (voluntary) contributions to make up gaps in your contribution record. However, any years when you were paying the married woman's reduced rate contributions do not count towards your state pension.

For more on national insurance contributions, see Chapter 12(4).

Credits – In certain circumstances you can be credited with contributions that will count towards your basic state pension. For example, you will normally be credited with a contribution for any week in which you have a limited capability for work due to illness or disability. From 6.4.10 'credits for parents and carers' replace HRP.

Some credits are given automatically, for instance if you have been awarded child benefit for a child under 12, but in other cases you will need to apply for them. For more on national insurance credits, see Box D.7, Chapter 12.

Your qualifying years

A *'qualifying year'* is a tax year in which you have paid, been treated as having paid, or been credited with, enough contributions for a basic state pension.

Prior to 1975, qualifying years were worked out by adding up all your stamps and dividing them by 50.

Since 1975, a qualifying year is one in which you have paid, been treated as having paid, or been credited with, contributions on earnings equivalent to 52 times the *'lower earnings limit'* for that year.

In the year April 2013 to April 2014, the lower earnings limit is £109 a week. However, people will only start to pay contributions on earnings above a higher level of £149 a week, the *'primary threshold'*. Although they will not be paying contributions, people with earnings between £109 and £149 will still be building up entitlement to a state pension and other contributory benefits. When we refer in this book to people who have 'paid contributions' we are also including those in this position who are treated in the same way as those paying contributions.

For self-employed people and those paying voluntary contributions, the test is the number of flat-rate contributions, as it was before 1975, but divided by 52.

A qualifying year can also be made up of a combination of credits and paid contributions.

Working out your state pension

In most cases, you won't need to work out your entitlement to a state pension. All your records should be on the computer in Newcastle, so all you have to do is put in a claim. If when you receive information about your state pension you think it is not correct, you can ask for more information about your contribution record and question any gaps in your record that you think should have been covered by contributions, credits or HRP. If you disagree with the information you are given, you may want to get advice to challenge this.

State pension statement – To check your contribution record, you can ask for a state pension statement if you are over 30 days away from your state pension age. The statement will show your current state pension entitlement based on records held by HMRC. It should allow you (with some help if necessary) to make the right decisions about your future contribution position. To get a statement, contact the Future Pension Centre (part of The Pension Service) (0845 300 0168; textphone 0845 300 0169; www.gov.uk/state-pension-statement).

Credited with earnings for S2P

Some disabled people, carers and people with low earnings will be credited with earnings into S2P. If you have annual qualifying earnings of at least the lower earnings limit (£5,668 in 2013/14) but less than the *'low earnings threshold'*, you will be treated for S2P purposes as though you have earnings at that level (£15,000 in 2013/14). You can also be treated as having earnings at the low earnings threshold if, throughout the year, you are:

■ paid carer's allowance, or would be paid it but for overlapping benefit rules; *or*
■ entitled to the 'credits for parents and carers' (from 6.4.10; see Box D.7, Chapter 12) or got home responsibilities protection because you were caring for a disabled person or a child under the age of six (prior to 6.4.10, see Box O.2); *or*
■ paid the long-term rate of incapacity benefit, or would be paid it but for overlapping benefit rules or because you do not fulfil the contribution conditions; *or*
■ paid contributory employment and support allowance (ESA) that:
　– has been payable for a continuous period of 52 weeks; *or*
　– includes a support component; *or*
　– (for a man born between 6.4.44 and 5.4.47 or a woman born between 6.4.49 and 5.4.51) has been payable for a continuous period of 13 weeks following a period on statutory sick pay,

or would be paid it but for the overlapping benefit rules or because you do not fulfil the contribution conditions; *or*
■ paid severe disablement allowance (SDA).

From 2010/11 onwards you can combine periods when you paid NI contributions with periods when any of the above conditions (or a combination of these conditions) apply. Prior to April 2010 you had to meet just one of these conditions throughout the year and periods when you had actually paid NI contributions could not be included; furthermore, in the case of incapacity benefit, contributory ESA and SDA, you need to have paid a certain number of years of contributions on retirement.

PA S.9(2) & Sch 1, Part 6, para 34(4)

Contracting out

For additional state pension earned up to 5.4.97, if you were contracted out of SERPS and were a member of a company salary-related scheme, all or part of your 'additional' pension will be paid, as a *'guaranteed minimum pension'* (GMP), via your employer. If your GMP is less than the SERPS you would have received had you remained contracted in, your state pension will include any increases needed to increase your GMP in line with inflation. For GMPs accruing after 6.4.88, the employer pays the first 3% of inflation proofing.

If you were contracted out of SERPS and belonged to your company's money purchase scheme or a personal pension scheme, you will receive a pension based on the value of the

---

O.2 Home responsibilities protection

Home responsibilities protection (HRP) can protect your basic state pension rights (and bereavement benefits for your spouse or civil partner) for tax years 1978/79 to 2009/10 if you had a child or you were looking after someone who was sick or disabled and you did not have enough credits or national insurance contributions in the tax year. From 2002/03 to 2009/10 it can also help you build up state second pension in certain cases.

On 6.4.10 HRP was replaced by 'credits for parents and carers', as explained in Box D.7 in Chapter 12. If you reach state pension age on or after that date, any years of HRP will be converted into a qualifying year of credits.

For people who reached state pension age before 6.4.10, HRP can help you satisfy the second condition for the full basic state pension (see Box O.1), which is that about nine out of every ten years in your working life must be qualifying years. The number of years in which you were awarded HRP will be deducted from the number of qualifying years you normally need for a full basic state pension. HRP cannot reduce the required number of qualifying years to less than 20 for a full pension.

SSCBA, Sch 3, para 5(7)

Do you qualify?

You qualify for HRP if, throughout a complete tax year between 1978/79 and 2009/10, you:

■ spent at least 35 hours a week looking after someone who got attendance allowance, disability living allowance middle or highest rate care component or constant attendance allowance, for 48 or more weeks in the year (52 weeks for tax years before 6.4.94); *or*
■ got income support and were substantially engaged in looking after a sick or disabled person; *or*
■ were paid child benefit for a child under 16; *or*
■ were a registered foster carer (for tax years 2003/04 onwards).

HR Regs, reg 2(1)-(4)

Does anything affect the provision of HRP?

Work – Work makes no practical difference. If you qualify for HRP, you will get it if you have not paid or been treated as having paid enough national insurance contributions that tax year to count for state pension.

Change of circumstances – If you were a foster carer, getting child benefit or income support for only part of the tax year but you were caring for a disabled person for the rest of the same year, you can apply for HRP for the basic state pension. But if you met the qualifying conditions for only part of that year, you will not get HRP for that year.

HR Regs, reg 2(1)(c)

Married women and widows – You cannot get HRP for any tax year in which you paid or were liable to pay reduced-rate contributions.

How do you apply?

If you are entitled to HRP for years when you were receiving child benefit or income support you do not have to apply. Your HRP should be recorded automatically.

If you reach state pension age on or after 6.4.08 and you discover you were not the child benefit claimant, although you were the one staying at home to look after a child, you may be able to have HRP put on your account if your partner whom you were living with cannot make use of it because they already have a qualifying year through paid contributions.

HR Regs, reg 2(2)(aa) & (5)(aza)

If you qualify for HRP in any of the other ways, or if you were covered partly by one of the conditions and partly by another, you will have to apply for each tax year you need HRP.

To apply, complete form CF411, available from your local Jobcentre Plus or HMRC office or download it from www. hmrc.gov.uk/forms/cf411.pdf. For tax years up to 2001/02, if HRP has not been awarded automatically, you can apply at any time up until your state pension age. The deadlines for claims for tax years 2002/03 to 2009/10 have all now passed.

HR Regs, reg 2(5)(b)-(c)

fund built up (through contributions and the investment return on these). The part of the fund intended to replace SERPS is known as your 'protected rights'. If you were contracted out prior to 5.4.97, your additional state pension will be reduced by an amount that may be more or less than the pension provided by your scheme.

Since 6.4.97 there has not been a link between additional state pension and contracted-out pension schemes. Instead of providing a GMP, a contracted-out salary-related scheme has to satisfy an overall test of quality. For contributions made from 6.4.97 you will either receive an additional state pension or, if you are contracted out, an occupational or personal pension based on the scheme's rules.

From 6.4.12, contracting out of the additional state pension for company money purchase schemes and personal pension schemes has ended, but the money paid into these schemes in previous years will stay there (see Box O.3).

7. Other state pension payments

Your Category A or B pension may also include:

Graduated retirement benefit
This is based on graduated contributions made between April 1961 and April 1975. However, levels of payment are low – typically less than £1 a week. Graduated retirement benefit can be paid on its own.

Invalidity addition
This may be paid if, within eight weeks before reaching state pension age, you were receiving:
- an invalidity allowance with your invalidity benefit; *or*
- incapacity benefit transitional invalidity allowance; *or*
- an age addition with long-term incapacity benefit.

Provided you get some additional state pension, you can get this even if you don't get any basic state pension. It is paid at

O.3 Private pensions and further information

Pension options

In addition to building up a basic state pension, employees earning more than the lower earnings limit (£109 a week from April 2013) will normally build up additional pension through the state second pension (S2P) (see Chapter 43(6)) unless they have *'contracted out'* and have joined their employers' occupational pension scheme or a personal pension instead.

If you contracted out of the state scheme through your employer's occupational pension, both you and your employer paid a lower rate of national insurance (NI).

If you contracted out with an appropriate personal pension or a stakeholder pension (a type of personal pension which meets certain conditions), HMRC paid a rebate of your NI contributions to your scheme provider. Not all private pension schemes are contracted out of S2P, so it is possible to build up entitlement to both types of pension at the same time.

From 6.4.12, contracting out of S2P for employers' money purchase pension schemes and personal pension schemes has been abolished, so no more rebates will be paid for years after the 2011/12 tax year. Instead, you will pay full rate NI and build up S2P from April 2012. The funds you built up in an existing scheme will stay invested in it and if you or your employer also put money into the scheme, you can continue to do so.

Employers' salary-related pension schemes can continue to contract out of S2P after April 2012.

If you are self-employed, you will not be able to build up S2P or join an occupational pension, but you could pay into a personal pension.

Often, the best way of building up a second pension for your retirement is to join an occupational pension scheme if your employer runs one. Your employer will provide details of the terms and conditions of the scheme.

All employers will eventually be required to automatically enrol eligible workers into a pension scheme. This is being phased in between October 2012 and February 2018, depending on the size of the organisation.

Private pensions and social security benefits

A private pension will be counted as income for means-tested benefits such as income support, income-related employment and support allowance (ESA), income-based jobseeker's allowance or housing benefit. It is also counted as income for pension credit, although it may help you

qualify for the savings credit element of pension credit. It will not normally affect your entitlement to non-means-tested benefits. However, an occupational or personal pension over certain levels may affect contributory ESA, incapacity benefit or contribution-based jobseeker's allowance and a private pension counts as earnings if your partner is claiming an increase for you as an adult dependant, or if they are claiming an increase for a child dependant. More information is given in the appropriate sections of this Handbook.

Problems with occupational, personal and stakeholder pensions

If you are a member of an occupational pension scheme or have a personal or stakeholder pension and you have a problem with your pension, ask your pension provider for details of their complaints procedure.

If you are not satisfied with the response or need further help or advice you can contact the Pensions Advisory Service (Helpline 0845 601 2923; www.pensionsadvisoryservice. org.uk/online-enquiry). They can give general information or individual advice about pension problems and may be able to help resolve the problem by taking up your case and negotiating with your provider. If the Pensions Advisory Service cannot solve your problem, they may recommend that you take your complaint to the Pensions Ombudsman.

The Pensions Advisory Service and the Pensions Ombudsman are both based at 11 Belgrave Road, London SW1V 1RB.

The Pensions Regulator is the body that regulates pension schemes. It is based at Napier House, Trafalgar Place, Brighton BN1 4DW (0845 600 0707).

The Pension Tracing Service provides a free tracing service for people who want to contact a scheme in which they may have pension rights but do not know the contact address: The Pension Tracing Service, The Pension Service, Whitley Road, Newcastle upon Tyne NE98 1BA (0845 600 2537; textphone 0845 300 0169).

DWP leaflets

The Pension Service publishes free leaflets covering the following topics:
- state pensions;
- pension credit;
- how to get extra state pension or a lump-sum payment (also known as state pension deferral).

You can order them by ringing 0845 731 3233 (textphone 0845 604 0210).

the same rate as your invalidity allowance or age addition but is offset against an additional state pension or contracted-out deduction.
SSCBA, S.47

Extra state pension for deferring retirement

If you do not draw your state pension at state pension age, you may get a higher pension or a lump sum when you start to draw it at a later date. This is called *'deferment'*.

For periods of deferment after 6.4.05, your state pension (including any graduated retirement benefit and additional state pension) is increased by 1% for each five weeks that you put off drawing your state pension, as long as you defer it for at least five weeks. Alternatively, if you defer your state pension for at least 12 consecutive months, instead of an increased state pension you can receive a one-off taxable lump sum based on the amount of pension you would have received plus interest. (This lump sum will be disregarded for income-related benefits such as pension credit or housing benefit.) If you defer for less than a year, you will not receive interest payments but you can have your backdated pension paid as a lump sum. You can defer your state pension for as long as you want to and receive extra pension or a lump sum in this way.

For periods of deferment of at least seven weeks before April 2005, your state pension (including any graduated retirement benefit and additional state pension) is increased by 1% for each seven weeks that you deferred drawing your state pension.
SSCBA, Sch 5

You cannot clock up extra state pension by keeping another income maintenance benefit (such as widow's pension) or pension credit after state pension age. An increase for an adult dependant will not be made if you defer claiming state pension. However, a married woman who has deferred her Category B pension may receive an increase to this as long as she was not receiving certain other state pensions or benefits in the meantime. Since April 2006 you can draw graduated retirement benefit without this affecting any increase for deferring a category B pension.
WBRP Regs, reg 4(1)

For more on deferring your state pension, see DWP leaflet SPD1.

Age addition

This is 25p a week for people aged 80 or over.
SSCBA, S.79

8. Non-contributory state pension

Category D pension is non-contributory and paid at £66 a week to people who do not have a contributory state pension.

If you have a contributory state pension of less than £66, you can receive a Category D pension to top up your state pension to a total of £66. To qualify, you must be aged 80 or over and satisfy certain residency conditions. To claim, ask The Pension Service for a claim-form for the Category D pension.
SSCBA, S.78

9. How do you claim state pension?

Normally, The Pension Service contacts you with details about claiming your pension about four months before you reach state pension age. However, this does not always happen; The Pension Service may not have your current address, especially if you have not worked for some time.

You can claim in different ways. You can ring 0800 731 7898 (textphone 0800 731 7339) to make a claim over the phone or ask for a claim-form. You can also download the claim-form or claim online (www.gov.uk/claim-state-pension-online).

From 2.11.10 you no longer need to make a claim for Category A or B state pension in certain circumstances, eg if you were getting employment and support allowance, income support, jobseeker's allowance, incapacity benefit or pension credit at some time within the eight weeks leading up to your state pension age. However, there are exceptions. If you qualify and so do not need to make a claim for state pension, you will be notified two weeks before state pension age.

If you have decided to defer drawing your state pension at state pension age, you should contact The Pension Service up to four months before you do wish to draw it. If you have already started to draw your state pension but now wish to defer it, contact The Pension Service. You can only give up your state pension once and you cannot backdate this choice.
C&P Regs, Sch 4, para 13

10. How is state pension paid?

State pension is normally paid directly into a Post Office, bank or building society account. See Chapter 57(5) for more on payments.

If you reached state pension age before 6.4.10, you will have been able to choose whether to receive it weekly in advance or in arrears every four or 13 weeks. If you reach state pension on or after 6.4.10, weekly payments will normally be made in arrears. However, if you were previously receiving a working age benefit that was paid two-weekly in arrears, your state pension will usually continue to be paid in that way.

Pay day for people claiming their state pension before 6.4.10 is generally Monday (or Thursday if you claimed in 1984 or earlier) but it can now be any weekday. If your state pension is £5 or less a week, it is normally paid in a lump sum with your Christmas bonus.

Special compensation schemes

This section of the Handbook looks at:

44 Industrial Injuries scheme

1. Who is covered by the scheme?

The Industrial Injuries scheme provides no-fault tax-free benefits for an employee who *'suffers personal injury caused after 4.7.48 by accident arising out of and in the course of'* work, or who contracts a prescribed disease while working.

SSCBA, S.94 for accidents & Ss.108-110 for prescribed diseases

You are covered by the Industrial Injuries scheme if you are working for an employer. It doesn't matter if you do not earn enough to pay national insurance (NI) contributions, or if you are too old or too young to pay them. Nor does it matter if the accident happens on your first day at work. What counts is that you are gainfully employed under a contract of service, or as an office-holder with taxable earnings.

You will not be covered if you are genuinely self-employed or if you are a volunteer, unless the accident happens while you are doing specified types of voluntary work, eg a special constable. There is a discretion to treat someone who is illegally employed as an employed earner.

SSCBA 1992, Ss.2(1) & 96-97; Social Security (Employed Earners' Employment for Industrial Injuries Purposes) Regs 1975, Sch 1, Part 1 & Sch 3

Working outside the UK – You are covered by the Industrial Injuries scheme if your accident occurred outside the UK if your employer was paying NI contributions for you while you were working abroad or if you were working in a European Community country or Norway or on the continental shelf of the UK, or as a mariner or airman, or as a volunteer development worker who continued to pay UK contributions.

SSCBA, Ss.117–120

Appeals – If there is any doubt over your status as an employed earner, your case is decided by an HMRC officer; you have a right to appeal to a First-tier Tribunal (Tax Chamber). It may be possible to show that you were an employee for benefit purposes (despite the tax and NI arrangements) if the real relationship between you and the contractor is that of an employee and employer. This applies in particular to building workers, who are very often categorised as self-employed. Your trade union may be able to advise you.

Pre-1948 cases – Before 5.12.12, there were separate benefit schemes for diseases, conditions and accidents which occurred or arose before 5.7.48. Since 5.12.12, awards of benefit under these old schemes have been transferred onto the Industrial Injuries scheme described in this chapter. A claim relating to this earlier period will be treated as a claim for industrial injuries benefit.

2. Industrial accidents

If you have an accident at work you should report the details as soon as possible to your employer. Do this even if things don't seem serious at first. A cut can turn septic. A pain in the stomach can turn out to be a hernia. (An accident book or an equivalent electronic record must be kept at any workplace where ten or more people usually work.)

In most cases it will be clear that an 'accident' has happened and that it was 'industrial', but case law has expanded these concepts to include less obvious situations. For example, a conversation or verbal harassment could constitute an accident. Box P.1 looks at these issues in more detail and at some of the problems that can arise.

If you are in any doubt about whether you are covered by the Industrial Injuries scheme you should seek advice and claim benefit anyway. Case law is complex so always get advice if you are turned down.

3. Prescribed industrial diseases

Benefit can be paid for around 60 different diseases or conditions that are prescribed as being risks of particular occupations and not risks common to the general population. These are listed in DWP guide DB1 (see Box P.4) along with the types of occupations you must have worked in to qualify for benefit.

For some diseases, there are rules about the length of time you must have worked in the occupation. For example:

❑ **Occupational deafness** – See 6 below.
❑ **Chronic bronchitis and emphysema** – To qualify, you must have worked underground in a coal mine for a total of 20 years or more (this includes periods of sickness absence) and have a defined reduction in lung capacity. In April 1997 the medical conditions were modified, so if your claim was refused under the old rules you should re-apply. In July 2008 coverage was extended so that each two years of work as a screen worker on the surface of a coal mine before 1.1.83 is equivalent to one year working underground.

IIPD Regs, Sch 1

❑ **Cataract** – To qualify, you must have worked in a listed job for at least five years.

IIPD Regs, reg 2(e)

P.1 Accidents at work: principles of entitlement

What is an accident?
You must first show that an 'accident' has occurred. While this is usually clear-cut, there are situations where it may not be immediately obvious. In CI/2414/98, for example, a conversation with a colleague causing the claimant to suffer stress and depression was accepted as an accident and the opinion given that words alone such as *'verbal sexual harassment at work [could] amount to an accident or series of accidents as might misinformation designed to shock or causing shock'*.

In most cases an accident will involve an unexpected event. But what if an expected event causes an unexpected injury? In *CAO v Faulds* (R(I)1/00), the claimant was a fireman suffering post-traumatic stress disorder after attending a series of horrific incidents. The House of Lords rejected the argument that attending such incidents was the job for which he had been trained and so could not constitute 'accidents' to him, and decided that an accident need not be an unexpected event but that the sustaining of an *unexpected* personal injury caused by an *expected* event or incident may itself amount to an accident.

Accident or process?
Problems can arise if the injury developed relatively slowly through the normal course of work. This is called injury by *'process'*. If your injury developed as a result of a continuous process at work you will not be entitled to industrial injuries benefits, unless your injury is listed as one of the prescribed industrial diseases.

However, the cumulative effect of a series of small incidents, each of which is separate and identifiable, that were slightly out of the ordinary can count as an accident. But each one must have led to some physiological or pathological change for the worse. For example, in R(I)43/55 the claimant developed a psychoneurotic condition and skin disorder. He had been working near a machine that irregularly produced loud explosive reports. Any one of them could have been the start of a major explosion. It was held that each explosion was an 'accident' with a cumulative effect on his condition.

If a process has been going on for only a short time, or you have just started a new job or have had a change in working conditions, it may be easier to show you have suffered injury by accident, but each case will be a matter of fact and degree.

What about other causes of injury?
If you have a condition that predisposes you to certain injuries you can still be covered by the scheme but some aspect of your employment must have caused the injury in question. For example, an asthma sufferer had an acute asthma attack due to fumes from a fire at work. He was covered, as it was probable that he would not have had that attack if it had not been for the fire at work.

Your claim will fail if it was pure coincidence that you had the heart attack, strain, fit, etc at work rather than somewhere else. However, this is not always clear-cut. In R(I)6/82, it was confirmed that even if an accident happens out of the blue it will count as an 'industrial' one if the activity you are doing represents a special danger to you because of something in yourself or you are also injured because of coming into contact with the employer's plant or premises (eg by falling onto the floor).

Is it an 'industrial' accident?
To count as an 'industrial' accident, it must have arisen *out of* and *in the course of* employment. The difference between these phrases is clearly shown in *CAO v Rhodes* (R(I)1/99). Here, a Benefits Agency worker was assaulted by a neighbour whom she had reported for undeclared earnings. As the worker was at home on sick leave, she was found to have had an accident out of her employment but not in the course of it. Had she been working at home on the day, the outcome might have been different.

If your accident happens during an early arrival, late stay or permitted break on the employer's premises you would probably be covered. But if you had got in early or overstayed the break purely for your own purposes (eg to have a game of snooker), you would have taken yourself outside the course of your employment.

Travelling to and from work
In the main, you are not covered if you have an accident while travelling to or from your regular workplace but you may be covered while travelling in the employer's time to an irregular workplace so that your journey can be accepted as having formed part of the work you were employed to do (see R(I)7/85). One important (but not conclusive) factor is whether you were being paid for the time spent on the journey or were able to claim overtime or time off in lieu for it. You will usually be covered if you are in transport provided by your employer. You will not be covered if your journey is for your own purposes, unconnected with your work (unless it is reasonably incidental to it).

Peripatetic workers, such as home helps, are normally accepted as covered when travelling between jobs but not when travelling to the first or from the last job.

Emergencies
If you have an accident while responding to an emergency, you will be covered if what you did was reasonably incidental to your normal duties and was a sensible reaction to the emergency. Besides the obvious emergencies of fire and flood, unexpected occurrences can also count.

In one case, a lorry driver delivering bricks helped move a concrete mixer out of the way and was injured. He was covered as, even though that was not a normal part of his duties, it was reasonably incidental to his work and it was in his employer's interests for him to complete his delivery quickly.

Accidents treated as 'industrial'
Some accidents can be 'treated as' arising out of work. If you have broken any rules but what you have done is for the purposes of, and in connection with, your employer's business, you will be covered if you have an accident. You may have problems if what you have done is not part of your job, but if you can show that your employer would not automatically have stopped you doing the activity in question you might succeed. You must also show that it was in your employer's interests.

You will be covered for an injury during the course of your work caused by someone else's misconduct, negligence or skylarking, by an animal or by being struck by an object or by lightning, provided you did not contribute directly or indirectly to the accident.

SSCBA 1992, Ss.98–101

❑ **Osteoarthritis of the hip** – To qualify, you must have worked in agriculture as a farmer or farm worker for a total of ten years or more.
IIPD Regs, Sch 1

❑ **Osteoarthritis of the knee** – This disease was added to the list in July 2009. To qualify, you must have worked for a total of ten years or more, made up of periods underground in a coal mine before 1986 and/or periods from 1986 in certain mining occupations.
IIPD Regs, Sch 1

It is up to you to claim benefit for a prescribed disease. If you have any reason to suspect that your illness is related to your work, ask Jobcentre Plus and your doctor for advice. If you do not, you may lose benefit. For example, few secretaries realise that they may be covered by prescribed disease A4 (task-specific focal dystonia) if they experience cramp of the hand or forearm. Similarly, welders or hairdressers with hay fever symptoms may have a claim for prescribed disease D4, allergic rhinitis.

If your disability arises from a non-listed condition that was contracted at work, you may still be able to claim under the 'accident' provisions. Case law has shown that the 'catching' of the condition can be accepted as an industrial accident; such cases include a nursery nurse who contracted poliomyelitis from an infected child (CI/159/50) and a tinner whose frequent burns on the hands caused cysts (R(I)24/54).

4. Common law compensation

As well as a claim for benefits under the Industrial Injuries scheme, you may have a civil claim for personal injury against your employer. With industrial diseases, this could apply even if you did the job years ago or the employer has ceased trading; in some cases an award can be significantly more than can be claimed in benefits. You may also claim

---

P.2 How is disablement assessed?

The legislation uses three different terms when considering disablement questions. These are:
■ loss of faculty;
■ disability;
■ disablement.

They are each used as different concepts and must not be confused. They are not defined in the law but have been considered by the Social Security Commissioners, particularly in R(I)1/81.

Loss of faculty

A *'loss of faculty'* is any pathological condition or any loss (including a reduction) of the normal physical or mental function of an organ or part of the body. This does include disfigurement, even though there may not actually be any loss of faculty. For industrial injuries disablement benefit (IIDB), the loss of faculty must be caused by an industrial accident or prescribed disease.

A loss of faculty is not itself a disability. It is the starting point for the assessment of disablement. It is a condition that is either an actual cause of one or more disabilities or a potential cause of disability. For example, the loss of one kidney is a 'loss of faculty'. If the other kidney works normally, you may not notice any problems. But you will have lost your back-up kidney, so this is a potential cause of disability in the future. Appeal tribunals have assessed the loss of one kidney (the other functioning properly) at between 5% and 10%.

Disability

A *'disability'* means an inability to perform a bodily or mental process. This can be a complete inability to do something (eg walking), or it can be a partial inability to do something (eg you can lift light weights but not heavy ones). The disability must result from the relevant 'loss of faculty' to count for IIDB. Note that the availability of artificial aids may reduce the actual disability. The only reported Commissioners' decisions on this, R(I)7/67 and R(I)7/63, concerned spectacles.

Disablement

'Disablement' is the sum total of all the separate disabilities you may experience. It represents your overall inability to perform the 'normal' activities of life – the loss of your health, strength and power to enjoy a 'normal' life. There is a complete scale of assessment from 1-100% disablement. Every case is decided individually, so it is possible to give only general guidelines. Some types of disability have a fixed percentage, which can be increased or decreased depending on the circumstances of the case. These 'scheduled assessments' are listed in Box P.3. Other disabilities are assessed in relation to this list.

What is taken into account?

The assessment is done by comparing your condition (all your disabilities due to the relevant loss of faculty) with that of a person of the same age and sex whose physical and mental condition is 'normal'. The decision maker, or in practice the DWP healthcare professional who assesses you, also has to make judgements about what is normal for someone of your age and sex. For example, how much hearing loss is normal for a man of 50? At what age does it become normal to lose teeth and wear false teeth?
SSCBA, Sch 6, paras 1–3

If your condition differed from normal prior to the accident and therefore the industrial injury is more disabling than it would otherwise be, the assessment may be increased to take account of this. For example, decision makers *'are entitled to increase the disablement percentage to take account of the fact that, when disaster struck, he was blind. They are not entitled to compensate him for the blindness itself, but they are entitled to take account of the fact that a particular happening to a blind man, or somebody suffering from some other disability, may be more serious of itself than it would be in the case of a man who suffered from no disability'* (Murrell v Secretary of State for Social Security (appendix to R(I)3/84)).

The decision maker also has to consider how your condition affects you, rather than just considering what is generally true of people with your condition or taking the same drugs. Inconvenience, genuine embarrassment, anxiety or depression can all increase the assessment.

If your disablement also has a mental element, R(I)4/94 provides a useful summary of the ways in which that might affect the assessment of disablement. R(I)13/75 discusses the differences between hysteria, malingering and functional overlay. See also CSI/1180/01 and CI/1756/02.

There have been a number of cases involving stress-related conditions, which are particularly difficult to assess in relation to the schedule. CI/1307/99 is useful in this respect, the Commissioner using the tariffs for facial disfigurement and loss of sight as bearing the closest comparison in that they interfere with interpersonal communications.

The fact of your loss of earning power, or incapacity for work, cannot be taken into account in the assessment. Nor can the fact that your disabilities may lead to extra expenses. But the disabilities that lead to incapacity for work (or extra expenses) are taken into account, along with disabilities that do not affect your working capacity at all.

for non-listed conditions. Normally, your employer has to be partly at fault, but for some industrial diseases (eg deafness) there are no-fault compensation schemes that have been negotiated between unions and employers. The time limit for filing civil claims is three years from the date of the accident. For diseases, the three years start from the date you became aware that your disease or condition was caused by work.

You will need a solicitor. Your union may help or you can contact Accident Line (see Box P.4). While many solicitors deal with personal injury claims, it is important to choose a solicitor who specialises in your specific condition, particularly if you have an asbestos-related disease. See Chapter 59(2).

For information about the way in which benefits and compensation payments affect each other, see Chapters 28(6), 46 and 48.

For certain dust diseases, including mesothelioma, byssinosis and pneumoconiosis, a lump-sum payment can be claimed under the Pneumoconiosis etc (Workers' Compensation) Act 1979 when a civil compensation claim may not be possible because the employer is no longer in business. If in doubt, claim anyway. Negligence need not be proved. You should make a claim under the Act at the same time as you claim industrial injuries disablement benefit (IIDB). Any payment made will be based on your age and the DWP percentage assessment of your disablement for IIDB purposes, but do not wait for an assessment before claiming under the Act. Posthumous claims can be made by dependants but any payment made is substantially less than is paid if the person with the disease makes the initial claim. For claim-forms and more information, ring 0844 984 0190. If you have mesothelioma, you can make a claim under the Mesothelioma Scheme 2008 even if your illness was not caused by work.

There are special schemes in particular industries, eg

The assessment doesn't just depend on your condition on the day (or time of day) you are examined. If your condition varies, the healthcare professional will work out an average assessment taking into account your good and bad spells. It is arguable that any loss of life expectancy should also be taken into account, as well as the effect of your knowledge of the nature of your disability on your life.

Scheduled and non-scheduled assessments

The scheduled assessments, listed in Box P.3, are fixed on the assumption that your condition has stabilised and there are no added complications. Other disabilities are assessed accordingly.

If your disability is not in the schedule, the decision maker '*may have such regard as may be appropriate to the prescribed degrees of disablement*'. They should try to assess your disabilities so that your percentage assessment looks right in relation to the scheduled assessments. R(I)2/06 sets out the approach to be taken by appeal tribunals to questions of assessment.
GB Regs, reg 11(8)

When you look at the schedule, remember that 100% is not total and absolute disablement. It is just the legal maximum assessment. If the scale could go higher, some people would be assessed as 200% disabled or more.

The schedule says that if you are totally deaf, or severely facially disfigured, the fixed assessment is 100%.

If you have had either arm amputated just below the shoulder, you will be assessed at 80% – even if you cope perfectly well. If the amputation has not yet stabilised, or there are other complications with it, a higher assessment can be made.

If you cannot use one arm at all, you may well be assessed at 80% – as if you had actually lost your arm. CI/1199/02 usefully illustrates this point in relation to vibration white finger (PD A11).

Several conditions

Four different disabilities due to the same accident or prescribed disease may each be assessed as causing 10% disablement, but the assessment will not always be the total of 40%. This is because the interaction of different conditions in one person may be far more disabling – so the final assessment could well be higher. If you have several of the minor scheduled conditions, the total percentage assessment could be less or more than the actual total of the percentages for each of the scheduled conditions. The healthcare professional will give their opinion on what is the appropriate assessment for you – given your age, sex and physical and mental condition as a whole. So even for the scheduled assessments, the healthcare professional may increase (or decrease) the percentage(s) if that is reasonable in a particular case. The formula for assessing disablement that has more than one cause is set out in CI/2183/2011, which makes the point that it is essential to establish accurately the dates of each accident and the onset of each disease.

Pre-existing condition

If your disability has some other cause, you may have problems – eg where a previous back injury is followed by an industrial injury to your back. However, your percentage assessment should only be cut, or offset, if there is evidence that a pre-existing condition would have led to a degree of disablement even if the accident had not happened. If there is no evidence for this, the offset should not be made. R(I)1/81 explains the concepts fully.

If an offset is justified, the net assessment (ie after the offset) should reflect any greater disablement because of the interaction between the two (or more) causes of the same disability. Note that a pre-existing condition may cause disablement later. Although the disablement you would have had from that pre-existing condition alone cannot be taken into account, its interaction with the effects of the industrial injury may lead to greater disablement. This could justify a request for a supersession on the grounds of a change of circumstances (see section 10 in this chapter).
GB Regs, reg 11(3)

Conditions arising afterwards

If a condition is 'directly attributable' to the industrial accident or disease, it is assessable in the normal way. If it is not 'directly attributable', but is also a cause of the same disability, then whether or not any greater disablement can be taken into account depends on the percentage assessment for the industrial accident or disease. If the disablement resulting from the industrial accident is assessed at 11% or more, that assessment can be increased to reflect the extent to which the industrial injury is worsened because of the later condition. This can be done at the time of the assessment, or later on an application for a supersession.

Note that in reaching the 11% benchmark, account is taken of any greater disablement because of the interaction with a pre-existing condition that is also an effective cause of the disability.

The 11% rule does not apply where one is considering the interaction between two or more industrial accidents or diseases (see R(I)3/91).
GB Regs, reg 11(4)

mining and the NHS. Trade unions should be able to advise members on these and on benefits and other types of compensation.

5. What benefits can you claim?

Industrial injuries disablement benefit – Industrial injuries disablement benefit (IIDB) is the main industrial injuries benefit and is paid to compensate those who have suffered disablement from a *'loss of physical or mental faculty'* caused by an industrial accident or prescribed disease (see Box P.2). Your employer does not have to be at fault in any way for you to get benefit.

You can claim whether or not you are incapable of work or have had any drop in earnings. IIDB is tax free and paid on top of earnings or other non-means-tested benefits. Benefit is payable from 15 weeks from the date of the accident or onset of the disease if your disablement is assessed at 14% or more. For some prescribed chest diseases you can get benefit if the assessment is from 1% to 13%. For occupational deafness you can get benefit only if your disablement is 20% or more.

If you are claiming for a prescribed disease (PD), the date of onset should be the date the disease started, not the date of claim. As benefit is only payable 15 weeks after this date, you should check this and challenge it if necessary. However, for occupational deafness, the date of onset must be the date a successful claim was made, and payment can start from that day. There is no 15-week waiting period for PD D3 (diffuse mesothelioma) or PD D8 and PD D8A (primary carcinoma of the lung). These three diseases are paid at the 100% rate from the date of claim.

SSCBA 1992, S.103; IIPD Regs, regs 20(4) & 28

Reduced earnings allowance – Reduced earnings allowance (which replaced special hardship allowance from 1.10.86) was abolished on 1.10.90 for accidents or diseases occurring after that date. If your accident or the onset of a prescribed disease (which must be listed before 10.10.94) occurred before 1.10.90, you can still claim reduced earnings allowance. It is tax free and paid on top of any earnings or other non-means-tested benefits you receive. See 14 below for more details.

Retirement allowance – Retirement allowance replaces reduced earnings allowance if you are already getting at least £2 a week reduced earnings allowance and not in regular employment when you reach state pension age. See 15 below for more details. Retirement allowance is tax free and paid on top of any earnings or other non-means-tested benefits you receive.

Industrial death benefit – Industrial death benefit was payable if the death occurred before 11.4.88. It was abolished on 5.12.12. Those widowed on or after 11.4.88 as a result of an industrial accident or prescribed disease are entitled to widows' benefits and, since 9.4.01, bereavement benefits, without having to satisfy any contribution conditions (see Chapter 53).

6. How do you claim industrial injuries disablement benefit (IIDB)?

To claim IIDB ring your Regional Call Centre: Scotland, North West England, East of England, South East England and London 0845 603 1358; Yorkshire and The Humber, North East England, East and West Midlands, South West England and Wales 0845 758 5433; use textphone 0845 605 8551 or go to www.gov.uk/industrial-injuries-disablement-benefit/how-to-claim. You need form BI100A for an accident or BI100PD for any of the prescribed industrial diseases.

Benefit cannot be backdated more than three months even if you have a good reason for not claiming earlier.

There are special time limits for these prescribed diseases:

❑ **Occupational deafness** – To qualify, you must have worked in one or more of the listed jobs as an employed earner for a total of at least ten years, and have a hearing loss of at least 50db in each ear, due, in the case of at least one ear, to occupational noise. If you qualify, you will be paid from the date your claim is received in an IIDB Delivery Centre – and that date must be within five years of the last day you worked in one of the jobs listed. There is no backdating of claims.

IIPD Regs, regs 2(c) & 34

❑ **Occupational asthma** – You cannot get IIDB for occupational asthma if you last worked as an employed earner in the listed job more than ten years before your date of claim. But this 10-year limit does not apply if you have asthma because of an industrial accident and have been awarded IIDB for life or for a period which includes your date of claim. If you are outside these time limits, a return to a listed occupation for just one day would start the period running again.

IIPD Regs, reg 36

7. How is your claim decided?

All decisions are made by a DWP decision maker acting on behalf of the Secretary of State.

Accident cases

The decision maker first decides whether you have had an industrial accident and, if so, whether it arose out of and in the course of your work. If the decision is in your favour, you will be asked to go for a medical examination.

You will be examined by one (or possibly two) DWP healthcare professionals. They will provide the decision maker with a report giving an opinion on whether you have a loss of faculty as a result of the accident and, if so, the extent to which that loss of faculty leads to disablement and the period over which it is likely to last. The percentage assessment of your disablement can cover a past period as well as a forward one.

The decision maker will then decide your claim based on this report as well as any other available evidence, such as a letter from your GP or hospital consultant. In practice, they will normally adopt the DWP healthcare professional's opinion.

Prescribed industrial diseases

The decision maker will decide if you have worked in one of the occupations listed for your particular disease or condition and whether the disease was caused by that occupation. For many prescribed diseases there is a presumption in law that, unless the contrary can be proved, the condition was caused by your job if you were working in the listed occupation on the date of onset or within one month of that date. If it is decided you do not satisfy these employment conditions, your claim will be refused. You have one month to appeal against the decision.

If the decision maker decides you satisfy the employment conditions, you will be asked to go for an examination by one (or possibly two) DWP healthcare professionals. They will send a report to the decision maker giving their opinion on whether you have the prescribed disease, any resulting loss of faculty, the level and period of your disablement, the date of onset and whether your disease is due to your employment. The healthcare professional(s) can obtain reports from your hospital consultant and GP if necessary. Although in deciding your claim the decision maker has to take into account all the available evidence, they will normally adopt the DWP healthcare professional's opinion.

If you are claiming for certain asbestos-related diseases or some prescribed cancers, your claim will be fast-tracked and you will be sent for an examination while the employment questions are being considered. If you have diffuse mesothelioma (PD D3) or primary carcinoma of the lung (PD D8 and D8A), an examination may not be necessary if your diagnosis is confirmed by your consultant, GP or specialist nurse. This is because, provided you meet the employment conditions, you are automatically assessed as 100% disabled once diagnosis is confirmed.

For some prescribed diseases you may be asked to have a particular test before being sent for an examination – for example, for occupational deafness, a hearing test, and for chronic bronchitis and emphysema, a breathing test. If the results of those tests show that you meet the particular criteria for those conditions you will be sent for an examination. If not, your claim will be disallowed. You have one month to appeal against a disallowance.

If you have had (or have) industrial injuries disablement benefit for the same disease, the decision maker may need to decide whether there has been a worsening of your condition or whether you have contracted the disease afresh. This is known as the recrudescence question.

P.3 Prescribed degrees of disablement

Description of injury	Degree
Loss of both hands or amputation at higher sites	100%
Loss of a hand and a foot	100%
Double amputation through leg or thigh, or amputation through leg or thigh on one side and loss of other foot	100%
Loss of sight to such an extent as to render the claimant unable to perform any work for which eyesight is essential	100%
Very severe facial disfiguration	100%
Absolute deafness	100%
Forequarter or hindquarter amputation	100%

Amputation cases – upper limbs (either arm)

Amputation through shoulder joint	90%
Amputation below shoulder with stump less than 20.5 centimetres from tip of acromion	80%
Amputation from 20.5 centimetres from tip of acromion to less than 11.5 centimetres below tip of olecranon	70%
Loss of a hand or of the thumb and four fingers of one hand or amputation from 11.5 centimetres below tip of olecranon	60%
Loss of thumb	30%
Loss of thumb and its metacarpal bone	40%
Loss of four fingers of one hand	50%
Loss of three fingers of one hand	30%
Loss of two fingers of one hand	20%
Loss of terminal phalanx of thumb	20%

Amputation cases – lower limbs

Amputation of both feet resulting in end-bearing stumps	90%
Amputation through both feet proximal to the metatarso-phalangeal joint	80%
Loss of all toes of both feet through the metatarso-phalangeal joint	40%
Loss of all toes of both feet proximal to the proximal inter-phalangeal joint	30%
Loss of all toes of both feet distal to the proximal inter-phalangeal joint	20%
Amputation at hip	90%
Amputation below hip with stump not exceeding 13 centimetres in length measured from tip of great trochanter	80%
Amputation below hip and above knee with stump exceeding 13 centimetres in length measured from tip of great trochanter, or at knee not resulting in end-bearing stump	70%
Amputation at knee resulting in end-bearing stump or below knee with stump not exceeding 9 centimetres	60%
Amputation below knee with stump exceeding 9 centimetres but not exceeding 13 centimetres	50%

Amputation below knee with stump exceeding 13 centimetres	40%
Amputation of one foot resulting in end-bearing stump	30%
Amputation through one foot proximal to the metatarso-phalangeal joint	30%
Loss of all toes of one foot through the metatarso-phalangeal joint	20%

Other injuries

Loss of one eye, without complications, the other being normal	40%
Loss of vision of one eye, without complications or disfigurement of the eyeball, the other being normal	30%

Loss of fingers of right or left hand

❏ **Index finger:**

Whole	14%
Two phalanges	11%
One phalanx	9%
Guillotine amputation of tip without loss of bone	5%

❏ **Middle finger:**

Whole	12%
Two phalanges	9%
One phalanx	7%
Guillotine amputation of tip without loss of bone	4%

❏ **Ring or little finger:**

Whole	7%
Two phalanges	6%
One phalanx	5%
Guillotine amputation of tip without loss of bone	2%

Loss of toes of right or left foot

❏ **Great toe:**

Through metatarso-phalangeal joint	14%
Part, with some loss of bone	3%

❏ **Any other toe:**

Through metatarso-phalangeal joint	3%
Part, with some loss of bone	1%

❏ **Two toes of one foot, excluding great toe:**

Through metatarso-phalangeal joint	5%
Part, with some loss of bone	2%

❏ **Three toes of one foot, excluding great toe:**

Through metatarso-phalangeal joint	6%
Part, with some loss of bone	3%

❏ **Four toes of one foot, excluding great toe:**

Through metatarso-phalangeal joint	9%
Part, with some loss of bone	3%

GB Regs, Sch 2

As the questions to be decided on your claim are often complex, try to get advice and help with an appeal if your claim is turned down. See Chapters 58 and 59.

How disablement is assessed

The DWP examining healthcare professionals(s) will give an opinion on the extent and likely duration of your disablement and must consider all the disabilities resulting from the accident or disease, including the worsening of pre-existing conditions. They will assess the disablement resulting from any *'loss of faculty'* by comparing your condition with that of a healthy person of the same age and sex. For this purpose, your job and other personal circumstances do not matter. See Box P.2 for details on the principles of assessment.

The decision maker can make a *'provisional'* or a *'final'* assessment. A provisional assessment is reviewed towards the end of a set period and reassessed, so if your condition is taking time to stabilise you may have a series of provisional assessments. If your disablement is less than 14% and it seems unlikely the current assessment can be added to any other assessments to reach the 14% minimum for payment, a final assessment will be made. A final assessment may be for life if your disablement is considered permanent and unlikely to change appreciably, or it may be for a fixed period. In the latter case, the decision maker is effectively saying you will no longer be affected by the accident or disease after a specified date. This is not the same as saying there is no longer any disablement but rather that the causative link has been broken.
SSCBA, Sch 6, para 6

Reduced earnings allowance is only payable during the period of a disablement assessment of at least 1%. If your assessment is a final one for a limited period, it cannot be paid beyond that period. To safeguard your award of reduced earnings allowance, you can either appeal against the period of the assessment or you can wait until near the end of the assessment period and ask for the decision to be superseded on the grounds of a change of circumstances (see 10 below). As either option could result in a nil assessment you might decide to wait. But, to be safe, you should apply for a supersession before your final assessment ends because if there is a break of even one day between assessment periods you could permanently lose the reduced earnings allowance (see 14 below).

8. How much do you get?

Lump-sum gratuities – pre-1.10.86 claims
If you claimed industrial injuries disablement benefit (IIDB) before 1.10.86 and your disablement was assessed at 1-19%, you were paid a lump-sum gratuity (unless you were claiming for certain chest diseases for which a pension was paid). The amount of gratuity paid depended on the percentage and duration of your assessment; if it was 20% or over, you were paid a weekly pension as now.

If you were entitled to special hardship allowance, you could choose to have the IIDB paid as a weekly pension on top instead of as a lump sum. This is no longer possible, but an existing pension in lieu of a gratuity can continue (if you remain entitled to reduced earnings allowance, which replaced special hardship allowance) until the end of the period of your assessment.
II&D(MP) Regs, reg 12

A gratuity for a final life assessment lasts for seven years (R(I)11/67) when deciding if any offset is appropriate against a further award for a subsequent accident or disease or an increase in the original assessment. (For an example of how this works in practice, see *Disability Rights Handbook* 23rd edition, page 151.)

Weekly pension – claims after 1.10.86
Since 1.10.86, you can get benefit only if your total disablement is assessed at 14% or more, or at least 1% for pneumoconiosis and byssinosis.

Benefit is paid as a weekly pension. Assessments of 14-19% disablement are paid at the 20% rate. Assessments of 24% (or 44%, etc) are rounded down and paid at the 20% rate (or 40%, etc). Assessments of 25% (or 45%, etc) are rounded up and paid at the 30% rate (or 50%, etc). For pneumoconiosis and byssinosis, assessments of 1-10% are paid at the 10% rate and assessments of 11-24% are paid at the 20% rate.
SSCBA, S.103(3); IIPD Regs, regs 15B & 20(1A)

Anyone diagnosed as having pneumoconiosis (PD D1) is automatically treated as at least 1% disabled and therefore entitled to benefit. It appears (from R(I)1/96) the DWP may have treated such claims incorrectly in the past, so you should contact them if you had a claim for pneumoconiosis rejected. Benefit can be paid back to 25.8.94 if appropriate and compensation paid for official error.

Percentages and amounts

20%	£32.32	50%	£80.80	80%	£129.28
30%	£48.48	60%	£96.96	90%	£145.44
40%	£64.64	70%	£113.12	100%	£161.60

Aggregation of assessments

Disablement assessments for more than one industrial injury or disease can be added together, or *'aggregated'*, if the assessment periods overlap. This can help you reach the minimum payment figure of 14% during a common core period, so it is worth claiming IIDB for even 'minor' injuries.

An assessment on a claim made on or after 1.10.86 can be aggregated with any assessment(s) on claim(s) for accidents or diseases before that date. Case law has established that this includes pre-1986 life awards for which a gratuity has been paid. Decision makers will aggregate only if you have at least one assessment that has been made after 1.10.86. So, for example, they would refuse to aggregate two pre-86 life awards of 11% and 9% but would aggregate them if either award was increased after 1.10.86, or a successful claim for a further accident/disease was made after 1.10.86, even if it occurred before this date. See R(I)4/03.

If you have had a gratuity in the past and think this percentage assessment is not being aggregated with any further assessment(s), you should ask Jobcentre Plus to supersede any previous decision and award you a weekly pension, if this brings you to at least 14%, or to increase your existing pension to take account of the earlier assessment. Decision makers are advised to revise on the grounds of official error or to supersede if the decision was made after 24.7.95. Arrears cannot be paid back to a date earlier than 24.7.95, the date of CI/522/93 (see R(I)1/03). Decision makers should also consider compensation (see Chapter 60(2)) but may need to be prompted. Assessments of under 20% for occupational deafness cannot be aggregated. Aggregation of assessments (at least in pneumoconiosis or byssinosis cases) is carried out only if it is to your advantage.
SSCBA, S.103(2); IIPD Regs, regs 15A, 15B & 20

9. How do you appeal?

You have the right of appeal to an appeal tribunal against the Secretary of State's decision on your claim. You have one month from the date the decision was sent to you. To appeal, complete the form in DWP leaflet GL24. Provide as much detail as possible as to why you disagree with the decision. As industrial injuries benefits are complex, you may need expert advice. Your trade union or an advice centre may help.

As an alternative to an appeal, you can ask Jobcentre Plus to look at your claim again; this is called a revision. However, if a medical question is involved, the decision maker is unlikely to change the original decision based on the DWP healthcare professional's report even if you provide your own medical evidence to support your claim. From October 2013, it will not be possible to lodge an appeal unless you have already gone through the revision process. See Chapter 58 for full details of the dispute procedure.

10. If your condition gets worse

To increase your assessment or extend the period it covers you must ask for a supersession on the grounds of a change in circumstances. Any new assessment could be lower rather than higher. It could even be reduced to nil, which could then also involve a loss of reduced earnings allowance. Retirement allowance is not affected because it is awarded for life and not linked to any disablement assessment.

Try to get advice before applying. You should be particularly careful if you have now developed arthritis or spondylosis, as this can often lead to your disability being assessed as 'constitutional' and not due to the effects of your injury or prescribed disease.

Payment and aggregation of assessments following a supersession

If your request for an increased assessment is successful and the new percentage is 14% or more, you will get a pension. If you had been paid a gratuity for that injury in the past, as this is likely to be more than seven years ago, no offset will be appropriate (see 8 above).

If your assessment is increased but remains under 14% you will not get benefit unless you can aggregate that percentage with another current assessment(s). In this case, the whole percentage assessment becomes available for aggregation, not just the actual increase in percentage gained. This can be added to any current assessments you have, including final life assessments for which you received a lump-sum gratuity.

However, the position is slightly different if you are currently getting a pension in lieu of a gratuity for the original assessment. In this case, your right to a pension in lieu will end and you will receive the balance (if any) of the original gratuity, plus the appropriate gratuity for the increase in the percentage assessment or period. Or, if your disablement is assessed at 14% or more, you will receive a pension at the appropriate rate.

II&D(MP) Regs, reg 12(3)

11. Extra allowances

The following additional allowances can be paid:

Additional allowances	per week
Constant attendance allowance	
– part time	£32.35
– normal maximum	£64.70
– intermediate rate	£97.05
– exceptional rate	£129.40
Exceptionally severe disablement allowance	£64.70
Unemployability supplement*	£99.90

(earnings limit £5,174 per year)
* This was abolished from 6.4.87 for new claims and is payable only to existing claimants.

12. Constant attendance allowance

Constant attendance allowance is automatically considered when your disablement assessment totals 95% or more. Your need for care and attention must be the result of an industrial accident/disease. If you think this has been missed, claim on form BI104, available from your Regional IIDB Delivery Centre. If you receive disability living allowance (care component), personal independence payment (daily living component) or attendance allowance, it will be reduced by the amount of constant attendance allowance you receive.

SSCBA 1992, S.104

There is no right of appeal if your claim is refused, but you can ask for the decision to be looked at again if you feel some facts were not taken into account.

13. Exceptionally severe disablement allowance

This is automatically considered if you qualify for one of the two higher rates of constant attendance allowance. However, your need for that level of attendance must be likely to be permanent. Again, there is no right of appeal if your claim is refused. For more details of this and constant attendance allowance, read DWP guide DB1.

SSCBA 1992, S.105

14. Reduced earnings allowance

You can claim reduced earnings allowance (REA) if your accident happened before 1.10.90 or your disease started before 1.10.90, provided the disease (or the extension to the prescribed disease category) was added to the prescribed list before 10.10.94. REA will not be paid for newly prescribed diseases or extensions to those already listed.

You must claim REA separately from industrial injuries disablement benefit (IIDB). To claim REA, ring 0845 758 5433; you need form BI103. A claim for REA cannot be backdated for more than three months. It is possible to have more than one award of REA if you have had more than one industrial accident or disease (R(I)2/02). However, you cannot be paid more than 140% of the maximum rate of disablement benefit when your IIDB and REA awards are added together.

Once you have made a successful claim for REA, you can make renewal claims, subject to the usual rules. But if you were entitled to REA immediately before 1.10.90 (ie on 30.9.90), a break in entitlement of just one day may mean you lose REA for good.

If you are getting REA when you reach state pension age and are not in regular employment, your REA will be replaced by retirement allowance, paid at a lower rate (see 15 below). However, at present there appears to be a loophole in the law

P.4 For more information

For reference use *Social Security: Legislation Volumes I and III* (published annually by Sweet & Maxwell) and *The Law of Social Security* by Wikeley, Ogus and Barendt (2005, Butterworths). *Compensation for Industrial Injury* by R Lewis (1987, published by Professional Books Ltd/ Butterworths; out of print but may be available in large libraries) is useful for case law prior to 1987. The DWP produces a technical guide for advisers – DB1 *A guide to Industrial Injuries Disablement Benefits*, available only online (www.dwp.gov.uk/publications/specialist-guides/ technical-guidance).

Accident Line – If you have been injured in an accident or have an industrial disease, you can arrange, through Accident Line, a free legal consultation with a local solicitor specialising in personal injury claims (www.accidentlinedirect.co.uk or 0800 192939 in England and Wales).

that allows anyone claiming REA for the first time after state pension age to be paid REA, provided they are not in regular employment at the time of claim, without ever having this converted to retirement allowance. So, if you are nearing state pension age and considering claiming REA, it may be worth seeking advice about the possibility of delaying your claim.
SSCBA, Sch 7, para 11

Who qualifies for REA?
To qualify for REA you must have a current assessment of at least 1% in respect of an accident or disease that occurred before 1.10.90 (see above). You must also be unable to return to your regular occupation or do work of an equivalent standard because of the effects of the disablement caused by your accident or disease.

The broad aim is to make up the difference between what you are capable of earning, as a result of the injury or disease, in any suitable alternative employment and what you would have been likely to earn now in your regular job if you had not had the accident or disease and were still in your regular job. There are two ways of qualifying for REA.
❏ **Under the continuous condition** – You must have been incapable of following both your *'regular occupation'* and any *'employment of an equivalent standard which is suitable in [your] case'* ever since 90 days after your accident happened or your disease began.
❏ **Under the permanent condition** – It is enough if you are now *'incapable, and likely to remain permanently incapable, of following [your] regular occupation'* and also incapable of any *'employment of an equivalent standard ...'*
SSCBA, Sch 7, para 11(1)

Earnings
On a first claim, your pre- and post-accident earnings are individually assessed. On subsequent claims for the same accident or disease, revisions may be linked to the general movement in earnings of broad occupational groups, depending on how the law applies to your situation.
Social Security (Industrial Injuries) (Reduced Earnings Allowance & Transitional) Regs 1987, reg 2

Broadly, if your post-accident earnings are less than your pre-accident earnings would be now, the difference is made up by REA, subject to a maximum payment of £64.40. This comparison may be totally hypothetical, eg if your regular job no longer exists or disabilities that cannot be taken into account in the REA assessment make you incapable of any work. If you are unable to do any work because of the accident or disease you should get maximum REA.

Tackling appeals
Case law on REA, much of which originally applied to the earlier special hardship allowance, is complex and extensive. For example, there may be arguments over what your 'regular' occupation is, particularly if your accident happened during lower-paid 'stop gap' work; or you may argue that your reasonable prospects of advancement should be taken into account. If your claim is turned down or you do not get maximum REA, do not give up without first getting expert advice. As well as depending on case law, your claim may rest on many detailed facts as well as medical evidence. It is quite possible that the decision maker made a decision in ignorance of some of the relevant facts.

You have a right of appeal against the refusal of REA or the amount awarded. See Chapter 58 for more on appeals.

No percentage assessment?
To get REA, you must have a current disablement assessment of at least 1%. You also need to be sure that the loss of faculty identified by the DWP healthcare professional(s) in the report covers all the disabilities caused by the industrial accident/disease and is sufficient to contribute materially to your being incapable of following your regular occupation. The DWP healthcare professional(s) give their opinion on the link between the accepted loss of faculty and your inability to follow your regular occupation. The decision maker is not bound to accept this but in practice usually does.

If you do not have a current percentage assessment or the loss of faculty needs to be more broadly identified, you have to tackle that side of things first, by appealing or by seeking a revision or supersession. An appeal may be the best choice if you need to broaden the loss of faculty. If you are out of time, make a late appeal (see Chapter 58(7)). In a separate letter, ask for a revision or supersession. If you are trying to cover a gap in your assessment period to re-qualify for REA, a late appeal may be a better option because of the restricted backdating on supersession.

If the decision on your disablement assessment is revised or changed at appeal, the decision maker can revise the decision on your REA if this is to your advantage. This precludes the need for a separate appeal on the REA question (see Chapter 58, Box T.5).

15. Retirement allowance
Retirement allowance is set at £16.16 maximum or 50p minimum a week. It is the lower of 10% of the maximum rate of disablement benefit or 25% of the reduced earnings allowance (REA) you received immediately before reaching state pension age (see Chapter 43(2)) or ceasing regular employment, if that was later. In practice, if you had maximum REA, your retirement allowance would be £16.16. If you had retired and claimed your state pension before 10.4.89, you do not get retirement allowance, but your REA is frozen for life.

Retirement allowance is payable for life and is not linked with any percentage assessment of disability. It is only payable if you are transferring from REA. If you want to stay on REA when you reach state pension age, you can only do so while you remain in regular employment (see below). However, if you are approaching state pension age and have not yet claimed REA, you should consider delaying your claim in order to keep it indefinitely (see 14 above).

Retirement allowance replaces REA if, when you have reached state pension age, you give up regular employment and on the day before you give up that employment your award(s) of REA add up to at least £2 a week. If you stopped work before reaching state pension age, you are treated as giving up regular employment in the week you reach state pension age. If you continue regular employment after state pension age, your REA will be replaced by retirement allowance when you stop work.
SSCBA, Sch 7, paras 12 & 13

Regular employment – This is defined as gainful employment under a contract of service that requires you to work for an average of at least ten hours a week over any 5-week period (not counting any week of permitted absence such as leave or sickness), or gainful employment (which may be self-employment) that you undertake for an average of at least ten hours a week over any 5-week period.
Social Security (Industrial Injuries) (Regular Employment) Regs 1990, as amended

45 Armed Forces Compensation scheme

1. Armed Forces Compensation scheme

The Armed Forces Compensation scheme (AFCS) replaces the War Pensions scheme for injuries, illnesses or death caused by service on or after 6.4.05. War disablement pensions and war widows' pensions awarded prior to 6.4.05 are not affected and claims can still be made in respect of disablement or death due to service before 6.4.05. For information about the War Pensions scheme, see Box P.5.

The AFCS provides higher awards for more severely disabled people than the War Pensions scheme. A claim can be made for any illness or injury caused, or exacerbated, by service.

As the AFCS is a 'no fault' scheme, an award would not preclude the recipient from making a civil claim for negligence against the Ministry of Defence. However, any award made by the AFCS would be taken into consideration by the courts when assessing damages.

If your AFCS claim is successful, you receive a tax-free lump sum, assessed under a 15-level tariff system. The tariff is based on guidelines used in civil personal injury cases, with the most serious injuries graded as Level 1 and attracting the highest payments, and the least severe injuries graded as Level 15. It is possible to receive the lump sum while still in service.

If your illness or injury is likely to cause a significant decrease in earning capacity, you will also receive a tax-free *'guaranteed income payment'* (see 3 below). A *'survivor's guaranteed income payment'* will be made to a surviving partner (including same-sex partners) where the service person's death was attributable to service. See 4 below.

2. Who can claim?

All members of HM armed forces (including Ghurkhas) are covered by the AFCS, even if they have chosen to remain in the 1975 Armed Forces Pension scheme. You can also claim under the AFCS if you are a member of the reserve forces (as defined in the Reserve Forces Act 1996). Serving personnel are also covered.

You can get compensation for disablement or death due to incidents which were the direct consequence of your duties in the armed forces, including terrorism and warlike activities, or negligence by the Ministry of Defence as an employer.

You or your dependants can claim compensation for death, injury or disease for an attributable:
- death in service;
- injury or illness in service (whether or not resulting in a medical discharge);
- illness or death occurring within seven years of leaving service; *or*
- condition(s) or death that develop at a later date (eg some cancers), with no time limit. For details of the exceptions list of illnesses, ring the Veterans UK Helpline (0800 169 2277).

You can also claim for a pre-existing condition that is significantly aggravated by service.

Generally, your injury, illness, death or disablement must occur while you are on duty. This can include injuries caused by service-related physical activities, including physical education, exercise and sport approved by the relevant service authorities.

You can get compensation in certain exceptional circumstances when you are off duty, eg if you were a victim of a terrorist attack and were targeted because of being a service person.

ARF(CS) Order, arts 7-13

3. How much can you get?

The level of an award is based on a tariff that lists the injuries for which compensation may be paid. The 15 tariff levels are graduated according to the seriousness of the condition.

Lump-sum payments

A lump sum may be paid for pain and suffering, paid according to which of the 15 tariff levels applies to you. It can be awarded while you are still in service.

Guaranteed income payment

A *'guaranteed income payment'* (GIP) for life, to compensate for loss of earnings, is payable to those whose injuries are assessed at tariff levels 1-11. It is calculated by multiplying your basic salary (excluding allowances) by a figure determined by your age. A younger claimant's pay would be multiplied by a higher figure, as they would have had longer until their retirement and their potential loss of earnings is therefore greater.

Once the GIP has been calculated, you will receive a percentage of the full GIP payment, depending on the tariff level of your illness or injury. The percentages fall into four bands, as follows:

Tariffs	percentage of the GIP calculation
1-4 (Band A)	100%
5-6 (Band B)	75%
7-8 (Band C)	50%
9-11 (Band D)	30%
12-15	No GIP payable

You cannot receive a GIP while in service, but it will be payable on discharge.

ARF(CS) Order, art 24

Length of GIP awards

There is no regular review mechanism once a decision has been made and awards are intended to be full and final, taking into account the expected deterioration in health and complications arising from the illness or injury. However, if the long-term effect of an illness or injury is unclear, an interim award will be made, based on the appropriate tariff level at that time. This can be paid for up to two years before the condition is re-assessed, at which time the award can be confirmed, increased or lowered. Awards can be reviewed in exceptional circumstances, eg if the condition becomes worse than expected.

ARF(CS) Order, art 26

4. Widows, widowers and other dependants

If your death is attributable to service, your surviving spouse, civil partner or any partner (including same-sex partners) who was in a *'substantial relationship'* with you will be entitled to make a claim under the Armed Forces Pension scheme (AFPS).

The Service Personnel and Veterans Agency will be notified of your death and will establish whether there is a surviving partner or eligible child. If this is established, a Veterans Welfare Manager will visit to advise the surviving partner on claiming a pension and other benefits to which they are entitled.

ARF(CS)Order, art 30

Survivor's guaranteed income payment

A widow or widower, civil partner or eligible partner will receive a *'survivor's guaranteed income payment'*, calculated by multiplying your salary at the time of your death by a factor based on your age at the time of death; 60% of this figure is paid as the survivor's guaranteed income payment, which is reduced by 75% of any AFPS benefits received.

ARF(CS) Order, arts 29(1)(a) & 34

Bereavement grant

The surviving partner may also receive a tax-free *'bereavement grant'*, which will vary depending on which pension scheme you were in (AFPS 75 or AFPS 05) and whether you were in service at the time of your death.

❑ If you die in service and were a member of AFPS 75, your widow, widower, civil partner or eligible partner will receive a grant of £25,000.

❑ If you die in service and were a member of AFPS 05, your partner will receive no grant if your salary was above £25,000. If your salary was below £25,000, your partner will receive a grant for the difference between your salary and £25,000.

❑ If your service ended prior to your death, your partner will receive a grant of £37,500, regardless of your pension scheme.

A bereavement grant can be paid to an eligible child if you do not leave a surviving spouse, civil partner or adult dependant. Where there is more than one eligible child, the grant will be divided equally between them.

ARF(CS)Order, arts 29(1)(b) & 35

Dependent children

Dependent children will qualify for a *'child's guaranteed income payment'*, which will stop when they reach 18. It can continue if they are in full-time education or vocational training and are under 23. They may also continue to qualify if they are unable to support themselves financially due to a mental or physical disability diagnosed before they reached 18.

ARF(CS) Order, arts 29(1)(c), 31, 32 & 36

5. Does anything affect what you get?

The level of your award is not affected by state benefits, capital or income (other than your salary, insofar as it is used to calculate your guaranteed income payment (GIP)). If you have already received compensation for the injury or illness through the civil courts, it will be taken into account when assessing your award. Payments received under the Armed Forces Pension scheme will also affect the amount of GIP.

P.5 War Pensions scheme

The War Pensions scheme remains in place for those with existing awards on 6.4.05, and for new claimants whose injury, ill health or bereavement was caused by service before 6.4.05. You do not need to have been on active service when the injury or illness was caused, providing it is linked to your time in service. You can also claim for illnesses suffered during service which have caused permanent damage, or pre-existing conditions which have worsened through service.

Who can claim?

You can claim for any present disablement resulting from:

■ an injury or condition caused or worsened by service in HM armed forces at any time including service in the Home Guard, Nursing and Auxiliary Services, the Ulster Defence Regiment from 1970 and the Territorial Army;

■ a physical injury or disease sustained as a civilian during World War 2 as a result of enemy action;

■ a physical injury or disease sustained while carrying out duties as a Civil Defence Volunteer in World War 2;

■ an injury or condition caused or worsened by service during World War 2 in the Polish Forces under British Command or while serving in the Polish Resettlement Forces;

■ certain injuries or illnesses sustained while serving in the Naval Auxiliary Services, Coastguard or Merchant Navy in World War 2, or conflicts in the Gulf, Falklands, Suez or Korea; or while being held prisoner.

How much can you get?

War disablement pension – The basic disablement pension depends on your degree of disability, assessed on a percentage basis as in the Industrial Injuries scheme (see Box P.2, Chapter 44). If your assessment is 20% or more, a weekly pension is paid. The maximum pension at the 100% rate is £171.50. If your assessment is less than 20%, you will receive a one-off lump-sum gratuity, unless the claim is for noise-induced sensorineural hearing loss. No payment can be made for sensorineural hearing loss alone, but if your assessment is 20% or more for the hearing loss, this can be added to your assessment for any other disability to increase the percentage you are awarded.

Supplementary allowances

Tax-free supplementary allowances can be paid on top of your basic war disablement pension or gratuity. Some allowances you have to claim, others are paid automatically. You need to make a claim for the following allowances:

❑ **War pensioners' mobility supplement*** – This is paid if your pensioned disablement is assessed at 40% or more and is the sole or main cause of your walking difficulties.

❑ **Constant attendance allowance*** – This is paid if your pensioned disablement is assessed at 80% or more and causes you to need a lot of care, attention or supervision. It is paid at four different rates, which depend on the level of care you require.

❑ **Unemployability supplement*** – This is paid if your pensioned disablement is assessed at 60% or more and consequently you are likely to be permanently unable to work. You must be under 65 when you first claim, but once awarded, it can continue to be paid after age 65.

❑ **Allowance for lowered standard of occupation*** – This is paid if your pensioned disablement is assessed at 40% or more and consequently you are unable to follow your regular occupation or do work of an equivalent standard.

❑ **Clothing allowance** – This is £221 a year, paid if your pensioned disablement is 20% or more and causes exceptional wear and tear to your clothing.

❑ **Treatment allowance** – This is paid if you have lost earnings due to having treatment at home or in hospital as a result of the pensioned disablement.

❑ **Rent allowance** – This can be paid to a surviving spouse or civil partner towards their accommodation costs if they are claiming a surviving spouse/civil partner's pension *and* a child allowance.

Social security benefits and tax credits

If you are receiving a GIP, your entitlement to other state benefits may be affected. For means-tested benefits, the first £10 of your GIP will be completely disregarded, but the rest will be treated as income. The same disregard applies to housing benefit, although local authorities have the discretion to apply a 100% disregard, which means that none of the GIP will be treated as income. Most authorities apply a 100% disregard, but this varies, as the matter is under constant review and revised from time to time. If your local authority applies only a 10% discount, The Royal British Legion (see Box P.7) should be informed, as this is currently the subject of a campaign.

For tax credits, the entire GIP is disregarded as income. However, a survivor's GIP attracts a disregard of £300 a year and the remaining amount is treated as income.

A lump sum paid under the AFCS is treated as capital for means-tested benefits and no disregard is applied.

When the benefit cap is introduced (see Box H.1 in Chapter 21), it will not apply to households where someone is in receipt of an AFCS GIP.

6. How do you claim?

To get a claim-form, ring the Veterans UK Helpline (0800 169 2277), write to the Service Personnel and Veterans Agency (SPVA), Norcross, Thornton-Cleveleys FY5 3WP, contact your local Veterans' Welfare Office (addresses in SPVA Leaflet 1) or go to www.veterans-uk.info.

You must complete a claim form within seven years of:
■ the incident that caused your injury; *or*
■ the date you sought medical advice for an illness; *or*
■ leaving the service, if the illness or injury was not attributable to a particular incident.

There are exceptions to these time limits if you have a late-onset condition. The scheme also allows for some discretion when dealing with exceptional circumstances.

Dependants' benefits are not normally awarded if your death occurs more than seven years after leaving service. If you die in service or within seven years of leaving service, the normal rule is that a claim must be made within three years of your death.

ARF(CS) Order, arts 46-49

What happens after you claim?

The SPVA will check your service records, if appropriate, to decide if you come within the scheme. If you do, the cause and the degree of your disability will be decided by SPVA doctors after medical evidence has been obtained. The cause of the illness or injury is decided using the 'balance of probabilities' standard of proof, meaning the claim will be successful if it is more likely than not that it was attributable to service. This is the same standard of proof used in civil personal injury claims.

The following allowances are paid automatically:
❑ **Exceptionally severe disablement allowance** – This is paid if you receive constant attendance allowance at one of the two highest rates.
❑ **Severe disablement occupational allowance*** – This is paid if you receive one of the two highest rates of constant attendance allowance, but you are normally in employment.
❑ **Comforts allowance** – This is paid if you receive unemployability supplement and/or constant attendance allowance.
❑ **Age allowance** – This is paid when you turn 65 if your disablement is assessed at 40% or more.
* These allowances overlap with state benefits of a similar nature, so you will not be paid both at the same time.

Widows, widowers and surviving civil partners

A pension can be paid if your spouse/civil partner's death was due to, or substantially hastened by, an illness or injury for which they were either receiving a war disablement pension or to which they would have been entitled had they claimed. You can also claim if your spouse/civil partner was receiving constant attendance allowance at any rate (or would have been had they not been in hospital) or if they were receiving unemployability supplement and their pensionable disablement was assessed at 80% or more.

You cannot be paid a surviving spouse/civil partner's pension as well as a national insurance bereavement benefit or widow's pension, but a surviving spouse/civil partner's pension is tax free and normally paid at a higher rate. You can also get benefits based on your own national insurance contributions, eg state pension or contributory employment and support allowance, on top.

Entitlement to the pension stops if you remarry, enter into a civil partnership or start cohabiting, but it can be reinstated if the new marriage or partnership ends.

The benefit cap

When the benefit cap (which limits the total weekly benefits that can be claimed; see Box H.1 in Chapter 21 for details) is introduced, it will not apply to households in which someone is receiving a war disablement pension or a surviving spouse/civil partner's pension.

How do you claim?

To make a claim, contact the Service Personnel and Veterans Agency (see Chapter 45(6)). There is no time limit for claiming and you can claim for any illness or injury, providing you can show a link between that illness or injury and your service. However, you will usually only receive an award from the date of your claim and, if your claim is made more than seven years after leaving the forces, the burden of proof will be on you to show that the illness or injury was caused by service. You cannot make a claim while still serving in the forces.

For illness or injury caused by service on or after 6.4.05, you need to claim under the Armed Forces Compensation scheme instead (see Chapter 45).

Reviews

Decisions on war pensions can be reviewed at any time, which means that if your condition deteriorates you can request a review of your assessment. However, the assessment could be reduced as well as increased, so you could end up with a smaller payment.

If you are not happy with the level of award, the date from which the award will run, the refusal of an award, or any changes to the amount or period of the award, you can appeal to a First-tier Tribunal in England and Wales. In Scotland and Northern Ireland, the appeal is made to the Pensions Appeal Tribunal of that country.

It is important that you get help with an appeal or a review. Some ex-service organisations like The Royal British Legion can help prepare your case and represent you at the tribunal (Legionline: 0845 772 5725). Alternatively, an advice centre may be able to help.

7. Appeals

Under the AFCS, you can appeal if you disagree with:
- the level of your award;
- a decision not to waive the time limits;
- the medical name given for a claimed condition;
- the date from which the award starts; *or*
- a decision on the grounds of deterioration.

You should always get advice when appealing, from either an ex-service organisation such as The Royal British Legion (see Box P.7) or an advice centre (see Chapter 59).

The AFCS has a 3-stage appeal process:

❏ **Internal review/reconsideration** – apply for a review within three months of your AFCS decision.

❏ **Appeal to an independent pensions appeal tribunal** – apply within six months of your AFCS decision or the date of a reconsidered decision.

❏ **Appeal to an Upper Tribunal** – on a point of law (in Northern Ireland appeals will go to the Pension Appeal Commissioners).

If you are challenging the level of your assessment, the tribunal may carry out a medical examination.

P.6 Far East prisoners of war

Tax-free lump-sum payments of £10,000 can be claimed by former prisoners of the Japanese during World War 2, or by their widows or widowers. Former members of the forces, civilians and some members of the colonial forces are included. The payment is disregarded indefinitely for means-tested benefits and there is no time limit for claiming. For details and claim-forms ring the Veterans UK Helpline (0800 169 2277) or go to www.veterans-uk.info.

How to appeal

To appeal a decision, first write to the Service Personnel and Veterans Agency (SPVA; see 6 above), giving details of the decision and why you disagree. The letter must include your name, address and reference number and must be signed and dated. The SPVA may reconsider the decision and amend the award, or may refer it to the tribunal. If the case goes to the tribunal, The Royal British Legion can provide representation and assistance.

Some decisions do not carry a right of appeal and, in such cases, the tribunal may decide the appeal cannot be heard. There is no further right of appeal.

The appeal decision

The tribunal may decide that:
- the decision was correct;
- the award should be increased or reduced;
- the award should be made from a different date;
- a condition previously rejected should be accepted; *or*
- the medical name for the condition should be changed.

Appeals to the Upper Tribunal

If you disagree with the tribunal's decision, you can appeal to the Upper Tribunal, but only on a point of law; that is, it is not sufficient that you think the tribunal made the wrong decision, you must be able to show there was a legal error in the way the decision was reached (see Box T.8, Chapter 58).

To appeal to the Upper Tribunal, contact the tribunal's office in writing within six weeks of the decision, explaining why you disagree with their decision. The tribunal can review the original decision, place the matter for appeal before the Upper Tribunal, or refuse your application to appeal further. If the tribunal turns down your application, you can apply directly to the Upper Tribunal. See Chapter 58(18) for more on appeals to the Upper Tribunal.

8. Extra help you can get

State benefits

Unlike the old War Pensions scheme, the AFCS does not carry supplementary allowances. However, this allows you to claim the corresponding social security benefits (see the benefits checklist on pages 4 and 5).

A guaranteed income payment will not affect contributory benefits. Therefore, if you are unable to work as a result of an injury incurred through service, you could claim contributory employment and support allowance (see Chapter 12).

Armed forces independence payment

In April 2013, alongside the introduction of personal independence payment (see Chapter 4), the Ministry of Defence introduced the armed forces independence payment (AFIP) scheme.

You will be eligible for the AFIP if you receive an AFCS award for an injury assessed at tariff 1-8, or if you receive a guaranteed income payment of 50% or more (see 3 above). If you are eligible, you will not need an additional medical assessment to receive the AFIP and you will not be required to undergo regular re-assessments to maintain eligibility.

The amount payable is £134.40 a week, which is equivalent to the enhanced rates of the mobility and daily living components of personal independence payment.

The AFIP is tax free and can be paid anywhere in the world. It is not stopped if you are in hospital (excepting the Royal Chelsea Hospital), a care home or prison.

AFIP is an alternative to the personal independence payment; if you are not eligible for AFIP, you can claim the personal independence payment. Contact the Veterans UK Helpline (0800 169 2277) for more on the AFIP.

ARF(CS) Order, arts 24A-24F

P.7 For more information

Veterans UK Helpline
Ring the Veterans UK Helpline (0800 169 2277) to enquire about your claim or the Armed Forces Compensation scheme and to get claim-forms and leaflets. Leaflets are also available at www.veterans-uk.info.

The Royal British Legion
The Royal British Legion provides advice and support in a number of areas including war pensions, benefits, debt advice, care homes, resettlement, training, employment and remembrance travel: Haig House,199 Borough High Street, London SE1 1AA (020 3207 2100; Helpline 0845 772 5725; www.britishlegion.org.uk).

46 Criminal injuries compensation

1. Who can claim?

You may be eligible for a payment from the Criminal Injuries Compensation Authority if you sustain an injury directly attributable to you being a direct victim of a crime of violence in Great Britain or in certain listed offshore situations.

Criminal Injuries Compensation Scheme, para 8 & Annex C

A crime of violence includes:

- a physical attack;
- any other violent act or omission which causes physical injury to you;
- a threat against you, which would make a reasonably firm person fear immediate violence;
- a sexual assault; *or*
- arson.

Criminal Injuries Compensation Scheme, para 4 & Annex B, para 2

You can claim compensation if you are injured when trying to stop someone from committing a crime, or trying to stop a suspected criminal, or helping the police to do so. In this case, the injury must be directly attributable to your taking an exceptional and justified risk; the risk will not be considered exceptional if it would normally be expected of you in the course of your work.

Criminal Injuries Compensation Scheme, para 5

You may be eligible to make a claim for a mental injury if you witnessed an incident in which a loved one sustained a criminal injury or if you were involved in the immediate aftermath of such an incident.

Criminal Injuries Compensation Scheme, para 6

You can claim compensation even if your attacker has not been convicted (eg they are immune from prosecution because of mental illness).

Criminal Injuries Compensation Scheme, para 9

Compensation may be reduced or withheld unless the Authority is satisfied that you:

- reported the incident to the police as soon as reasonably practicable, taking into consideration your age, capacity and the effect of the incident on you;
- co-operated as far as reasonably practicable in bringing the assailant to justice;
- took all reasonable steps to assist with the application; *and*
- are of good character and have no unspent convictions.

Compensation may be reduced or withheld if your conduct before, during or after the incident makes it inappropriate to make an award or a full award. In this case, conduct does not include intoxication through alcohol or drugs to the extent that such intoxication made you more vulnerable to becoming a victim of a crime of violence.

Criminal Injuries Compensation Scheme, paras 22-27 & Annex D

Violence within the family – If you and your assailant were living together as members of the same family, you can apply for compensation provided that:

- you were injured on or after 1.10.79; *and*
- you and your assailant no longer live together and are unlikely to do so again.

Compensation will not be payable unless the Authority is satisfied that the assailant will not benefit from the award.

Criminal Injuries Compensation Scheme, paras 19, 20 & 21

2. How do you claim?

You can complete an application over the phone using the Helpline (0300 003 3601), or you can apply online at www.justice.gov.uk/victims-and-witnesses/cica/apply-online. You can apply for compensation even if your attacker is unknown or has not yet been arrested.

Applications should be made as soon as possible after the incident and must be received by the Authority within two years of the date of the incident. This time limit may be waived only in exceptional circumstances and where it is clear that the application can be determined without further extensive enquiries; reasons for any delay should be provided with the application.

Criminal Injuries Compensation Scheme, paras 87 & 89

3. How much do you get?

Compensation is made up of several possible elements.

- **For the injury itself** – A fixed sum assessed by reference to a tariff that groups together injuries of comparable severity and allocates a sum of compensation to them. The Authority will consider the medical information on your injury and decide where in the tariff your injury features.

Criminal Injuries Compensation Scheme, paras 32-41 & Annex E

- **Loss of earnings** – No compensation is paid for the first 28 weeks of lost earnings. Any loss of earnings and/or earning potential incurred as a direct consequence of the injury beyond that will be compensated, subject to certain limits.

Criminal Injuries Compensation Scheme, paras 42-49 & Annex F

- **Special expenses** – Examples of these include care and supervision costs or equipment such as a wheelchair, or towards expenses for medical, dental or optical treatment. To qualify, you must have lost earnings or earnings capacity (or if not normally employed, be incapacitated to a similar extent) for more than 28 weeks and if so, the award will be calculated from the date of injury. You must also be able to prove that the goods or services are not available free of charge from another source.

Criminal Injuries Compensation Scheme, paras 50-56

Compensation if the victim has died

If someone has died as a result of a criminal injury, compensation may be made to a qualifying relative in the form of a 'bereavement payment', a 'child's payment' or a 'dependency payment'. A *'qualifying relative'* is a person who, at the time of the deceased's death, was their:

- spouse or civil partner, living with them in the same household;*
- partner (other than a spouse or civil partner), living with them in the same household and had done so for a continuous period of at least two years immediately before the date of the death;*
- spouse or civil partner, or a former spouse or civil partner, who was financially dependent on them;
- parent; *or*
- child.

* Or who did not live with the deceased because of either person's ill-health or infirmity.

Criminal Injuries Compensation Scheme, paras 57 & 59

Bereavement payment – If you are a qualifying relative and were not divorced or estranged from the deceased at the time of death, you may be eligible for a bereavement payment. This is a fixed sum of £11,000 if you are the only qualifying relative, or £5,500 for each person who qualifies.

Criminal Injuries Compensation Scheme, paras 61-62

Child's payment – You may be eligible for a child's payment if the child is a qualifying relative who was under 18 at the time of the deceased's death and dependent on them for parental services. The amount of a child's payment is £2,000 for each year, proportionally reduced for part years, up to the child's 18th birthday. The Authority may also pay an

additional amount for such 'reasonable' expenses suffered by the child as a direct result of the loss of parental services.
Criminal Injuries Compensation Scheme, paras 63-66 & Annex F

Dependency payment – A dependency payment may be made to a qualifying relative who at the time of the deceased's death was financially or physically dependent on them. The award should be set to reflect the extent of financial dependency, subject to a maximum amount.
Criminal Injuries Compensation Scheme, paras 67-74 & Annex F

Funeral expenses
If a person has died as a result of a criminal injury, a funeral payment may be made in respect of their funeral expenses for the benefit of their estate. This is normally set at £2,500 but may be increased to cover 'expenses reasonably incurred', up to a further £2,500.
Criminal Injuries Compensation Scheme, paras 75-77

Compensation from the courts
The full amount of a compensation payment for personal injury or damages made by a civil or criminal court in respect of the same injury (less any amount of 'recoverable' benefit – see Chapter 48) is deducted from an award under the Criminal Injuries Compensation scheme.
Criminal Injuries Compensation Scheme, para 85

4. How is your claim decided?
The Authority's staff will look at your application to check that the information you have given is correct. On a consent form, you are asked to give them authority to contact the police, your doctor, your employer or any other relevant person, to obtain confirmation of the incident, your injuries, loss of earnings, etc. They may ask you for other details. In some cases, you might be asked to undergo a medical examination by a doctor chosen by the Authority.

The Authority's staff will decide if you come within the scheme, and, if so, will assess the amount of compensation. You will be sent a written decision. You must reply in writing within 56 days and accept the decision before any payment is

made. If the award has been reduced or disallowed, you will be given reasons.

5. If you don't agree with the decision
If you are unhappy with the decision, you can apply, in writing, for a review. The Authority must receive your request within 56 days of the date of the letter notifying you of the decision. The 56-day time limit can be extended if you can show there are exceptional circumstances that justify the granting of an extension; the request must be made in writing.

Your review application must be supported by reasons, together with any additional evidence. After the review, if you are still dissatisfied with the decision, you can appeal to a First-tier Tribunal (see Chapter 58).

Both reviews and appeals involve a full reconsideration of eligibility and the amount of the award, which could result in your award being increased, unchanged, reduced or withdrawn.
Criminal Injuries Compensation Scheme, paras 117-134

6. If your condition changes
The Authority can re-open your case if your medical condition has deteriorated to the extent that the original assessment is unjust given your present condition. It can also re-open a case where a person has since died as a result of the injury. If you apply more than two years after the original decision, it is important to give as much information and medical evidence as you can with your application. The Authority will only consider the application if it has enough evidence without needing to make further extensive enquiries.
Criminal Injuries Compensation Scheme, paras 109-116

47 Vaccine damage payments

1. What is the Vaccine Damage scheme?
This scheme provides a tax-free lump sum of £120,000 for someone who is (or was immediately before death) severely disabled as a result of vaccination against specific diseases. It is described in *Vaccine Damage Payments* (see 4 below).

2. Who qualifies?
Payments can be made to someone who has been severely disabled as a result of vaccination against:
- diphtheria;
- tetanus;
- pertussis (whooping cough);
- poliomyelitis;
- measles;
- rubella (German measles);
- mumps;
- tuberculosis;
- meningococcal group C (meningitis C);
- haemophilus influenzae-type B (Hib);
- smallpox (vaccination up to 1.8.71);
- human papillomavirus;
- pandemic influenza A (H1N1) 2009 virus (swine flu; vaccination up to 31.8.10); *or*
- pneumococcal infection.

P.8 For more information

The Criminal Injuries Compensation Authority publishes a general guide to the Criminal Injuries Compensation scheme. Free copies of this guide and the scheme are available from the Criminal Injuries Compensation Authority, Tay House, 300 Bath Street, Glasgow G2 4LN (0300 003 3601) or they can be downloaded from www.justice.gov.uk/downloads/victims-and-witnesses/cic-a/how-to-apply/cica-guide.pdf.

Victim Support is an independent national charity for people affected by crime. You can contact your local Victim Support scheme for help (0845 303 0900).

Traffic accidents
If you are the victim of an uninsured or untraced motorist, there is a different scheme for compensation for personal injuries. This is run by the Motor Insurers' Bureau (MIB), established by motor insurers, which has agreements with the government to provide that compensation. Compensation is worked out in the same way as for common law damages. If the driver cannot be traced, you should report the accident to the police within 14 days for personal injury or five days for damage to personal property. You must apply to the MIB within three years of the accident for personal injury or nine months for damage to personal property. For details, call 0190 883 0001 (www.mib.org.uk).

Claims can be made on the basis of combination vaccines, eg diphtheria, tetanus and pertussis (DTP), measles and rubella (MR), measles, mumps and rubella (MMR), and the five-in-one vaccine. People damaged before birth as a result of vaccinations given to their mothers during pregnancy are included in the scheme, as are those who have contracted polio through contact with someone who was vaccinated against it using an orally administered vaccine.

The claimant must also satisfy the following conditions.

❑ The vaccination must have been given in the UK or Isle of Man (except for serving members of the armed forces and their immediate families vaccinated outside the UK as part of service medical facilities).

❑ The vaccination must have been given either when the claimant was under 18 (except for rubella, poliomyelitis, meningococcal group C, pandemic influenza A (H1N1) 2009 virus and human papillomavirus) or at a time of an outbreak of the disease within the UK or Isle of Man.

❑ The claimant must also be over the age of 2 on the date of the claim, or, if they have died, they must have been over the age of 2 when they died.

❑ The claim can be made at any time before the claimant's 21st birthday, or, if they have died, the date on which they would have attained that age, or up to six years after the date of the vaccination, whichever date is later.

❑ In the case of someone who contracted polio through contact with someone who was vaccinated against it, they must have been *'in close physical contact'* with the other person during the period of 60 days that began on the 4th day after the vaccination. They must also have been *'looking after'* the vaccinated person or been looked after jointly with them.

VDPA, Ss.1-3 & VDP Regs, regs 5-5A

3. What is 'severe disablement'?
A person is considered severely disabled if the disablement due to vaccination damage is assessed at 60% or more. Disablement is assessed in the same way as for industrial injuries disablement benefit (see Box P.2, Chapter 44).

VDPA, S.1(4)

4. How do you claim?
You can get the leaflet *Vaccine Damage Payments* and a claim-form from the Vaccine Damage Payments Unit, Palatine House, Lancaster Road, Preston, Lancashire PR1 1HB (01772 899 944; textphone: 0845 604 5312; www.gov. uk/vaccine-damage-payment).

Don't delay claiming. If you have supporting medical evidence send a copy with the claim, otherwise the Vaccine Damage Payments Unit will obtain medical evidence on your behalf. If the disabled person is under 18, the claim should be made by the parents or guardian.

5. What if you are refused?
If your claim is refused, you will be sent a written decision with reasons. If you disagree with this decision, you can ask the DWP to consider a reversal of the decision or you can appeal to a First-tier Tribunal. There is no time limit for making your appeal. The appeals process is described in Chapter 58.

Reversals – If you want the DWP to consider a reversal of their decision or the decision of a tribunal, write to the Vaccine Damage Payments Unit requesting a reversal, giving reasons why you think the decision is wrong, within six years of the date you were notified of the original decision or within two years of the date you were notified of the tribunal decision, if that is later. You may provide new evidence in support of your request.

Reconsiderations – If the DWP has made a payment, the decision can be reconsidered at any time if they have reason to believe there was a misrepresentation or non-disclosure of relevant information.

VDPA, Ss.3A-5 & VDP Regs, reg 11

6. Does it affect other benefits?
The capital value of a vaccine damage payment held in a trust fund is disregarded for the purposes of income-related employment and support allowance (ESA), income support, income-based jobseeker's allowance (JSA) and housing benefit. If the payment is not held in a trust fund, its capital value can be disregarded for up to 52 weeks from the date of receipt (to allow you time to set up a trust). After that it will be taken fully into account.

Any regular payments made out of the trust fund to or for the disabled person are disregarded for the purposes of income-related ESA, income support, income-based JSA and housing benefit. Other lump-sum payments will be treated as capital and will reduce benefit if the payments bring the total capital above the lower capital limit (see Chapter 28(4)).

48 Compensation recovery

1. Compensation recovery
If, as a result of an accident, injury or disease, you claim compensation, the *'compensator'* (the person or organisation that pays the compensation) is liable to pay damages to you and repay benefits to the DWP via the Compensation Recovery Unit (CRU). The compensator can deduct some or all of the amount they have to pay to you from the gross compensation award, a practice known as *'offsetting'*.

It is not the actual benefits that are recovered, but an amount equivalent to the total amount of *'recoverable'* benefits paid as a result of your accident, injury or disease. Not all social security benefits are recoverable, as some are paid for reasons that have no connection to the compensation claim. Recoverable benefits are listed in 2 below.

Social security benefits are not paid in respect of pain, suffering, personal inconvenience and so on, and therefore no offsetting can be made against the general damages element of your compensation award.

In cases involving accidents and injuries, benefits are recoverable from the day following the accident or injury for a period of five years or up to the date the claim is settled, whichever is earlier. In disease cases, the 5-year recovery period begins on the date on which a recoverable benefit is first claimed as a consequence of the disease.

Social Security (Recovery of Benefits) Act 1997

The certificate
Before a compensation payment is made, the compensator must request a certificate from the CRU. This certificate lists the recoverable benefits that have been paid. The CRU will issue a certificate to the compensator and send a copy to you (or your solicitor), so that both parties can estimate the extent of any potential offsetting.

Since offsetting can greatly affect the size of the net compensation award, both sides should take it into account when conducting negotiations.

You and the compensator have the right to request a review of a certificate at any time if either of you believe that the calculation shown on the certificate is incorrect or that benefits not paid as a consequence of the accident, injury or disease have been included. However, an appeal against a certificate can be made only after the final compensation payment has been made and the total amount of recoverable benefit has been repaid to the CRU. See 5 below for details on appeals.

2. Benefits that can be recovered

Compensation can be reduced to take account of benefits paid in respect of the following:

■ **loss of earnings** – employment and support allowance, industrial injuries disablement benefit, incapacity benefit, income support, invalidity benefit, jobseeker's allowance, reduced earnings allowance, severe disablement allowance, sickness benefit, statutory sick pay (paid before 6.4.94), unemployment benefit, unemployability supplement, universal credit;

■ **cost of care** – attendance allowance, disability living allowance (DLA) care component, personal independence payment (PIP) daily living component, constant attendance allowance, exceptionally severe disablement allowance;

■ **loss of mobility** – DLA and PIP mobility component, mobility allowance.

In making an order for a compensation payment, the court must specify how much is to be awarded under each of these three headings.

Social Security (Recovery of Benefits) Act 1997, Sch 2

Example of offsetting: an award of compensation is agreed:

Compensation award:	£100,000
consisting of:	
General damages	£40,000
Loss of earnings	£30,000
Loss of mobility	£30,000

The CRU certificate lists the following recoverable benefits:

Employment and support allowance totalling	£15,000
DLA mobility component totalling	£10,000

The compensator cannot offset against the general damages element of the award, but may offset the employment and support allowance paid against the loss of earnings heading. They therefore deduct £15,000 from this, leaving £15,000 to be paid to the injured person. Similarly, the compensator may offset the £10,000 of DLA paid against the loss of mobility heading, leaving £20,000 to be paid to the injured person. The injured person has settled their claim for a total of £100,000. Following offsetting, they receive £75,000 from the compensator, having already received £25,000 in recoverable benefits from the DWP.

P.9 For more information

Further information can be found in the guide CRU27, *Compensation, social security benefits and or lump sum payments,* which can be downloaded from the Compensation Recovery Unit (CRU) website (www.dwp. gov.uk/cru).

For enquiries regarding the relevant law, ring the CRU Policy Liaison Section (0191 225 2485).

For information regarding a similar scheme in Northern Ireland, contact the Compensation Recovery Unit, Social Security Agency, Magnet House, 81-93 York Street, Belfast BT15 1SS (028 9054 5890).

---

3. Exempted payments

Some compensation payments are exempt from the recovery rules. They are:

■ vaccine damage payments;
■ Criminal Injuries Compensation scheme payments (but see Chapter 46(3));
■ payments from the Macfarlane and Eileen Trusts, MFET Ltd, the Caxton Foundation and the Skipton Fund;
■ payments from the government-funded trust for people with variant Creutzfeldt-Jakob disease;
■ payments from the UK Asbestos and EL Scheme Trusts;
■ payments from the London Bombings Relief Charitable Fund;
■ payments under the Fatal Accidents Act 1976;
■ contractual sick pay from an employer;
■ payments made under the NHS industrial injuries scheme;
■ payments made to the injured person by an insurer under the terms of an insurance contract agreed before:
  – the date on which the injured person first claims a recoverable benefit in consequence of the disease in question; *or*
  – the occurrence of the accident or injury in question;
■ payments under the NCB Pneumoconiosis Compensation scheme; *and*
■ payments in respect of sensorineural hearing loss of less than 50dB in one or both ears.

Social Security (Recovery of Benefits) Act 1997, Sch 1(5); The Social Security (Recovery of Benefits) Regs, reg 2

4. Lump-sum payments

The compensator can reduce any part of your compensation award (including damages paid for pain and suffering) if you have had a lump-sum payment under:

■ the Pneumoconiosis etc. (Workers' Compensation) Act 1979 (including any extra-statutory payments made following the rejection of a claim under that Act); *or*
■ the 2008 Diffuse Mesothelioma scheme.

The Social Security (Recovery of Benefits)(Lump Sum Payments) Regs 2008

5. Appeals

If your compensation payment has been reduced to take account of benefit recovery and you think the certificate is wrong, you can appeal. You must attach letters you have received from the compensator telling you the compensation payment has been reduced. You must state under which of the four following grounds you are making your appeal:

■ an amount, rate or period specified in the certificate is incorrect; *or*
■ the certificate shows benefits or lump sums that were not paid as a result of the accident, injury or disease in respect of which compensation was paid; *or*
■ benefits or lump sums listed that have not been, and are not likely to be, paid to you have been brought into account; *or*
■ the compensation payment made was not as a consequence of the accident, injury or disease.

You must appeal within one month of the date the compensator pays the Compensation Recovery Unit (CRU). If you apply late, you must show there are special circumstances for the delay. Appeal forms can be downloaded from the CRU website (www.dwp.gov.uk/cru).

Social Security (Recovery of Benefits) Act 1997, S.11

Warning: A tribunal dealing with an appeal against recovery is entitled to decide whether or not the benefits recovered were in fact paid in respect of the accident, injury or disease in question. Both the tribunal's decision and the evidence on which it is based can potentially raise doubts about entitlement to those benefits. Consequently, it would be wise to seek advice before lodging an appeal.

R(CR)2/02

This section of the Handbook looks at:

Coming to or leaving the UK

49 Coming to the UK

1. Introduction

To qualify for most benefits you must satisfy the rules about residence and presence in Great Britain (GB). Your right to benefit may also be affected by your immigration status. GB means England, Scotland and Wales. The United Kingdom (UK) means GB plus Northern Ireland. In Northern Ireland and the Isle of Man social security benefits come under separate but similar legislation to that in GB, and periods of residence may count for UK benefits. In the Channel Islands the system is different but a reciprocal agreement allows periods of residence there to count for UK benefits. Periods of residence in another European Economic Area (EEA) country may count as residence in GB for those covered by European Union (EU) rules, and reciprocal agreements with some non-EEA countries include similar rules.

EEA countries – The EEA consists of the EU member states: Austria, Belgium, Bulgaria, (Croatia from 1.7.13), Cyprus, *Czech Republic, Denmark, *Estonia, Finland, France, Germany, Greece, *Hungary, Italy, *Latvia, *Lithuania, Luxembourg, Malta, Netherlands, *Poland, Portugal, Republic of Ireland, Romania, *Slovakia, *Slovenia, Spain, Sweden, UK (including Gibraltar, but not the Channel Islands or Isle of Man), together with Iceland, Norway and Liechtenstein. Rules applying to EEA nationals also generally apply to Swiss nationals.

A8 – This term refers to the eight countries marked * above.
A2 – This term refers to Bulgaria and Romania.

EEA co-ordination rules

If you (or a family member) have moved between EEA states, are an EEA or Swiss national (or a refugee or stateless person resident in an EEA state) *and* have been employed, self-employed, studying or claiming certain benefits, you may be covered by more favourable EEA social security co-ordination rules, including being able to use periods of residence, employment and national insurance contributions paid in another EEA country to satisfy requirements for UK benefits.
EC Regulations 883/04

Reciprocal agreements

Reciprocal social security agreements with some countries (including Switzerland and all EEA countries except A8 and A2 countries, Greece and Liechtenstein – the reciprocal agreement applies if you are not covered by EU rules) may help you receive benefit. Non-EEA countries covered by reciprocal agreements are Barbados, Bermuda, Canada, Isle of Man, Israel, Jamaica, Jersey & Guernsey, Mauritius, New Zealand, Philippines, Turkey, USA and former Yugoslavia. Agreements differ and not all benefits are covered. There are 'association' and 'co-operation' agreements with Algeria, Morocco, San Marino, Slovenia, Tunisia and Turkey.

2. Residence and presence tests

Entitlement to many benefits depends on satisfying residence and presence tests for that benefit.

Meaning of terms

Present – This means physically present in GB throughout the whole day. (See Chapter 50 for when you can be treated as present in GB while you are abroad.)
Resident – You are usually 'resident' in the country where you have your home for the time being.
Ordinarily resident – This term is not defined in regulations. You should be *'ordinarily resident'* in the place where you normally live for the time being if there is a degree of continuity about your stay such that it can be described as settled.
Right to reside – This term does not have a single statutory definition. See below for how this test is applied.
Habitually resident – This term is not defined in regulations. See below for how this test is applied.
Common Travel Area – The UK, Channel Islands, Isle of Man and the Republic of Ireland.

Disability benefits

Attendance allowance, carer's allowance, disability living allowance and personal independence payment – For attendance allowance, carer's allowance and disability living allowance (DLA) claimed on or after 8.4.13 and personal independence payment (PIP), you must be habitually resident in the Common Travel Area (see above), present in GB and have been present in GB for not less than 104 weeks in the last 156 weeks.

If you were entitled to attendance allowance, carer's allowance or DLA on 7.4.13, there are more generous rules: you must be present and ordinarily resident in GB, and have been present in GB for not less than 26 weeks in the last 52 weeks. These are continuing requirements that apply to any day for which you are claiming benefit. These rules will continue to apply to you until your award is terminated or (for ordinary residence) revised or superseded or (for the shorter past presence test) until 7.4.15.
Exceptions – For attendance allowance, carer's allowance, DLA care component, and PIP, the past presence test does not apply if you are covered by the EEA co-ordination rules (see 1 above), and you are habitually resident in GB, and you can demonstrate a genuine and sufficient link to the UK social security system.

If DLA is claimed for a baby under 6 months old, a 13-week presence test applies until their 1st birthday. If DLA is claimed for a baby aged 6-36 months, the test is 26-weeks in the last 156 weeks.

The 104-, 26- or 13-week presence tests do not apply if you are terminally ill.
AA Regs, reg 2-2B; DLA Regs, reg 2-2B; ICA Regs, reg 9-9B; PIP Regs, reg 16

Employment and support allowance 'in youth', incapacity benefit 'in youth' and severe disablement allowance – For contributory employment and support allowance 'in youth' (CESA(Y)), incapacity benefit 'in youth' and severe disablement allowance, you must be present and ordinarily resident in GB, and have been present for not less than 26 of the last 52 weeks. These are continuing requirements that apply to any day for which you are claiming benefit (except for CESA(Y)).

ESA Regs, reg 11; SDA Regs, reg 3; IB Regs, reg 16

Tax credits and child benefit

For working tax credit and child tax credit you (and your partner if make a joint claim) must be present and ordinarily resident in the UK and, for new child tax credit claims made on or after 1.5.04, have a right to reside in the UK (see below).

TCA s.3(3); TC(R) Regs, reg 3

To be entitled to child benefit you *and* the child must be present in GB (or Northern Ireland if claiming there), be ordinarily resident in the UK and, for new claims made on or after 1.5.04, have a right to reside in the UK (see below).

SSCBA s.146; CB Regs, reg 23 & 27

Means-tested benefits

For housing benefit, income-related employment and support allowance (ESA), income-based jobseeker's allowance (JSA), income support, pension credit and universal credit, you must satisfy the habitual residence test (see below) and, except for housing benefit, be present in GB.

Partner abroad – If you used to live in GB or abroad with your partner who is now abroad, they will be treated as your partner (with their income and capital affecting your entitlement to benefit) unless you do not intend to resume living together or the absence is likely to exceed 52 weeks (or six months for universal credit).

IS Regs, reg 16(2); ESA Regs, reg 156(3); JSA Regs, reg 78(2); SPC Regs, reg 5(1)(a); HB Regs, reg 21(2); UC Regs, reg 3(6)

Habitual residence test (HRT)

For means-tested and disability benefits, unless you are exempt (see below), you must be habitually resident in the Common Travel Area (see above). For means-tested benefits, this includes having a right to reside (see below) in the Common Travel Area. Only the claimant is subject to the HRT. For universal credit, if your partner fails the HRT, you can still claim universal credit as a single person with a single person's maximum amount but your partner's income and capital will affect your entitlement.

If you are not accepted as habitually resident for income-related ESA, income-based JSA, income support or pension credit, the housing benefit office must make its own decision, not just follow the DWP decision.

Exemptions – For means-tested benefits, you are exempt from the HRT if you:

- have refugee status, humanitarian protection, or exceptional leave to enter/remain (eg if you have been granted up to three months' exceptional leave as a victim of domestic violence); *or*
- (except for universal credit) left Montserrat after 1.11.95 because of the volcano; *or*
- arrived in the UK from Zimbabwe between 27.2.09 and 18.3.11 under a UK government assistance scheme; *or*
- are an EEA national (see 1 above and restrictions for A8/A2/Croatian nationals below) classified as a *'worker'* (you must be employed in the UK doing *'genuine and effective'* work) or self-employed – including if you have retained either status because you are temporarily unable to work due to an illness or accident, or have retained 'worker' status while involuntarily unemployed and registered as a jobseeker with Jobcentre Plus, or while engaged in vocational training (connected to your former work if you are voluntarily unemployed); *or*
- are a family member (ie spouse, civil partner or dependent (grand)parent or (grand)child (who is either under 21 or dependent)) of someone in the group above; *or*

- are an EEA national with a right to reside permanently in the UK under Article 17 of Directive 2004/38/EC (eg if you worked in the UK and then retired, or became permanently incapable of work, in certain circumstances), or living with a family member in this group; *or*
- are an A2 national subject to authorisation working in accordance with the conditions of your accession worker authorisation document; *or*
- are not a *'person subject to immigration control'* (see 3 below) and have been deported, expelled or otherwise legally removed from another country; *or*
- (housing benefit only) are in receipt of income-based JSA, income-related ESA, income support or pension credit; *or*
- (income-related ESA only) are being transferred from an award of income support that is part of a continuous period of entitlement to one or more of: income-based JSA, income support, pension credit, housing benefit or council tax benefit that included 30.4.04.

At the time of writing there are no exemptions from the HRT for attendance allowance, DLA and PIP other than for serving members of HM Armed Forces and their families.

The test – If you are not exempt, you must show you are habitually resident (including, for means-tested benefits, that you have a right to reside). There is no definitive list of factors that determine habitual residence, but you must show a *'settled intention'* to stay here. In most cases, you also need to be actually resident for an *'appreciable period'* of time, which is not a fixed period of time and will depend on your circumstances. However, you may be accepted as habitually resident from your first day of residence if you are:

- returning to the Common Travel Area (see above) and you were previously habitually resident here; *or*
- covered by the EEA co-ordination rules (for income-based JSA, income-related ESA or pension credit only) – see 1 above.

Seek specialist advice for help completing the HRT questionnaire or if you need to appeal against a decision that you are not habitually resident.

IS Regs, reg 21-21AA; ESA Regs, reg 69-70; JSA Regs, reg 85-85A; SPC Regs, reg 2; HB Regs, reg 10; UC Regs, reg 9; PIP Regs, regs 16(c) & 20

Right to reside test

For new claims made on or after 1.5.04, you must have a *'right to reside'* for child tax credit, child benefit and (to satisfy the HRT) each of the means-tested benefits. However, this requirement does not apply to a new claim for housing benefit, income-based JSA, income support, pension credit or, since 31.10.11, income-related ESA, if it is part of a continuous period of entitlement to one or more of these benefits (or council tax benefit) that included 30.4.04.

The Social Security (Habitual Residence) Amendment Regs 2004, reg 6

Circumstances when you will have a right to reside include if you are in one of the groups exempt from the HRT (listed above; with the exception of the last three groups) or if you are a British or Irish citizen, or have leave to enter/remain in the UK or you are (or your family member is) an EEA national and you (or they):

- have a permanent right to reside because of having 'resided legally' in the UK for five years or in limited circumstances if you have retired or become permanently incapable of work after having worked in the UK; *or*
- are self-sufficient (including while enrolled as a student); *or*
- (for child benefit, child tax credit and income-based JSA only) are registered as a jobseeker.

In some circumstances if you have a right to reside as a family member you can retain this right to reside if the EEA national dies, leaves the UK or your marriage or civil partnership to them is ended with divorce or dissolution.

You also have a right to reside if you are the primary carer of a child in education in the UK where one of the child's parents is, or was, an EEA 'worker' (see above).

Others can have a right to reside, depending on their circumstances.

The Immigration (EEA) Regs 2006; Directive 2004/38/EC

A2/A8/Croatian nationals – Until 31.12.13 most A2 nationals can take employment only if they hold, and work in accordance with, an accession worker authorisation document. Limited categories are exempt from these requirements including those who have completed a year of authorised work. While subject to authorisation, an A2 national:

■ has no right to reside as a jobseeker;
■ cannot retain their 'worker' status in the ways listed in the fourth HRT exempt group (see above); *and*
■ is only defined as a 'worker' (see above) if their work is authorised.

It is expected that from 1.7.13 most Croatian nationals will be subject to similar restrictions to A2 nationals.

Until 30.4.11, most A8 nationals were subject to similar restrictions and required to work for an 'authorised employer' (this includes employment either during the first month or registered under the Worker's Registration scheme). These restrictions no longer apply but can be relevant when establishing the permanent right to reside of an A8 national or their family member or the residence right of the primary carer of an A8 national's child in education.

The Accession (Immigration & Worker Registration) Regs 2004; The Accession (Immigration & Worker Authorisation) Regs 2006

3. Immigration status

If you are defined as a *'person subject to immigration control'*, unless you come under one of the exemptions below, you will be excluded from possible entitlement to the following benefits:

■ attendance allowance, disability living allowance (DLA) and personal independence payment (PIP);
■ carer's allowance;
■ child benefit;
■ child tax credit and working tax credit;
■ contributory employment and support allowance 'in youth' (CESA(Y)) and incapacity benefit 'in youth' (IB(Y));
■ housing benefit;
■ income-based jobseeker's allowance (JSA);
■ income-related employment and support allowance (ESA);
■ income support;
■ pension credit;
■ severe disablement allowance (SDA);
■ social fund;
■ universal credit.

You are defined as a 'person subject to immigration control' if you are not an EEA national (see 1 above) and you:

■ require leave to enter/remain in the UK but do not have it; *or*
■ have leave to enter/remain in the UK subject to a condition that you do not have recourse to public funds; *or*
■ are a sponsored immigrant – ie you have been given leave to enter or remain as a result of a maintenance undertaking (a written undertaking given by someone else in pursuance of the immigration rules, to be responsible for your maintenance and accommodation).

Immigration and Asylum Act 1999, S.115; ESA Regs, reg 11; IB Regs, reg 16; TCA, S.42; TC(I) Regs, reg 3

Exemptions: who can still get benefits?

You are not excluded from benefit entitlement if you are not defined as a person subject to immigration control. Examples include: people with refugee status, humanitarian protection, discretionary leave or indefinite leave to enter/remain (unless given as the result of a maintenance undertaking) and family members of EEA nationals who have a right to reside in the UK.

Some groups of people (listed below) can be entitled to benefit despite being defined as a person subject to immigration control.

Warning: All the benefits listed above are classed (and PIP and universal credit are expected to be classed) as *'public funds'* except CESA(Y) and IB(Y). If your immigration status is subject to a *'no recourse to public funds'* condition, receiving one of these benefits (or if your partner is paid benefit on your behalf) may jeopardise your right to stay in the UK or undermine applications to the Home Office. However, the Home Office does not regard you as having 'recourse to public funds' if benefit is paid because you fall into one of the exempt groups below.

Immigration Rules, para 6, 6A, 6B & 6C

Get expert advice (see Box Q.1) before making a claim if you have concerns over public funds or do not have leave to enter/remain, have overstayed your leave or are unsure about your immigration status, since information is exchanged between the benefit authorities and the Home Office.

The government intends to make it a condition of entitlement to contributory ESA, contribution-based JSA, maternity allowance and statutory maternity/paternity/adoption/sickness pay that you have an entitlement to work in the UK.

Who can get means-tested benefits?

Even if you are defined as a person subject to immigration control, you are not excluded from entitlement to housing benefit, income-related ESA, income-based JSA, income support, pension credit, universal credit or the social fund if you are:

■ a national of Croatia (until 1.7.13, when you will become an EEA national anyway), Macedonia or Turkey and you are lawfully present in the UK; *or*
■ a sponsored immigrant and either you have been resident in the UK for at least five years (beginning on the later date of either your entry to the UK or the signing of the maintenance undertaking) or your sponsor has (or, if more than one, they have all) died; *or*
■ (except for universal credit) on limited leave with the condition that you do not have recourse to public funds, and you have not yet had such recourse other than under this provision, and you are dependent on funds from abroad that are temporarily disrupted, but which are reasonably expected to resume (maximum of 42 days' payment per period of leave); *or*
■ an asylum seeker who claimed asylum before 3.4.00 and are covered by transitional protection rules. Entitlement will end on the date your asylum claim is abandoned or decided and notified to you.

(IA)CA Regs, reg 2(1), (4)(c), (5)-(8) & 12

If your partner is subject to immigration control – If you are entitled to income-based JSA, income-related ESA, income support, pension credit or universal credit, you cannot be paid for a partner who is subject to immigration control (unless, except for pension credit, they are in one of the exempt groups above).

IS Regs, regs 21(3) & Sch 7, para 16A; JSA Regs, regs 85(4) & Sch 5, para 13A; ESA Regs, regs 69 & Sch 5, para 10; SPC Regs, reg 5; UC Regs, regs 3(3), 18(2), 22(3) & 36(3)

Who can get tax credits?

Even if you are defined as a person subject to immigration control you are not excluded from tax credits if either the second or third bullet in the list relating to means-tested benefits (above) applies to you. You are also not excluded from tax credits if you are:

■ (child tax credit only) a national of Algeria, Morocco, San

Marino, Tunisia or Turkey and lawfully working (or have lawfully worked) in UK; *or*

■ (working tax credit only) a national of Croatia (until 1.7.13, when you become an EEA national anyway), Macedonia or Turkey and you are lawfully present in the UK; *or*

■ (child tax credit only) awarded child tax credit immediately following an award of income support or income-based JSA for a child while you are an asylum seeker with transitional protection who claimed asylum before 3.4.00 or a lawfully present national of Croatia (until 1.7.13, when you become an EEA national anyway), Macedonia or Turkey.

TC(I) Regs, reg 3 & 5;

If your partner is subject to immigration control – and you are not (or you are but are in one of the exempt groups above) your joint claim will be treated as if your partner were not subject to immigration control (except that the couple element of WTC is not paid unless you or your partner have a child or your partner is a national of Croatia, Macedonia or Turkey and they are lawfully present in the UK).

WTC(E&MR) Regs, reg 11(4)(b) & (5)

Who can get disability benefits and child benefit?

Even if you are defined as a person subject to immigration control you are not excluded from attendance allowance, DLA, PIP, carer's allowance, child benefit, CESA(Y), IB(Y) and SDA if:

■ you are the family member of an EEA (including UK) national; *or*

■ either you, or a member of your family who you are living with, are a national of Algeria, Morocco, San Marino, Tunisia or Turkey and lawfully working (or have lawfully worked) in GB; *or*

■ you are a sponsored immigrant; *or*

■ (for attendance allowance, DLA and child benefit only) you are covered by a reciprocal agreement (see 1 above); *or*

■ you were in receipt of the benefit immediately before 5.2.96 (or 7.10.96 for child benefit). Your entitlement will end if:

– your benefit is revised or superseded. Claiming child benefit for an additional child does not give rise to a revision or supersession of your existing entitlement; *or*

– you break your claim, or your fixed-period award comes to an end; *or*

– your claim for asylum (if any) is recorded as having been decided or abandoned.

(IA)CA Regs, reg 2(2), (3) & (4)(b)

If you get a positive decision on your asylum claim

If you are granted refugee status you may be able to claim tax credits and child benefit backdated to the date of your asylum application (or, for tax credits, 6.4.03 if this is later). You must claim tax credits within one month and child benefit within three months of receiving the letter notifying you of your refugee status. However, the amount of tax credits paid will be net of any subsistence payments of asylum support you have received.

TC(I) Regs, reg 3(4)-(9); Child Benefit & Guardian's Allowance (Admin) Regs 2003, reg 6(2)(d)

If you are aged 18 or over and have (or someone you are a dependant of has) been granted refugee status or humanitarian protection since 11.6.07, you can apply for an 'integration loan'; details and application forms are available at www.ukba.homeoffice.gov.uk.

Once you are granted refugee status, humanitarian protection or discretionary leave, you are no longer subject to immigration control while you have that leave, and you can claim all benefits.

4. Other forms of support

Asylum support – If you (or someone you are a dependant of) are aged 18 or over, have an outstanding asylum claim or appeal and are destitute, you may be able to get asylum support (accommodation and/or subsistence payments). If your asylum claim and appeal have been refused, you may be eligible for 'section 4' support. Seek advice for details (see Box Q.1).

Help from social care – You may be eligible for assistance from the local authority social care department under certain legal provisions (see Chapter 29(4)). If you have needs that are not solely a consequence of destitution or its physical effects (eg needs due to age or disability) you may be entitled to accommodation and other assistance under the National Assistance Act 1948. If you are an unaccompanied child aged under 18 or you have a dependent child, you may be able to get assistance under the Children Act 1989. Remember that information is exchanged between social care departments and the Home Office. If you are refused assistance from your local authority, seek independent advice.

50 Leaving the UK

1. Introduction

You may be able to receive benefits while you are travelling or living abroad. Some benefits (eg state pension) can be paid no matter how long you are away, while the conditions for others are more complex. The rules vary depending on the country you go to. You may benefit from social security co-ordination rules if you go to a European Economic Area (EEA) country, or from a reciprocal agreement – see Chapter 49(1). However, if you are not covered by EEA co-ordination rules or a reciprocal agreement, the general rules on payment of benefits abroad apply. There are also rules treating you as being in Great Britain (GB) for the purposes of certain benefits if you (or a family member you live with) are a member of the armed forces serving abroad, a crown servant posted overseas (or your partner is) or one of certain categories of airmen, mariners and continental-shelf workers.

This chapter covers general rules and indicates benefits payable in EEA countries. EEA co-ordination rules and reciprocal agreements are too varied to cover here, so if you plan to go abroad get specialist advice. Contact the International Pension Centre (see inside back cover) for information about receiving state pension abroad; for other benefits, contact the office that pays them. In each case, they will need to know the purpose, destination and intended length of your visit.

Temporary absence – For many benefits, one condition for payment while abroad is that your absence is temporary. For attendance allowance, disability living allowance, personal independence payment, child benefit and tax credits this means the absence is unlikely to exceed 52 weeks. For other benefits, the term is not defined in law and in deciding whether your absence is temporary, the DWP should consider all the circumstances, including your intentions and the purpose and length of your absence. If the decision maker decides your absence is not temporary, you have a right of appeal.

2. Incapacity and maternity benefits

General rules – If you are temporarily absent from GB, you can continue to be paid incapacity benefit, severe disablement allowance (SDA) or maternity allowance for the first 26 weeks of the absence if Jobcentre Plus agrees. There is no right of appeal if they refuse; your only recourse is judicial review. You are not subject to the 26-week limit and do not require Jobcentre Plus agreement if you are receiving attendance allowance, disability living allowance, personal independence payment or armed forces independence payment. However, in all cases you must satisfy one of the following conditions:
- at the time you go abroad you have been continuously incapable of work for at least six months and remain continuously incapable while abroad; *or*
- you have gone abroad *'for the specific purpose of being treated'* for an illness or disability that began before you left. The treatment does not need to be your only reason for going abroad. However, going abroad to convalesce or for a change of air, even on your doctor's advice, is not enough. *'Being treated'* must involve some activity by another person. It does not matter whether the treatment is available in the UK or not. In some cases claimants did not receive any treatment, but did go abroad specifically to try to get it.

PA Regs, reg 2

EEA – You may be able to get maternity allowance if you get agreement from Jobcentre Plus before you go to another EEA country to live or for medical treatment. Long-term incapacity benefit and SDA can continue to be paid in another EEA country.

3. Employment and support allowance (ESA)

4-week rule – You can continue to be entitled to ESA for the first four weeks of a temporary absence from GB if the period of absence is unlikely to exceed 52 weeks and you continue to satisfy the other conditions of entitlement.

ESA Regs, reg 152

26-week rule – You can continue to be entitled to ESA during the first 26 weeks of a temporary absence from GB if the absence is solely:
- in connection with arrangements made for treatment for a condition directly related to your limited capability for work, which began before you left GB; *or*
- because you are accompanying a dependent child in connection with arrangements made for treatment of their condition.

In either case, the period of absence must be unlikely to exceed 52 weeks and you must continue to satisfy the other conditions of entitlement. The treatment must take place outside GB and must be by, or under the supervision of, a person appropriately qualified to carry out that treatment.

ESA Regs, reg 153

NHS treatment abroad – You can continue to be entitled to ESA during any period of temporary absence from GB, provided you continue to satisfy the other conditions of entitlement, if the absence is for the purpose of receiving treatment by the NHS outside GB.

ESA Regs, reg 154

Partner abroad – If you are claiming income-related ESA and you stay in GB, you will get benefit for your partner for the first four weeks. If they are accompanying a dependent child abroad for treatment (as under the 26-week rule above) you will get benefit for them for the first 26 weeks. After this,

benefit will be reduced. Your partner's income and capital will affect your entitlement unless you do not intend to resume living together or the absence is likely to exceed 52 weeks.

ESA Regs, reg 156(1)&(3) & Sch 5, paras 6-7

EEA – Contributory ESA can continue to be paid in another EEA country.

4. Employer-paid benefits

You can receive statutory sick/maternity/paternity/adoption pay while abroad, unless your employer is not required to pay Class 1 national insurance contributions for you – eg because they are not present or resident, and do not have a place of business, in the UK.

5. Income support

If you are entitled immediately before you leave, you can continue receiving income support during a temporary absence abroad if:
- you are receiving NHS treatment outside GB; *or*
- the absence is unlikely to exceed 52 weeks and you continue to satisfy the other entitlement conditions and satisfy the 4- or 8-week rule below.

4-week rule – You can be paid income support for the first four weeks if:
- you are in Northern Ireland; *or*
- you and your partner are both abroad and a disability premium, severe disability premium or pensioner premium is applicable for the partner of the claimant; *or*
- you have been continuously incapable of work during the 364 days before the day you leave GB, or 196 days if you are terminally ill or entitled to personal independence payment enhanced rate of daily living component, disability living allowance highest rate care component or armed forces independence payment (two or more periods of incapacity are treated as continuous if the break between them is not more than 56 days each time); *or*
- you are incapable of work and your absence is *'for the sole purpose of receiving treatment from an appropriately qualified person for the incapacity by reason of which'* you are eligible for income support; *or*
- you are in one of the groups that can claim income support (see Box E.1, Chapter 15) other than if you are entitled to statutory sick pay, or are incapable of work (unless you are covered by one of the last two groups), or are appealing against an incapacity for work decision, or are a 'person subject to immigration control' (unless you are covered by either of the last two groups listed under 'Who can get means-tested benefits?' in Chapter 49(3)), or are in full-time education, or involved in a trade dispute.

8-week rule – You can get income support for the first eight weeks abroad if you are taking your dependent child abroad for medical treatment by an appropriately qualified person.

IS Regs, reg 4

Partner abroad – If you are the income support claimant and you stay in GB, your income support will include benefit for your partner for the first four weeks (or eight weeks if they

Q.1 For more information

For further information on benefits for people entering and leaving the UK, see *Welfare Benefits and Tax Credits Handbook* (2013/14), Part 12 (Child Poverty Action Group).

For immigration advice, contact a law centre (see Chapter 59(2)). DWP and HMRC leaflets (including some in languages other than English) for countries covered by a reciprocal agreement with the UK are available from the International Pension Centre (see inside back cover).

meet the conditions of the 8-week rule above). After this, benefit will be reduced. However, your partner's income and capital will affect your income support entitlement unless you do not intend to resume living together or the absence is likely to exceed 52 weeks.

IS Regs, reg 16(1)&(2) and Sch 7, paras 11 & 11A

6. Pension credit

You continue to be entitled to pension credit during a temporary absence from GB if you are receiving NHS treatment outside GB. Otherwise, as long as you continue to satisfy the other conditions of entitlement and the absence is unlikely to exceed 52 weeks, it continues for 13 weeks.

SPC Regs, regs 3 & 4

Partner abroad – If one of these circumstances applies to your partner, your pension credit will include benefit for them for the relevant period of their temporary absence. After this, they cease to be treated as your partner and your benefit will be reduced.

SPC Regs, regs 4 & 5

7. Jobseeker's allowance

General rules – If you are entitled immediately before you leave, you can continue receiving jobseeker's allowance (JSA) during a temporary absence abroad if you are receiving NHS treatment outside GB or the absence is unlikely to exceed 52 weeks and you satisfy one of the following rules:

❑ You can be paid for the first four weeks if you are in Northern Ireland and continue to satisfy the conditions of entitlement while there, or you are abroad with your partner and a disability premium, severe disability premium or pensioner premium is payable in respect of your partner and you are the claimant. You can also be paid for up to four weeks if you are under 25 and receive a government training allowance but are not receiving training (although certain training courses are excluded).

❑ You can be paid for the first eight weeks if you are taking your dependent child abroad for medical treatment by an appropriately qualified person.

❑ If you go abroad for a job interview and are away for no more than seven consecutive days, you can be paid for your days abroad if you give notice (written, if required) to the Jobcentre Plus office and on your return you satisfy the employment officer that you attended the interview.

❑ You can be paid for the first 15 days if you go abroad to take part in annual continuous training as a member of a territorial or reserve force.

JSA Regs, reg 50

Partner abroad – The rules for income-based JSA are similar to income support (see 5 above). However, if you are claiming as a joint-claim couple and on the date you make your claim your partner is abroad, you will only be paid for them for the first four weeks if they are in Northern

Ireland (and the absence is unlikely to exceed 52 weeks) or they are in receipt of a training allowance (as above) or for up to seven days if they are attending a job interview. Otherwise you will be paid as a single person.

JSA Regs, reg 78(1)&(2), Sch 5, paras 10-11 and Sch 5A, para 7

EEA – For contribution-based JSA, if you go to an EEA country to look for work, have been registered with the Jobcentre Plus office for (normally) four weeks and satisfy the conditions of entitlement up to the date you leave the UK, you can usually get benefit in the EEA country for up to three months. You must register as unemployed in the country where you are seeking work within seven days and comply with their procedures. For income-based JSA, seek advice to argue the same rules should apply.

8. Disability benefits

You continue to be entitled to personal independence payment (PIP) and (unless you are still covered by the more generous transitional absence rules – see below) attendance allowance and disability living allowance (DLA) during a temporary absence abroad for:

■ the first 13 weeks; *or*

■ the first 26 weeks if the absence is solely in connection with medical treatment for your illness or disability that began before you left GB.

In each case your absence must be unlikely to exceed 52 weeks.

AA Regs, reg 2; DLA Regs, reg 2; PIP Regs, regs 17 & 18

Transitional absence rules – If you were entitled to attendance allowance or DLA on 7.4.13, you can continue to be paid it during a temporary absence abroad:

■ for the first 26 weeks; *or*

■ longer if the absence is for the specific purpose of being treated for an illness or disability that began before you left GB, and the DWP agrees to pay you for longer.

These rules cease to apply when your award is terminated or on 7.10.13 if this is earlier. However, if you were already abroad on 8.4.13 under the second group above, you can continue to be paid until either you return or your award is revised or superseded.

AA Regs, reg 2(2); DLA Regs, reg 2(2)

EEA – You can be paid attendance allowance or DLA in another EEA country indefinitely if your entitlement to the benefit began before 1.6.92 and you (or a family member) were last employed or self-employed in the UK.

If you move to another EEA country you can continue to be paid, or make a new claim for, attendance allowance, DLA care component or PIP daily living component if you:

■ are habitually resident in another EEA state or Switzerland; *and*

■ are covered by the EEA co-ordination rules (see Chapter 49(1)); *and*

■ can demonstrate a genuine and sufficient link to the UK social security system.

AA Regs, reg 2B; DLA Regs, reg 2B; PIP Regs, reg 23

The DWP accepts that attendance allowance or DLA care component should have been paid if, since 18.10.07, you went to another EEA country and the UK continued to be responsible for paying your benefits. If your attendance allowance or DLA care component was stopped in these circumstances, arrears should be paid from the date that the benefit stopped (seek specialist advice if this was before 18.10.07). For details, write to: Exportability Co-ordinator, Room C201, DCS, Warbreck House, Warbreck Hill Road, Blackpool FY2 0YE (0125 333 1044).

C&P Regs, reg 6(35-37); D&A Regs, Reg 7(9A)

DLA mobility component cannot be exported to another EEA country.

ECJ, Case C-537/09 Bartlett

9. Universal credit

If you are entitled immediately before you leave, you can continue receiving universal credit during a temporary absence abroad for:

- **one month,** if the absence is not expected to exceed and does not exceed one month; *or*
- **two months,** if the absence is in connection with the death of your partner or child (or qualifying young person; see Chapter 38(1)) or a close relative of you, your partner or child (or qualifying young person) and it would be unreasonable for you to return to GB within the first month; *or*
- **six months,** if the absence is not expected to exceed and does not exceed six months and is solely in connection with the medically approved care, convalescence or treatment of you, your partner or your child (or qualifying young person).

If you have a joint claim for universal credit the rules above must apply to both you and your partner.

Partner or child abroad – If you stay in GB while your partner is abroad, your entitlement will not be affected while one of the groups above applies to them. If none of these apply, you will cease to be entitled to universal credit as joint claimants; you must claim as a single person. Your award will be the maximum for a single person but your partner's income and capital will still affect your entitlement until your partner has been, or is expected to be, apart from you for six months, when you will cease to be treated as a couple.

If your child (or qualifying young person) is abroad, you are entitled for them while one of the groups above applies to them.

UC Regs, reg 3(6), 4(7) & 11

10. Carer's allowance

General rules – This will be paid during a temporary absence abroad for up to four weeks (this could be without the disabled person during a 'break in care' – see Chapter 7(10)). If you go abroad temporarily specifically to care for that person, you will receive carer's allowance for as long as they continue to receive a qualifying benefit (see Chapter 7(2)).

ICA Regs, reg 9

EEA – The rules are the same as for attendance allowance/DLA (care component) (see 8 above).

11. Child benefit

If you are ordinarily resident in the UK and temporarily absent (see 1 above) from the UK you continue to be entitled to child benefit for the first eight weeks, or for the first 12 weeks if the absence is in connection with:

- your treatment for a disability or illness; *or*
- the treatment (for a disability or illness), or death, of your partner, or the sibling, parent, (great)grandparent, child (including a child you are responsible for), (great)grandchild of you or your partner.

If a woman gives birth while absent from the UK in accordance with this 8/12-week rule, the baby will be treated as being in the UK for up to 12 weeks from the start of the mother's absence.

Child benefit can be paid for the first 12 weeks of your child's temporary absence abroad. It may be paid for longer if your child goes abroad:

- for the specific purpose of being treated for an illness or disability that began before they left the UK; *or*
- solely in order to receive full-time education in another EEA country (or Switzerland) or on an educational exchange or visit.

CB Regs, Part 6

The same rules apply to guardian's allowance.

EEA – You may be paid benefit for a child resident in another EEA country and also if you go to another EU country.

12. Industrial injuries disablement benefit

A basic disablement pension and retirement allowance are both payable while you are abroad. However, there are time limits for other industrial injuries benefits.

Reduced earnings allowance (REA) – REA is payable for the first three months of a temporary absence abroad if you were entitled before you left and your absence is not connected with work, or for longer if the DWP agrees. If you lose REA for one day, you may lose it for good.

Constant attendance allowance and exceptionally severe disablement allowance – These are payable for the first six months of a temporary absence abroad, or longer if the DWP agrees.

PA Regs, reg 9

EEA – Any industrial injuries benefit (including those above) can be paid without time limit in an EEA country.

13. Retirement, widows' and bereavement benefits

These are payable no matter how long you are away. If you intend to go for longer than six months, inform Jobcentre Plus so arrangements can be made for paying your benefit abroad. If you are living permanently in a country outside the EEA, you can only receive annual upratings if that country has a reciprocal agreement with the UK covering the payment of annual increases or you are covered by a co-operation and association agreement.

You will be disqualified from a bereavement payment if you are abroad both when you claim and at the time of your spouse/civil partner's death unless they were in GB when they died, or you returned within four weeks of their death, or their national insurance contribution record satisfies the contribution condition of a widowed parent's allowance or bereavement allowance.

PA Regs, reg 4

EEA – If you are living in another EEA country, you will get annual benefit increases as if you were in the UK.

14. Tax credits

If you are ordinarily resident in, but temporarily absent (see 1 above) from, the UK you are treated as present and can therefore either claim or continue to be entitled to tax credits for the first eight weeks, or for the first 12 weeks if the absence is in connection with:

- your treatment for a disability; *or*
- the treatment (for a disability), or death, of your partner or the sibling, parent, (great)grandparent, child (including a child you are responsible for), (great)grandchild of you or your partner.

TC(R) Regs, reg 4

EEA – If you are in the UK, child tax credit can be paid for family members living in another EEA country. It can also be paid if you go to another EU country.

Tax

51 Income tax

1. Introduction

This chapter briefly outlines income tax, but applies only to incomes up to £100,000, above which allowances may be withdrawn. Contact details for HMRC are on their website (www.hmrc.gov.uk). HMRC has a taxes helpline: 0845 300 0627; textphone 0845 302 1408 and a self-assessment helpline: 0845 900 0444. For independent advice, contact TaxAid (0345 120 3779 or www.taxaid.org.uk) or, for the over-60s, Tax Help for Older People (0845 601 3321 and 01308 488066 or www.taxvol.org.uk).

To check if you are paying the right amount of tax you need to know what income is taxable, the allowances you are entitled to and the appropriate rate of tax. Allowances and tax rates change each year (from 6 April). The figures and allowances in this chapter are for 6.4.13 to 5.4.14.

2. Income

Many types of income (eg earnings and state benefits) are taxable, but some are exempt (eg interest on an Individual Savings Account or 'ISA') and ignored for tax. Tax relief is allowed on certain outgoings (eg pension contributions).

The following are the only taxable benefits:

- adult dependants' additions paid with certain benefits (but not additions for children);
- bereavement allowance, widowed mother's/parent's allowance and widow's pension;
- carer's allowance;
- contributory employment and support allowance and long-term incapacity benefit (but not if you transferred from invalidity benefit – see Box D.10, Chapter 14);
- income support (if you are directly involved in a trade dispute);
- invalidity allowance (paid with a state pension);
- industrial death benefit;
- jobseeker's allowance;
- state pension;
- statutory adoption pay, statutory maternity pay, statutory paternity pay and statutory sick pay.

3. Tax allowances

Tax allowances are amounts of annual income on which you do not have to pay tax. You are entitled to a *'personal allowance'*; you may also be entitled to a *'blind person's allowance'* or *'married couple's allowance'* (see below). If you think you have not had the correct allowances, a refund may be due (see 7 below). Everyone has a personal allowance that can be set against all taxable income:

- born after 5.4.48 (the *'basic level'*), it is £9,440;
- born between 6.4.38 and 5.4.48, it is £10,500;
- born before 6.4.38, it is £10,660.

The higher age allowances are reduced if your adjustable net income (ie your income less things like pension contributions) is more than £26,100. For each £2 extra income over £26,100, £1 of allowance is lost. Your allowance will not be reduced below the basic level of £9,440. Spouses/civil partners each have their own income limit. If you don't use your full personal allowance, you cannot transfer it to a partner or carry it forward to a future year.

In some circumstances personal allowances are not available (eg if your income is over £100,000 or you are not 'domiciled' in the UK).

Entitlement to the higher age allowances was different before 5.4.13.

Blind person's allowance – You will get an extra allowance of £2,160 if you are registered blind (but not if registered as partially sighted). In Scotland and Northern Ireland, you must be unable to do any work for which eyesight is essential. Spouses or civil partners can transfer surplus allowance from one to the other. If both spouses/civil partners are registered blind, one of them can get both their own blind person's allowance and the other's surplus allowance. You can receive the allowance for the tax year before the one in which you are registered as blind if you had obtained the evidence for registration (eg ophthalmologist's certificate) before the end of that tax year.

Married couple's allowance – This is for married couples or civil partners who live together if at least one of them was born before 6.4.35; the allowance for 2013/14 is £7,915. Tax relief on married couple's allowance is restricted to 10% and this amount is taken off tax due for the year. Married couple's allowance may be reduced if the income of the higher-earning partner is above the £26,100 income limit (by £1 for every £2 over the limit). It only starts to be reduced if the personal allowance has been reduced to the basic level (see above) and it cannot be reduced below a minimum of £3,040.

4. Income tax rates (non-savings income)

Taxable income	rate for tax year 2013/14
The first £32,010	20% (basic rate)
Between £32,011 and £150,000	40% (higher rate)
Over £150,000	45% (additional rate)

For further details, see www.hmrc.gov.uk/rates/it.htm.

5. Working out your tax

Step 1: Work out your taxable income

Add up income from all sources for the tax year (6 April to 5 April). Include taxable state benefits, but not exempt income (to see what income is exempt go to www.litrg.org.uk/pensioners/tax-essentials/TaxFreeTypes).

Step 2: Deduct personal allowances

Deduct your personal allowance (plus the blind person's allowance if you qualify) from your taxable income in Step 1. If your taxable income exceeds £100,000, the basic personal allowance is reduced by £1 for every £2 of income over £100,000 until it is reduced to nil (for 2013/14, this will be the case for incomes over £118,880). Blind person's allowance is not reduced whatever the income level.

Step 3: Work out your tax

a) Work out the tax on the result from Step 2 using the income limits and tax rates in the table above. Different tax rates may apply on savings income from banks and building societies (see 7 below).

b) If you get married couple's allowance (MCA), work out 10% of it and deduct the result from the tax payable in (a). This is the tax you are due to pay (before taking off any tax already paid at source).

Example: James, aged 78, is married to Annie, 72. James is registered blind. He gets a private pension of £10,514 for this tax year and state pension of £7,035.

Step 1: James's taxable income

Private pension	£10,514
State pension	£7,035
All taxable income	*£17,549*

Step 2: Deduct personal allowances

Personal allowance, aged 75+	£10,660
Blind person's allowance	£2,160
Total personal allowances	*£12,820*
Subtract allowances from income	
Taxable income	*£4,729*

Step 3: James's tax

a) 20% of £4,729	£945.80
b) Less 10% of MCA of £7,915	£791.50
Tax due to be paid	*£154.30*

James will see if he has tax to pay or be refunded by checking his P60 (issued by the pension company after the tax year end) to see how much tax he paid on his private pension through PAYE (see 6 below) against tax due of £154.30.

6. Notice of coding

If you have earnings or private pension income you will generally have tax deducted under PAYE (Pay As You Earn). For each pension or source of earnings, HMRC should send you a notice of coding (form P2), setting out your allowances and any necessary deductions. Contact HMRC if you think they are incorrect. The contact details will be on the coding notice.

For example, a single person under 65 and registered blind would get allowances of £11,600 (personal allowance £9,440 plus blind person's allowance £2,160). Their code would be 1160L; the final digit of the allowance is replaced by the letter L if the basic personal allowance applies. Other letters (P, Y or T) may be used; the first two indicate certain age allowances and the last is used in most other cases. In some cases a code BR will be used; this is a basic rate of 20% on earnings with no personal allowances.

7. Tax refunds

You can only claim a refund of overpaid tax for four years following the end of the tax year (eg a claim for the 2009/10 tax year expires on 5.4.14). The time limit can be extended if tax was overpaid due to HMRC or other government department error and there is no dispute or doubt as to the facts (extra-statutory concession B41). To claim a refund, write to HMRC with the details or, for savings tax refunds, ask for form R40.

If you are unemployed and do not expect to go back to work, or have retired permanently (and do not get a pension from your old employer) or have returned to full-time study, a tax refund can be claimed on form P50 four weeks or more after leaving work. Send your P45 (which your former employer should give you when you leave), with the completed P50, to HMRC. You need to estimate your income for the rest of the tax year. If you leave work and claim jobseeker's allowance, you cannot get a tax refund until the end of the tax year.

Savings income from banks and building societies – Tax of 20% is deducted by banks, building societies, etc from most interest on savings. If all your taxable income, including interest before tax is taken off (the *'gross'* amount), is less than your total personal allowances, you can receive interest without deduction of tax. Ask your bank or building society for form R85. You need to complete a separate form for each bank or building society.

The tax rate on savings income depends on the level of your income. If all your taxable income is less than your personal allowances, no tax is due. (You may be able to claim a refund of any tax paid at source; ring HMRC on 0845 300 0627; textphone: 0845 302 1408). If your taxable income, including interest but after deducting personal allowances, is less than £2,790 you are liable for tax on the interest at 10%; if 20% tax has been deducted at source, you will be due a refund. If you are a basic-rate taxpayer and your taxable income is over £2,790, tax is due on savings income at 20%; if 20% tax has been deducted at source, there is no more to pay. Higher-rate taxpayers pay 40% tax on interest, ie an extra 20%, which may be paid through their PAYE coding or self-assessment (see 9 below). Additional-rate taxpayers pay an extra 25%.

Dividends – The basic tax rate on dividends is 10%. The tax deducted at source (the *'tax credit'*) covers tax due at 10%, but is not refundable, so even non-taxpayers cannot claim back the dividend's tax credit. The tax credit can, however, be used to reduce the amount of tax due for the year. Higher and additional rates are 32.5% and 37.5% respectively but the tax actually payable will be net of the tax credit, so rates of 22.5% and 27.5% will apply.

8. Arrears of tax

If you have not paid enough tax, HMRC can claim it from you, usually within four years. In some circumstances (eg deliberate tax evasion) the time limit is 20 years. HMRC could charge penalties if you are at fault.

Arrears of tax may be wholly or partly waived if they have arisen because HMRC failed to take account of information they have about you and you reasonably believed your affairs were in order. This concession may be given if you are notified of the arrears after the end of the tax year following that in which HMRC received information indicating you had underpaid tax or if HMRC failed repeatedly and arrears have built up over two or more tax years. If you believe this applies to you, write to HMRC claiming a waiver under extra statutory concession A19.

9. Self-assessment

You may be asked to complete a tax return if you have income that is not taxed at source (eg untaxed interest or rents) or if your circumstances have changed. Some taxpayers (eg self-employed people) are asked to do this annually. If in any tax year you receive taxable income or taxable capital gains which HMRC does not know about, you must notify them within six months of the end of the tax year (eg by 5.10.14 for 2013/14).

Keep records of your income and capital gains to enable you to complete a tax return. Records should usually be kept for 22 months after the end of the relevant tax year. If you are self-employed or have rental income, that period is extended by four years.

If you regularly file a tax return, you will be sent a blank form (or notice to complete one if you normally file online) shortly after the end of the tax year. Paper returns must be filed by 31 October. HMRC will calculate your tax and let you know by 31 January how much to pay. Tax returns filed online are due by 31 January. If you want HMRC to collect tax due (of amounts less than £3,000) through your PAYE code for the following year, complete and file paper returns by 31 October or online returns by 30 December. Tax should be paid in full by 31 January or you may be charged interest or a penalty. There is also an immediate penalty if the return is filed late and further penalties can arise depending on how late you file the return or pay the tax due. In some circumstances, you may be able to claim you had a reasonable excuse for late filing or payment, or otherwise be able to appeal against penalties.

10. Self-employment

Register with HMRC as soon as possible after you become self-employed. A penalty may be charged if you fail to do so by 5 October (for tax purposes) or 31 January (for national insurance contributions) after the end of the tax year in which you started the business. To register, use form CWF1 (www. hmrc.gov.uk/forms/cwf1.pdf or ring 0845 900 0404) or ring the newly self-employed helpline (0845 915 4515, textphone 0845 915 3296). You will be sent a tax return to complete each year. HMRC booklet SE1 has more information (www. hmrc.gov.uk/leaflets/se1.pdf or ring 0845 900 0404).

52 VAT relief

1. Introduction

This is a brief summary of VAT relief on items purchased to help with your disability or for works carried out to adapt your home to your needs. More information is in *VAT reliefs for disabled people* (Notice 701/7) and the helpsheet *About purchasing zero rated adapted vehicles (Guidance for customers)*. These are available at www.hmrc.gov.uk, or you can request them and get advice by:

- ringing the HMRC Charities and VAT Helpline: 0845 302 0203 (select option 1);
- writing to HMRC VAT reliefs for disabled people, St John's House, Merton Road, Liverpool, L75 1BB;
- emailing via a form on the HMRC website: www.hmrc. gov.uk/charities/vat-relief-disabled.htm.

If you are eligible for relief, the items (*'goods'*) or works (*'services'*) qualify and you inform the supplier (and provide an eligibility certificate), VAT is charged at zero rate rather than at 20%.

Note: VAT law uses terms no longer in use, which may cause offence. When we use them here we do so to reflect accurately the wording of the law.

2. Do you qualify?

To qualify for relief, the law states you must be *'chronically sick or disabled'*. HMRC guidance defines this as a person:

- with a physical or mental impairment that has a long-term and substantial adverse effect upon his/her ability to carry out everyday activities;
- with a condition that the medical profession treats as a chronic sickness, such as diabetes; *or*
- who is terminally ill.

3. What items or works qualify?

Goods – Some items you purchase or hire to help with your condition qualify for relief. Here are some examples:

- medical appliances designed solely for relief of 'severe abnormality or injury';
- adjustable beds designed for invalids;
- commode chairs, stools and similar devices to aid bathing;
- chair and stair lifts for invalid wheelchairs, hoists and other lifting equipment designed for use by disabled people, and the cost of installation;
- boats designed or substantially adapted for use by a disabled person;
- items designed solely for use by a disabled person. Examples in HMRC guidance include low-vision aids, Braille embossers, long-handled pick-up sticks, text telephones, whistling cups for blind people and vibrating

pillows for the deaf or hard-of-hearing.

Services – Some alterations to items or to your home can qualify for relief, for example:

- the cost of adapting general-purpose goods to suit your particular needs (but not the cost of the goods themselves);
- constructing ramps or widening doorways or passages in your home (but not constructing new doorways or passages);
- extending or adapting a bathroom, washroom or lavatory in your home if necessary because of your condition;
- installing a lift in your home so you can move between floors;
- installing an alarm system so you can call for assistance.

Relief given for alterations to your home is strictly defined. Some common examples of works that do *not* qualify are:

- alterations resulting from the installation of special equipment (eg to house a renal dialysis unit). The equipment might qualify for relief, the alterations do not;
- altering the layout of your home to accommodate a downstairs bedroom.

Cars and motor vehicles – Your hire, lease or purchase of a motor vehicle with a maximum capacity of 12 people qualifies for relief in any of the following circumstances:

- the vehicle was designed or substantially modified before it was supplied to carry a person in a wheelchair or on a stretcher;
- the vehicle was designed or substantially modified before it was supplied to enable you to enter, drive or be carried in it. A vehicle does not meet this condition merely because it has automatic transmission. To qualify, you must usually use a wheelchair or be carried on a stretcher;
- the vehicle contains features designed solely to enable you to be carried in a wheelchair. To qualify, you must usually use a wheelchair or be carried on a stretcher.

Relief applies if you lease an unused motor vehicle under the Motability scheme for a minimum of three years or you buy a vehicle that has previously been hired under the Motability scheme (the vehicle must be purchased from a person operating the scheme without any intervening supply).

Other costs – Parts and accessories for qualifying goods are generally zero rated when supplied to you, as are the installation, repair or maintenance of those goods. However, parts and accessories for qualifying goods must be designed solely to go with the item concerned. For example, a generator purchased to run a stair lift in the event of a power cut does not qualify because it is a general-purpose item that could have other uses.

Bathrooms are specifically mentioned in the law, but kitchens are not. This may mean VAT relief is confined to kitchen equipment designed specially to suit your disability.

VAT Act 1994, Sch 8, Group 12

4. How do you claim?

Suppliers must ensure their goods or services qualify for zero rating and that you qualify as a 'disabled person'. When making a purchase you think might qualify, ask the supplier about zero rating. If the goods or services qualify, the supplier will ask you to make a declaration (eg by signing a form or by electronic means if buying over the internet) that you are an eligible disabled person.

5. Decisions and reviews

Suppliers decide whether or not to zero-rate their goods or services, according to their interpretation of the rules. If there is uncertainty, the manufacturer can obtain a ruling from HMRC. If a decision is still in doubt, an appeal can be made to the First-tier Tribunal (Tax Chamber).

Other matters

53 After a death

1. What to do after a death

Following a death there can be many practical issues to deal with. This process, combined with the emotional effects of bereavement, can be difficult to cope with. DWP leaflets *What to do after a death in England and Wales* or *What to do after a death in Scotland* give advice and information on all aspects of bereavement.

You can get practical help and advice from a funeral director, GP, solicitor, religious organisation, social care department or Citizens Advice Bureau. A health visitor or district nurse may help if the death was at home. If it was in hospital, the ward sister or hospital chaplain might help. One of the first things you may need to do is transfer insurance policies (eg car and home insurance) into your name.

If you need support and comfort, organisations such as Cruse Bereavement Care (helpline: 0844 477 9400; www. cruse.org.uk) and Winston's Wish, which offers a service to bereaved families and young people (0845 203 0405), can help.

Social fund funeral expenses – If you receive income-related employment and support allowance, income support, income-based jobseeker's allowance, housing benefit, pension credit, working tax credit (if it includes either disability element) or child tax credit (at any rate greater than the family element), you may be able to get a payment from the social fund for funeral expenses (see Chapter 23(3)).

2. Income-related benefits

If you are below the qualifying age for pension credit and on a low income you may be able to get income-related employment and support allowance (ESA), income support or income-based jobseeker's allowance (JSA), depending on your circumstances. See Chapters 13, 15 and 16 respectively. For each of these benefits, £10 a week of widowed parent's or widowed mother's allowance is disregarded in the assessment of your income. If you have reached the qualifying age for pension credit, see Chapter 42 for details of that benefit.

Late claims – If your claim for income support or JSA is late and it was not reasonable to expect you to claim earlier because of the death of a partner, parent, son, daughter, brother or sister, your claim can be backdated for up to one month (see Chapter 57(3)).

Carers – If you are getting carer's allowance or income support because you were caring for the person who has died, your benefit can continue for up to eight weeks following their death (see Chapter 8(8)). The carer premium in other means-tested benefits may also continue for up to eight weeks (see Chapter 25(6)).

Housing costs – If you have a mortgage and are claiming income-related ESA, income support, income-based JSA or pension credit, you may be entitled to help with mortgage interest payments. If you are eligible for pension credit you can get this help straightaway; for other benefits there is a 13-week waiting period. See Chapter 26.

Rent and council tax – Housing benefit helps towards rent if you are on a low income. In the assessment of your income, £15 a week of widowed parent's or widowed mother's allowance is ignored. See Chapter 21. For help towards council tax, see Chapter 22.

Pension arrears – If your spouse or civil partner was receiving pension credit or state pension (or any other benefit combined for payment with these), arrears of these benefits can be paid automatically to you on their death without the need for a claim.

3. Bereavement benefits

Bereavement benefits are available to people whose spouse died on or after 9.4.01 or whose registered civil partner died on or after 5.12.05. Women whose husbands died before 9.4.01 continue to claim widow's benefits.

There are three bereavement benefits:

- bereavement payment: a lump-sum payment of £2,000 (see 4 below);
- bereavement allowance: payable for up to 52 weeks for those aged 45 or over (but under state pension age) when their spouse or civil partner died (see 5 below);
- widowed parent's allowance (WPA): payable if you have dependent children or are pregnant (see 6 below).

You must have been legally married or in a registered civil partnership. If you were in the process of divorcing or of dissolving a civil partnership, you would still qualify for bereavement benefits if your spouse or civil partner died before the decree absolute or final dissolution was issued.

Bereavement allowance, WPA and widow's benefits under the old scheme are suspended for any period when you are cohabiting with a same/opposite-sex partner. If you remarry or form a civil partnership, the benefit ceases.

SSCBA, Ss.37(3)-(4), 38(2)-(3), 39A(4)-(5) & 39B(4A)-(5)

Claims and time limits

To claim bereavement benefits, ring the DWP Bereavement Service (0845 606 0265; textphone 0845 606 0285). The time limit for claiming a bereavement payment is normally 12 months from the date of death of your spouse or civil partner. If you were receiving state pension when they died, you do not need to claim bereavement payment to become entitled to it, so the time limit will not apply. There is no time limit for claiming bereavement allowance or WPA, and claims can normally be backdated for three months.

The 12-month time limit for claiming the bereavement payment and the 3-month backdating limit for bereavement allowance and WPA can be extended if you were unaware of your spouse or civil partner's death.

❑ If your spouse or civil partner's body has not been found or identified, and you claim any of the bereavement benefits within 12 months of the date the death was *presumed* to have occurred, the claim can be backdated to this date.

❑ If more than 12 months have passed since death was presumed to have occurred, and you claim any of the bereavement benefits within 12 months of the date that a decision maker decides that your spouse or civil partner can be presumed to have died, the claim can be backdated to the date the death was presumed to have occurred.

❑ If the body is discovered or identified more than 12 months after the known or presumed date of death, you are made aware of the discovery or identification within 12 months and you claim any of the bereavement benefits within 12 months of the date on which you first knew of the discovery or identification, the claim can be backdated to the date of the discovery or notification of the body.

C&P Regs, regs 3(da), 19(2)-(3B) & SSAA, S.3

For help available to widows, widowers and surviving civil partners of those whose death is attributable to service in HM Armed Forces, see Chapter 45(4).

The benefit cap

Bereavement allowance and WPA are both included in the list of benefits to which the 'benefit cap' applies (as are widowed mother's allowance and widow's pension). This cap limits the total weekly benefits that can be claimed to £500 for lone parents and couples and £350 for single claimants. See Box H.1 Chapter 21 for details (including exemptions).

Future changes

The government is considering replacing the three bereavement benefits with a single payment structure for all claimants, the *'bereavement support payment'*. This would be paid in instalments over 12 months, during which the payment would be disregarded in the universal credit (see Box J.1, Chapter 25) and benefit cap (see above) calculations. The changes are planned to take place from April 2016.

4. Bereavement payment

This is a tax-free, lump-sum payment of £2,000 for spouses bereaved on or after 9.4.01 and for civil partners bereaved on or after 5.12.05. You must have been under state pension age when your spouse or civil partner died, unless they were not entitled to a Category A state pension. If you were living with another person as part of a couple at the time of your late partner's death, you will not qualify.

To qualify, your spouse or civil partner must have paid Class 1, 2 or 3 national insurance contributions on earnings in any one tax year equal to 25 times the lower earnings limit for that year (see Chapter 12(7)). For tax years before 6.4.75, 25 flat-rate contributions will be sufficient. If your spouse or civil partner died as a result of an industrial accident or prescribed industrial disease, the contribution conditions are treated as satisfied.

SSCBA, Ss.36 & 60(2)&(3) & Sch 3, para 4

5. Bereavement allowance

Bereavement allowance is payable if you were aged 45 or over when your spouse/civil partner died and is payable for up to 52 weeks following their death. You cannot get the allowance at the same time as widowed parent's allowance, but can claim it for the remainder of the 52 weeks if your widowed parent's allowance ends during that time. Bereavement allowance cannot be paid beyond state pension age (see 8 below).

SSCBA, S.39B

The amount you are paid is related to your age when your spouse or civil partner died; payments range from £32.49 a week if you were 45, to £108.30 if you were 55 or over.

SSCBA, S.39C(5)

The contribution conditions for bereavement allowance are the same as those for the basic state pension for people who reached state pension age before 6.4.10 (see Box O.1, Chapter 43).

SSCBA, Sch 3, para 5(2)&(3)

If your spouse or civil partner's national insurance contribution record was incomplete, the amount payable is reduced, unless they died as a result of an industrial accident or prescribed industrial disease.

WBRP Regs, reg 6 & SSCBA, S.60(2)&(3)

A bereavement allowance is taxable.

6. Widowed parent's allowance

Widowed parent's allowance (WPA) is a regular payment for men and women bereaved on or after 9.4.01 (5.12.05 for civil partners) who have at least one dependent child or 'qualifying young person' under 20 (see Chapter 38(1)). Men widowed before 9.4.01 who have dependent children can also qualify. Women pregnant by their late husband can qualify, including those who become pregnant following certain fertility treatments, including the donation of eggs, sperm or embryos. This rule also applies to a woman whose late partner was a registered civil partner. Women whose husbands died before 9.4.01 can continue to claim widowed mother's allowance (see 7 below). WPA cannot be paid beyond state pension age (see 8 below).

SSCBA, S.39A

The contribution conditions for WPA are the same as those for the basic state pension for people who reached state pension age before 6.4.10 (see Box O.1, Chapter 43).

SSCBA, Sch 3, para 5(2)&(3)

If your spouse or civil partner met the national insurance (NI) contribution conditions, the full rate of £108.30 a week is payable. If your spouse or civil partner's NI contribution record was incomplete, you will receive a proportionately reduced amount of WPA, unless they died as a result of an industrial accident or prescribed industrial disease.

WBRP Regs, reg 6 & SSCBA, S.60(2)&(3)

If you have dependent children, you should claim child tax credit at the same time as WPA (see Chapter 19).

You may get an additional state pension (SERPS, or state second pension – see Chapter 43(6)) based on your spouse/ civil partner's earnings. The maximum amount of additional pension that you can inherit is restricted. You may only inherit a maximum of 50% of your partner's state second pension. You may be able to inherit a greater percentage of your partner's SERPS, depending on their date of birth.

WPA for yourself is taxable. Increases for children payable on claims made before 6.4.03 are tax free.

7. Widowed before 9.4.01

The following benefits are for women widowed before 9.4.01.

❑ **Widow's pension** – You may get a reduced, age-related widow's pension if you were aged 45-54 on the day your husband died or when your widowed mother's allowance ended. If you were aged 55-64 on that day, you may get a full-rate pension. The amount is the same as bereavement allowance (see 5 above) except that an additional state pension may be payable with widow's pension.

SSCBA, Ss.38 & 39

❑ **Widowed mother's allowance** – This is usually payable if you have dependent children. The amounts and qualifying conditions are the same as those for widowed parent's allowance (see 6 above).

SSCBA, Ss.37 & 39

Widow's pension and widowed mother's allowance are both included in the list of benefits to which the 'benefit cap' applies (see 3 above).

8. What happens to other benefits?

Overlapping benefits – Bereavement and widows' benefits overlap with contributory employment and support allowance, incapacity benefit, carer's allowance, severe disablement allowance, contribution-based jobseeker's allowance, maternity allowance, unemployability supplement and state pension. You cannot receive two overlapping benefits at the same time; you'll receive the higher of the overlapped benefits.

OB Regs, reg 4

Industrial death benefit – If your husband died before 11.4.88 and you get industrial death benefit, it is paid in full on top of any transitional incapacity benefit (see Box D.10, Chapter 14) or state pension you are entitled to based on your own national insurance (NI) contributions.

When you reach state pension age

Bereavement allowance, widowed parent's allowance and widow's pension cannot be paid beyond state pension age (see Chapter 43(2)). Widowed mother's allowance can be paid indefinitely if you have dependent children (but overlaps with state pension – see above).

SSCBA, Ss.39A(4)(b), 39B(4)(a), 38(2) & 37(3)

State pension – When you reach state pension age, if you have not remarried or formed a civil partnership, you will be entitled to a Category B state pension based on your late spouse/civil partner's NI contributions, or to a Category A state pension based on your own NI contributions record and including your spouse/civil partner's record if that would give you a higher state pension. See Chapter 43(4)-(6) for details.

9. Death of a child

Benefits will be affected by the death of your child, but dealing with different agencies after such a loss may be unbearable. Since the agencies concerned do need to be informed quickly, you could ask someone to make the calls on your behalf, perhaps an advice worker or a good friend.

Some benefits will continue for eight weeks after the death of a child. These include carer's allowance, child benefit, child tax credit and any carer premium, disabled child premium, enhanced disability premium and child allowances paid in means-tested benefits.

The National Child Death Helpline (0800 282 986) and the Compassionate Friends Helpline (0845 123 2304) can provide support and comfort to bereaved parents and families.

54 Health benefits

1. Who qualifies for help?

Some people qualify for help with NHS charges, vouchers for glasses or contact lenses and hospital travel fares because of their circumstances. You qualify automatically if you:

■ or a member of your family, receive income-related employment and support allowance, income support, income-based jobseeker's allowance or pension credit guarantee credit;

■ or a member of your family, receive child tax credit *or*

working tax credit and child tax credit *or* working tax credit with a disability or severe disability element, and your relevant income for tax credit purposes is £15,276 or less, and you are named on a valid NHS tax credit exemption certificate;

■ are a war/service pensioner and have been issued with an exemption certificate (the need must be due to your accepted war disablement).

If you qualify for a tax credit exemption certificate, the NHS Business Services Authority will send it to you when your award has been confirmed by HMRC. This may take several weeks, so if you need chargeable treatment while waiting, you may be able to use your tax credit award notice as evidence of entitlement. If you have to pay, get a receipt from the pharmacist, dentist, optician or hospital and claim a refund later. Your exemption certificate is valid until the date specified on the certificate, regardless of changes to your tax credit entitlement.

Some people qualify for an HC2 (full) or HC3 (partial) certificate for help with NHS charges, hospital travel costs and vouchers for glasses on the basis of low income. If you qualify on low-income grounds, your partner and dependent children also qualify. See 5 below.

Young care leavers maintained by an English or Welsh local authority and people residing permanently in a care home funded wholly or partly by a local authority are entitled to an HC2 certificate by making a claim under the low income scheme without having to satisfy a further means test. Asylum seekers (and their dependants) supported by the government should automatically be issued with HC2 certificates; those not supported by the government need to apply under the low income scheme (but will not have to satisfy the means test).

The NHS Business Services Authority manages the health benefits scheme. For details, see NHS leaflets HC11 and HC12, available from the NHS forms-line (0845 610 1112) or website (www.nhsbsa.nhs.uk). See Chapter 35(2) for details of the hospital travel fares scheme.

NHS(TERC) Regs, reg 5

2. Prescription charges

Prescriptions are free in Northern Ireland, Scotland and Wales but cost £7.85 in England (2013/14) for each item, so it is important to take advantage of exemptions and prepayment certificates that save money on frequent prescriptions. If you are a hospital outpatient, exemptions from charges made by hospitals for prescribed drugs are the same as those listed below. Patients who live in Scotland or Wales but registered with an English GP can apply for an free '*entitlement card*' that confirms their entitlement to free prescriptions.

Exemptions

Who is automatically exempt? – Your prescriptions are free if you are in any of the groups listed in 1 above or:

■ are under 16, or under 19 and in full-time education; *or*

■ are aged 60 or over.

Who can get an exemption certificate? – You can get an exemption certificate for free NHS prescriptions if you:

■ are pregnant or have given birth in the previous 12 months. Get form FW8 from your doctor, midwife or health visitor;

■ are undergoing treatment for cancer, the effects of cancer or the effects of cancer treatment; *or*

■ have a specified condition (see below).

NHS(CDA) Regs, reg 7

What are the specified conditions? – If you have one of the conditions listed below, you are entitled to an exemption certificate:

■ a continuing physical disability that prevents you leaving home without help from another person (a temporary disability is excluded even if it is likely to last a few months);

- a permanent fistula (eg caecostomy, colostomy, laryngostomy or ileostomy) requiring continuous surgical dressing or an appliance;
- diabetes mellitus (except where treatment is by diet alone), myxoedema, hypoparathyroidism, diabetes insipidus or other forms of hypopituitarism, forms of hypoadrenalism (including Addison's disease) for which specific substitution therapy is essential, and myasthenia gravis;
- epilepsy, requiring continuous anti-convulsive therapy.

Claim on form FP92A, available from your doctor.

NHS(CDA) Regs, reg 7(1)(e)

How to claim
Complete the declaration on the back of the prescription form. The pharmacist will ask for evidence that you are eligible for free prescriptions. When you collect your prescription take your exemption certificate, prepayment certificate or benefit award notice. You should not be refused the prescription if you do not have the evidence but your entitlement may be checked later and if you were not exempt you will be asked to pay the prescription charge. You may also be charged a penalty of up to five times the cost of the prescription, subject to a £100 maximum.

Refunds – You can claim a refund within three months (later if you have good cause) of the date you paid for treatment if you should have been entitled to help. When you pay, ask your pharmacist for receipt form FP57 and follow the instructions on the form.

NHS(CDA) Regs, reg 10

What is a prescription prepayment certificate?
If you are not exempt from charges, or your income is too high to get the HC2 certificate (see 5 below), a prepayment certificate saves money if you need four or more items in three months or 14 or more items in a year. A 3-month certificate costs £29.10, a year's certificate £104 (2013/14). Apply on form FP95, available from pharmacists or the NHS Business Services Authority (0845 850 0030 or www.nhsbsa.nhs.uk/HelpWithHealthCosts.aspx).

NHS(CDA) Regs, reg 9

3. Sight tests and glasses
You and your partner qualify for free NHS eyesight tests and vouchers for glasses or contact lenses if you:
- are in any of the groups listed in 1 above;
- are under 16, or under 19 and in full-time education; *or*
- need complex or powerful lenses with one lens that has a power in any one meridian of plus or minus 10 or more dioptres, or is a prism-controlled bifocal lens.

NHS eyesight tests or examinations are also free if you are:
- aged 60 or over;
- living in Scotland;
- registered blind, severely sight-impaired, sight-impaired or partially sighted; *or*
- diagnosed as having diabetes or glaucoma, or considered to be at risk of glaucoma, or aged 40 or over and the parent, brother, sister or child of a person with glaucoma.

NHS (Optical Charges & Payments) Regs 1997, regs 3 & 8

You may qualify for vouchers for glasses or contact lenses and help towards the cost of sight tests if your income is low (see 5 below). Ask for a voucher when you have your eyes tested. The value of the voucher depends on the strength of the lenses you need, with additions for clinically necessary prisms or tints. You will usually be asked for evidence that you qualify. When you buy the glasses, give the supplier the voucher. If the glasses cost more, you must pay the extra.

Refunds – You can claim a refund within three months (later if you have good cause) of the date you paid for treatment if you should have been entitled to help. When you pay, ask

your optician for a receipt. Ring 0845 850 1166 to get an HC5 refund claim-form.

4. Free NHS dental treatment
You qualify for free NHS dental treatment if you:
- are in any of the groups listed in 1 above;
- are aged under 18, or under 19 and in full-time education;
- are pregnant – if you were pregnant when the dentist accepted you for treatment;
- have given birth in the past year – if you start a course of dental treatment before your child's first birthday;
- are an NHS inpatient and the treatment is carried out by a hospital dentist; *or*
- are an NHS Hospital Dental Service outpatient (but there may be a charge for dentures and bridges).

NHS (Dental Charges) Regs 2005, regs 3(2) & 7; Sch 5

For information on the low income scheme, see 5 below.

In Scotland, oral health and dental examinations are free for everyone, and in Wales are free for those aged under 25 or over 60. In Wales, certain dental treatments, such as post-operative cancer treatment or suture removal, are also free.

Tell your dentist you qualify (you will usually be asked for evidence) and fill in the declaration on the form they give you.

Refunds – You can claim a refund within three months (later if you have good cause) of the date you paid for treatment if you should have been entitled to help. When you pay, ask your dentist for a receipt. Ring 0845 850 1166 to get an HC5 refund claim-form.

5. Low income scheme
The NHS low income scheme for help with NHS charges and optical vouchers is operated by the NHS Business Services Authority (NHSBSA). If your capital is £16,000 or less, you may be eligible for help. In the low income scheme, a comparison is made between your income and your requirements (see below).

If your income is less than or equal to your requirements (plus 50% of the current cost of a prescription), you are entitled to full help with NHS charges, vouchers towards the cost of glasses and free eye tests. The NHSBSA will send you an HC2 certificate.

NHS(TERC) Regs, reg 5(2)(e)

If your income is higher than your requirements by more than 50% of the prescription charge (the difference is called your *'excess income'*), you cannot get help with the cost of NHS prescriptions but may get help with travel expenses (see Chapter 35(2)) and other NHS charges. The NHSBSA will send you an HC3 certificate (partial help) to show how much you have to contribute towards the charges.

For sight tests, your maximum contribution is the excess income figure. For glasses or lenses, the maximum voucher value is reduced by twice your excess income. For dental charges, your maximum contribution is three times your excess income.

NHS(TERC) Regs, reg 6

The low income assessment
Income and capital – The assessment of income and capital is broadly the same as for income support (see Chapters 27 and 28) but there are differences.
- Assumed tariff income is £1 a week for every £250 (or part thereof) of capital in excess of £6,000, up to the upper capital limit of £16,000. This applies even if you or your partner are aged 60 or over.
- If you live permanently in a care home, the upper capital limit is £23,250.
- If you receive employment and support allowance (ESA), earnings from exempt work (see Chapter 17(3)) are ignored as income.
- If you are on strike, your pre-strike income is taken into

account.

❑ If you are receiving contributory ESA that is being reduced (see Chapter 10(17)), this is taken into account as if the reduction had not been applied.

❑ Pension credit savings credit is ignored as income.

❑ Some Scottish student maintenance loans are disregarded in England and Wales. The £10 disregard for other student loans only applies if your assessment includes any premiums, or you or your partner get a disabled students' allowance because of deafness. Loans are calculated over 52 weeks, unless it is the final year of study or a one-year or sandwich course. Student maintenance grants in excess of the normal maximum are disregarded.

❑ If you have a lodger (without board), the standard disregard in rental income is £20.

Requirements – Your *'requirements'* are worked out in the same way as the income support applicable amount (see Chapter 15(8)), with significant differences.

❑ A disability premium is included if you receive ESA with a component (support/work-related activity) or you have been continuously incapable of work for 28 weeks; the premium is not included if you (and your partner) are aged 60 or over.

❑ If you are under 25 you are entitled to the personal allowance applicable to someone aged 25 or over if you receive ESA with a component (support/work-related activity) or you have been continuously incapable of work for 28 weeks.

❑ Generally, net weekly housing costs are taken into account including: mortgage capital repayments; payments on an endowment policy or hire purchase agreement in connection with buying your home; repayments of interest and capital on a loan to adapt your home for the special needs of a disabled person; rent and council tax less housing benefit and council tax reduction. Amounts for non-dependants are deducted (see Chapter 21(21)).

❑ If you live permanently in a care home, your requirements are the total amount of weekly charge for the accommodation (including all meals and services provided) plus the amount for personal expenses (see Chapter 34(7)).

NHS(TERC) Regs, regs 16 & 17 & Sch 1

How do you claim?
Claim on form HC1, available from Jobcentre Plus offices or the NHSBSA (www.nhsbsa.nhs.uk/HealthCosts/1128.aspx; 0845 850 1166). Hospitals, GPs, dentists, opticians and advice agencies may also have the form. If you are unable to act for yourself, someone else can claim for you. Claim on form HC1(SC) if you live in a care home and the local authority helps with the fees, or if you are a 16/17-year-old care leaver and a local authority supports you. The NHSBSA will send its decision to you. If you are entitled to full help, they will send an HC2 certificate. If you are entitled to partial help, they will send an HC3 certificate. HC2 and HC3 certificates are usually valid for periods of between six months and five years, depending on your circumstances.

If you are not happy with the decision – There is no right of appeal but you can write and ask the NHSBSA to reconsider its decision (Review Section, Help with Health Costs, Sandyford House, Newcastle upon Tyne NE2 1BF).

6. Healthy Start vouchers and vitamins
Healthy Start provides vouchers for fresh milk, infant formula milk and plain fresh or frozen fruit and vegetables. It also provides coupons to claim free vitamin supplements locally without a prescription. You are eligible if:

■ you are at least ten weeks pregnant, aged under 18 and not subject to immigration control (see Chapter 49(3)); *or*

■ you are at least ten weeks pregnant, or have a child aged under four, and you or a member of your family receive

income-related employment and support allowance, income support, income-based jobseeker's allowance or child tax credit (but not working tax credit, unless paid during the 4-week run-on period – see Chapter 19(6)) and your relevant income is less than £16,190 (2013/14).

You can get more information and an application leaflet (HS01) from the website (www.healthystart.nhs.uk) or by ringing the Healthy Start helpline (0845 607 6823). You might also get an application leaflet from your GP surgery or baby clinic. All applications to the scheme must be supported by a registered health professional.

Healthy Start Scheme and Welfare Food (Amendment) Regs 2005

Nursery Milk scheme – Children under 5 who attend approved daycare facilities (including registered childminders) for two hours or more a day, and some 4-year olds in reception classes, are eligible for free milk. Babies under one year may be given infant formula instead. For more information, see www.nurserymilk.co.uk.

55 Protection against discrimination

1. What protection is there and who is covered?
The Equality Act 2010 brings together and replaces previous discrimination laws, including the Disability Discrimination Act. The Equality Act prohibits discrimination against disabled people, as well as discrimination on the grounds of age, gender, gender-reassignment, marriage or civil partnership, race, religion or belief, or sexual orientation. It applies to Great Britain only; the Disability Discrimination Acts still apply in Northern Ireland.

The Equality Act treats disability discrimination in distinctive ways, in particular by requiring *'reasonable adjustments'*. There are some improvements in rights, such as: protection against indirect discrimination, restrictions on health and disability questions in recruitment, and protection against discrimination because of perceived and associated disability. The Act makes it unlawful to discriminate against anyone who has, or has had, a disability in connection with employment, education, the provision of services, the exercise of public functions, and premises.

2. Disability
Disability is defined as *'a physical or mental impairment which has a substantial and long-term adverse effect on [your] ability to carry out normal day-to-day activities'*. If you can show that you come within this definition, you will have the protection of the disability provisions. People who have had a disability within the meaning of the law in the past are protected from discrimination even if they no longer have the disability.

Impairment – This includes sensory impairments (eg blindness), learning disabilities, mental health conditions and long-term health conditions such as heart disease or diabetes. Any steps taken to treat or correct your disability (eg hearing aid, artificial limb or medication) are ignored when considering whether your impairment has a substantial

adverse effect. However, if you wear glasses or contact lenses, it is the effect on your vision with the lenses that is considered.
Substantial – This means *'more than minor or trivial'*.
Long term – This means effects that have lasted at least 12 months, or are likely to last at least 12 months, or are likely to last for the rest of your life (if that is less than 12 months). Conditions likely to recur, eg epilepsy, will be considered as long term if it is more likely than not that their substantial adverse effects will recur beyond 12 months.

Equality Act 2010, s 6; Sch 1 and Guidance on matters to be taken into account in determining questions relating to the definition of disability, http://odi.dwp. gov.uk/docs/wor/new/ea-guide.pdf

Special provision
Some conditions, namely cancer, multiple sclerosis and HIV infection, count as a disability from when you first develop the condition; others are covered as soon as they affect your ability to carry out normal activities. Severe disfigurements are covered, even if they do not affect your ability to carry out normal activities. You automatically meet the disability definition if you are registered with your local authority as blind or partially sighted, or if a consultant ophthalmologist has certified you as such.

Wider protections
Discrimination by association – The Equality Act gives you the right not to be subjected to direct discrimination or harassment on the grounds of your association with a disabled person (eg if you care for a disabled child).
Discrimination by perception – The Equality Act protects people from direct discrimination or harassment because they are wrongly perceived to be a disabled person.
Dual discrimination – The government has decided not to commence protection against *'dual discrimination'* in the Equality Act. Dual discrimination refers to direct discrimination or harassment experienced because of a combination of protected characteristics, eg because you are a disabled woman.

3. Employment rights
It is unlawful for an employer to discriminate against you, as outlined below. The Equality Act covers almost all employment except the armed forces. It covers temporary, contract and permanent staff and all employment matters, including recruitment, training, promotion, dismissal and redundancy and discrimination against former employees. Volunteers are not covered unless they have a volunteering agreement that might be construed as a contract of employment.

Employers are legally responsible for the actions of their employees and agents (eg a recruitment agency that discriminates while working for the employer). You need not be employed for a minimum period of time to bring a discrimination claim, and compensation is unlimited.

Equality Act 2010, Part 5

Types
There are four types of employment discrimination:
- **direct discrimination** – occurs where, because of their disability, a person receives worse treatment than someone else without that particular disability;
- **discrimination arising from disability** – occurs when a disabled person is treated unfavourably because of something connected to their disability; it only applies if employers or service providers know, or could reasonably be expected to know, that you are a disabled person;
- **indirect discrimination** – occurs when there is a rule, policy or practice that applies to everyone but particularly disadvantages disabled people compared to other employees;
- **failure to make reasonable adjustments** – see below.

Equality Act 2010, Ss.13, 15, 19 & 21

Victimisation and harassment
The Equality Act protects people who make a complaint under it and anyone victimised for helping a disabled person to make a complaint. You do not have to be a disabled person to claim victimisation.

Harassment occurs if an employer, or someone working for an employer, engages in unwanted behaviour that has the purpose or effect of violating the disabled person's dignity, or creating an intimidating or offensive environment.

Equality Act 2010, Ss.26-27

Reasonable adjustments
The Equality Act requires employers to make *'reasonable adjustments'* to the workplace and to employment arrangements, including recruitment, so that a disabled employee or job applicant is not at a substantial disadvantage. Reasonable adjustments include changes to the physical environment, eg widening a doorway for wheelchair access or allocating a parking space for a disabled person. The term includes changes to working arrangements, eg allowing flexible working hours, providing additional training, allowing time off for medical appointments or treatment and providing auxiliary aids and services (eg purchasing specialised equipment or providing communication support). Employers only need to make an adjustment if they know, or could reasonably be expected to know, that you need an adjustment.

Equality Act 2010, Sch 8

Rented premises – If your employer rents premises, the landlord cannot unreasonably refuse permission for the premises to be altered to accommodate you, although they may attach reasonable conditions to their permission (eg returning the premises to the original condition when vacating them). If your employer does not make a reasonable adjustment because the landlord unreasonably refuses permission, you could take your employer to the Employment Tribunal, and you or your employer could ask the Tribunal to make the landlord a party to the case. The landlord would then have to go to the Tribunal.

Justification
Employers can legally justify discrimination arising from disability and indirect discrimination only if they can show that the treatment is a proportionate means of achieving a legitimate aim. This requires a balance to be struck between the needs of an employer and those of the disabled person; the more serious the effect on the disabled person the more substantial the reason for the treatment must be. Justification must be considered after reasonable adjustments have been made.

Pre-employment questions
The Equality Act makes it unlawful for employers to enquire about your health or disability before making a job offer. Sole exceptions are to:
- ask if you need reasonable adjustments to take part in an interview;
- conduct anonymous diversity monitoring;
- ask questions relating to your ability to carry out specific job functions, with reasonable adjustments if need be;
- conduct positive action.

It is lawful to ask for medical information after offering the job. However, if, on the basis of this information, the employer withdraws the job offer, they will need to ensure that this is non-discriminatory, including that they have considered reasonable adjustments.

If you think an employer has flouted the law by asking questions about health or disability that are not permitted, you can complain to the Equality and Human Rights Commission (EHRC), which can take enforcement action. Disabled people themselves can seek redress in Employment Tribunals if an employer has asked prohibited health or disability questions *and* used the information to discriminate against them. More information is available from the government Equalities Office and the EHRC (see Box S.1).

Equality Act 2010, S. 60

Specific provisions
There are specific provisions against discrimination in relation to:
- occupational pension schemes and insurance obtained through employers (eg health insurance);
- work experience done as part of vocational training (eg an NVQ in plumbing);
- occupations such as police officer, barrister, partnerships and office holders (eg judges and members of non-departmental public bodies);
- membership of trade organisations;
- employment services (eg employment agencies and careers guidance services);
- qualifying bodies that regulate entry into a profession (eg the Nursing and Midwifery Council).

4. Access to goods and services
It is unlawful for organisations that provide goods, facilities or services in the UK directly to the public to discriminate against disabled people. It does not matter whether the services are free or paid for, or whether they are provided by the public or private sector. Service providers include: shops, hotels, banks, cinemas, restaurants, courts and solicitors, private education and training providers, schools, colleges and universities (as far as non-education activities are concerned, eg parents' evenings), students' unions, telecommunication companies, libraries, leisure facilities, healthcare, social/housing services, government offices and voluntary services (eg advice centres). Airports, stations and booking facilities are covered. Insurance companies are covered but special rules apply.

Service providers are legally responsible for any discrimination on the part of their employees or anyone else who works as part of their business (eg contractors).

The Equality Act does not cover the manufacture and design of products.

Equality Act 2010, Part 3

Use of transport
The use and provision of transport vehicles such as buses, taxis, minicabs, trains, trams, car hire and breakdown services are covered by the Equality Act. Disabled people have protection against less favourable treatment and rights to reasonable adjustments to help use services. These duties do not cover changes to physical features (see 7 below for accessibility requirements for public transport vehicles) except in respect of rental vehicles and breakdown recovery vehicles (the latter must overcome physical features that present barriers to disabled people, by providing the service in a reasonable alternative way). Ships and aircraft remain exempt from the Equality Act, although EC Regulation 1107/2006 on air travel gives disabled people and those with reduced mobility certain rights. See Box S.1 for details of guides on transport.

Private clubs and political parties
Private clubs and political parties with 25 or more members cannot discriminate against, and have duties to make reasonable adjustments for, current and potential disabled members, associates and guests.

Equality Act 2010, Part 7

Types of unlawful discrimination
Under the Equality Act it is illegal for a service provider or a public body to discriminate against disabled people. There are four types of unlawful discrimination (as defined in 3 above):
- direct discrimination;
- indirect discrimination;
- discrimination arising from a disability;
- failure to make a reasonable adjustment.

Not only is the refusal of service prohibited, but also providing service of a lower standard or in a worse manner (eg a cafe tells someone with a facial disfigurement to sit apart from others) or providing a service on worse terms (eg a travel agent asks for a larger deposit because they think you are more likely to cancel due to disability).

Victimisation and harassment
Victimisation and harassment (as defined in 3 above) are prohibited in relation to goods and services.

Justification
Service providers can legally justify discrimination arising from disability and indirect discrimination only if they can show that the treatment is a proportionate means of achieving a legitimate aim.

Reasonable adjustments
Providers must make adjustments to their service(s) if, without the adjustments, disabled people would be at a *'substantial disadvantage'*. There are three types of reasonable adjustment:
- changing the way a service is provided (*'provision, criterion or practice'*), eg changing a 'no dogs' policy to allow for assistance dogs;
- providing an additional aid or service if it will help you access the service, eg communication support;
- removing or altering physical features (eg doors, lighting or glass screens) if they create barriers to the service, or providing a reasonable means of avoiding them, or providing the service in an alternative way, eg if premises are inaccessible, the provider could offer home visits.

The Equality Act clarifies that the provision of information includes a duty to provide it in accessible formats.

Service providers need only do what is reasonable. *'Reasonable'* is not defined, but can depend on several factors, including how practicable it is to make the adjustment, and the cost. Service providers must plan ahead to meet these duties, and must comply even if they do not know that someone is disabled – this is known as an 'anticipatory duty'. Providers must not charge disabled people for making reasonable adjustments.

Equality Act 2010, Sch 2

5. Housing
It is unlawful for anyone letting, selling or managing rented property (be it houses, flats or offices) to discriminate against disabled people. The same four types of discrimination as set out in 3 above apply (although the reasonable adjustment provisions are narrower). Harassment of disabled people is also unlawful.

The rules apply to most agencies involved in letting, selling or managing rented property, including local authorities, housing associations, private landlords, estate agents, accommodation agencies, banks, building societies, property developers and owner occupiers.

Landlords who let rooms in their own homes to six or fewer people are exempted. There is no obligation on anyone selling or letting property to alter the premises to make them accessible. The law does not cover sales arranged without an estate agent.

Landlords and management companies must make reasonable adjustments to policies and procedures, and take reasonable steps to provide additional aids and services. The duty does not apply to physical features. However, some features do not count as 'physical features' in this sense (including signs, adapted doorbells/entry phones and changes to taps/door handles) and therefore are covered by the reasonable adjustment duty.

Landlords cannot refuse, unreasonably, to allow tenants to make changes to a property because of a disability. But you must pay for the alterations (or seek a grant) and must ask permission first. The relevant provisions of the Equality Act would apply this right to 'common parts', eg hallways or stairs. However, the government has not yet said when, or even if, this section of the Act will be implemented. In Scotland, the right already applies to common parts but other tenants and the landlord need to agree to the changes.

For more information, see the Equality and Human Rights Commission Code of Practice on services, public functions and associations (see Box S.1).

Equality Act 2010, Part 4 & S.190 & Sch 4

S.1 For more information

❏ The Equality Advisory and Support Service provides free advice, information and guidance to individuals on equality and human rights issues (helpline: 0808 800 0082; textphone 0808 800 0084; www. equalityadvisoryservice.com). Information and advice is also on the Citizens Advice website (www.adviceguide.org.uk).

❏ Information and advice is on the Citizens Advice website (www.adviceguide.org.uk).

❏ Codes of practice and guidance are on the Equality and Human Rights Commission website (www.equalityhumanrights.com/advice-and-guidance) and the government's Equalities Office website (www.equalities.gov.uk).

❏ The Equality Commission for Northern Ireland publishes codes of practice, guidance and advisory leaflets (Equality House, 7-9 Shaftesbury Square, Belfast BT2 7DP; 028 9050 0600; textphone 028 9050 0589; enquiry line 028 9089 0890; www.equalityni. org).

❏ The regulator Ofqual provides guidance on reasonable adjustments in qualifications: Specifications in Relation to the Reasonable Adjustment of General Qualifications (www.ofqual.gov.uk/files/2011-12-15-specifications-in-relation-to-the-reasonable-adjustment-of-general-qualifications.pdf).

❏ Information about Equality Act transport provisions and the Access to Air Travel for Disabled Persons and Persons with Reduced Mobility: Code of Practice are available from the Equality and Human Rights Commission website (www.equalityhumanrights.com) and from www.gov.uk/transport-disabled.

❏ Information about taking an employment case and about court fees is available from the Ministry of Justice (www.justice.gov.uk/tribunals/employment and www.justice.gov.uk/courts/fees).

Information on the Equality Act is in a number of publications, including:

❏ Blackstone's Guide to the Equality Act 2010 edited by Wadham, Ruebain, Robinson and Uppal

❏ Equality and Discrimination – The New Law by Brian J Doyle (Jordans)

❏ Employment Law: An Adviser's Handbook by Tamara Lewis (Legal Action Group).

---

6. Education

It is unlawful for education providers to discriminate against or harass disabled students. This applies to admissions, education and related services and exclusions. Discrimination is not unlawful if it complies with a permitted form of selection.

Schools must ensure disabled pupils are not treated less favourably and must make reasonable adjustments to avoid putting them at a substantial disadvantage. There is no right to reasonable adjustments to premises, as these are covered by 'accessibility plans'.

The duties apply to all schools, including publicly funded, independent and mainstream schools, special schools, pupil referral units, local authority-maintained nursery schools and classes, and nursery provision at independent and grant-aided schools. Private, voluntary and statutory providers of nursery education not constituted as schools are covered by the services provisions of the law (see 4 above).

It is unlawful for bodies that provide general qualifications such as GCSEs, A and AS levels and other non-vocational exams (including Scottish and Welsh equivalents) to discriminate against disabled people (see Box S.1). Exam candidates can expect such bodies to make reasonable adjustments, eg providing extra time or exam materials in alternative formats.

Local authorities and schools are required to publish accessibility strategies and plans, respectively, to improve access to school education for disabled pupils, monitored by Ofsted (England) and ESTYN (Wales). Similar duties exist under Scottish education law.

Post-16 education providers include further, higher, adult and community education and the statutory youth service. It is unlawful to discriminate against or harass disabled students. Providers have a duty to make reasonable adjustments to avoid putting disabled students at a substantial disadvantage. Providers must provide auxiliary aids and services, and make physical alterations to premises.

Services provided by student unions and institutions of further/higher education to members of the public other than students, and private/voluntary sector education providers are covered by the services provisions (see 4 above).

Equality Act 2010, Part 6 & Sch 13

7. Transport

The Equality Act gives the government power to make accessibility regulations for public transport vehicles. New buses, coaches and trains must comply with specified accessibility standards, eg width of doors or colour contrast. All buses and coaches must comply with the regulations by 2017 and 2020 respectively. All trains must comply by 2020 at the latest. The government has not yet made taxi accessibility regulations. Licensed taxis and minicabs cannot refuse to carry and cannot charge more for a disabled person accompanied by an assistance dog. Drivers can ask to be exempt from this duty on medical grounds.

Equality Act 2010, Part 12

8. Enforcing your rights

You should always try to seek advice. In first instance, you can look at the Equality and Human Rights Commission website, Citizens Advice website, or contact the Equality Advisory and Support Service (see Box S.1). Be aware of time limits, as you must make a claim within a certain time after the alleged discriminatory act.

Employment – If you think you have been discriminated against under the employment provisions, you can make a complaint to an Employment Tribunal. The complaint must be registered with the Tribunal within three months of the discriminatory act, eg the date you were dismissed. At present there is no charge to take a claim to an Employment Tribunal, but this will change from summer 2013. People on low incomes may not have to pay the full fees. The changes will cover England, Scotland and Wales.

A *'Questions Procedure'* enables you to ask the employer questions. This can help you decide whether you have a strong case. You could ask your trade union for help if you are a member of one. However, the government is legislating to remove the questions procedure.

Goods and services – Rights under the goods and services and post-16 education provisions are enforceable through the County Court (the Sheriff Court in Scotland). You must take the case to court within six months of the discriminatory act, eg the date you were refused service. You can use the questions procedure for goods and services cases. You can make a complaint to the Pensions Ombudsman if you think the managers of a pension scheme have discriminated against you (see Box O.3, Chapter 43).

Education – Rights under the education provisions that apply to schools are enforceable in England through the First-tier Tribunal and in Wales through the Special Educational Needs Tribunal. There are similar tribunals in Northern Ireland. Claims of unlawful discrimination in respect of a refusal to admit to, and permanent exclusions from, maintained schools and city academies are heard by admissions appeal panels or independent appeals panels. Disability discrimination claims against schools in Scotland are enforceable through the Sheriff Court but the Equality Act provides for these to be heard in the Additional Support Needs Tribunal. You must take a case to court or the tribunal within six months of the date of the discriminatory act.

Equality Act 2010, Part 9

What you can expect
If you are successful in a tribunal or court, you can obtain damages for financial loss or hurt feelings. The tribunals and Sheriff Court cannot award financial compensation in claims against schools, but can make other orders including: that staff receive training or guidance; policy changes; insisting on school admissions; and demanding apologies. Courts can order service providers to make adjustments in some circumstances, and tribunals can recommend that an employer makes an adjustment. Tribunals can recommend action that benefits the wider workforce, not just the individual claimant. Courts and tribunals can make a public declaration that you were discriminated against because of your disability.

Other remedies
As an alternative to legal action, you can use a mediation service. For employment cases, free conciliation is available from ACAS (Advisory, Conciliation and Arbitration Service). A similar service is available from the Labour Relations Agency for Northern Ireland. For education cases, local authorities in England and Wales must provide independent disagreement resolution services to deal with disputes between parents and schools (and in Wales between pupils and schools).

56 TV licence concessions

1. Do you need a TV licence?
You need a TV licence to install or use television receiving equipment to watch or record TV programmes as they are being shown on TV. This is irrespective of what channel you watch, what device you use (TV, computer, laptop, mobile phone, etc) or how you receive it (terrestrial, satellite, cable, internet, etc). You do not need a licence if you use a digital set-top box solely to listen to TV programmes through a hi-fi or stereo system (the box must be incapable of recording and must not be connected to a device capable of showing images).

A licence covers you and anyone else who normally lives with you at the address on the licence. A colour TV licence is £145.50 a year; for a black and white TV it is £49. For concessions, see 2, 3 and 4 below.

For further information, go to www.tvlicensing.co.uk or ring 0300 790 6115 (Mincom 0300 790 6050).

2. Aged 75 or over
If you are aged 75 or over the TV licence is free for your main home but not for a second home. Although free, you must apply for the over-75 licence. You will need to provide TV Licensing with your date of birth and national insurance number. You can do this online (www.tvlicensing.co.uk) or by phone (0300 790 6131). If TV Licensing can verify these details, the over-75 licence is renewed automatically and you will only receive a new licence every three years. If you do not have a national insurance number, ring TV Licensing (0300 790 6131) to arrange other proof of your date of birth. If the over-75 licence-holder dies, the licence continues to cover your household until it runs out.

If your 75th birthday will fall in the year covered by the next licence, you can buy a short-term licence to cover you until your birthday, or you can claim a refund on an existing licence for the months since you reached the age of 75.

3. Concession for those who are blind/severely sight impaired
There is a 50% discount on the licence fee if you are blind or severely sight impaired (not partially sighted). Anyone in the household who is blind or severely sight impaired (including children) can apply for the 50% discount, but the licence must be transferred into that person's name. You can apply for a discount for a second residence as well as your main home.

When your licence is due for renewal, send your renewal form and a photocopy of the certificate from your local authority or ophthalmologist indicating that you are blind or severely sight impaired to: TV Licensing, Blind Concession Group, Bristol BS98 1TL. Once you have proved your eligibility, you should not need to do so again for another five years. For further details, ring 0300 790 6115.

4. Care homes
The concessionary Accommodation for Residential Care licence costs £7.50. It is available if you live in certain types of care home and are retired (if you are still in paid work, this must be no more than 15 hours a week) and are aged 60 or over, or disabled. The person in charge of your accommodation can enquire about your eligibility for the concession and apply for it on your behalf by ringing 0300 790 6131. You will only need a TV licence if you watch TV in your own separate living area. If you watch TV only in communal areas, the person in charge of your accommodation must ensure those areas are properly licensed.

If you are aged 75 or over, the warden will apply for your free licence. When you move into a care home, you may get a refund for the remainder of your existing licence at your previous home. The warden should apply for you. Write to TV Licensing, Bristol BS98 1TL (or ring 0300 790 6131).

Communications (Television Licensing) Regulations 2004

Claims and appeals

This section of the Handbook looks at:

57 Claims and payments

1. Making a claim

Traditionally, you had to complete claim-forms for most social security benefits. But now, for many benefits (including employment and support allowance, income support, jobseeker's allowance, state pension and pension credit), you are encouraged to make first contact by telephone. Details of your claim can be taken on the phone and a statement may be sent to you to check that the details are correct. Claims for many benefits can also be made online.

For details about how to claim each benefit, see the relevant chapter. Here we look at some of the common rules about, and problems with, claiming.

Who should claim? – You should claim (or ask the DWP for advice) as soon as you think you might qualify. If you cannot make enquiries or claim yourself, get someone else to do so; the DWP can accept a claim made by someone else on your behalf as long as you have signed it. The DWP can appoint someone to act on behalf of anyone who cannot act for themselves (see 4 below).

Defective claims – If you make a *'defective'* claim (ie one not completed in accordance with DWP instructions) or you don't use the correct form, the claim should be referred back to you or you should be given the correct form. If it is referred back, and you return the properly completed claim-form within one month of it being sent to you (or longer if an extension is agreed), your claim must be treated as though the original claim had been properly made. A similar rule applies to claims made by phone. See 2 below for the rules on income support and jobseeker's allowance. You can appeal against a decision to disallow benefit on the basis that the claim was defective.

C&P Regs, reg 4(7), 4G(3)-(5) & 4H(6)-(7); Novitskaya V London Borough of Brent & Anon [2009] EWCA Civ 1260

National insurance (NI) numbers – For most benefits, you must give your NI number when you claim (and your partner's if you are claiming for them) and enough information to confirm the number is yours. If you don't know your number, give the DWP sufficient information to allow them to trace it. Normally, the details you provide when you make the claim are enough. If the DWP wants more evidence, they will let you know. If you don't have an NI number, you are still entitled to benefit if you apply for a number and provide enough information and evidence for one to be allocated to you. Contact Jobcentre Plus to apply.

SSAA, S.1(1A) & (1B)

2. Date of claim

The date your claim is *'made'* is usually the day it is received, properly completed, in a DWP office, DWP-approved office or (for tax credits) HMRC office. Sometimes your claim can be treated as though it were made on an earlier date.

❏ For disability living allowance and attendance allowance, your date of claim is the date you requested a claim-form from the DWP or Benefit Enquiry Line if you return the completed claim-form within six weeks.

C&P Regs, reg 6(8) & (9)

❏ For personal independence payment, your date of claim is the date you telephoned the DWP's PIP claim-line, provided you return the completed form *How your disability affects you* within one month (see Chapter 4(14)).

UCPIP(C&P) Regs, reg 12

❏ For employment and support allowance, your date of claim is the date you informed the Jobcentre Plus office of your intention to claim, as long as that office receives a properly completed claim-form from you within a month of your first contact (unless an extension is agreed). For telephone claims, see Chapter 10(11).

C&P Regs, reg 6(1F)(c)

❏ For pension credit, your date of claim is the date you informed the DWP or local authority office of your intention to claim pension credit if you provide all the information and evidence they require within one month (unless an extension is agreed).

C&P Regs, reg 4F(3)

Claims for income support

Your date of claim for income support is the date you first told Jobcentre Plus you wanted to claim, as long as you return the claim-form (or signed statement if the claim was made over the phone) fully completed with all the information and supporting documents required within one month. Until you do this, you have not made your claim, unless you can show that one of the following situations applies.

❏ You have a *'physical, learning, mental or communication difficulty'* and it is not reasonably practicable for you to get help with your claim or get the required information or evidence.

❏ The information or evidence required:
  – does not exist; *or*
  – can only be obtained at serious risk of physical or mental harm to you and it is not reasonably practicable for you to get it by other means; *or*
  – can only be obtained from a third party and it is not reasonably practicable for you to get it from them.

C&P Regs, regs 4(1B) & 6(1A)

Send in your claim-form or signed statement explaining your difficulties, or ring Jobcentre Plus (or get someone else to contact them for you). If you do this within one month and they accept your reasons, your date of claim will be the date you first told Jobcentre Plus you wanted to claim.

If there is other evidence needed to decide your claim but it is not specified in the claim-form, it does not affect your date of claim if you can't provide it with your claim.

Claims for JSA
Your date of claim is the date you first contacted Jobcentre Plus, as long as you provide a fully completed claim-form or signed customer statement and all the required evidence by the time you attend your 'work-focused interview' (or during the interview). If either member of a joint-claim couple does not attend the interview with their claim-form or statement and evidence, the date of claim is the date one of them eventually does so.

C&P Regs, reg 6(4ZB) & (4A)

If you cannot get all the evidence for one of the reasons outlined above for income support, contact Jobcentre Plus explaining your difficulties. If you do this within one month and they accept your reasons, your date of claim will be the date you first told Jobcentre Plus you wanted to claim.

C&P Regs, regs 4(1B) & 6(4AB)

3. Backdating delayed claims
The time limits for claiming benefits are given in Box T.3.

Income support and jobseeker's allowance (JSA) can be backdated for up to one month or three months in the limited circumstances described below.

T.1 Work-focused interviews

You are required to take part in one or more *'work-focused interviews'* if you are claiming one of the following:
- employment and support allowance (ESA);
- incapacity benefit;
- income support; *or*
- severe disablement allowance (SDA).

You are also required to take part in a work-focused interview if your partner is claiming extra for you in one of the last three benefits listed above.

In the work-focused interview a personal adviser will discuss your work prospects. We describe what happens at a work-focused interview in Chapter 10(15); the process is similar for each benefit. See Chapter 16(3) for details of the work-focused interview for jobseeker's allowance (JSA).

An interview for one benefit counts for all others, so you don't have to go through interviews for each benefit you claim.

The requirement to attend a work-focused interview may be deferred to a later date at the discretion of the personal adviser. Some claimants may have their interview waived if it would not be of any assistance or appropriate. This waiver facility has been removed for the majority of claimants of incapacity benefits. You are not required to attend a work-focused interview if you have reached pension credit qualifying age (see Chapter 42(2)).

When will they take place?
Initial interviews – For income support, the first work-focused interview will normally take place shortly after you first contact Jobcentre Plus.

For ESA, the first work-focused interview will normally take place after the initial work capability assessment if you have been placed in the work-related activity group (see Chapter 10(6)).

If you are required to attend a work-focused interview as the partner of a claimant, the interview will normally take place after they have been entitled to the benefit for at least 26 weeks.

Follow-up interviews – If you are claiming ESA (and have been placed in the work-related activity group), incapacity benefit or income support on the grounds of incapacity, you must usually attend a series of further work-focused interviews.

For other benefits, follow-up interviews are required only at 'trigger points', such as:
- carer's allowance entitlement stops but you continue to be entitled to income support, incapacity benefit or SDA;
- you start or stop part-time work of less than 16 hours a week;
- you finish an education or training course arranged by your personal adviser;

- your partner is claiming extra for you in income-based JSA, you are responsible for a child or qualifying young person (see Chapter 38(1)) and six months have passed since your last interview;
- you have not had an interview in the last three years.

JPI Regs, reg 4(4)-(5) & JPIP Regs, reg 3A

What if you don't attend or take part in the interview?
The reductions for not taking part in an ESA work-focused interview are described in Chapter 10(17). If you are claiming incapacity benefit, SDA or income support on the grounds of incapacity, *'sanctions'* are applied as follows: for the first four weeks an amount equal to 50% of the ESA work-related activity component is deducted from your benefit (£14.22), thereafter an amount equal to the ESA work-related activity component is deducted (£28.45).

Social Security (Incapacity Benefit Work-focused Interviews) Regs 2008, reg 9

For other benefits, the rules are as follows.

New claims – Unless you can show you had good cause for not attending or taking part in a work-focused interview, your claim will not proceed. If the interview had been deferred, with the result that benefit was already in payment, then entitlement will stop. In either case, you should claim again, and appeal against the decision if you think it is wrong (see below).

JPI Regs, reg 12(2)(a)&(b)

Benefit in payment – If you are already claiming benefit and you fail to attend or take part in a work-focused interview without good cause, a deduction of £14.34 a week is made from your benefit. The deduction continues until you do take part in a work-focused interview or reach pension credit qualifying age.

JPI Regs, reg 12(2)(c), 12(9) & 13

If your partner fails to attend or take part in a work-focused interview when required to do so without good cause, £14.34 a week is deducted from your benefit. This deduction continues until they take part in a work-focused interview.

JPIP Regs, reg 11

Challenging a decision
Personal advisers (or, in the case of ESA, the private or voluntary sector equivalents) make decisions on whether you have complied with the requirement to take part in an interview and whether you have good cause for failing to do so. You can appeal against their decision within one month of the decision being posted to you (see Chapter 58(7)). Alternatively, you can ask them to reconsider and revise the decision – within one month for any reason, or outside of one month if it arose from an official error (see Box T.5). In each case, any arrears due are paid back in full if you are successful. There is no right of appeal about waivers and deferrals, although you can ask the personal adviser to reconsider.

If you are under the qualifying age for pension credit (see Chapter 42(2)), housing benefit can be backdated for up to six months if you formally request it and have continuous *'good cause'* for the delay in claiming. If you have reached the qualifying age for pension credit (and are not claiming income support, income-related employment and support allowance (ESA) or income-based JSA), housing benefit can normally be backdated for up to three months without you having to formally request it or show good cause. See Chapter 21(16) for details.

For other benefits, there is no extension to the time limits for claiming, no matter how good your reasons are for not applying earlier – unless, in some cases, it is because of a delay in the award of a qualifying benefit (see below).

If you want to claim benefit for an earlier period, make sure you state this on the claim-form (or when you claim over the phone).

Delays in qualifying benefits

Entitlement to some benefits may depend on you, a member of your family or someone else getting another qualifying benefit, eg carer's allowance depends on the person you care for receiving the appropriate rate of personal independence payment (PIP), disability living allowance (DLA) or attendance allowance (see Chapter 7(2)).

The general rule – Claim straight away; do not wait for a decision on a qualifying benefit. If your first claim is refused because the qualifying benefit has not yet been awarded, claim again once you get a decision awarding the qualifying benefit. If you do this within three months of the decision awarding the qualifying benefit (which might be after a revision or appeal if the qualifying benefit is refused initially), the second claim can be backdated to the date of the first claim, or to the date from which the qualifying benefit is awarded, if that

T.2 Interchange of claims

If you make a claim for one benefit, then find you should have claimed a different benefit instead, or you were also entitled to another benefit, the rules on interchanging benefit claims may help you get arrears of benefit beyond the usual limits. Your original claim may be treated as a claim for another benefit, either as an alternative to the original claim or in addition. But not all benefits can count as a claim for any other. Within each group below, the benefits listed are interchangeable with each other:

■ employment and support allowance, maternity allowance;
■ state pension of any category, widow's benefit/ bereavement benefit;
■ disability living allowance, attendance allowance, industrial injuries constant attendance allowance;
■ child benefit, guardian's allowance, an addition for a child dependant (with non-means-tested benefits prior to April 2003), maternity allowance claimed after confinement;
■ a claim for income support can be treated as a claim for carer's allowance, but not the other way round.

C&P Regs, reg 9 & Sch 1

If the decision maker treats one claim as another, then the date of the original claim counts as the date of claim for the alternative benefit and arrears may be payable from then. However, the overlapping benefit rules could prevent some or all of the arrears being payable.

You cannot appeal against a decision on whether to treat a claim for one benefit as a claim for another but you can ask the decision maker to look at the decision again (see 'Ground 9' in Box T.5).

is later. On the date you first claim, if you have not already claimed the qualifying benefit you have another ten days to do so. If you wait longer than ten days, a second claim made once the qualifying benefit is awarded cannot be backdated in this way.
C&P Regs, reg 6(16)-(18)

Qualifying benefit re-instatements – Where entitlement to one benefit depends on another, if one stops the other stops too. If you challenge the decision on the qualifying benefit and it is reinstated, make a fresh claim for the other benefit within three months of the date of the decision to reinstate the qualifying benefit – the other benefit will then be fully backdated. For example, if your PIP is stopped you may lose entitlement to income-related ESA. If you get back your PIP after a successful appeal, make a fresh claim for income-related ESA and it will be paid again from when it was stopped.
C&P Regs, reg 6(19)-(21)

Income support/income-based JSA additional rule – When you are in receipt of income support or income-based JSA and make a claim for a benefit that could provide access to a premium, eg carer's allowance, it is possible that while you are waiting for the carer's allowance to be awarded the income support/JSA might be stopped for some other reason, eg a small increase in your income. In this case, when the carer's allowance is eventually awarded, make a fresh claim for the income support/JSA within three months of the date of this award and the income support/JSA can be paid from the time the previous claim for it ended.
C&P Regs, reg 6(30)

Carer's allowance – If you have been waiting for the person for whom you are caring to be awarded a qualifying benefit (see Chapter 7(2)), and you claim carer's allowance within three months of the date of a decision to award the qualifying benefit, your claim for carer's allowance can be treated as having been made on the first day of the benefit week in which the qualifying benefit became payable.
C&P Regs, reg 6(33)

Backdating income support and JSA
Administrative reasons: one-month backdating – Income support and JSA can be backdated for up to one month if any one or more of the following administrative reasons apply, as a result of which you could not reasonably have been expected to make the claim earlier.
❑ You couldn't attend the Jobcentre Plus office to make your claim because it was closed or because of transport difficulties, and there were no alternative arrangements available.
❑ You tried to ring the Jobcentre Plus office to let them know of your intention to claim, but could not get through because their lines were busy or inoperable.
❑ There were adverse postal conditions.
❑ You were not sent notice of the end of entitlement to a previous benefit until after it actually ended.
❑ You stopped being part of a couple within one month before claiming.
❑ You claimed JSA after your partner had failed to attend a work-focused interview.
❑ Your partner, parent, son, daughter, brother or sister died within one month before you claimed.
C&P Regs, reg 19(6) & (7)

Special reasons: 3-month backdating – Income support and JSA can be backdated for up to three months if one or more of the special reasons below apply, as a result of which you could not reasonably have been expected to make the claim earlier.
❑ You were given information by a DWP official that led you to believe your claim would not succeed. What you understood from the information you were given may

have been affected by your disability or communication difficulties and this should be taken into account.

❑ You were given written advice by a solicitor or other professional adviser, a medical practitioner, a local authority, or a person working in a Citizens Advice Bureau or similar advice agency, which led you to believe your claim would not succeed.

❑ You or your partner were given written information about your income or capital by an employer or ex-employer, or a bank or building society, which led you to believe your claim would not succeed.

❑ You were prevented by bad weather from attending the Jobcentre Plus office.

❑ You have difficulty communicating because you are deaf or blind, or you have learning, language or literacy difficulties.

❑ You are ill or disabled (this is not accepted as a special reason for JSA). There is no definition of 'ill' or 'disabled' in the regulations.

❑ You were caring for someone who is ill or disabled. You do not have to live with the person or be related to them.

❑ You were required to deal with a domestic emergency affecting you.

In the last four cases, you will also need to show it was not reasonably practicable for you to get help to make your claim. The test is about your ability to get help, not whether someone should have offered it (CIS/2057/1998).

C&P Regs, reg 19(4) & (5)

You should give full details of your reasons for claiming late on your claim-form (or when you make the call if the claim is made over the phone). You can appeal if you disagree with the decision on backdating.

Test cases
If you are claiming following a test case, any backdating that might apply under the normal rules is generally limited to the date the test case decision was given. See Chapter 58(6).

4. Appointees
If a person is or might be entitled to benefit and cannot act for themselves, the decision maker can appoint someone aged 18 or over, an *'appointee'*, to act on their behalf. An appointee is usually a relative or friend, but can also be a body of people such as a firm of solicitors or a housing association. An appointment may be appropriate, for example, if the claimant is unable to act for themselves because of a severe learning disability, mental illness or dementia. Contact the office dealing with the claim and they will make the arrangements.

If you are the appointee, it is your responsibility to deal with the claim, including, for example, notifying changes of circumstances. The appointee is responsible for claiming on time and their own circumstances will be relevant in deciding whether there are special reasons for backdating a delayed claim, or for not providing all the documentary evidence required for a claim.

If you are appointed to act for the claimant in relation to one benefit, that appointment can cover all social security benefits, including tax credits and payments from the social fund. A separate appointment must be made for housing benefit.

C&P Regs, reg 33

The DWP is arranging to review individual appointments to ensure they are still appropriate. Appointees for children and pension-age claimants will be reviewed every five years, and appointees for working-age claimants every eight years.

5. Payments
Benefit payments are normally paid into a bank, building society or credit union account. They can also be paid into a Post Office card account, which accepts payment of benefits

T.3 Time limits for claiming benefit

Time limits are not generally cut-off points for claiming benefit, but limit the extent to which your benefit can be backdated: eg if you claim carer's allowance it can be automatically backdated for three months.

However, in the case of industrial injuries disablement benefit, you must claim within five years of working in the listed occupation for occupational deafness, or ten years for occupational asthma, otherwise you lose entitlement completely (see Chapter 44(6)).

For some benefits time limits can be extended in certain circumstances (see 3).

Benefit	Time limit
Disability living allowance, personal independence payment, attendance allowance	
■ initial claim	immediate
■ renewal claim	immediate
Income support, jobseeker's allowance	immediate
Social fund	
■ Sure Start maternity grant	from 11 weeks before expected week of birth, up to 3 months after date of birth, or adoption, guardianship, residence or parental order
■ funeral expenses	from the date of death to 3 months after date of funeral
Carer's allowance	3 months
Employment and support allowance	3 months
State pension	12 months
Pension credit	3 months
Tax credits	1 month
Child benefit, guardian's allowance, maternity allowance	3 months
Bereavement allowance, widowed parents' allowance	3 months (or 12 months when death has been difficult to establish)
Bereavement payment	12 months
Industrial injuries disablement benefit	3 months from the first day you were entitled to benefit (15 weeks after date of accident/accepted date of onset of disease)

C&P Regs, reg 19 & Sch 4

or tax credits but only allows cash withdrawals at Post Office counters or Bank of Ireland ATMs situated at some Post Office branches. You can nominate someone else to withdraw your money for you and they will be issued with the card.

If for some reason you are unable to open or use any of the above accounts, you will be paid by 'Simple Payments' instead. This is a system run by Citybank, in which claimants are issued with cards that can be used (with proof of identity) to collect payments at PayPoint outlets.

Certain benefits are paid through wages – ie statutory sick, maternity, paternity and adoption pay.

Compensation for delays – You may be due compensation if payments are delayed (see Chapter 60(2)).

Forgotten PIN – If you have forgotten your PIN, ask for a replacement. Contact the bank or building society into which your benefit is paid. If your benefit is paid into a Post Office card account, call their helpline (0845 7223 344; textphone 0845 7223 355).

6. Short-term advances

From 1.4.13 *'short-term advances'* of benefit are available to claimants of any contributory or income-related benefit (including universal credit, when it is introduced).

Short-term advances of benefit are intended to help you:

- through the period before benefit is paid by providing an advance of your future benefit award, which will then be recovered from subsequent payments of benefit;
- if you have experienced a change of circumstances that will increase the amount of benefit to which you are entitled;
- where your first payment of benefit is made in respect of a period shorter than that in respect of which subsequent payments will be made (eg the first payment is made in respect of a week and the next payment is due to be paid in two weeks' time and will be made in respect of those two weeks); *or*
- if it is impractical for benefit to be paid to you on the due date (eg because of a technical problem in processing the claim or payment).

To be eligible for a short-term advance, you must be able to demonstrate that you are in financial need. Guidance will assist decision makers in applying this to applicants. There will be a maximum repayment period of three months, which may be extended to six months in exceptional circumstances.

Social Security (Payments on Account of Benefit) Regs 2013, regs 3-10

7. Overpayments

An overpayment of benefit is recoverable if it was overpaid because you misrepresented, or failed to disclose, a *'material fact'*, even if you acted in all innocence.

A 'material' fact is one that would have affected the amount of your benefit. A 'fact' is not the same as a conclusion drawn from fact. For example, the conclusion that you have a 'limited capability for work' is drawn from the facts of your case.

A Court of Appeal judgment held that once a fact is 'known' to you and the duty to report it has been made clear to you, you cannot argue that due to the particular circumstances of your case (eg mental disability) disclosure of the fact could not reasonably have been expected.

CoA: 'B' (upheld recently by the European Court of Human Rights)

A House of Lords judgment held that a claimant failed to disclose a material fact by not informing one DWP office of a benefit decision taken by another DWP office. Consequently, when a decision is made on one benefit that could affect entitlement to another, you have a duty to inform the office dealing with the potentially affected benefit.

HoL: 'Hinchy'

In deciding whether there has been a recoverable overpayment, the decision maker must first revise or supersede your entitlement to benefit and decide how much you should have been paid. Then they must identify the material fact that you failed to disclose or misrepresented. Finally, they need to ascertain how much of the overpayment is recoverable.

SSAA, S.71

The Supreme Court has ruled that the DWP (and local authorities for housing benefit) does not have the right to recover overpayments if you are subject to a debt relief order.

SC: 'Payne & Anor'

The overpayment test is common to employment and support allowance (ESA), income support, income-based jobseeker's allowance (JSA), pension credit, social fund grants, and to almost all non-means-tested benefits. There is a different test for housing benefit (see Chapter 21(18)). Generally, HMRC has greater flexibility in dealing with changes of circumstances in respect of tax credits, with a continual process of adjusting what they overpaid or underpaid you one year with what they will pay you in the next year (see Chapter 20(5)-(9)). Notwithstanding this flexibility, overpayments due to fraud or negligence can be dealt with by a penalty system (see Chapter 19(12)).

If the overpayment is not recoverable

If an overpayment is not recoverable under legislation, you do not need to pay back the overpayment. Nevertheless, the DWP may ask you to pay it back; you should not feel under pressure to do so. The Supreme Court has ruled that the DWP does not have the power under common law to recover overpayments arising from their official error.

CPAG v Secretary of State [2010] UKSC 54

A clause in the Welfare Reform Act 2012 allows such overpayments of universal credit, employment and support allowance and jobseeker's allowance to be recoverable. There will be some exceptions in the case of housing credit for pensioners. The government is currently drawing up a new code of practice on recovery.

SSAA, Ss.71ZB-7!ZF; Social Security (Overpayments & Recovery) Regs 2013

The DWP can offset arrears of entitlement in a later award against the irrecoverable overpayment. However, if disability living allowance has been suspended due to an overpayment, arrears awarded following a new decision should not be offset against the overpayment in this way.

PAOR Regs, reg 5(1) and R(DLA)2/07 (CoA 'Brown')

Incapacity and disability benefits

If there has been an improvement in your condition and you did not know you should have reported it, you should not be left with an overpayment. Similarly, if the effect of your incapacity or disability proves not to be as severe as it was originally believed, and you did not know you should have reported the mistake in the original information, you should not be left with an overpayment. Any reduction in your benefit in either case should thus not be backdated. See Chapter 58(5) under 'What if your benefit goes down' for details.

Appointees and others

Overpayments can be recovered from third parties if it is they who have misrepresented or failed to disclose a material fact. If it is an appointee acting on behalf of the claimant, the decision maker may decide that the overpayment is recoverable from both the claimant and the appointee. Alternatively, the decision maker may decide the overpayment is recoverable from either one or the other. In general, if the appointee has retained the benefit instead of paying it to, or applying it for the benefit of, the claimant, only the appointee is liable. If the appointee has acted with due care and diligence, only the claimant is liable.

R(IS)5/03

Appeals

You can appeal against a decision that you were paid the wrong amount of benefit. You can also appeal against a decision that the overpayment is recoverable and against decisions relating to the period of the overpayment, from whom it is recoverable and the amount owed.

Amount of the overpayment

The recoverable overpayment is the difference between the amount of benefit you actually received and the amount you should have received, had the decision maker known the correct facts from the beginning of the period of overpayment. The overpayment amount is reduced by:

- any amount of the overpayment of benefit that has been offset against arrears of entitlement in a later award of a different benefit;
- any extra income support, income-related ESA, income-based JSA or pension credit you (or your partner) should have been paid, not necessarily for the same period as the overpayment (R(IS)5/92, CSIS/8/95).

PAOR Regs, regs 5 & 13

If you had not claimed any benefit (eg income support), but would have been entitled to it had you not been overpaid another benefit, put in a claim and ask for it to be backdated if you have 'special reasons' (see 3 above). If successful, you can ask for an abatement of the overpayment against what you should have received under the other benefit.

For more details about the nature of the overpayment test, read the notes to section 71 of the Social Security Administration Act 1992 in *Social Security: Legislation 2012/13 Volume III* (see page 6).

Diminution of capital

If you have been overpaid income support, income-related ESA, income-based JSA or pension credit because you did not tell the DWP about all your capital resources, or you misrepresented the nature of your capital, allowance is made for capital you would have spent had you not been paid benefit. At the end of each 13-week period, starting with the first day of the overpayment, your capital is treated as having been reduced by the amount of benefit you were overpaid during that quarter. At the same time, any tariff income (see Chapter 28(4)) will be recalculated.

Your capital cannot be treated as diminished in this way over any period shorter than 13 weeks. However, if you spent any of that undeclared capital during the overpayment period, the overpayment would end on the day your capital reached the appropriate limit, assuming the notional capital rules do not apply (see Chapter 28(9)). The treatment of diminution of capital under this rule would also apply to the reduced amount.

PAOR Regs, reg 14

A similar diminution of capital principle applies to housing benefit. The diminution of capital principle is different from the diminishing notional capital rule explained in Chapter 28(9).

HB Regs, reg 103

8. Civil penalties and fraud

Civil penalties

A decision maker may impose a civil penalty of £50 if they consider that you have negligently made an incorrect statement or representation or given incorrect information or evidence that has resulted in an overpayment of benefit. The decision maker must be satisfied that you failed to take reasonable steps to correct the error (the DWP interprets this as *'taking sensible or practicable actions or interventions to correct an error'*).

A civil penalty can also be imposed if you failed, without reasonable excuse, to provide information or evidence, as required to do so, or failed to notify of a relevant change of circumstances, in connection with a claim or award of benefit, that has resulted in an overpayment. The DWP interprets *'reasonable excuse'* as meaning that *'there is a credible reason or justification for [you] failing to do what was required of [you], or for doing it late'*.

In each case, the decision maker cannot impose a penalty if you have been charged with an offence, cautioned or given a legal notice, in respect of the overpayment (see below).

WRA 2012, S.116; The Social Security (Civil Penalties) Regulations 2012

The civil penalty will be added to the overpayment amount and will be recovered in the same manner. You can appeal against a decision to impose a civil penalty.

Fraud

Fraud is dishonestly or knowingly making a false statement or providing a false document or information to get benefit or more benefit. It is also fraud if:

- there has been a change of circumstances affecting entitlement to your or another person's benefit; *and*
- the change is not excluded by regulations from changes that are required to be notified; *and*
- you know the change affects your own or the other person's entitlement; *and*
- you fail to give a prompt notification of the change in *'the prescribed manner to the prescribed person'* (eg giving notice in writing to the relevant authority).

These rules apply to appointees or to anyone else with a right to receive benefit on behalf of another person. They also apply to third parties such as landlords, if they know, or would be expected to know, of changes with respect to a tenant's occupation of a dwelling or a tenant's liability to make payments in respect of that dwelling.

SSAA, S.112

Fraud interviews – If fraud is suspected, the DWP (or local authority for housing benefit) may ask you to attend an interview with a fraud officer. Seek advice beforehand and if possible take a friend with you who is not involved in the matter. Following the interview, the DWP may decide it is more appropriate to offer an administrative penalty or a formal caution as an alternative to prosecution, even if it believes you have committed fraud. If you are prosecuted and found guilty of fraud, the court can fine you or imprison you, or both.

Alternatives to prosecution – If the DWP or local authority believe they have enough evidence to successfully prosecute, they may give you the option of paying an administrative penalty as an alternative to prosecution. The administrative penalty is a minimum of £350, which rises to an equivalent of 50% of the overpayment (whichever is greater); the maximum is £2,000. You also have to repay the overpayment. You have 28 days to change your mind if you have agreed to pay an administrative penalty.

SSAA, S.115A; WRA 2012, S.114

A formal caution may be offered as an alternative to prosecution. This is a DWP administrative practice, not a criminal conviction. But if you are later found guilty of another offence, the formal caution may be used in court for sentencing purposes (in England and Wales, but not in Scotland).

Different rules apply to tax credits, which have a penalty system in place (see Chapter 19(12)). If HMRC believes fraud is involved, it may prosecute in the courts.

If you are accused of fraud, get legal advice as soon as you can (see Chapter 59).

58 Decisions, revisions and appeals

1. Who makes decisions?

The Secretary of State for Work and Pensions is responsible for decision making for most social security benefits, but in practice decisions are made on their behalf by an officer called a decision maker. Decisions on appeal are made by a Social Security and Child Support First-tier Tribunal (a tribunal) in the Social Entitlement Chamber within the Ministry of Justice. Appeals against decisions of tribunals are made to the Upper Tribunal in the Administrative Appeals Chamber. Administration for both of these tribunals is carried out by HM Courts & Tribunals Service.

Housing benefit has a similar decisions and appeals system. Decisions are made by a local authority officer. The ways of changing decisions described in this chapter apply equally to housing benefit decisions unless otherwise stated. Decisions on appeal are made by a tribunal.

Some HMRC decisions use the same appeal system.
❏ **Working tax credit, child tax credit, child benefit and guardian's allowance** – Decisions are made by an officer of HMRC. The tax credits decision-making process is different from that for social security benefits (see Chapter 19(13)). Decisions on appeal are made by a Social Security and Child Support tribunal.
❏ **National insurance credits** – Decisions are made by HMRC officers based in the National Insurance Contributions Office. The decision-making process is the same as that for social security benefits. Decisions on appeal are made by a Social Security and Child Support tribunal.

Decisions on national insurance contributions and employed earner status are made by HMRC. Appeals are usually made to a tribunal in the Tax Chamber.

There are separate systems for statutory sick pay (Chapter 9(10)), statutory maternity, paternity and adoption pay (Chapter 36) and the Armed Forces Compensation scheme (Chapter 45). There are modified rules for vaccine damage payments (Chapter 47(5)).

Council tax reductions and discounts are administered by local authorities. Decisions are made by a local authority officer. Each authority has its own procedure to consider disputes. Appeals are made to a Valuation Tribunal.

2. Ways of changing decisions

Once a decision is made, it stands and is binding until one of the methods given in the law for changing decisions is set in motion. Even a decision given without legal authority counts as an effective decision until it is challenged.

Changing a decision made by a decision maker
There are four ways of changing a decision made by a decision maker on behalf of the Secretary of State:
■ correct an accidental error (see below);
■ revise the decision;
■ supersede the decision;
■ appeal against the decision.
Revisions, supersessions and appeals are covered in 3 to 16 below.

Correcting an accidental error – An 'accidental' error in a decision can be corrected by the decision maker at any time. Arithmetical or clerical errors can be corrected in this way. Correction is discretionary and there is no appeal against a refusal to correct.

If the decision is corrected, the dispute period (see 3 below) starts from when notice of the correction is sent. If a decision is not corrected, the original dispute period remains in place; so if you ask for a decision to be corrected, make sure you also ask for a revision or lodge an appeal before the end of the time limit in case the decision is not corrected.

D&A Regs, reg 9A; UCPIP(D&A) Regs, reg 38

Changing a decision made by a tribunal
There are four ways to change a decision made by a tribunal:
■ correct an accidental error;
■ set aside the decision;
■ supersede the decision;
■ appeal against the decision.
These are covered in more detail in 17 and 18 below.

3. 'Any grounds' revisions

Dispute period – There is a *'dispute period'* of one month from the date a decision maker's decision is sent to you, during which you can ask for the decision to be revised on *'any grounds'* or appeal against it. The decision can be revised for any reason other than for a change of circumstances occurring after the decision was made (in which case you must make a fresh claim or ask for the award to be superseded – see Box T.5). The time limit can be extended in special circumstances (see below). Outside the dispute period, a decision can be revised only if certain grounds are satisfied (see 4 below and Box T.5).

D&A Regs, reg 3(1); UCPIP(D&A) Regs, reg 5(1); TP(FTT)SEC Rules, Sch 1

A decision of a tribunal cannot be changed by an 'any grounds' revision. See 17 below for what to do if you disagree with a tribunal decision.

Mandatory revisions – Universal credit and personal independent payment decisions cannot be appealed unless the decision has first been reconsidered by a decision maker under the revision process. This mandatory revision will be introduced for other benefits on 28.10.13. The decision notice will tell you whether you must ask for a revision before you can appeal.

SSA s 12(3A); UCPIP(D&A) Regs, reg 7

Time limit
Unless you have requested a written statement of reasons (see below), your request to revise the decision must be received no later than one calendar month from the day after the date the decision was posted to you. Make the request to the office address on the decision letter.

D&A Regs, reg 3(1)(b), UCPIP(D&A) Regs, reg 5(1)(b) & TP(FTT)SEC Rules, Sch 1

The date the decision is posted is taken to be the date on the decision letter. For example, if the decision letter is dated 10 October 2013, your request must be received on or before 10 November 2013. If there is no corresponding date in the next month, your request must be received by the last day of that month; for example, if a decision is dated 31 May 2013, your request must be received by 30 June 2013.

Keep a record of the date you make your request. If you take a letter into the office, ask for a dated receipt.

DWP guidance says that decision makers should accept requests received one day late unless they are certain the decision letter was actually posted on the day it is dated.

Decision Makers Guide, Vol 1, para 03063

'Any grounds' revision or appeal?
The decision letter should explain your right either to ask for an 'any grounds' revision or to appeal. (The letter might not use the word 'revision' but may instead ask if you want the decision looked at again or reconsidered; it means the same thing.) Normally you have a choice, although some decisions cannot be appealed (see 7 below) and sometimes the revision process is mandatory (see above).

Asking for a decision to be revised is usually a quicker way of changing a decision than appealing. If you appeal straight away, you lose this chance of having the case looked at again by the DWP (although a separate revision can happen as part of the appeal process – see 9 below). For the revision, the DWP simply has another look at the decision, taking into account any further information or evidence you supply. Normally, a different decision maker looks at the case. You will have a further month to appeal if you are not satisfied with the revised decision. For more on appeals, see 7-17 below.

How do you ask for a revision?
It is important to act within the one-month time limit, otherwise you could lose arrears of benefit or even find you cannot challenge the decision at all. You can ask for a revision over the phone, but you should confirm your request in writing and keep a copy of it. If you are near the deadline for requesting a revision, phone to register the revision and say you will write with more details, otherwise a postal delay could result in your request being out of time. For housing benefit, your request must be in writing to the local authority. A few days after posting your revision request, ring the office you sent it to, to make sure they have received it.

You can ask for an 'any grounds' revision for any reason, but you should explain why you think the decision is wrong. If you can, get evidence to back up your argument. If you cannot send this straight away, say so. You should be given a month to send in extra evidence; this time limit can extended at the decision maker's discretion.

Written statement of reasons for the decision
If the decision letter did not include reasons, you can ask for a 'written statement of reasons'. You must do this within one month of the date of the decision. If you ask for the written statement within one month and it is provided within that time, the one-month dispute period is extended by 14 days; if it is provided after one month, the dispute period is extended

to 14 days from the date it is provided. Unfortunately, you cannot always tell from the decision letter whether reasons are included, and the written statement you are sent might not explain the decision fully; so try to ask for a revision within the one-month time limit, even if you are also asking for written reasons.

D&A Regs, regs 3(1)(b)(ii)-(iii); UCPIP(D&A) Regs, reg 5(1)(b)(ii)-(iii) & TP(FTT)SEC Rules, Sch 1

Extending the time limit for revision
If you have missed the deadline, there are two options.
❑ Ask for a late 'any grounds' revision. The dispute period can be extended if strict conditions are met (see below). If the application is accepted, the decision can still be revised for any reason – you are not limited to certain grounds – and benefit can be fully backdated.
❑ Look for grounds to revise or supersede the decision outside the dispute period. Grounds are limited and, for a supersession, arrears of benefit are normally paid only from the date you apply. See 4 and 5 below and Box T.5.

T.4   Backdating

A *revised* decision takes effect from the date the original decision took effect, so benefit is fully backdated. A *superseded* decision generally takes effect from the date you apply for the decision to be superseded, so benefit can only be backdated to this date. Exceptions to the rule are listed below.

Event	Date change takes effect
Award of a qualifying benefit	full backdating to the start of existing award or, if later, date qualifying benefit starts
Following a reinterpretation of the law in a test case	the date of test case decision
Change of circumstances	
■ notified within one month	the date of change
■ for universal credit – notified during an assessment period (see Chapter 58(5))	the start of the assessment period
■ for disability living allowance, personal independence payment or attendance allowance – notified within one month of completing 3- or 6-month qualifying period for new rate or component	the end of qualifying period
■ notified after one month	the date notified – no backdating
■ notified after one month (but within 13 months) – special circumstances for the delay	the date of change or, for universal credit, the start of the assessment period in which the change occurred
Official error	
■ all benefits	full backdating to the date of the original decision

If you request a late revision, consider asking the decision maker to treat the request as a late appeal (see 7 below) if it is rejected. You can also ask for the revision request to be treated as a request for a supersession, so you can be paid from now while you are waiting for the tribunal to decide on the past period.

Late revisions – An application for a late 'any grounds' revision may be accepted if:
- it is reasonable to grant the application;
- the application for revision has 'merit' – this is not defined but if there is no prospect of success, the application for a

late revision will probably be refused; *and*
- the delay was caused by special circumstances – you must show that it was not practicable for you to apply in time. The longer the delay, the better the reason must be. It will not be enough that you simply did not know or understand the law or the time limits involved.

A reinterpretation of the law by an Upper Tribunal or court is not a ground for a late 'any grounds' revision (but it may allow a supersession for error of law – see Box T.5).

Apply for a late 'any grounds' revision in writing; include the name of the benefit, the date of the decision, why you

---

T.5 Grounds for revising or superseding a decision

Outside the dispute period, a decision can only be reconsidered for specific reasons, or *'grounds'*. If at least one of the grounds outlined in this box is met, a decision can be either revised or superseded. We have called them 'Ground 1', 'Ground 2', etc for convenience, but these numbers are not used officially, so you must clearly state the grounds in your application. We include only the main grounds here; the full list is contained within the appropriate regulations: D&A Regs, regs 3 & 6; UCPIP(D&A) Regs, parts 2 & 3; HB&CTB(D&A) Regs, regs 4 & 7; Child Benefit & Guardian's Allowance (D&A) Regs, regs 5-13. In the footnotes we refer only to the first two sets of these regulations, which cover most social security benefits.

If you ask for a decision to be looked at again, you must show that one of the grounds is met. Similarly, if the decision maker decides for themselves to revise or supersede the decision, they must show that a ground is met. If no ground is met, the decision cannot be changed no matter how wrong it may be (CDLA/3875/2001).
Note: A decision made by a First-tier or Upper Tribunal cannot be revised on any ground and cannot be superseded because of an 'error of law'; so Grounds 2 and 4 cannot be used.

Ground 1: Change of circumstances
Any decision can be *superseded* if there has been a *'relevant change of circumstances since [it] had effect'*, or such a change is anticipated.
D&A Regs, reg 6(2)(a); UCPIP(D&A) Regs, reg 23(1)

What changes are 'relevant'? – A change of circumstances is *'relevant'* if it calls for serious consideration by the decision maker and could (but not necessarily would) change some aspect of the award, such as the amount or length of the award.

For example, if you receive the standard rate of the daily living component of personal independence payment (PIP) and your condition deteriorates so that your care needs increase, this is a relevant change of circumstances because it could lead to entitlement to the enhanced rate.

Note the following points:
- ❏ A decision to refuse benefit cannot be superseded due to a later change of circumstances. You must make a fresh benefit claim.
- ❏ For work capability assessment decisions, a new report from a DWP-approved healthcare professional enables a decision to be superseded (see Ground 3 below). For other benefits, such as disability living allowance or PIP, a different medical opinion is not in itself a relevant change of circumstances. However, a new medical report may provide evidence of a change of circumstances – eg the report may indicate that your condition has deteriorated (R(DLA)6/01).

❏ A change in legislation is a relevant change of circumstances and a supersession can take effect from the date on which the law changes. However, new case law (a decision of a court or Upper Tribunal) does not count as a relevant change of circumstances (R(I)2/94).

The backdating rules following a change of circumstances are described in Chapter 58(5).

Ground 2: Error of law
A decision can be *superseded* if it was based on a mistake about the law (eg the decision maker misinterpreted the relevant law). In practice, supersession of a decision maker's decision should take place only if the legal error comes to light because of an Upper Tribunal's or court's decision on another claim – a test case decision (see Chapter 58(6)). In this case, extra benefit can be paid only from the date of the test case decision. For any other error of law, the decision should be *revised* as an official error, with full backdating of benefit (see 'Ground 4').
D&A Regs, reg 6(2)(b)(i); UCPIP(D&A) Regs, reg 24(a)
Note: A decision of a First-tier or Upper Tribunal cannot be superseded because of an error of law. You may, however, be able to appeal further (see Chapter 58(17)).

Ground 3: New medical report
A new medical report from a DWP-approved healthcare professional is grounds for a decision maker to *supersede* a decision (including a tribunal's decision):
- awarding a personal independence payment; *or*
- that you have a limited capability for work or limited capability for work-related activity (for employment and support allowance (ESA) or universal credit).

The decision maker must look at all the relevant evidence, including the medical evidence used for earlier decisions (CIB/3985/2001).
D&A Regs, reg 6(2)(g) & (r); UCPIP(D&A) Regs, reg 26

Ground 4: Official error
A decision can be *revised* if it arose from an official error by the DWP, HMRC or local authority (or a body designated to act on their behalf), as long as no one outside the department or authority caused or materially contributed to the error.
D&A Regs, regs 1 & 3(5)(a); UCPIP(D&A) Regs, reg 9(a)

The revised decision generally takes effect from the same date as the original decision, so benefit is fully backdated no matter how long ago the original decision was made; but see Ground 2 for errors that come to light because of a test case.

Ground 5: Award of a qualifying benefit
If you, your partner or a dependent child become entitled to another *'qualifying'* benefit, or to an increase in such a benefit, and as a result your existing award should be increased, your award can be *revised* or *superseded*. Benefit is fully backdated to the start of the existing award (by revision) or to the start of the award of the qualifying benefit (by supersession), if that is later, eg if you apply for both income-related ESA and PIP daily

think it should be revised and your reasons for the delay. You cannot get a late revision more than 13 months (plus any extension because you asked for a written statement of reasons – see above) after the date the decision was sent to you. If you are refused a late revision once, you cannot apply again.
D&A Regs, reg 4

Late appeals – The rules are different (see 7 below).

The revised decision

You will get a written decision following your application for a revision. The revised decision takes effect from the date of the earlier decision, so benefit is backdated to that date.
SSA, S.9(3)

Appeal rights – You can appeal within one month of being sent a revised decision. If the decision maker decides not to revise the decision, they will write to tell you. You have one month to appeal against the original decision from the date of the letter.
TP(FTT)SEC Rules, Sch 1

If a mandatory revision must take place before an appeal can be made (see above), you will have no right to appeal

living component, but the PIP is awarded only after a delay, your income-related ESA award can be revised or superseded to backdate the severe disability premium to the date the PIP award started. For universal credit, any extra benefit is payable from the start of the assessment period (see Chapter 58(5)) in which the award of the qualifying benefit was made.
D&A Regs, regs 3(7), 6(2)(e) & 7(7); UCPIP(D&A) Regs, reg 12 & Sch 1, para 31

This rule can increase entitlement only to a benefit you already have. If you don't have an existing award, see Chapter 57(3) for rules on backdating claims. See also Chapter 15(12).

A decision maker can *revise* a decision disallowing reduced earnings allowance because it has been decided that you do not have a prescribed disease or a loss of faculty (see Chapter 44(14), and the latter decision is either revised by a decision maker or changed at appeal.
D&A Regs, regs 3(7A)

A decision maker can *revise* or *supersede* an income support, income-related ESA, income-based jobseeker's allowance or pension credit decision if a non-dependant living with you is awarded backdated benefit (eg attendance allowance) so that you become entitled to the severe disability premium or the pension credit equivalent.
D&A Regs, regs 3(7ZA), 6(2)(ee) & 7(7)

Ground 6: Incorrect facts

Any decision (including a First-tier or Upper Tribunal's decision) can be *superseded* if it was made in ignorance of a material fact or was based on a mistake about a material fact, eg when you filled in your PIP claim form you may have underestimated the help you need with personal care. If you give the DWP this information now, they can supersede the decision.
D&A Regs, regs 6(2)(b)(i) & (c); UCPIP(D&A) Regs, reg 24(a) & 31

A decision favourable to you (eg to increase your benefit) can only take effect from the day you apply for the original decision to be superseded. There is generally no backdating (see Box T.4).
SSA, S.10(5)

If you think the DWP, HMRC or local authority made a mistake and neither you nor anyone else outside the department or authority contributed to the mistake, this may be an official error (see 'Ground 4' above). You can get full backdating of arrears if there has been an official error.

Mistakes in your favour – The general rule is that if you were paid more benefit than you were entitled to because a decision was made in ignorance of a relevant fact, or was based on a mistake about a fact, a decision maker can *revise* the decision at any time (but only *supersede* the decision if it was made by a First-tier or Upper Tribunal).
D&A Regs, regs 3(5)(b) & 6(2)(c); UCPIP(D&A) Regs, regs 9 & 31

The new decision takes effect from the same date as the original decision took effect (even if it is a decision superseding that of a First-tier or Upper Tribunal). If there is any overpayment, the decision maker must consider whether it is recoverable under the normal overpayment rules (see Chapter 57(7)).
D&A Regs, regs 5(1) & 7(5); UCPIP(D&A) Regs, regs 35 & 37

The same rule applies whenever the original decision was more advantageous to you than it should have been (see Chapter 58(9)). However, a cut in benefit will not be backdated if the decision involves an assessment of disability or limited capability for work and the decision maker is satisfied that at the time of the original decision you didn't know and couldn't *'reasonably have been expected to know'* of the fact in question and that it was relevant. For more about this rule, see Chapter 58(5) under 'What if your benefit goes down?'
D&A Regs, reg 3(5)(b),(c)&(d); UCPIP(D&A) Regs, Sch 1

Ground 7: Revision during the appeal process

If a valid appeal has been lodged, a decision maker can *revise* a decision at any time before the appeal is decided. This means, for example, if an appeal tribunal is adjourned for further evidence, the decision maker can revise the original decision once that evidence is produced, making a further hearing unnecessary.
D&A Regs, reg 3(4A)

Ground 8: Following the outcome of an earlier appeal

A decision can be *revised* at any time following a successful appeal against an earlier, related decision. For example: you appeal against a decision that you do not satisfy one of the disability tests for PIP. You also make a second claim for PIP, which is unsuccessful. If the appeal against the first decision is successful, benefit is paid up to the date of the decision refusing the new claim. The decision maker can now *revise* the second decision so that payment of the benefit can continue.
D&A Regs, reg 3(5A); UCPIP(D&A Regs), reg 11(2)

Ground 9: No appeal rights

A decision that carries no right of appeal can be either *revised* or *superseded* at any time, without needing specific grounds. These decisions include most administrative decisions about claims and payment of benefit (see Chapter 58(7)).
D&A Regs, regs 3(8) & 6(2)(d); UCPIP(D&A) Regs, regs 10 & 25

Ground 10: Sanctions

If a decision maker wishes to impose a benefit reduction or sanction, any decision that ESA, jobseeker's allowance or universal credit is payable can be *superseded*, including one made by a First-tier or Upper Tribunal. A decision to apply a sanction to your jobseeker's allowance can, in turn, be *revised* at any time. So if you are outside the dispute period, you can still challenge a sanction. The new decision takes effect from the same date as the original decision. If the sanction is lifted, arrears of benefit can be fully backdated.
D&A Regs, regs 3(5C), (6) & 6(2)(f); UCPIP(D&A) Regs, regs 14 & 27

if special circumstances for a late revision are not accepted and the application to revise is refused. If the application is refused you cannot apply again for the decision to be revised.
SSA, S.12(3A); UCPIP(D&A) Regs, reg 6

4. 'Any time' revisions and supersessions
It is best to challenge a decision within the dispute period if you can. However, this may not be possible; your circumstances might change later or you might only realise later that the decision was wrong. You can go back to the DWP or local authority at any time to ask them to reconsider a decision, however long ago the decision was made, but you must first show that certain grounds are satisfied (see Box T.5). If the grounds are satisfied, the decision maker will revise or supersede the decision as appropriate.
The difference between revising and superseding a decision – A decision can be revised only if it was wrong at the time it was made. A revised decision replaces the original decision, so its effect is fully backdated. Generally, a decision is superseded if there is a later change. A supersession creates a new decision that takes effect from a later date and leaves the original decision unchanged; backdating is usually limited to that later date. Sometimes when a decision is wrong, it can be replaced only by supersession and not by revision, so arrears are limited. Box T.4 summarises the backdating rules.
SSA, ss 9 & 10;

Whether a decision is revised or superseded depends on which grounds (listed in Box T.5) apply. If you are not sure what to ask for, just explain why you think the decision is wrong. The decision maker can treat a request to supersede as one to revise and vice versa. If there are grounds to both revise and supersede, the decision should be revised.
D&A Regs, regs 3(10) & 6(5); UCPIP(D&A) Regs, regs 20(1) & 33(1)

Applying for a decision to be revised or superseded
It is best to ask in writing for a decision to be revised or superseded. For housing benefit this is the only option, but with other benefits you can ring or go to the appropriate office in person. However, if you do this, you should confirm your request in writing. Check which one or more of the grounds (listed in Box T.5) apply and say why you think those grounds are satisfied. The decision maker need not take into account anything not raised in your application. If you can, provide evidence to back up your argument. If you cannot send this straight away, say that you are sending it soon. Keep a copy of your letter and any evidence you send.

Appeal rights
If one of the grounds in Box T.5 is satisfied, the original decision can be either revised or superseded. The result may be to confirm the original decision or change it. If the decision maker makes a decision to revise, supersede or not to supersede, you have a right of appeal (if the decision maker decides not to supersede they will confirm the original decision as correct). If the decision maker refuses to revise, you do not have a right of appeal. Rarely, if the application to supersede is obviously hopeless and could not alter the benefit award, the decision maker can refuse to make a decision. As no decision is made, there is no right of appeal.
R(DLA)1/03

For appeal rights within the dispute period, see 3 above.

5. Backdating after a change of circumstances
Whether benefit can be backdated following a change of circumstances depends on the precise nature of the change. Tell the DWP or local authority about the change as soon as you can. For most benefits, if you tell them about the change within one month, benefit is fully backdated to the date of the change.
D&A Regs, reg 7(2)(a); UCPIP(D&A) Regs, Sch 1

For universal credit, a change that is favourable to you will usually take effect from the first day of the assessment period in which you told the DWP of the change. An *'assessment period'* is a period of one month beginning with the first day of entitlement to universal credit and each subsequent period of one month following this, for the duration of the award.
UCPIP(D&A) Regs, Sch 1, para 21

For personal independence payment (PIP), disability living allowance (DLA) and attendance allowance, an increase can be paid from the first pay day after you first satisfy the 3- or 6-month qualifying period (see Chapters 3(4), 4(4) and 5(3)) if you tell the DWP about the change within one month of completing the qualifying period. If you can only give the month and not the day that you would have first satisfied the disability test, the decision maker is told to assume you satisfied it on the last day of that month.
D&A Regs, reg 7(9)(b); UCPIP(D&A) Regs, Sch 1, para 15; Decision Makers Guide, Vol 1, paras 04396 & 04400

Late notification – If the change of circumstances happened more than a month ago, you may still be able to get benefit backdated to the date of the change if you apply within 13 months of the change (or, in the case of PIP, DLA or attendance allowance, within 13 months of the date on which the conditions of entitlement were satisfied). Write to the appropriate office giving details of the change of circumstances and reasons for not telling them earlier. To backdate benefit, the decision maker must be satisfied that:
- it is reasonable to grant the application; *and*
- the change is relevant to the decision that is to be superseded (see 'Ground 1' in Box T.5); *and*
- there are special circumstances that are relevant to the application (eg a serious illness); *and*
- because of the special circumstances it was not practicable for you to notify the change of circumstances within one month of the date of change.

The longer the delay, the better the reason must be. The decision maker will not take account of the fact that you did not know the time limits or the law, or that an Upper Tribunal or court has reinterpreted the law.
D&A Regs, reg 8; UCPIP(D&A) Regs, reg 36

What if your benefit goes down?
If your circumstances change, and as a result your benefit goes down or stops, the general rule is that the new decision takes effect from the date of the change, no matter when you reported it. The same applies whenever the decision is not advantageous to you (see 9 below). If the DWP or local authority decides you have been paid too much benefit, they may try to recover the overpayment (see Chapter 57(7)).

There are exceptions, however, for the following:
- the disability tests for PIP, DLA or attendance allowance;
- limited capability for work for employment and support allowance (ESA) and universal credit;
- disablement for severe disablement allowance or industrial injuries benefits.

For these benefits, the reduction is backdated only if you knew or could reasonably have been expected to know that the change should have been reported. In this case, the reduction is backdated to the date you should have told them.
D&A Regs, reg 7(2)(c); UCPIP(D&A) Regs, Sch 1, paras 7-8, 16-17 & 23-24

The same applies to a decision made on another benefit as a result of one of the above disability or limited capability for work decisions. For example, if DLA stops following a Right Payment Programme check, both DLA entitlement and any severe disability premium included in income-related ESA will stop from the date the DLA decision is made if you could not reasonably have been expected to know that you should have reported a reduction in your care needs.
D&A Regs, reg 7A(2); UCPIP(D&A) Regs, Sch 1, para 31

In deciding whether you *'reasonably could have been expected to know'* that you should have reported the change, decision makers should take into account:

- how much you knew about the reasons for awarding you benefit;
- what information was given to you about reporting changes of circumstances;
- your ability to recognise when a gradual improvement results in a relevant change of circumstances. A slight change in your care or mobility needs, or your ability to carry out activities in the ESA work capability assessment, would not normally be a change that you could reasonably be expected to report. However, even if the change is gradual there may still be a point at which you could reasonably be expected to know it should be reported.

Decision Makers Guide, Vol 1, para 04237/40

6. When a test case is pending

A decision on your claim may be affected by a matter of law that is under appeal in the courts in another case – ie a *'test case'*. A decision maker can postpone making a decision in your case until the test case has been decided. Alternatively, they can make the decision in your case as though the test case has been decided in a way that is unfavourable to you. If the test case turns out to be favourable, the decision maker must then go back and revise the decision.

SSA, S.25 & D&A Regs, reg 21; UCPIP(D&A) Regs, reg 44(2)(c)

When the decision maker makes a decision in your case after a test case decision, any arrears of benefit are restricted to the date the test case was decided.

SSA, S.27(3)

If you have appealed – The outcome of your appeal may depend on the result of another case pending at the courts. If this happens, the decision maker may ask a First-tier or Upper Tribunal to do one of the following:

- not to decide the appeal, but to refer it back to them. The appeal will be held until the test case is decided. The decision maker will then revise or supersede the decision as appropriate;
- deal with the appeal. The First-tier or Upper Tribunal can either hold the appeal until the test case has been decided or determine it as if the test case has been decided in a way that is unfavourable to you. If the result of the test case is then favourable, the decision can be superseded by a decision maker.

SSA, S.26

7. Appeals

You have the right to appeal to a tribunal against any decision on a claim for benefit or against any decision that revises or supersedes another decision, unless it is specifically listed in law as one with no right of appeal. When a decision is made about your benefit, you must be given a written decision notice that says whether you have a right to appeal.

No right of appeal – There is no right of appeal against:

- most administrative decisions about claims and payment of benefit (but you can appeal against a decision that a claim is 'defective' (see Chapter 57(1));
- entitlement to constant attendance allowance or exceptionally severe disablement allowance (both paid with industrial injuries disablement benefit), or to the Christmas bonus; *or*
- any part of a housing benefit decision that adopts a rent officer's determination (see Chapter 21(10)); *or*
- decisions to postpone or make temporary unfavourable determinations when a test case is pending (see 6 above); *or*
- a universal credit or personal independence payment decision if that decision has not first been reconsidered by a decision maker (this will apply to other benefits from 28.10.13).

The full list is in SSA, Sch 2; D&A Regs, reg 27 & Sch 2; HB&CTB(D&A) Regs, Sch; UCPIP(D&A) Regs, Sch 3

If you do not have a right to appeal, you can ask for the decision to be revised or superseded (see 'Ground 9' in Box T.5). Judicial review by the High Court or Upper Tribunal may be possible; seek advice from a law centre or solicitor.

Tribunal rules – Tribunals must act within a set of rules whose stated overriding objective is to deal with appeals *'fairly and justly'*. Parties to the appeal must co-operate with the tribunal and help it fulfil this objective.

A tribunal can overlook a failure to comply with the rules or ask you to remedy a failure to comply. The tribunal cannot overlook a failure to appeal within 12 months of the end of the normal appeal time limit.

TP(FTT)SEC Rules, rules 2, 5, 7 & 23

Time limits for appeals

Usually, an appeal request must be received by the office that sent you the decision within one calendar month of the date it was sent to you (see 3 above). Appeals against personal independence payment and universal credit decisions, and other decisions subject to a 'mandatory revision' (see 3 above), are sent to HM Courts & Tribunals Service (HMCTS) directly.

Asking for written reasons – You can ask for written reasons for the decision if they are not included with the decision notice. You must do this within one month of the day the decision is sent to you. Asking for written reasons can extend the appeal time limit (see 3 above).

Tax credit decision notifications do not contain reasons and asking for reasons will not extend the appeal time limit.

Late appeal

If you miss the deadline, a late appeal can be treated as made in time in specified circumstances. A late appeal must be made in writing and state the reasons why it is late. For most benefits, a decision maker first decides whether to accept the appeal. They decide whether it is in the interests of justice to treat the appeal as made in time and in doing so will consider whether there are *'special circumstances'* relevant to the delay. These are:

- you, your partner or a dependant has suffered serious illness; *or*
- your partner, a dependant or the person who appealed has died (and you are pursuing the appeal on behalf of the deceased person); *or*
- you live outside the UK; *or*
- normal postal services were disrupted; *or*
- some other *'wholly exceptional and relevant'* circumstances exist.

The longer the delay, the better the reasons must be. No account is taken of whether you did not know or understand the law or time limits involved, nor that the Upper Tribunal or a court has reinterpreted the law.

If the decision maker cannot treat the appeal as made in time, they must refer it to HMCTS, where a tribunal judge decides whether to accept it. The judge can accept the late appeal and waive the requirement that it is made in time, but appeals made more than 12 months after the time limit cannot be accepted. The judge will usually allow the appeal unless the decision maker objects, in which case the judge will consider whether the objection is reasonable.

D&A Regs, reg 32; TP(FTT)SEC Rules, rules 5(3)(a) & 23(5)

For personal independence payment and universal credit decisions and any other decisions subject to a mandatory revision, late appeals are sent to HMCTS directly where a tribunal judge decides whether to accept it.

TP(FTT)SEC Rules, rule 22

8. Making an appeal

For most benefit decisions, appeals are made to the office that made the decision you are appealing against. For universal credit and personal independence payment decisions, appeals are made directly to HM Courts and Tribunals Service (HMCTS). The requirement for appeals to be made to HMCTS will be extended to other benefits from 28.10.13.

You or your representative must apply in writing, in English or Welsh. There are forms on which appeals can be made, or you can appeal in a letter. For most benefits the form is GL24, which you get from the DWP. HMRC provides the WTC/AP appeal form for tax credits and the CH24A appeal form for child benefit and guardian's allowance. For housing benefit, your local authority will provide its own appeal form. HMCTS has its own form, the SSCS1, for the appeals that must be made to it directly.

Your appeal must give your name and address and that of your representative if you have one. It must give an address where documents can be sent to you if your own address is inappropriate. You must give details of the decision being appealed (date, name of the benefit, what the decision is about) and grounds for your appeal.

TP(FTT)SEC Rules, rule 23(6)

9. What happens when you appeal?

When they receive your appeal, the decision maker will check to see if they can revise the decision you are appealing against. If your appeal is made to HM Courts and Tribunals Service directly, a copy is sent to the DWP and a decision maker will decide whether to revise it at this stage.

If it is revised, your appeal lapses if the new decision is more advantageous to you – even if it does not give you everything you wanted. If you wish to continue with your appeal, you must now make a new appeal within one month of the date of the revised decision.

SSA, S.9(6)

If the decision is revised but the new decision is not more advantageous to you, your appeal will go ahead against the revised decision.

The decision maker can decide to revise the decision again at any time until the appeal is decided (see Ground 7 in Box T.5). Otherwise, the appeal will go forward to tribunal.

D&A Regs, reg 30(3)-(5)

When is a decision more advantageous? – A decision is more advantageous to you if:
■ more benefit is paid (or would be but for a restriction, suspension or disqualification);
■ the award is for a longer period;
■ a denial or disqualification of benefit is lifted wholly or partly;
■ an amount of recoverable overpaid benefit is reduced or it is decided that it is not recoverable;
■ it reverses a decision to pay benefit to a third party;
■ it reverses a decision that an accident was not an industrial accident;

T.6 Human Rights Act

The Human Rights Act 1998 incorporates into UK law the rights guaranteed under the European Convention on Human Rights. Arguments based on Convention rights can be made in social security appeals. Decision makers and tribunals must interpret the law in a way that is consistent with the Act as far as they are able. You should seek legal advice if you think it may apply in your case.

You can find the Human Rights Act and detailed commentary on its provisions in *Social Security: Legislation 2012 Volume III* (Sweet & Maxwell).

■ you will get some financial gain.
This list is not exhaustive.

D&A Regs, reg 30(2)

Tax credits
When they receive your appeal, an HMRC officer will look at your appeal grounds and decide whether or not it can be settled without having to go to tribunal. They will contact you to discuss the decision first and propose the terms of a possible settlement. If you provisionally agree to these, they will send you a copy of the terms. You will have 30 days in which to write to HMRC if you do not agree with the terms they suggest or do not want to settle. If you do not do this, the settlement will come into force and the appeal will lapse. There is no further right to appeal against a decision settled in this way.

Taxes Management Act 1970, S.54

10. Opting for a hearing

When your appeal is lodged, you will get an acknowledgement letter.

If your appeal was not made to HM Courts & Tribunals Service (HMCTS) directly, the DWP, HMRC or local authority will send your appeal to HMCTS, together with a copy of their response to the appeal and all the documents they have that are relevant to the decision. You will be sent copies of these.

If your appeal was made to HMCTS directly, a copy of your appeal is sent to the DWP for comment. They will write a response to the appeal and return it to HMCTS together with the documents relevant to the decision. You will be sent copies of these.

TP(FTT)SEC Rules, rule 24

HMCTS will send you a pre-hearing enquiry form. This asks whether you want your appeal to be decided with or without a hearing. Be sure to return this form within 14 days, otherwise the tribunal could think you don't want to continue with your appeal and may strike it out (see 12 below).

In most cases, it is better to ask for a hearing. In some cases, it will be crucial for the success of your appeal; particularly if your case involves medical or disability questions (eg decisions about the work capability assessment or personal independence payment).

Decisions without a hearing – An appeal is decided without a hearing only if all parties consent (or none objects) and the tribunal agrees that a hearing is unnecessary.

TP(FTT)SEC Rules, rule 27

If there is no hearing, the tribunal will study all the appeal papers and come to a decision based on these papers alone. The tribunal will be made up in the same way as for a hearing (see 16 below). You can send comments or extra evidence to the tribunal to consider at any time before they make their decision. You will not be told when the decision is due to be made, so send your evidence or comments as soon as possible. If you need time to prepare your information, contact the clerk to the appeal tribunal. Say when you expect to send the information and ask for the decision to be delayed until it has been received.

11. Withdrawing an appeal

You can withdraw your appeal at any time before the hearing. You do not need to give a reason and do not need the agreement of the DWP, local authority or tribunal judge (unless the tribunal has specifically directed that its consent is required). You must write to HM Courts & Tribunals Service (HMCTS) stating that you wish to withdraw the appeal. You can withdraw the appeal at the hearing itself, but only with the consent of the tribunal. A withdrawn appeal can be reinstated if you apply within one month of the date HMCTS received your withdrawal notice or within one month of the date of the

hearing at which your appeal was withdrawn.
TP(FTT)SEC Rules, rule 17; CDLA/1780/2010 & CDLA/1781/2010 [2011] UKUT 228 (AAC)

12. Striking out an appeal

Your appeal, or any part of it, can be struck out if:

■ the tribunal does not have jurisdiction to deal with the appeal (eg it is about a decision that does not carry a right of appeal or should be dealt with by a different tribunal or court);
■ you have failed to co-operate with the tribunal to the extent that it feels it can no longer deal with your appeal fairly or justly;
■ the tribunal feels that your appeal, or part of it, has no reasonable prospects of success; *or*
■ you fail to comply with a direction given to you (eg to provide additional evidence).

If a decision maker thinks the tribunal does not have jurisdiction or your appeal has no prospects of success, they can write to HM Courts & Tribunals Service (HMCTS) asking a judge to strike out the appeal. If the judge is considering striking out the appeal, they will ask you to comment on the matter before deciding whether to do so.

If a tribunal issues a direction saying your appeal will be struck out if you fail to comply, it can strike out your appeal automatically if you fail to comply within the given time limit. It can decide any of the questions under appeal against you and bar you from further proceedings. HMCTS will write to you if your appeal has been struck out.

Reinstatement – If your appeal is struck out because of a failure to comply with a direction, you can ask for your appeal to be reinstated and any decision made to be set aside. You must do so in writing within one month of the date of issue of the order to strike out. If you are barred from further proceedings, the tribunal can ignore an application to reinstate the appeal unless you ask for the bar to be lifted.
TP(FTT)SEC Rules, rule 8

If the tribunal decides that another type of court or tribunal has jurisdiction to deal with your appeal, it can transfer your appeal to it instead of striking out your appeal.
TP(FTT)SEC Rules, rule 5(3)(k)

13. Preparing your case

Read the decision maker's response to the appeal to see where you disagree with it and might need to dispute it. Find out if there is a local advice centre that can advise you and maybe support you at the hearing itself (see Chapter 59).

The tribunal need not consider any issue not raised by the appeal. It is important to give as much detail as you can about why and how you think the decision is wrong. If you are happy with part of your award, you should say so and ask the tribunal not to look at it. The tribunal can only look at circumstances existing at the time of the decision you are appealing against, so if your circumstances change while you are waiting for the appeal to be heard, you should consider making another claim or asking for a supersession (see 14 below).
SSA, S.12(8)

T.7 Upper Tribunal and Commissioners' decisions

Decisions of the Upper Tribunal are binding on First-tier Tribunals and decision makers. In 2008 the Upper Tribunal replaced the Social Security Commissioners (the Commissioners). Decisions of the Commissioners are also binding on First-tier Tribunal and decision makers.

To use decisions of the Upper Tribunal and Commissioners effectively they should be cited correctly, using the appropriate referencing system.

Decisions of the Upper Tribunal

Some Upper Tribunal decisions carry greater legal weight than others. Most decisions are made by a single judge. If an appeal is thought to be particularly complex or likely to affect a large number of other claims, a tribunal of three judges decides the appeal. Decisions made by three judges carry more weight that those of a single judge.

A decision may be reported by publication in bound volumes produced by the Administrative Appeals Chamber. The decision will have been circulated to the Upper Tribunal judges who hear Social Security and Child Support appeals. These judges must broadly agree with the decision's reasoning before it can be reported. A reported decision carries more weight than an unreported decision.

Unreported decisions – When an appeal is first lodged with the Upper Tribunal it is given a reference number in the form CJSA/2280/2009, where: 'C' indicates the decision is unreported; the initials following indicate the benefit claimed (in this case jobseeker's allowance); the first set of numbers is a specific reference for the case and 2009 is the year that the appeal was lodged. The decision will keep this reference unless it is published on the HM Courts & Tribunals Service (HMCTS) website or is reported.

Published on the website – If a decision is thought to be of importance it is published on the HMCTS website. The decision then acquires a reference in the form *Secretary*

of State for Work and Pensions v JB (JSA) [2010] UKUT 4 (AAC), where: *Secretary of State for Work and Pensions v JB (JSA)* are the parties to the appeal (JB is the initials of the person who claimed the benefit) and JSA indicates the benefit claimed (in this case, jobseeker's allowance); [2010] UKUT indicates a decision published on the website in 2010 and made by the UK Upper Tribunal; 4 is the reference number and AAC the Administrative Appeals Chamber. Decisions published on the website carry no more legal weight than any other decision.

Reported decisions – If a decision goes on to be reported, an additional reference is added. In this instance it becomes *Secretary of State for Work and Pensions v JB (JSA)* [2010] UKUT 4 (AAC); [2010] AACR 25. The reference [2010] AACR 25 indicates it is the 25th decision reported in the Administrative Appeals Chamber Reports of 2010. The first time the decision is referred to it should be cited in full. Thereafter, abbreviations for the parties and benefit can be used, eg *SSWP v JB (JSA)*.

Decisions of the Commissioners

Decisions of the Commissioners are still binding on decision makers and First-tier Tribunals. As with decisions of the Upper Tribunal, a decision made by three Commissioners carries more weight than that of a single Commissioner and a reported decision carries more weight than an unreported decision.

When an appeal was first registered with the Commissioners' office it was given a reference number in the form CDLA/1234/2002 – the same form as for unreported decisions of the Upper Tribunal (see above). This reference remained unless the decision was reported.

Slightly different reference systems were used by the Scottish and Northern Irish Commissioners (see *Disability Rights Handbook* 34th edition, page 260).

On reporting, the decision was given a new reference in the form R(DLA)5/06 – the fifth DLA decision reported in 2006.

Check the law

Tribunals must make decisions by applying the particular facts of your case to relevant legislation and case law.

Legislation – Legislation is made up of Acts of Parliament and Regulations. The appeal papers should refer to the parts of the legislation relevant to your appeal. You can see these in *The Law Relating to Social Security* (see page 6).

Case law – Case law is found in decisions of the Upper Tribunal (formerly the Social Security Commissioners (see Box T.7)) and the courts. The appeal papers may refer you to some relevant decisions, but other decisions may be helpful too. We produce case law summaries covering disability living allowance (DLA) and attendance allowance, employment and support allowance and adjudication (decision-making and appeals). Summaries of reported decisions are also available in *Neligan's Digest* (see page 6). Our factsheet *Finding the Law* provides general advice on finding the relevant law to support your appeal (www.disabilityrightsuk.org/finding-law).

Sort out the facts and evidence

After looking at legislation and case law, you may have a clearer idea of which facts are important for your appeal and what extra evidence you need. Most appeals concern a dispute about facts or different interpretations of the same facts. If you do not understand the law, just concentrate on the facts. Read the chapter in this Handbook on the benefit you are appealing about to get an idea of what facts will be important.

You do not have to prove any fact 'beyond all reasonable doubt'. You must prove your case on a balance of probabilities – ie show that your version of the facts is the most likely. Your word is just as much 'evidence' as any document. However, try to get as much other evidence as you can to back up what you are saying, as this helps tip the balance of probabilities your way.

You might need to call witnesses, and will need to get their agreement beforehand. Try to ensure their account will back up your case. If a witness cannot attend the hearing, ask them to give you a written statement for the tribunal.

If you can, send further evidence or comments on the appeal to HM Courts & Tribunals Service well before the hearing. Make a copy of your evidence and take it with you to the hearing.

Getting medical evidence

If your appeal involves a disability question, try to get supportive medical evidence. The tribunal can only consider your circumstances up to the date of the decision you are appealing against (see 14 below). You can get medical evidence later but it should relate to the time covered by the decision under appeal.

The evidence can come from medical professionals such as your GP, specialist nurse, physiotherapist or hospital consultant. When you request a letter or statement from them, ask specific questions. Try to get information directly relevant to the case, rather than vague comments about your general condition. Make sure they are aware of your condition and how it relates to the question under appeal; if you have kept a diary of your care needs, give them a copy.

If the appeal papers contain a report from a healthcare professional assigned to your case, read it carefully to see where you might need to get your own medical evidence to counter what is said in the report. Make sure you ask for comments specifically on the points in dispute. For example, if you disagree with a healthcare professional's report that says you can walk 100 metres without severe discomfort, ask your GP or physiotherapist for an opinion about how far you can walk without severe discomfort.

The tribunal should not automatically treat a report from a DWP-approved healthcare professional as more reliable or accurate than that of any other medical professional, eg your GP. The tribunal should consider all the evidence in a case and decide which it accepts and which it rejects.
R(DLA)3/99; see also R(M)1/93 & CIB/3074/2003

Difficulties obtaining evidence? – If you think you will be unable to get supportive medical evidence by the time of the hearing, you can ask for a postponement to allow you more time to obtain it (see 16 below). If you do not think you can get the evidence you need, you can ask the tribunal to ask for a copy of your medical records or refer you for a medical examination. It will do this if it thinks it cannot decide the appeal without further medical evidence. If you think a medical report needs to answer specific questions, ask the tribunal to put them to the healthcare professional who is to see you at the examination.
SSA, S.20 & TP(FTT)SEC Rules, rule 25(3)

There is no rule that says you must have corroborating medical or other evidence. You can go ahead with your appeal even if you cannot get supporting evidence.

14. If your circumstances change before the appeal

It can take some months for your appeal to be heard and your circumstances may change in the meantime. The tribunal can only look at your situation as it was up to the time of the decision you are appealing against. It decides whether the decision was correct at the time it was made, based on your circumstances at that time. If your situation has changed between the decision and the tribunal hearing, it cannot take that into account.
SSA, S.12(8)(b)

For disability living allowance renewals, this is the case even if a change takes place after a renewal decision is made but before it takes effect. The only exception is if the change is one that is almost certain to occur, such as a child reaching a particular age (eg 3, when the mobility component becomes payable).
R(DLA)4/05 & CDLA/4331/2002

If your circumstances change while your appeal is pending and you think it is now clearer that you qualify for the benefit concerned, you should make a fresh claim. If you already get the benefit, ask the DWP or local authority to supersede the award decision because your circumstances have changed. If you don't and your appeal is unsuccessful, you could lose out because of the rules on backdating.

If the new claim or request to supersede is unsuccessful, it is important to put in a second appeal because your first appeal cannot take into account the period covered by the second decision. The benefit may be put into payment by a successful outcome in the first appeal then stopped from the date of the unfavourable second decision. The decision maker can revise the second decision following a successful appeal against the first decision (see 'Ground 8' in Box T.5), but there is no guarantee this will happen. To be safe, lodge a second appeal. Ask for a single tribunal to hear the appeals together. For appeals on limited capability for work, see also Chapter 11(11) and (12).

Tax credits – Tax credit appeals have similar rules. If your circumstances change after the date of the decision you are appealing against, you should tell HMRC, who may then issue a new decision reflecting your new circumstances. If you are not satisfied with that decision, lodge a further appeal. If you have more than one appeal ongoing, ask for a single tribunal to hear all the appeals together.

15. Special needs, access to the hearing and expenses

If you have any special needs, check with the tribunal clerk beforehand about accessibility, what facilities are available and how your needs can be met to enable you to be present at your hearing and get home again within a reasonable time. You should ask for whatever you need. If HM Courts & Tribunals Service (HMCTS) cannot provide it, seek advice.

For example, if it is too far for you to walk easily to the tribunal room from the nearest point at which a car can set you down, ask for a wheelchair to be waiting for you. If you need breaks during a hearing (eg to go to the toilet, take food or medication, stretch your legs or change position), ask for them. It helps if the tribunal knows what you might need; contact the tribunal clerk before the hearing.

If you arrive to find the premises are not accessible to you, the tribunal should adjourn to a time and place where you can be present (CI/112/84).

Out-of-centre and domiciliary tribunals – HMCTS can arrange for the tribunal to take place nearer to you than their usual venues (at an 'out-of-centre' venue) or in your home (a 'domiciliary hearing'). You should provide medical evidence of your need for an alternative venue.

The tribunal may hold a preliminary hearing to decide whether to adjourn for an alternative venue – you can send a representative to this hearing. If the tribunal refuses your request for an alternative venue and decides to deal with your appeal in your absence, it must be satisfied that it already has enough evidence to make a decision. Otherwise, it must adjourn and make arrangements to get further evidence (eg by referring you for a medical report or arranging a video link to your home).
CIB/2751/2002

A local disability group may know of a suitable and fully accessible venue near your home that could be used instead of a HMCTS office.

Claiming expenses – You can claim travelling expenses for yourself and a travelling companion if you need one. If you cannot travel by public transport you can claim for taxi fares or a private ambulance. You can get compensation for loss of earnings and for childminding expenses up to set maximums. You can claim for a basic meal if you are away from home or work for more than a specified time.

If you are not sure what you, or someone with you, can claim, ask the tribunal clerk: ring the number on the hearing notice. If you need anything other than travel expenses for yourself by public transport, agree the expenses with the clerk well before the hearing.

16. At the hearing

You must be given at least 14 days' notice of the time and place of a hearing, starting from the day the hearing notice is sent to you. In practice, you are usually given much more notice than this. You can be given shorter notice if you consent, or in urgent or exceptional circumstances.
TP(FTT)SEC Rules, rule 29

Asking for a postponement – If the date is inconvenient or it does not give you enough time to prepare your case, write to the clerk to the tribunal and ask if the hearing can be postponed. If time is short, you can ring the clerk (the phone number will be at the top of the hearing notice) but you should also write to confirm your request. The same applies if you are ill on the day or have a domestic emergency. A tribunal judge will decide whether to grant a postponement. If you have not had the postponement confirmed, it is best to go along to the hearing if you can in case your request is refused and the appeal is decided in your absence.
TP(FTT)SEC Rules, rule 5(3)(h)

Who is at the hearing?
You and your representative – It is always best to attend the hearing yourself; see 15 above if there is a problem with access. You are entitled to have someone with you to represent you (see Chapter 59) and you can also bring a companion for support. Both you and your representative have the right to speak, and you can call witnesses.
TP(FTT)SEC Rules, rules 11 & 28

Tribunal members – The tribunal is made up of a legally qualified tribunal judge and possibly one or two other people, depending on the type of appeal:
- for personal independence payment, disability living allowance and attendance allowance – a judge, a doctor and a 'disability member' (see below);
- for limited capability for work assessments and limited capability for work-related activity assessments – a judge and a doctor;
- for severe disablement allowance, industrial injuries benefit – a judge and a doctor;
- for difficult financial matters about trust funds or business accounts – a judge and an accountant;
- for any other matter (including a declaration of industrial accident) – a judge alone.

The hearing cannot go ahead unless all the tribunal members are present (except in exceptional circumstances and only if you and/or your representative agree). Members are drawn from a panel appointed by the Judicial Appointments Commission.

To avoid a conflict of interest, the tribunal must not include a doctor who has ever provided advice or prepared a report about you, or has ever been your regular doctor.

The disability member is a person who is 'experienced in dealing with the physical or mental needs of disabled persons because they work with disabled persons in a professional or voluntary capacity or are themselves disabled'. They cannot be a medical practitioner but can be a paramedic, physiotherapist or nurse.

Where the tribunal would normally consists of a judge and one doctor, a second doctor can be appointed if 'the complexity of the medical issues' demands it.

Although an additional member may be appointed to a particular tribunal, there can never be more than three tribunal members. The appeal tribunal can ask an expert to attend the hearing or give a written report, but this expert cannot take part in the appeal tribunal's decision making.
TCEA, s. 4 & Schedules 2 & 6; Qualifications for Appointment of Members to the First-tier Tribunal & Upper Tribunal Order 2008; First-tier & Upper Tribunal (Composition of Tribunal) Order 2008

Others – Apart from tribunal members, there may be a presenting officer to put the decision maker's case. The presenting officer is there to help the tribunal and so may also identify any points in your favour.

A clerk is present to deal with the administration of the hearing. They may have an assistant.

If the tribunal judge agrees, any other person can be present during the hearing. The hearing will be open to the public unless the tribunal judge decides otherwise. You can ask for a private hearing. The decision is made at the discretion of the judge. In practice, the only members of the public who are likely to be present are other claimants (to see what happens before their own appeal is heard) or advisers (to help them in their work).
TCEA, s. 40; TP(FTT)SEC Rules, rules 2, 5, 28 & 30

What happens at the hearing?
The hearing itself should be fairly informal. The tribunal is inquisitorial: its job is to investigate the appeal – so it is likely to ask lots of questions (in contrast to adversarial courts that mainly hear arguments).

There is no set procedure, so the tribunal judge decides which procedure will most effectively determine each appeal. The judge will begin by introducing the members of the tribunal and explaining its role. Often, the judge then clarifies what they understand to be the issues before them to make sure that everyone understands what the appeal is about.

If there is a presenting officer, the judge often asks them

to present the decision maker's case first. Other tribunals may begin by asking you direct factual questions. A common procedure for disability-related appeals is to ask you to describe what you do on an average day.

At some point in the hearing you will be asked to explain your case. Put your main points in writing so you don't forget anything. If you are interrupted, you can ask tactfully to make all your points before answering questions. Where possible, back up your argument with documentary evidence (eg bills, bank statements, doctor's letters). At the end of your statement, repeat the decision you want the tribunal to make. You can question the presenting officer, if there is one, and any witnesses. Listen carefully, and ask questions if you think anything is being misunderstood or misrepresented.

Once the tribunal is satisfied that each party has had the opportunity to present its case, the judge will ask everyone (except the clerk) to leave the tribunal room while the tribunal makes its decision.

Medical examinations – For severe disablement allowance or industrial injuries appeals involving an assessment of the extent of your disability, the doctor on the tribunal will examine you in private, usually towards the end of the hearing. After the examination, the hearing may start again to discuss the doctor's findings.

The tribunal cannot carry out a physical examination for any other benefit. It cannot ask you to undergo a walking test for the mobility component of personal independence payment or disability living allowance. It will, however, watch how you walk into and out of the room and how you cope with what might be a lengthy hearing. The tribunal can refer you for an examination so that a healthcare professional can provide a report (see 13 above).
TP(FTT)SEC Rules, rule 25

17. The appeal decision

You will get a decision notice on the day of the hearing or soon after. A copy of the decision notice is sent to the department that made the original decision so they can put the tribunal decision into effect and pay you any benefit owed.

If the appeal is unsuccessful, you can ask for a more detailed explanation, the *'statement of reasons'* for the decision. If you want to appeal to the Upper Tribunal, you need this statement. Make sure you write and ask for it within the one-month time limit (see 18 below). Once you have read the statement of reasons, it should be clear to you how and why you have been unsuccessful. If it is not, this may be an error of law (see Box T.8) and it may be possible to appeal further to the Upper Tribunal.

If you disagree with the decision

A decision of an appeal tribunal can be changed in the following ways:

■ apply to the tribunal to correct an accidental error (see below);
■ apply for the decision to be set aside (see below);
■ appeal to the Upper Tribunal if there is an error of law – see 18 below (if you cannot appeal, see below for some ideas of what to do);
■ apply to the DWP or local authority to supersede the decision if there has been a relevant change of circumstances or such a change is anticipated (see 'Ground 1' in Box T.5). This can include a change of circumstances that occurred after the decision under appeal was made but which only came to light during the appeal process (the tribunal itself would have been prevented from taking the change into account);
■ apply to the DWP or local authority to supersede the decision if it was made in ignorance of a material fact, or was based on a mistake about a material fact (see 'Ground 6' in Box T.5).

Correcting an accidental error – An 'accidental' error in the decision of an appeal tribunal can be corrected at any time. Arithmetical or clerical errors can be corrected in this way (eg if it is clear the tribunal accidentally gave the wrong starting date for an award of benefit). Write to HM Courts & Tribunals Service. There is no right to appeal against a refusal to correct the decision.
TP(FTT)SEC Rules, rule 36

Setting aside for procedural reasons – A decision may be set aside by a tribunal judge, if it 'appears just' to do so because:

■ a document relevant to the appeal wasn't sent to, or received in sufficient time by, any party to the proceedings, their representative or the tribunal; *or*
■ a party to the proceedings or a representative wasn't present at the hearing; *or*
■ there has been some other procedural irregularity.

You must apply in writing to have the decision set aside within one month of the date the decision was given or sent to you. The tribunal judge can extend the time limit.
TP(FTT)SEC Rules, rules 37 & 5

Setting aside wipes out all or part of the tribunal's decision. There must be a fresh hearing before a new appeal tribunal. You cannot appeal against a refusal to set aside. A refusal to set aside starts afresh the time limits for asking for permission to appeal to the Upper Tribunal. This does not apply, however, if the application to set aside was made late (unless the tribunal granted an extension to the time limit).
TCEA, s.11; TP(FTT)SEC Rules, rule 38(3)(c)&(4)

T.8 Errors of law

Can you understand the decision?

The statement of reasons for the tribunal's decision must set out clearly what it decided and why it made that decision. If you had put forward specific arguments, the statement must show clearly how the tribunal dealt with them. It must also show that the tribunal understood and correctly applied the relevant law. If the statement is not clear on any of the above, the decision may contain an error of law.

Identifying an error of law is essential if you wish to appeal to an Upper Tribunal from a First-tier Tribunal decision. It will also be helpful if you want to change a decision using 'Ground 2' or 'Ground 4' in Box T.5.

Identifying errors of law

Several Commissioners' decisions, including R(A)1/72, R(IS)11/99 and R(I)2/06, set out what might constitute an error of law. A decision might be wrong in law if any of the following apply:

❑ The decision contains a misdirection about, or misunderstanding of, the relevant law (including not taking into account relevant case law).
❑ There has been a breach of the rules of natural justice (ie the procedures followed were incorrect or unfair).
❑ The tribunal has failed to make the findings of fact needed to apply the law correctly.
❑ The evidence does not support the decision.
❑ The tribunal has failed to give adequate reasons for the decision (including failing to explain clearly how it resolved disputes about relevant facts or evidence or interpretation of the law).
❑ The tribunal took irrelevant matters into account.
❑ The decision is perverse: there is such a clear inconsistency between the law, the facts of the case and the decision, that no tribunal acting reasonably could have made the decision.

If you cannot appeal to the Upper Tribunal – If you think there is an error of law in the decision but you are out of time for appealing, are refused permission (or leave) to appeal or your appeal fails, you may want to try one of the following.

❏ If no benefit is being paid, make a fresh claim. Normal backdating rules will apply.

❏ If some benefit is being paid, the decision can be superseded if it was made in ignorance of a material fact or was based on a mistake about a material fact (see 'Ground 6' in Box T.5). Often what counts as a material fact depends on how the test required by the law is interpreted. If an error of law has been made, it is possible that the tribunal did not explore the relevant facts correctly. If a supersession takes place the law may be applied differently, as it must reconsider all aspects of the decision.

❏ If some benefit is being paid and there has been a change of circumstances since the tribunal's decision, the decision maker can correct the error of law when they supersede the decision. This is because the supersession must reconsider all aspects of the decision.

18. Appeals to the Upper Tribunal

You can appeal to the Upper Tribunal only if there is an error of law in the First-tier Tribunal decision (see Box T.8). You cannot appeal about the facts. As it is sometimes hard to separate the law from the facts, ask an experienced adviser to check the decision. Do not delay, as strict deadlines must be met. To appeal you must take the following steps.

Step 1: Ask for a *'statement of reasons'* for the decision within one month of the date the tribunal sends a decision notice that finally disposes of all issues in the appeal proceedings. The time limit can be extended under the tribunal's general case management powers.
TP(FTT)SEC Rules, rules 34 & 5(3)(a)

Step 2: Apply for permission (or, in Scotland, leave) to appeal to the tribunal within one month of being sent:

■ the statement of reasons; *or*

■ notification of amended or corrected reasons following a review (see below); *or*

■ notification that an application to set aside is unsuccessful.

Write a letter stating why you think the decision was legally wrong and what result you seek. Head it *'Application for permission to appeal to the Upper Tribunal'*. Make a copy, and send it to the clerk to the tribunal with copies of the tribunal's decision notice and its statement of reasons. If there is no statement of reasons, the tribunal has discretion to treat the application as a request for one. An application can only be allowed without a statement of reasons if the tribunal thinks it is in the interests of justice to do so.
TP(FTT)SEC Rules, rule 38

Reviewing the decision – On receiving your application for permission to appeal, the tribunal can review its decision. In particular, the tribunal can:

■ correct an accidental error in the decision;

■ amend the reasons for the decision; *or*

■ set aside the decision.

If it sets aside the decision, it must make a new decision or refer the appeal to the Upper Tribunal. You must be sent a notification of any new or amended decision.

You may be given the opportunity to comment before the review takes place. If you are not, the notification must state that you can ask for the new decision to be set aside and a further review made.

If you think the new or amended First-tier Tribunal decision contains an error of law, you have one month from the date the notification is sent to ask again for permission to appeal to the Upper Tribunal (repeating Step 2).
TCEA, s. 9; TP(FTT)SEC Rules, rules 39 & 40

Step 3: If the judge refuses permission to appeal, you can apply for permission from the Upper Tribunal directly. You must do so within one month of being sent the notice refusing permission. You should be sent a form to do this. Enclose a copy of the tribunal decision notice, the tribunal's statement of reasons and the notice refusing permission to appeal. Send these to the Upper Tribunal (see inside back cover). If you are posting them and you are close to the time limit, send them by recorded delivery.
TCEA, s. 11; TP(UT) Rules, rule 21

Step 4: If permission to appeal is granted by the tribunal, you must make a formal appeal to the Upper Tribunal within one month of being sent the notice granting permission. You will be sent a form on which to do this. If permission is granted by the Upper Tribunal, you will not have to appeal formally unless the Upper Tribunal specifically directs you to do so, as your application for permission will be treated as the appeal.
TCEA, s. 11; TP(UT) Rules, rule 23

If you miss any deadline, the Upper Tribunal can allow your application if it thinks it is fair and just to do so. Your late application must contain details of why it was late.
TP(UT) Rules, rules 5, 7 & 21

The decision maker has the same rights of appeal as you. If the decision maker asks for permission to appeal, you will be sent a copy of their application and asked to comment.

Payment pending appeal

If you appeal to the Upper Tribunal, the DWP, HMRC or local authority will put the decision of the tribunal into effect until your appeal is settled. If the decision maker appeals (or intends to appeal), the tribunal's decision may be suspended and you will not be paid until the appeal is finally decided. If this causes hardship, ask the relevant office to consider lifting the suspension.

The Upper Tribunal's decision

If the Upper Tribunal finds that a First-tier Tribunal's decision is wrong in law (see Box T.8):

■ it can give the decision that the tribunal should have given, if it can do so without making fresh or further findings of fact; *or*

■ if it thinks it expedient, the Upper Tribunal can make fresh or further findings of fact and then give a decision; *or*

■ if there are not enough findings of fact, and the Upper Tribunal does not make new findings, the case is referred to a new First-tier Tribunal. The Upper Tribunal may give directions to the new tribunal to make sure the error of law is not repeated.
TCEA, s.12

There is a quicker procedure: if both you and the decision maker agree on an outcome, the Upper Tribunal can set aside the First-tier tribunal's decision by consent, making the provisions necessary to put into effect what has been agreed.
TP(UT) Rules, rule 39

A
B
C
D
E
F
G
H
I
J
K
L
M
N
O
P
Q
R
S
T
U

Help and information

59 Getting advice

1. Who can help you?

Your local Citizens Advice Bureau (CAB) can help with benefits advice and many other matters. You can also get application forms and leaflets from them. The CAB may be able to represent you if you have a problem or are making an appeal. If not, they may be able to tell you if another local organisation could help; other independent advice centres may provide similar services. Your local authority might have a welfare rights service or a list of local advice centres. Contact your town hall for information. A local DIAL (Disability Information and Advice Line) group or other disablement advice centre may be able to offer advice and, in some cases, may be willing to represent you.

2. Free legal help

Most solicitors will not be familiar with the social security system, so you should normally first seek advice from your local CAB, DIAL or other advice agency. Some firms of solicitors, however, employ welfare rights specialists.

If you live or work in the catchment area of a law centre, contact them to see if they can help. Law centres can sometimes give benefits advice as well as help in other areas of the law such as housing, employment and immigration. For details of your nearest law centre in England, Northern Ireland and Wales, contact the Law Centres Network (020 7749 9120; www.lawcentres.org.uk).

Your CAB may have volunteer lawyers and can possibly refer you to one at a special advice session. Many trade unions offer free legal advice to their members.

Free legal advice is available from the Community Legal Advice (CLA) helpline (0845 345 4345; textphone 0845 609 6677).

Legal Aid – In England and Wales, free legal advice or 'Legal Aid' is no longer available for most types of welfare benefits advice. From April 2013, it is now only available for benefit appeals to the Upper Tribunal (see Chapter 58(18)) and higher courts and for First-tier Tribunals where the tribunal itself has identified an error of law in its own decision (see Box T.8 in Chapter 58).

Disability Rights UK membership

Become a member

Join Disability Rights UK to help shape the disability rights picture and get your voice heard. We encourage members to share experiences and we will include you in our work to ensure our policy, research and campaigns genuinely reflect the lives of disabled people.

To find out more about membership visit
www.disabilityrightsuk.org/membership

Advice and assistance through participating solicitors and advice agencies in such cases is available to anyone who receives income-related employment and support allowance, income support, income-based jobseeker's allowance or pension credit (guarantee credit). Other people, in or out of work, may qualify if their savings and income are low enough; use http://legalaidcalculator.justice.gov.uk to work out if you qualify. Not all solicitors are part of the scheme; ring the CLA helpline (see above) for details of participating solicitors and advice agencies.

The Scottish Legal Aid Board manages a Legal Aid scheme that covers a much broader range of welfare benefits advice. Ring 0845 122 8686 or look at the website (www.slab.org.uk) for details of participating solicitors. In Northern Ireland, contact the Legal Services Commission (028 9040 8888; www.nilsc.org.uk) for details of the scheme there.

Injured in an accident – If you have been injured in an accident in England and Wales, you can arrange for a free legal consultation with a local solicitor specialising in injury claims by ringing the Accident Line (Freephone 0800 192 939). If you belong to a union, they may be able to arrange a solicitor for you.

Making a will – A free Legal Aid scheme covers making a will for specific groups of people only, including most people with disabilities, people aged 70 or over, the parent of a disabled person who wants to provide for that person in their will, and a lone parent wishing to appoint a guardian for their child in a will.

60 Making a complaint

1. Complaints about the DWP

When a DWP agency has made a mistake you can expect them to explain what went wrong and why, and to apologise. They should not treat you any differently just because you have complained. To make a complaint, start by contacting the person you dealt with, or that person's manager. It may be possible to sort things out easily. Complain as soon as something goes wrong; don't wait until you get a decision on your claim.

If the problem is not resolved, take the following steps.

❏ Contact the manager at the office dealing with your claim, telling them what happened, how it has affected you and what you want to happen to put things right. They should resolve the issue over the phone, or deal with your complaint within 15 working days.

❏ If you are not satisfied with the response from the manager, you should be asked if you want your complaint sent to the Director General of Operations for the DWP. They aim to deal with your complaint within 15 working days.

❑ If you are not satisfied with Director General's response, you can ask the Independent Case Examiner (Jupiter Drive, Chester CH70 8DR, 0845 606 0777) to look into your complaint. They can only look at your complaint if it relates to maladministration; they cannot look at disputes relating to legislation (you should challenge these through the normal revisions and appeals process – see Chapter 58).

❑ If you are not satisfied with the Independent Case Examiner's response, contact your MP, who can, if the complaint is on the grounds of maladministration, refer your case to the Ombudsman (see 5 below).

If your complaint is about a DWP medical examination, see 3 below. If your complaint is with a company providing services to the DWP (such as a Work Programme provider), you should go through their complaints procedure first. If you are not satisfied with the result of this, the case should be referred to the Independent Case Examiner (see above).

2. Financial redress for maladministration: the Special Payment scheme

You can claim compensation or *'financial redress'* through the Special Payment scheme when you have lost money due to DWP maladministration (be it a mistake or a delay) or because you have received wrong or misleading advice from them. There are three categories of payment within the scheme: loss of statutory entitlement, actual financial loss or costs and consolatory payments.

Guidance on the scheme is in DWP guide *Financial Redress for Maladministration*, available via our website (www.disabilityrights.uk.org/links-government-departments).

Loss of statutory entitlement

If DWP maladministration has resulted in you losing entitlement to a benefit, and the normal statutory channels are not available to you, the DWP should consider awarding a special payment to cover the loss.

Actual financial loss or costs

Where DWP maladministration has resulted in you incurring additional expenditure or losses, the DWP should consider awarding a special payment to cover these. If you have incurred professional fees trying to resolve the matter, these will usually be met only if you can show that:

■ you made all reasonable attempts to engage with the complaint resolution process before engaging professional help;

■ the issue would not have been resolved within a reasonable timescale had you not sought professional help; *and*

■ the fees are reasonable.

Interest for delay – An additional element can be included in the special payment if there has been a significant delay in paying benefit arrears. The additional element will be calculated as if it were simple interest (generally with reference to the HMRC standard interest rate).

Consolatory payments

If you have suffered an injustice or hardship arising from DWP maladministration, the DWP should consider awarding a consolatory payment. In making such a payment, the DWP should consider your circumstances and the impact any maladministration has had on them (eg the impact if you have a pre-existing health condition may be more severe than for someone with no health problems). Consolatory payments normally range between £25 and £500, although higher amounts can be considered given your circumstances.

Claiming special payments

Write to the office handling your claim to ask for a special payment. You should explain fully the circumstances of the case and provide copies of any evidence that you have showing that you have incurred losses or expenses due to the maladministration.

3. Complaints about DWP medical examinations

If you disagree with a benefit decision that was based on medical advice provided by an Atos Healthcare or Capita professional who carried out a medical examination on behalf of the DWP, you should challenge this through the normal DWP revisions and appeals process (see Chapter 58).

However, if you wish to make a complaint about the conduct or professionalism of such a person, or about the appointment arrangements or facilities at the medical examination, you will need to contact Atos Healthcare or Capita directly and follow their complaints procedure. For Atos, write to Atos Healthcare, Customer Relations, Wing G, Government Buildings, Lawnswood, Leeds LS16 5PU or email customer-relations@atoshealthcare.com. For Capita, use the contact details on letters they have sent to you.

If you have been through the Atos Healthcare or Capita complaints process and the problem remains unresolved and involves maladministration, you can complain to the Independent Case Examiner (Jupiter Drive, Chester CH70 8DR, 0845 606 0777). The Independent Case Examiner cannot concern itself with a healthcare professional's clinical findings, but can examine complaints about the way a medical examination was conducted – eg the healthcare professional was rude or insensitive.

If you are not satisfied with the Independent Case Examiner's response, contact your MP, who can, if the complaint is on the grounds of maladministration, refer your case to the Parliamentary and Health Service Ombudsman (see 5 below).

4. Health and social care

In England there is a standard complaints procedure to use if you are not happy with care services provided by local authorities or with health services provided by the NHS. See Chapter 29(6) for details.

For complaints in the rest of the UK about hospitals, GPs and NHS services, the best starting point is your local Community Health Council in Wales, the Patient Advice and Support Service (delivered by Citizens Advice) in Scotland, or the Patient and Client Council in Northern Ireland. They can advise you on the correct procedure and might be able to help you make your complaint.

Patients detained in hospitals or care homes under the Mental Health Act can contact the Care Quality Commission (030 0061 6161; www.cqc.org.uk), who will look into the complaint. In Scotland, contact the Mental Welfare Commission for Scotland (0800 389 6809; www.mwcscot. org.uk).

Disability Rights UK services

Independent Living Advice Line

Provides advice and information on funding from social services in relation to the care needs of disabled people including direct payments, personal budgets, and general advice on employing a personal assistant.

Telephone: 0845 026 4748
Opening hours: Monday and Thursday 9am-1pm
Email: independentliving@disabilityrightsuk.org

This advice line does not provide benefits information
For information visit www.disabilityrightsuk.org

5. Complaining to the Ombudsman

Complaining to an Ombudsman is not an alternative to the normal appeals process, nor an extension of that process. You complain to an Ombudsman about the way a decision was taken or the way you were treated, rather than the decision itself. Before you can complain to an Ombudsman, you should first exhaust the normal complaints procedure, and where appropriate, contact the Independent Case Examiner (see 1 above). Keep a copy of your complaint letter and anything connected with it. There is no fee for making a complaint to an Ombudsman.

An Ombudsman investigates whether maladministration has caused injustice. Ombudsmen do not generally investigate personnel matters, although the Northern Ireland Ombudsman does so in some cases.

❏ **Maladministration** – This includes matters such as bias, prejudice, incorrect action, unreasonable delay and failure to follow (or have) proper procedures and rules.

❏ **Injustice** – This covers not only financial and other material or tangible loss but also inconvenience, anxiety or stress, and even a sense of outrage about the way in which something has been done.

Ombudsmen have powers similar to those of the High Court (Court of Session in Scotland) for obtaining evidence.

If an Ombudsman upholds your complaint, they will expect the body against which you have complained to provide you with some remedy. This may be an apology, a change in procedures, financial compensation, or any combination of these or similar measures.

Which Ombudsman?

In England you complain to:

■ the Parliamentary and Health Service Ombudsman (PHSO; 0345 015 4033; www.ombudsman.org.uk) about central government (eg the DWP), health authorities and trusts, doctors, dentists and opticians, etc. The PHSO can also investigate health-related cases where maladministration has caused hardship, and complaints about clinical judgements and refusal of access to official information;

■ the Local Government Ombudsman (030 0061 0614; www.lgo.org.uk) about local government, eg local authority housing benefit offices or social care departments (but not complaints about the internal management of schools).

In Scotland and Wales, you complain to the PHSO about central government. For devolved matters, the Scottish Public Services Ombudsman (0800 377 7330; www.spso.org.uk) deals with complaints about the Scottish Government and its agencies, and the Public Services Ombudsman for Wales (0845 601 0987; www.ombudsman-wales.org.uk) deals with complaints about the Welsh Government. Each also deals with complaints about other public bodies in Scotland and Wales, including health, housing and social care. In Northern Ireland there is just one government Ombudsman (0800 343424; www.ni-ombudsman.org.uk).

You can ask your local Citizens Advice Bureau (CAB) to check with the Ombudsman first to make sure that an Ombudsman can investigate a complaint against a particular government body, such as a quango.

How to complain

You can complain directly to any of the Ombudsmen except the PHSO and, in cases concerning central government, the Northern Ireland Ombudsman. Only an MP can refer a complaint to the PHSO. You should normally approach your own MP; approach an MP for another constituency only if yours refuses to refer your complaint. If you approach another MP, they will usually contact your own MP before deciding whether to refer your complaint.

Other Ombudsmen

As well as the government Ombudsmen, there are several others, including the Financial Ombudsman, Housing Ombudsman and Legal Ombudsman. For details check the website (www.bioa.org.uk) or ask your local CAB. For information about the Pensions Ombudsman, see Box O.3 in Chapter 43.

61 Useful publications

1. Benefits guides

In many chapters in this Handbook we suggest other sources of information, including guidance and reference books. Look in boxes called 'For more information'.

Listed below is a selection of other guides, the publishers and the prices.

❏ *Guide to Housing Benefit and Council Tax Benefit 2013/2014*, Chartered Institute of Housing and Shelter, £32

❏ *Welfare Benefits and Tax Credits Handbook 2013/2014*, Child Poverty Action Group (CPAG), £45 (£12 for benefit claimants)

❏ *Child Support Handbook 2013/2014*, CPAG, £29 (£9 for benefit claimants)

❏ *Council Tax Handbook 2011, 9th edition*, CPAG, £17

❏ *Paying for Care Handbook 2009, 6th edition*, CPAG, £19.50

❏ *Fuel Rights Handbook 2013, 16th edition*, CPAG, £21

2. DWP leaflets and guidance

DWP leaflets and official guidance should be available from your local Jobcentre Plus. You can download official DWP guidance, such as the *Decision Makers Guide*, via our website (www.disabilityrightsuk.org/links-government-departments).

3. Disability Rights UK publications

We produce a range of guides and publications to promote independent living. They can be ordered from our webste (www.disabilityrightsuk.org).

❏ *If only I'd known that a year ago*, £12.99
❏ *National Key Scheme Guide 2013*, £12.99
❏ *Holiday Guide 2013*, £12.99
❏ *Doing Life Differently* (set of six: Careers, Information Technology, Money, Sport, Transport and Work), £14.99

Factsheets

We have produced over 60 factsheets covering a range of benefits and care issues. They are free to download from: www.disabilityrights.uk.org/how-we-can-help/benefits-information/factsheets.

Index